# Mapping Applied Linguistics

*Mapping Applied Linguistics: A guide for students and practitioners* provides an innovative and wide-ranging introduction to the full scope of applied linguistics.

Incorporating both socio-cultural and cognitive perspectives, the book maps the diverse and constantly expanding range of theories, methods and issues faced by students and practitioners alike. Practically oriented and ideally suited to students new to the subject area, each chapter demonstrates how applied linguists can investigate the role of language in an individual's or group's real-world problem, and the potential solutions available.

The book provides in-depth coverage of:

- Language teaching and education, literacy and language disorders
- Language variation and World Englishes
- Language policy and planning
- Lexicography and forensic linguistics
- Multilingualism and translation

Including real data and international examples from Latin America, South-East Asia, the US and the UK, the book features further reading and exercises in each chapter, fieldwork suggestions and a full glossary of key terms. An interactive companion website also provides a wealth of additional resources, including ideas for research projects, links to key websites and sample answers to the chapter exercises. A reader forum allows students and practitioners to share experiences and concerns.

Providing a dynamic and thorough overview of the rapidly growing field of applied linguistics, this book will be essential reading for students studying applied linguistics, TESOL, general linguistics and education at the advanced undergraduate or master's degree level. It is also the ideal gateway for practitioners to better understand the wider scope of their work.

**Christopher J. Hall** is a Senior Le̶    ̶k St John University, UK and currently teaches on the BA in Eng̶      and the MA in TESOL.

**Patrick H. Smith** is Associate Profe̶      ̶Literacy/Biliteracy at The University of Texas at El Paso, USA.

**Rachel Wicaksono** is a Senior Lecturer at York St John University, UK and Head of Programme for the MA in TESOL.

# Mapping Applied Linguistics

## A guide for students and practitioners

**CHRISTOPHER J. HALL, PATRICK H. SMITH AND RACHEL WICAKSONO**

Routledge
Taylor & Francis Group

LONDON AND NEW YORK

First published 2011
by Routledge
2 Park Square, Milton Park, Abingdon, Oxon OX14 4RN

Simultaneously published in the USA and Canada
by Routledge
270 Madison Ave, New York, NY 10016

*Routledge is an imprint of the Taylor & Francis Group, an informa business*

© 2011 Christopher J. Hall, Patrick H. Smith and Rachel Wicaksono

Typeset in Akzidenz Grotesk and Eurostile by
Keystroke, Station Road, Codsall, Wolverhampton

Printed and bound in Great Britain by
MPG Books Group, UK

*British Library Cataloguing in Publication Data*
A catalogue record for this book is available from the British Library

*Library of Congress Cataloging-in-Publication Data*
Hall, Christopher J., 1961–
    Mapping applied linguistics : a guide for students and practitioners /
    Christopher J Hall, Patrick H Smith, Rachel Wicaksono.
        p. cm.
    Includes bibliographical references and index.
    1. Applied linguistics.  2. Language and languages—Study and teaching.
    I. Smith, Patrick H.  II. Wicaksono, Rachel.  III. Title.
    P129.H27 2011
    418—dc22                                                      2010031444

ISBN13: 978–0–415–55912–6 (hbk)
ISBN13: 978–0–415–55913–3 (pbk)
ISBN13: 978–0–203–83242–4 (ebk)

# Dedications

For Juan always (CJH)
Para la Luz de mi vida (PHS)
For Rian and Clara (RW)

# Contents

# Figures

We are indebted to the people and archives below for permission to reproduce illustrations. Every effort has been made to trace copyright holders, but in a few cases this has not been possible. Any omissions brought to our attention will be remedied in future editions.

# Tables

# Preface

A map is a representation, an abstraction, 'a surface that can be dealt with'.
    It is the product of an exacting rationality, and it furthers the conquest of system-making over the melange of the everyday.

> (Ralph Cintron, *Angels' Town: Chero ways,*
> *gang life, and rhetorics of the everyday*)

This book presents the complex and shifting field of applied linguistics as 'a surface that can be dealt with'. Scholars and practitioners in the field are concerned with the language-related needs of individuals and groups in 'the melange of the everyday', all the way from foreign language learning to literacy skills, from translation to trademark disputes, from the protection of endangered languages to the detection of dyslexia. The map we provide here systematically plots the landscapes of applied linguistics at the opening of the second decade of the twenty-first century. It's a time of unparalleled changes, including unprecedented flows of people, goods and services across linguistic and national boundaries, the increased interconnectedness of global capital and economic systems, and a staggering array of new and ever faster forms of digital technology. These technologies have direct relevance for identifying, and attempting to resolve, the language needs faced by language users (and applied linguists), and they feature prominently in all chapters of the book. Indeed, just as we get directions now from GPS systems and online maps, this book is part of a broader online applied linguistics project anchored in its companion website at www.routledge.com/textbooks/hall/.

 **www.0.1**

We have written the book to be a map of current knowledge and contemporary practices in the field, as well as a guide to this dynamic world for practitioners and students – current and future applied linguists. It goes without saying that this book is not the only map. We have also tried to encourage and envision maps that our students and readers will (re)create as they read the book. Mapmakers Maribel Casas-Cortes and Sebastian Cobarrubios comment that 'to make maps is to organize oneself, to generate new connections and to be able to transform the material and immaterial conditions in which we are immersed. It isn't the territory but it definitely produces territory' (Casas-Cortes and Cobarrubios, 2008, p. 62). In this sense, we regard readers as cartographers who will use the individual chapters, activities and discussions with instructors and classmates on- and offline to begin or continue, as the case may be, to create their maps of applied linguistics. Because maps are ongoing projects, we've provided recommendations for further readings in each area.

## WHY MAPPING?

There are many reasons for the mapping metaphor. Here are a few of the most compelling. First, maps can be read from any starting point. Although they can be made and read using dominant orientations (North as top of the world), maps are also technologies for expressing other orientations (e.g. Figures 1.6 and 1.7 on p. 20). This map in book form assumes certain features that will be familiar to our audience of highly practised readers: the left-to-right and top-to-bottom convention for presenting written text; the distribution of knowledge in separate chapters and thematically related parts (Parts A, B and C); a glossary of specialized vocabulary; an index; etc. A common feature of textbooks is that the chapters are written to be read in a rigid sequence, from first to last. This book is like a map in that you can find your way around from whichever chapter you choose as a starting point. We do, however, recommend beginning at Chapter 1, because this is where we introduce some basic concepts and outline our vision of the scope and essential ingredients of the field, all of which inform the rest of the book. Otherwise, you can wander around between specific points of departure and arrival, depending on your own interests. This feature is further enhanced on the companion website.

Like the dictionaries we discuss in Chapter 10, textbooks and maps are often regarded as authoritative texts. Although they are perceived as 'objective' or 'neutral' and free from ideological bias, they are in fact conceived by human authors and so necessarily, although not always explicitly, convey the theoretical or ideological stances of their authors. As Baghat and Mogel (2008, p. 6) write, 'all maps have an inherent politics that often lies hidden beneath an "objective" surface'. Karrow (2007, p. 13) adds, 'Maps depict the physical characteristics and spatial organization of our planet. But the content of maps is also determined by, and expresses, the culture, historical circumstances, and ideas and interests of mapmakers and map users'. We try to be alert to the implicit theories, ideas and interests of the linguists and applied linguists we mention in this book, as well as to our own. We ask you to evaluate our success in this endeavour as you read.

Maps are intimately connected with the notion of guiding. Tourist guides often include maps of regions and streets, and interactive maps can guide map readers to their particular areas of interest. We have chosen the subtitle of the book, *A guide for students and practitioners*, because we are aware of the complexities and diversities of issues that applied linguists will face in their careers. The field has become so broad and at the same time deeply specialized, in the sense that students and professionals usually concentrate their areas of practice in a single, or no more than a few, domain(s). We argue that most language and language-related problems can benefit from the expertise of applied linguists with different disciplinary orientations, knowledge and tools. The answers to the most vexing problems will be generated, we think, through collaboration between practitioners from different sub-fields. We hope that this guide will be of service in this enterprise.

## HOW IS THE BOOK ORGANIZED?

The book contains twelve chapters organized into three parts, together with introductory and closing chapters at either end, to set the scene and point to the future, respectively. We introduce some of the fundamental themes, tools and participants of applied linguistics in Part A, before moving on to the different specialist areas in Parts B and C. Part A starts out with Chapter 2, 'Language varieties', in which we consider the fundamental but seldom fully appreciated fact that all language is fluid and dynamic, constantly morphing through time and space, across speakers and situations. Chapter 3, 'Key populations', presents the people behind the discourse: the centrally important 'clients' with whom applied linguistics engages. The next two chapters focus on language in its social contexts, with Chapter 4, 'Discourse analysis', discussing one of applied linguists' major tools for understanding inter-actions between language uses and users, and Chapter 5, 'Language policy and planning', assessing our ability to shape language structures and uses through deliberate actions performed on or by their users.

Part B reflects the central role of language as a tool of learning, starting with the culture of written texts in Chapter 6, 'Literacy', and then turning to the more spe-cific issue of language-mediated schooling in Chapter 7, 'Language and education'. The next two chapters explore some of the educational problems and opportunities presented by our multilingual world, with Chapter 8, 'Bilingual and multilingual education' examining the practice of schooling in more than one language, and then Chapter 9, 'Additional language education' zeroing in on learning and teaching a second or subsequent language (the historical focus of applied linguistics). In Part C we cast our net wider and review a range of more specialized language needs, such as: communication between users of different languages in Chapter 10, 'Translation'; dictionary-making in Chapter 11, 'Lexicography'; language and the law in Chapter 12, 'Forensic linguistics'; and the assessment and treatment of language disorders in Chapter 13, 'Language pathology'.

Running through the whole book is a series of core issues which we believe are so important to applied linguistics that they can't be dealt with in a single chapter. These strands are as follows:

- Applied Linguistics as *critical practice*, inherently political;
- language at the heart of issues of *freedom and inequality*;
- language as a *cognitive*, as well as a *social*, phenomenon;
- *methodological best practice* for applied linguistic research;
- *IT and corpus-based enquiry* as forces in applied linguistics;
- *Englishes* across the world, as resources (and threats).

Language is sometimes confused with, or used as a symbol of, many facets of the human condition, including identity, ethnicity, intelligence, development and opportunity. In fact, language, in and of itself, is none of these things. The six strands reflect our view of language as essentially a functional *instrument* serving varied mental and social uses for individuals and groups of people in the contemporary world, rather than as an ideal or idealized decontextualized system governed either by rigid social orthodoxies or by immutable cognitive laws. Rather unfashionably in some quarters of the field, we also stress throughout that language must be seen as residing both in communities and in brains/minds simultaneously. We don't believe that it's in the interests of our client populations to align ourselves exclusively with intellectual traditions which pit nature against nurture or biology against society.

## WHO ARE THE AUTHORS?

Like all applied linguists, we are interested in, and excited by, variation in language structures and uses wherever such variation may occur: across and within cultures and communities, political borders, demographic groups, socioeconomic levels, ethnic identities and modalities of use. The three of us represent a mix of professional, academic and personal backgrounds. But as native English-speaking 'Anglos' who struggled with 'foreign' languages at school and inherited a great deal of cultural baggage around notions of the value of 'good English', we are all very driven to understand and challenge the simplistic and harmful monolingual, monolithic views of language competence we have grown up with. To our way of thinking, these views haven't been adequately resolved in mainstream general linguistics, despite much passionate championing of linguistic equality from most linguistics scholars, whatever their intellectual persuasion.

**www.0.2**  Briefly, this is who we are and what we bring to this book. Chris is from the north of England, where he studied English language (at Newcastle University) and general linguistics (at the University of York). He did his PhD on the psychology and historical development of word parts across languages at the University of Southern California (Los Angeles), before turning to second language acquisition and applied linguistics more generally during two decades teaching and doing research in Mexico. His main interests and expertise continue to be in the psychology of language and multilingualism, especially at the lexical (word) level, but he's recently become obsessed with how cognitive work in this area shares many ideas and goals with primarily sociologically oriented work and thinking in the 'World Englishes' paradigm.

**www.0.3**  Patrick hails from the northern US, growing up in Michigan and Maine. In New England he studied history (at Bowdoin College) and TESOL (at the School for International Training). Turning east and south, he then developed an interest in language and literacy in social contexts by teaching elementary school pupils in Kenya and adolescents and young adults in Mexico. He did his PhD in Language, Reading and Culture with a minor in English language and linguistics at the University of Arizona. His research focuses on literacy and biliteracy development in schools and multilingual communities in Mexico and in the US–Mexico borderlands. At the University of Texas at El Paso, he is studying the literacy practices of transnational immigrants.

**www.0.4**  Rachel is also from the north of England. She studied English Language and Literature at Oxford University, and TESOL (teaching English to speakers of other languages) at the University of London's Institute of Education. She has spent a lot of time in Asia, leading courses in EFL (English as a foreign language) and teacher training in India and Indonesia, and in cyberspace, including blogging for the BBC World Service on its Learning English website. Rachel runs the MA in TESOL at York St John University, where Chris is now one of her colleagues. She is especially interested in the use of English as a lingua franca in mixed language groups of university students, and in ways of sensitizing students to their own use of language and the effects this has on the achievement of mutual understanding.

We hope that readers will enjoy and learn from the international flavours that we bring to the study of applied linguistics. Chris and Patrick use examples of work they have engaged in together and with colleagues from the Spanish-speaking world, reflecting the *mole* sauce of rich linguistic diversity of Latin America. Rachel has added South-East Asian examples to the mixture, creating even more of a *gado gado* flavour for this guide. As the field of applied linguistics grows quickly beyond a traditional focus on English and predominantly English-speaking contexts, we believe knowledge of international contexts and problems is an indispensable ingredient in the successful preparation of future applied linguists. A map on the companion website will show the location of the places we mention in this book. We predict that many readers will find themselves working with learners and other clients from these and other regions, and perhaps studying or working there.

## WHO IS THIS BOOK FOR?

We have written this book for students of applied linguistics and allied disciplines (like TESOL, general linguistics and education) at the advanced undergraduate or master's degree level. Students from all over the world will be able to gain essential information and a wealth of additional insight from the material presented here, independently of their language background, cultural identities or the educational system they've experienced. As we mentioned in the previous section, we have a great deal of experience interacting with students from diverse backgrounds and in diverse world contexts. Applied Linguistics has developed specifically to address different individual and group identities in contact and in conflict, and its practitioners are for that reason inherently international and intercultural in outlook, especially attuned to these different needs.

Apart from students, we also think that practising language professionals will get a great deal out of the book, by appreciating how scholarship from a variety of complementary perspectives may enrich their daily practice, reaffirm their expertise and unique 'feel' for language, and create new spaces for professional alliance and dialogue by revealing the extent to which their work faces similar challenges in quite distinct arenas. For example, how many speech therapists have considered that foreign language testers may have struggled with some of the same assessment challenges as they do when they develop tests of productive vs receptive vocabulary knowledge? How many teachers developing activities for reading and writing in a foreign language are aware of the various competencies associated with literacy skills beyond the basic ability to read and spell? How many lexicographers, language teachers, translators, forensic linguists and language planners are aware of their overlapping and rapidly converging needs in the development of online resources such as multilingual corpus databases? These are just a few of the transdisciplinary perspectives and understandings that can be developed from a foundation in applied linguistics.

For general readers who want to learn about the field out of curiosity or because they work with applied linguists (lawyers with forensic linguists, for example), this book ought to provide some enjoyment, as well as considerable enlightenment. We don't use technical vocabulary where we can avoid it, and when we do it's for the sake of precision: language is so central in our lives it has its own folk terminology, which is not always appropriate or helpful when we want to make subtle, and often surprising, points about it. But the book is not for the faint-hearted either: we don't dumb down or trivialize the complexity of language problems in the world. Indeed, we'll probably leave you with more questions than answers, but we've also provided plenty of additional examples on the companion website.

## HOW CAN THE BOOK BE USED?

If, as we noted above, applied linguists can't agree on precisely how their field is constituted, then how can we provide a book which represents their collective visions and that targets their collective students in different academic traditions around the globe? Well, the way we've structured the book means that, however applied linguistics is construed in your context of study, it can be used to deliver a flexible but coherent synthesis. The book is readily adaptable to most international course structures for use as a required or recommended text. Most universities and colleges operate either a ten-week academic term/quarter/trimester (give or take a couple of weeks), or a fifteen- to sixteen-week semester. The book's twelve core topics, plus opening and closing chapters, fit comfortably into a semester, with room for other readings or activities if desired. For those on a term/quarter/trimester system, tutors and their students might want to cover most of the nine core chapters in Parts A and B, and then choose to look at only one or two of the four specialized themes of Part C as a class, or cover all the themes in smaller groups and then report to the whole class. Alternatively, for those who wish to have a broader view of applied linguistics without the educational focus (for example those studying the subject as part of a general linguistics or sociology course), Part B could be used only selectively, leaving time for fuller coverage of Part C.

The book will probably be read most profitably in sequence, given the serial nature of all linguistic expression as it streams through time. But the chapters were not originally written in the order they appear here, so they all make a lot of sense on their own, if the dipping-in reader is willing to consistently ignore (or consistently follow up) the cross-referencing to other chapters. The glossary, which is woven into the text as well as listed alphabetically at the end, can serve as a useful alternative or complement to the cross-references.

Complementing the bibliographical references to electronic and print sources that we give throughout the text, and the further reading included at the end of each chapter, we have provided an annotated selection of internet resources on the companion website. Where these are referred to in chapters, we have marked them with the 🌍 icon and a number indicating their place in our online list. So instead of laboriously copying out URLs, you can easily locate the resource you want on our website and, if you're interested, click the link to go straight to the resource.

Finally, we've provided end-of-chapter activities, which might be assigned as homework and followed up in class discussion, written up on an online class discussion board or even submitted for assessment. Some of the end-of-chapter activities may inspire you to think about doing a more structured research project, something that could turn into your final dissertation or thesis (there are more research ideas on the companion website). Alternatively, if you are reading this book as part of a course of self-study, or out of general curiosity, you might want to use the activities as a way of exploring your favourite topics in more detail. Rather than simple comprehension checks, the activities are designed to help you extend your understanding of the key points in each chapter by exploring them in real-life contexts. Some activities involve fieldwork in your own community, and others will lead you to explore new contexts of applied linguistics practice via the internet and other digital technologies. Example responses for many activities can be found (and posted) on the companion website. We hope that you will contribute your thoughts, findings and experiences to the website from wherever in the world you are reading this book; participating in the ongoing process of mapping applied linguistics.

So, whatever format you're reading in, whatever your particular interests and whatever your current location: *selamat datang*, *bienvenidos*, welcome! We invite you to join us on this guided tour of the exciting and rapidly growing field of applied linguistics.

# Acknowledgements

The authors would like to thank our editors, Russell George and Nadia Seemungal, for their encouragement and sound advice in bringing this project to fruition. We are also grateful to the anonymous reviewers who shared their expertise with us, making so many excellent suggestions for improving the book.

We are indebted to the following colleagues and students who kindly read and offered helpful comments on chapters and activities, and/or provided us with useful information: Jennifer Alvarez, Lilia Barrios, Chandy Charlton, Debbie Cole, Rocio Gallardo, Terrie Garcia, Stephen Gibson, Heriberto Godina, Carmen González, Ann Gregory, Mandy Holzrichter, Muhammad Ilyas, Anne Lafeber, Shu Liu, Rubilí Loredo, Andrew Merrison, Sally Merrison, Cindy Mireles, Luz Murillo, Gerardo Ortega, Cynthia Prado, Shirley Reay, Craig Salminen, Ulrike Sperr, Guadalupe Tijerina, Amabilia Valenzuela, Mónica Urbina and Saffron Walkling.

We especially appreciate invaluable contributions from Khawla Badwan, Chandy Charlton, Duan Yan, Liliana Fernández and Melissa Vasquez, practising applied linguists whose perspectives have added much to our map of the field.

# CHAPTER 1

# Introduction

Truth is the summit of being; justice is the application of it to affairs.
(Ralph Waldo Emerson)

A book about applied linguistics is inevitably a book about language, its users and uses. Because the number of language users includes all 6.8 billion of us and language uses encompass almost all our myriad activities, from the most banal to the truly momentous, the subject we're covering in this and the following thirteen chapters is remarkably wide-ranging. It's a big topic to fit between the covers of a book made of paper and enclosed between covers of card, so it's inevitably going to spill over onto the companion website, get expanded in the recommended readings, well up and multiply in classroom discussion or discussion boards, and it won't be contained.

This first chapter is designed to provide some fixed points on our map of applied linguistics, describing points of departure, characteristic features of the terrain and ways *not* to go. In the chapter we do three things. First, we outline a broad perspective on human language which knits together its social and cognitive strands. The account, based on ideas from our sister discipline of general linguistics, informs all the other chapters in the book. Second, we identify ten fundamentally misguided ideas in everyday thinking about language, but argue that applied linguists need to acknowledge and respect them, because they are firmly embedded in most people's world views and determine many of their language-related decisions and practices. In other words, they are part of the territory. Our third and last goal here is to characterize the discipline of applied linguistics as we map it in this book. We won't try to reach Emerson's summit of the 'truth', of course, because applied linguistics is a mountain range of many truths. We do, however, hope to give an initial flavour of how the discipline is united in its 'application to affairs' and show that we all share the ultimate destination of social justice.

## 1.1 WHY DO WE USE DIFFERENT LANGUAGES?

According to some estimates, people speak as many as 7,000 different languages on the planet today, belonging to more than a hundred distinct families (Lewis, 2010; see Figure 1.1). One of the central problems that applied linguists seek to address is how to meet the challenges and promote the opportunities of this diversity through education, policy-making, translation and activism at local and global levels. The existence of so many different languages means that most of us  **www.1.1**

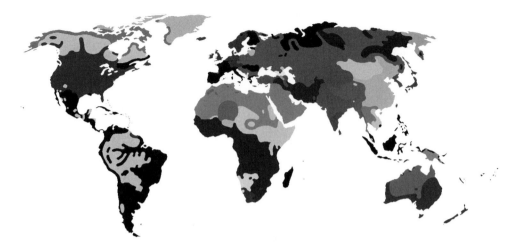

Figure 1.1    Geographical distribution of some of the world's major language families with each area of shading representing a distinct language family (Source: Wikimedia Commons)

can't communicate in any sustained and significant way with most of our fellow human beings. As many as one-third of us are monolingual, and even though the majority of the world's population know and use more than one language, no one, of course, speaks *all* the languages! There is, perhaps, a tiny number of people who are able to converse, read and write in the ten languages that have the largest number of native speakers, but even these polyglots can't communicate with half the world's population.

Here's a question that may not have occurred to you before: why is it that we speak different languages, rather than having just one way to communicate our thoughts to all members of our species? After all, that's more or less the way other animals do it: the birds and the bees basically inherit their 'languages' directly through the genes of their parents. Since modern *homo sapiens* is thought to have originated in southern Africa around 200,000 years ago, why haven't we all inherited, say, an ancient version of Zulu, in the same way that we inherit the heart, the ability to walk on two legs or the capacity to distinguish a certain range of frequencies of sound?

The answer is that, unlike the heart, language is both a biological and a social property of the species. It has evolved not just to serve the individual user, but also to serve the group. This means it must have a way to escape the confines of the human body, allowing us to connect with others around us. Since telepathy is impossible, language originally found its external medium in sound, and so speech was born. Given that language is mediated by speech in society, and not only through the genes in the biological system, infants don't reproduce an identical copy of their parents' system as they acquire their language. Thus language inevitably changes. After many generations, the system will be transformed into a completely different language, as Latin has developed into Spanish, French and the other Romance languages.

We live in a multilingual world because speakers move, lose contact with their ancestral groups and encounter new language communities. When the first bands of *homo sapiens* migrated from southern Africa around 100,000 years ago, generational changes must first have resulted in different dialects and then different languages. This scenario has been played out over and over again around the planet, resulting in a cacophony of different tongues, each one merging with the ones surrounding it. Current figures, of course, represent only a tiny fraction of the languages that have existed through the millennia; the globalizing forces of transport, trade, exploration and conquest over the last thousand years have caused the abrupt disappearance of many of them: currently at about two a month according to commonly accepted estimates (e.g. Krauss, 1992). More recently, these globalizing forces have been abetted by mass communication through radio, TV and the internet. The result is language decline and death at unprecedented rates.

**www.1.2**

But human language is not just characterized by its astonishing (if dwindling) diversity. Although it is transmitted through speech in social and cultural contexts, it is also a biological phenomenon, and many linguists believe that children are born with brain systems which allow them to acquire languages (and may be used for other cognitive functions too). To this extent, language is like the heart and other physical properties: it develops in infancy, may be damaged through injury or inherited impairment and breaks down in old age, in ways which are very similar to other aspects of our biological endowment. Our common linguistic inheritance as members of the species of *homo sapiens* is attested also in underlying similarities between the structures of all languages: universal patterns which defy the pressures of generational change because they are fixed by our brains, ultimately by the way human language has evolved in the species. For example, all phonological systems use at least the three vowels /i/, /a/ and /u/ (as in *key*, *car* and *coo*). And all grammars use pronouns (at least for first and second person).

So we have an apparent paradox: language is biological, a property of the species, but language*s* (and the dialects which constitute them) are social, associated with groups of individual speakers defined by culture rather than chromosomes. This paradox is not apparent to us in our everyday lives: most human beings are normally aware of only the social element of the equation, of language as a maker and marker of group identity and as a way of getting things done together. And this is surely a sensible arrangement. Language is not an end in itself, but rather a social tool, allowing us to influence and understand each other in sophisticated ways, and so enhance our survival through pooled resources and concerted actions. Our language mechanisms have evolved to operate in the background, to mimic as closely as possible the fiction of telepathy. While we get on with whatever it is we are doing (hanging out with friends, negotiating with a business partner, watching the TV news or whatever), the brain's language circuits are hard at work, transforming sound into meaning and meaning into sound. The job description for language is a long one, involving an array of specialized linguistic tasks as well as teamwork with other cognitive systems dedicated to moving muscles, negotiating social contexts, etc. Tasks include:

- choreographing complex arrays of muscle contractions for speaking, signing, writing and typing;
- encoding and decoding tens of thousands of nouns, verbs, adjectives and adverbs;
- working out grammatical relations to encode and decode information on who's doing what to whom, even when they're not physically present;

- detecting non-literal meanings, including metaphor, sarcasm and humour;
- encoding social variables like deference, courtesy or disrespect.

Most of the time these processes are happening at lightning speed and without us exercising any conscious control over them. It's as natural as walking, eating and breathing. We tend to become aware of language use only under certain circumstances: when old age, an accident or illness begins to hamper our ability to communicate; when a misunderstanding occurs; or when we are confronted with individuals who speak differently from us (in a different dialect, a foreign accent or another language completely). The result of this general lack of awareness of language is twofold: we tend to equate language with thought itself, because we can't see the join between them, and we identify languages with the groups who speak them, because that's what's mostly visible to us. It's as though language has us under a spell, making its use almost invisible, like telepathy, and throwing to the fore its physical manifestations, the actual speech patterns which identify people as 'one of us' or 'one of them' (Hall, 2005).

This lack of awareness of the dual biological and social nature of language has important consequences for both ordinary language users and the applied linguists whose job it is to help them find solutions to language problems. Our inability to break the spell of language – to unwrap its social trappings at one end and unravel it from thought at the other – means that some language problems go unrecognized and others are rendered intractable. To understand why, we need to acknowledge a series of dead ends in the mapping of language and applied linguistics.

## 1.2 TEN WAYS WE'RE LED ASTRAY IN LANGUAGE AND APPLIED LINGUISTICS

A 'folk' theory of language, capturing 'common sense' beliefs, is a natural consequence of the 'Language Spell' we mentioned in the previous section. All communities and cultures have deeply held beliefs about the nature of language and languages, which applied linguists ignore at their peril. But research in linguistics and allied fields allows us to bring new perspectives on the practical problems facing language users, which we must also be aware of if we are not to be led astray by tempting, but misleading, courses of belief and practice. Sometimes the most level path or the straightest-looking route doesn't lead to new territory, but ultimately sends us round in circles or soon dries up altogether. Here are our top ten 'dead ends'. Although you might have your doubts right now (especially if you're new to linguistics), we'll try to convince you, as we map applied linguistics in the chapters to come, that these dead ends are not the way to go.

## DEAD END 1: PEOPLE THINK IN LANGUAGE

In the previous section, we noted that people commonly identify language with thought itself, believing that we 'think' in language. If you have ever studied another language, you may recall your teacher telling you to try to 'think in French' or – even harder – 'try not to think in English' or whatever first language(s) you acquired as an infant. Most cognitively oriented linguists (e.g. Jackendoff, 1992; Pinker, 1994) argue that humans think in a non-linguistic format (Pinker calls it **mentalese**) which we map automatically and without conscious control onto the structures of particular languages like English or French. We then use these structures, either in our heads to regulate our thoughts consciously (**inner speech**), or in the external modalities of speech, writing or sign, for communication with others. You may have had the experience of dreaming in a language you're learning, and perhaps you can even recall dreamed conversations in it. Again, although these impressions can seem very vivid, they are not evidence that we think in language. We can wrap our thought in language, and this is clearly how we co-construct many of our beliefs about the world with other speakers, as psychologists such as Lev Vygotsky (1986) have pointed out. But this doesn't mean that language and thought are the same thing.

Because we are so caught up in the 'spell' of language, the only way to really appreciate this point is to consider other mental phenomena which we use thought to make or manipulate, but which don't require language. Take, for example, the James Bond movie theme: you can 'think' it in your head, but not with words or syntax. And 'think' about how you would get from where you are now to the closest bathroom: you don't need words in order to plan your route. Finally, look at Figure 1.2. You'll 'see' a white triangle above a black-edged triangle and three solid black circles. But none of these objects are actually there: you 'think' them into existence, and, again, the languages you know are not involved.

**Mentalese** is the abstract 'language of thought' in the mind: *what we are consciously or unconsciously thinking*, independent of whether it is expressible or expressed using the 'linguistic language' of speech, writing and sign.

**Inner speech** is spoken (or signed) language that doesn't get expressed.

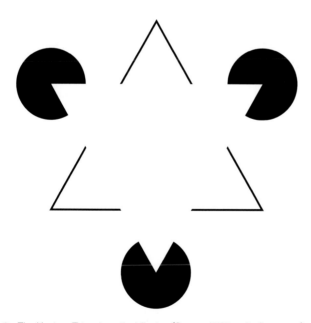

Figure 1.2    The Kanizsa Triangle optical illusion (Source: Wikimedia Commons)

In the course of the book we'll encounter plenty of tangible, practical evidence for the limited value of equating thought with language, including from applied linguistics itself:

- research in bilingualism demonstrates that bilinguals do not have two separate sets of thoughts for the two languages they speak;
- research in language pathology shows case after case of speakers with impaired language but perfectly intact thoughts and thinking processes.

Another major piece of evidence comes from children: if thought equals language, this seems to imply that before they acquire language children can't think. If they can't think, then how on earth do they do the *learning*? This leads us to our next dead end.

## DEAD END 2: CHILDREN ARE TAUGHT THEIR FIRST LANGUAGE(S)

Most people don't think much or at all about how they came to be fluent language users. When asked, they will often mention being taught by their parents (especially mothers) or through early schooling, and/or will assume that they imitated the adults around them. Children, to their great amusement, often do imitate adults, and often we deserve it. And parents and teachers do teach us some of the words we come to know. But the evidence from first language acquisition studies doesn't support the claim that instruction and imitation are the only or even the most important strategies involved in acquiring our first language(s). Imitation is crucially important for certain aspects of language development, especially at the level of its physical manifestations (speech sounds, word forms, intonation contours, handshapes and movements in sign, etc.), but imitation can't explain how those symbolic devices come to represent meanings and social functions in the child's mind. And neither can it explain why children try out grammar they haven't heard from adults, like 'That's she's Mom' or 'What do you think what's in that box?' (Foster-Cohen, 1999).

An unexpected research finding for most non-linguists is the sheer insignificance of explicit correction of non-adult, non-conventional forms like these. Ways of correcting children and the importance of doing so vary culturally, but it's quite clear that explicit attempts to get kids to say the adult form don't work. Children can be berated, sometimes, to reproduce the parentally desired form, but they stick with their preferred phrasing until their emerging grammar fits adult conventions. Additionally, although **child-directed speech** plays an important role in language development in most cultures, a great deal of the language input children receive comes from conversations not addressed to them and without any instructional intent by parents and caretakers. Children build their first language mentally, by making sense of (and with) the language they're exposed to, which is almost never accompanied by explicit explanations of its structure.

There is a great deal of evidence for a critical period during which your brain is 'biologically ready' for learning your first language(s). Even though talk of a 'grammar gene' is wildly inaccurate, we know that language development and use are biologically constrained, and indeed some elements of the neural structures implicated, like the protein FOXP2 (see Figure 1.3), are being studied in laboratories around the world. Closer to everyday experience, though, linguists have shown that people who don't get exposed to sufficient amounts of contextualized input (talk situated in context) before a certain age (around puberty), don't end up attaining

**Child-directed speech** is the linguist's term for the distinctive patterning of language used by some care-givers with babies. It is characterized by cooing intonation and short, simplified words. It's also known as *motherese*, even though fathers and non-parents use it too (with pets as well as babies).

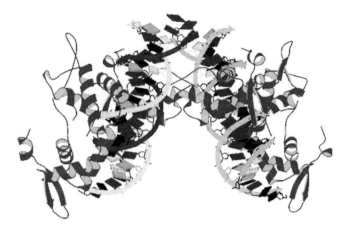

Figure 1.3    A representation of the structure of FOXP2, a protein implicated in the development and use of human language (Source: RCSB Protein Data Bank)

the full spectrum of linguistic resources. This has happened, for example, in cases of children who are deaf but are mistakenly thought to be mentally retarded, and are not exposed to sign language. It's not surprising, then, that children tend to get closer to native-like competence in a second language than adult L2 learners. These facts do not mean, however, that older people cannot learn additional languages. Researchers looking at the differences between child and adult learners have found unique advantages in each group. Children are able to hear salient differences in form better than ageing ears (an evident advantage in word-learning), as well as benefiting from factors including more time in the second language in informal, non-school contexts. But adult learners have different advantages that make them good language learners, too. They have the advantage of a fully formed first language to draw on and make comparisons with, as well as more developed cognitive systems and social competencies.

In most contemporary societies, much of adults' more advanced socialization comes through the educational process, of course. It is schooling, therefore, which develops access to print through consolidated literacy ability, as well as familiarizing pupils with strategies for studying, both of which can be critical for additional language development. It is important to be aware of how inextricably linked the three concepts have become in the modern imagination. Roughly, the string of assumptions goes as follows:

- languages as they are written constitute their most fulfilled form;
- literacy is the product of institutionalized education;
- only the educated are fully competent in the languages they use;
- uneducated parents are bad models and teachers for their children.

The social consequences of this mainstream set of beliefs are grievous for individuals and groups. We turn now to the dead-end belief which lies at the beginning of this unproductive way of thinking.

# DEAD END 3: WRITTEN LANGUAGE IS SUPERIOR TO SPOKEN LANGUAGE

Written language is probably the most important human development of the last five or six millennia. But for the fifty or sixty millennia before that humans were speaking languages that were in essence just like the ones we speak today (though with very different words, of course!). The relatively recent appearance of written forms of language means that language acquisition, for virtually all of our history as a species, has taken place in the absence of written language. In fact, even the notion of the 'recency' of writing in the species is thoroughly deceptive, since the vast majority of the species didn't have access to it until less than a hundred and fifty years ago, when public education became generally accessible. For over 97 per cent of the time writing systems have existed, they've been the almost unique property of the privileged elites from royal, aristocratic and priestly classes.

Since you are reading this book, you are obviously highly literate. It is probably hard for you to imagine your life without reading and writing. But although we now take these skills so much for granted, we are still regularly judged on the basis of our command of different forms of literacy. Increasingly, education and job opportunities are closely tied to evaluations of candidates' skill as readers and writers, and the economic prospects for those who have not mastered desired forms are not ideal. And while the presence of print literacy, in physical and virtual forms, has greatly increased around the world, demands on written language abilities have also increased, and so it is still the case that over 770 million adults are categorized as illiterate, according to UNESCO figures.

Despite its obvious importance in our lives, however, we need to keep in mind that writing is a way of making language physical, a modality of expression like sign and speech, rather than constituting language itself. Of course, its durability and wider scope of audience give it many advantages as a modality, but these very features also make it a powerful tool of social coercion and control. And given that access to the modality has been so long in the hands of those with power, this leads to a belief that their way of representing the language *is* the language. In fact, written texts have only very recently had an influence on how the language faculty is transmitted in our species, and only in some societies. As children develop the spoken, signed and written language practices of those around them, many of them do so independently of the great dictionaries, style manuals and usage guides of their national elites. Which leads us to the next dead end.

# DEAD END 4: SOME GROUPS OF PEOPLE DON'T USE THEIR LANGUAGE PROPERLY

You can substitute several adjectives here for variations on the same myth. Among the most common: some ways of using your language are more beautiful, more complex, more pleasant, more efficient, more logical, more civilized . . . Many such beliefs arise naturally because of mistrust of 'the Other', but in large part language judgements follow from the notion of a 'standard' form of the language against which all other varieties can be measured – and found wanting. But in what sense do standard languages exist? They certainly seem to exist in forms of discourse such as newspaper editorials, national language policies and school textbooks. Standard forms of language are appealed to, often when people feel that their national or regional identities or interests are being threatened. Despite the social power of the belief, standard languages don't exist in the minds of individual speakers; rather, groups of speakers share different degrees of awareness of a set of conventions about what is acceptable, prestigious and desirable. Written language has played perhaps the most important role in 'fixing' these conventions as the basis for how others should write and speak.

An extension of this dead end is the belief that some *languages* are better than others, for example that some are harder or easier to learn, some are closer to God(s), some are more beautiful, more complex, more pleasant, more efficient, more logical, more civilized, etc. Descriptive linguistics and sociolinguistics are useful here to expose the patent nonsense of such beliefs, by comparing the same linguistic unit in different languages or dialects. This allows us to see how the same or a similar element of phonology, for example, can have different linguistic value in different languages, without requiring or entailing any measurement of efficiency, complexity, logic or aesthetics. The /l/ and /r/ sounds of English and many other languages are not differentiated by Chinese speakers, for example, just as the tonal features of Chinese can seem indistinguishable to speakers of atonal languages, such as English. And the 'illogical' double negative of many English dialects ('I ain't got none') is part of the 'standard' versions of French and Spanish.

One of the fundamental tenets of general linguistics is that such differences should not be attributed to the inherent superiority of one language or dialectal variety over another, but rather are rooted in issues of identity and feelings about other linguistic groups. As the linguist Dennis Preston puts it:

> Some groups are believed to be decent, hard-working, and intelligent (and so is their language or variety); some groups are believed to be laid-back, romantic, and devil-may-care (and so is their language or variety); some groups are believed to be lazy, insolent, and procrastinating (and so is their language or variety); some groups are believed to be hard-nosed, aloof, and unsympathetic (and so is their language or variety), and so on. . . . Germans are harsh; just listen to their harsh, guttural consonants; US Southerners are laid-back and lazy; just listen to their lazy, drawled vowels. Lower-status speakers are unintelligent; they don't even understand that two negatives make a positive, and so on.
>
> (Preston, 2002, pp. 40–41)

## DEAD END 5: SOME PEOPLE SPEAK THEIR LANGUAGE WITHOUT AN ACCENT

Everybody has an accent. It's just that we typically don't notice or think about our own or those of our immediate speech community until we have been exposed to new varieties. Moving across language boundaries, physically and virtually, people realize that not everyone sounds the same. For over a hundred years, voices have been projected across borders through broadcasting, and so the 'written standard' developed through control of literacy education has been able to dominate the airwaves as well as the printed page. In the UK, almost all official broadcast speech in the first six or seven decades of the twentieth century was in 'Received Pronunciation', the audible version of the Queen's English. If you didn't sound like them, you had an accent.

Some people, like Peter Sellers' character Inspector Clouseau in the *Pink Panther* movies, make us laugh with their impressions of 'foreign accents' (where a room with a phone is 'a rim with a fern'), and this pleasure in recognizing language differences may be universal. Foreign accents, unfortunately, are also considered by some native speakers to be a sign of general incompetence, lack of intelligence or unwillingness to assimilate into the majority group. Routinely, pronunciation differences, or people's perceptions of them, are associated with social identities, as Dennis Preston makes clear in the passage quoted on p. 9. The myth of the non-accent is also about power: those with power are the ones to emulate; they are the norm.

 ## DEAD END 6: THE WAY GROUPS USE THEIR LANGUAGE REFLECTS THEIR INTELLIGENCE

The IQ tests we all know about from the media, school and/or internet sites typically confuse general intelligence with vocabulary knowledge, competence in the grammar of the standard version of the language in which the test is presented, and familiarity with the linguistic discourse of tests. None of these attributes are present in the test-taker because of her intelligence. Intelligence is often construed so as to fit the characteristics of the standard version of a language. So, when intellectuals like Simone de Beauvoir and Jean-Paul Sartre use the double negative, considered part of 'standard' French ('Mon roman *ne* valait *rien*'), their intelligence is left unquestioned. On the other hand, working-class Londoners and African Americans saying something similar in their own dialects ('What I wrote was*n't* worth *nothing*') are judged to be of flawed intelligence (unless of course there's a market for it, like the Rolling Stones' 'I ca*n't* get *no* satisfaction', surely the most lucrative of all double negatives).

The popular conflation of intelligence with language ability is further confirmed by the fact that measures of language proficiency for second language learners, such as the International English Language Testing System (IELTS) or the Test of English as a Foreign Language (TOEFL), are used to predict their academic success, a variable commonly associated with intelligence. Because these tests are normed on native speakers of the 'standard' version of the language, it is probably more accurate to say that what is really being measured here is the forms of knowledge valued by the users of standard English, and that language is thus a key variable in social constructions of intelligence. Additionally, and importantly, the role of literacy and culture in these tests is fundamental to a full understanding of what is actually being measured.

# DEAD END 7: PEOPLE WITH TWO LANGUAGES ARE CONFUSED

Like their monolingual counterparts, many bilinguals may well be confused about lots of things. But not because they speak more than one language. This myth, reflected in a great deal of educational material in different periods, has at least two parts. On the cognitive side, there is the notion of the mind-as-finite-container, incapable of holding two or more languages simultaneously. There is a related notion that having to process more than one language slows us down or otherwise impedes the development of conventional forms of speaking. Since we can point to well-known polyglots such as Nelson Mandela (Xhosa, English, Afrikaans and Zulu) and numerous other examples of bilingual and multilingual people who are respected, prosperous and who learned multiple languages from an early age, it's clear that bilingual children's brains have no particular difficulty in negotiating language acquisition or the world beyond it. Indeed, a great deal of research in experimental psychology suggests that, once socioeconomic variables are controlled for, early bilingualism brings big cognitive advantages, including early mastery of some of the abilities involved in reading (see Chapter 6). This relates back, of course, to dead end 1, according to which language and thought are one and the same. If they're not, and language is separate from thought, then those who have two versions of the former have got two ways of acquiring, expressing and linguistically regulating the latter (see Figure 1.4).

There is also a sociolinguistic reason why this belief is a dead end. In bilingual communities, speakers know (at an unconscious level) which language to use and which contexts to use it in. Thus, Korean American children living in the US may use Korean at home and English at school, and a combination of the two languages in the broader community. Bilinguals who mix elements of more than one language are often denigrated, but upon closer inspection the speech of fluent **code-switchers** shows that switches from one to the other often follow highly systematic constraints that are consistent with core principles of both grammatical systems and do not happen because of 'incompetence' in one or both of the languages. Switching also follows socioculturally acceptable patterns depending on who's talking about what with whom. Not all bilinguals do it, but for those that do, code-switching is far from 'word salad'. Instead, the highly organized way in which it

**Code-switching** is the ability to form utterances using elements of multiple languages in real-time discourse, and the practice of doing so.

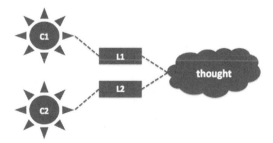

Figure 1.4    Two languages (L1 and L2) allow speakers to acquire concepts from different cultural contexts (C1 and C2) and to express and internally regulate one body of thought in two different ways

interweaves elements from two languages into a single coherent discourse resembles fusion cuisine in its most sophisticated form.

## DEAD END 8: LANGUAGES GET CONTAMINATED BY INFLUENCE FROM OTHER LANGUAGES

It's one thing, perhaps, to accept that individual speakers mix two or more languages, but surely the 'languages themselves' should maintain their own integrity? Is it right and good that the English words *laptop* or *roaming* are now regularly used in Swahili, Turkish, Spanish and so many other languages around the globe? That Russian words are still prevalent in Estonian and Georgian, twenty years after the fall of the Soviet Union? That Japanese has a huge number of Chinese words and that English vocabulary was fundamentally Latinized by Norman French in the first centuries of the last millennium? To most linguists these are absurd questions, because languages are not monoliths, pure 'Platonic' systems somehow separate from their spatio-temporal users and uses.

We've tried to show so far in this chapter that the following ways of thinking will allow us to make progress in applied linguistics, both as academics and as practitioners:

- there's no telepathy to directly share our thoughts, so concerted beliefs, concepts, actions and identities take shape largely through language;
- language is locally modulated, so we end up with different 'languages' which mould different sets of concerted beliefs, concepts, actions and identities;
- languages are mental systems that are independent of 'thoughts' in individual minds;
- they are at the same time social systems that exist independently of the named 'standard varieties' used by elite groups and reified in educated written usage;
- actual users of languages use their linguistic resources for their own purposes in their own ways, and may well be unaware of how these resources compare with the 'standard variety' (if indeed one has been promoted for their language).

What emerges from this view is that 'languages' are not monolithic systems existing as ideal systems in grammar books and dictionaries, but neither are they the products solely of individual minds. Rather, they are sociocognitive systems, mediating between isolated individuals and named groups living within and across regional or national borders. Because of this, their own borders, in both the minds of individuals and communities of speakers, are *very* fluid indeed. Believing that governments and academies can ring-fence a language from outside influence is as naive as believing that everyone outside the borders of Italy can be prevented from eating pizza, or that everyone outside the borders of China can be forced to celebrate the new year without fireworks.

And yet language groups feeling economic and other social pressures from others often try to legislate or otherwise mandate restrictions on the public use of forms of language that originate beyond their national borders. Famously, for example, signs in English were banned in French-speaking Quebec in 1977 after the electoral triumph of the Parti Québécois, as part of their campaign for separate sovereignty from the rest of Canada. Likewise, the 1994 Toubon Law in France legislated against other languages being used in government, commerce, education and broadcasting. Similar actions have been taken in Estonia to repel lexical invaders from Russia after independence from the USSR, and in Iran to replace foreign words with Persian ones after the Islamic revolution (Spolsky, 2004). All these efforts to maintain the fiction of monolithic languages share an underlying political intention: to assert national identity through national language.

## DEAD END 9: A NATION HAS, OR SHOULD HAVE, ONE LANGUAGE

It's no coincidence that the historic language of the English people is called *English*, that the main language of the Japanese people is called *Japanese* and that the principal language of the Icelandic people is called *Icelandic*. The fact that a single language can have different names according to who's speaking it should also come as no surprise: for example, Swedish, Norwegian and Danish are basically the same language, spoken in three separate nations called *Sweden*, *Norway* and *Denmark*. This state of affairs seems natural to the populations of countries like England, Japan, Iceland, Sweden, Norway and Denmark, where monolingualism is, on the whole, the norm. Conversely, in many of the nations of Africa, Asia and Oceania, where the imposition of European monolingualism has been impeded by the much greater linguistic diversity of peoples living in these formerly colonized regions, this dead end is much better signposted.

But for most of the former colonial powers, there is a major confusion between language, nationality and place in the minds of linguists and laypeople alike. Thus, English people are English speakers, foreigners are speakers of foreign languages, and each country has its language. The myth is so strong that it's perfectly natural for linguistics students to write sentences like the following (taken from real under-graduate essays):

1   Only around half of some European countries can actually speak another language, so how do they communicate with other countries?
2   Different countries have alternative rules of grammar.

Such imprecision is very easy to commit, and we the authors are often guilty of it. We are in good company, too. David Crystal in the UK, for example, states (2002, p. 1): 'No one knows how many foreign people have learned English to a reasonable standard of fluency – or to any standard at all, for that matter.' (By foreign people, he presumably means non-native speakers, which would include UK citizens whose first language is British Sign Language or Bengali). And Elaine Chaika in the USA (2008, p. 28) writes as part of a textbook exercise: 'Listen to a foreign person speak English, and write down every word for which the English word sounds foreign because the wrong [speech sound] was used.' (We're assuming she doesn't have Canadians in mind.)

The myth that each nation has only one language is a rather recent one, beginning with the rise of the nation state after the Middle Ages. Clearly tied to the political and economic identities of post-Renaissance Europe (see Barbour and

Carmichael, 2000), language became an important policy tool in the drive to centralization of power in the new nation states and to successful domination in the colonization and administration of Africa, Asia, the Americas and Oceania. The myth, interpreted as a policy whereby a prestigious language was elevated over others that were denigrated or banned outright, led to dire consequences for minority groups in the home countries and for the established populations of the new colonies. Despite its durability, the future of this myth is uncertain given the increased contact among previously unconnected groups of language users through new media (e.g. television, movies and music videos), digital information exchange (through the internet, e-mail, chat, social networking, etc.) and massive surges in migration.

 **DEAD END 10: LANGUAGES EXIST INDEPENDENTLY OF USERS AND USES**

All of these dead ends lead to one big bridge to nowhere: the belief that English and all other languages have objective existence outside our imaginations. From the belief that English is *out there* it follows that:

- 'it' exists in the *Oxford English Dictionary*, in good literature, on the BBC, in the mouths of educated people;
- children can have different degrees of success at acquiring 'it' and many people don't acquire 'it' properly;
- you think with 'it', so if you haven't acquired 'it' properly you'll be less intelligent;
- if your mind shares 'it' with another language you'll be confused, and mixing 'it' with another language sullies 'it', and possibly you;
- 'it' belongs to England and, by inheritance, also to Australia, Canada, New Zealand, the USA and other national communities of native speakers;
- 'it' can treated as a tangible good, a commodity, to be exported, promoted, marketed and sold in order to advance certain interests.

We'll contest all these views in the chapters to come, but we'll also continually bear in mind that most language users (the clients of applied linguistics), hold them to be self-evident; and, furthermore, that the beliefs of users can have profound effects on language *uses*. Finally, we'll remember that all those who work professionally with language, including linguists, will succumb to the lure of these attractive avenues of belief . . . even if they do lead nowhere except to fewer spirited discussions at family holidays, the dinner table, the pub or the coffee house.

## 1.3 APPLIED LINGUISTICS

We should perhaps first clarify that *general linguistics* is different from 'applied linguistics'. General linguistics describes and theorizes about language and languages, and is an umbrella term for a number of sub-disciplines. General linguistics analyses the sound systems, grammars, vocabularies and discourse-organizing principles and practices of different languages, classifying various features, and identifying universal patterns as well as distinctive localized phenomena (this is the province of mainstream **descriptive** or **theoretical linguistics**). General linguistics also explores how these systems vary in time and space and context of use, and tries to describe and explain their acquisition and cognitive functioning. **Sociolinguistic** research explores variation, by collecting and analysing data from different groups of users and in different situations, including bi- and multilinguals. **Psycholinguistic** experiments try to tap into mind-internal processes of learning, memory and use of one or more languages. General linguists use a range of methods, including speakers' intuitions, language data collected from informants, non-linguistic data which correlates with language use (e.g. brain scans or translation times) and the analysis of massive computerized samples of language expression in writing and speech (**corpus linguistics**).

That, extremely briefly, is general linguistics. You might think that a definition of applied linguistics would follow on quite naturally as another sub-discipline of general linguistics, presumably like applied physics follows from pure physics, where, for example, the latter can be used in seismology and engineering for the very practical purposes of earthquake detection and damage limitation. Hence, applied physics could be defined as 'physics applied for practical use'. By analogy, then, the term 'applied linguistics' should refer to the application of general linguistics to practical use in additional language teaching, translation, speech therapy, etc. And indeed the findings, descriptions and theoretical models of general linguistics were originally so applied (almost exclusively to language learning and teaching). But that's not what a good many present-day applied linguists believe their discipline is about, or what they themselves actually do.

For many, applied linguistics is a sister (rather than a sub-)discipline of general linguistics. It is 'applied' in the 'applied physics' sense in that it deals with 'practical use', but it is not limited to applying the findings of general linguistics. Henry Widdowson (2000) has called early conceptualizations of the field 'linguistics applied', placing the emphasis on (general) *linguistics*. For the moment, let's use the term 'autonomous applied linguistics' for the contrasting conceptualization of applied linguistics as a sister discipline to general linguistics. We should point out, though, that despite the impression given by the many pages dedicated to the relationship in applied linguistics books and journals, not all teachers and researchers in the area have been preoccupied with the field's legacy of association with general linguistics: indeed, many *have* no association with that field, don't see a sharp division between them and/or don't think it matters much. Christopher Brumfit (1995, p. 27) takes the focus off linguistics in his definition of the field as 'the theoretical and empirical investigation of real-world problems in which language is a central issue', and we think that's a sensible move.

Autonomous applied linguistics is a discipline concerned with the role language and languages play in perceived problems of communication, social identity, education, health, economics, politics and justice, *and* in the development of ways to remediate or resolve these problems. Scholars in autonomous applied linguistics address an increasingly broad range of language-related issues. Here's a random sample of four topics to illustrate the scope of the subject:

- the assessment of language proficiency and consequent social processes (e.g. identity construction) in sign language learners;

**Descriptive linguistics** documents and describes what people say, sign and write, and the grammatical, lexical and phonological systems they use to do so.

**Theoretical linguistics** builds theories about the nature and limits of grammatical, lexical and phonological systems.

**Sociolinguistics** is the study of language in social contexts.

**Psycholinguistics** is the study of the psychology of language and the nexus of language and mind/brain.

**Corpus linguistics** is the creation and analysis of (normally large, computerized) collections of language composed of actual texts (speech and writing), and their application to problems in descriptive and applied linguistics.

- the analysis of the social, professional and economic impact of IT resources for translators;
- the study of treatment and educational options for those minority language children who also happen to have language deficits;
- the development of literacy norms for use in dictionaries as part of actions to maintain endangered languages.

Because of this broad scope, autonomous applied linguistics draws on theory, findings and method from many other scholarly fields aside from general linguistics, including education, anthropology, sociology, public policy, health sciences, information technology and others. 'Autonomous applied linguistics' thus differs from 'linguistics applied' largely in terms of the scope of its objectives, methods and inputs (see Figure 1.5). Note that the autonomous view actually subsumes linguistics applied. Since this book is designed to map the whole territory, we'll adopt the broader view, and – now we've got the inevitable academic tribalism out of the way – we'll henceforth drop the 'autonomous' tag.

But if you ask ten applied linguists to write down the major component areas of their field, each list will most likely differ from all the others, to a greater or lesser extent, in both contents and ordering. Probably everyone would include additional language education in some guise, and for some this area would be the principal one, around which others (like language testing, language for specific purposes, bilingual education) would naturally cluster. Some would include areas which for others would be part of general linguistics proper, like sociolinguistics and psycholinguistics. Some might include (or exclude) typical applied linguistic tools and resources, such as corpus linguistics and discourse analysis. Some might list all areas which may be informed by linguistics, such as language pathology and forensic linguistics; others might see these areas as only peripheral, especially where scholars from these areas do not consider themselves to be applied linguists. Our choices are not the same as those of many other mappers of the field, given

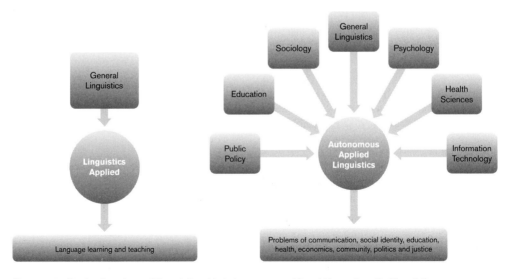

**Figure 1.5**  Contrasting views of the relationship between general linguistics and applied linguistics

our problem- and practice-oriented conception of it. For example, we see theories of second language acquisition and of language impairment as part of the domain of general linguistics, because they are not 'about' solutions to problems and associated professional practice.

We could spend more time here describing historical and contemporary top-down debates on the extent of the territory, where to draw borders on the map, and how to label the resulting parts and their dependencies (see, for example, Part One of Cook and North, 2010; Davies, 2007; Schmitt and Celce-Murcia, 2010; Waters, 2009). However, we are interested here in an approach to applied linguistics that 'disinvents', or at least calls into question, some of the assumptions of previous approaches (e.g. the centrality of either cognitive or sociocultural concerns to the exclusion of the other; the privileging of academic agendas over practitioner and client needs; the balkanization of areas within the field). Therefore, we now draw on our own experience and that of our colleagues, as well as scholarship in the field, to identify five essential ingredients of applied linguistics as we currently see it. These ingredients are evident in every chapter of the book, and in Chapter 14 the experiences of five practitioner colleagues provide examples of them in action.

**Centrality of client needs**    First and foremost, applied linguistics is concerned with individuals' and groups' language-related *needs*. We have, so far, used the words *problem*, *need* and *issue* in an unprincipled fashion, but we recognize that they are not synonyms. *Problem* clearly has the potential to stigmatize when associated with the people involved in the matter at hand, so we use the word *need* here. But problems are definitely addressed (and sometimes solved) in applied linguistics; furthermore, the term is regularly used in many sub-fields of the discipline, so we will be using it in the chapters to come. *Issue* is problematic. For some speakers of English, the word now means the same as *problem*, but is thought to be less stigmatizing. For others, an issue is an abstract question or matter which may be discussed but doesn't necessarily need solving. We use it in this more general sense throughout the book.

Brumfit (1995) reminds us that the identification and definition of a 'real-world' problem must be informed by the people who experience it: only then does it become a need. For an applied linguist to claim that something is a problem thus requires consultation with the people involved in the problem. Disagreements about what 'counts' as a problem are extremely likely, even (or especially?) between people involved *in* the problem. So the question 'Is this is a problem?' needs to be answered by the 'clients' involved, as much as by the academics who analyse their situations and the practitioners who deal with them. Furthermore, Brumfit reminds us that applied linguists should not make assumptions about the relationship between a client's problem and the language resources and practices which co-occur with it. Defining the *nature* of the problem, as well as deciding whether there actually *is* a problem, is a process which should be informed by the experiences of the people who are involved in it.

The *raison d'être* of applied linguistics is its promise of a real-world response to the problems it tackles. Applied linguistics is, above all, a problem-solving discipline, and while any project in applied linguistics may *begin* with a description or empirical investigation of the role of language in a real-world problem, it should aim to *end* with the planning, testing and evaluation of a potential solution. This, we believe, should be conducted in close collaboration with the people who are experiencing the problem or whose needs are to be met.

***Pragmatic orientation***    Second, applied linguistics is *pragmatically oriented*, drawing on whatever expertise is necessary to address the problems identified. This means that applied linguistics is not associated with a particular set of ideals or political beliefs (that is, it isn't bound to any particular **ideology**); nor is it restricted by a particular theory of knowledge or methodological paradigm (that is, it isn't bound to any particular **epistemology**). This doesn't, of course, mean that applied linguists don't or shouldn't have strongly held ideological or epistemological commitments (we actually think they do and should). Or that we wish to marginalize strands of applied linguistics which *are* so committed (such as **critical applied linguistics**; see also Chapter 9 on critical pedagogy and Chapter 4 on critical discourse analysis). Finally, it doesn't mean that we think applied linguistic issues and practices are ideologically neutral or can be investigated in an epistemologically neutral fashion. We see it as part of the work of applied linguistics to expose and explore the ideological and epistemological commitments and positions inherent in all our language-related beliefs, states of mind and social activity.

***Social and cognitive embeddedness***    Third, applied linguistics recognizes the inevitable *social embeddedness* of all language needs, but at the same time acknowledges that language exists in sociocultural as well as cognitive spaces simultaneously. A focus on one of these aspects can be useful for some specific purposes in applied linguistics, of course. Take language and speech pathology. If you want to diagnose and design treatment for a language comprehension problem in someone who has suffered a head injury, you might need to conduct a carefully controlled psycholinguistic test as part of the assessment procedure, to establish what kinds of words or structures the person can/does understand (rather than simply hoping to observe them in interaction with others). Conversely, the way the mind works might seem completely irrelevant for a language planner tasked with developing policy and resources for citizens and public services in areas with large minority language communities. But the person recovering from the head injury will want practical advice about coping with social situations; members of her family and community will need advice on how to support and interact with her. In other words, the pathologist must be able to appreciate the person in their social context and not just the language deficit. And the language planner should, conversely, be aware of some of the tenacious, dead-end thinking about multilingual minds that we explored in section 1.1.

***Role-shifting and collaboration***    The fourth ingredient we see as special in contemporary applied linguistics is its *role-shifting* and *collaborative* nature. As we've already suggested, applied linguists read about theory and practice in a wide range of disciplines (those in Figure 1.5 and more), but, moreover, they actually work with a broader group of 'stakeholders' than their colleagues in general linguistics and other, less 'applied', academic fields. They work with:

■   *practitioners*, that is, those whose primary activity is undertaken directly with clients in a professional (non-academic) capacity, as speech–language pathologists, language teachers, lexicographers, interpreters, etc.;

**Ideologies** are shifting and sometimes contradictory sets of ideas about power and social structures that shape the way we view the world, including the ways we use and talk about language.

**Epistemology** is the study of forms of knowledge and how we come to know them.

**Critical applied linguistics** is the practice of applied linguistics grounded in a concern for addressing and resolving problems of inequality.

- *client populations* (as we dub them in Chapter 3) and the communities they live and work in;
- *colleagues* in related academic disciplines;
- *students* of applied linguistics and related academic disciplines, including practitioners in continuing professional development.

As the last point here makes explicit, we are not necessarily talking about separate groups of people here, but rather of *roles*. Many will play more than one of these roles and, additionally, may or may not identify themselves as general or applied linguists. Some may be all at once. Hence, collaboration in applied linguistics can be intrapersonal, between different activities of the same individual: theory-building before breakfast; theory interpretation, mediation and application until lunchtime; professional practice in the afternoon; and then on to your evening class.

**Mode of enquiry**    Finally, when the four essential ingredients listed above are combined, what happens? We suggest that the field of applied linguistics resulting from such a combination is much more than simply a collection of topics (lexicography, language pathology, translation, etc.). In fact, we would argue that contemporary applied linguistics is not so much a *field* as *a way of exploring*; it's a process, a 'mode of enquiry' for working with language-related problems and needs. By mode of enquiry we mean that our four ingredients – (1) starting and finishing with our clients' needs, (2) being pragmatic, responsive and critically aware, (3) considering both the social and cognitive nature of language, and (4) collaborating on the design and evaluation of solutions – provide a way of thinking and acting as an applied linguist that is fundamentally richer and ultimately more useful than saying, for example, 'I'm an additional language teacher' or 'I'm a translator'. As with any mode of enquiry, thinking of our practices as connected with those of other applied linguists is a means of expanding the resources available for teaching and learning within and without formal classroom settings (González *et al.*, 2005).

## 1.4  BOTTOM-UP APPLIED LINGUISTICS

It's important to stress that, in presenting this characterization of applied linguistics to students and practitioners, we do not mean to say prescriptively what practice should look like in every setting. In our experience, a great deal of the teaching (and at least some of the learning!) that has taken place in applied linguistics study involves a top-down transmission model, from professor to student; from academic and scholarly centres of power to institutions and individuals on the peripheries of academia; and from native speakers of languages of wider communication to those who have learned them for purposes of education. Our goal is therefore to be more descriptive and, we hope, more inclusive than prescriptive. We mean to give a sense of what contemporary applied linguistic practice around the world looks like to us, but we acknowledge that our map is one projection among many, just as the different maps in Figures 1.1, 1.6 and 1.7 all give very different but equally legitimate views of the Earth's continents.

The approach we adopt in the chapters to come seeks to capitalize on this diversity of views and practices. We argue that an applied linguistics that fosters

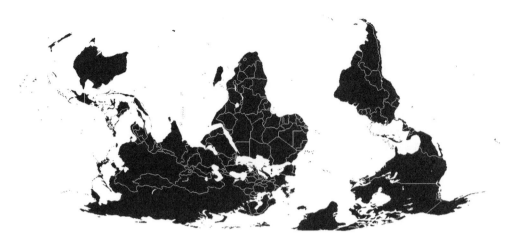

Figure 1.6    Reversed world map (Source: Wikimedia Commons)

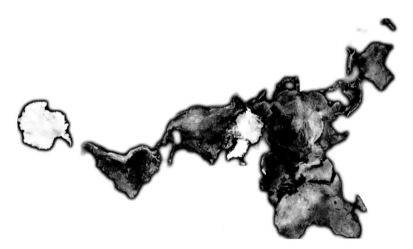

Figure 1.7    World map using the Dymaxion (or Fuller) projection (Source: Wikimedia Commons)

unbridgeable polarities and intellectual territoriality compromises the discipline's successful dynamism and hybridity. Hence we propose that our common enterprise will benefit from full and open recognition of the dual social and cognitive realities of language, full engagement with colleagues in sister areas of applied linguistics and in other disciplines, and thorough exposition and exploration of all our ideological and epistemological commitments and positions.

activities

1 We've argued that the dead ends described in this chapter are wide-spread and persistent. But don't take our word for it. To discover whether these folk understandings of language are operating in the minds of people in your context, conduct an informal survey by converting the dead ends into ten statements and asking people you interact with to register their agreement or disagreement with each. You could also ask your respondents to provide an example that supports their thinking. Compare your results with what your classmates or others have found. If you are working in the same geographic region or in similar areas of applied linguistics, do you find similar patterns of belief about language?

2 As a follow-up activity to activity 1, analyse a language artefact (for example: a primary school language arts or literacy textbook; an English as an additional language textbook and any teachers' notes accompanying it; a language test; a school language policy). Can you identify any examples of 'dead-end thinking'? What problems might these assumptions produce in application with the intended clients?

3 In this chapter we've provided a particular view of applied linguistics. How does this view fit with your previous understanding and perhaps formal study of linguistics and language? Which notions do you find most surprising? Which do you think will be most useful for your current or intended area of practice? If you are using this as a course book, you might want to save your answers to this question and revisit them at the end of the course to see how your thinking changes as a result of thinking with us about applied linguistics.

## FURTHER READING

Bauer, L. and Trudgill, P. (1998). *Language myths*. Harmondsworth: Penguin.

Coffin, C., Lillis, T. and O'Halloran, K. (eds) (2010). *Applied linguistics methods: A reader*. London: Routledge.

Cook, G. and North, S. (eds) (2010). *Applied linguistics in action: A reader*. London: Routledge.

Davies, A. and Elder, C. (eds) (2004). *The handbook of applied linguistics*. Oxford: Blackwell.

Hall, C. J. (2005). *An introduction to language and linguistics: Breaking the language spell*. London: Continuum.

Pinker, S. (1994). *The language instinct*. New York: HarperCollins.

# Language in everyday use

We start mapping the field of applied linguistics with a bird's-eye view of the general terrain, which we've organized into four chapters, each of which explores a different dimension of language in everyday use, and each of which highlights issues which are at the heart of the sub-fields of the discipline described in Parts B and C.

Chapter 2, on *language variation*, tackles the troublesome truisms that we all speak different versions of the language(s) we share with others, and that these versions differ in different ways on different occasions and with different people. This variation in structure and use is invisible to most of us, most of the time, and is at the root of many of the problems applied linguists are called upon to address. The different individuals and groups experiencing these problems are the topic of Chapter 3, on *key populations*. Here we count some of the ways that language is implicated in the everyday lives of all of us, whoever we are and whatever our circumstances may be, and we forefront some of the significant features of 'client' groups that applied linguists need to be aware of and sensitive to.

Chapter 4 is dedicated to a method – we might call it also a philosophical tool – which has the potential to penetrate the meanings and assumptions *behind* everyday language use. *Discourse analysis*, although not the only way to do applied linguistics, is used in most of the sub-fields of the discipline, and is relevant to all of them. We outline in this chapter the various ways in which it may be used to bring to the surface the unconscious beliefs and practices, as well as the more deliberate purposes, underlying talk and text. The final dimension of everyday language use that we explore in this part relates to the extent to which we can influence it. Chapter 5, dealing with *language policy and planning*, recognizes that as students and scholars in an applied discipline we are inevitably involved in making *decisions* about language. But our role and influence in the linguistically modulated world around us is (alas!) limited, to say the least. It is, of course, *non*-specialists who make most of the language-related decisions, all the way from immigrant parents deciding which language to use with their children to legislators voting on funding for bilingual education. All these decisions affect the everyday language practices of ordinary people. We argue in this chapter that applied linguists from every sub-field must seek to influence, understand and inform the decision-makers, and must ensure that their own decisions and advice on policy are responsive to the needs of the populations affected by them.

There are some common themes in all of the chapters in Part A. One is the danger of 'monolithic' thinking: about language, languages and linguistics. We stress throughout these chapters that although the *sociocultural* interfaces and manifestations of language are often the primary sites in which applied linguistic work is relevant, we must acknowledge and address also the *cognitive* underpinning of all language use, even when these are less accessible to us and have no, or only a superficial, place in many scholarly approaches. The broad approach we take in Part A also suggests we need to abandon, or at least problematize, monolithic views of languages – questioning the objective reality of English and all the other named languages, and embracing, instead, a conception of language hybridity, played out simultaneously within individual minds and across socially constructed communities of practice, identity and belief.

In advocating such a *plurilithic* approach to language(s), we are inevitably and transparently articulating a *critical* perspective on the non-linguistic forces which mould everyday language use: essentially, the sociopsychological motives of power, prestige and identity which hijack the language capacity for their (our) own ends. In Chapter 2 we demonstrate how these factors determine the values we attach to our own and others' ways of speaking, and how these values, in turn, influence the ways in which the clients described in Chapter 3 (and often more powerful outside agents) treat their diverse language practices and needs. Chapter 4 presents a flawed but still potent antidote to the often harmful assumption that language 'says what it means', independently of the diversity of its users and of the circumstances in which it is used. The critical strand continues in Chapter 5, where we address the tensions between policy-makers and policy-proposers, between the privileged and the marginalized, between those 'in the know' and those 'on the outside'.

More mundanely, perhaps, the four chapters in Part A illustrate the diverse nature of the data and evidence which inform the various sub-fields of applied linguistics, but at the same time they demonstrate the fundamental unity of purpose between what may appear, on the surface, to be a heterogeneous collection of callings. So, for example, our understanding of variation in language in Chapter 2 comes from meticulous linguistic descriptions of language data, as well as from surveys of attitudes and ethnographies of speaking. Chapters 3 and 4 juxtapose scholarship from a broad range of cross-disciplinary perspectives in the former, with a common, but technically and philosophically diverse, focus on one linguistic interface level (*discourse*) in the latter. The topic of Chapter 5, policy and planning, is characterized by methodogical eclecticism: clients and applied linguists alike must use the methods and data they have available in order to make the most effective decisions and monitor their effectiveness.

So, in each chapter, we:

- critically examine a central dimension of language in everyday use which is relevant to applied linguistic scholarship and practice;
- identify and explain key concepts, terms and references;
- provide representative examples of applied linguistic theory and practice;
- emphasize the attitudes, abilities and roles of applied linguists in the consideration of these issues.

At the end of each chapter, we suggest a series of activities designed primarily to encourage you to reflect on, and engage with, what we've had to say, from the different perspectives that each reader brings to the text. We know that each reader is different, so we invite you to adapt each activity to your own circumstances, interests and abilities, and to visit our companion website to share your ideas and check for more detailed content.

**CHAPTER 2**

# Language variation

Correct spelling, correct punctuation, correct grammar. Hundreds of itsy-bitsy rules
for itsy-bitsy people.

(Robert Pirsig, 1974)

Most of the 'dead ends' discussed in Chapter 1 are rooted in our unfortunate inability
to recognize that languages always exist in a multitude of forms. We see them as
single objects, like rocks, but they are in fact more like sandy beaches, rain clouds
or galaxies: collections with no one central point and no sharply defined borders.
Our misperception leads to firmly held beliefs about how language(s) may be used
and abused, and to intractable positions when these beliefs are questioned or
threatened. But it's a palpable fact that we don't all speak the same way, even when
we happen to share what we regard as the same language. The variation in and
between languages has profound but often hidden consequences for the whole
spectrum of enterprises we call applied linguistics, only some of which have begun
to be understood and revealed. In this chapter we look more closely at the notion
of language variation and varieties, asking how some of them come to be regarded
as 'standard' while others are viewed as 'non-standard' or even 'incorrect'. We'll also
address the distinction between native and non-native varieties of a language,
and issues of language authority and linguistic insecurity. Implicit in all this are
underlying issues of power, prestige and identity, making language variation one
of the thorniest issues applied linguists deal with.

    The chapter is organized as follows. In the opening sections we tackle the
'monolithic myth' which dominates folk belief, namely that there is, or ought to be,
one correct, standard language, from which departure is inevitable but lamentable.
We discuss the identification of variation in language with the social construction
and valuation of one's own and especially *others'* identities in section 2.1, and briefly
illustrate the main dimensions of monolingual variation in 2.2. We then turn to the
process of standardization and the distinction between 'standard' and 'non-standard'
varieties in 2.3. Of particular interest to many applied linguists, and increasingly
relevant in our ever more globalized world, is the newly contested ground of 'non-
native' varieties, and this is the focus of 2.4, where the topic of **World Englishes**
is introduced as a strand which will be developed throughout the book. The notion
of linguistic insecurity, fostered by ideologies of intolerance for language variation,
is discussed in 2.5, and its role in the very survival of linguistic diversity is stressed.
In the last couple of sections, we present an applied linguistic view of variation as
a function of situated practice (2.6) and close with a comment on what we think
may be *the* key responsibility for all applied linguists (2.7).

**World Englishes**
refers to the
phenomenon of
English as an
international
language, spoken in
different ways by
perhaps one-third of
the world's population
spread across every
continent. The term
also indicates a view
of English which
embraces diversity
and questions the
assumption that
contemporary native
speakers have
inherent stewardship
of, or competence in,
the language.

## 2.1 LANGUAGE VARIATION AND SOCIAL JUDGEMENT

In introductory linguistics classes around the world, first-year students undergo the ritual process of what we might call *de-prescriptivization* (or, more candidly, 'linguistic reprogramming'). Outside linguistics and applied linguistics, the unquestioned assumption is that there is *one* form of the language(s) of the state, the so-called 'standard' form, variation from which may be inevitable but is generally undesirable and must be kept in check. It is the job of schools and other (official or self-appointed) guardians to *prescribe* the 'standard' forms and *proscribe* the 'non-standard' ones. Rather perversely to some lay commentators, general linguistics seeks to *describe* linguistic systems and how they vary through space, time and context, without judging the so-called 'varieties' corresponding to each different system. Routinely, the process of de-prescriptivization is at most only a partial success, and more often it fails completely. We introduced in Chapter 1 the notion of the Language Spell (Hall, 2005) as a metaphor for our incapacity to penetrate the sociocognitive reality of language: that it's actually located in six billion brains, interacting in dynamic and fluid communities, and not in a few thousand grammar books, dictionaries and usage guides. We are normally impotent before the power of the Spell, and even when we do become aware of it, as students of linguistics (and linguists ourselves), it tests us mightily. Take, for example, English in England: the almost universally held belief is that there is *one* English language, against which other national varieties (spoken in the USA, Australia, Scotland, etc.) are measured and (mostly) tolerated; in comparison with which regional dialects are treasured, ridiculed or deplored; and foreigners' attempts to reproduce which are judged correct or (more often than not) *wrong* (see Figure 2.1).

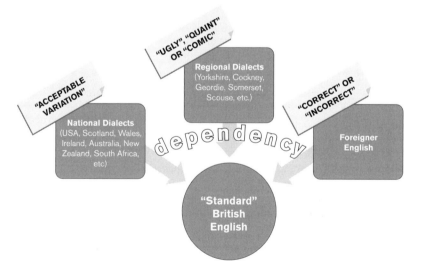

Figure 2.1  'Standard British English' and some varieties supposedly deriving from or dependent on it

This is the myth of 'Monolithic English' (Hall, 2005, p. 252; Pennycook, 2007), which we can summarize in the following two folk maxims:

- 'the' English language is a monolithic social entity, characterized by the 'standard variety' spoken by educated native speakers;
- English learners learn and English teachers teach 'the' English language, analogous to the way 'proper' table manners may be learned, taught and prescribed.

The power and pervasive damage of the myth can't be underestimated. It underlies our conceptions of social value and the power of class and privilege. The quotation from Robert Pirsig about the pettiness of 'correct English' in the epigraph on p. 25 continues as follows:

> It was all table manners, not derived from any sense of kindness or decency or humanity, but originally from an egotistic desire to look like gentlemen and ladies. Gentlemen and ladies had good table manners and spoke and wrote grammatically. It was what identified one with the upper classes.
>
> (Pirsig, 1974, p. 183)

And with the educated, reading classes, who should know better: in a letter to a newspaper, a North Carolinian upset with the linguist Walt Wolfram's recommendations to teachers working with language minority children, fulminated: 'To not know the forms of proper English usage is ignorance; to know and then still not use them because of your desire to be "culturally diverse" is attempted murder upon the English language' (quoted in Wolfram *et al.*, 1999, p. 30). The effects of the monolithic myth and the associated belief in a 'standard' language are so much more important than the effects of bad table manners, as the next section, on authority in language, shows.

## Authority in language

The notion of language standards is closely tied to the notion of public or private 'authorities' that set and seek to maintain those standards, however arbitrary and far from the 'linguistic facts' they may be. Such efforts are typically not really about language at all, but rather about establishing or protecting the power of a group through the language or variety they speak. The monolithic myth underlying such efforts holds that language is essentially a static entity rather than a dynamic system which is capable of – indeed, dependent on – constant change and diversification. Policies and recommendations by language academies to exclude foreign words from public use, and workplace language policies promoting one language over others, are essentially attempts to gain or maintain power and control over individuals and groups who are perceived as threatening and whose language or variety is thus a target for public criticism and even legislation. Like Ron Unz, the anti-bilingual education activist in the US, language authorities are often self-nominated, legislating norms for the rest of us. Rosina Lippi-Green (1997, p. 73) describes how rules about 'standard' language can be used to justify restrictions on less powerful

 www.2.1

**Table 2.1**  Lippi-Green's 'language subordination model' (Source: adapted from Lippi-Green, 1997, p. 68)

| Language subordination process | Message |
| --- | --- |
| Language is mystified | You can never hope to comprehend the difficulties and complexities of your mother tongue without expert guidance. |
| Authority is claimed | Talk like me/us. We know what we are doing because we have studied language, because we write well. |
| Misinformation is generated | That usage you are so attached to is inaccurate. The variant I prefer is superior on historical, aesthetic or logical grounds. |
| Non-mainstream language is trivialized | Look how cute, how homey, how funny. |
| Conformers are held up as positive examples | See what you can accomplish if you only try, how far you can get if you see the light. |
| Explicit promises are made | Employers will take you seriously; doors will open. |
| Threats are made | No one important will take you seriously; doors will close. |
| Non-conformers are vilified or marginalized | See how willfully stupid, arrogant, unknowing, uninformed and/or deviant and unrepresentative these speakers are. |

peoples' individuality and their right to participate on equal terms, and calls the criticism of some accents 'the last back door to discrimination' (see section 2.2 below for more on accent). She describes a process of language subordination by which certain varieties become thought of – even by the people who speak them – as ugly or illogical or incoherent. The process operates, she argues, through the repetition of messages in the education and judicial systems (Table 2.1), the broadcast and print media, the entertainment industry and the corporate sector (Lippi-Green, 1997, p. 68).

And even linguists fall for the myth, or at least fail to acknowledge the difficulties associated with it. In his pivotal work *Aspects of the Theory of Syntax*, for example, Noam Chomsky (in)famously posited 'an ideal speaker-listener, in a completely homogenous speech-community, who knows its language perfectly and is unaffected by . . . grammatically irrelevant conditions . . . in applying his knowledge of the language in actual performance' (Chomsky, 1965, p. 3). Accounts of English and other languages in Chomskyan theoretical linguistics are largely constructed from data sets which really don't represent the rich linguistic resources deployed by the majority of their speakers spread across vast heterogeneous networks of user groups and uses. The 'intuitions of grammaticality' collected to form data sets for analysis (by asking questions such as 'How does *John's seeming to be intelligent* sound to you?') are provided by educated language users whose deliberate judgements are naturally and inevitably constrained by socialization processes. In the case of English at least, these processes are the cultural legacy of centuries of explicit and implicit privileging of certain ways of using and thinking about language, especially as it's been codified through written texts.

Grave as these methodological shortcomings may be, however, it's unwise to dismiss Chomsky's mentalist approach to language out of hand. An acknowledgement of the cognitive basis of linguistic systems requires the kind of descriptive detail and theoretical rigour that will allow accounts of language to be compatible with theory in cognitive neuropsychology, as applied, for example, to language disorders like aphasia (see Chapter 13). Such an approach can provide sophisticated tools to explore variation between individuals, and some descriptive linguists following the Chomskyan tradition use dialect and 'non-standard' data as a matter of course (e.g. Henry, 1995; Green, 1998; Kayne, 2000; Mesthrie and Bhatt, 2008, ch. 3). Others specifically highlight the potential contribution of Chomskyan theory to an understanding of 'socially realistic linguistics' (Wilson and Henry, 1998). But for the most part it has been sociolinguists who have focused on variation within a language, albeit concentrating on the level of groups, rather than individual minds. One of the pioneers of modern sociolinguistics, William Labov, acknowledged the theoretical and empirical richness of Chomsky's approach, while exposing its methodological limitations (e.g. Labov, 1972, ch. 8). He even attempted to modify Chomskyan-style grammatical rules by incorporating probabilities of occurrence as influenced by non-linguistic variables (such as gender and class). But this notion of 'variable rule' proved to be ultimately unworkable in the opinion of most sociolinguists (Wardhaugh, 2006, p. 187). The work of Labov and others extending linguistic theory beyond the analytical ideal of homogeneity in the speech community has had a profound influence on the development of applied linguistics, and underlies much of the thinking mapped out in the chapters to come.

## Language judgements

Linguists' use of the term **variety** (e.g. Ferguson, 1971) to describe a linguistic system shared by a geographically or socially defined group (covering both dialect and language) reflects the centrality of the notion of variation in language study. For prescriptivists, the term 'standard variety' must look like quite an oxymoron, given that *standard* suggests an accepted norm but *variety* suggests that languages come in different versions. Furthermore, the word *variety* suggests, and rightfully so, that the standard is really just another dialect, at least linguistically speaking. In Chapter 1 we said that the notion of a single standard version of a language is a dead end for applied linguists, but it remains a powerful one in the minds of language users. Thus, while the differences between varieties can be empirically described by linguists, users imbue these differences simultaneously with two fundamentally different forms of meaning: linguistic and social significance. Here is an example of these different interpretations, based on a fragment of a variety that greatly surprised one of the authors who as a child moved from the Midwestern state of Michigan to Maine in New England on the East Coast of the USA.

> *Smith*:          I really liked that movie.
> *Maine resident*:  So didn't I. It was wicked good.

Like the young Smith, readers unfamiliar with this variety can probably negotiate the unfamiliar linguistic expression and understand that the Maine resident here is actually agreeing with Smith that the movie was a good one rather than expressing disagreement. Embedded in non-linguistic and other contextual clues, this example of 'non-standard' use of *didn't* doesn't cause any breakdown in

In linguistics, a **variety** refers to the systematic ways in which an identified group of speakers uses a language's sounds, structures and senses. The term allows linguists to recognize the distinctiveness of a group's shared linguistic system and usage, without making claims about its status as a 'full language' or 'just a dialect'.

 **www.2.2**

communication. As is typical of instances of intralinguistic dialect contact, speakers work out the message without much difficulty. Note another question raised by such contact: just who is speaking with appropriate norms here? The young Smith, whose usage may be closer to the variety this book is written in, or his counterpart, into whose linguistic territory Smith has just moved? Thus, we could argue that all varieties function as the standard (the norm for the context) somewhere, usually in the geographic location(s) or social contexts in which the speakers who speak them are situated, but also in text-types or in cyberspace.

**www.2.3**

At the same time as speakers successfully negotiate a linguistic message, we are also unconsciously assigning social meaning. In the case of our 'wicked good' moviegoers, the Maine resident may have wondered why Smith sounded like a teacher or someone on the television news, and Smith no doubt formed some opinions of his own about his interlocutor's social background and identity. If the teenage Hall and Wicaksono were to join the conversation at this point, speaking about *films* as opposed to movies, the other kids might assign them class- and education-related identities based solely on their 'posh' or 'cool' British accents. Such judgements, based on the ways people talk, result in hearers' constructions of identity, which the speakers themselves may or may not share, and which are often informed by general stereotypes. Recall Preston's words from p. 9:

> Some groups are believed to be decent, hard-working, and intelligent (and so is their language or variety); some groups are believed to be laid-back, romantic, and devil-may-care (and so is their language or variety); some groups are believed to be lazy, insolent, and procrastinating (and so is their language or variety); some groups are believed to be hard-nosed, aloof, and unsympathetic (and so is their language or variety), and so on.
>
> (Preston, 2002, pp. 40–41)

The words we use, the way we pronounce them and the way we string them together have far-reaching social significance, leading to swift and often very harsh judgements not only of individual identity but of situational appropriacy (see the sub-section on register variation on p. 35). Take taboo words, for example. An iconic national ritual on the BBC's prestigious Radio 4 in the UK is the marking of the hour with three pips, preceded by a solemn continuity announcement spoken in solid **Received Pronunciation** (RP). In 2009 the seasoned professional Peter Jefferson was reported to have lost his job after mixing up his words and saying the 'F-word' *during the sacred pips* (Adetunji, 2009). This particular word (otherwise written as *f\*\*k*) is fast losing its taboo status in many English-speaking social groups (it does, for example, appear in the national newspaper article where we read about the story); but its use can still cause shock and/or offence if uttered in the wrong social context or by the wrong person, as our example illustrates. We will be using a word from the *f\*\*k* family later in this chapter and in future chapters, but for purely scientific purposes, so we hope no offence will be taken.

That the way a person uses language is such a powerful factor in social judgements has been neatly demonstrated by the 'matched guise' technique, originally employed in Canada by Wallace Lambert. Lambert had been struck by the judgements people made about the language choices and uses of others in bilingual Montreal. In an early article summarizing the technique, Lambert shared an anecdote

**Received Pronunciation** (RP) is a way of pronouncing English which emerged in the late nineteenth century as the accent of England's privileged classes. It is considered by many to have very high prestige and is still used as a target for teaching and a benchmark for phonetic description of other accents, despite its rarity.

about his twelve-year-old daughter to illustrate how strong language attitudes can be and how sensitive we are to them, from a very early age. After they have stopped to pick up one of her friends on the way to school, she excitedly tells her father *not* to pick up a second friend they subsequently encounter:

> At school I asked what the trouble was and she explained that there actually was no trouble although there might have been if the second girl, who was from France, and who spoke another dialect of French, had got in the car because then my daughter would have been forced to show a linguistic preference for one girl or the other. Normally she could escape this conflict by interacting with each girl separately, and, inadvertently, I had almost put her on the spot.
>
> (Lambert, 2003 [1967], p. 306)

On the basis of such experiences, Lambert developed a technique for assessing attitudes to language varieties by having people judge the speaker of utterances spoken in different accents or languages on traits such as sincerity, intelligence, friendliness and confidence. Unbeknownst to the judges, the utterances were produced by a single voice, that of a bidialectal or bilingual actor. In the UK, Howard Giles used the technique to assess attitudes to regional accents of English. Although there are drawbacks to the technique (cf. Agheyisi and Fishman, 1970), the results are consistent and striking. In a series of studies, Giles and colleagues showed how accents in the UK were regularly associated with stereotypical regional characteristics, with the use of 'standard' forms like RP normally judged more positively than that of 'nonstandard' forms like Brummie (from Birmingham) or Cockney (from London) (Giles and Billings, 2004).

 **www.2.4**

**www.2.5**

## 2.2  KINDS OF VARIATION

### Accent

Perhaps the most immediate and overt parameter of variation in language is its principal external modality, either speech or sign. Babies *perceive* speech or sign before they *understand* and *produce* it in structured ways. When you're exposed to a language you don't know, all you get is the speech sounds or signs, not the sense they are intended to communicate. It is speech and sign which make languages observable; you can't *perceive* grammar or semantics. Variation at this level is largely a matter of accent, and we all have one (including signers: see, for example, Johnston and Schembri, 2007). Lippi-Green likens the development of accent to the construction of a house to live in. Although all hearing children are born with the ability to acquire the phonology of any language variety, the immediate environment inevitably determines the system they build:

 **www.2.6. 2.7**

> At birth the child is in the Sound House warehouse, where a full inventory of all possible materials is available to her. She looks at the Sound Houses built by her parents, her brothers and sisters, by other people around her, and she starts to pick out those materials, those bricks she sees they have used to build their Sound Houses . . . [She] starts to socialize with other children. Her

best friend has a slightly different layout, although he has built his Sound House with the exact same inventory of building materials. Another friend has a Sound House which is missing the back staircase. She wants to be like her friends, and so she makes renovations to her Sound House. It begins to look somewhat different than her parents' Sound Houses; it is more her own.

(Lippi-Green, 1997, pp. 46–47)

The child settles into an accent which is not identical to those of her parents or friends, but extremely similar to them. For example, many young people from the east of Yorkshire in England share with their parents a distinctive pronunciation of the vowel sound /o/ in words like *foam* or *both*, such that they sound to other British English speakers like *firm* and the French word *boeuf*, respectively. But some young speakers from the same communities have picked up an innovation from the south of England, known as *th*-fronting, whereby words like *thin* are pronounced the same as *fin*, and *writhe* the same as *rive* (with '*th*' consonants produced at the front of the mouth). So a young person from this area might pronounce *both* with their parents' vowel and their peers' final *f*. Young people regularly move to or between different groups and can operate with different phonologies, sometimes losing, sometimes maintaining them. Lippi-Green continues:

> Maybe she [becomes] embarrassed by [her] A[frican] A[merican] V[ernacular] E[nglish] Sound House and never goes there anymore, never has a chance to see what is happening to it. Maybe in a few years she will want to go there and find it structurally unable to bear her weight.

(Lippi-Green, 1997, p. 47)

Taken together, the different accents within and across individuals and groups reflect the degree of variation in the **phonology** of their language.

## Dialectal variation

People sometimes confuse **dialect** with accent. But from a linguistic perspective, accent is just one of several features that distinguish one variety from another; vocabulary, syntax and **morphology** are other features of language that vary across groups of speakers. Dialects, then, *include* accent, and linguists use the term to refer to varieties that share with others sufficient linguistic elements for them to be called a single language. So, many varieties of Scottish English, for example, are perfectly intelligible to speakers of other varieties spoken outside of Scotland, even though they vary in accent, vocabulary and syntax. An example of lexical variation in Scottish Englishes is the use of *outwith* as a preposition meaning 'outside', as in this example from the British National Corpus:

> *there is already a determination that schools outwith Scotland's central belt should be the beneficiaries.*

Just as everyone has an accent, so too everyone has a dialect. The 'standard' is just one among others. Outwith linguistics, the term is normally used for 'non-standard'

---

The **phonology** of a spoken language is the system of sounds that it uses, both individual units (consonants and vowels) and combinations of these units (stress and intonation). The phonology of a sign language is the system of manual and facial gestures that it employs.

A **dialect** is a variety of a language determined normally by geographical and/or social factors. The term is normally used in the context of languages which have been extensively documented and have a recognized 'standard' dialect against which others are compared.

**Morphology** is the systematic patterning of meaningful word parts, including prefixes and suffixes.

regional varieties: the 'ugly', 'quaint' or 'comic' ways that urban underclasses or rustic peasantry speak. But speech communities are not only determined by region. Just as Lippi-Green's Sound House builder starts her phonology at home with the family and then adjusts it when she moves outside to participate in larger social groupings, so she builds a new grammar and lexicon which reflect her age group and lifestyle choices.

The cartoon in Figure 2.2 reflects non-linguists' awareness of social dialects, especially how linguistic stereotypes (word choice, writing style and literacy practices) dovetail with stereotypes about age, dress and behaviour. The humour of the cartoon stems from its overlapping sets of parallel incongruities between language form and language practice:

1   (a) The speaker wears a bow tie and smokes a pipe; but (b) he also sprays graffiti on walls.
2   (a) The speaker sprays graffiti on walls; but (b) the graffiti uses the writing and punctuation of the educated.
3   (a) The speaker uses words like *yes* (not *yeah*), *legibility* and *punctuation* in the first line; but (b) he uses *street*, *roll* and *motherfucker* in the second.

This strong connection between dialect and non-linguistic group identity is seen especially clearly at the level of 'nation', where dialects associated with national identities regularly get called languages in their own right, despite their mutual intelligibility with other dialects beyond the national borders. So, for example, there is Dutch in the Netherlands, called Flemish in Belgium; Hindi in India, called Urdu  **www.2.8**

'*Yes well, legibility and correct punctuation might not be "street"... but that's how I roll, motherfucker.*'

Figure 2.2   How language is perceived as correlating with age, dress and behaviour (copyright Philip Selby)

www.2.9,
2.10

www.2.11

in Pakistan; Norwegian, Swedish and Danish in Scandinavia, but basically varieties of the same language. Within nation states, dialects of the majority language spoken by minority groups with power are often recognized as languages, whereas those of other significant minorities without power remain dialects. For example, Scots, which is claimed as a separate language from English in Scotland, is no more unintelligible to speakers of neighbouring 'Geordie' than African American English is to speakers of Mexican American English. Scots gets more legitimacy as a language because Scotland is a proud nation in its own right within the UK, whereas African American English is the stateless dialect of a relatively powerless minority group.

A particularly notorious case is that of the Catalan and Valencian translations of the proposed EU Constitution, submitted to the European Commission by the Spanish government in 2005. The linguistic legacy of the Roman invasion of the Iberian peninsula over two millennia ago resulted in a broad spectrum of related languages, all the way from Portuguese in the south-west to Castilian, the national standard of Spain, in the centre, and to Galician and Catalan in the semi-autonomous regions of the north-west and north-east. After the forty-year fascist dictatorship of Franco in Spain, in which the linguistic minorities were brutally oppressed, most regions achieved a significant degree of autonomy, leading to the official recognition of their languages. Valencian is quite clearly a sister variety of Catalan, but Valencia is a major regional player, and when its authorities failed to reach agreement with neighbouring Catalonia on norms for their shared language, Catalonia decided to submit the Valencian version of the constitution as its own, as a sign of common political cause with Valencia, as the national daily *El País* reported (Valls, 2004).

www.2.12

From Table 2.2 you can appreciate why eyebrows were raised in Brussels, and anger and embarrassment was felt in different parts of Spain, when the central government in Madrid submitted 'both' versions, along with Galician, Basque and Castilian (Maragall rectifica . . . , 2004).

The flip-side of this dialect–language jousting between powerful players is the widespread disparagement of what are clearly languages by calling them *dialects*. In Peru, for example, the education ministry only considers Ashaninka, Awajún, Shipibo and Quechua as languages; other Indigenous languages are treated as dialects, and not considered worthy of their own curriculum or textbooks (see Chapter 14 for more on this point).

Table 2.2   Excerpts from the Valencia and Catalan versions of the EU Constitution

| *Catalan* | *Valencian* |
| --- | --- |
| La present Constitució, que naix de la voluntat dels ciutadans i dels Estats d'Europa de construir un futur comú, crea la Unió Europea, a la qual els Estats membres atribuïxen competències per a assolir els seus objectius comuns. La Unió coordinarà les polítiques dels Estats membres encaminades a assolir estos objectius i exercirà, de forma comunitària, les competències que estos li atribuïsquen. | La present Constitució, que naix de la voluntat dels ciutadans i dels Estats d'Europa de construir un futur comú, crea la Unió Europea, a la qual els Estats membres atribuïxen competències per a assolir els seus objectius comuns. La Unió coordinarà les polítiques dels Estats membres encaminades a assolir estos objectius i exercirà, de forma comunitària, les competències que estos li atribuïsquen. |

# Registers

There is also a great deal of authentic variation in the ways a single speaker uses the linguistic resources at their disposal. Imagine for a moment a bailiff in family court, paying close attention to the proceedings. His friend the clerk is reading legal papers and she has momentarily lost the plot. She whispers to the bailiff to find out what she has missed. The bailiff tells her, *soto voce*, that

> They've asked what the other guy thinks 'bout the kid.

If we rewind the scene and replace the clerk with a judge, however, the bailiff might give her the same message using very distinct linguistic encoding:

> A second professional opinion regarding the infant has been requested by counsel, Your Honour.

The style of the first is informal and concise, relying on shared knowledge and reflecting greater intimacy. The second is much more formal and elaborated, taking little for granted and explicitly encoding the power relations. Linguists use the term **register** to refer to an individual's styles as they vary with situation and interlocutor. Table 2.3 summarizes some of the differences in register illustrated by our invented courtroom discourse. Note how there are differences at every level, and that we assemble and interpret language in *bundles* of elements from each level. Together, these elements constitute registers from a shared social repertoire.

For bilingual or multilingual speakers, different languages may serve the same purpose as registers do for monolinguals (a phenomenon known as **diglossia**). See Chapter 8 (on bilingual and multilingual education).

Table 2.3  Comparison of formal and informal registers

| Level | Informal | Formal |
|---|---|---|
| Sound | ■ consonant cluster reductions (absence of /k/ and /d/ from *asked*); contractions (*They've*; *'bout*) | ■ fewer reductions or contractions |
| Vocabulary | ■ shorter, high frequency, Germanic words (*ask*; *about*; *kid*)<br>■ circumlocution (*what the other guy thinks*) | ■ longer, low frequency, Romance words (*request*; *regarding*; *infant*)<br>■ specialist term (*professional opinion*) |
| Grammar | ■ active voice (*asked*) | ■ passive voice (*has been requested*) |
| Discourse | ■ contextually determined reference (*They've*; *the other guy*)<br>■ no honorifics | ■ context-free reference (*counsel*; *second professional opinion*)<br>■ honorifics (*Your Honour*) |

A **register** is a way of using the language in certain contexts and situations, often varying according to formality of expression, choice of vocabulary and degree of explicitness. Register variation is intrapersonal because individual speakers normally control a repertoire of registers which they deploy according to circumstances.

**Diglossia** is the (perhaps universal) use of (normally two) different languages, varieties or registers of differing levels of prestige for different situations and/or purposes. So, for example, in a Welsh bank the cashiers might use Welsh with their customers but English when requesting approval for leave from the area manager.

## 2.3  STANDARDIZATION AND 'NON-STANDARD' VARIETIES

If some dialects become recognized as the 'standard' for their respective languages, how does this happen? As we pointed out in Chapter 1, the ability to recognize differences in the ways people speak is perhaps part of our biological endowment as 'the linguistic species'. But how do we go from recognizing that people from the next town or village (or on the other side of the hill or river) speak differently, to widely shared perceptions of the relative value of the multiple varieties we come into contact with? To a neutral observer, the kind of visceral reaction to language variation we cited at the beginning of the chapter may appear surprising, given the linguistically arbitrary nature of the distinction between 'standard' and 'non-standard' varieties. A variety can become regarded as the standard through a series of events and conditions that favour its acceptance and spread, not because it is linguistically more complex, inherently more effective as a vehicle for communication, 'purer' or more logical than other varieties (all 'dead ends' we met in Chapter 1). It may be that as more people come into contact with the standard as a result of its use in literacy, school or the mass media (more on this on pp. 38–9) they will come to regard it as more accessible or easier to understand than other dialects of the same language, but that is a feature of circumstances of its *use* (who speaks it where) rather than an inherent property of its form.

Preston (2002, pp. 62–64) argues that the identification in most people's minds between attitudes to *speaker* and attitudes to *speech* can only be fully explained if we acknowledge the fundamental opposition between linguistic and non-linguistic theories of language. His characterization of the 'folk theory' (Figure 2.3) echoes our 'monolithic myth', with 'the language' seen as an ideal object, abstracted from 'good usage' and distinct from 'ordinary language [use]', which is

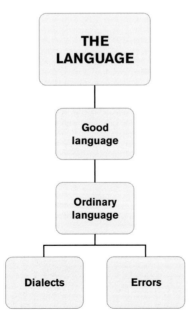

Figure 2.3  A folk theory of language (adapted from Preston, 2002, p. 64)

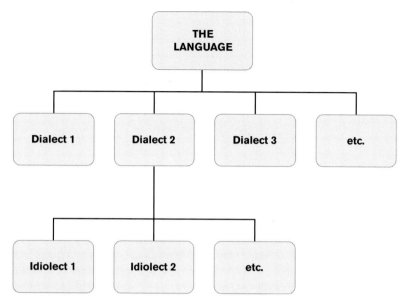

Figure 2.4   A linguistic theory of language (adapted from Preston, 2002, p. 64)

itself either 'dialect' or 'wrong'. Whereas the folk theory defines 'the language' in terms of value, a *linguistic* theory (Figure 2.4) views 'the language' as a collection of dialects, which themselves are viewed as collections of overlapping but distinct realizations of cognitive systems in individual minds (known as **idiolects** in socio-linguistics). No value judgements are made, no dialect is privileged over any other. 'The language' is not the same thing as 'the standard variety', which is one dialect among others.

www.2.13

An **idiolect** is the unique form of a language represented in an individual user's mind and attested in their discourse.

As we argued in Chapter 1, we believe that a linguistic view of language informed by psycho- and sociolinguistics makes a fundamental contribution to applied linguistics. By adopting this view, applied linguists can understand and contest the monolithic myth of the 'standard' version of languages, and all the prescriptivist baggage that comes with it. Without it, we are prone to fall victims to what Lippi-Green calls *standard language ideology*:

> a bias toward an abstracted, idealized, homogenous spoken language which is imposed and maintained by dominant bloc institutions and which names as its model the written language, but which is drawn primarily from the spoken language of the upper middle class.
>
> (Lippi-Green, 1997, p. 64)

## Writing and technology

It is often argued that written language serves as a sort of fixative, analogous to the chemical process of 'fixing' just the right shades of black and white on a photograph in a darkroom. Thus, in the case of English, the dialect 'frozen' by print was that spoken where the earliest English printers worked, in the power triangle between Oxford, Cambridge and London (but not the 'Cockney' variety of the capital spoken by Shaw's *Fair Lidy*). The idea of 'fixing' through print is even more explicit in the policies and practices of the major European language academies, those official organizations which regulate how the national language is to be used in public domains. The stated purpose of the *Dictionnaire de l'Académie Française* (founded 1694), for example, is to 'fix the usage of the language' (*Fixe l'usage de la langue*). Similarly, the motto of the *Real Academia Española,* which published its first dictionary in 1780, is 'Limpia, fija y da esplendor' (*cleanse, fix and make resplendent*). Hence, physical fixing became social fixing, with print serving to maintain the status of one variety over others.

It's worth pointing out that systems which function by representing the sounds of a particular language, like alphabets and other forms of **glottographic** writing, lend themselves especially to this fixing process (see Chapter 6). In contrast, the spread of **logographic** writing systems that convey messages primarily via word-images, such as Chinese characters and the systems developed by Mesoamerican groups, can be read in different language varieties, without favouring one over others. This doesn't mean that such systems were not highly stylized or that they didn't promote certain (visual) conventions over others, but due to their nature their effect on establishing standard varieties of speech was likely very limited. The flip-side of this is that because they are largely meaning-based, rather than pronunciation-based, such systems can be used to claim unity around a standard where in fact there is diversity, even multilingual diversity. Such is the situation with written Chinese, called *Zhÿngwén*, literally 'Writing of the Middle Kingdom', but often used to refer to Standard Mandarin Chinese (*Putonghua*, or 'common speech', based on the Beijing dialect). Although non-linguists both inside and outside China think of the nation as having a single national language with many dialects (together with some minority languages like Uighur or Mongolian), linguists normally deny the existence of a single Chinese language, recognizing instead members of a Chinese language *family*, which includes Mandarin and Cantonese. The fact that Mandarin and Cantonese and all the other 'dialects' of Chinese can be written with the same logographic system licenses politically convenient assertions of a single Chinese language. A logographic system also similarly lends itself to use as a tool of cultural assimilation, e.g. in Hong Kong, where Cantonese is spoken. During the twentieth century, however, Cantonese developed its own written form, but it is not yet standard, despite its increasing use in chat rooms and SMS messaging.

In addition to writing, the spread of sound-based communications technologies such as radio and television has helped fix the sound of certain varieties as the 'standard' in the minds of listeners. But there is a perpetual tension between innovation and standardization, given changing social dynamics and increased contact between speakers of different languages and varieties. The central pull of the prestigious broadcast accent in the UK seems to be losing its power, for example. BBC news readers historically have been speakers of RP, but today's listeners and viewers can hear a much broader range of regional accents. Furthermore, the rapid spread of digital and interactive technologies, such as smart-phones and personal computers, and broadening access to them, means that users are potentially receiving input in a much greater range of language varieties. They are also able to produce and send messages in their preferred varieties through the social networking, podcasts, blogs and chat functions of virtual, computer-based

**www.2.14**

**www.2.15**

**Glottographic** writing systems use symbols which represent sounds, either individual phonemes (as in alphabetic codes like the one used for English) or syllables (as in the syllabary used for Inuktitut in Canada or the Japanese hiragana and katakana scripts).

**www.2.16**

**Logographic** writing systems use symbols which represent whole words or ideas. They normally encode no (or only limited) information about how the symbols are

**www.2.17**

pronounced (compare the logographic symbol & with **alphabetic** *and*) and no (or only limited) iconic information about what the symbol *means* (so ☺ is not a logographic symbol, but 面 is – it's a word for 'face' in Chinese script).

communication. But perhaps the key word here is *potential*, as given the greater number and range of broadcasting options and the increased ease of access to them, listeners are also able to choose to *decrease* the range of voices they are exposed to. Certainly the picture is a very complicated one; while technology can provide an outlet for frequently unheard language varieties, it also facilitates contact and standardization, as well as the fracturing of the audience into smaller and more specialized groups who can choose to avoid language varieties other than their own.

## 2.4  NON-NATIVE VARIETIES AND WORLD ENGLISHES

The spread of languages of wider communication, including Chinese, Arabic, English and Spanish, means that many of us live in ever richer speech communities in which multiple languages are present. This contact leads, in many cases, to speakers learning and using additional languages, that is, retaining their first language while gaining another or others (see Chapters 9 and 10). While theoretical and descriptive linguists have traditionally focused on people's knowledge of their first language, interest in language use by non-native speakers is growing rapidly. This is particularly true for the growing numbers of non-native users of English, estimated at over one-third of the world's population (Graddol, 2006; Crystal, 2008). Thus, applied linguists and language professionals working in education, translation and other areas face decisions about whether it is right or realistic to expect non-native speakers to attain native speaker 'status' – to perform, at least in certain contexts of use, like native speakers (see Chapter 9 on the notion of *native-speakerism*).

 **www.2.18**

    There are at least two ways of looking at this issue. From an *individual* perspective, applied linguists devise and interpret tests, tasks and other means of measuring language learners' abilities in certain aspects of language use. The IELTS (International English Language Testing System) and the TOEFL (Test of English as a Foreign Language) are good examples of tools which attempt to assess whether an individual has mastered the elements of English needed to perform successfully in an English-speaking university. Likewise, professional standards developed by the organization Teachers of English to Speakers of Other Languages (TESOL) are intended to gauge which teacher candidates have developed levels of proficiency that will allow them to be effective teachers of that language. Such measures are ways of operationalizing the minimal threshold of non-native speaker proficiency (in this case, of English) to satisfy the linguistic requirements of learning and teaching that language at scholarly and professional levels. All attempts to measure language proficiency face a number of problems, however, including what to test and how to test it in a way that is accurate and fair, a topic we return to in Chapter 9. The question of 'what to test' is relevant here, as the answer to this question will involve making a decision about the relevant *variety* of the language to be tested and a rejection of those varieties considered irrelevant to the target situation (see Davies *et al.*, 2003).

 **www.2.19**

    Non-native varieties can also be viewed *collectively*, as in the case of World Englishes, an approach to English which highlights the historic diversification that the language has undergone as a result of successive 'diasporas' (dispersions) of its speakers (see Kachru *et al.*, 2006; Kirkpatrick, 2007). The term *pluricentric* is regularly employed in this paradigm, to suggest that English is a collection of national or regional varieties, both in the 'Anglo' countries of colonist England and colonized Scotland, USA, New Zealand, etc. and in the non-Anglo colonized nations of the Indian subcontinent, Africa, South-East Asia, etc. In the first, there are national standard varieties spoken by native speakers (Scottish English, Australian English, etc.). In the second, emerging non-native standard varieties of English (Indian English, Nigerian English, etc.) vie with other native languages, such as (predominantly) Hindi-Urdu in South Asia, or Yoruba, Igbo and Hausa in Nigeria. These 'new Englishes', also called *indigenized* or *nativized Englishes* (see Kachru, 1992, pt II), face a struggle for recognition both in the 'Anglo' countries and in the countries in which they arose, because as **second languages**, they are unquestioningly valued less.

Additional languages may be classified as **second languages** when they are routinely *used* in a country outside the context in which they are *learned* (for example in bilingual countries) and as **foreign languages** when they are not so used. English is learned extensively as a second as well as a foreign language, whereas Icelandic is always learned as foreign language, unless the learner is in Iceland.

The 'norms' of the native varieties are pretty much established, codified in dictionaries and descriptive grammars, and rendered as models in education and writing. So, for example, when mentioning the first and last items of a list, the norm for British English is to use the preposition *to* (*vegetarian recipes: from apples to courgettes*), whereas the norm for US English is to use the preposition *through* (*apples through zucchinis*). The 'norms' of the new varieties, however, are only beginning to be accorded similar status within their local domains, and codification itself is not yet prevalent. For example, 'Standard Nigerian English' lacks a dictionary, usage guide or pedagogical grammar, but does satisfy other indicators of its 'standardized' status. Bambgose's measures of the status of innovations in nativized varieties (Bambgose, 1998) can help here (see Table 2.4). Some Nigerian English usages, such as *I don't mind to go*, are used by most speakers, but are stigmatized by users of the prestige variety, and so are not, on Bambgose's 'demographic' measure, part of Standard Nigerian English. Other usages, such as the homophony of *beat* and *bit*, *cord* and *cod*, and *cart* and *cat*, are common to almost all speakers, including teachers, and so are standard on his 'authoritative' measure. But they are not yet codified in pronouncing dictionaries, even though the contrast between the vowel sounds is still tested in Nigerian high schools, as Bambgose reported in 1998

**Table 2.4**   Factors for determining the status of innovations in nativized Englishes (Source: adapted from Bambgose, 1998, pp. 3–5)

| Factor | Measure |
| --- | --- |
| *Demographic*: How many people use the innovation? | Number of users within the local variety with the most prestige. |
| *Geographical*: How widely dispersed is the innovation? | Usage across L1 backgrounds and geographical areas. |
| *Authoritative*: Who uses the innovation? | Usage in literature, education, media, publishing. |
| *Codification*: Where is the usage sanctioned? | Appearance in written form, especially in dictionaries and manuals. |
| *Acceptability*: What is the attitude of users and non-users to it? | Degree of awareness and favourable attitudes. |

(p. 8). (There is more on the role of dictionaries in codifying norms in Chapter 11, on lexicography.)

The multiple native and nativized Englishes can be contrasted with those developing in countries where the language has no official status and are first encountered in classrooms rather than in the institutions left by conquest and colonization by England or one of its 'Anglo' daughters. In such contexts English is truly a **foreign language**. In effect, given the English-learning boom of the past half-century (Graddol, 2006), this means all the other nations on Earth, but typified by Europe, where English is increasingly used as a **lingua franca**, and China, where the number of people learning English is larger than the total number of native speakers on the planet. In Kachru's model of World Englishes, representing the three domains we've just discussed in concentric circles (see Figure 2.5), this last domain is called the **Expanding Circle**, but it's fairly clear that he's using *expanding* here to refer to individual learners and users, rather than nations, as in the **Inner Circle** of native English speakers or the **Outer Circle** of ESL speakers.

 **www.2.20**

When a language is used as a medium of communication between speakers of different languages, it is known as a **lingua franca**.

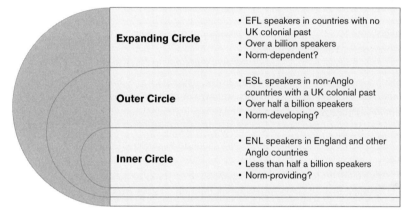

| Expanding Circle | • EFL speakers in countries with no UK colonial past<br>• Over a billion speakers<br>• Norm-dependent? |
| --- | --- |
| Outer Circle | • ESL speakers in non-Anglo countries with a UK colonial past<br>• Over half a billion speakers<br>• Norm-developing? |
| Inner Circle | • ENL speakers in England and other Anglo countries<br>• Less than half a billion speakers<br>• Norm-providing? |

Figure 2.5   A model of World Englishes (Source: adapted from Kachru, 1985) (*Note*: *ENL* = English as a Native Language; *ESL* = English as a Second Language; *EFL* = English as a Foreign Language)

The **Expanding Circle** is Braj Kachru's (1985) term for the regions where English is used mainly as a foreign language, and where most of its users may now be found. The **Outer Circle** is his term for where English is used mainly as a second language, in former colonies of the UK and USA, where new norms may be developing. English is used mainly as a native language in the **Inner Circle**: the British Isles and the regions where English native speakers effectively displaced local populations.

English was originally imposed on the ancestors of many current speakers around the world, often through military force. Unsurprisingly, there are therefore ambivalent attitudes towards English in these countries. Some view the language as a symbol of continuing subjugation to foreign powers through cultural (rather than military) imperialism or of a lack of national self-confidence, sometimes perpetuating an inferiority complex. For others it represents the loss of cultural diversity and ancestral culture. The writer Vikram Seth's poem *Diwali* illustrates this ambivalence. In it, he describes English in India as a 'Six-armed god / Key to a job, to power / Snobbery, the good life / This separateness, this fear'. After independence, the 'conqueror's tongue', as Seth calls it, did not, of course, disappear, and the legacy continued to be both a blessing and a curse. One response to the problem was to eliminate it. For example, the newly independent government of Malaysia replaced English with a variety of Malay as the only official language (known as Bahasa Malaysia), to give voice to the Indigenous peoples of the new republic and to

 **www.2.21**

 **www.2.22**

promote national unity. Malaysia was bucking the postcolonial trend, however, and English remains an official language for around fifty nation states (Bangladesh and Sri Lanka are the only others to have struck English off the list, although for all three nations English maintains a prominent role in national affairs).

But when we talk of 'English' here, what variety of English exactly do we mean? Clearly the millions of users of English in the Outer Circle don't all use the same variety, the one promoted as the only valid version by the teachers and textbooks imported from the USA and the UK and promoted by the British Council and agencies of the US Department of State. Although the snobbery mentioned by Seth ensures that most users in the Outer Circle value the same dialects considered 'correct' by Inner Circle speakers, the reality on the ground is just the same as in the Inner Circle: users of English in the Outer Circle represent a rich collection of many different varieties, clustering together as usual on the basis of geographical or social factors, and also influences from local languages. So, for example, terms like *cousin-sister* ('female cousin'), *big father* ('father's elder brother') and *co-brother* ('wife's sister's husband') in the Englishes of Africa and Asia reflect regional kinship systems (Mesthrie and Bhatt, 2008, pp. 112–113). And the extensive plural use of mass nouns in Sri Lankan English (like *equipments* and *advices*) is undoubtedly due to the fact that their translation equivalents in Sinhala, the dominant national language, are inherently plural.

www.2.23

The feelings of separateness and fear that Vikram Seth associates with English in India begin to dissipate when, as always happens, users appropriate the colonial language for themselves. The consequence of this is that they effectively *refit* it for their own purposes, just as every child does as they acquire their native language from exposure to the situated speech around them. The applied linguist Henry Widdowson has articulated this reality most persuasively, claiming that

> [y]ou are proficient in a language to the extent you possess it, make it your own, bend it to your will, assert yourself through it rather than simply submit to the dictates of its form. . . . So in a way, proficiency only comes with non-conformity.
> (Widdowson, 1994, p. 384)

Just as infants forge changes in their 'mother tongue' by creatively reconstructing the system in each generation, and just as these changes fade or spread to the extent that they are generalized across the members of a speech community, so non-native speakers use the materials of the other language(s) they are exposed to to innovate, and these innovations too become distinctive features of non-native varieties, despite the power of the 'standard language ideology'.

## Pidgins and creoles

The concept of national varieties and learner varieties still suggests that English is a self-contained collection of overlapping systems, independent of all the other languages being spoken by the same people or others around them. This rather oversimplifies the nature of actual language use around the globe, and so is not going to be sufficient for user-oriented applied linguists who wish to fully understand their clients' problems. The untenable fiction of 'separate' languages is particularly well exposed by the existence of **pidgins** and **creoles** (see, for example, Holm, 2000). Pidgins tend to rely on a powerful (typically European) language, known as the **superstrate**, for their vocabulary, but use these words in grammatical frames influenced more by speakers' (normally less prestigious) mother tongues, known as **substrates**. In Nigerian Pidgin, for example, the source of most words is English, but much of the syntax and morphology is supplied by Nigerian languages like Hausa, Igbo and Yoruba.

Once a pidgin is acquired as a native tongue by children it evolves into a creole. Creoles are full language systems, endowed over the course of a few generations with complete grammars and extensive vocabularies, through the rich psycholinguistic events unfolding in children's minds as they participate in the social world around them. Pidgins and creoles typically arise in contexts such as the following:

- trade, especially at ports and along shipping lanes;
- slave plantations, especially in the Caribbean islands;
- multilingual states, as a result of colonial invasion or postcolonial union;
- sign language, through creative construction by children.

The likelihood of creolization varies in each context. So, for example, it's less likely in trade contexts, because these are utilitarian and temporary, and more likely where social cohesion is favoured by common cause, such as slave plantations or new nations. The emergence of creoles in sign language contexts will depend on the uniquely variable dimension of generational continuity: most (more than 90 per cent) of deaf children are born to speaking parents (Mitchell and Karchmer, 2004). But there are cases where creoles have arisen from interaction between pidgin signers, the best-documented of which is Nicaraguan Sign Language (Kegl and Iwata, 1989).

Something similar can happen in reverse with spoken creoles, in what linguists call the **decreolization** process (Holm, 2000, p. 49 ff.). Often, regular contact between creole speakers and monolingual speakers of the superstrate language increases over time. The superstrate language normally has greater prestige and is used in educational and other 'official' contexts, so with increased access to education and the media, and with creole speakers' social aspirations finding linguistic expression through the acquisition of desirable superstrate features, the creole may gradually lose elements from the original substrate language and gradually come to resemble the superstrate. Since the superstrate is very commonly English, the decreolized variety often becomes a variety or dialect of English. Some linguists claim that this is the case of African American English and Hawaiian Creole. Figure 2.6 illustrates the pervasive nature of the pidginization–creolization process in the linguistic history and diversity of our world.

As in so many areas of the sociolinguistic reality of our planet, the monolithic myth has overwhelmingly negative power in the case of pidgins and creoles too. Creoles are seen as inherently 'mongrel' or 'half-breed', and so are consistently disparaged. Hawaiian Creole, for example, was vilified for much of the last century, as the following passage starkly describes:

One elementary teacher . . . claimed that children should be taught contrasting images to associate with Pidgin and good speech. 'Words spoken correctly and

**Pidgins** are very basic linguistic systems which sometimes emerge in situations in which speakers of different languages find themselves in frequent contact and need to communicate.

**Creoles** are complete languages that have evolved from more basic pidgin languages, in some cases in a matter of two or three generations.

In a language contact situation, the **superstrate** language is the one spoken by the politically and socioeconomically dominant group. The **substrate** language is spoken by less powerful speakers, and influences the development of grammatical features in an emerging variety based on superstrate vocabulary.

**Decreolization** occurs when a creole begins to merge with varieties of the superstrate language through (renewed) contact with it.

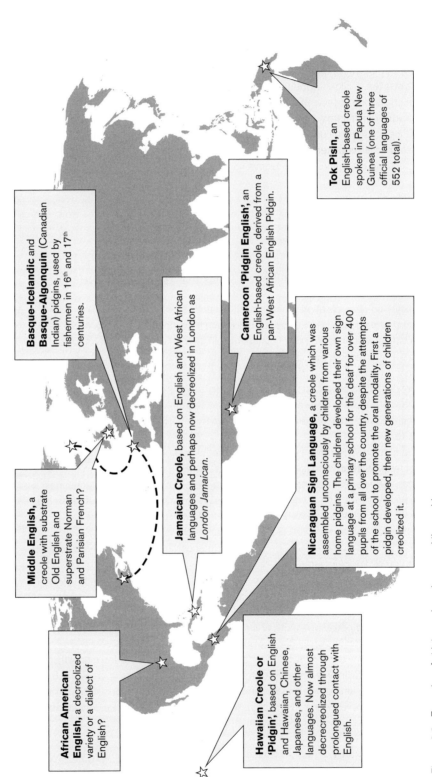

**Tok Pisin,** an English-based creole spoken in Papua New Guinea (one of three official languages of 552 total).

**Basque-Icelandic** and **Basque-Algonquin** (Canadian Indian) pidgins, used by fishermen in 16th and 17th centuries.

**Cameroon 'Pidgin English',** an English-based creole, derived from a pan-West African English Pidgin.

**Middle English,** a creole with substrate Old English and superstrate Norman and Parisian French?

**Jamaican Creole,** based on English and West African languages and perhaps now decreolized in London as *London Jamaican.*

**Nicaraguan Sign Language,** a creole which was assembled unconsciously by children from various home pidgins. The children developed their own sign language at a primary school for the deaf for over 400 pupils from all over the country, despite the attempts of the school to promote the oral modality. First a pidgin developed, then new generations of children creolized it.

**African American English,** a decreolized variety or a dialect of English?

**Hawaiian Creole or 'Pidgin',** based on English and Hawaiian, Chinese, Japanese, and other languages. Now almost decreolized through prolongued contact with English.

Figure 2.6  Examples of pidgins and creoles around the world

pleasingly pronounced,' she wrote, 'are jewels, but grammatical errors and Pidgin are ugly.' She urged teachers to tell children that Pidgin was like the 'frogs, toads, and snakes' in the fairy tales they were reading. Good speech was like the roses, pearls, and diamonds that dropped from the lips of the good sister who helped people and was beautiful. As speech sounds came into fashion as a topic of scientific study in the 1930s, 40s, and 50s in American universities, there was a trend in Hawai'i toward identifying Pidgin as incorrect sounds and as evidence of speech defect. In 1939–40, newly trained speech specialists tested for speech defects in 21 schools. They found them in 675 of the 800 children they tested.

(Da Pigin Coup, 1999)

 **www.2.24**

The monolithic myth is still strong, even in core areas of applied linguistics like language pathology, as we see in the next section.

## 2.5  LINGUISTIC INSECURITY AND LANGUAGE LOSS

For an automatic communication device that operates mostly under the level of consciousness, it is actually quite startling to realize how language is also such a powerful component of people's sense of themselves and the ways they relate to others. The discourses of prescriptivism, the monolithic myth, the standard/non-standard distinction and the inbuilt defectiveness of the non-native speaker all reflect the ways people believe language should be used by themselves and by others. It's no surprise, then, that those socialized into a particular speech community share conventions for representing social hierarchies through language. The myth of a single 'correct' or proper form of speaking, and the fact that it is actually enforced through schooling, language academies and official language policies, contributes to a strong sense of what Labov termed linguistic insecurity in many speakers lower down the hierarchies (e.g. Labov, 1972, chs 4 and 5). One can think of numerous examples of cases in which individuals and groups act in the belief that their language variety is inadequate or that their own speech and writing are somehow inferior. Labov himself concentrated on New York City, just over the Hudson from where he was born. In a number of influential publications in the 1960s he showed how many lower-middle-class New Yorkers exhibited not only insecurity about the way they talked but even linguistic 'self-hatred'.

A Google search in January 2010 for 'accent reduction' businesses in New York yielded over 600 hits, showing that this insecurity is still alive. Although most of these are aimed at the millions of ESL (English as a Second Language) learners and users in the city, many are designed also for native speakers. Some are qualified language pathologists, and although the USA's leading professional body (ASHA, 2010) clearly states that 'accents are NOT a speech or language disorder', it does include accent reduction as one of the services offered by holders of its Certificate of Clinical Competence. The following excerpt from an online message board illustrates how strong the insecurity is, how it's guided by a desire to conform to local conditions as much as to be 'correct', but how the association with speech defects prevails.

### Accent Reduction Help!!!?

i was born in new york and have never left the cpuntry but i have a haitain accent for sum reason. anyway i need sum help reducing the accent and prefer- ably changing it to a new york accent (though i really jus want to lose my accent . . . any tips, websites, or anything else would help

. . .

All I can say is good luck! I also have an accent and I've learned to just live with it. I can't say some words like Sheet because it sounds like Sh*t. And when I say Beach it sounds like B*tch.

. . .

if you can afford it – go to a speech therapist – this is something tehy work on

Once more, here we are witnessing broad parallels between 'standard' vs 'non-standard' forms on the one hand and 'native' vs 'non-native' on the other. The notions of status, solidarity and power underlying 'folk theories' of language variation pervade applied linguistic issues, in both mono- and multilingual contexts. And it's the hegemony (dominance) of native-speaking 'standard' code users which is at the heart of many problems applied linguists are called upon to address. In language policy and planning, for example (Chapter 5), the prevalence of ideologically induced linguistic insecurity at the language level (as opposed to accent or dialect level) is a major contributory factor in language loss. In a seminal study of Hungarian/ German bilingualism in Oberwort in the east of Austria in the 1970s, Susan Gal found that use of Hungarian was falling off quite rapidly, with younger women spearheading the shift. Of these women she noted:

When discussing life choices they especially dwell on the dirtyness and heaviness of peasant work. Rejection of the use of local Hungarian, the symbol of peasant status, can be seen as part of the rejection, by young women, of peasant status and life generally. They do not want to be peasants; they do not present themselves as peasants in speech.

(Gal, 1978, p. 13)

Language choice is being used here in the same way that many newly urbanized young peasants in Mexico, and no doubt other countries, will allow their fingernails to grow to indicate that they are not farm labourers.

Linguistic insecurity is thus a significant barrier to efforts to maintain or revitalize threatened languages and varieties. Unlike the women in Gal's (1978) study, many people view language change negatively, an example of decline rather than the inevitable result of language use over time. This assumption underlies the concept of a 'golden age' of language use, a time when people really spoke or wrote the language well. Speakers of vital and endangered languages alike can hold such views, of course, but the effects can be especially damaging in the case of languages that are losing native speakers. Take, for example, the case of Mohave, a Native American language indigenous to north-western Arizona and western California, now spoken as a first language by perhaps fifty elderly people. Clearly, the only viable means of survival for Mohave and countless other endangered languages is for elders to begin speaking it with younger speakers. And yet, language revitalization efforts are often stymied by grumbling elders, bemoaning how younger speakers can't speak correctly. This leads, unsurprisingly, to younger speakers preferring not to speak the language for which they are criticized.

Personal and group linguistic *security* can thus be undermined by a monolithic view of language and by prescriptivist attitudes to language variation and change. And yet the very notions of 'standardization' and codification that in part give rise to such attitudes can, paradoxically, be instrumental in language maintenance and the development of pride in localized language(s). Acceptance and codification go hand in hand, as we saw earlier with Bambgose's (1998) measures of the status of innovations in Outer Circle Englishes. So *fixing* a standard version of a minority or endangered language in writing, and especially through dictionaries, can be a powerful booster to the status of the language. (We discuss this further in Chapter 5, on language policy and planning, Chapter 6, on literacy, and Chapter 11, on lexicography.) The importance of ensuring that linguistic insecurity does not inhibit the transmission of localized languages is emphasized in this extract from the Manifesto of the Foundation for Endangered Languages:

 **www.2.25**

> the success of humanity in colonizing the planet has been due to our ability to develop cultures suited for survival in a variety of environments. These cultures have everywhere been transmitted by languages, in oral traditions and latterly in written literatures. So when language transmission itself breaks down, especially before the advent of literacy in a culture, there is always a large loss of inherited knowledge.
>
> (Foundation for Endangered Languages, 2009)

The Rosetta Project (n.d.) is one of a number of initiatives which aim to document the planet's linguistic diversity before its inevitable and drastic reduction over the next few generations (as much as a 90 per cent reduction by 2100 according to linguists' estimates, e.g. Krauss, 1992). The Rosetta Project is assembling a publicly accessible digital library of over 2,500 languages, and has produced a disk (Figure 2.7) on which 13,000 pages of documentation for over 1,500 languages have been microetched at a magnification of 1,000 times.

 **www.2.26**

Figure 2.7    Image of the Rosetta Project disk (Source: www.rosettaproject.org/)

But one may argue that 'diversity fixed' like this is more a linguistic than an applied linguistic project. Essential as this record of languages is, essential also is the acceptance of variation in language as an inevitable, and fundamentally dynamic, process. Applied linguists, both those who work at the level of language policy and planning and those who work with individual users, face the challenge of trying to balance the needs and desires of the individual language user, who may have aspirations which don't coincide with those of local activists or well-meaning outsiders (like us). When linguistic insecurity and language loss are at stake, careful thinking about how best to achieve this balancing act is an essential, but subtle, challenge for applied linguists.

## 2.6  CONTEXT AND LANGUAGE PRACTICES

**Convergence** in talk is when a person changes the way they speak in order to sound more like the person they are talking to (or more like the way they *think* the other person speaks). For example, an additional language teacher may use less complex syntax when she is talking to a group of beginning learners.

**Divergence** occurs when a person changes the way they speak to sound less like the person they are talking to, like the local who exaggerates his accent in order to differentiate himself from the incomer.

**www.2.27**

Language variation happens or is made to happen in particular contexts and practices, a passive result of circumstances or an active result of purposes, at the level of both individuals and groups. In other words, we speak differently to different people, at different times and places, during different types of activities, to achieve different outcomes. One way to think about this is to see all speakers as dialect shifters, switching varieties and registers to suit the communicative and social demands of the situations they find themselves in. The ability to modify your style of speaking as a way of attending to your interlocutor's presumed interpretative competence, conversational needs and role/status is called 'accommodation'. The study of accommodation focuses on **convergence** and **divergence** in talk; for example the tendency for locals working in the tourist industry to adjust their talk when speaking to foreign visitors (Giles *et al.*, 1991). There are complexities involved in making these adjustments, as full convergence by one speaker can also be negatively evaluated by the person being spoken to, as an identity-threatening act ('I can see that you're not one of us, so why are you pretending?'). Switching of languages, varieties and registers actually unfolds within talk in very complex ways: the extent and frequency of convergence or divergence can vary within a conversation; speakers may express a desire to converge/diverge but not have the linguistic competence to achieve their aims; or specific task-based motivations may override the need for social approval/distance. In addition, a speaker's assessment of another person's speech is inevitably subjective, and involves all the judgements about interpretative competence, conversational needs and role/status that we have been talking about in this chapter.

Those of us for whom contact with other varieties is fairly limited are unlikely to have the same need to cross variety boundaries. In other words, our actual repertoire of language varieties is limited by experience. Those who live in multilingual communities or who have travelled to new speech communities for work, study and other purposes will have had some practice in monitoring other people's language variety, and are likely to have developed at least receptive competence in the varieties to which they are exposed. The following dialogue from the movie *Airplane* illustrates this to comic effect. In it, the *jive* speech of two African American passengers is translated into Standard American English (SAE) for the flight attendant by an interpreter (earlier in the film their dialogue has subtitles). The interpreter is berated by one of the *jivemen* for assuming that he can't understand SAE ('I dug her rap').

*Jiveman 1*:   Mnnnnnnnnnnnnnnnnnnnn, hmmmmmmmmmmmmmmm.
*Attendant*:   Can I get you something?
*Jiveman 1*:   S'mo fo butter layin' to the bone. Jackin' me up. Tightly.
*Attendant*:   I'm sorry I don't understand.
*Jiveman 2*:   Cutty say he cant hang.
*Woman*:       Oh stewardess, I speak jive.
*Attendant*:   Ohhhh, good.
*Woman*:       He said that he's in great pain and he wants to know if you can
               help him.
*Attendant*:   Would you tell him to just relax and I'll be back as soon as I can
               with some medicine.
*Woman*:       Jus' hang loose blooood. She goonna catch up on the rebound a
               de medcide.
*Jiveman 1*:   What it is big mamma, my mamma didn't raise no dummy, I dug
               her rap.
*Woman*:       Cut me som' slac' jak! Chump don wan no help, chump don git no
               help. Jive ass dude don got no brains anyhow.

Exposure to multiple languages and varieties of a language may mean that convergence on other peoples' ways of speaking is more likely but it doesn't, on its own,
ensure that convergence is always received as appropriate ('[M]y mamma didn't
raise no dummy') or associated with a positive assessment of the speaker ('Jive ass
dude don got no brains anyhow'). The implication here for applied linguists is that
raising awareness of language variation, not just protecting or facilitating switching
between varieties, is key.

## 2.7  CASTING AHEAD

Understanding that language difference is not equivalent to language deficit is a
mainspring of applied linguistics, with relevance to all areas of professional practice.
So we come back to the topic of (attitudes to) language varieties again and again
in the chapters which follow, especially Chapter 7, on the language of education,
and in our final chapter, Chapter 14, on future directions. Applied linguists understand that when a speaker of another variety 'sounds' different to us when she
signs, speaks or writes, this is – as often as not – a result of our unfamiliarity with
her variety of language and our suspicion of her as part of the unknown 'other'. The
responsibility of the applied linguist is to protect varieties and languages, as well
as to raise awareness of the inevitability and usefulness of variety. In the climate of
prescriptivism which we've grown to assume is normal, with its petty but popular
fetish of language 'standards' and unquestioning belief in languages as monoliths,
this responsibility is likely to prove a heavy burden.

activities

1   Do you speak the variety of English that is sometimes referred to as 'standard' British English? What other (national and regional) varieties of English do you speak? If you speak more than one language, what variety(ies) of your additional language(s) do you speak? What are the attitudes within your family, school, workplace or the wider community to the different varieties of the languages you speak?

2   Compare the sounds, vocabulary, grammar and discourse of an *informal* and a *formal* register of any language that you speak well. Are there any similarities between your findings and the example illustrated by Table 2.3 in section 2.2? What are they?

3   In this chapter, we differentiate between linguistic theories and folk theories of language variation. In order to explore the latter in your language context, choose a non-linguist and ask them to draw a diagram showing the varieties of language that they encounter daily and the relationship between these varieties. Do they draw a mainly horizontal diagram like the one in Figure 2.4 or is their diagram mainly vertical, like the one in Figure 2.3? Ask them to tell you what they think about each of the varieties in the diagram, including who the typical speakers of each variety are and where the variety is (or should or shouldn't be) spoken. How do your interviewee's ideas compare with other local, regional and national ideas about language variation?

4   Bearing in mind the languages, the varieties and registers of language(s) that you and others around you speak, and the local, regional and national attitudes to those varieties, what might be some of the possible consequences of language varieties for practitioners of applied linguistics and their clients in your context? You could consider: language policies and practices in local schools (see the Hawaiian Creole example on pp. 43–5); professional development training for workers in call centres, import/export businesses, multinational companies who communicate with speakers of different varieties from their own (see the accent reduction example on p. 46); additional language learners (see the World Englishes example on pp. 39–42). How might applied linguists in your language context attempt to raise their clients', and other language professionals', awareness of language varieties? What might be some of the potential problems of your plans to raise awareness?

## FURTHER READING

Adger, C. T., Wolfram, W. and Christian, D. (2007). *Dialects in schools and communities*, 2nd edn. London: Routledge.

Chambers, J. K., Trudgill, P. and Schilling-Estes, N. (eds) (2002). *The handbook of language variation and change*. Oxford: Blackwell.

Kirkpatrick, A. (ed.) (2010). *The Routledge handbook of World Englishes*. London: Routledge.

Makoni, S. and Pennycook, A. (eds) (2007). *Disinventing and reconstituting languages*. Clevedon, UK: Multilingual Matters.

Wardhaugh, R. (2006). *An introduction to sociolinguistics*, 5th edn. Oxford: Blackwell.

# CHAPTER 3

# Key populations

> Within any society . . . both linguistic and non-linguistic groups will form; stereo-
> types will jell, and subsequently may decay; and the roles played by each kind of
> group in the formation and maintenance of the other are complex and of great
> variety.
>
> (Le Page and Tabouret-Keller, 1985, p. 249)

We pointed out in Chapter 1 that applied linguists can play different, overlapping roles, as theorists, applied scientists and practitioners. Although they can and do develop theory in their multiple domains of interest, most will want to get to grips with the real needs and concerns of language users, working with practitioners by mediating theory or working with clients by doing professional practice. In this chapter we profile some of the key 'clients' and point out some of the ways applied linguists directly or indirectly address their needs. Figure 3.1 depicts the overlapping and (more or less) homogenous groups we'll be looking at in this chapter.

All the populations share a potential to benefit from applied linguistic services of some kind, at the individual or group level, and, more often than not, at both. For example, an elderly person recovering from a stroke will need language therapy to help him or her recover lost language abilities. A village community where most residents can't read or write may need a literacy education programme. But the stroke recoverer forms part of a wider community, including carers, fellow patients in a health centre or clinic, and family members, all of whom will benefit from research and practice in language pathology. And in the village, individual members of the community might need special attention because of particular learning difficulties, physical incapacity, age, occupation or gender. It's the responsibility of the applied linguist to balance the needs of the majority with the needs of the few, and ultimately to consider solutions for all.

We conceptualize these individuals and groups as the major 'clients' of applied linguistics, even though they may not necessarily identify themselves as such (in the same way that many specialists working in the areas we discuss in this book may not identify themselves as applied linguists; see Chapter 1). Furthermore, by using the word 'clients' we don't mean to imply that applied linguistic services should be approached or viewed from the perspective of market forces. Of course, somebody has to pay somewhere down the line: there is no such thing as a free linguistic lunch. But, as we suggested in Chapter 1, we should try to keep separate the research work of applied linguists and the actual paid professional practice of teachers, translators, speech therapists and the like, even though in practice many academic applied linguists are also language professionals, and many language

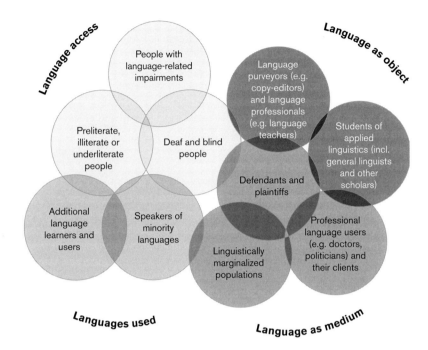

Figure 3.1    Some of the key populations in applied linguistics, roughly organized according to dimension of relationship with language

professionals are involved in applied linguistic research. In any event, most applied linguistic research is financed by government agencies or philanthropic foundations, rather than directly by the ultimate clients. So when we talk of 'clients of applied linguistics', we mean users and beneficiaries of the theoretical knowledge and practical know-how yielded by research in linguistics and applied linguistics. As we saw in Chapter 1, one of the major characteristics that distinguishes applied linguistics from general linguistics is precisely the focus in applied linguistics on people's *needs* in real contexts.

There is a great deal of variation in the profiles and needs of the populations discussed in this chapter. For some, such as the blind and the deaf, people with aphasia or dyslexic children, biological factors underlie the issues applied linguists might be called upon to help resolve. Other clients may have largely socially based areas of need, such as the non-literate, additional language learners, immigrant speakers of a minority language or women in some contexts. And still others may have purely professional needs, like translators, lawyers and copy-editors, and scholars from neighbouring or seemingly unconnected disciplines. By placing all these groups together, we don't want to suggest that they are necessarily defined by their needs. We realize that we must tread carefully, to avoid unintentionally antagonizing or alienating readers who see themselves in these groups but perhaps resent their inclusion or disagree with the labels we are using here. Rather than running the risk of appearing to marginalize or stigmatize through pigeonholing, our intention here is simply to group our client populations in terms of the language issues they face and the potential benefits and services they can derive from applied linguistic research and practice.

The chapter is organized as follows. In the first two sections, we consider some general issues about our client populations, before characterizing the groups in the body of the chapter. In section 3.1 we look at the quintessentially linguistic, but very culturally sensitive, issue of naming practices for our client groups, and in 3.2 we make some observations regarding the overlapping nature of our client groups and the factors which characterize them. We then look at a succession of key populations, organizing them according to their relationship to language, on four general dimensions: 3.3 considers clients' relationships with languages themselves, as users and learners; 3.4 focuses on questions of normal and impaired access to language, through writing, speech, sign and Braille; 3.5 concerns language as the essential social medium through which many non-linguistic problems are played out, like gender stereotyping or the conduct of legal processes; and 3.6 addresses the involvement of language as an object or objective in professional (including academic) practice, from theatre direction to lexicography. The chapter ends (3.7) with some key roles for applied linguists arising from this survey.

## 3.1  ISSUES IN THE NAMING OF POPULATIONS

The problem of group labelling is itself an important theme for applied linguists working in the areas of **critical discourse analysis** and **language maintenance** (see Chapters 4 and 5). As we saw in Chapter 2, language is a principal marker of group identity: think of regional accents, business jargon or the distinctive speech patterns of some gay men, for example. And group names are perhaps the most public and prominent linguistic indices of group membership. In recent decades, western governments, political parties, professional associations, intellectuals and others have questioned many of the traditional names uncritically used for 'minority' groups by non-members of these groups. The earliest targets were unmistakably offensive terms such as *nigger*, *kike*, *queer* and *cripple*. Later the debate became both more subtle and, unfortunately, more open to abuse and ridicule. Pronouncements from government agencies often seemed to reflect the uncritical assumption that most traditional patterns of language use imply negative beliefs and attitudes, and that members of minority groups would always welcome new 'politically correct' ways of labelling them. Comics, parodists and the popular press then made a mockery of these good intentions, bringing the whole healthy process into disrepute (we've all chortled or smirked at some of the proposals, from 'vertically challenged' for short people, to 'sanitation technician' for toilet cleaner).

A case in point is the client group we label in this book as 'the blind' or 'blind people.' In 1993, the US Education Department's Office of Civil Rights (OCR) stated in a memorandum:

> OCR recognizes the preference of individuals with disabilities to use phraseology that stresses the individuality of all children, youth, and adults, and then the incidence of a disability. In all our written and oral communications, care should be given to avoid expressions that many persons find offensive.
>
> (quoted in Jernigan, 2009)

The intention was that government employees should use phraseology which expressed the individual before the disability, so that 'people who are blind' would be preferred over 'blind people', and even the word *blind* would become almost taboo, with the euphemism 'visually impaired' being perceived as more neutral. It seems not to have occurred to them that English grammar places an attributive adjective *before* the noun it modifies, and that the word *blind* may not be deemed offensive by many of the people whose visual status it has traditionally been used to label.

Later the same year, the National Federation of the Blind passed a resolution at its annual conference which stated:

 **www.3.1**

> We believe that it is respectable to be blind, and although we have no particular pride in the fact of our blindness, neither do we have any shame in it. To the extent that euphemisms are used to convey any other concept or image, we deplore such use. We can make our own way in the world on equal terms with others, and we intend to do it.
>
> (National Federation of the Blind, 1993)

Research on the opinions of blind people suggests that most either have no preference or favour the disability-first nomenclature (cf. Bickford, 2004).

There is similar controversy around the naming of deaf people, but here the use of a lower-case or upper-case *d* is the main focus. We follow the widely accepted practice in the Deaf community clearly set out on the California-based *Inside Deaf Culture* website:

 **www.3.2**

■ The use of the lowercase *d* indicates *what* you are. *deafness* is a physical description. It is the inability to hear for whatever reason. There are different levels of *deafness*.

■ The use of the uppercase *D* indicates *who* you are. *Deafness* is an identity, a community, a culture, a mode of being. You can be *deaf* and not *Deaf*, or alternatively, considered *Deaf* but not *deaf*.

> (EpiGenesis, 2007)

Another relevant naming domain is ethnicity. Does she call herself – and do we call her – *Lapp* or *Sámi*? Is he *Berber* or *Amazigh*? Is it *Black* or *African American* or *Afro-Caribbean*? *Roma*, *Traveller* or *Gypsy*? *Chicano* or *Latino* or *Hispanic*? *American Indian*, *First Nation* or *Native American*? Here are some opinions expressed by members of this last group in a 1992 newspaper article:

■ 'The word Indian identifies us,' [Joseph] Brown [a Lakota elder] says. 'Indian covers a lot. A lot of Indians don't like to be called Indian because they're trying to be white men and they're prejudiced against themselves.' But for others, especially those who are younger, Native American is the preferred label because it rejects the tragic historical associations that the word Indian carries.

■ 'The idea of calling people Native Americans appeals to me because we are native – more so than any other group,' says Allethia Allen, an assistant professor of social work at the U[niversity of] W[ashington]. 'I would prefer that because the name Indian comes from Columbus.'

■    Others say there are no right or wrong choices. 'I think the majority feels comfortable with the word Indian,' says Cecil James, a resource-management worker for the Yakima fisheries. 'Each individual has their own definition of how they want to be called. When I talk in public, I identify myself as an Indian of the Yakima Nation, but it should be up to each person to decide.'

(de Leon and Macdonald, 1992)

There is no single or clear answer to the question of how to name groups of people who are perceived, rightly or wrongly, to be vulnerable. While it is certainly not the case that changing the label will automatically change the attitudes and behaviours of the labeller, it is also very clear that use of terms which many or most of the labelled themselves find objectionable will not be in the interests of anybody involved.

In any event, it is salutary to reflect that *everyone* is a potential user of the services of applied linguistics, however we carve up and name our client group. We probably all fall under one or more of the categories listed, even if only temporarily: even white adult males among the western elites learn languages at school and are susceptible to aphasia in old age. (Likewise, once marginalized individuals may break through socially imposed linguistic ceilings or recover from language-damaging illnesses and return to the 'mainstream'.)

## 3.2    ISSUES IN THE CATEGORIZING OF POPULATIONS

Our list of key populations is, necessarily, an initial idealization. In fact, as we recognized on p. 52, many clients of applied linguistics fall into more than one category. In the village literacy case, for example, we mentioned gender as one of the special cases. In many contexts, women in traditional communities do not have the same access to communal life and opportunities as men. This inequality is normally founded in deep-rooted cultural values and practices, and is often played out in part through limits on women's access to discourse opportunities, such as village meetings or other forums for local talk. Thus, a woman whose life is restricted by community norms to the home and hearth may be doubly disadvantaged, being denied access to national life through her inability to use publicly preferred forms of language, including the written code, and also having little or no voice in her own future at the local level. And such examples abound: most deaf children who have acquired a sign language in infancy are expected to learn the spoken language of the majority community as a *second* language; immigrants who do not speak the language of the host community face additional problems if they become plaintiffs or defendants in court cases; dyslexics will have special needs in bilingual education classes; blind children require literacy education in Braille; etc.

Moreover, we must stress that the biological and social factors which define different group memberships are, in fact, constantly in intimate interaction. Poverty, for example, correlates highly with the incidence of many of the biologically based language-related problems we look at in this chapter. It is not a coincidence that higher proportions of the populations of underdeveloped or developing nations are affected by avoidable or treatable blindness and deafness, especially in children. This can be a result of one or more of the following factors:

- poor educational provision (leading to lack of early detection of deafness, abuse of certain medicines which provoke hearing and vision loss, use of risky traditional remedies, ignorance of viable treatments, etc.);
- inadequate and underfunded healthcare (including lack of surgeons, health checks and drugs);
- the prevalence of disease and infection (such as AIDS, meningitis and, in parts of Africa, 'river blindness');
- vitamin deficiencies due to poor nutrition;
- unhealthy working conditions (which may cause or aggravate conditions through prolonged contact with toxic substances or increased risk of injury).

Age is another sociobiological factor that crops up again and again in applied linguistics. Longer life spans, for example, have led to a marked rise in cases of hearing and vision loss in older people. Living longer also brings with it increased risk of stroke, dementia and other conditions that may affect language ability. At the other end of our lives, infancy is a critical time for care-givers and language pathologists to detect and treat developmental language disorders. And age can also be a critical factor in language and literacy learning (see dead end 2 in Chapter 1, pp. 6–7). Some scholars argue, for example, that there is a biologically dictated 'critical age' for language learning: a window of opportunity which closes around puberty. On the socio-psychological plane, school-age children may lack the attention-span, motivation, social strategies and confidence that adults might deploy to learn an additional language or literacy skills more successfully. We will stress this interdependence between biology and culture, nature and nurture, in the chapters to come.

## 3.3 POPULATIONS CHARACTERIZED BY THE LANGUAGE(S) USED

### Learners and users of additional languages

Most of us have, at some stage in our lives, wanted, or been forced, to learn a language in addition to the language(s) we learned at home. What language this was, how we went about learning it and our definition of 'successful' learning will have depended on a number of interlocking variables, including: where in the world we live; our age; our (and our teachers', schools' and government's) beliefs about language learning and teaching; the resources we have access to; and our reasons for wanting to be able to communicate in the additional language.

Where additional language learners have some control over their learning, they will need to decide what language to learn (and what variety of that language), what level of proficiency to aim for (and how this will be measured) and how best to learn the additional language. Inevitably, however, many school-age learners will have little, if any, control over their language learning. The treatment of additional languages as an academic subject, like geography or biology, is likely to encourage teachers and students to teach and study to the end-of-year test, rather than for the actual communication of meaningful messages (though where 'a good mark in the test' is the goal of both learners and teachers, this treatment shouldn't be a

**www.3.3**

problem). Having said this, in recent decades the proliferation of texts in many languages on the World Wide Web and increased access to internet-based communication have provided many language students with opportunities for non-classroom-based interaction. This has meant that learners, whose needs might previously have been easily diagnosed by a teacher as 'to pass the test', may now have a more complicated set of needs and wants ranging from the very specific, such as to be able to contribute to a *Stop Global Warming* Facebook group, to the more general, to 'be like a native speaker'.

For language teachers, there are several problems with the learner needs exposed in this particular example, including: underfamiliarity with the variety of language typical of social networking sites such as Facebook; and overfamiliarity with the native speakerism (see Chapter 9) which assumes that native-speaker competence is the only desirable or achievable goal. One option for language teachers faced with these problems is to decide to ignore our students' definition of their needs, and teach whatever and however we think best. As we say in the conclusion to this chapter (section 3.7), however, including our clients in the design and execution of solutions to their language problems is one of the defining characteristics of the field and we ignore their definition of their own needs at our peril. Even in teaching and learning contexts where the consideration, observation and discussion of 'needs' might be an unfamiliar activity, we think that it is part of an applied linguist's job to (begin to) raise awareness of the range of possible language learning goals and the different ways of achieving them (see Chapter 9).

In previous chapters we made the point that being multilingual, not monolingual, is the *rule*, not the exception, in the past, present and (even more so, perhaps) the future of human beings. We have also said that contact and interaction with speakers of other languages is, and always has been, an inevitable and rich resource, with many communicative, cultural and cognitive advantages to being bi- or multi-lingual, compared to being monolingual. Unfortunately, the precise nature of some of these advantages will depend on the social status of the languages spoken by the individual and on the context in which they are operating. In Chapter 2, we stressed how such attitudes to (varieties of) different languages are often very strong; a fact that inevitably has a sometimes unhelpful impact on the planning of bilingual services, media and education (see Chapters 5 and 8 for more information on the controversies surrounding the latter).

Multilingual clients of applied linguists, and those of us who work with these clients, should be aware that language proficiency (in a first or additional language) is not the same thing as intelligence, and that judgements of, for example, school pupils' or workers' abilities should be based on general cognitive or developmental criteria rather than on language proficiency. Without such awareness, there is the danger of over-representation of non-dominant language speakers in special programmes for people with learning difficulties and of under-representation in 'fast track' or 'gifted and talented' programmes. Multilingual clients need to be consulted, where possible, on the languages they prefer to use in different social and institutional contexts, with support from applied linguists for the provision of materials and services in the language of their choice.

# Speakers of minority languages

Bilingual or multilingual contexts regularly exhibit an imbalance between the languages spoken, according to the number of speakers of each in the local or broader regional/national domain, and their relative status, including official recognition, etc. Often one language is called the majority (or dominant) language and the other the minority (or subordinate) language. The term *minority* has, of course, two dimensions of meaning: the literal one of 'smaller number' and the extended, social one of 'groups of people who are disadvantaged or discriminated against'. Although a minority language is spoken by a minority group in this second sense, the group doesn't necessarily represent a smaller number of people within a broader population. Indeed, the numbers game in world languages is not at all straightforward. According to *Ethnologue* (Lewis, 2010), of the 6,909 living languages, there are 172 with over three million native speakers. The top twenty are listed in Table 3.1. This includes what are, linguistically speaking, macrofamilies: 'multiple, closely related individual languages that are deemed in some usage contexts to be a single language'. So in fact, *Chinese* here includes 12 of the 13 members of the macrofamily; *Arabic* embraces 16 of 30; and *Lahnda*, 2 of 8.

 www.3.4

We saw in Chapter 2, on language variation, that counting languages is a perilous occupation (recall that Hindi and Urdu are treated as separate languages by most descriptive linguists). Counting speakers of languages is just as hard, given the multiple challenges facing official census offices, and even when a number can be more or less agreed upon, it will not always have immediate significance without further contextualization. But if we compare speaker numbers for these twenty 'big'

Table 3.1   Top twenty languages by number of speakers (Source: Lewis, 2010)

| Language or *macrolanguage | Speakers (millions) |
| --- | --- |
| *Chinese | 1,213 |
| Spanish | 329 |
| English | 328 |
| *Arabic | 221 |
| Hindi | 182 |
| Bengali | 181 |
| Portuguese | 178 |
| Russian | 144 |
| Japanese | 122 |
| Standard German | 90.3 |
| Javanese | 84.6 |
| *Lahnda | 78.3 |
| Telugu | 69.8 |
| Vietnamese | 68.6 |
| Marathi | 68.1 |
| French | 67.8 |
| Korean | 66.3 |
| Tamil | 65.7 |
| Italian | 61.7 |
| Urdu | 60.6 |

languages with those for 'smaller' languages, the differences are stark and significant. Let's take as 'smaller' languages those with fewer than 10,000 native speakers. The number of languages is 3,524, that is, over half of the world's languages. The total number of speakers for the twenty 'big' languages is 3,680 million. Together, the 3,524 'smaller' languages are spoken by a tiny 8.2 million. At these orders of magnitude, numbers do matter, and many of the small languages are endangered. While the major responsibility of general linguists is to *document* these languages and thus help preserve fragments of the unique cultural knowledge and experience expressed through them, applied linguists are at the forefront of efforts to maintain or revitalize the languages as integral components of the lives of minority communities. This issue is taken up in greater depth in Chapter 5, on language policy and planning.

But there are minority language speakers who are not numerical minorities and yet may still be clients of applied linguistics. Let's revisit the case of Pakistan, discussed briefly in Chapter 2. Its official languages are Urdu and English, but *Ethnologue* lists over sixty languages for this nation of over 150 million. It's not perhaps surprising that the number of native English speakers has been estimated at around 1 per cent, given the postcolonial status of that language (Abbas, 1993). But that the most recent census figures indicate that only 7.5 per cent are Urdu speakers is unexpected to those used to the 'one nation – one language' fallacy (Population Census Office, 1998). According to the census data, the language with the largest number of native speakers is Panjabi, with 44 per cent of the population. Western Panjabi and Seraiki, counted in the Lahnda macrolanguage by *Ethnologue*, are amongst the top twenty of the world in size, but speakers of the latter accuse the dominant Panjabi speakers of linguistic imperialism, and are campaigning for autonomy and linguistic rights (Asif, 2005).

 **www.3.5**

 **www.3.6**    According to the European Charter for Regional or Minority Languages, designed to protect and promote minority languages and adopted by the Council of Europe in 1992, such languages are defined as those which are:

1    traditionally used within a given territory of a State by nationals of that State who form a group numerically smaller than the rest of the State's population; and
2    different from the official language(s) of that State.

Significantly, it adds the restriction that this 'does not include either dialects of the official language(s) of the State or the languages of migrants'. For applied linguists, we would argue that the concept of minority language must be defined from the perspective of the speakers, our clients. If the speakers are disadvantaged or discriminated against for reasons that include (one of) the language(s) they speak, then that language is a minority language, regardless of the number of native speakers, its status within the nation where the group of speakers resides, and its numerical or social status in other countries or globally. Figure 3.2 gives an example of this principle in action for overlapping pairs of languages centred around French and Moroccan Spoken Arabic (MSA) in France.

In France, French is the majority language and Arabic a minority language. But in Morocco, Standard Arabic (and its local spoken counterpart MSA) is the majority language, in accordance with official Arabization policies after independence from

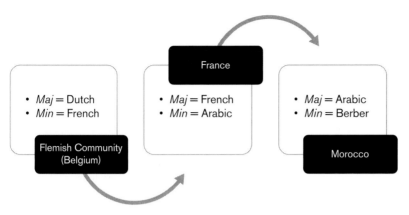

Figure 3.2    An example of the mutable status of the concept *minority language*

France in 1956. The non-Arab Berber languages have been largely suppressed until very recently, and don't have a consistently used, or standard, written version. But powerful French can be a minority language too, even in countries where it has official status and is very widely used. In Belgium, there has been linguistic conflict between the numerical Dutch-speaking Flemish majority and the French-speaking Walloon minority since the modern state was founded following the revolution of 1830. In the autonomous Flemish Community, French is not much spoken and is widely disparaged, especially around the isolated pockets of the community that do use it. For instance, a few years ago in the Flemish town of Wezembeek-Oppem, 'a Roman Catholic priest . . . was removed from his parish by the cardinal for refusing to allow French-speakers to celebrate Mass in his church' (cited in Spolsky 2004, p. 3). The rights of French speakers in the Flemish Community are as much the concern of applied linguists as those of Berber speakers in Morocco. Chapter 5 explores in detail the work of applied linguistics in such areas.

## 3.4  POPULATIONS CHARACTERIZED BY ISSUES OF ACCESS TO LANGUAGE

### Preliterate children and non- or underliterate adults

This may seem like an odd pairing to make (and just in case any reader is unsure, we *don't*, of course, mean to characterize non- or underliterate adults as childlike!). But there is the commonality that these potential clients of applied linguistics lack (full) access to written language and the discourses that depend on literacy. Applied linguists need to overcome their inevitable assumptions about the primacy of written language in all areas of their activity: in some these assumptions may mislead (e.g. diagnosing language deficits in children), whereas in others they could be more or less irrelevant (e.g. teaching English for Academic Purposes, where the genre is inherently written). In Chapter 6 we explore applied linguistic approaches to literacy in some depth, showing how the topic must be understood in a vastly broader context than that of merely learning the mechanical writing conventions that are used to represent spoken language. Here we'll just highlight the issue with an example and give an idea of the scope of the continuing challenges of literacy around the world.

First, a simple demonstration of the *literate biases* we rather bluntly called 'inevitable' in the previous paragraph. We can assume that if you are reading this book you are highly literate, and that for most readers this is probably an ability that has been developing from the earliest school years (and, for many, even before). Since writing is more permanent than speech, and encodes the 'standard' variety of most languages, our socialization leads most of us to tend to assume that the written language *is* the language (as discussed in Chapter 2). Even cognitive psychologists interested in the mental representation of language fall under the 'Language Spell' (see Chapter 1) when it comes to the effects of literacy. In a psycholinguistics textbook review of research on reading, discussing English spelling patterns like those in words ending in the letters *o, v, e*, words like *cove* are presented as having 'regular pronunciation with many irregular exemplars' (e.g. *dove* or *move*), compared with words like *love*, which have 'irregular pronunciation with many regular exemplars' (e.g. *stove* or *wove*) (Harley, 2008, p. 215). Few note the fundamental error here: by *pronunciation*, the author means *spelling*. An irregular pronunciation of *love*, for example, would make it rhyme with *wove*. We so easily invert the dependency of writing on speech, for example when we talk of *h*-dropping for speakers who pronounce *hat* the same as *at*, or *hill* the same as *ill*. But for applied linguists in so many situations, these differences are fundamental: *h*-dropping is not 'wrong' but 'different'. Writing systems which encode sound (like the alphabetic one used by English) often represent the socially privileged accent, rather than the *right* one, and we need to see through these artefacts of writing if we are to fully understand the scope of many of the problems some of our clients face.

Children learning to manage writing systems have not undergone this socialization process, of course. But many adults we encounter in applied linguistic professional practice have not had these literacy experiences either. Statistics from the UNESCO Institute for Statistics (2010) suggest that although there has been improvement over the past decade or so in both overall literacy rates and the elimination of illiteracy (UNESCO Institute for Statistics, 2008), there are still 796 million non-literate adults around the world, concentrated in the most populated nations of Bangladesh, Brazil, China, Egypt, India, Indonesia, Mexico, Nigeria and Pakistan. And still there is a major gender gap, with illiteracy rates among women at around 64 per cent compared with 36 per cent among men. Of course, a binary literate–illiterate distinction grossly oversimplifies the reality of access to literacy skills, as UNESCO recognizes through the Literacy Assessment and Monitoring Programme (LAMP), successfully piloted now in five countries. LAMP recognizes five basic levels of literacy, which it summarizes as follows:

**www.3.7**

**www.3.8**

- *Level 1*: the individual has very poor skills and may, for example, be unable to determine the correct amount of medicine to give a child from the label on a package.
- *Level 2*: respondents can only deal with simple, clearly laid-out reading tasks. At this level, people can read but test poorly. They may have developed coping skills to manage everyday literacy demands, but they find it difficult to face new challenges, such as job skills.

- *Level 3*: considered a suitable minimum for coping with demands of daily life and work in a complex society. This skill level is generally required to successfully complete secondary school and access tertiary education.
- *Levels 4 and 5*: respondents demonstrate command of higher-order information processing skills.

So literacy goes way beyond knowing how to read and write (and is not just an issue in the underdeveloped and developing nations). Literacy skills are increasingly being recognized as a major factor in excluding vulnerable groups from full participation in developed countries, sometimes leading to antisocial or even criminal behaviour. In the UK, for example, Clark and Dugdale, citing work by the Every Child a Chance Trust, reported that

 **www.3.9**

> 70 per cent of pupils permanently excluded from school have difficulties in basic literacy skills. 25 per cent of young offenders are said to have reading skills below those of the average seven-year-old. 60 per cent of the prison population is said to have difficulties in basic literacy skills.
>
> (Clark and Dugdale, 2008, p. 4)

Competence in and control of the paraphernalia of language in society thus saturate issues of social inclusion, social justice and social harmony.

## Deaf people and blind people

Human language must rely on some kind of external channel or modality in order to communicate meanings or messages. There are four principal channels: speech, writing, Braille and sign. For most, speech is the default: all human beings have a genetically built-in potential for acoustically based phonology. Additionally, as we've just seen, those who are literate can also use *writing* to mediate the same underlying language systems, giving us a massive social advantage. But two important groups of individuals don't have equal access to speech and/or writing: the deaf with the spoken modality, and the blind with reading and writing. Given the inherently psycholinguistic and sociolinguistic issues implicated in the experiences of deaf and blind people, and their marginalization in the applied linguistics literature (including, alas necessarily, in this book), we address these clients in slightly more depth in this chapter than other groups who are treated more fully in subsequent chapters.

### Blind people

According to World Health Organization statistics, there are around the world over 35 million blind people, and around 125 million with low vision (although the numbers have decreased since the 1990s, due in no small part to the World Health Organization's 'Vision 2020' campaign to eliminate the causes of avoidable blindness (Rao and Raman, 2005). Echoing the gender imbalance evident in other key populations discussed here, women are affected more than men, and of the

 **www.3.10**

completely blind, more than 80 per cent are over fifty years old. The age factor reflects longer life expectancy, especially in the more developed nations, but in fact more than 90 per cent of the visually impaired live in underdeveloped or developing countries, for reasons we discussed earlier (pp. 56–7). The appearance of Braille in the early nineteenth century (thanks to its eponymous inventor, Louis Braille) gave blind people access to text through the tactile modality. Although the National Foundation of the Blind has been reporting decreasing Braille literacy in the US for over a decade (NFB, 2009), it is increasingly common to encounter Braille in public places, and the 2009 bicentenary gave it greater prominence in the seeing public's mind in many parts of the world (Figure 3.3).

**www.3.11**

Furthermore, recent advances in simulated voice technology will have a massive impact on blind people's access to visually based literacy once the software becomes more readily available. These systems automatically turn written printed text or Braille into speech and Braille into printed text, meaning that blind students will be able to interact fully with texts and teachers, and any blind person with access to the internet will be able to navigate the World Wide Web. One such system is the *Braille Lite* note-taking device, which may be used, for example, to help blind or visually impaired learners of an additional language make their written assignments accessible to non-blind language teachers who do not read Braille (Kapperman and Sticken, 2003).

The way in which language acquisition happens in blind children will be influenced by the lack of visual input: sighted infants rely on visual input in their construction of the many perceptually based concepts (meanings) that language is used to express, but blind children will need to compensate using the other sensory systems. (The problem is doubly challenging for the deaf–blind, as eloquently described in Helen Keller's books and articles.) The evidence seems to suggest that although language development in blind children may be initially slower in comparison with sighted children, the disparity disappears completely with age, and indeed blind adults can become 'better' (more sensitive) hearers than their hearing counterparts, a development which will, in part, compensate for the lack of visual input.

Applied linguists work with blind people and their family and social networks in the following ways:

- informing parents and other care-givers (in preschool or daycare, for example) about the language development patterns of their children;
- devising, implementing and promoting Braille literacy programmes;
- promoting acquisition of, and access to, materials in Braille for libraries, schools, government departments, etc.;

**www.3.12**

Figure 3.3   The front of a London bus in Braille, part of the UK's Royal National Institute of Blind People's 2009 bicentenary campaign

■   advising educational authorities and professional organizations about appro-
    priate strategies for teaching additional languages to blind students.

As we saw in Chapter 1, general linguists also often assume the mantle of applied
linguists when their scholarship is used directly or indirectly in the development of
practical solutions for language problems. So we can add a further area of involvement, this time from computational linguistics:

■   advising software developers on the design of speech synthesis tools.

## Deaf people

Around 250 million people have a disabling hearing impairment, of whom two-
thirds live in underdeveloped or developing nations. Next to depression, hearing loss
in old age is the second leading cause of YLDs (years lived with a disability). It is
important to recognize that what we call deafness is not normally an absolute             **www.3.13**
inability to hear, but rather a continuum of hearing impairment that may range from
insensitivity to certain frequencies and intensities as we age, to absence of any
response at all to auditory input in the more extreme cases. In fact, 95 per cent of
babies born deaf (i.e. diagnosed with congenital deafness) actually have some
residual hearing.

According to the World Health Organization, 50 per cent of cases of deafness
or hearing impairment are avoidable (WHO, 2006). Early diagnosis is crucial for
prevention or rehabilitation. Again, underdeveloped and developing nations often
lack the resources for widespread screening and treatment by otologists and
audiologists. Applied linguists working in speech pathology (see the sub-section
on people with language-related impairments on pp. 66–7 and Chapter 13) will
be concerned with any case in which communicative ability is disrupted, designing
and implementing treatment and support programmes. But the nature of their
recommendations for deaf individuals will depend on the kind of deafness involved.
In cases where there is residual hearing or the condition is acquired after exposure
to or use of spoken language, lip-reading and finger-spelling (based on the alphabets of spoken languages) may be indicated. In other cases, especially with infants
and children who have never been exposed to spoken languages, instruction in a
sign language might be the best way to unlock the individual's language faculty and
provide him or her with the ability to engage in the same range of discourse available
to speaker-hearers.

There has been considerable debate about the advisability of exposing infants
to sign language, and about the teaching of such a language to older children.
Some have argued that this 'ghettoizes' deaf children, cutting them off from the orally
monopolized discourses of the majority communities they are part of. Some who
hold this view are perhaps unaware or unconvinced that established sign languages
with native signers have the same complexity and range of expressive potential as
spoken languages. Descriptive linguistic and psycholinguistic research over the
past few years has demonstrated that sign languages such as American Sign
Language (ASL), Mexican Sign Language (MSL) and Quebecois Sign Language
(LSQ) have phonological, morphosyntactic, semantic and pragmatic systems which

follow the same fundamental design plans as spoken languages. They are acquired in infancy at the same pace and in the same basic sequence as spoken languages (Petitto, 1997). You can whisper and shout in sign, write poetry or sign with a regional or foreign 'accent' (see, for example, Johnston and Schembri, 2007, pp. 43–50, on variation in Australian Sign Language). And yet they are not mimed versions of spoken languages: MSL has nothing to do with Spanish, and is unintelligible to users of Spanish Sign Language; ASL and British Sign Language are unconnected; a Canadian who uses LSQ, Canadian Sign Language and French is trilingual. In short, they are real, separate languages.

Native signers (or anyone who has acquired a sign language within the 'critical period') therefore have a full linguistic system with which to communicate. They will never have complete access to a spoken language, since by definition they cannot hear it, and they will not be able to speak it either. For a deaf person to have greater access to the full social reality of the hearing people around them, then, they will need to acquire the relevant spoken language, through its written modality, as we pointed out above in our section on bilinguals (pp. 57–8). Once more, then, we are seeing overlapping client populations, and once more the applied linguist can be a major source of guidance, since it is applied linguists who have tried to alert politicians and educators to the naturalness of bilingualism, and the benefits it provides to both the individual and the communities he or she acts in and upon.

Applied linguists may work with deaf people and members of Deaf communities in the following activities relating to language and the deaf:

- promoting awareness of sign language among the general public and educational authorities;
- developing instructional materials and techniques for teaching sign language as a first or additional language;
- developing instructional materials and techniques for teaching a spoken language to the deaf through its written modality.

Notice again that general linguists play a major, but indirect, applied role in the promotion of sign languages by providing rigorous descriptive and explanatory accounts of their structure and use. In so doing, they furnish educators, deaf rights groups and other lobbyists with a greater appreciation of the status of sign languages as full linguistic systems (see, for example, Valli and Lucas, 2000, on American Sign Language).

## People with language-related impairments

Many readers may be familiar with **autism** or, more accurately, **autism spectrum disorder (ASD)**, from claims reported in the press a few years ago which named the measles, mumps and rubella (MMR) vaccine as a major cause (a claim rejected by most medical professionals and health departments). ASD affects 3–6 children out of every 1,000 (NINDS, 2009). It manifests itself typically around the age of two to three in a spectrum of behavioural abnormalities, especially difficulties in interpersonal relations, obsessive and repetitive behaviour, and communication problems,

**Autism** is a complex developmental condition that typically appears during the first three years of life and is the result of a neurological disorder which affects the normal functioning of the brain, impacting development in the areas of social interaction and communication skills.

**Autism spectrum disorder** (ASD) refers to an array of related disabilities (such as Asperger's syndrome) that share many of the core characteristics of the classical form of **autism**. The term is now used more frequently than autism alone, in order to emphasize the diverse nature and extent of individuals' symptoms and experiences.

including apparent mutism in a considerable number of cases. People with ASD have problems interacting with the world, perhaps because of genetic abnormalities in the part of the brain responsible for the understanding that others have their own thoughts and intentions (the ability known as **theory of mind**). It is not surprising, then, that such individuals have language problems, since it is largely through language that we engage with others and interpret their states of mind. But although many autistic people don't speak, others talk a lot, repeating phrases they hear or even engaging in lengthy monologues on topics that interest them. There is no evidence that autistic individuals have a specifically linguistic disorder, but language pathologists, working with psychologists, may contribute greatly to treating them through verbal communication therapy.

The previous sections have addressed client groups who have needs relating to language modalities and propensities. But *language itself* – the computational system of phonology, morphology, syntax and lexicon linked with conceptual systems – is also a biological faculty, instantiated in speakers' brain circuitry. When you comprehend, your neural hardware (or 'wetware' as it's sometimes called) receives information from the auditory system for listening, from the visual system for reading and sign, and from the tactile system for Braille. When you produce a linguistic message, the language circuits send information to the muscular system of the vocal tract for speech, and the arms and hands for writing and sign. Language problems thus arise for some people when part of this complicated biological system is compromised, by developmental or acquired impairment. People who are born with normal language circuits but later go on to acquire some kind of impairment are said to have **aphasia** (see p. 306). People who are born with neurological disorders which affect only language are said to have **Specific Language Impairment** (SLI). Additionally, the probably more familiar condition called **dyslexia** appears to be a phonologically based impairment, affecting people's reading, writing and symbolic processing in general.

There are no statistics on the incidence of aphasia in the world population, because of variation in classification criteria, difficulties in detection and inconsistent reporting. But based on a generally accepted figure of one million aphasics in the US (NICDC, 2004), we can hazard a guess that around 4 per cent of the world population have some kind of aphasic disorder. US estimates for SLI range from 2 to 8 per cent of children, with boys affected more than girls (NICDC, 2004). A British study suggests 4 per cent and 6 per cent (Snowling, 2008, cited in Rose, 2009). Chapter 13 will deal with all these populations in much greater detail.

## 3.5 POPULATIONS CHARACTERIZED BY THE SOCIAL ROLE OF LANGUAGE

### Linguistically marginalized populations

There are individuals and groups in all nations who are explicitly or implicitly, officially or unofficially, perceived as being inferior, insignificant or somehow threatening to the dominant or mainstream population. Often, such people may be marginalized through the language beliefs and practices imposed or perpetuated by dominant or mainstream groups. In this extremely heterogeneous client group we might count

**Theory of mind** refers to humans' (and perhaps other primates') innate knowledge that the minds of other members of the species have intentional states, including beliefs and desires. In other words: the mental faculty of *empathy*.

 **www.3.14**

 **www.3.15**

 **www.3.16**

**Specific Language Impairment** (SLI) refers to problems in the acquisition and use (production and comprehension) of language, typically in the situations where there are no other developmental disorders, hearing loss or acquired brain injury.

**Dyslexia** is a heritable, neurodevelopmental condition involving impairment or loss of phonological awareness, which shows up as a range of difficulties in learning to read, write and spell, especially in languages which use **logographic** systems or have significant opacity in phonetic-based spelling (like English). These difficulties tend to persist despite the provision of appropriate learning opportunities. They do not reflect an individual's general cognitive abilities and may not be typical of performance in other areas.

women and sexual orientation minorities, the educationally and economically disadvantaged, the politically oppressed, the disabled, the functionally non-literate and minority language speakers. We have already profiled some of these groups separately, because they have independent and widely recognized language needs. The other groups mentioned here are not necessarily seen as being defined or characterized principally on linguistic grounds. And yet members of these populations are very often confronted with social and political circumstances in which their different language practices become, or are converted into, obstacles to their full and equal participation in the broader communities they live in.

Surprisingly, the link between language and economic marginalization has only recently come to assume a more prominent place in applied linguistic studies. Poverty plays a central role in language loss, as speakers move from rural areas to urban centres and shift to dominant languages (see Chapter 5). But it is also a medium through which poverty is perpetuated, when the language spoken represents an obstacle to accessing resources and, more abstractly but just as critically, a symbol of community insecurity and even shame (as we saw at the end of Chapter 2). Batibo (2009) recounts a salutary case which highlights the potential importance of applied linguistics for the empowerment and ultimately economic improvement of speakers of minority languages in Africa. He describes the case of the Naro speech community, with around 9,000 members, in western Botswana. The development trust established by NGOs a couple of decades ago followed a strategy built around the revitalization of the Naro language, starting with description and codification, as described in Figure 3.4. The results reported by Batibo are most promising:

> [T]he per-capita income of the Naro has increased substantially . . . The
> number of youth reaching higher education has increased, as the younger

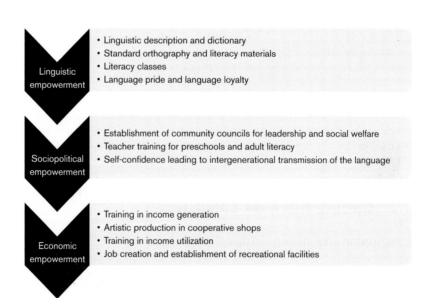

Figure 3.4  Language, sociopolitical and economic empowerment of Naro speakers in Botswana (Batibo, 2009, pp. 31–33)

generation has not only a solid educational base in the mother-tongue-medium school, but also self-confidence . . . The functional literacy of the Naro has increased . . . [They] are now able to live healthier lifestyles because of access to information about health and social hazards. At the same time, it has been reported that with a solid mother tongue base, they are able to learn the other languages like Setswana, Shekgalagarghi and English more easily. Also, they are now ready to co-operate with the majority groups in matters of nation building as they see themselves being valued and respected.

(Batibo, 2009, p. 33)

The painful, gradual process of empowerment being experienced by groups like the Naro in Africa, faces – at very different levels – economically disadvantaged groups in the developed world too: recall the case of Hungarian speakers in Austria from Chapter 2. Wherever poverty hurts people, sociolinguistic processes are at work, and combating it will involve potential contributions from many of the applied linguistic domains covered in subsequent chapters of this book.

## Women

From this language-as-medium perspective, a major client population for applied linguistics is also women. Women and men are generally conditioned from early infancy to assume social roles which, to a considerable extent, are articulated through language. A number of publications claiming to show the differences between men's and women's talk have become best-sellers in some countries over the past couple of decades. In these popular books 'Martian' men and 'Venusian' women are presented as talking differently (and behaving differently in other ways) either because they have evolved different brains or because they have been socialized into different 'cultures'. The results of these presumed cognitive and social differences are used to 'explain' why:

■   women talk more than men (Figure 3.5);
■   women are more verbally skilled than men;
■   men talk more about things and facts, women talk more about people, rela-
    tionships and their feelings;
■   misunderstandings between men and women are a frequent occurrence.

Although there do seem to be some differences between men's and women's brains, a number of the claims that have been enthusiastically reported by the news media are not supported by research in this area. The social conditioning girls and boys receive about 'appropriate' ways of talking has been found to vary around the world, meaning that the stereotypes listed above are assumed to be evidence of 'natural' behaviour by *some* people, but not by others. Whereas the cartoon in Figure 3.5 implies that men talk less than women, in fact a number of studies have shown that men actually talk *more*, and that the significant variable is not gender, but *status* (people considered to be more important than others in any given situation talk more than people who are considered less important; Cameron 2007, p. 118). Where the home and its related work are considered the responsibility of women,

Figure 3.5   A miscommunicating man and woman being assisted by a (male) applied linguist? (© Mark Parisi)

women are indeed likely to be observed in domestic situations talking more than men. This is not *because* they are women, however, but because members of such societies are socialized into believing that the home is a 'natural' environment for women. Dale Spender (1980) suggests that where women are criticized for talking too much, it is because, in the minds of those doing the criticizing, they shouldn't really be allowed to talk at all!

Other language practices which contribute to women's marginalization are those which encode male dominance in the shared resources of the language. A much-commented upon example is the so-called 'generic' use of masculine forms, including the English pronouns *he* and *him* and terms like *man* and, in other languages, masculine gender on nouns, to refer to professionals and people in general. Women can be linguistically disadvantaged for other reasons too. As we have seen in previous sections, they are disproportionately represented among the blind, the deaf and the non-literate. In many societies, women also tend to have limited or zero access to the policy-making process and to educational opportunities.

## Defendants and plaintiffs

Language features prominently in the world of legal affairs. Perhaps most importantly, it is the principal medium through which laws are drafted, encoded,
promulgated, exercised and enforced. In both criminal and civil cases, language
makes possible the dispensation of justice and the redress of grievances through
the prosecution, defence, judgement and sentencing of those accused of breaking
the law. It also makes possible the abuse of the law for the advantage of the privileged and powerful. Given that people's liberties and livelihoods may be affected
by legal action, the language of the law must be as precise and unambiguous as
possible, and this has given rise to often highly esoteric technical vocabulary and
discourse practices. Unfortunately, this specialized language of the law, together
with lawyers' legitimate needs for verbal dexterity and rhetorical skill, often represents a barrier to those outside the profession, especially linguistically vulnerable
or marginalized groups like some of the populations discussed above. This danger
is especially keen for plaintiffs and defendants if more unscrupulous members of
the profession use language as a weapon or smokescreen. As the eighteenth-
century English poet John Gay wrote in his fable *The Dog and the Fox*:

> I know you lawyers can, with ease,
> Twist words and meanings as you please;
> That language, by your skill made pliant,
> Will bend to favour ev'ry client.

Applied linguists have, as a consequence, been occupied by the needs of people
involved in judicial proceedings to have effective access to the code. They have been
involved in campaigns for language clarity and simplification, some sponsored by
governments and the profession itself, and have also addressed the rights and
needs of minority language speakers in the witness box, dock and jury box, as we'll
see in Chapter 12. Discourse analysis (Chapter 4) has been a major recent tool in
these endeavours.

 **www.3.17**

But language is not only the medium of the law. It is also a frequent object of
legal proceedings, appearing as the major issue in some court cases (for example
in trademark disputes and defamation or obscenity proceedings), and even more
often in a supporting role, as evidence for the prosecution or defence. If you are
accused of a crime or accuse someone else, lawyers and the police will take statements, record interrogations and cross-examine witnesses and defendants. These
texts and discourses constitute evidence that judges and juries will use to adjudicate
guilt or innocence, so it is important that alternative interpretations are revealed and
analysed (through linguists' use of the tools of sociolinguistics, pragmatics and
discourse analysis). Chapter 12, on forensic linguistics, discusses these issues
further.

## 3.6  POPULATIONS CHARACTERIZED BY THEIR PROFESSIONAL OR ACADEMIC  INTEREST IN LANGUAGE

### Professional language users and their clients

With the exception perhaps of Trappist monks in their kitchens and gardens, all human beings use language in the workplace. But for many, language is also a principal work tool. For some, like language teachers or interpreters, language constitutes also the sole, or major, objective or product of their professional activities. These are discussed in the following section. For others, however, language is used to achieve their non-linguistic professional goals. Lawyers, priests, journalists, advertisers, politicians, spin doctors, psychiatrists, social workers, teachers and broadcasters – to name but a few – get paid for the ideas they communicate through keyboards and vocal tracts. We have already mentioned the need for lawyers to use clear, client-friendly language as well as the specifically legal language they speak to each other. There is a similar need for such 'register adjustment' in other professionals who must deal fairly and openly with their (lay) clients. Christian priests are old hands at this, having forsaken the Latin mass and bible in favour of vernacular translation many centuries ago. But others, such as doctors and social workers, may benefit from the fruits of research on professional discourse and the dynamics of professional–client interaction in order to allay the fears of increasingly savvy users of their services.

A good example of this is job interviews. Roberts and Campbell (2006) studied videos of over sixty real job interviews in the UK, using discourse analysis (see Chapter 4). They found that first generation ethnic minorities (i.e. interviewees born abroad) were less successful than ethnic minority members born in the UK not because of language proficiency, but due to problems acting and interacting in culturally appropriate ways. This kind of applied linguistic work can contribute greatly to professional training programmes for effective communication, in this instance to help interviewers penetrate or work around issues of cross-cultural talk in order to identify key skills that match the job specifications. The applied linguist Celia Roberts has done a lot of work in this area, leading to the production of audiovisual training tools for general medical practitioners, for example.

### Language purveyors and language professionals

The term 'language purveyor' is not a generally accepted term in applied linguistics (it was used in Hall, 2005), but seems an appropriate way to refer to those for whom language itself forms the essential material for their professional activities. Some of these, such as novelists, screenplay writers, theatre directors, copy-editors and language-related software developers, will not generally associate themselves with the field of applied linguistics. But many will make use of applied linguistic expertise, from dialect coaching to discourse analysis in the creation of screen or stage dialogue, to grammar-checkers and natural language search engines on computers. As professional barriers become increasingly blurred, we predict increased collaborations and overlaps between applied linguists and language purveyors in the future.

Other occupations (more usually known as 'language professions') may be identified more closely with applied linguistics or indeed welcome or require some professional training in the area. They include lexicographers, translators and interpreters, language teachers, language pathologists and language planners. Unlike those who teach applied linguistics and (some of) those who conduct research in the area, they work directly with the client populations we have described here. The needs of these clients are discussed throughout the book.

## Students of applied linguistics

Even if you're reading this book to *teach* from, this means you (and us)! Some study applied linguistics formally as part of a general undergraduate degree in linguistics. Others may elect to continue their linguistic education by taking a (post)graduate qualification in applied linguistics, perhaps as a way of deciding which branch of the profession they would most like to work in. Many study applied linguistics at this level after some years of practising as a language professional; the advantage of this route being the opportunity to learn from other areas of the profession. But in a very real sense, we're all students. One of the characteristics of any language professional, we would argue, is a research orientation to their work – each client more than likely having a unique set of overlapping needs for which, given the resources, unique programmes of treatment are devised. Applied linguists should, therefore, be willing to learn from and about their clients, their professional contexts and each other, face to face, online and in print, permanently.

 **www.3.18**

 **www.3.19**

Equally, scholars in other disciplines will recognize themselves as permanent students, and some will wish to be, or may profit from being, students of applied linguistics. Take for example *general* linguists: we saw in Chapter 1 that applied linguistics is not simply linguistics applied. Applied linguistics is more usefully seen as a sister discipline to linguistics unapplied, but often the interests and objectives of both coincide. A clear example is in the support of endangered languages. Field linguists documenting these languages are increasingly recognizing the need to understand and use research models, methods and findings from additional language teaching, language policy and planning, bilingual education, literacy and various other specialities in the field. And applied linguistic expertise is being used too by scholars in fields where language is definitely not the focus. For example, in the area of international development, restocking has been proposed as a response to livestock loss as a result of disaster in sub-Saharan Africa, but the effectiveness of the policy is not assured. A research project for the UK's Department for International Development Livestock Production Programme examining thirty pastoralist communities in Kenya used discourse analysis techniques from applied linguistics to evaluate local perceptions of restocking practices (Heffernan *et al.*, 2001). This is by no means an isolated instance.

## 3.7  ROLES FOR APPLIED LINGUISTS

Each chapter in Parts B and C of this book ends with a brief summary of roles for applied linguists. We anticipate this feature here, by listing some general roles arising from the nature of our work with clients:

■   A hundred years ago the famous hotelier César Ritz said, 'Le client n'a jamais tort' (*The customer is never wrong*). Although applied linguistics is not a commercial enterprise, we should take care to listen to our clients and work with them to address the language problems they face. Of course, clients are often wrong, but their wrongness is a distinctive part of the problem and so ought to be recognized and addressed in any possible solution. Our role here is as *listeners* and *partners* with our clients.

■   Applied linguists also have a responsibility to be aware of research in general linguistics, in order to be able to 'break the Language Spell' (in the words of Hall, 2005) and so reveal and be able to challenge our own and our clients' linguistic prejudices and misunderstandings. Here we are *advocates* and *consciousness-raisers*, exploring the issues not only with clients, but also with policy-makers, practitioners, institutional authorities, colleagues and students.

■   The diversity, complexity and ever-changing nature of our client populations requires applied linguists to understand their contexts and needs from as close to 'the inside' as possible, resisting top-down, theory-determined solutions which may be completely inappropriate for local requirements. We act here as **ethnographers** and *mediators* between general theories and local practices.

■   The multifaceted nature of our clients and their membership in overlapping population groups means also that applied linguists need to bear in mind the whole person, be it student or patient, professional or labourer, academic or non-literate, young or old. In doing so, we're *noticers* and *empathizers*.

■   As we hope this book will show, the landscape of applied linguistics is very varied, but certain topographical features, both opportunities to be taken advantage of and challenges to be met, recur again and again. We can learn a lot from each other: teacher from pathologist, translator from teacher, planner from translator, discourse analyst from forensic phonetician. So we're inevitably *collaborators* and *students* across professional and philosophical boundaries.

**Ethnographic** enquiry seeks to understand cultural situations and activities from the richly contextualized perspectives of the participants themselves. Ethnographers record what they observe from a holistic perspective, with no preconceived expectations about what to look for and what to ignore. Can't get there in person? Try 'virtual ethnography':

**www.3.20**

---

*activities*

1   Look back at the client groups named in Figure 3.1 at the beginning of the chapter. Are you (or a friend or relative of yours) a member of any of these groups? As a client of applied linguistics, what language services have you received? What labels are available for the groups you belong to? Which labels do you prefer and why?

2   Read the section of this chapter which talks about the client group(s) you, or your friend or relative, belong to. Make a list of obligations and activities for applied linguists in this area and rank them in order of importance for you as a client.

3    Type the name of a client group from Figure 3.1 and the name of a country in which you are interested into an internet search engine (to make sure you get a local view you can use your national Google domain, unless you want to look at the USA). What are the issues facing the client group in the country you chose? For example, when we tried *minority language speakers* and *Russia*, we found a European Union report on regional and minority languages in new EU member states. The report mentions the need for more resources on the World Wide Web in minority languages to avoid the deepening of a 'digital divide' between speakers of minority and majority languages.

4    Repeat activities 1 and 2 with someone who is a member of a different client group and compare your findings with your own experience.

## FURTHER READING

Harbert, W., McConnell-Ginet, S., Miller, A. and Whitman, A. (eds) (2009). *Language and poverty*. Clevedon, UK: Multilingual Matters.

Heller, M. (2006). *Linguistic minorities and modernity: A sociolinguistic ethnography*, 2nd edn. London: Continuum.

Long, M. H. (2005). *Second language needs analysis*. Cambridge: Cambridge University Press.

# CHAPTER 4

# Discourse analysis

> [D]iscourse Analysis is one way to engage in a very important human task. The task is this: to think more deeply about the meanings we give people's words so as to make ourselves better, more humane people and the world a better, more humane place ... If such talk [seems] too grandiose to you, then, I suggest, you've been reading – and doing – the wrong academic work.
>
> (Gee, 2005, p. xii)

Discourse surrounds us in everyday life, often in ways that seem so normal we barely notice them: from the combining of texts and images in school books, on food packaging and road signs; to greetings between friends and between strangers; to the writing of emails and academic essays. As these examples imply, the word *discourse* refers to spoken or written language (perhaps in combination with images) used to communicate particular meanings. Discourse *analysis* is the practice of exploring what kinds of speaking, writing and images are treated as 'normal' (and 'abnormal') in real situations, and the proportions, combinations and purposes of discourse that are conventionally acceptable (or not) in these situations.

The aims and methods of discourse analysts have varied over time and across a broad range of academic disciplines. Aims have included, for example: the description of contextualized language use, the explanation of how discourse is processed in the mind, and the consideration of how discourse can both reflect and create a particular version of events, objects or people (Pennycook, 1994a). Broadly, analysts interested in achieving the first two of these three aims have tended to conceptualize discourse from a linguistic or psycholinguistic perspective, in which language provides the components of discourse and the mind is the ultimate seat of language. In contrast, analysts interested in achieving the third of the three aims have tended to conceptualize discourse from a sociolinguistic perspective, in which understanding of the mind (and, more generally, what it means to be a person, or a member of a particular group or culture) is created (not just expressed) in and through discourse. In other words, for discourse analysts working within a social rather than a cognitive tradition, mind, people and cultures are the product of discourse, not its source (though see the section on discursive psychology on pp. 87–8 for a new approach to the relationship between mind and language). For a brief historical overview of developments and a discussion of definitions of discourse analysis, see Jaworski and Coupland (1999, pp. 1–44).

As an applied linguist, you may be called upon to deal with problems which are conceptualized by your clients, and the language professionals who work with them, as *either* or *both* cognitive and social. Therefore we think that it's important to be aware of all possible dimensions of discourse. With this in mind, we map a variety of approaches to discourse analysis, but with our focus firmly on those which have already proved useful to applied linguists. The usefulness of each of these approaches is important, so in addition to briefly describing its aims and methods and mentioning some of the scholars associated with an approach, we have given an example of a study which uses the approach to illuminate a language problem faced by an individual (or groups of) user(s).

If you think that analysing discourse in your own professional context, or for a course of study you're engaged in, is something that you would like to do, how do you know which of the approaches described in this chapter to choose? Unfortunately, there isn't an easy answer to this question, and before you make your decision you will probably read a lot of research reports (published in the usual places: academic journals, books, profession-specific newsletters and websites) on the topics and client groups you are interested in. While you're reading these reports and comparing the context and the clients with your own, you may also want to consider the approach to discourse analysis used by the practitioner/ researcher and whether such an approach would be feasible in your own context. One way of starting to think about an approach is to look up the study we mention at the end of each sub-section (in 4.2 and 4.3) and consider how the context being researched is similar to or different from your own. Another way of choosing an approach to discourse analysis is to think about which topics or themes (as mentioned in each of the sub-sections in 4.2 and 4.3) the various approaches have been associated with, and whether these are topics or themes which interest you. For example, if you are a teacher interested in error correction in classroom discourse it would be useful to look at conversation analysis (see p. 87) and the considerable body of work by conversation analysts on **repair** (see, for example, Seedhouse, 2004).

Choosing an approach to discourse analysis that other practitioners/ researchers have used to explore the topic/theme/context/client group you are interested in has the obvious benefit of facilitating comparisons between your own findings and those of other discourse analysts. On the other hand, you could con- sider using an approach to analysis that has been used in a context that is similar to yours in some ways and different in others (a possibility we'll come back to in section 4.4). For details of the techniques associated with each of the approaches to discourse analysis described in sections 4.2 and 4.3 and demonstrations of how these techniques work on actual data, you could look up the studies that are mentioned as examples or check any of the books in the list of further reading at the end of this chapter. Many of the approaches also have frequently updated websites, often maintained by users of the different approaches, and, where relevant, these are noted in the text and included as links on the companion website.

It's important to remember that discourse analysis, just like all other kinds of analysis, is not a neutral, objective method for describing language use as it 'really is' (though the proponents of certain approaches to discourse analysis may claim otherwise). All the different approaches are underpinned by assumptions about:

- language (especially the relationship between language, thought and society);
- relationships between the practice of analysis and 'real life';
- the kind of changes we, as applied linguists, should be helping our clients make.

In conversation analysis, **repair** refers to the ways in which speakers correct unintended forms and non-understandings, misunderstandings or errors (or what they perceive to be such) during a conversation. A self-initiated repair is when the speaker corrects themself: 'You know Jim, *erm, what's his name,* John?' An example of an *other*-initiated repair is when the listener replies: '*Hmm?*'

In most cases, discourse analysts are likely to bring these assumptions to the surface rather than pretending that they don't exist. Often, as part of the process of selecting and justifying their analytical choices, analysts will make their assumptions accessible for inspection (and challenge) by the participants in their analysis. Ultimately, what approach to the analysis of discourse you take will depend on the types of questions you and your clients are asking about your situation and the types of text that are available for analysis. No one approach is necessarily better than any of the others; none of the approaches is an end in itself – all are simply tools in our quest to understand the real language issues encountered by our clients.

Here's the route we'll be taking in this part of the applied linguistics map. In the next section, 4.1, we stress the centrality of discourse in social processes as a prelude to describing some of the approaches to discourse analysis which have proved useful to applied linguists, briefly reviewing the typical aims, methods and principal scholars associated with each approach. We have divided up the approaches into two sections, 4.2 for those approaches whose origins are most closely tied to linguistics and 4.3 for those approaches whose origins are most closely associated with sociology, ethnography and cultural theory. (Treating the various ways of doing discourse analysis as separate sub-sections has the unintended side-effect of implying clear-cut differences between a complex and interrelated set of approaches which, in addition, can be mixed and matched to suit an applied linguist's specific needs. This is an issue to which we give further thought at several points in this chapter.) After our tour of approaches, we draw out some of the major themes that discourse analysts have explored, in section 4.4, and then conclude, in section 4.5, with some final thoughts about how doing discourse analysis can help applied linguists in their work.

## 4.1  THE PERVASIVE RELEVANCE OF DISCOURSE (ANALYSIS)

As we have already said, discourse is analysed in a variety of disciplinary fields, including (but not limited to) linguistics, anthropology, sociology, philosophy, literature and psychology, by people with a wide variety of aims, methods, theories and topics. What all these discourse analysts have in common is an interest in the following question: how does the study of discourse illuminate cultural and social processes? As applied linguists, we can probably narrow down this general question to: how does the study of discourse illuminate the cultural and social processes that can lead to language-related problems, and solutions, for our clients (the key populations of Chapter 3)? But perhaps this is too narrow a question, in that it doesn't acknowledge the contribution that sensitivity to language issues, a sensitivity characteristic of applied linguists, can make to the study of general cultural and social processes. Although the focus of this book is indeed language-related problems and solutions, this chapter is an appropriate place to remind ourselves of the importance of language in cultural and social *processes* as well as its importance as a *product* of culture and society (an interdependence we come back to later in this chapter in a section on texts and contexts, on pp. 91–2).

In an early study of the management of social relationships through discourse, the anthropologist Bronislaw Malinowski (1999 [1923]) observed how the meaning of much small talk is almost entirely context-defined. Employing the phrase **phatic communion**, he showed how these predictable patterns of ritual text help create positive feeling between speakers – not because of what the words *mean*, but because of what they *do*. By filling in silences or helping to start and end new topics, the meaning of these patterns of text is created by the context in which the words occur. Changing the context can change the meaning of the text, as the following example shows. In Scotland, 'greeters' employed by a supermarket to stand at the entrance to the shop and tell customers to *Enjoy your shopping experience* were ridiculed by the very customers the shop was trying to create a relationship with. In this case, the supermarket customers implicitly recognized the social bonding work being attempted by use of ritual text and resisted the exploitation of phatic communion for commercial purposes (Cameron, 2002). The relevance for applied linguists of the judgements all language users make about text, context and appropriacy is very clear: in situations where we are called on to give advice, we should be sensitive to local norms and be disdainful of global prescriptions for effective communication (like the self-help guides that insist we 'be direct' and 'be clear'). Each context is different, and all contexts have their own discourses. We have had enlightening conversations with academic colleagues about the role of discourse in a wide variety of fields, including education, theology, marine biology, geography and business management. The combination of a problem-solving orientation and a sensitivity to local contexts/discourses makes an applied linguist a useful person to have on any team tasked with the investigation of real-world issues.

> **Phatic communion** is a term used by Malinowski to refer to communication which is not intended to convey information but which functions as a way of creating or maintaining social contact. In English 'How are you?', 'Have a nice day!' and 'Terrible weather!' are examples of phatic communion.

 **www.4.1**

## 4.2 LINGUISTIC APPROACHES TO DISCOURSE ANALYSIS

 **www.4.2**

### Corpus linguistics

Corpus linguists amass (sometimes extremely large) electronic collections of naturally occurring written and transcribed texts (a **corpus**). The texts are usually chosen to represent a particular variety (or set of varieties) of language, genre or type of language user. By tagging (electronically labelling) selected features of the texts and then using a search engine to sort through the collection of tagged texts, corpus linguistics (CL) aims to explore the extent to which certain features of language use are associated with contextual factors (which could include variety of language, genre or type of language user). By counting how many times a selected feature occurs in the corpus, CL aims to uncover characteristic patterns of language use and to generalize from the collected texts to other texts of a similar type, or to the language as a whole. CL has been used to analyse language by a variety of applied linguists, including those working in forensic linguistics (Wools and Coulthard, 1998; also see Chapter 12), the preparation of bilingual dictionaries (Clear, 1996; see also Chapter 11) and additional language learning (Carter and McCarthy, 2006; O'Keeffe *et al.*, 2007; see also Chapter 9). Taking additional language learners as a type of language user, CL studies have suggested that learners of English tend to overuse adjective modifiers like *very* (Lorenz, 1998) and high generality words like *people* and *things* (Ringbom, 1998), and underuse hedging

> A **corpus** (plural **corpora**) is a digital collection of authentic spoken or written language. Corpora are used for the analysis of grammatical patterns and estimations of the frequency of words, word combinations and grammatical structures. The results are useful in, for example, additional language education, translation, lexicography and forensic linguistics.

 **www.4.3, 4.4**

devices like *perhaps* and *possibly* (Flowerdew, 2000). In CL, the features of the linguistic patterns under study are assumed to be 'in' the variety, genre or type of language user, independent of the context-specific processes of writing or speaking, or the processes of constructing and analysing the corpus.

There are applied linguists who dispute the validity and methods of CL for solving real-world language problems (for example Widdowson, 2000), though there are also those who argue that CL can be used to investigate not just patterns of linguistic structure and deployment, but also the role of language in social and cultural processes, making CL a possible tool in **critical discourse analysis** (Baker, 2006), of which more on pp. 88–9. The role of CL in studies of English as a **lingua franca** is an interesting and a controversial case, with some scholars using CL to try and discover grammar and lexis which are 'core' to (typically associated with) all lingua franca talk, regardless of setting, participants, etc. (see Seidlhofer, 2001; and the online *VOICE* English as a lingua franca corpus). Other scholars have argued for a more ethnographic approach to the analysis of lingua franca talk, emphasizing the importance of methods which are sensitive to the context-specific ways in which speakers adjust their talk to achieve specific goals (Canagarajah, 2007).

## Speech act theory

Speech act theory is part of the wider discipline of **pragmatics**. The work of philosopher J. L. Austin provided pragmatics with a theoretical framework for understanding the relationship between speaker, hearer, utterance and context (Austin, 1975). Using the concept of **speech act** as the principal object of study, Austin distinguished between the *words* used in the act (**locution**), the *intention* or force of the speaker (**illocution**) and the *effect* of the utterance on the listener (**perlocution**).

Speech act theory recognizes that language is not only a way of communicating ideas, but can also be used, depending on the participants and their sociocultural contexts, to transform their reality. In other words, we say things that not only are judgeable as true or false, but can also perform an action that impacts on the world. A speaker who says, 'It's hot in here' may simply mean to observe that it's hot (the propositional meaning, or, using Austin's term, the locutionary force); but they might also be making a *request* for a window to be opened (the illocutionary force), with the effect that the listener opens a window (the perlocutionary force). In an example of how speech act theory has been used in applied linguistics, Myers (2005) explores the role of language in public opinion research by corporate and government institutions. The study demonstrates how speech act theory can help us to understand the comments of a group of people living very close to a nuclear power plant, a choice of location that might be considered risky or dangerous. The local residents tell an interviewer appointed by the government body responsible for dealing with nuclear waste that, on the one hand, they feel safe, despite their close proximity, but, on the other hand, they don't want the by-products of the plant, the nuclear waste, to be disposed of near their homes.

Myers points out that one possible interpretation of these seemingly contradictory comments is that a statement of trust in a person or institution can have the

**www.4.5**

**Pragmatics** aims to understand what spoken (or signed) language means in specific contexts of use, through a description of the relationship between speaker, hearer, utterance and context.

**www.4.6**

**Speech acts** are utterances which operate as a functional unit in communication; for example: promises, requests, commands and complaints. In additional language education (especially lesson planning and syllabus design), speech acts are often referred to as *functions*.

In speech act theory, utterances involve two kinds of meaning: a **locutionary** meaning, which is the literal meaning of the words and structures being used; and an

perlocutionary force (the effect on the listener) of creating an *obligation* to be trustworthy. In stating that the nuclear plant is safe to a person they identity with the plant, the locals may be doing something about making the plant safe: via the interviewer, the managers of the plant and the government are reminded that they have an obligation to ensure safety if they are not to fail in the trust bestowed by the local residents. Speech act theory, in this example, helps to show how the meaning of the locals' comments about safety is more richly interpretable from the perspective of the specific relationship between the speakers, hearers and places involved. The application of speech act theory also helps to explain why other data collection methods, such as surveys, which are not as context-sensitive as a face-to-face interview, have failed to generate much insight into general public opinion (other than the very obvious, like 'nuclear waste should be disposed of, but not near us').

**illocutionary**
meaning, which is the effect the utterance is intended to have on the listener. A **perlocutionary** act is the effect or result of the utterance.

## The Birmingham School

An early use of discourse analysis in applied linguistics was the description of classroom discourse by John Sinclair and Malcolm Coulthard (1975). Developed out of an approach to structural analysis in linguistics, Sinclair and Coulthard's groundbreaking work identified twenty-two combinable speech acts that typified the verbal behaviours of primary school teachers and their pupils in traditional, teacher-centred lessons. Their model involved a discourse hierarchy composed of units of discourse from the largest unit, *lesson*; down to *transaction* (episodes within the lesson usually bounded by discourse markers such as 'right' and 'now then'); then *exchange,* a unit of discourse comprising combinations of question–answer–feedback *moves*; and finally the smallest unit, *act* (nominating students, getting them to put their hands up and so on) (see Figure 4.1).

Sinclair and Coulthard suggested that typical of classroom discourse was the 'eliciting exchange', comprising the three core moves of teacher initiation, followed

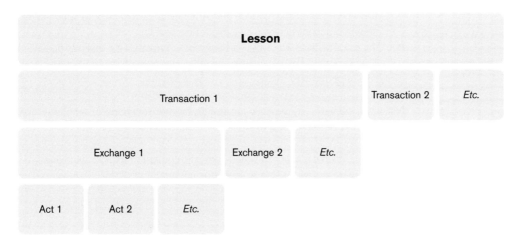

Figure 4.1    Sinclair and Coulthard's discourse hierarchy for traditional teacher-centred lessons (Sinclair and Coulthard, 1975)

by student response, followed by teacher feedback or evaluation (IRF/E). For example:

> *Teacher:*   What's the past form of the verb 'swim'? *Initiation*
> *Student:*   Swam *Response*
> *Teacher:*   Swam, good! *Feedback and evaluation*

Whilst it is extremely important for raising awareness of teacher talk in general (and starting the debate about the effectiveness of different patterns of talk), the practical difficulty of identifying a one-to-one relationship between moves and speech acts has been identified as a possible threat to the validity of the Birmingham School's approach to discourse analysis, as has the problem of over-generalization and lack of sensitivity to local context (Seedhouse, 2004).

## Systemic functional linguistics

**www.4.7**

**Systemic functional linguistics** (SFL) is interested in the social context of language. In SFL, language is analysed as a resource used in communication, as opposed to a decontextualized set of rules. It is an approach which focuses on functions (what language is being used to *do*), rather than on forms.

Drawing on the work of linguist J. R. Firth and Dell Hymes (of whom more in the next section), **systemic functional linguistics** (SFL) is most closely associated with M. A. K. Halliday (1978, 1994). SFL aims to explore the systematic relationship between the contexts of everyday life and the *functional organization* of language; that is, what language does in, and for, the situation in which it is spoken or written – in other words, its social purpose. The central claim of SFL is that the structural choices made in the construction of texts are ultimately derived from the functions that language serves in a context of use. Halliday's framework for describing texts and their social contexts comprises three elements, which together reflect the concept of **register** we introduced in Chapter 2:

- The *field* of discourse: what is happening? What is the nature of the social action that is accomplished by the text?
- The *tenor* of discourse: who is taking part? What kinds of temporary and permanent status and roles do the participants have in the interaction and in other interactions in which they might take part?
- The *mode* of discourse: what part does the language of the text play (including whether the discourse is spoken or written, and its rhetorical mode: persuasive, didactic, expository, etc.)?

Halliday's semantic framework for identifying the functions of language also consists of three categories, which are (in a rather simplified form):

- The *ideational* function: how the semantic content of a text is expressed.
- The *interpersonal* function: how the semantic content is exchanged or negotiated.
- The *textual* function: how the semantic content is structured in the text.

SFL uses these two frameworks (which are more detailed and intricate than our summary implies) to explore the relationships between social contexts and functions of language, paying attention to how:

- *experiential* meanings are activated by features of the *field*;
- *interpersonal* meanings are activated by features of the *tenor*;
- *textual* meanings are activated by features of the *mode*.

The consequence of SFL's functional approach is a theory of meaning in which text and context are inseparable; language operates in contexts of situation, and social contexts are created by the range of texts that are produced within a community. In an example of how SFL can be used in applied linguistics, Young and Nguyen (2002) compare how a scientific topic is presented in interactive teacher talk with how the same topic is presented in a textbook. The study identifies three aspects of scientific meaning-making: representations of physical and mental reality, lexical packaging and the rhetorical structure of reasoning. The comparative analysis of teacher talk and textbook illustrates the different ways in which students are socialized into thinking and talking about science, as well as making some recommendations for the design of school textbooks.

## The ethnography of communication

Ethnographic approaches to discourse analysis are part of a sociolinguistic tradition and are closely associated with the work of Hymes (1972) (see also Saville-Troike, 2003). With the intention of extending Chomsky's linguistic competence/performance model, discussed in Chapter 1, Hymes proposed the construct of **communicative competence**: knowledge of whether and to what degree an utterance is considered by a specific community or group to be grammatical, socially appropriate, cognitively feasible and observable in practice. Figure 4.2 illustrates some of the elements of communicative competence.

Hymes developed a framework which analysed communication at three different levels: speech *situations* (sports events, ceremonies, trips, evenings out, etc.); speech *events* (ordering a meal, making a political speech, giving a lecture, etc.);

**Communicative competence** is not only the ability to form utterances using grammar, but also the knowledge of when, where and with whom it is appropriate to use these utterances in order to achieve a desired effect. Communicative competence includes the following knowledge: grammar and vocabulary; the rules of speaking (how to begin and end a conversation, how to interrupt, what topics are allowed, how to address people and so on); how to use and respond to different speech acts; and what kind of utterances are considered appropriate.

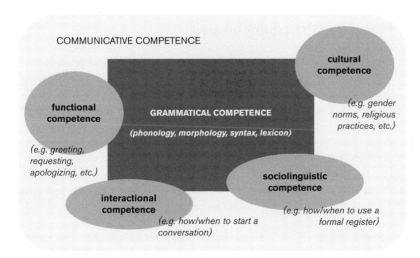

Figure 4.2    Aspects of communicative competence

The **communicative approach** in additional language teaching stresses that the aim of learning a language is communicative competence. Teachers who base their lessons on a communicative approach may follow a syllabus based on functions or topics, teaching the language needed to perform a variety of authentic tasks and to communicate appropriately in different situations.

The work of **interactional sociolinguists** focuses on the fleeting, unconscious and culturally variable conventions for signalling and interpreting meaning in social interaction. Using audio or video recordings, analysts pay attention to the words, prosody and register shifts in talk, and what speakers and listeners understand themselves to be doing with these structures and processes. Gumperz, the founder of interactional sociolinguistics, was mainly interested in contexts of intercultural miscommunication, where unconscious cultural expectations and practices for conveying and understanding meaning are not necessarily shared between speakers.

and speech *acts* (greetings, compliments, etc.: see pp. 80–1). Speech events (the middle category) rely on speech for their existence (without speech it would, for example, be difficult, though not impossible, to insult someone effectively). The components of speech events can, according to Hymes (1974), be described using the following eight-part list based on the word *speaking*:

- **s**ituation (physical, temporal, psychological setting defining the speech event);
- **p**articipants (for example, speaker, hearer, addressee, audience);
- **e**nds (purposes, goals and outcomes);
- **a**ct sequence (message form and content);
- **k**ey (manner of speaking, tone, for example serious, joking, tentative);
- **i**nstrumentalities (spoken or written, use of dialects, registers, etc.);
- **n**orms of interaction (for example turn-taking) and interpretation (local conventions of understanding);
- **g**enre (for example poems, academic essays, myths, casual speech, etc.).

One important impact on applied linguistics of the ethnography of communication has been in the inspiration of the **communicative approach** to teaching additional languages (Howatt and Widdowson, 2004; see also Chapter 9). Applied linguists use ethnographic approaches to understanding the discourse of specific communities or groups with which they are closely involved, either through participation in the communities' usual activities and/or very careful observation. A community could be, for example, people in a courtroom, a family, participants in an online discussion board, a department or team at work, and students and teachers in a classroom. In an example of the latter, Duff (2002) illustrates the use of an ethnographic approach to communication in a study of a UK high school classroom with a high proportion of pupils who are speakers of English as an additional language. A detailed analysis of the classroom talk, from the point of view of the participants, highlights the contradictions and tensions in a teacher's attempt to encourage her students to respect each other's cultural identity and difference.

## Interactional sociolinguistics

The approach to discourse known as **interactional sociolinguistics** was established by a close associate of Hymes, the anthropological linguist John Gumperz (for example Gumperz, 1982), drawing on the work of Erving Goffman (for example Goffman, 1981). Much of Gumperz's work focuses on intercultural communication and misunderstanding (see pp. 92–4) and aims to show that our understanding of what a person is saying depends not just on the content of their talk but on our ability to notice and evaluate what he calls *contextualization cues*, which include: intonation, tempo, rhythm, pauses, lexical and syntactic choices and non-verbal signals. Gumperz adapted and extended Hymes' ethnographic framework by examining how interactants with different first languages apply different rules of speaking in face-to-face interaction.

How this happens, and the subconscious nature of the interpretive processes involved, is suggested by the following example (Gumperz, 1982). Newly hired South Asian airport canteen staff were perceived as surly and uncooperative by their

British supervisors and the British cargo handlers they served food to. Observation of the canteen staff at work showed that they didn't exchange many words with their colleagues, but when they did, the way in which they pronounced these words was interpreted negatively. For instance, instead of saying *Gravy?*, with rising intonation, as a way of offering gravy, the South Asian staff used falling intonation.

Gumperz describes how the researchers recorded the canteen interaction and played it to both British and South Asian employees, asking them to paraphrase what they meant by each utterance. After several such data sessions, the British employees could see that the South Asian canteen staff were not intending to show rudeness or indifference, but using their normal way of asking questions in that situation. The South Asian employees had sensed for some time that they were being misunderstood but explained this as a reaction to their national origins. Gumperz claims that the discussion sessions, by focusing not on stereotypes or attitudes but on context-bound interpretative preferences, resulted in the acquisition by the staff of strategies for the self-diagnosis of communicative problems (for a similar study of discrimination in the workplace based on a misunderstanding of contextualization cues, see Roberts, 2005).

## Contrastive rhetoric

So far, we have been concerned with the organization of discourse *within* languages. In a much discussed paper, the applied linguist Robert Kaplan claimed that there were differences in the way that discourse was organized *between* languages. Kaplan (1966) suggested that written texts were organized in ways that corresponded to the 'thought patterns' of the following five 'cultures': Semitic, Russian, Romance, European and Oriental. For example, 'European' writing was supposed to be organized in a linear, hierarchical pattern, whereas 'Oriental' writing was spiral and non-hierarchical. Kaplan's original article has been challenged (including by Kaplan himself) on various grounds (Connor, 2002), including:

- its research methods (Kaplan mainly used texts written in English by students studying English in the US);
- its simplistic generalizations about language and writing within 'cultures', and its underdeveloped concept of 'culture';
- its view of writing as a product, not a process;
- its implication that other cultures need to learn to avoid 'bad' writing;
- its conflation of 'thought patterns' with the way written texts are organized;
- its use of the paragraph, not the whole text, as the unit of analysis;
- its lack of attention to the writing styles of different genres within languages or to differences between the many languages in each category;
- its lack of sensitivity to the way writers actually shuttle between local and target language practices in their writing.

Despite these criticisms, applied linguists working in a number of areas, including how to teach academic or business writing to first and second language writers, may find the analysis of differences in the organization of texts (**contrastive rhetoric**) a productive exercise. For example, in a comparative study of English

**Contrastive rhetoric** compares the organization of texts written in different languages, based on the assumption that there are characteristic patterns of writing associated with culturally determined ways of thinking.

Language **processing** research investigates how the linguistic knowledge that is stored in the mind/brain is used in real time (as the cognitive events unfold) to produce and understand utterances.

**Cognitive discourse analysis** is an approach which takes into account the mental representations and processes involved in the production and comprehension of discourse, including the role of socially shared knowledge stored in individuals' long-term memory and the capacity and limitations of their short-term (working) memory.

**Mental models** are representations of situations in the mind which are constructed on the basis of sensory and linguistic input, general knowledge, beliefs, attitudes and intentions. They are the starting point for writing and speaking and the endpoint for listening and reading. Mental models contain far more detailed information than can be mapped onto the linguistic expressions we use to produce (encode) and comprehend (decode) them.

language business correspondence in Hong Kong, writers with Cantonese as a first language tended to delay and justify their requests more than those writers with English as a first language (Kong, 1998).

## Cognitive discourse analysis

A cognitive approach to discourse analysis is one which aims to describe language use with reference to the knowledge schemas and memory structures that are activated or constructed in language users' minds as they engage with discourse, both in production and comprehension. The **processing** of discourse is a major topic in psycholinguistics, where the moment-by-moment cognitive events of language use are tracked using experimental techniques such as measurements of pause times in speaking or eye-tracking in reading. But real context is absent in such laboratory work. As a result, cognitive approaches are often viewed as philosophically, epistemologically, methodologically and even ideologically incompatible with an interest in the actual use of language by specific users in authentic contexts. Despite this, and in keeping with our belief that applied linguists are in the business of opening doors and crossing bridges in the pursuit of understanding and aiding client populations, we take seriously the view that cognitive and social processes are always co-present, and implicate each other, even if the conceptualization of the relationship between them is still confused and incomplete.

The work of Teun van Dijk provides an example of **cognitive discourse analysis** that demonstrates possible overlap between cognitive and social processes. He takes cognition as both personal and social, involving memory structures and mental representations such as beliefs, emotions, evaluations and goals, and links it with society, which he defines in terms of both context-specific, face-to-face interaction between individuals, and the global, social and political organization of groups and relationships between them. Van Dijk (2001) suggests that a socio-cognitive analysis can help us understand, for example, the effect of a petition against the US government's prosecution of Microsoft for monopolistic business practices. Van Dijk argues that the writers of the text use words such as *rights*, *freedom* and *individual* to connect their own neo-liberal anti-interventionist stance with their readers' **mental models** of positive political and social goals. An analysis of an advertisement for a political party broadcast on television during a US presidential election campaign uses **conceptual blending theory** to explain the mental operations involved in persuading the audience that there was a causal relationship between the actions of one of the candidates, George W. Bush, and a horrific race hate crime two years earlier (Coulson and Oakley, 2000). This kind of work, drawing on the tools of linguistics and psycholinguistics, has the potential to show how individual minds are, ultimately, the place where the meanings and effects of discourse are created, and so provides an important basis for building links with apparently irreconcilable scholarly world views, such as critical discourse analysis, discussed in section 4.3.

## 4.3  SOCIAL APPROACHES TO DISCOURSE ANALYSIS

### Conversation analysis

The origins of **conversation analysis** (CA) lie in the sociological approach to language and communication known as ethnomethodology (associated with Harold Garfinkel, 1967): the study of social order and the (actually very complex) ways in which people coordinate their everyday lives in interaction with others. CA was initially developed into a distinctive field of enquiry by, amongst others, Harvey Sacks, Emmanuel Schegloff and Gail Jefferson, and looks both at (usually) short segments of ordinary, mundane conversation and at the institutional forms of talk found in, for example, suicide prevention centres, group therapy sessions and classrooms. The analysis aims to show the intricate ways in which interlocutors mutually organize their talk and what these tell us about socially preferred patterns of interaction, including: turn-taking, opening and closing an interaction, introducing and changing topics, managing misunderstanding, introducing bad news, agreeing and disagreeing, eliciting a response by asking a question, and so on.

CA has been used in applied linguistics to evaluate and inform the practice of language professionals and their clients in a wide range of types of interaction, including: students doing group work at university, medical examinations, service encounters and business meetings (for accounts of the relationship between CA and applied linguistics, see Drew, 2005; Schegloff *et al.*, 2002). For example, a study comparing the interaction of a mother and a speech therapist with a child experiencing phonetic problems (Gardner, 2005) shows how, amongst other things, the mother uses a much greater number of turns in dealing with a problem word than the therapist, with less success and with the unintended result of provoking new errors. Gardner suggests that the findings of this study could be used to demonstrate to the mother the need to reduce her number of turns per problem word, increasing the amount of positive intervention available to the child and the likelihood of progress.

### Discursive psychology

Who hasn't spent time listening to another person talk and trying to work out what they 'really' want, or what kind of person they 'really' are? Cognitive traditions in psychology have tended to focus on inner mental states as the *causes* of what people say (and how they say it) and concentrate on talk as *reflective* of what a person thinks, believes, feels or wants (see the sub-section on cognitive discourse analysis on the previous page). **Discursive psychology**, in contrast, is interested in how people *perform* emotions, attitudes and beliefs in their talk, and how this performance can bring mental states into being. In other words, instead of thinking of talk as a reflection of what people are 'really' feeling or their 'real' attitudes to a topic, discursive psychologists think of talk as *constituting* these feelings and attitudes. For example, imagine someone you know who you believe to be shy or arrogant or happy or forgetful; a discursive psychologist would say that these are judgements you make based on *how* this person expresses him/herself (in specific

 **www.4.9**

**Conceptual blending theory** looks at how the meaning of texts is comprehended in real time by a listener or reader prompted by linguistic cues to activate mental models. These models allow speaker-listeners to distinguish between different elements of a text and understand where there is a relationship ('blending') between these elements.

 **www.4.8**

**Conversation analysts** are interested in the organizational structure of spoken interaction, including how speakers decide when to speak in a conversation (rules of turn-taking) and how the utterances of two or more speakers are related (adjacency pairs like A: 'How are you?' B: 'Fine thanks.'). As well as describing structures and looking for patterns of interaction, some analysts are also interested in how these structures relate to the 'doing of' social and institutional roles, politeness, intimacy, etc. What conversation analysts want to know is: why that now?

Traditionally, psychology has understood the cognitive and emotional states of individuals to be the source of interactive phenomena such as friendship, aggression and the influence of one person's beliefs on another. **Discursive psychologists**, on the other hand, are interested in how (and which) ways of talking and behaving are understood by people to mean that a person is (being) friendly, aggressive, loving and so on: how we 'do' friendliness, for example, and what we recognize as friendliness when we see and hear it.

situations in which s/he is interacting with particular people). Traditionally, psychologists have asked people about their attitudes, beliefs and emotions using surveys which aim to discover clear and stable patterns common to large groups of people. Discursive psychologists, in contrast, observe the interactional business that is performed by these accounts of attitudes etc., using recordings, transcriptions and detailed analysis of actual accounts, focusing on variability and inconsistency (Edwards and Potter, 1992; te Molder and Potter, 2005).

The topic of classroom-based additional language learners' 'motivation' is an illustrative one. On the whole, motivation has traditionally been thought of by teachers and researchers as an individual phenomenon reflecting an internal mental state. A discursive psychologist, on the other hand, might focus on how students and teachers actually demonstrate, through physical activity and talk, what gets *recognized* as motivation, rather than asking a student whether he or she is motivated.

Discursive psychology has its disciplinary roots in the sociology of scientific knowledge (Gilbert and Mulkay, 1984) and has used analytical methods typical of *conversation analysis* (see Park, 2007, for a study of the construction of native and non-native speaker identities), *critical discourse analysis* and *speech act theory* (see Cameron, 2005, for an account of the role of discourse in how we experience our gender and sexuality).

## Critical discourse analysis

Critical discourse analysts study the ways in which social power, dominance and inequality are enacted, reproduced and resisted by text and talk in social and political contexts.

**Critical discourse analysis** (CDA) is a way of thinking about texts, talk and visual imagery that is sensitive to the relationship between discourse and our beliefs about ourselves, other people, relationships and things that surround us. It is committed to exposing social and political unfairness. In this context, then, *critical* means being interested in uncovering the role of discourse in the creation, description and solution of social problems, the acquisition and use of power and the justifications provided for change or the maintenance of the status quo. Critical discourse analysts don't assume that the relationship between discourse and beliefs, objects, people and relationships should be taken for granted (for example, that teachers/doctors just 'naturally' treat students/patients in a particular way). Instead, they look in detail at the role of texts and talk in how our beliefs about our social world (for example gender roles) and physical world (for example animal welfare) come about, how our beliefs change over time and between places, who is advantaged or disadvantaged by our texts and talk, and how any disadvantage could be avoided or corrected.

The aims, theory and methods of CDA are drawn from a wide variety of sources, including sociology, literary criticism and linguistics, and are influenced by Halliday's systemic functional linguistics (Fairclough, 1995, 2001). Topics investigated have included gender, racism, identity, political and media discourse; research designs and methods have included small-scale qualitative case studies, as well as large amounts of data collected during ethnographic fieldwork (Wodak and Meyer, 2001). In an example of how CDA can be used to investigate real-world language problems, Blommaert (2005) reports a case study of interview talk between African asylum seekers and Belgian immigration officials, showing how judgements about incoherence, irrelevance and untrustworthiness can be a function of low levels of familiarity on the part of the interviewer and/or the interviewee with the language(s) used in the interview.

One problem with the way we have chosen to organize sections 4.1 and 4.2 is that we have perhaps made the differences between the approaches look greater than they actually are. While some methods may be more homogenous in their theories and practices than others, none have rule-books and all are used in slightly different ways by different analysts at different times. The challenge for an applied linguist is to understand the assumptions about language, cognition and society that their chosen approach(es) are based on, and to have the confidence to adapt techniques to suit their own and their clients' needs, while being transparent about these choices. We come back to this challenge in the final section of this chapter (4.4).

## 4.4  THEMES IN CONTEMPORARY DISCOURSE ANALYSIS

### Multi-modal texts

It's probably true to say that discourse analysis has tended to focus on the linguistic elements of texts. If you are reading a printed copy of this book, take a moment to look at the object you are holding; think about how the size of the font, the use of chapters, sub-headings and quotations, the glossary, the artwork, the back-cover blurb and the publishing company's logo encourage you treat this as an academic, authoritative text, one which you can legitimately quote in your own academic writing. Think also about how quoting a text, as we have done throughout the book, alters its meaning. Take the epigraph at the very beginning of this chapter, from James Gee. You, as the reader of this chapter, have encountered Gee's sixty-five-word text not in its original environment on page xii of the Preface to his book, but in another book (this one). This new position transforms the text into a *quotation*, and by implication makes it a quotable text. In its new position, the text is participating in the creation of a new piece of academic writing, a genre which is characterized by quotations. The text has, in addition, been transformed into an *advertisement* for the original object in which it was embedded.

In addition to images embedded in primarily *written* texts like this book and the book from which our epigraph was taken, there are also *image-heavy* texts which may use very few words. An example is given in Figure 4.3: a multi-modal roadside sign protesting against the construction of a perimeter fence along the US–Mexico border to keep migrants from crossing illegally. Note that much of the message is conveyed by imagery rather than words (the skeleton soldier in a US military uniform and Nazi helmet and the borderline represented by a furled Mexican flag). The meaning of the sign is signalled by the combination of words, shapes, colours and its physical location (in Brownsville, Texas, USA). In an example of multi-modal discourse analysis, Piety (2004) shows how an approach to discourse that is both cognitive and social (see the sub-section on cognitive discourse analysis on p. 86) can help language professionals describe and compare different ways of doing audio description (inserting extra spoken information about the action or

Figure 4.3   A hand-painted sign displayed on the US side of the US–Mexico border

scene of a play, film or TV programme for the benefit of visually impaired people). Multi-modal discourse, then, can use any way of communicating meaning, including design of everyday objects, sculpture, still or moving images and sounds.

Texts can also be oral, of course, such as conversations, service encounters and classroom discourse, although their analysis often involves transcription into written formats. Sometimes texts that reach the public via the auditory channel are first prepared in writing, such as teachers' lesson plans and the lectures of university instructors (or at least the well prepared among them!). Some are then preserved in written texts: think of the Swiss linguist Saussure's lectures *Course in General Linguistics* (1983, published posthumously by his students in 1916) or the script for a play that began with actors improvising their lines. Recent developments in communication technology favour the creation and display of multi-modal texts which combine oral and written forms of language along with music, images and other non-linguistic elements. A search of YouTube for 'Gandhi speeches' will provide many examples of multi-modal texts. In a typical YouTube Gandhi video, you can hear a speech, read the transcript, watch a rolling display of photos, drawings and posters of Gandhi, and perhaps listen to some lead-in music – all in one 'text'. New forms of digital literacy are pushing us to rethink the connections between the modality and meaning of texts, particularly with respect to the possibilities for authorship and shared design that can develop in online communities.

## Multi-voiced texts

As well as drawing on more than one semiotic system, texts can be multiply struc-tured in other ways, including the recycling of the language and genre-specific features of *other* texts. A multi-modal text like the Gandhi videos mentioned above might, for example, have different 'voices' associated with the different modalities; in one example from YouTube, extracts from his speeches are heard over a succession of connected images relating to recent government restrictions on freedoms in the UK and USA, including press photos, newspaper headlines, movie clips, posters and text. At one point, Gandhi's words 'we have no secrets' are accompanied by a camera zoom-in on the Masonic pyramid symbol on a dollar bill. At another, his words of protest against the fingerprinting of Indians in South Africa in the 1930s are heard over photos of the UK's new ID cards, US Social Security cards and a still image of Nazi guards checking identity papers during World War II.

 **www.4.10**

Multiple voicing or **heteroglossia** is a concept associated with Mikhail Bakhtin (e.g. 1981), who suggested that all spoken and written texts echo aspects of all the other texts that have been experienced by the speaker or writer, and all the ways in which the texts have been subsequently interpreted. The job of the discourse analyst becomes one of tracing the influences and interpretations of different genres and ideologies in a text, as well as their associated values, assump-tions and effects. In applied linguistics, the recognition that everyday speaking and writing require the constant stretching and twisting of communicative resources, rather than simply the reproduction of fixed, unchanging rules of language, has led analysts to focus on the creative styling in language of identities, histories and social relationships (e.g. Moss, 1989; Maybin and Swann, 2007).

Bakhtin's theory of **heteroglossia** suggests that a text can't be reduced to a single, fixed, self-enclosed, 'true' meaning which is determined by the intention of its author. Instead, the meanings of the words in the text, and the ways in which these words are combined, are linked to conditions of cultural production and reception. What texts mean, therefore, depends on the multitude of understandings, values, social discourses, cultural codes and so on of all their potential readers and hearers.

## Texts and contexts

In the introduction to this chapter, we defined discourse as text that is understood to relate to context. This definition, however, raises the obvious (and difficult) question: what is context? Definitions of context abound, but they are also notoriously slippery. Minimally, context comprises the linguistic, proximal, temporal, geographical, interpersonal and ideological dimensions of the situation in which a text is produced and interpreted (Figure 4.4). Because these dimensions exist simultaneously, it's inevitable that certain elements will be foregrounded in any given analysis, while others receive less attention.

But what are these dimensional labels, if not a collection of more texts, modifying the meaning of, and being modified by, each other? James Gee (2005, p. 57) describes the relationship between text and context as 'reflexive'; where the meaning of text and context is created by interaction between both. So how do we know which dimensions of a context are relevant? In their introduction to an edited collection of papers on language and context, Alessandro Duranti and Charles Goodwin (1992) claim that although an overarching definition of context may *never* be possible, it really doesn't matter. The absence of a definitive answer to the ques-tion provides impetus for the ongoing study of language in specific contexts of use, study which asks the question: what dimensions of the situation *are being made*

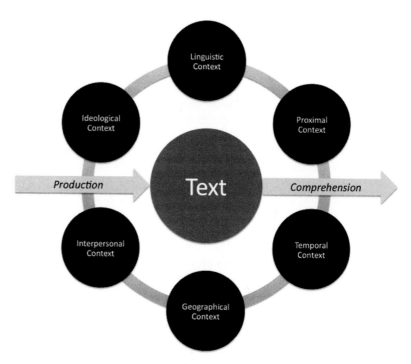

Figure 4.4   Some dimensions of context determining the situation in which text is produced and comprehended

*relevant here*? In other words, rather than proposing that analysts decide in advance on what aspects of the context help make sense of a text, Duranti and Goodwin take an interactionist view, suggesting that analysis should focus on 'how the participants attend to, construct, and manipulate aspects of context as a constitutive feature of the activities they are engaged in. Context is thus analyzed as an inter-actively constituted mode of **praxis**' (Duranti and Goodwin, 1992, p. 9). So, while your conversation with a classmate might take place within a classroom, the classroom context (with all its typical constraints on 'acceptable' ways of talking and behaving) might not be made relevant in talk between pupils after the teacher has left the room, when jokes about, for example, gender difference make 'girl' and 'boy' a more noticeable aspect of the context than 'pupil'.

**Praxis** is educational jargon for 'practice' or 'enaction', from the Greek verb *prattein*, 'to do'.

Particularly salient contexts for studying discourse as praxis are those contexts in which participants come to the interaction *without* shared cultural norms, a common feature of settings in which applied linguists work. There are several ways of thinking about the issue, and the next sub-section, on intercultural communi-cation, sketches some of them.

## Intercultural communication

It is possible to think about intercultural communication from a number of different points of view. A descriptive social-psychological approach (see, for example, Spencer-Oatey and Franklin, 2009) tends to assume that:

- cultural and linguistic factors are inextricably linked (we communicate the way we do because of our culture);
- cultural and linguistic factors precede interaction (in contrast to the assumptions of discursive psychology, critical discourse analysis and Duranti and Goodwin's (1992) proposal);
- cultural and linguistic factors are likely to be the cause of frequent difficulties in intercultural communication.

Critical approaches may be based on similar assumptions, except that communication is assumed to be the product not of culture, but of the institutions that regulate peoples' lives, imposing their ideologies on the discourses of individual speakers (see Blommaert, 2005, for a blend of CDA and interactionist approaches). Interactionist approaches are less likely to essentialize cultural group characteristics and equate individuals with a single culture or institution. They are more likely to pay attention to the features of actual samples of discourse in an attempt to show how culture is created in interaction. Such features could include: choice of (national) language or language variety; topic management; use or avoidance of repair strategies; elicitation of preferred responses; use of phonological features to emphasize certain information; and so on (see Bremer *et al.*, 1996, for a social-interactionist approach; and chapters in Richards and Seedhouse, 2005, for an interactionist, conversation-analytic approach).

Applied linguists are perhaps most likely to work with clients or in professional environments where the links between culture and communication are believed to be fixed and to precede specific instances of interaction, simply because the popular view of culture assumes it to be something everyone has before they start to speak (in culturally predictable ways). The direction of **causality** described above as social-psychological is assumed to be *from* culture *to* language; we communicate in certain ways *because* of our culture. This is an explanation we have frequently heard in conversations between additional language teachers (where nationality labels are used to imply cultural patterns) – along the lines of 'The Chinese students in my class hardly ever speak, but I can't shut the Italians up.' Causality in the opposite direction (i.e. from language to culture) has been observed in studies of legal language, where the language spoken by an appellant is assumed to determine his or her cultural patterns of thought. In an analysis of US case law materials, Mertz (1982) shows how a policy requiring immigrants to the US to speak English is based on an assumption that the ability to understand US political concepts is dependent on fluency in English (the 'native language' of the law). The relationship between language and legal rights is a central concern of applied linguists, as we explore in more detail in Chapter 12.

Good applied linguists are aware that there are many possible approaches to the analysis of intercultural discourse. Moreover, they realize that specific problems can be created, and also diffused, by the very approaches that are adopted to understand them. The acknowledgement of this awareness leads us to what might seem a surprising conclusion to a discussion premised on the idea of communication problems. Intercultural communication, we suggest, is no different from communication in general. This is not to say that there are no differences between the ways in which groups of people and individuals think and behave: indeed there are. But the impact of these differences on communication can be grossly

**Causality** is the relationship between causes and effects. The causality of two events describes the extent to which one event happens as a result of the other.

exaggerated. More important than itemizing the differences is an exploration of how these differences are used and who benefits (or loses out) when a difference is assumed. Successful communication, in our opinion, is not so much dependent on similarities or differences in language and culture, but on willingness to listen, to empathize and to negotiate. These qualities are less to do with language and more to do with attitudes and practice. To assume the inevitable existence of essential differences between individuals or groups results in the creation of many fictional barriers. To use these barriers to exclude people on the grounds of their difference is common practice, profitable for the party with the most power, and difficult or dangerous for the party with the least.

## 4.5 HOW CAN DOING DISCOURSE ANALYSIS HELP THE CLIENTS OF APPLIED LINGUISTS?

One of our most important jobs as applied linguists is to describe precisely how our clients' lives are affected by language, based not on folk beliefs, but on the systematic collection and analysis of relevant evidence, central to which are language data. In some cases, individual clients will benefit from interventions designed to help them in their specific situation. In other cases, we may choose to focus on interventions that seek to bring about a fundamental shift in our clients', and other peoples', *perceptions* of their situation. These interventions include or combine attempts to effect a move from a prescriptive (deficit) perspective on language use (in which 'non-standard' groups and practices are seen as inferior), to a descriptive perspective which demonstrates the integrity of our clients' use of language, or to a critical perspective which exposes discrimination against our clients, or to an interactionist perspective which attempts to show how language problems are locally constructed in specific contexts of use.

Wherever we think that solutions to a language problem might lie within an individual client and/or in the people, institutions and talk that surround them, some kind of discourse analysis is likely to be useful. At the beginning of this chapter (p. 77), we mentioned the benefits of choosing an approach that has a history of being used in your area of interest, as well as the benefits of taking an approach (and associated methods) from a different area to your own. Going back to the topic of additional language teachers' treatment of student errors, we could, for example, look at a recently published study (which uses critical discourse analysis and corpus linguistics) of how *newspaper reports* use language to create very specific reader responses to political events, by 'positioning' their readers in a certain way (Coffin and O'Halloran, 2010). A teacher could collect examples of their own and other teachers' correction of students' written work and, using the same approach and methods as the Coffin and O'Halloran study, consider how the language of these corrections might position students in a certain way, perhaps as novice language users, with the reduced rights to creative self-expression apportioned to the not-yet-competent.

The Coffin and O'Halloran study successfully combines two *different* approaches to discourse analysis: critical discourse analysis and a corpus-based approach. Combinations of approaches are another possibility when making your choice but it is important to bear in mind that some of the approaches described above are based on a range of different, sometimes contradictory, ideas about language, culture, context, identity and power. Perhaps it could be argued that, in order to fully understand an approach and the techniques associated with it, the applied linguist should aim to specialize. On the other hand, the use of multiple approaches to the analysis of what our clients say and write (and what is said and written about them) may help illuminate multiple aspects of their language problems and therefore indicate the best range of solutions. Perhaps the ideal situation is one in which applied linguists work in teams of analysts; providing ways of seeing, and avoiding prescriptions of what to see, through discussion and collaboration with fellow practitioners. Certainly, any solution we design for our clients or action we undertake on their behalf, based on discourse analysis (or any other research method), needs to be carefully evaluated as part of an ongoing cycle of observation, analysis, reflection and action, in other words an **action research** approach (McNiff, 2002; Burns, 2009).

We may have given the impression in this chapter that discourse analysis is the only tool that a good applied linguist needs to know how to use. Indeed, where a detailed analysis of single instances of interaction or a small collection of texts is what's needed, discourse analysis is likely to be entirely valid and appropriate. But of course many language problems might require other, very different, kinds of analytical tools (for example **spectrograms**, for speech sounds: see Chapters 12 and 13). It's also important to note that discourse analysis is not necessarily suited to situations in which we are being asked, or would like, to generalize our diagnosis or proposed solution across large populations and over time. Because discourse analysis (like other kinds of qualitative analysis) usually deals with short extracts of text or talk, it is often impossible to say whether, or how, these extracts are representative even of the client groups we are working with, never mind all similar client groups, at all times. Where such generalizations are required, we might be better off using much larger data samples and associated quantitative approaches to analysis, for example from language corpora, while reminding ourselves that even well-designed quantitative studies risk over-essentializing very complex processes of social difference or change.

It's tempting to say that where we have the resources to collect data from large groups of people we should combine qualitative and quantitative approaches to analysis. But individual applied linguists may not have such resources, and care must be taken when combining approaches that are based on potentially incompatible ideas about language, culture and the relationship between research and practice. Again, perhaps one solution to providing the best combination of qualitative and quantitative approaches is teamwork.

As applied linguists, it is our job to be constantly aware of the opportunities and constraints of discourse as they are experienced and produced by our clients. Moreover, to adapt a phrase from the epigraph (p. 76), we must be unrelenting in our efforts to 'think more deeply about the meanings we give [their] words' and unrelenting in our attempts to reveal these meanings to others.

**Action research**
is a form of self-reflective enquiry (which may include discussion and reading) undertaken by participants in social contexts with the aim of improving their situation in some way. Action researchers often organize their activities in ongoing cycles of reflection and action.

 **www.4.11**

activities

1   Are there examples online of studies in your area of interest in applied linguistics which use discourse analysis? To find out, type the words *discourse analysis* plus one of the chapter titles in this book, for example *literacy*, into an internet search engine and try to find either the full text or an abstract of three different studies.

2   Are discourse analytic studies being carried out in your country (or a country of your choice)? To find out, type the words *discourse analysis* followed by the country name into an internet search engine and try to find either the full text or an abstract of three different studies (to make sure you get a local view you can use your national Google domain, unless you want to look at the USA). We found studies in Australia, Singapore, Kenya, India and China that use discourse analysis to improve understanding of: local government recreation and sports plans for people with disabilities; posters used in a government HIV/AIDS awareness campaign; community-level beliefs about poverty and livestock raising; urban and rural sign language; and Chinese and English language sales letters.

3   Read two of the abstracts or full-length articles you found for activities 1 and 2. Do(es) the writer(s) of the study name their chosen approach to discourse analysis? If the approach is identified, do any of the assumptions it makes, or ideas it states, about language, culture, the client and the relationship between research and practice seem consistent with the information in the chapter? If not, how do they differ? If the approach to discourse analysis is not named in the study, does the chapter help you identity the approach, its methods and disciplinary origins?

4   With the consent of the participants, are you able to collect any spoken or written data from an applied linguistic context in which you are interested? If your data are spoken, you will need to make a recording so that you can listen to them repeatedly and perhaps write down (transcribe) a short extract to make it easier to analyse them in detail. Once you have your spoken or written data, look again at sections 4.2 and 4.3 and consider which of the different approaches to discourse analysis could be used to explore the relationship between your text and the context in which you collected it. If you could use more than one approach, consider how the diagnosis and treatment of any language problem occurring in the text, or in the relationship between the text and context, might be different, depending on your choice of approach to discourse analysis.

## FURTHER READING

Coffin, C., Lillis, T. and O'Halloran, K. (eds) (2010). *Applied linguistics methods: A reader.* London: Routledge.

Gee, J. P. (2005). *An introduction to discourse analysis: Theory and method.* London: Routledge.

Jaworski, A. and Coupland, N. (eds) (1999). *The discourse reader*. London: Routledge.

Johnstone, B. (2002). *Discourse analysis*. Oxford: Blackwell.

Schiffrin, D., Tannen, D. and Hamilton, H. E. (eds) (2003). *The handbook of discourse analysis*. Oxford: Blackwell.

Walsh, S. (2006). *Investigating classroom discourse*. London: Routledge.

**CHAPTER 5**

# Language policy and planning

The best laid schemes o' mice an' men
Gang aft a-gley,*
An' lea'e us nought but grief an' pain,
For promised joy.
> (Robert Burns, *To a Mouse, on Turning Her Up in Her Nest, with a Plough*)

(*often go awry)

In Chapter 4 we explored discourse analysis as a tool that applied linguists use to understand how speakers, signers and writers employ language to represent themselves and others in given contexts. In this chapter we focus on the area of applied linguistics known as language policy and planning, defined by Robert Cooper (1989, p. 45) as 'deliberate attempts to influence the behaviour of others with respect to the acquisition, structure, or functional allocation of their language "code"'. Thus, language planners are concerned with decisions about language use by, and on behalf of, a wide range of clients of applied linguistics. Like the students and practitioners whose concerns we've discussed in the rest of Part A, language planners and policy-makers are concerned with aspects of language in everyday use, and in understanding and solving a broad range of contemporary problems in which language is sometimes the target or end and sometimes the means or tool by which other (non-linguistic) issues can be resolved. An example of the former is the government of China's decree that Mandarin Chinese be the obligatory language of schooling across the nation:

> Article 10 of the Law of the People's Republic of China on Use of Language and Script . . . ordains that all schools and other educational institutions in China must adopt Mandarin and standard Chinese written characters as their primary teaching language and written form.
>
> (Chen, n.d.)

**Orthographies** are symbolic systems for representing language in visual form (or tactile form, in the case of Braille). They can include alphabetic and syllabic elements, and are the focus of applied linguists working with literacy development in written and previously unwritten languages.

Language planning aimed at language as an end includes also the work of:

- national language academies to establish, standardize and compel adherence to policies on terminology and orthography;
- lexicographers to provide a useful record of common usage of words;
- applied linguists who devise **orthographies** for previously unwritten languages.

Echoing the concern of the last two chapters to distinguish between language as end and language as means, we recognize here that planners and policy-makers at various levels seek to solve problems in which language is not the ultimate goal or target, but is a key variable or factor in some other social issue. A great deal of official language planning, for example, aims to provide citizens and clients with access to opportunities to participate in public institutions, and to receive services in legal, medical, work and religious domains. And at the individual level, a well-meaning parent or teacher might discourage a child from speaking the local language, promoting instead a more dominant or prestigious language or variety, not from a wish to influence the use of a particular language, but from a desire to shape the child's social aspirations, educational attainment and economic well-being.

Language policy and planning involve decisions made by individuals (about their own language use and often about the language use of others), as well as decisions made by and for members of certain groups. In this, it is similar to additional language education (Chapter 9) and literacy (Chapter 6), because non-specialists often take leading roles in decision-making processes. Indeed, as we'll see in numerous cases, the disciplinary knowledge and expertise of applied linguists are very often only one factor to be considered in complex problems. For this reason, some scholars have categorized language planning as a 'wicked problem' (Ricento and Hornberger, 1996) – one which, due to its complexity, may be inherently unsolvable, at least from the vantage point of current scholarly and professional knowledge. Throughout this chapter, we bear in mind that the success and effectiveness of language policy and planning efforts will depend on the ability of applied linguists to collaborate with other stakeholders, and (to tamper with Burns' epigraph) that the best laid schemes of applied linguists *gang aft a-gley* for reasons that are not linguistic. Our intention is to map the current state of language planning as an area of applied linguistics practice, giving due consideration to the diverse and interrelated social, economic, linguistic and environmental issues that are involved.

We begin the chapter in section 5.1 by describing language decisions, distinguishing between those which are aimed at language as an end and those in which language figures as a tool or means to other (non-linguistic) ends. We go on to consider the work of language decision-makers and the question of who decides what, for whom, in whose interests, and then end the section with a discussion of the work of professional and scholarly language planners and policy-makers. In 5.2 we take up the formal categories of **corpus planning**, **status planning** and **acquisition planning.** In 5.3 we look at issues involved in efforts to keep languages alive – **language vitality, language maintenance** and **language revitalization** – as well as considering the aspects of planning and policy in which language is a tool rather than a goal. Section 5.4 outlines language policy and planning for access to services in domains such as education, health care, the law and the workplace. Section 5.5 considers two key aspects of language policy and globalization: language and poverty and language and immigration, using **linguistic landscapes** as a tool for mapping this corner of the field of applied linguistics. We conclude (5.6) with a discussion of roles for applied linguists.

 **www.5.1, 5.2, 5.3**

 **www.5.4**

## 5.1 LANGUAGE DECISIONS

All people make numerous decisions involving language use in their daily lives. As we saw in Chapter 1, however, much of our use of everyday language takes place so quickly as to seem instantaneous, meaning that many choices about how we use language are not made consciously and are, therefore, not really decisions at all. Choice in this sense is probably more accurately thought of as processing, since the real-time constraints of language in use do not lend themselves to the type of policy and planning we are concerned with in this chapter. Other decisions, such as which words convey just the right shade of meaning in an apology or a request, the most appropriate register or form of address when talking with a respected elder, or a sign interpreter translating English into British Sign Language during a university lecture, are more available to conscious reflection, but constant attention and attempts to control them too closely would be inefficient and would soon impede communication. Fortunately, as we outlined in Chapter 4, members of speech communities share linguistically enacted cultural routines – the stuff of pragmatics – that allow us to perform effectively most of the time without having to devote too much attention to language form.

Table 5.1  Pupil interaction table (Source: adapted from Grima, 2005)

| Lesson | Language X | Language Y | Code-switching |
|---|---|---|---|
| Teacher addresses whole class | | | |
| Teacher addresses individual pupil | | | |
| Pupil asks question of teacher | | | |
| Pupil asks question of another pupil while the whole class is listening | | | |
| Pupil talks to another pupil while the teacher continues with the lesson | | | |
| Pupils talk during group work | | | |
| Pupil talks to a visitor | | | |
| Visitor addresses pupil(s) | | | |
| A pupil from an other classroom comes to class and addresses the teacher | | | |
| A pupil from another classroom comes to class and addresses pupil(s) | | | |
| Parent comes to class and talks to pupil | | | |
| Pupils listen to a broadcast | | | |
| Pupils work on a computer | | | |
| Pupils listen/use a tape-recorder | | | |
| Other | | | |

Other kinds of decision involve deliberate choices, based on awareness, even *monitoring*, of language practices in a given situation. Grima's (2005) guidelines for developing school language policy, for example, include a checklist for recording the language(s) children and teachers use with different interlocutors and for different purposes as they interact in a bilingual classroom (Table 5.1). Notice the choices include either of two languages of instruction and a third option, **code-switching** between languages.

## Language decision-makers

In this chapter, we take the position that everyone is a language decision-maker in that we all make decisions about our personal use of language. These decisions can influence the ways we speak, sign and write language and even, as we showed in Chapter 2, the judgements we form about others' intelligence, character, trust-worthiness and morality. As important as such decisions can be in the lives of individuals and in how people interact within and outside social groups and institutions, we wish to contrast this broad and informal sense of language decision-making with more conscious efforts to modify and regulate the way others use language, including stipulations concerning the languages and varieties that are privileged, permitted, discouraged and even forbidden in settings such as schools, courts of law, hospitals, government offices and other institutions and workplaces. Language decision-makers at this second level include teachers, textbook writers and material developers, language therapists, lexicographers and translators, as we describe in Parts B and C. Although these language professionals may not consider themselves language planners, we argue that their decisions about language and the actions they take based upon such decisions are examples of language planning in action. Indeed, although less heralded than announcements of government policy, their overall effects may be more important, although less coordinated and even less predictable, than the outcomes of official or formal language policies (Eggington, 2002). The third level of language decision-making considers the work of applied linguists whose work is explicitly aimed at formulating and implementing language policy and at monitoring the outcomes of language plans and policies. In this chapter we are primarily concerned with language decisions made at these last two levels.

## Language policy, language planning and language practices

Thus far we have discussed different levels of language decision and whether poli-cies are implicit or explicit, but what is it exactly that is being planned when language planners plan? Joan Rubin (1983) makes a useful distinction between language policy and language planning, in which policy is the legal or statutory measures intended to regulate language use, and planning is the practical implementation of these policies, i.e. the associated goals, strategies and means of assessing progress and outcomes. Here's an example, from the Bibliothèque et Archives Canada (Library and Archives Canada; LAC), which is charged with collecting and preserving Canada's documentary heritage and making it accessible to all Canadians.

LAC respects the *Official Languages Act* . . . and relevant Treasury Board policies. All LAC information is available in both English and French. Visitors should be aware that some information from other organizations is available only in the language in which it was provided. Original materials presented on the LAC website, such as documents, and audio and video recordings, remain in their language of origin. LAC creates archival descriptions and catalogue records only in the original language of the item.

(LAC, 2008)

**www.5.5**

So the Library's language planning process is set by Canadian national language policy, the Official Languages Act (Figure 5.1). You can read this and (apparently) all other official information in French or in English.

To enact the policy in a systematic way, the Library has developed a plan for documentation and public access of the materials it collects, preserves and displays digitally and in manuscript form. Its language planners have also set limits on the institution's linguistic responsibilities under the plan: visitors to the website are advised that materials are presented in their original language (thereby cutting out their applied linguistic translator colleagues!).

Spolsky (2004, p. 222) also distinguishes between language policies and language practices, observing that 'the real language policy of a community is more likely to be found in its practices than in its management'. Together with Rubin's (1983) definition, this suggests a hierarchy in which actors with diverse and sometimes competing interests do language planning work at one or more of three different levels. Indeed, a significant challenge for language policy and planning efforts is that policy, planning and practices are seldom in neat alignment. For example, Baquedano-López (2004) describes a case in Los Angeles, where the passage of an anti-bilingual education referendum by California voters (policy) in 2000 led the Catholic Diocese in that city to stop offering catechism and other religious services in Spanish (planning) in local churches, despite the fact that the great majority of parishioners were immigrants from Mexico, El Salvador and other Latin American countries who had originally joined the church because of its Spanish-language services. In *practice*, however, church workers, many of them immigrants themselves, continued to use Spanish, and the ban proved unworkable. This case is illustrative because it shows how a language policy, in this case an electoral

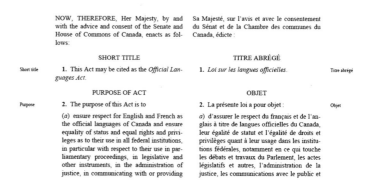

Figure 5.1   Extract from the Official Languages Act of Canada

decision to restrict the use of languages other than English in the domain of public education, was applied in a different domain (religion) and resulted in a language plan that was ultimately resisted by local people.

## Language planning orientations

One of the best-known and most frequently cited notions in the field of language planning is the model proposed by Richard Ruiz (1984), who described three primary **language orientations**:

1    language as problem;
2    language as right;
3    language as resource.

For example, the Chinese language planners who made Mandarin Chinese and Putonghua script obligatory in school presumably viewed both the spoken language and the written script as useful resources for all students. In contrast, as Ruiz and many others have since noted, while dominant languages and **languages of wider communication** (LWC) tend to be viewed, including by many speakers of minority languages, as *resources*, minority languages are often regarded as *problems*. This distinction helps explain the remarkable successes of some government-led or government-backed efforts, such as the revitalization of Hebrew in Israel, and the more modest gains in others, such as Welsh (Huws, 2009; Romaine, 2009). For many Israelis, Hebrew has been perceived as a resource, necessary for connecting to sacred texts and religious practices and for communicating across the language differences of newly arrived immigrants. However, in the case of Welsh (banned altogether from official affairs between 1536 and 1942), the right to use Welsh in court was not initially absolute but rather allowed only when a speaker admitted to being unable to use English well enough to stand trial in that language. Even under subsequent legislation guaranteeing the right of Welsh speakers to use Welsh in the courts without restriction, court workers report that

> [w]hat tends to happen with defendants and witnesses too, is that they feel that they don't want to cause any bother for the court, and they think that by asking for something in Welsh, they're being difficult, you see, so they're like, 'no, it doesn't matter, I'll do it in English' even though the offer's there and the court, the police and the prosecutors are quite willing to conduct cases in Welsh, people feel they're putting someone out by asking for that.
>
> (Huws, 2009, p. 68)

Thus, even in cases where courts and other government institutions have adopted a language-as-*right* orientation, the clients who could presumably benefit may avoid the minority language, based on a language-as-*problem* orientation.

**Language orientations** refers to the idea that language planning efforts of all types can be characterized as approaching language from one or more of three primary stances: language as problem, language as right and language as resource. Conflicts in orientation can explain why language policy and plans are so difficult to implement.

**Language of wider communication** (LWC) refers to a language or variety that is used across communities and regions. The term is completely relative and context dependent, of course; Kiswahili is an LWC in East Africa, but not in Asia or Europe. Similar to **lingua franca**.

## Implicit and explicit language policies

Another way to think about language planning is to consider the scope of decisions, whether they are made in, and with reference to, public spheres, such as government, schooling, health care and other basic services, or about more private spaces, such as a multilingual couple's decision to raise their children in a particular language or languages. Language decisions made about public spheres and spaces may seem to automatically qualify as examples of explicit policies, but this is not always the case. Consider the case of Tigrinya, the dominant language in the federal region of Tigray in northern Ethiopia. Policy decisions to support Tigrinya as the language of instruction from primary school have had the unplanned consequence of reducing teaching in other regional languages (such as Afar, Saho, Agew, Oromo and Kunama). The introduction of English in the first year of primary school before Amharic, the language of the Ethiopian state since the thirteenth century, in year three, is also a matter of controversy and an example of implicit policy (Lanza and Woldemariam, 2009).

An example of an explicit language policy in a professional sphere comes from a statement by the International Association of Schools of Social Work:

> IASSW is a member organisation which is open to all social work educational programmes from all over the world. Therefore its aim is to practise an inclusive language policy, and refrain from becoming an elite organisation dominated by member institutions from the Western world. The language policy and practise is an important factor for deciding whether this is an attractive organisation for a global target.
>
> (IASSW, 2009)

In practice, IASSW's language policy supports four languages of publication and presentation, English, French, Spanish and Japanese. The Association's language policy continues:

> To make sure a real exchange is taking place and that people from various cultures and language groups have fair opportunities, we need to organise our congresses and meetings in ways so that not the same people are always in an inferior position. Thus, sometimes minority languages might even become dominant ones. People from the dominating languages may have to realise that international communication is a challenge for all of us.
>
> (IASSW, 2009)

This is an example of an explicit policy that acknowledges the intellectual gains that can be developed through collaboration across languages, that recognizes that the spread of English serves some interests better than others, and that seeks more equitable conditions for members.

Conversely, one may imagine that language decisions made in private domains such as the family are more likely to be implicit, unwritten and perhaps even unstated. Perhaps. But think back to your own childhood and see if you can remember any parental or family controls on features of language use in your home. We certainly can: Chris remembers being admonished not to 'speak common'. For

Patrick, there was clear separation (nearly always conscientiously observed) between the acceptable uses of profanity at home and at school. Rachel recalls losing an argument about whether her use of a certain word 'counted' as rude and deserved to be punished, or not.

With strong pressures on migrant and minority language children to give up their first language in order to learn a dominant language of wider communication, immigrants and other multilingual families face particularly difficult choices. We know parents who make strong pronouncements on language use in the home, such as: 'This is a Bangladeshi-speaking home. You will speak Bangladeshi at home'; or, conversely: 'We have to speak only English at home now. This is the best way to learn English and if we don't learn English we won't make it here.' An informal but powerful statement of a family language policy comes from *Turtle Pictures*, a work by Mexican American author Ray González describing an adolescent's frustration with his younger brother's refusal to speak Spanish – and his plan for remediation:

> I don't know how it happened, but Tony quit speaking Spanish. One day, he just lost it and couldn't get it back. He grew up in our house listening to Mom and Papa talk Spanish all the time, but Tony's friends just spoke English. The stupid kid can't even talk to his grandmother Josefina, who doesn't speak English. I can't believe my dumb brother doesn't want to say a single word in Spanish. Hell, even if he wanted to, he can't say the words. I'm glad I can speak, read, and write it. When I talk to Tony, who is now thirteen, I cuss him out in Spanish. He knows those words and gets mad at me. He calls me a motherfucker, just like all his rapping friends. They listen to rap CDs where every other word is motherfucker. If Tony doesn't start speaking Spanish to me, I'm going to steal his stupid music and make him ask for it back in Spanish.
>
> (González, 2000, p. 48)

As these examples suggest, decisions about language use almost always involve much more than language. They are also about identity, communication across and within generations, and the long-term vitality and ultimately the existence of a language or variety in competition with other forms.

Other explicit language decisions are made in the electoral sphere, such as voter referendums that seek to regulate the use of language in public spheres and which minority languages may be used for official purposes. It is worth pointing out that, in the English-speaking world at least, the great majority of legislative and electoral efforts to outlaw the official use of languages occur in the USA. Take, for example, the case of Nashville, Tennessee, a city better known for country music stars than for ethnic neighbourhoods and restaurants, but where the population of immigrants was projected to double between 2000 and 2010 (Mendoza, 2004). Like other communities in the 'New South', this historically Euro-American and African American city is the new home of refugees and immigrants from Iraq, Korea, Ethiopia, Sudan, Latin America and especially Mexico. In response to these rapidly changing demographics, a recent referendum asked voters whether the City charter should be amended to specify English as the official language of local government. The proposal read as follows:

English is the official language of the Metropolitan Government of Nashville and Davidson County, Tennessee. Official actions which bind or commit the government shall be taken only in the English language, and all official government communications and publications shall be in English. No person shall have a right to government services in any other language. All meetings of the Metro Council, Boards, and Commissions of the Metropolitan Government shall be conducted in English. The Metro Council may make specific exceptions to protect public health and safety. Nothing in this measure shall be interpreted to conflict with federal or state law.

(Nashville English First Charter Amendment, 2009)

In Figure 5.2, an editorial cartoon mocks the Nashville effort to regulate the use of English, contrasting the 'non-standard' English spoken by a stereotypical southerner (complete with beer belly and baseball cap bearing the Confederate flag) with the formal variety (and prescriptive grammar lesson) provided by a professionally attired immigrant.

Supporters of the measure claimed that it was necessary to maintain civic unity and to avoid the financial costs of providing translation and interpreting services for non-English speakers. Business leaders opposed it on the grounds that the English-only message was divisive rather than unifying, and would undermine the city's efforts to present itself as a cosmopolitan centre and attract international labour and capital to the region (Brown, 2009). A coalition of immigrant groups, led by Kurdish and Spanish speakers and also African American leaders, argued that the proposed ban on languages other than English would harm non-English speakers by limiting their access to health, education and legal services. To the surprise of many observers – and unlike the results in US cities such as

Figure 5.2   Mocking an English-only policy in Nashville, Tennessee (copyright Political Graffiti – Independent Political Cartoons; politicalgraffiti.wordpress.com. All rights reserved)

Green Bay, Wisconsin and Lowell, Massachusetts – Nashville voters rejected the option of making English their Official and Only Language of local government. The economic argument in favour of multilingualism seemed to carry the day and in January 2009 Nashville voters rejected the English-only measure by a margin of 57 per cent to 43 per cent.

Similar attempts to restrict or ban outright the use of other languages in government have enjoyed robust support at the state level, with thirty US states (including Tennessee, California, Arizona and Florida) adopting English-only statutes since 1981 and another (Oklahoma) currently considering it. Advocates of English-only policies are also extremely active at the national level, with numerous (but as yet unsuccessful) proposals to amend the US constitution to stipulate English as the (sole) official national language. You can learn more about this always fascinating area of language policy and planning from ProEnglish, whose slogans (*Protecting our nation's unity in English* and *Tired of 'press 1 for English'?*) appear routinely in English-only literature. For a pro-linguistic diversity and language rights perspective, you can consult the Institute for Language and Education Policy.

 **www.5.6**

 **www.5.7**

Before we leave our discussion of this contentious issue, two final points are worth making. First, although the US situation is somewhat atypical, the underlying conditions are certainly not unknown elsewhere. Migration across linguistic borders is on the rise around the globe, as is attention to the legal and human rights of immigrants and other linguistic minorities. These factors play out differently in different contexts, and even relatively enlightened national constitutions, such as India's, which recognizes twenty-two official languages, effectively limit access to power and privilege for speakers of other languages (Mohanty, 2009). Second, comparative language policy and planning studies suggest that, across contexts, attempts to limit language rights typically originate with, and are supported primarily by, non-(applied) linguists (Johnson, 2009). Applied linguists generally favour plurilingual policies and language plans that support, rather than limit, the rights of minority speakers.

## 5.2  CORPUS, STATUS AND ACQUISITION PLANNING

Cooper (1989) distinguished between three types of language planning: corpus planning, status planning and language acquisition planning. This classification has become a dominant framework for language planning over the past twenty years, so we'll map the associated territory in some detail here. But we'll see later, in section 5.5, that there is still much to explore that falls beyond or between the borders of these three domains.

## Corpus planning

**Corpus planning** is the attempt to modify the code itself, including the development of terms for new technologies, processes and services. Changes in computer technologies have been especially productive in motivating the creation of new terms across languages (see Chapter 11). Since many such terms are currently

**Corpus planning** refers to language planning that attempts to modify in some way the code of a given variety. Not to be confused with **corpus** as a digital collection of authentic language.

**Status planning** refers to efforts to increase or decrease the prestige of a particular language or variety.

**www.5.8**

**Diacritics** are the 'extra' marks required in many orthographies, including the alphabets of French, German, Spanish and the consonantal writing system of Arabic. Placed over, under, next to and even through individual letters or syllabic elements, diacritics change the phonetic value of what they mark, occasionally with important semantic consequences, for example *año* ('year') and *ano* ('anus') in Spanish.

**www.5.9**

introduced in English, a logical question is whether the term will be borrowed from English or whether an alternative, Indigenous term will emerge or be proposed. Whether Spanish-speaking computer users in Buenos Aires, for example, develop a linguistic preference for a *wireless mouse*, *un ratón inalámbrico*, *un mouse inalámbrico* or some other term depends in part on the efficacy of efforts by national language academies to suggest an attractive alternative term to compete with the English translation (perhaps unsurprisingly, *mouse* doesn't appear in the *Registro de Lexicografía Argentina* or the *Diccionario de la Lengua Española*, available on the website of the Academia Argentina de Letras).

Technology is not the only engine driving the generation of new words, however. As we saw in Chapter 2, languages and language varieties are carried in the minds and literate artefacts of immigrants across regional and national boundaries, and rebuilt, although never exactly the same way, in new 'host' communities. When power relations are reversed, former colonial powers may resist language changes that they associate with their former colonies; for example the popular resistance in Portugal to orthographic changes that added three letters (*k*, *w* and *y*) which favoured Brazilian conventions. The reduction in the use of **diacritics** is also seen to favour Brazilian and African countries, where they are viewed as unnecessary hindrances for mass literacy (Beninatto, 2009). Political boundaries, marked linguistically on maps, are also cause for new words when boundaries change dramatically. For example, the political reunification of East Germany and West Germany into a single state following the fall of the Berlin Wall resulted in the creation of new words, including *Mauerspecht*, to describe people who chipped chunks off the Wall to sell (Braber, 2006, p. 161), but reunification also led to the loss of some words created and used by East Germans and to a new pattern of one-way movement of new terms from West to East.

## Status planning

**Status planning** refers to efforts to increase or decrease the perceived status or prestige of a language in a given sphere, for non-linguistic purposes. In the case of the larger languages, status planning is generally conducted by government agencies. For example, although nowadays there is apparently little need to promote the status of English around the world, this has not always been the case. Phillipson (1992) describes linguistic lobbying by the British Council and other government agencies to ensure that English became and remained the language of post-war Europe. Similar actions have been taken to fortify French as a language of international communication and counter the dominance of English. The main player here has been the intergovernmental organization of *La Francophonie*, with fifty-six member states, set up largely at the instigation of Quebec and France's former African colonies in the mid-1970s (Dilevko, 2001). The harnessing of language for political and commercial ends is evident in this case: according to the official website, '[t]he French language and its humanist values represent the two cornerstones on which the International Organisation of La Francophonie is based'.

In status planning, the establishment, promotion and defence of a 'standard variety' and its codification are essential ingredients for government agencies (especially through dictionaries; see Chapter 11). But, as we saw in Chapter 2, languages of wider communication like English have travelled far from the traditional lands of their earliest speakers and are regularly used alongside many other tongues, as additional languages (see Chapters 2 and 9). Indigenized or nativized versions of English therefore compete with Inner Circle standard varieties, with government agencies most often on the side of the latter. Singapore provides a clear example. The government launched a massive 'Speak Good English' campaign in order to suppress the local 'Singlish' variety, which it sees as an obstacle to the small nation's continued trade-based economic growth. In a typical scenario in this ongoing debate, officials of the Ministry of Education responded to linguists, stating in an open letter:

 **www.5.10**

> While Singlish may be a fascinating academic topic for linguists to write papers about, Singapore has no interest in becoming a curious zoo specimen to be dissected and described by scholars. Singaporeans' overriding interest is to master a useful language which will maximize our competitive advantage, and that means concentrating on standard English rather than Singlish.
>
> (Ministry of Education, Singapore, 2008)

While national language policies have concentrated on the economic pragmatism of standard English as a lingua franca, thus greatly diminishing the vitality of Hokkien, Malay and Tamil (Rubdy, 2006), many Singaporeans continue to take pride in the **covert prestige** of Singlish, and have done some impressive status planning of their own, including publishing the *Coxford Singlish Dictionary* and maintaining an entertaining and informative website called *Talking Cock* (a Singlish term for 'idle banter'). The page's logo reflects campaigners' belief that they're being linguistically repressed (see Figure 5 3).

 **www.5.11**

**www.5.12**

**Covert prestige** is a term describing instances in which language pride goes underground due to social pressures. For example, when schools and other institutions frown upon the use of a certain language or variety, speakers often continue to use it as an expression of in-group solidarity and resistance to authority, and it often spreads widely as a result.

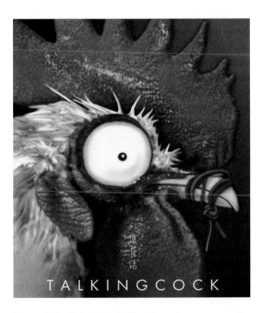

Figure 5.3  'Talking Cock': Resistance to government language policy in Singapore (copyright TalkingCock.com. All rights reserved)

The increasing presence of English around the globe has led to calls to support the language it is seen to displace or is perceived as disfiguring. For example, defenders of Portuguese in Brazil sponsor legislation banning the use of English words on billboards, public signs and advertisements. Rajagopalan reports the arguments of the city government official in San Carlos, Brazil against 'extraigner-ismos' (*foreignisms*):

> How can one explain this undesirable phenomenon [the transformation of Portuguese by the introduction of foreignisms], a potential threat to one of the most vital elements of our cultural heritage, the mother-tongue, which has been underway with growing intensity in the last 10 to 20 years? How can one explain it except by pointing to [a] state of ignorance, to [an] absence of critical and aesthetic sense, and even to [a] lack of self-respect.
>
> (Rajagopalan, 2005, p. 107)

An example of status planning on a more local scale is the decision by a bilingual school to conduct its business in both languages or to privilege the minority language in ways that are not normally seen outside school. Thus, bilingual schools (see Chapter 8 for examples) may decide to conduct public presentations in the non-dominant language or to provide instruction primarily in that language, even though it is not a language of power in that community. Or they may reject the non-dominant language in favour of a dominant one. In many cases the decision is out of schools' hands. In the largely Uyghur-speaking Xinjiang province of China, use of Han (Mandarin) Chinese in schools is mandated by the central government in Beijing, independently of local concerns. A teacher who works with both local Uyghur and majority-Chinese Han students told a language planning researcher that schools should teach all students in both languages and that the current policy undermined the status of Uyghur people:

> If you want to live in our area, Uyghur should be learnt and taught to Han stu-dents in schools. The majority of people here are Uyghurs. Of course we need to learn the Han language. Everyone knows that it is important to use the Han language but our Uyghur language is also important. The policy makes our Uyghur students feel our language is not important, so the Han students do not have to learn it. We Uyghurs often regard people who speak our language as friends because they respect our culture – like the Uygur saying, 'recognize the language not the face to be friends'.
>
> (Tsung, 2009, p. 136)

# Acquisition planning

**Acquisition planning** involves direct instruction, independent language study and other efforts to motivate people to acquire or learn a particular language or variety.

Language **acquisition planning** (LAP) describes efforts to promote the acqui-sition of additional languages. Cooper (1989) describes the careful planning and extensive financial and human resources devoted to the delivery of Hebrew language classes for new immigrants in Israel. There are many contemporary exam-ples of immigrants studying the language and literacies of their adopted countries. Bilingual education programmes (see Chapter 8) are prominent examples of LAP, and the choice of instructional methods and materials they employ can also be viewed from a language planning perspective. In the case of languages in which a standard orthography has not (yet) been established, bilingual educators who select a particular orthography for teaching literacy, or a particular variety of a language for developing materials, need to consider the implications of choosing one variety over others. In Peru, for example, applied linguists involved in the development of an orthography for Ashaninka, an Indigenous language spoken in the Amazon region, must attend not only to the selection or elaboration of symbols to best represent the sounds of that language, but also to disagreements among speakers about which variety should be encoded orthographically. Since the Summer Institute of Linguistics proposed the first orthography of Ashaninka around 1960, at least eight different alphabets have been developed (Fernández, personal communication, February 2010). An example of the most recent orthography is shown in Figure 5.4, displayed on the wall behind the applied linguist Liliana Fernández and the Indigenous teachers she worked with to develop teaching materials and grammatical understanding for bilingual teachers teaching in Ashaninka and Spanish.

The decision to publish a textbook in a dominant language such as Arabic, English or French would probably not have major implications for the present vitality of those languages on a global scale. However, a decision to use such a book could have very important consequences in schools and small language communities. For example, a Cameroonian school's decision to adopt a science textbook written in Fulfulde rather than one written in English or French would add massive prestige to the local language, and could be considered an example of status planning. Furthermore, by making available a text in Fulfulde, including the possible creation of new terms (say, in the area of computers and information technology), the

Figure 5.4   A class of bilingual educators studies the grammar and orthography of the Ashaninka language in Peru

decision to educate bilingually or in mother tongue would have implications for corpus planning as textbook writers select terms, consciously or not, that reflect and reinforce certain ways of speaking and writing that are highly valued. Likewise, on the other side of the African continent, the current Kenyan education policy of providing textbooks in English has pedagogical implications: Glewwe, Kremer and Moulin (2007) suggest that the dominant use of English, the third language of many students, in national textbooks limits access to knowledge and that no single curriculum can serve equitably the linguistically diverse peoples of Kenya.

As we've already suggested, the forms of bilingual education and additional language teaching we describe in Chapters 8 and 9 are major sites of LAP. To the extent that teachers, teacher educators, administrators, curriculum writers and materials developers are directly involved in helping students become more proficient and accomplished speakers and writers of other languages, the applied linguists who hold these jobs can be regarded as language acquisition planners. The term **language-in-education planning** is sometimes used to describe language decisions that take place in educational settings but are not primarily aimed at language acquisition (Paulston and McLaughlin, 1994). Regardless of the language of instruction, the decision to base assessment of student learning on student writing (essays) vs performance on multiple-choice tests is one example of language-in-education planning (see Chapter 7). Another is the language that is used for testing content knowledge (e.g. which of South Africa's eleven official languages should be used for national exams?). Faced with the need to make decisions on such issues, teachers and other language professionals often act as *de facto* planners, responsible for implementing (or resisting) elements of language policies on a daily basis within a particular context.

## 5.3 KEEPING LANGUAGES ALIVE

In Chapter 1 we made the bleak observation that, based on current estimates, languages are being lost at the rate of about two a month. Painfully, especially for those who love language and languages, the convergence of increased scholarly and public consciousness about language loss and the spread of internet technologies makes it possible for us to witness **language death**, or at least be informed of it, as it happens in a way that has not been possible before now. For example, as we wrote this chapter, new stories appeared on the BBC, Yahoo and other internet news services announcing the death of Boa Senior, the last living speaker of Bo, a tribal language from the Andaman Islands in the Indian Ocean. Anvita Abbi, the linguist who worked with Boa to document Bo, said that she had outlived all other speakers of Bo by at least thirty years and that 'she was often very lonely and had to learn an Andamanese version of Hindi in order to communicate with people' (Lawson, 2010). You can hear a recording of Boa speaking Bo on the BBC News website. (You can monitor **endangered language** 'hot spots' around the globe at the Enduring Voices project, sponsored by National Geographic.)

**www.5.13**

**Language-in-education planning** refers to instances of language planning that take place within the domain of education and schooling.

**Language death** is the dramatic and unfortunate fate currently facing most of the world's smallest languages. Linguists sometimes view language death as a process (a language is said to be 'dying' when people stop using it) and sometimes as a final state of linguistic rest (i.e. the last living native speaker has died).

**www.5.14**

**www.5.15**

# Language vitality, maintenance and revitalization

In Chapter 3 we briefly discussed the concept of language death, noting that the accelerating rate of loss was mostly due to the shift to languages of wider communication such as Chinese, English and Spanish. One of the most compelling (and an increasingly widely studied) aspect of language planning involves the **vitality** or health of a language or language variety. Although there are many other factors involved, as we'll see, a key factor in the health of a language is the extent to which parents pass it on to their children. In circumstances of extensive shift away from one language to another, a language is said to become 'endangered' as the next generation stops acquiring it from dwindling numbers of older speakers. Many Indigenous communities around the world are losing speakers faster than they are raising children in their language(s), and many communities have proposed and carried out schemes for **maintaining their language**.

Schooling is often a component of **language revitalization** plans, and the role and effectiveness of schools in keeping languages vital have been much studied and debated by applied linguists and the clients they are serving. In Joshua Fishman's (1991) much-used *Graded Intergenerational Disruption Scale* for evaluating language vitality, being schooled in the **endangered language** has important effects in favour of language growth. But languages can also be maintained without being taught in school. Intergenerational language transmission is the *sine qua non* of Fishman's model: there is little the school can do if children are not already developing their proficiency in the threatened language (whether monolingually or bilingually) by the onset of schooling. With severely threatened languages, of course, this disruption has already happened and there are no school-age speakers. Table 5.2 shows the rubric used by UNESCO in assessing the degree of language endangerment, with Fishman's metric of uninterrupted intergenerational transmission as the core criterion.

Table 5.2   Degree of language endangerment, UNESCO Framework (Source: adapted from Lewis and Simons, 2010)

| Status | Indicators |
| --- | --- |
| Safe | The language is spoken by all generations; intergenerational transmission is uninterrupted |
| Vulnerable | Most children speak the language, but it may be restricted to certain domains (e.g. home) |
| Definitely endangered | Children no longer learn the language as mother tongue in the home |
| Severely endangered | The language is spoken by grandparents and older generations; while the parent generation may understand it, they do not speak it to children or among themselves |
| Critically endangered | The youngest speakers are grandparents and older, and they speak the language partially and infrequently |
| Extinct | There are no speakers left |

**Language vitality** is a construct used by language planners to gauge the long-term health of a language or variety. Although there are many ways to operationalize this construct, the central feature concerns the transmission of a language from one generation to the next.

**Language maintenance** implies a focus on keeping a language vital within a given speech community or region. This term is sometimes used to describe bilingual education programmes that aim for learners to retain or further develop their home language

 **www.5.16**

while gaining an additional language.

**Endangered languages** are those which are at risk of being lost due to massive language shift or the death of their remaining speakers.

**Language revitalization** is the name given to efforts to stop or slow down language loss and simultaneously increase the vitality of a language in a given community or region. Because the social forces motivating language loss are typically beyond the control of individuals, applied linguists engaged in these efforts are often swimming against the current.

Of course, because languages are not uniformly distributed across generations, households or communities, it is true that a language can be vital in the life of some users while others in the same community are losing or regaining their ability to communicate in that language. This is the case in Ika-speaking communities of Arhuaco Indians living in the Sierra Nevada de Santa Marta mountains in northern coastal Colombia. With snow-capped mountain peaks rising within view of the Caribbean, this region is home to a remarkable linguistic and biological diversity. Trillos (1998) described the language and cultural vitality of Kogui, Kankuamo and Ika speakers living in the Sierra Nevada, and found that all three languages are under stress from Spanish and that the Indigenous languages are most vital in the towns at the highest elevations. Murillo (2009) describes an example of local language planning in an Arhuaco community. Her ethnography of language and literacy in an Ika/Spanish bilingual school and community revealed an issue in language planning that has received little attention: the role of Indigenous cosmology and world view as influences in a decision to support mother tongue education. Murillo concluded that, in a community where language use is guided by spiritual leaders who remind people how to be Arhuaco, some speakers strongly support the use of their first language for literacy instruction, but their goal is not to promote widespread literacy in Ika, nor to use Ika as a bridge to development of Spanish literacy. Rather, this local language policy – specifically the decision to teach reading and writing in Ika in the village of Simunurwa – is attributed to the elders' desire to maintain and affirm Arhuaco identity among the youth, and also because Indigenous identity offers some protection against being drafted into the paramilitary forces and, consequently, the violence surrounding the Sierra Nevada.

## Evaluating language maintenance efforts

Can language really be planned? This question was posed in the title of a now classic work in the field of language planning (Rubin and Jernudd, 1971), written during the nation-building period that former European colonies in Africa and Asia were engaged in during the 1960s and 1970s. In those heady days for the emerging field of language planning, applied linguists consulted with education leaders of emerging and newly independent governments on the question of which languages would be taught in schools and universities, with obvious consequences for teacher preparation, the creation of textbooks, tests and other learning resources, and the development of the corpus (via lexicography, for example; see Chapter 11).

The difficulty of predicting, much less directing, changes in language use with any degree of certainty has led language planners to consider factors in addition to language. For example, in parallel with the social sciences generally, there is a consensus that understanding the material and social conditions in which language problems are embedded is fundamental to effective planning for change. And scholars have become interested in, and now understand, more about how people's beliefs about language (their language ideologies) influence how they take to, comply with or resist government proposals for language change, such as changes in the language of schooling. The linguist Colin Williams (2009) has identified thirteen reasons why language policies suffer in implementation, ranging from team competence (the ability of language planners to work with team members with other disciplinary expertise), to limitations in software and technical vocabulary, to lack of financial resources to pay translators, interpreters and teachers. So, with this greater sophistication, are we closer to determining whether language maintenance can be planned?

At the risk of not answering the question, perhaps it is best to say that some aspects of language are easier to plan for than others. For example, from studying the effects of outright bans on certain languages in schools (Hawaiian for most of the previous century; the 'Russification' of the former Soviet Union beginning in 1938; virtually all Indigenous languages in Canada and the United States for most of the histories of those countries) language planners know that the imposition of monolingual language policies on multilingual groups can cause great and lasting harm. On the other hand, undoing or reversing **language shift** seems to be much more difficult to plan effectively, even though planners apparently have years in which to try to stave off language death for endangered languages. UNESCO's language endangerment scale (Table 5.2), which pinpoints the language of childhood as the most important difference between 'safe' and 'vulnerable' status, suggests that the language policies and practices of schools have the potential to support or undermine the vitality of non-dominant language. The history of Indigenous languages in schools is such that, in many cases, people are under-standably reluctant to bring them into schools now. Bessy Waco, a Chemehuevi speaker in Arizona who taught a white linguist to speak her language in the 1960s, explained why some community members would not speak Chemehuevi with whites: 'When I was a little girl they whipped me for speaking Chemehuevi. Now a white man comes and wants to learn my language. White men are crazy' (Major, 2005, p. 525).

> **Language shift** refers to the process in which speakers, individually or collectively, abandon one language in favour of another. 'Reversing language shift' entails efforts to change the conditions that contribute to language loss (in other words, **revitalization**).

Language policy and planning is still a young discipline compared to some other areas of applied linguistics such as language teaching, translation and lexicography. Like its sister disciplines, it is thoroughly grounded in eurocentric ideas about language and knowledge that guided the 'discovery' and cataloguing of non-European languages. Makoni and Pennycook (2007, p. 13) remind us that the names of many of the languages and language groups that planners and policy makers work with today are the products of European colonial rule and the imperial desire for order: 'From the muddled masses of speech styles they saw around them, languages needed identification, codification and control: they needed to be invented: African languages were thus historically European scripts.' This ontology produces a paradox for the field: 'If the notions of language that form the basis of language planning are artefacts of European thinking, language policies are therefore (albeit unintentionally) agents of the very values which they are seeking to challenge' (Makoni and Pennycook, 2007, p. 12).

Similarly, early language planning efforts have been critiqued for assuming a rational model of language decision-making, that is, for projecting language policy outcomes on the assumption that people would make language choices and support policies that (so many planners and policy-makers believed) were in their own economic and other interests. Thus, applied linguists and others involved in these efforts often operated in the belief that specific recommendations (for example to select and codify the dialect spoken in national capitals or centres of economic power) made economic sense and would be accepted by speakers, over time, as the most appropriate route to national economic development. Similarly, newly independent governments' decisions to maintain colonial languages such as English and French over Indigenous languages for the purposes of education and government were regarded as 'neutral' or 'common sense'.

The flip-side of this unwritten corollary was, of course, that the choice of Indigenous language is deemed 'marked' and unwise. This sentiment is still heard. Suzanne Romaine (2009, p. 129) points to remarks by the applied linguist Henry Widdowson that the government of Nunavut, a federal territory in northern Canada, had erred in choosing Inuktitut to be the language of government: '[Inuktitut] creates tremendous problems because it is a pre-literate language not suited for use in complex legal and bureaucratic procedures.' Romaine further reminds us that Welsh, Indonesian and Basque are among the languages that have recently expanded to meet the needs of government as a language of state. Tollefson (2002, p. 5) summarizes this critique by noting that 'traditional' language policies are assumed 'to enhance communication, to encourage feelings of national unity and group cooperation, and to bring about greater social and economic equality'. A critical approach to language policy and planning places front and centre the question of who decides what, for whom and in whose interests?

## 5.4 PLANNING FOR ACCESS TO SERVICES

Fostering access to public services is another arena of action for language planners and policy-makers. It is commonplace these days to see signs like that in Figure 5.5 on local authority websites and in printed information. In Chapter 3 we saw an example from a London-based public information campaign to raise awareness of Braille, the writing system for the blind. If you live in a city, depending on its material resources, a quick survey of public access points such as public signage for bathrooms in airports and other public buildings, and the instructions written on automatic bank tellers, vending machines, etc. may reveal that Braille, in addition to notices written in spoken languages, is being planned into the design of these service-oriented texts. Public announcements for services in multiple languages are

---

**This information can be provided in your own language.**

我們也用您們的語言提供這個信息 (Cantonese)

এই তথ্য আপনার নিজের ভাষায় দেয়া যেতে পারে । (Bengali)

Ta informacja może być dostarczona w twoim  (Polish)
własnym języku.

Bu bilgiyi kendi dilinizde almanız mümkündür.  (Turkish)

(Urdu) یہ معلومات آپ کی اپنی زبان ( بولی ) میں بھی مہیا کی جاسکتی ہیں۔

☎ **01904 551550**

---

**www.5.17**  Figure 5.5   Multilingual services on the York City Council website in the UK

adding to the linguistic landscapes of multilingual cities, an idea we'll return to at the end of the chapter (see pp. 121–2).

Ensuring that language differences don't limit clients' access to education, literacy, health, legal services, employment and technology can challenge the abilities of even linguistically enlightened governments. Recall the English Only referendum facing voters in Nashville, Tennessee, that we described at the beginning of this chapter (pp. 105–7), which was opposed by immigrant groups on the grounds that English-only legislation would undermine the ability of immigrants and other non-fluent speakers of English to obtain access to quality health care services. In Wales, the National Health Proposal calls for health care professionals to learn the Welsh language to be able to care for elderly speakers (Bellin, 2009). But in Peru the lack of Quechua-speaking health care professionals has been identified as a grave flaw in the provision of reproductive and maternal care for Indigenous women and infants. Amnesty International reported the following testimony from a twenty-four-year-old woman who was pregnant for the fifth time, after two of her children had died:

 www.5.18

> The first time she [the doctor] didn't understand what I said to her. I went back and again she didn't understand. The third time she asked me for my family planning card and I went back with it . . . I couldn't speak [to her] . . . When we went with my husband, then he got the doctor to understand [that I was pregnant]. We're scared when they speak to us in Spanish and we can't reply . . . I start sweating from fear and I can't speak Spanish . . . what am I going to answer if I don't understand Spanish? It would be really good [if they could speak in Quechua]. My husband, when he goes to Lima, leaves me with the health promoters so that they can accompany me. They take me to my check ups and speak to the doctor.
>
> (Amnesty, 2009, p. 30)

To protect the health of Quechua-speaking women and their families, the authors of the report recommend that language support be provided in all health facilities attended by Indigenous women, either through training community members in the health professions or by providing medical interpreters for Quechua/Spanish communication.

This brings us to another vital aspect of planning for access to services: translation and interpreting. If constitutionally guaranteed, how available are they in practice? Arturo Tosi (2006) contrasts the importance of translation in the European Parliament and the limited role professional translators are allowed to play in the translation process. The 1958 Language Charter, the legal basis for European Union language policy, states that all European citizens must be able to read and understand documents and legislation in their own languages (Tosi, 2006, p. 13). This has created a 'massive' industry within the EU, 'the largest translation agency in the world' (Tosi, 2006, p. 15), in which translators work individually on sections of texts rather than on whole texts or through collaboration. Translators often work through translations rather than from original documents in the source language.

Furthermore, 'translators are not encouraged to act as mediators between the intentions of writers and the effect of the translation on the readers. Quite the contrary, the rather "mechanistic" procedures they are trained to adopt encourage the straightforward substitution of all items in a text, and the direct transfer of its format and punctuation, from one language to another' (Tosi, 2006, pp. 14–15). According to Tosi, problems of quality under this arrangement threaten the access to equivalent information for all language groups. Although his proposed solution – to fully involve translators in a badly needed revision of EU translation policy – seems sound, it raises other questions, such as:

■ How do we determine or certify a person's qualifications to translate and interpret for official and legal purposes?
■ What sort of education is needed and available?
■ Who should pay for the education of these language professionals and how much should they be paid?

We explore legal translation and ethical considerations further in Chapters 10 and 12.

## 5.5  LANGUAGE POLICY AND PLANNING IN GLOBALIZING TIMES

In this final section, we raise the question of how language policy and planning have been affected by the weakening of national economies and movement toward global integration. For lack of a more precise term, we'll call on the overworked but useful notion of *globalization*. Following Castles (2007, p. 39), we'll use the term to refer to 'flows across borders, flows of capital, commodities, ideas, and people'. We'll examine an ongoing shift in the field, from a concern with describing what governments, institutions and individuals do with language within national boundaries to a more politically conscious, less place-based version. This move has also been described as **critical language planning** (see Johnson, 2009; Tollefson, 2002):

> A critical perspective toward language policy emphasizes the importance of understanding how public debates about policies often have the effect of precluding alternatives, making state policies seem to be the natural condition of social systems ... Moreover, a critical perspective aggressively investigates how language policies affect the lives of individuals and groups that have little influence over the policy making process.
>
> (Tollefson, 2002, p. 4)

**Critical language planning** involves questioning the social causes and ramifications of language plans and policies and their implementation. In line with critical applied linguistics generally, language planning from a critical perspective means asking why and in whose interests decisions about language(s) are made.

From this perspective, we consider two interrelated areas that are rapidly growing beyond state control: language and poverty, and language and immigration.

## Language planning and poverty

The study of the connections between language and poverty is a rapidly developing area. Because applied linguists often serve clients who live in conditions of poverty (see Chapter 3), our work is regularly shaped by the economic and non-linguistic needs of the individuals and communities we serve. Grenoble, Rice and Richards

(2009) point out that while rural poverty associated with linguistic isolation is consistent with maintenance of some Indigenous languages, people who are struggling to meet their basic human needs generally have little energy or time for responding to language shift. Furthermore, there is great inequality of access to public language services such as bilingual education, mother-tongue instruction and community interpreting (see Chapter 10). If such services are not provided by the state, the poor are unlikely to be able to afford them.

As scholars from various disciplines consider the interrelationship between economics and language, they can stumble over, and be misled by, some of the dead ends we presented in Chapter 1. For example, there remains a strong tendency to assume that the lower levels of formal education and the 'non-standard' ways of speaking and writing that are associated with communities living in poverty are a strong index – or, worse, predictor – of their intelligence (see dead ends 4 and 6, pp. 8–9 and 10). While conditions of poverty can indeed truncate or otherwise limit our exposure to certain experiences and discourses, making it more difficult to develop academic literacy, it's an oversimplification to see economic status as *inevitably* associated with **linguistic deficit**. And yet the assumption is highly resistant to correction, as can be seen in the US educationalist Ruby Payne's (2008) claim that the vocabulary and language development of children living in poverty in the urban US is slower than that of middle-class children. When incorporated through language planning into curriculum and instruction, such claims would be problematic for learners in any group, but they may be especially harmful for the educational futures of children who are also linguistically marginalized. Although scholars have provided empirical evidence to discount so-called language deficits for the poor (Dworin and Bomer, 2008), the belief that poverty causes significant linguistic problems is a persistent barrier to equitable education for language minority students.

**Linguistic deficit** is a fictional creature that has, nonetheless, been the subject of much discussion and lament by non-linguists, particularly when applied to the language abilities of children from marginalized groups.

Another angle from which language planners consider language and poverty is to ask how income relates to an individual's 'language attributes' (Vaillancourt, 2009, p. 153). Planners use language and economic data from government census records and large-scale surveys on economic well-being and educational attainment. Because these data are reported rather than observed or independently confirmed, and because questions about language attributes are not consistent across measures, it's important to remember that they're only getting a part of the picture. It's also important to keep in mind that any relationship found would be correlational (e.g. *French/English bilingualism could be co-present with high levels of income*) rather than causal (*French/English bilingualism helps make people well off*).

So with these caveats, and understanding the limitations of the data, what do we know? The Canadian province of Quebec has been a focal point for this type of language and poverty research, where language planners are interested in the connections between language spoken, income and gender. Setting aside the effects of education, François Vaillancourt (2009) and colleagues examined the income of Anglophone and Francophone men and women, and found that men of all language backgrounds earn more than women of comparable language backgrounds. In other words, language does not offset gender bias in the pay of women workers. However, within gender, French/English bilingualism in Quebec correlates highly with higher incomes for Francophile men and women and for

Anglophile women. English monolingualism correlates highly with higher incomes for Anglophile men. Although these findings do not explain why these factors co-occur, they highlight the fact that the economic advantage of bilingualism is shared by some groups, but not Anglophile men. This information could be useful to politicians and policy-makers who are gauging support for public policy that privileges or fosters bilingualism, and who want to know how key demographic groups may vote on a referendum.

Specialists who study the relationship between language and poverty have pointed out that there are other measures of poverty in addition to the economic measures of interest to governments and international aid organizations. Among other non-monetary measures, Vaillancourt (2009) highlights nutrition, access to health care and educational poverty. In this chapter we've seen examples of how language policy-makers and planners are involved in efforts to influence the level and quality of people's formal education, to shape qualifications for employment and to provide access to health care. In line with Ruiz's (1984) Orientations model (discussed on p. 103), language planners interested in poverty can view language diversity as a resource. For example, scholarship on the relationship between linguistic diversity and biodiversity suggests that human and plant and animal diversity is put at risk when the lands and economies of Indigenous communities are threatened, and the way of life that supports the intergenerational transmission of the Indigenous language is stressed and disappearing (Murillo, 2009; Romaine, 2009). While there may be value in determining a formula to calculate the economic dimensions of language loss within a larger pattern of diversity loss, there are also human costs that are difficult to calculate and to understand, but which language planners must reflect on.

## Language planning and immigration

The field of language planning emerged as a result of the formation of postcolonial states, but the most dramatic events driving it today are related to migration and immigration across linguistic and national borders. There are patterns in these movements: at unprecedented levels, migrants are moving from poor areas to the former colonial centres, from south to north, and from rural to urban areas. Increasingly, these movements are intergenerational, and involve men, women and children. Along with the explosion in digital communication technologies, the flow of people to new homes within and across national boundaries stretches previous understandings that the locus of language planning work is the state. How to plan for Tagalog/Filipino, for example, when more than two million speakers are living outside the Philippines? Or keep up with Arabic, with 220 million speakers spread across nearly sixty countries (Lewis, 2010)? Immigration increases multilingualism in communities, sometimes very rapidly. Language is one of immigrants' primary resources and tools for making it in their new society, but how will host communities receive speakers of their language(s)?

As the result of mass internal and international migration, there is a pressing need to provide language classes for child and adult learners, and also for basic services such as public education, health care, and legal and public information in non-dominant languages. White and Glick (2009, p. 58) distinguish between *immigration policy* and *immigrant policy*, the former regulating 'who gets in' and the latter concerned with what kind of treatment they get. Two areas where applied linguists participate in, or challenge, immigration policy are the use of language analysis to determine national origin (see Eades, 2005; and Chapter 12) and language testing to manage immigrant numbers (see Shohamy and McNamara, 2009). Immigrant policy, which includes language classes, access to services and naturalization, is the site of more applied linguistic work. Eva Codó (2008), for example, analysed language use in a state immigration office in Barcelona, finding that Spanish was the only 'legitimate language' immigrants could effectively use in seeking Spanish citizenship. She described how the hiring of only Spanish-born interpreters led to a staff of specialists in languages that were not spoken by South Asian clients: predominantly Arabic (but not the variety spoken by Moroccan immigrants served by the Barcelona immigration office) and Russian. Immigration officials would sometimes use English and French with immigrants, but Codó found that most clients either attempted to speak Spanish or obtained the services of another immigrant who could speak Spanish with immigration officials on their behalf.

Each immigration context is unique, with key variables including the language(s) spoken in the sending and host community; the immigrants' level of formal education; and the reception that immigrants receive from officials and the host community. Family experience with migration/immigration has also been identified as a factor in the decision to migrate and the choice of a new community; pathways to migration seem less daunting if family support awaits migrants in the host country. The move to an urban area usually signifies increased access to education, employment, housing and health care, services through which migrants may also become clients involved in or affected by language policy and planning. Educating immigrant children is a challenge that faces schools in many countries (although migration often signals the end of formal schooling for young adults). Because of the increasing numbers of immigrant youth, bilingual education is perhaps the area of applied linguistics and language planning most influenced by immigration, and in Chapters 7 and 8 we look at language-in-education policies designed to serve migrant students.

We close this section with a brief look at the concept of **linguistic landscape** (LL) as an emerging methodological and conceptual approach for understanding how migrants contribute to language use in their adopted communities. The term originated with Landry and Bourhis' (1997) study of the distribution of languages on public signage in Canada and the reactions of Francophone high school students, the notion being that the positioning and density of texts in a specific language were an index of its vitality in that particular setting. Spolsky (2004) comments that 'linguistic cityscapes' might be a more accurate term, given that studies have mainly taken place in multilingual cities such as Quebec, Jerusalem and Brussels. Shohamy and Gorter (2009, p. 6) write that 'the connection of linguistic landscape with language policy is a natural one, given that linguistic landscape refers to language in public spaces, open, exposed, and shared by all'.

As a means of recording and understanding the written language that is visible in the public space, LL is well suited to capturing the linguistic contributions of immigrants and the hybrid linguistic outcomes achieved through contact between immigrant languages and the dominant language(s) in the host country. The

 www.5.19

**Linguistic landscapes** are visual representations of language use in a community. By mapping the presence of signs, posters and other publicly displayed texts, applied linguists form a picture of the relative vitality of languages at a particular place and point in time.

Figure 5.6   A bilingual advertisement for cleaning services

approach is based on the premise that migrants are agents, that is, they are 'not isolated individuals who react to market stimuli and bureaucratic rules but social beings who seek to achieve better outcomes for themselves, their families and their communities by actively shaping the migratory process' (Castles, 2007, p. 37).

Figure 5.6 shows an apparently homemade advertisement for a cleaning service. We found this ad taped to a supermarket window in a Chicago suburb that is home to many immigrants from the Mexican state of Puebla. The sign for this cleaning service contains several words with unconventional spelling in English and in Spanish, and yet it contains other elements suggesting that the author is familiar with design and is an experienced computer user. Aurora's poster was surrounded by similar texts, some handwritten and others more professionally produced. There were photographs, mostly photocopied, of cars, washing machines and other items for sale, and descriptions of homes for sale and rent. All of the advertisements contained elements of English and Spanish.

Advertisements like this one can be analysed on two levels. From the bottom up and on the level of the individual decision-maker, we can consider the author and anyone she may have enlisted to help her produce her poster. Photographing and analysing advertisements and publicly displayed texts can tell us something about the new ways immigrants are using language to support themselves in the host country. Additionally, we can ask residents for their interpretations of locally produced advertisements. For example, Collins and Slembroucke (2007) asked Turkish immigrants and Dutch-speaking Belgians in Belgium to interpret photographs of bilingual signs in shop windows in Ghent, and reported that immigrants and non-immigrants had very different interpretations of these texts and different opinions regarding the use of non-conventional spelling and other non-prestige forms of language use.

Language planners are also beginning to use LL at the level of community to measure the (co-)occurrence and positioning of languages in multilingual cities. For example, Lanza and Woldemariam (2009) mapped the linguistic landscape of the northern Ethiopian city of Mekele to study language ideologies surrounding Tigrinya (the regional language), Amharic (the dominant national language in Ethiopia) and English. Their corpus consisted of 375 signs displayed in a shopping district, approximately two-thirds of which were bilingual. Nearly all bilingual signs involved English, and only a very few simultaneously displayed Tigrinya and Amharic. None of the other regional languages spoken in Mekele were attested on signs. These written data can be collected easily and compared over relatively short periods of time, for example to see if the recent adoption of an ethnic federalism policy tilts public signage in favour of Tigrinya. At this level, LL data complement census data about what languages immigrants are speaking and where.

## 5.6   ROLES FOR APPLIED LINGUISTS

If it is true, as we have argued here, that languages are inherently difficult to plan with precision, it is also true that language policy and planning in the absence of applied linguistics constitute an unappealing choice. Language planners have responded to language problems that result from political events on the scale of independence movements and the realignment of nations following the end of the Cold War, the accelerated loss of Indigenous cultures and language, and mass migration from rural to urban communities. As we'll see in greater detail in Parts B and C, applied linguists have much to contribute to the design and implementation of bilingual education, additional language education and other language choice issues in schools, such as the language chosen for initial literacy instruction, the age of the onset and cessation of home and additional language instruction, and decisions concerning the languages in which language minority children should be tested. The explosion in the development and accessibility of new forms of technology also opens new avenues for language planners. The same digital technologies that are driving methodological advances in other areas of applied linguistics are also making possible levels of description and documentation that were unknown to earlier generations of linguists. With these changing conditions in mind, here are some of the roles we foresee for applied linguists.

■   One of the primary roles applied linguists can play in the development and evaluation of language policies and planning efforts is to assist the non-linguists who are involved in understanding basic issues of first and second language acquisition. For example, in assessing the literacy abilities of bilingual students, an applied linguist could help educators gain a fuller understanding of a learner's abilities in literacy by ensuring that students complete a writing sample and take a reading comprehension test in *both* their languages before literacy ability is determined.

- Applied linguists can select and develop books and other pedagogical materials for learning and teaching to follow (or resist) language policies and plans. If you are a classroom teacher, you might be the applied linguist or you might be an applied linguist collaborating with a team of teachers to develop a textbook or a curriculum. Strong digital literacy and multimedia skills would complement applied linguistic knowledge in this job.

- In documentation projects for language revitalization and maintenance, applied linguists work with individuals or small groups of speakers whose linguistic knowledge creates the data that become the codified 'grammar' of the language. Applied linguists also help train Indigenous teachers and other community members to become field linguists. Many linguists are from the Indigenous groups they work with, and this has been an important factor in the shift to community-based collaborative projects. Whether originally from inside or outside the community, applied linguists rethink their (and our) understandings of some of the core elements of applied linguistics: first and second language acquisition, literacy development, additional language teaching, translation and lexicography.

- Language planning is also practised in the publishing industry. For example, the authors, editors and translators of novels are all involved in the issue of which languages and varieties to work in. Kenyan author James Ngugi began his career writing and publishing novels in English, with little opportunity to publish in African languages . He began writing and publishing in Kikuyu and Kiswahili as Ngugi wa Thiong'o (2009 [1986]), and his books are translated into English and other languages for sale to international readers. Some publishers specialize in publishing books in multiple languages. The growth of the genre of children's literature around the world presents a special opportunity for authors and publishers of bilingual and multilingual books. (Interesting sites include *Language Lizard*, whose slogan *Inspiring kids through language* advertises that it sells bilingual books (English plus another language) in forty languages; and Cinco Puntos Press.)

**www.5.20**

**www.5.21**

As the epigraph at the beginning of the chapter (p. 98) suggests, language plans are fragile enterprises, and the ability to shape future language use is an uncertain science. Applied linguists with experience in this area understand the limitations of language planning that is overdependent on linguistic knowledge and neglectful of the desires of those who would be affected by proposed change. Experience also teaches that language policies imposed from the top seldom achieve the desired effects, although they may succeed in causing dramatic changes in language use in schools and other institutions. Collaborative and participatory projects which involve consulting and developing locally relevant policy with community members are more likely to reveal ideological barriers and beliefs about language that could hinder effective language planning. They also offer the possibility of obtaining feedback on how a language policy is affecting clients. To fully understand the contributions and knowledge generated 'from the bottom up', the applied linguist who engages in some form of language planning must study the demographics, history, geography and political economy of the groups involved.

1   What are the language policies of the country, region or community you are living in? Does the national constitution stipulate an official or national language(s)? What legislation or public policy guides language choices in the domains of education and health care? If you are studying or teaching abroad, how do the language policies of your host country compare to those of your home country? How are the linguistic needs of minorities addressed? What differences do you observe between policy and everyday practice?

2   Map the linguistic landscape of the community where you live. Take digital photographs of the advertisements and publicly displayed texts that use elements of multiple languages and images. In terms of the presence of English and other languages, how do the texts in your community compare to the linguistic landscape of Ghent or Mekele described in this chapter? Another take on the same activity is to show photographs of multilingual texts to residents of the community and ask them to interpret the signs. Do immigrants and non-immigrants differ in their interpretations?

3   As a (future) practitioner of applied linguistics, which of the aspects of language policy and planning discussed in this chapter is most closely related to the work you intend to do? Who are the language planning clients you plan to work with? Will this work involve clients from marginalized or impoverished communities? What are the explicit and implicit language policies you will likely encounter? For example, will you be expected or required to use particular language(s) and avoid using others? Will you be involved in top-down or bottom-up policies, or both?

4   If you are a practising teacher, what are the language-in-education policies at your school? Are they stated explicitly or simply understood? How did they become policy? How are these policies made known to students and teachers, and are there differences between the official policy and how it is enacted or practised? If you are not currently teaching, imagine that you are a language teacher in a school that is receiving an increasing number of immigrant students whose first language in not English. Knowing of your background in applied linguistics, your head of school has invited you to form a committee to design a school-wide language policy. Who else would you include on your committee? What would your policy look like?

activities

## FURTHER READING

Canagarajah, A. S. (ed.) (2005). *Reclaiming the local in language policy and practice.* Mahwah, NJ: Lawrence Erlbaum.

Ferguson, G. (2006). *Language planning and education.* Edinburgh: Edinburgh University Press.

Hornberger, N. H. and Pütz, M. (eds) (2006). *Language loyalty, language planning and language revitalization: Recent writings and reflections from Joshua A. Fishman.* Clevedon, UK: Multilingual Matters.

Spolsky, B. (2009). *Language management.* Cambridge: Cambridge University Press.

Tsung, L. (2009). *Minority languages, education and communities in China.* New York: Palgrave Macmillan.

**PART B**

# Language, learning and education

Part B, the central part of the book, is also central to the practice of applied linguistics in that the topics we address here include many of the most important and most studied aspects of the discipline. In Chapter 6, we tackle the key problem of *literacy*; a collection of learned behaviours which underpin how we judge the ability of (ourselves and) others to perform any task involving reading or writing, and yet which often remain a largely unrecognized element of the task. In this chapter, we hope to show how the written forms of language, and associated practices developed by readers and writers, are not static or universal, but rather highly diverse and shaped to fit particular purposes and uses in different contexts. Chapter 7, on *language and education*, considers language in one of its most studied and controversial domains, that of formal schooling. We probably all have strong opinions about which language(s) are suitable for the purposes of education and how they ought and ought not to be used in schools. As applied linguists, however, it is our role to show how notions of 'standard varieties', 'norms' and 'correctness' are socially constructed, and may bring both benefit and harm when used to judge the language of individuals and groups.

Chapter 8, on *bilingual and multilingual education*, examines the problem of schooling in multiple languages, a pressing and equally controversial, yet poorly understood, issue in many communities around the world. In Chapter 9 we investigate the area of applied linguistics which has received the most attention from both scholars and practitioners to date, *additional language education*. In keeping with our intention to map areas which have only recently come to be regarded as squarely within the field of applied linguistics, and unlike other introductory texts, we devote only one chapter to the rapidly evolving (but instantly and extensively mapped) concerns of this area.

All the chapters in Part B deal with the important issue of variation within (and between) languages, and to attitudes to these varieties. Chapter 6, for example, looks at how multiple forms of reading and writing have evolved over time and are manifested within contemporary societies and individuals. Chapter 7 explores controversies over which languages and varieties of language are suitable for use in schools, as well as how socially sanctioned varieties may differ from the varieties used in pupils' homes. Chapter 8 shows how the choice and balance of languages in bilingual education settings arise from often hidden ideas about an additional language as a resource, a right and/or a problem. The question of which variety of an additional language to teach has, until recently, been overlooked, with learners encouraged to believe (by materials publishing companies, standardized tests, private language schools and national governments) in monolithic correct versions and 'one-size-fits-all' targets. Chapter 9 addresses some of these issues and how language teachers can raise their students' awareness of them.

Closely connected to the issue of variation within and between languages are problems of (lack of) freedom and (in)equality. Taken collectively, the topics addressed in Part B highlight how language policies and practices in education can benefit but also harm student speakers and writers. Education practitioners are often encouraged by their training to see their role as *enforcing* (with students as subjects) one, or a limited range of, language variety(ies), rather than *exploring* them (with students as co-researchers). This always raises the danger that, by ignoring or repressing the literacies and language varieties that students bring to class (or that they may need in future), the range of linguistic expression they are able to deploy is narrowed rather than expanded. Similarly, where only prestigious languages, varieties of a language or literacy practices are promoted, the prestige of students who already have these languages/varieties/practices is reinforced and the gap between 'approved' and 'not approved' becomes wider.

The chapters in Part B raise many of the concerns of critical applied linguistics. All of the topics here challenge us to think very carefully about the connections between why (and how) language is learned (especially in educational institutions), and the social, economic and political contexts of language use (and assessment). As applied linguists we are faced with the responsibility of going further than thinking, towards taking action to encourage and facilitate the thinking of our students and the policy-makers who guide (and control?) our decisions about teaching and assessing languages.

We are aware, despite a strong emphasis of the social aspects of language learning in Part B, that the complex problems faced by applied linguists can be solved only through attention to the cognitive and sociocultural dimensions of language. As a result, in line with our practice in the rest of the book, we stress the transdisciplinary nature of applied linguistic practice, as applied linguists in one field rely on knowledge and tools developed in other fields. Similarly, while professionals and scholars in bilingual and additional language education have long recognized the necessary centrality of language in their work, this part of the book aims to show the importance of language for education in general, and for judgements about the educational achievements of individuals and groups.

In each chapter, we:

- present some of the main problems faced by applied linguists and language practitioners in educational contexts;
- identify and explain key concepts and terms;
- exemplify and explain solutions proposed by applied linguists;
- describe the roles currently, and potentially, played by applied linguists.

At the end of each chapter, we provide activities to encourage you to think about applied linguistics learning and practice in your own contexts and those you may be preparing to work in: at home, in class, in professional contexts; locally, regionally, internationally and virtually. These activities invite you to reflect on, and apply, the concepts presented by identifying similar problems and proposing possible solutions. For updated examples, additional and interactive activities, and further reading related to Part B, check the companion website.

# CHAPTER 6

# Literacy

> Literacy is a curious thing. It seems to envelop our lives and be central to modern
> living, and yet most of humanity has done without it for most of human existence.
> (Collins and Blot, 2003, p. 1)

This chapter takes up the applied linguistics of literacy – the written forms of
language and associated practices developed by readers and writers. As human
inventions go, writing systems are quite recent, dating back perhaps 5,000 or 6,000
years – roughly the same length of time that humans have been cultivating staple
crops like corn and wheat, but not as long as rice (10,000 years) or other key human
inventions:

■ beer (first brewed some 10,000 years ago in China);
■ human portraits and fish hooks (Italy, 14,000 years);
■ woven clothing (about 25,000 years);
■ musical instruments (the flute, 35,000 years, in Germany);
■ home decorating (the earliest known cave paintings, in Australia, date back
  nearly 40,000 years);
■ lipstick (70,000 years, Blombos Cave, South Africa).

(Morton, 2002)

Although the contemporary applied linguist can perhaps get by without fish hooks,
lipstick and possibly even beer, from our vantage point as modern-day literate
beings it is difficult to imagine our lives without reading and writing. Think email, text
messages and chat, shopping lists, cookbooks, novels, horoscopes, newspapers,
magazines, dictionaries, job notices, lottery tickets, course schedules and train time-
tables, to name but a few. And the literacy technologies we use to produce, transmit
and receive information: pens, pencils, books, personal computers, mobile phones,
iPads, e-books, etc.

Perhaps not surprisingly, we are often most aware of literacy when using the
very newest of technologies. The forms and practices involved in sending text
messages, twittering and chatting online may be anathema to writing instructors
and prescriptive citizens worldwide, but they are thrilling to many youths and to the
literate young-at-heart. Yet consider the myriad daily tasks we engage in without
being aware of the modality we're using; for example: reading the newspaper while
talking over breakfast with your partner; taking notes during a lecture; or teaching
a class and writing on the SMART Board. As Collins and Blot suggest in our epigraph, although literacy is a relative newcomer in the span of human invention, the

spell that language casts over us now clearly extends to the written as well as to the oral modality.

We begin our discussion of literacy with an examination of how scope and definitions of the term have expanded in recent years (section 6.1). We next consider the role written language has played in the historical development of human societies (6.2); the social or collective development of contemporary human communities (6.3); and literacy as developed and used by children and adults individually and in groups (6.4). The penultimate section is devoted to a consideration of literacy and academic achievement, including assessment issues. We end with roles for applied linguists (6.6).

## 6.1  THE EXPANDING SCOPE OF LITERACY

Written language hasn't always been a central concern for linguists. Although, historically, general linguists and their predecessors had focused mainly on the meanings of written texts, during most of the twentieth century speech was regarded as the only legitimate object of linguistic study. The linguist Leonard Bloomfield (1984 [1933], p. 21) famously described writing as 'merely a way of recording language by visible means'. Florian Coulmas (1989, p. 273) summed up this position in his influential book *The Writing Systems of the World*: 'Writing is not language. That is the axiom of modern linguistics.' Over the past two decades or so, however, views of written language have changed as the field has moved from modality-dominant views of language to the notion of an underlying language competence which we can externalize through four channels (speech, sign, writing and Braille). Robin Tolmach Lakoff captures nicely this shift away from modality-specific views of language and toward a more inclusive view:

> Any claim that some forms our language takes are 'realer' or more legitimate objects of analysis than others is misguided. The question to ask is, how do all the forms language takes in our time work together to produce the results that we see around us?
>
> (Lakoff, 2000, p. 14)

Studies in applied linguistics have paralleled this refocus on written language, and it seems safe to say that research and practice in such areas as discourse analysis, language planning, bilingual education, additional language education, translation, lexicography, among others, are now likely to include an explicit focus on the written aspects of language.

A by-product of this interdisciplinary cross-pollination is that the field of literacy studies has been enriched by the ideas of thinkers in other fields. Perhaps more than any other sub-field within applied linguistics, literacy has been interpreted and practised from the perspective of other disciplines, including psychology, history, anthropology, sociology, education, and visual and graphic design. For example, as we'll see in section 6.2, visual design theory has influenced views about what constitutes a written text and how the linguistic and non-linguistic elements it is composed of can be arranged and displayed. Eye movement studies of reading, as we'll see in 6.4, draw on knowledge of how the eyes receive linguistic and semiotic information that is interpreted by the brain. While demographers and sociologists view literacy as a quality that is distributed across groups and populations, anthropologists have contributed close ethnographic portraits of literate lives in certain locales, including schools and the literacy practices of those communities. Psychologists have shown that assessing levels of literacy is partly a factor of the instruments and tasks used. Many fine books have been written about literacy from each of these perspectives, and so the present chapter will thus inevitably omit or give short shrift to key notions of literacy as mapped by those disciplines. We note significant overlaps with and contributions from them but focus in this chapter on the topic of literacy for and from within applied linguistics. As in other chapters, we acknowledge that this is one of many possible maps of the topic; at the end of the chapter we suggest some other maps (further readings) that we think are important.

Literacy is also growing in scope due to recognition that literacy development and attainment remain stratified along the lines of gender, ethnicity, class and home language background, among other factors. Governments, non-governmental organizations and human rights groups attempt to address these inequalities through programmes to promote reading and writing as a human right for mar-ginalized individuals and groups, such as speakers of Indigenous languages, immigrants, people with language impairments and especially women. The United Nations Literacy Decade campaign estimates that one in five adults (about 780 million people) cannot read or write, and that about two-thirds of these are women. And people who are blind or have a visual impairment face additional challenges, despite the enormous contributions of new technology to Braille literacy (Hartz, 2000). Even where children have uninterrupted access to formal schooling, many struggle to learn to read and write at the rate or level that will allow them to succeed in higher education or handle the literacy demands of well-paying jobs. For all these reasons, interest in written language is increasing, with the result that many projects undertaken by applied linguists and teachers, language planners and other language professionals with a background in applied linguistics are directly related to literacy in some way.

 **www.6.1**

 **www.6.2**

## (Re)Defining literacy: new wine in an old bottle?

One consequence of the increased scope of literacy is that definitions are very much in flux, perhaps to the chagrin of the lexicographers whose work we'll get to know in Chapter 11. Compared with the terms *reading* and *writing* (both Anglo-Saxon), *literacy* is a distinct newcomer. David Barton (2007, p. 20) has traced the development of the word *literacy* and members of its word family (*literate, illiterate, illiteracy*) from their earliest appearance in English language dictionaries (an entry for *illiterate* in Samuel Johnson's dictionary, 1755) through to increasingly numerous and lengthier entries for *literacy*, from 1924 on, in the *Oxford English Dictionary*. Barton notes that the earliest entries carried the sense of being an educated person. What many might regard as the 'core' meaning of literacy, that is, the ability to encode (write) and decode (read) written text, did not appear until much later.

Something similar has been happening in other European languages, including Spanish, the language with the second largest number of websites, published books and academic journals in print after English (Hamel, 2003). Here we find:

- *alfabetismo/alfabetización* (Spain and Latin America, knowing, or not knowing, the alphabet and learning how to use it);
- *letrada* (from Latin *litterātus*, to be 'lettered' or educated);
- *lectoescritura* (Argentina and Mexico, a recent amalgam of *lectura* [reading] and *escritura* [writing]);
- *literacidad* (Peru, a direct translation of *literacy* that has appeared only very recently and seems to be gaining acceptance across the Spanish-speaking world).

This quick cross-linguistic glance provides some interesting insights: clearly, there is regional variation in the way Spanish speakers talk (and write) about literacy. We can see language change and language contact in action too; *alfabetismo* and other forms of *alfabetizar* came to the Americas courtesy of the Spanish conquest (through enforced conversions and Bible instruction), quickly displacing the words for 'reading' in Indigenous languages such as Nahuatl and Maya (more on these in 6.2), which can be translated as 'painting' and 'viewing'. Perhaps because of the purist stance often taken by Spain's Royal Language Academy (see Chapter 11), *lectoescritura* appeared in the Academy's dictionary for the first time in 2001; time will tell whether it will eventually accept or reject *literacidad*.

The semantic domain of literacy is also expanding as a result of its use in the formation of new compound nouns in English. Early forms from the 1970s included *mathematics literacy* (now being replaced by *numeracy*), *consumer literacy*, *financial literacy*, *media literacy* and *music literacy*. Ecological concerns have prompted a similar profusion of terms. Consider the following, taken from the mission statement of the Campaign for Environmental Literacy: 'Life on this planet as we know it cannot be sustained unless greater *environmental literacy* informs all human endeavours' (Environmental Literacy Council, n.d.) (see Figure 6.1); and recommended reading for government officials and especially for BP executives: 'Ocean literacy: an understanding of the ocean's influence on you and your influence on the ocean' (Ocean Literacy Network, 2009).

**www.6.3**

**www.6.4**

As we'll see in Chapters 7, 8 and 9, educators have not been immune to the trend of developing new terms (*cultural literacy*, *family literacy*, *emergent literacy*, *biliteracy* and *L2 literacy*, for example). Recent technological developments have also clearly contributed, with *digital literacy*, *computer literacy*, *information literacy* and even a proposed antidote to digital information overload, *bit literacy* ('a new set of skills for managing bits' [Hurst, 2007]).

The impressive generative capacity of the word *literacy* may have its drawbacks. The linguist M. A. K. Halliday makes this point:

> The problem is that if we call all these things literacy, then we shall have to find another term for what we called literacy before because it is still necessary to distinguish reading and writing practices from listening and speaking practices.
> (Halliday, 2007 [1979], p.98)

As authors distinguish between the more restricted sense of literacy as reading and writing and a newer, more generative use of the term to refer to knowing about or how to do something in a specialized area of knowledge, you get examples like the following, taken from the website of the Maia Foundation, a charity organization

Figure 6.1   Environmental literacy (Source: Environmental Literacy Council)

 **www.6.3**

# ENVIRONMENTAL LITERACY

## join me.

promoting women's health and health literacy in sub-Saharan Africa: 'The high death rate of teachers [in South Africa, Zimbabwe and Nigeria] shows clearly that *general literacy* and *health literacy* do not necessarily go hand in hand'.

 **www.6.6**

Finally, the scope of literacy has grown, like other areas of applied linguistics study and practice, through consideration of multiple languages and varieties. The conditions of increased migration and transnational exchanges introduced in the previous chapter and taken up again in Chapter 14; the fact that schooling and work around the world are being conducted in multiple languages, discussed in Chapters 7 and 8; the rapid development of compelling new literacy technologies and practices that emerge from their use; and questions about the role of literacy in the workings of globalization and rapidly changing economies are all factors leading scholars and practitioners to deal with multiliteracies rather than a monolithic, generic literacy. This shift to a concern with the plurilithic forms and practices of literacy is motivating much new research that many now recognize under the umbrella of the 'New Literacy Studies'. Following James Gee, one of the earliest architects of the New Literacy Studies, we won't use this term, on the grounds that it is already out of date (Clair and Phipps, 2008) and also because each of the topics we now turn to is worthy of discussion in its own right.

## Literacy as cognitive process and social practice

Despite these developments, for applied linguistics literacy remains fundamentally tied up with the ability to read and write printed texts and, increasingly, digitally mediated forms of text. In the remainder of this chapter, we'll concentrate mainly on this core meaning of literacy – reading and writing – and how readers and writers learn, process and communicate via written forms of language. To do this, we'll keep in mind our view that applied linguistics is most powerful as a means of finding solutions to language-related problems when it integrates cognitive and sociocultural aspects of language rather than emphasizing one to the exclusion of the other. This has particular implications for thinking about literacy because it is a topic within applied linguistics which is usually tackled from one paradigm or the other, with unfortunate consequences for fuller understanding and particularly for educational applications, as we discuss in section 6.5 and Chapter 7. Psychologists, for example, have tended to describe reading and writing as discrete skills to be learned on a more or less linear basis. Walmsley (1981, p. 82) observed that, within a cognitive development model, reading is conceived of as an intellectual process achieved 'through a series of fixed, value-free, and universal stages of development', with the implication that learners everywhere can be taught to read and write in the same way.

In a classic study of adult literacy education in Iran, the anthropologist Brian Street (1984) compared the forms of literacy promoted in UNESCO adult education programmes with those he observed in rural villages, including literacy instruction in Islamic schools. Reflecting on these differences and how they mapped onto understandings of literacy developed by literacy scholars, Street described a binary distinction between two views of literacy: (1) an earlier and (then) dominant view that he termed the **autonomous model** of literacy, in which reading and writing were conceived of and taught as a set of specific skills (for example decoding letters in **alphabetic writing systems**); and (2) the **ideological model**, which, he proposed, leads to a view of reading and writing as communicative practices that are developed in particular social contexts, but which cannot be assumed to hold in others. The latter view has become increasingly influential over the past three decades, because it is useful for examining literacy practices *in situ* and also because it allows us to consider emerging forms of literacy, including the digital varieties examined in 6.2. Barton's (2007, p. 32) definition encapsulates the ideological view of literacy as 'a set of social practices associated with particular symbol systems and their related technologies. To be literate is to be active; it is to be confident within these practices'. Although we favour this move to a situated view of literacy, we prefer another term, also proposed by Barton, the *ecological model*, because it allows applied linguists to attend to the sociocultural aspects of literacy without excluding the obvious cognitive dimensions that are inherent in the acts of reading and writing (Smith, 2004).

According to Brian Street's **autonomous model**, literacy is a set of skills for encoding and decoding language in the written modality. According to his **ideological model**, it is viewed as competence in forms of social practice.

An **alphabetic writing system** uses (ideally) single symbols for each phoneme (speech sound) in the language.

Given the evolving nature and growing scope of literacy, how, then, should we determine who is literate? Simpler definitions of literacy are attractive to governments, schools and other institutions because this enables them to estimate the percentage of literate people in a given region or country or group. For example, early counts of literates in mediaeval Europe were based on a (male landowning) person's ability to sign their name or, in Sweden, an ability to read aloud from the Bible, measures that wouldn't count for much today. Contemporary literacy counts, including those conducted by national census-takers, ask respondents to self-report answers to questions such as 'Can you write a short note to a family member?' More commonly, countries calculate literacy rates based on the number of people who report that they can read and write by a certain age. These calculations are troublesome for a number of reasons, including the problems inherent in self-reported data; the lack of consistency in defining 'reading' and 'writing'; and the fact that empirically based measures, such as reading tests, often suggest substantially lower rates. For this reason, and perhaps to avoid the misleading distinction between 'literates' and 'illiterates', international organizations such as UNESCO have moved to a system of literacy levels, further discussed in 6.5.

Critics of attempts to gauge mass literacy point out that while such criteria avoid the binary (yes/no) distinction between literates and non-literates, without actual testing it remains impossible to establish whether a person actually meets the criteria. An additional problem is that terms used in functional definitions, such as *everyday literacy demands* and *complex society*, are vague and can vary substantially across regional and national contexts. Finally, as anyone who has ever retrained for employment in a new field is aware, the specific literacy skills needed for work can vary a great deal in different jobs. In the face of such complexities, it's easy to see why the US *CIA World Factbook* shows comparative data for world literacy rates simply by listing the percentage of people that countries report can read by a certain age (fifteen years being the most common).

 **www.6.7**

## 6.2  WRITING SYSTEMS AND CULTURE

As we have noted, writing is a relatively recent human invention. Current scholarship on the origins of written language suggests that this new and transformative technology appeared separately in three regions of the world:

- Sumer (present-day Iraq) about 5,500 years ago;
- China about 3,300 years ago;
- Meso-America (the region from central Mexico to Nicaragua) about 2,600 years ago.

Although further research could certainly prove otherwise, at present there is no evidence for a single 'Eureka!' moment in which writing was invented by a single person and subsequently transmitted to other places (e.g. from Sumer to China and then Mexico). Archaeologists working in these three regions continue to uncover new texts, thus giving their **epigrapher** colleagues plenty of work for the foreseeable future. As John F. Kennedy once noted (in a speech at Rice University in 1962), if we were to compress the past 50,000 years of human existence into

**Epigraphers** study and interpret written inscriptions on hard surfaces, such as stone. To get an idea of what they do, visit Oxford University's *Curse Tablets of Roman Britain* site, which has a section on Cursing for Beginners.

 **www.6.8**

a fifty-year period, then people began to write the equivalent of only about five years ago. We can extend this temporal experiment to observe that literacy began to spread beyond a few highly trained specialists (scribes and teachers of the elite) to everyday people less than six months ago on Kennedy's fifty-year scale, and to all schoolchildren (at least in the wealthier nations) within the past three weeks or less. Even in this brief time, however, the ability to read and write has come to be regarded as an essential indicator of both 'civilization' and individual development.

Because literacy has become central to our understanding of collective and individual human development, and to the work of applied linguists, as we shall see in subsequent chapters, it behoves us to take a closer look at writing systems as technologies and at the cognitive, physical and cultural assumptions they rest on. Because definitions of written language are fluid, it's difficult if not impossible to fix the starting date. However, as Liliana Tolchinsky has observed,

> human beings have been involved in notational activities for the last 30,000 years – from daubs on a cave wall to clicking a mouse on a computer to produce a mark on a screen, every imaginable surface and instrument has been exploited in leaving traces. Even then, only a fraction of materials will have withstood the test of time.
>
> (Tolchinsky, 2003, p. 26)

Thus, it seems likely that people were inscribing organic materials such as bone, seashells, leather or wood long before the dates we now believe that Sumerian scribes were first writing on clay tablets. Unfortunately, due to the organic nature of these materials, the earliest of these inscriptions are lost, perhaps forever.

Acknowledging these limitations, we argue that literacy is best understood as an open, rather than a closed, set of practices. In linguistic terms, written language is more like an open class of words (such as nouns, which are growing in number all the time as new objects and concepts need to be talked and written about) and less like a closed class of words (such as prepositions, where not much new is going on). Joseph Lo Bianco (2000) observes that some forms of literacy that are very new, such as e-mail and multi-modal texts, actually draw on and make use of pre-existing 'available designs' to achieve new meanings. For example, the symbols for punctuation have long co-existed on the **QWERTY** keyboard, but it wasn't until electronic communication that writers routinely began to join them up to produce online smiles, winks, sad faces and the like. In following generations, such **emoticons** would automatically get converted into punctuation-free icons (Figure 6.2).

Or consider the more involved and evolving features of *leetspeak* (also known as *leet* or *elite*), a code in which letter substitutions (like l337 instead of leet) are used systematically to produce in-group messages. Here's an example, from English to two levels of leet, using ioyu's English to leet translator (ioyu.com, 2006):

*English*:
Sumerian scribes first wrote on clay tablets 5,500 years ago.

*Normal Leet*:
Sum3r14n scr1b3z f1rst wr0t3 0n cL4y t4bL3tz 5,500 y34rz 4g0.

**QWERTY** is the name of the standard keyboard layout devised by Christopher Sholes in Milwaukee, Wisconsin, in the USA in 1878, so called because of the order of the first six letters.

An **emoticon** is a representation of a facial expression using the punctuation marks and letters available on a keyboard. They range in complexity from the simple :) to the rather more elaborate Japanese d(˘ ▽ ˘)b, both of which mean 'happy'.

**www.6.9**

Figure 6.2   The emoticons grow up

*Extreme Leet:*
S|_||\/|3r14|\| scr1b32 |=1rs7 \/\/r073 0|\| c|_4'/ 74b|_372 5,500 '/34r2
460.

At the same time as innovating, written language also constrains. One of the clearest effects of mass literacy has been the fixing or slowing of language change, through the creation of standardized orthographies and preferred spelling conventions based on a specific oral variety. In the case of English, the decision by William Caxton and other early printers to encode a variety of English spoken in and around London was an economic one, aimed at the greatest number of potential readers. The printing press also greatly influenced the form of texts that readers had available for reading and, through literacy instruction at school, the conventions they learned to write with. The conservative brake on variation in spelling wasn't automatic, of course. In Chapter 7, 'Language and education', you'll read a fragment of an early English language textbook in which the author (Edmund Coote, 1997 [1596]) calls for improved spelling while spelling the word *schoolmaster* three different ways in just a few short paragraphs. As Kenneth Goodman (1993) observes in *Phonics Phacts*, phonetic regularity has not yet been completely achieved, at least not to the satisfaction of scholemaisters, publishers, editors and others charged with minding our orthographic Ps and Qs. These examples remind us that technologies associated with new forms of literacy can simultaneously have innovative and conservative influences on our use of language.

Cross-linguistic studies of written language can also teach applied linguists a great deal because they force us to consider new ways of thinking about reading and writing. One common and persistent idea about literacy held by many people in the English-speaking world and throughout much of Europe and the Americas is that writing is synonymous with the alphabet. If you first learned to read in English, French, Spanish, Portuguese or another language written with the Latin alphabet it's difficult to see beyond the confines of alphabetic thinking, in which readers use symbols to represent individual phonemes. Although the alphabets they employ look quite different from the Latin alphabet, Greek, Russian and Korean also use symbols to represent the individual phonemes of their respective spoken languages. And speakers of Thai, Arabic and Hebrew learn to read alphabetic texts in which only the consonants are represented in writing and in which they must insert the vowels mentally (**consonantal** writing systems). Texters and tweeters who omit vowels (*k* for okay, *plz* for please, etc.) will readily see the utility of this design feature.

Readers of Japanese, Cherokee and Vai (spoken in Liberia and south-eastern Sierra Leone) must learn to read a **syllabary**, in which each individual grapheme represents a syllable rather than an individual phoneme. When reading Chinese, readers are accessing and constructing meaning through **logographs** which represent specific words or ideas rather sounds or groups of sounds. These systemic differences, illustrated in Table 6.1, help explain the cognitive challenges facing adult readers who are already literate in one language and are learning to make sense of written language encoded in another alphabet or a distinct writing system, and especially children and non-literate adults (in an L2) who are learning to read symbols that represent phonemic or syllabic values in a language they are still learning to *speak*.

One important way in which oral language and written language are similar is that they are not pure. Just as oral languages borrow elements from others through different types of language contact, written languages are inevitably mixed systems which combine elements of sound and image. Perhaps the best-known example of a mixed system is Japanese, which combines three different types of scripts: *kanji* (based on Chinese characters); *hiragana* (a syllabary); and *katakana* (a second type

**www.6.10**

**Consonantal** writing systems have symbols for the consonants but not for the vowels. Context supplies the words' identities. (For example, *Cn y rd ths*?)

A **syllabary** is a writing system in which each symbol represents a syllable (in English we can simulate this by using *Q* for monosyllabic *cue*, *I-V* for bisyllabic *i.vy*, *F-E-G* for trisyllabic *e.ffi.gy*, etc.

Table 6.1   Examples of writing systems

| Writing system | Example | | |
|---|---|---|---|
| | *Language* | *Script* | *Sample* |
| Alphabetic | Russian | Cyrillic | Всеобщая декларация прав человека |
| Consonantal | Thai | Thai | ปฏิญญาสากลว่าด้วยสิทธิมนุษยชน |
| Syllabic | Yi (China) | Yi | ꆈꌠꁱꂷ |
| Logographic | Chinese | Báihuà | 世界人权宣言 |

of syllabary used to refer to non-Japanese names and words borrowed from other languages). Due to increased contact with non-Japanese speakers, the practice of writing imported words, such as the names of international companies and institutions, and particularly acronyms using the Latin alphabet, has also increased. Mayan is another writing system which combined elements of phonetic writing (**glyphs** representing individual syllables) with images representing ideas rather than sound. And although English is usually described as a language that is written phonetically, bits of it regularly get expressed using non-sound based symbols, such as $ and %, or the well-known example in Figure 6.3.

Here we focus more on the similarities and interplay between written and oral language than on their differences. This follows from the view that, along with sign and Braille, each is a modality that externalizes language, but it is also because the differences are discussed thoroughly elsewhere (cf. Chafe and Danielewicz, 1987; Halliday, 2007 [1979]). Of course, these differences, similarities and links are not generic across all languages in written and oral forms; as we have suggested, the task for a child of learning to read in a language that is written in alphabetic form differs in some important ways from that of learning to read in a language that is primarily logographic or non-glottographic.

Having taken a few tentative steps beyond the limits of an alphabet-only view, let's look briefly at a set of writing systems that have challenged scholars of written language and historians of language. Recall that Meso-America was the site of what is believed to be the third and final time that writing was 'invented', some two and a half millennia ago, independently of developments in Asia and Europe (Jiménez and Smith, 2008). Numerous writing systems were in use in the Americas at the time of the European conquest in the early sixteenth century, and older systems (e.g. Mayan and Zapotec) had left substantial written records. Tragically, most pre-Hispanic texts were destroyed by the invading Europeans, but sufficient examples and descriptions, together with engravings on stone stela and other

A **glyph** is a symbol or character used in a writing system, especially that of the ancient Mayan civilization in what is now Mexico. Ancient Egyptian hiero*glyphics* provide another example.

Figure 6.3   I love New York

monuments, remain to allow for at least partial interpretation. The reaction of the Spanish missionaries and soldiers to these unfamiliar forms of 'picture writing' was interesting to say the least. The Spaniards (only barely literate themselves) were already firmly of the 'alphabet mindset', and thus found it difficult to fathom the complexities of the Indigenous writing systems they encountered. Fray Toribio de Motolinía, one of the earliest Franciscan missionaries in the region, wrote:

> This land of Anahuac or New Spain, so named by our Lord the Emperor, according to the ancient books of these people, had characters and figures, and this was their writing because they had no letters, but only characters, and the memory of men was weak and of little substance.

(Motolinía, 1969)

**www.6.11**

So little substance, evidently, that the Spanish thought it necessary to burn many **codices** as 'works of the devil'. Figure 6.4 shows a page from one of the very few surviving pre-conquest codices, the Codex Vaticanus B, a divinatory calendar book from the Puebla region used to select propitious dates for marriages, planting, going to war and other events. Such texts were produced by a *tlacuilo* (a scribe, often working as part of a team of scribes) and probably read aloud by a priest for a client seeking advice on when to engage in a certain action.

A **codex** (plural **codices**) is an ancient manuscript in book form. The Mexican codices were painted on deerskin or bark paper. You can inspect facsimiles at the Foundation for the Advancement of Mesoamerican Studies.

Aside from illustrating – dramatically, we think – that complex written texts can be produced by societies that did not possess an alphabet, the Meso-American codices exemplify writing that suited the purposes of users in a specific time and

**www.6.12**

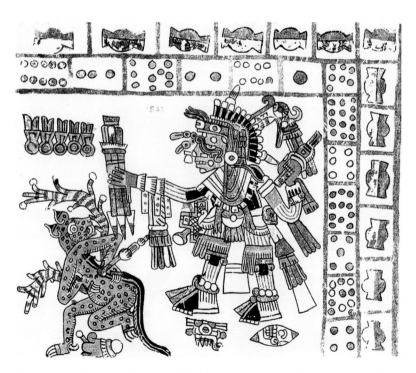

Figure 6.4   A divinatory calendar from Puebla, Mexico (Source: Wikimedia Commons)

place. Because their lives and needs were quite different from our ways of life, Meso-Americans generated writing and practices of writing and reading that we might dismiss, as Motolinía did, as 'pictures' and not real writing at all. Thinking about the codices and other ancient texts, those that have been recovered and are subject to contemporary interpretation and those that are lost and cannot be recovered, reminds us that our own views about literacy are very much bound up in our present circumstances and beliefs. They are useful for rethinking assumptions about the relationship of speech to written language, and of images to 'written' texts, and deeply ingrained views about the superiority of alphabets over other writing systems; and for applied linguists who encounter and work with forms of written language that are new to them but may actually be very old, such as the academic writing of Chinese students studying in English language universities and some of the forms employed in the digital literacies enjoyed and produced by young people.

## 6.3  LITERACY AND INDIVIDUALS

In section 6.2 we explored literacy as a social phenomenon, as a means of viewing peoples and cultures that produce and practise particular forms of reading and writing. But societies are composed of individuals, of course, and the idea that literacy is capable of transforming individual lives also has a long history. Concerns with the effects of writing on the mind of the individual go back at least as far as Plato, who argued in *The Phaedrus* (in writing, ironically) that writing fundamentally altered the way the pupil approached learning:

> [Writing] will introduce forgetfulness into the soul of those who learn it: they will not practise using their memory because they will put their trust in writing, which is external and depends on signs that belong to others, instead of trying to remember from the inside, completely on their own.
>
> (*The Phaedrus*, 275a–b)

Plato's concerns notwithstanding, the invention of literacy clearly has made a remarkable impression on the minds of the individuals who are taught to use it. Analysing writings by Plato and other classical philosophers and poets, Walter Ong argues that becoming literate restructures our ways of thinking:

> Without writing, the literate mind could not and would not think as it does. Not only when it is engaged in writing but normally even when it is composing its thoughts in oral form. More than any single invention, writing has transformed human consciousness.
>
> (Ong, 1982, p. 78)

As evidence, Ong offers the decline of some forms of oral expression, including the ability to commit to memory long stretches of oral poetry and saga through the use of mnemonics, or memory aides, and the spread of others, such as the ability to structure complex propositions and provide supporting evidence.

This argument in favour of the literate mind as the (only) architect of 'modern' thinking is obviously compelling for people who have already developed advanced literacy skills. However, by drawing on knowledge from psycholinguistics, anthropology and other fields, applied linguists can spot flaws inherent in this assumption. First, as we saw in Chapter 1, we don't *think* in language at all (although what Ong meant by the phrase 'composing thoughts in oral form' is open to interpretation), and it is important to keep in mind that while literates may indeed consciously structure what comes out of their mouths (and hands and keyboards) differently from non-literates, thought itself remains alinguistic and therefore non-literate. Second, we would want to reject any claim that societies (or their individual members) are inherently primitive and less 'advanced' by virtue of their (lack of) writing. Some have critiqued Ong's argument as a 'great divide' theory, with pre-literates on one side of history and literates on the other (see Jack Goody's fascinating discussion in the book *The Domestication of the Savage Mind* [1977]). Note also that the argument considers only alphabetic scripts as the potential engines of mental transformation, ignoring the logographic and ideographic scripts we looked at in section 6.2. From this logic, it would follow that there are no literate minds at all without the alphabet, an assertion that is as unfounded as it is discriminatory.

A related avenue into thinking about literacy and the individual comes from research on differences in perception, memory and problem solving among literates and non-literates. Building on learning theories proposed by Vygotsky, research by the Russian psychologist Alexander Luria with literate and non-literate peasants in Central Asia suggested a basic equation: literacy promotes intelligence (Cole *et al.*, 2005). This position was explored and ultimately challenged by literacy research among the Vai in Liberia in the 1970s. The cultural psychologists Sylvia Scribner and Michael Cole (1981) were interested in the psychology of literacy in this unique multilingual and multiliterate setting. Literacy among the Vai was particularly compelling due to the fact that the three written languages used in Vai communities are written in different scripts and are acquired and used in distinct circumstances and for distinct purposes:

- *Vai* syllabic script, invented around 1830, was originally taught in special schools by its inventor, Momolu Duwalu Bukele. By the time of Scribner and Cole's study, Vai script was being transmitted informally among men, including from father to son, and was used mainly for letter-writing among friends and acquaintances.
- *English* literacy, used in commerce and in the public domain, was taught in government schools open to boys and girls.
- *Arabic* literacy was taught in Qur'anic schools open only to boys, and used almost exclusively for religious purposes.

In this context, the literacy picture was not only highly complex, but also markedly different for males and females. Through close ethnographic work in which they explored each of the three transmission systems and the functions of literate communications that took place in each script, Scribner and Cole developed literacy tests and other tasks that were meaningful in this specific research context. By assigning the approximately 1,000 participants to groups on the basis of conditions of literacy acquisition and use, they were able to tease apart the effects of formal schooling and literacy achieved without formal schooling. They found that the highest scores on measures of categorization, abstract reasoning and forms of problem solving were obtained by subjects with greater exposure to school literacy (in this case in English). Alphabetic literacy (for example in Arabic) *per se* did not lead to higher scores, nor did syllabic literacy (in Vai). This led the researchers to conclude that it was the school activities that Vai learners encountered – rather than literacy on its own – which accounted for their superior performance on cognitive tasks.

## 6.4  CHILD AND ADULT LITERACIES

In this section we discuss literacy from the vantage points of childhood and adulthood, considering how reading and writing are developed and used before and after puberty. As we'll see, young children become very interested in cracking the literacy code they observe adults using because they sense that something important is going on. Parents, reading teachers and other adults are challenged to understand what children do when learning to read, because in becoming readers ourselves we have gone through a sort of transformation that it is difficult to look back on with clarity. Volumes have been written on literacy development in children and attention to adolescent and adult literacies is also growing. In each case, instruction continues to be a matter of heated debate in many contexts. There isn't space here to do full justice to the range of literacies across the lifespan, so we'll concentrate on a few main points and point you to important sources for further reading. We'll focus primarily on English literacy, in part because this is the language that has been most widely studied and also because it's a language that many children and adults are learning to read and write in today. We'll begin at the beginning, that is, with the literacies of children.

## Emergent literacies

For many children, literacy begins well before the first year of schooling. If you thought that you first learned to read and write in school, this idea may seem counterintuitive, even unsettling, but with the spread of print and electronic communications to virtually every corner of the globe, children observe a diverse range of texts and literacy practices in the course of their daily lives, simply by living and participating in their homes and in their communities. As they watch parents, siblings and others engage with the household and work-related forms of reading and writing of the sort we listed at the beginning of this chapter (p. 129), children begin to form nascent theories (ideas) about what literacy is, how it's done and the purposes it serves. In this sense, children develop literacy as they do **oracy** (although they are very different in some ways), by interacting with others through language. Thus, it's often more useful to consider language development without explicit reference to modality, especially in highly literate homes.

Research by Emilia Ferreiro and her colleagues focusing on the developmental nature of children's early writing has shown that learning to write is a complex psychological problem (Ferreiro and Gómez, 1997 [1982]). Rather than as fixed stages that all children go through in lockstep, this work presents early or **emergent literacy** as a process in which children encounter three fundamental problems:

**Oracy** is communicative competence in spoken interaction. The word was coined by analogy with *literacy* in the 1960s. The ORACY Australia Association has rich online resources for teaching and assessing oracy skills.

 **www.6.13**

The term **emergent literacy** refers to knowledge and behaviours involving reading and writing that children develop before formal schooling.

- What is the difference between drawing (pictures) and writing?
- How does writing relate to oral language?
- What are the conventions required to communicate in different genres, contexts, etc.?

In solving these problems, children form temporary theories about writing and how it works, and they revise and reform them as they encounter more input, face the problem of encoding what they want to say, learn from others and, most importantly, as they mature cognitively. Research with speakers of Spanish, French, English, Italian and Portuguese shows that, given input, children begin to form theories about written language even before the age of two (Ferreiro *et al.*,1996). Thus, what the untrained adult eye sees as scribbling or rows of figures which look like dots and sticks is actually a representation of the beginning of a child's 'thinking' about written language.

Working mainly with alphabetic scripts, literacy researchers have created specialized tasks to elicit responses from young children that will, in turn, tell them what the child currently knows about:

- the difference between pictures and writing ('Which one of these things is a picture?');
- the difference between numbers and letters ('Which of these things is good for counting?');
- the difference between letters and syllables;
- what individual letters represent (whole words first, usually concrete nouns);
- whether letters can be repeated in a word;
- the number of letters that are possible in a written word;
- what words represent;
- the number of words in a written phrase or sentence;
- where writing on a page can begin and end (directionality, layout).

Over the past thirty years or so, research with children learning to read an alphabetic language has provided the broad outlines (and, in some cases, very specific strokes) of a picture of early literacy development. Cross-linguistic research shows that some features of early writing have language-specific characteristics; for example, the unit of syllable is very robust across languages, but children learning to write in Portuguese, Italian and Spanish tend to produce first words composed mainly of vowels, while the first words produced by English-speaking children typically feature more consonants (Ferreiro *et al.*, 1996).

Another strong finding is that as children move towards adult-like conventions their literacy development is recursive rather than absolute. Thus, instances of children's invented spelling, such as the example in Figure 6.5 of a letter written by a five-year-old girl to her grandfather, can display multiple solutions to a single problem (our adult translation is on the right). On comparison, we see some characteristics of the child's writing that are quite adult-like (word segmentation, with a few exceptions, and end punctuation) and others that are clearly still in development (the lack of capitalization, and the spelling of *Maine* as *mayne* and *man*). Instead of viewing them as 'errors', we would regard such features as evidence that this writer is moving towards the contemporary norms expected of literate adult writers. It is

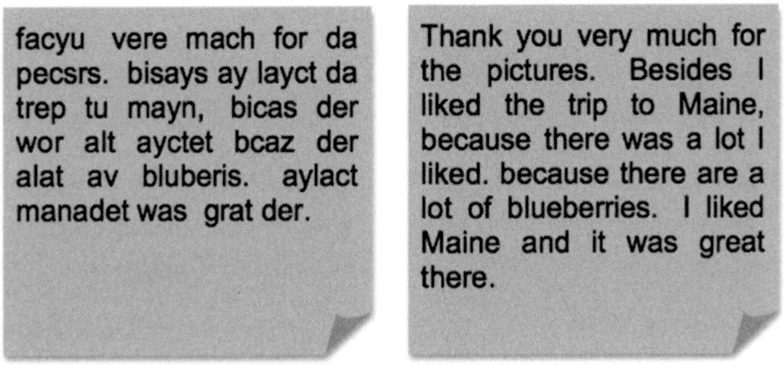

facyu  vere  mach  for  da
pecsrs.  bisays  ay  layct  da
trep  tu  mayn,  bicas  der
wor  alt  ayctet  bcaz  der
alat  av  bluberis.  aylact
manadet was  grat der.

Thank  you  very  much  for
the  pictures.  Besides  I
liked  the  trip  to  Maine,
because  there  was  a  lot  I
liked.  because  there  are  a
lot  of  blueberries.  I  liked
Maine  and  it  was  great
there.

Figure 6.5   A child's creative spelling

also instructive to recall the example of Coote's varied spellings of *scholemaister* in section 6.2, as well as the lack of concern with segmentation by adult writers in earlier times.

In this brief review of key issues in children's literacy we've focused mainly on writing rather than reading, a topic we return to in 6.5 and again in Chapter 7. There is a great deal of information available online; some of our favourites include the *Bank Street Guide to Literacy for Volunteers and Tutors*, a collection of user-friendly resources on child literacy for tutors and teachers, and *The Literacy Web* at the University of Connecticut.

 **www.6.14, 6.15**

## Adult literacies

In this section we examine the topic of literacy in adulthood from two directions: the information that proficient readers use as they read and the teaching of literacy to adults. Ken Goodman, following study with Noam Chomsky, described reading as a 'psycholinguistic guessing game' in which readers must simultaneously attend to and process the **graphophonic**, syntactic and semantic information available in texts. In this theory of reading, the reader's objective is to construct meaning from the text. Views differ on whether the goal here is (only) to reconstruct the meaning intended by an author or rather to create one's own meaning, which will differ from reader to reader. **Transactional** notions of adult reading (Rosenblatt, 2005) favour the latter view, based on the idea that adults have more life experience (semantic information), including previous experience with different formats and genres, and (usually but not always) greater memory recall than young children. Another advantage that adult readers have over children is that they have more fully formed grammars (syntactic information) and a larger lexicon; thus they are generally quicker at processing information in written form.

Further support for Goodman's model (1996) comes from eye movement studies, in which researchers use lasers to track the points at which the eye fixes on particular letters and words in a text, and the duration of those fixation points (typically about 200–250 milliseconds) before moving on. This technique allows researchers to obtain a better understanding of the connection between eyes and the brain in real-time reading. Figure 6.6 provides a graphic representation. As you might expect, proficient readers' eyes move more quickly over texts, stopping less

**Graphophonic** relations hold between the symbols of glottographic writing systems (the *grapho-* bit) and the sounds they represent (the *-phonic* bit).

In **transactional** views of reading, the process involves not simply the passive extraction of meaning encoded in the text, but also the active contribution of the reader's own knowledge and beliefs in constructing meaning.

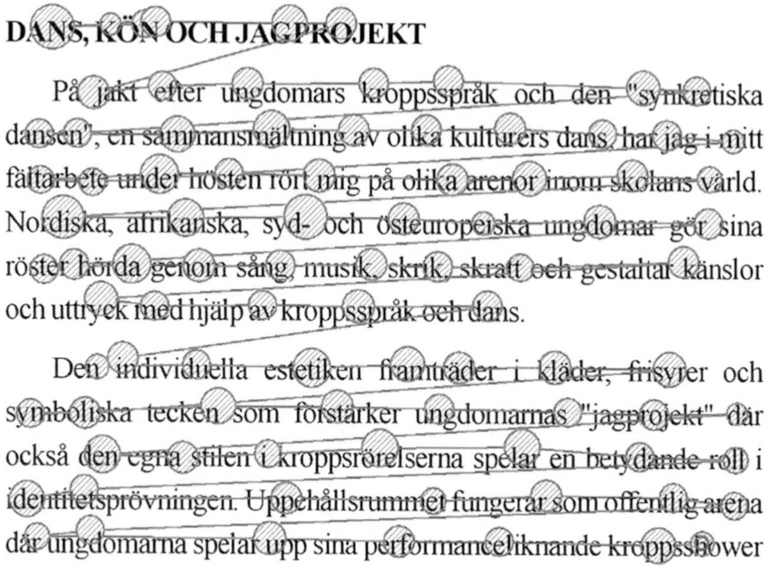

## DANS, KÖN OCH JAGPROJEKT

På jakt efter ungdomars kroppsspråk och den "synkretiska dansen", en sammansmältning av olika kulturers dans, har jag i mitt fältarbete under hösten rört mig på olika arenor inom skolans värld. Nordiska, afrikanska, syd- och östeuropeiska ungdomar gör sina röster hörda genom sång, musik, skrik, skratt och gestaltar känslor och uttryck med hjälp av kroppsspråk och dans.

Den individuella estetiken framträder i kläder, frisyrer och symboliska tecken som förstärker ungdomarnas "jagprojekt" där också den egna stilen i kroppsrörelserna spelar en betydande roll i identitetsprövningen. Uppehållsrummet fungerar som offentlig arena där ungdomarna spelar upp sina performanceliknande kroppsshower

Figure 6.6   Representation of eye movement during reading (Source: Wikipedia Commons)

often and for less time, thus debunking the folk belief that readers must decode every word they read. In fact, these experiments show that proficient readers often 'jump over' some words, slowing down and often jumping back again to confirm a working hypothesis (Paulson, 2005). These findings support the claim that readers seek to make meaning from texts but they also allow us to fine-tune the metaphor of reading as a psycholinguistic guessing game: rather than guessing, proficient adult readers are actually predicting what the text will 'say' and must slow down when their predictions are not supported. This helps to explain why we can skim quickly through some texts but feel we need to go more slowly and re-read others with which we are less familiar.

Adult literacy is also considered from the perspective of those who haven't (yet) developed it. In 6.1 we noted that about one in five adults cannot read and that as many as two-thirds of these non-readers are women. Concern for adult illiteracy is a relatively new social phenomenon, and the earliest widespread efforts to achieve mass literacy outside schools were led by national governments seeking, in some cases, to improve their standing among the nations of the world as much as to help their citizens. Figure 6.7 shows an early example from a government programme to end the literacy gender gap. In this 1923 poster from a Soviet literacy campaign advocating female literacy, the top section urges: 'Woman! Learn to read and write!' The text along the bottom has her daughter saying: 'Oh, mommy! If you were literate, you could help me!'

National literacy campaigns such as the Soviet effort also grew from aware-ness of the growing imbalances of power and wealth between urban, educated classes and rural, less educated populations. A common feature of national efforts has been the practice of sending secondary and university students from cities to rural areas to teach basic literacy skills to adults. The Nicaraguan literacy campaign

Figure 6.7   Poster from a Soviet literacy campaign aimed at women (Source: Wikipedia Commons)

of 1980, for example, trained 60,000 young people who formed a literacy 'army' that spent five months 'eradicating' illiteracy in mountainous areas with few schools. The metaphor of illiteracy as a 'disease' suffered by individuals and societies and therefore 'curable' through literacy training and education remains a powerful one.

In the past three decades, much of the responsibility for adult literacy has shifted to the international level. Since its founding, UNESCO has devoted a major part of its resources to improving access to literacy for underserved populations, and this concern is reflected in a proliferation of programmes. In 2003 UNESCO announced the Literacy Decade (2003–2012), complete with prizes to reward successful programmes and a Special Envoy for Literacy Development (currently HRH Princess Laurentien of the Netherlands), and the goal of reducing illiteracy by 50 per cent by 2015. Under the slogan 'Literacy is Freedom', UNESCO's Literacy Assessment and Monitoring Programme (LAMP) has identified five levels of adult literacy repeated here from p. 62:

 **www.6.16**

- Level I: The individual has very poor skills and may, for example, be unable to determine the correct amount of medicine to give a child from the label on a package.
- Level 2: Respondents can only deal with simple, clearly laid-out reading material and tasks. At this level, people can read but test poorly. They may have developed coping skills to manage everyday literacy demands but they find it difficult to face new challenges, such as job skills.
- Level 3: Considered a suitable minimum for coping with the demands of daily life and work in a complex society. This skill level is generally required to successfully complete secondary school and to enter college.
- Levels 4 and 5: Respondents demonstrate command of higher-order information processing skills.

Whether they are run by national or international organizations, a common criticism of mass literacy campaigns is that while they may be conceived with the best of intentions, implementation has tended to reinforce existing inequities rather than dispel them. Some scholars have questioned whether the training that literacy volunteers and tutors receive is adequate to allow them to effectively teach literacy, and have critiqued literacy materials as irrelevant to the lives of adult students, promoting a 'development agenda' featuring consumerism and orienting the newly literate toward certain types of (sub)employment (Street, 2001). An exception is perhaps **Braille literacy**, which, according to a recent report (NFB, 2009) faces crisis in the USA as fewer than 10 per cent of blind children are learning it, despite studies (e.g. Ryles, 1996) which demonstrate that Braille readers are far less likely to figure among the 70 per cent unemployment rate among blind adult Americans. As these examples show, enormous challenges remain for applied linguists and others committed to the ideal that literacy really can be about human freedom. Although it has not always found favour with sponsors of official literacy efforts, we think there is much promise, as yet unfulfilled, in Paulo Freire's proposal that adult literacy programmes teach the 'world' in addition to the 'word' (Freire and Macedo, 2001 [1987]).

**Braille literacy** is the ability to read and write using the tactile system of raised dots that represent the Roman alphabet, as well as other alphabetic writing systems such as Korean. The Braille Institute in California has resources for English-speaking teachers.

**www.6.17**

## 6.5  ACADEMIC ACHIEVEMENT AND THE MEASUREMENT OF LITERACY

How, then, should we determine who has satisfactorily met contemporary expectations of literacy? Let's begin with the observation that members of literate societies, whether or not we are highly literate ourselves, form impressions of who is and who isn't a good reader/writer. Just as we make initial judgements about a person's social class, level of formal education and even intelligence based on the way they speak, we form opinions about individuals and groups of people based on the ways they read and write. These impressions are often based on our perceptions of a person's mastery of formal aspects of literacy rather than on communicating and interpreting the meanings of texts. Thus, rapid evaluations of writing ability based on fragmentary evidence of, say, a person's handwriting on a job application form or unconventional spelling in an e-mail at work, and estimates of someone's' reading abilities based on how she navigates the dinner menu at a new restaurant, obviously won't do as formal measures of literacy.

Because popular understandings of literacy reflect school-based definitions, many people's view of 'what counts' as reading and writing will depend on the literacy practices and forms they learned at school and folk beliefs about the act of reading; that is, the view that reading entails a focus on and decoding of every single word rather than the reading for meaning which allows us to skip over words that conform to our predictions. This is doubly unfortunate, given that, as we've seen, school practices have not always been especially effective, and proficient adult readers don't actually read like they are popularly thought to.

A similar conflation of ideas can be observed in the relationship between literacy and education, specifically how academic achievement and school literacies are attained and assessed. National and international desires for accountability in education have contributed to what some educators and observers feel is an obsession with testing literacy, to the point that teachers may feel they have little time to teach it. The thinking behind this shift towards an emphasis on literacy assessment and away from actual literacy learning was captured by US President George W. Bush's observation that 'You teach a child to read and he or she will be able to pass a literacy test' (BBC World News, 2009). Presidential pronouns aside, the emphasis on assessing literacy through standardized measures reflects public concerns that increased access to schooling has not led to advanced literacy achievement for all and that some children are being 'left behind', eventually dropping out of school as a result.

In the US and UK especially, but also in Australia, New Zealand and elsewhere, curricula may acknowledge the need for the sort of broad understandings of reading, writing and literacy emphasized in this chapter, but literacy assessment has become heavily weighted towards a strong emphasis on sound and the decoding of individual phonemes. The National Curriculum of England, Wales and Northern Ireland (QCA, 2009), for example, requires government primary schools to assess pupils' knowledge of phonics, the idealized one-to-one correspondence between individual phonemes and the letters they 'stand for'. Thus, literacy is increasingly assessed on the basis of the learner's ability to:

- hear, identify, segment, and blend phonemes in words;
- sound and name the letters of the alphabet;
- link sound and letter patterns, exploring rhyme, alliteration and other sound patterns;
- identify syllables in words;
- recognise that the same sounds may have different spellings and that the same spellings may relate to different words;
- write each letter of the alphabet;
- use their knowledge of the sound symbol relationships and phonological patterns (for example, consonant clusters and vowel phonemes).

(Rose, 2006, pp. 10–11)

A heavy reliance on sound as the main component of school literacy programmes has a number of implications for literacy learning. One is that the other elements of reading (e.g. semantic and syntactic cues) are not as available to students when individual letters and words are presented in isolation and with insufficient context. Another major criticism, and one that is well founded, we believe, is that by treating reading mainly as decoding sound and writing as encoding it, reading instruction and assessment ignore the fact that literacy is, for children and adults alike, first and foremost a means of communication and of making meaning.

A further concern, with important consequences for the additional language and bilingual learners we'll meet in Chapters 7, 8 and 9, is that the phonology of pupils (and teachers) varies depending on dialect and home language(s). Instruction and assessment based exclusively on sound-based approaches to literacy can cause undue problems for learners who don't sound like their teacher. For example, the New Zealand Ministry of Education has produced a series of early literacy materials, *Kiwi Phonics*, based on the sounds of an idealized New Zealand English. The goal, 'introducing written sounds to new readers in a logical progression', sounds well enough, but we are sceptical that there exists a single 'logical' progression of sounds for new readers from different home language backgrounds.

 **www.6.18**

An area in which sound-based instruction seems to be especially appropriate is instruction designed for students who have been identified as having a form of **dyslexia**, a learning difficulty that primarily affects the skills involved in accurate and fluent word reading and spelling. As we'll see in further detail in Chapter 13, characteristic features of dyslexia include difficulties in phonological awareness, verbal memory and verbal processing speed. These are especially important in the decoding/encoding aspects of alphabetic reading and writing, and it follows that children and adults with these difficulties are less likely to read for pleasure and more likely to have trouble extracting meaning from and expressing meaning in written form. A young person interviewed in a recent study recalled the experience of reading in school:

> I just knew that something was wrong inside of me when it came to reading. Every time that the teacher got out the reading books I used to hope like crazy that she wouldn't call on me because I knew my reading was rubbish . . . I just felt so helpless.
>
> (Rose, 2009, p. 56)

Evidence is emerging that 'dyslexia occurs across the range of intellectual abilities [and is] best thought of as a continuum, not a distinct category [with] clear cut-off points' (Rose, 2009. p. 29), and this has led to an increase in testing for dyslexia and the number of pupils identified as having some form of this difficulty. The British Dyslexia Association estimates that as many as 5 per cent of school pupils are dyslexic, but because definitions vary by country it is difficult to know how this compares with other national populations. Dyslexia International provides information on how dyslexia is tested and remediated in different world contexts, and the World Health Organization has recently adopted a definition that may lead to more standard assessments.

**www.6.19**

**www.6.20**

**www.6.21**

In contrast to this context-independent view of literacy, instruction in university-level literacy, known in the UK as English for Academic Purposes (EAP), is increasingly focused on raising students' awareness as apprentices and new members of an academic community with a particular set of literacy practices. These include specific and sometimes unique uses of written language, for example justifying a worthwhile study, judging an effective argument and selecting relevant evidence. A context-dependent approach to academic adult literacies requires students and their language teachers to be knowledgeable about how language is used in appropriate ways, both within academic disciplines and within the institutions of higher education where they are studying or working. Genre analysis and studies of academic language corpora have helped teachers and students explore discipline-specific language. EAP tutors may, as applied linguists, be aware of how academic writing that is acceptable to, say, chemistry teachers requires both discipline-specific writing practices and subject knowledge. But there is still much work to be done in convincing the subject area teachers themselves, a point we return to in the following, final section.

**www.6.22**

## 6.6  ROLES FOR APPLIED LINGUISTS

Throughout this chapter, we have seen that literacy activities are not static or universal, but instead highly diverse, fluid and shaped to fit the particular purposes and needs of users in different contexts. If we have managed to convince you of this, then what might you, as an applied linguist, do in real-world situations in which literacy is an issue? Perhaps one (or more) of the following:

- Work with teachers in schools to identify instances in which students' specific literacy activities could easily be confused with having, or not having, subject knowledge or intelligence.
- Work with subject tutors in higher education to raise awareness of the fact that academic writing involves discipline-specific writing practices, as well as subject knowledge, and that different approaches to the development and assessment of these in students' writing are needed.
- Develop literacy materials that are culturally and linguistically appropriate for learners, especially those that involve reading and writing with digitally medi-ated forms of literacy.
- Train youth to produce texts using digitally mediated literacy technologies, in language labs, writing centres, after-school programmes or at an internet café.
- Conduct research on emergent literacies and biliteracy development in con-texts in which one or more of the child's languages is not a European (widely studied) language or is written in a writing system other than the Latin alphabet.
- Conduct research on your own and your family's and community's (including your professional community's) literacy practices and reflect on how these have evolved to suit particular purposes and uses in different situations.

Literacy is indeed a curious thing, as Collins and Blot suggest in the epigraph to this chapter (p. 129), and mapping this constantly changing territory will continue to be a real challenge for applied linguists. We are convinced, however, that an understanding of the fundamentals of literacy will be key to solving many of the language-related problems encountered by applied linguists, including those which take place in and around school, the topic of Chapter 7.

1   Type the words *literacy* and *definition* into an internet search engine and compile a list of at least six definitions from different sources. Remember to make a note of your sources. What are the similarities and differences between the definitions you have found? Is there one definition you like best? Re-read section 6.1, 'The expanding scope of literacy'. Do your definitions cover the all the points we make in this section?

2   Find examples of multilingual and multi-modal texts, in which elements of print, images, video and sound are incorporated. You might focus on texts advertising a particular type of product (beer, clothing, automobiles, beauty products, perfume, etc.) or service (online dating services,

activities

university programmes of study, travel agencies, etc.). How do these texts employ traditional and newer forms of literacy to convey their message? What new skills and abilities are required to produce and understand these kinds of texts?

3    Consider the various events in which you participate with your friends or family members, such as birthday parties, religious ceremonies, shopping trips, sporting events, cultural events or games. Choose an event and make a list of all the texts that are used to plan and carry it out. Collect as many event-related texts as you can (originals, copies or photos). If possible, record an interview with one or more of the participants, in which you show them the texts you have collected and ask them to talk about how they produced or used the texts to prepare and conduct the event. Review the texts, the interviews and your own thinking about your production and use of these event-related texts. Then, consider any of the following questions:

(a)    How were the texts you collected used in planning and carrying out this event; for example: as a replacement for spoken language; as a memory aid; as a way of solving a practical problem; to communicate information between participants; as part of a ritual; as a way of displaying something to the participants or those outside the event; to provide evidence relevant to, or about, the event; as a way of welcoming, threatening or otherwise involving those not present at the event; etc.?

(b)    How were different media (printed text, images, audio, video, etc.) used in the event-related texts? Was more than one language used? How and for what purpose(s)?

(c)    What roles in the production and use of texts were taken by the different participants in the literacy event? Was one person in charge, or was a team of people responsible for deciding how the texts would be created and used?

(d)    Did you observe any gender- or age-related differences in the way different people participated in the literacy event? What were they?

(e)    Were any new literacy forms or practices learned by any of the participants during the planning or carrying out of the event? Who was teaching and who was learning? How did this learning take place?

(f)    What institutions were involved in supporting and structuring the event (for example, TV companies, transport providers, schools, government, religious authorities, etc.)?

(g)    Has the way you produce or use event-related texts changed over time? Is this something the participants in the event know about? Is there any research into changes in the literacy practices that are involved in such events? What does this research suggest about your own literacy practices and those of your friends and family?

4    If you or any of your friends or family members has a child who is just learning to write, ask her to write something for you. The text can be a letter or note, a shopping list, a story, a photograph or picture they have captioned, or work they have done at school. Compare the features of the child's writing with the examples discussed in the emergent literacies section (pp. 143–5) of this chapter. Does your child author use invented spelling? What conventions of adult writing does she seem to use confidently and what features is she still developing? If you can, ask the child to talk about what she has written. What 'theories' of print and writing does she display in her writing or her talk about text?

## FURTHER READING

Cope, B. and Kalantzis, M. (eds) (2000). Multiliteracies: Literacy learning and the design of social futures. London: Routledge.

Fisher, S. R. (2001). *A history of writing.* London: Reaktion Books.

Freire, P. and Macedo, D. (2001 [1987]). *Literacy: Reading the word and the world.* London: Routledge.

Kress, G. and van Leeuwen, T. (2006). *Reading images: The grammar of visual design*, 2nd edn. London: Routledge.

Smith, F. (2004). *Understanding reading*, 6th edn. Mahwah, NJ: Lawrence Erlbaum.

Tolchinsky, L. (2003). *The cradle of culture and what children know about writing and numbers before being taught.* Mahwah, NJ: Lawrence Erlbaum.

**CHAPTER 7**

# Language and education

We are fed the crumbs of ignorance with Afrikaans as a poisonous spoon.
(Sign carried at the 16 June 1976 student uprising in
Soweto, South Africa; Pohlandt-McCormick, 2000)

This chapter considers language in one of its most studied and controversial domains, that of education. As users of different languages, varieties and registers, most of us are quite linguistically opinionated to begin with. Add to this our own school experiences, and we have the necessary ingredients for strong opinions about which language(s) are suitable for the purposes of education and how they ought to be used in schools. This was the case in Soweto, where the apartheid government imposed Afrikaans as a language of schooling for South African students and police shot dozens of teenage students for staging protests against this language-in-education policy. Strong opinions continue to be expressed in less repressive contexts, such as the Japanese Ministry of Education's policy of educating Brazilian Nikkei immigrants, who are speakers of Portuguese, only in Japanese (Riordan, 2005) and Singapore's 'Speak Good English Movement', the government campaign against the use of Singlish (Singapore English) in school. As we pointed out in Chapter 2, on language varieties, and Chapter 5, on language planning, the notions of 'standard varieties', 'norms' and 'correctness' are central to the work of applied linguists, and perhaps nowhere more so than in the area of education.

**www.7.1**  The normative role of schools in children's language development has a very long history. Edmund Coote's *The English Schoole-Maister* (1997 [1596]) is perhaps the first-ever English language textbook (although it's actually closer to a dictionary). On the title page, Coote, at the time headmaster of King Edward VI Grammar School in Bury St Edmunds, claimed that 'he which hath this booke only, needeth buy no other to make him fit, from his letters, vnto the Grammar schoole, for an apprentise, or any other his owne priuate vse, so farre as concerneth English'. Figure 7.1 shows the first page. Within a year of the publication of his book, Coote resigned from the school, probably at the request of the governors. According to Hutjens:

> School regulations . . . explicitly forbade instruction in basic English literacy, a standard requirement for admission to grammar schools in England: 'Let them seek elsewhere the ability to read and write. Let ours [?our masters] give nothing but the rules of grammar and the learning of the Latin and Greek tongue.' Coote's authorship of The English Schoole-Maister may have

### *The Schoole-maister his*
### profession.

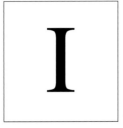

*profESse to teach thee, that art vtterly
ignorant, to reade perfectly, to write
truly, and with iudgement to vnder
stand the reason of our English tongue
with great expedition, ease, and pleasure.*

*I will teach thee that art vnperfect
in either of them, to perfect thy skill in
few dayes with great ease.*

*I vndertake to teach all my scholers, that shall be trayned vp for
any grammar schoole, that they shall neuer erre in writing the true
orthography of any word truly pronounced: which what ease and
benefite it will bring vnto Scholemaisters, they best know : and the
same profit doe I offer vnto all other both men & women, that now
for want hereof are ashamed to write vnto their best friends : for
which I haue heard many gentlewomen offer much.*

*I assure all Schoolemaisters of the English tongue, that they shall
not onely teach their scholers with greater perfection : but also they
shal with more ease and profit, and in shorter time teach a hundreth
scholers, then before they could teach forty.*

The preface
will shew you
how this may
certainely and
easely be done.

*I hope by this plaine and short kinde of teaching to encourage
many to read, that neuer otherwise would haue learned. And so
more knowledge will be brought into this Land, and moe bookes
bought, then otherwise would haue been.*

*I shall ease the poorer sort, of much charge that they haue been at
in maintayning their children long at Schoole and in buying many
Bookes.*

*Strangers that now blame our tongue of difficultie and vncer
taintie, shall by me plainly see and vnderstand those thinges which
they haue thought hard.*

Figure 7.1    Simplified transcription of the first page of Coote's *The English Schoole-Maister*
(1596)

embarrassed the governors of a school which prided itself on exclusive instruction in classical languages.

(Hutjens, 1997)

Over three hundred years after Coote, things hadn't changed very much. In their
literacy history of London's Spitalfields area, Eve Gregory and Ann Williams report
the case of Aumie, a Jewish immigrant who grew up there in the 1920s:

In our school, the headmaster was . . . particularly keen on good speech. And
so we had a speech choir as distinct from a singing choir. Bearing in mind we
were 12- to 13-year olds, for us it seemed so odd that we would have to recite

'Hickory, Dickory, Dock, the mouse ran up the clock. The clock struck one, the mouse ran down, Hickory, Dickory, Dock'. We would go to other schools and recite various poems as examples of good speech . . . It was an oddity . . . Looking back, it could have been a political gesture on the headmaster's part to establish his contribution in a so-called Cockney area . . . to improve the quality of speech.

(Gregory and Williams, 2000, pp. 96–7)

Almost a century after Aumie, we still find that, for many people, the way that language is currently taught in schools is a very serious problem (even a royal pain). Indeed, Britain's Prince Charles has been one of the most vocal critics of schools in the UK, as in the following lament on the quality of instruction: 'All the people I have in my office, they can't speak English properly, they can't write English properly. All the letters sent from my office I have to correct myself, and that is because English is taught so bloody badly' (30 June 1989, quoted in Carter, 1997, p. 7).

We begin our discussion of language in education by contrasting language as it is first used and developed – in the context of students' families, homes and communities – with how it is used in school (section 7.1). We then turn to an examination of language as a medium of education (7.2) and an object in contexts of formal schooling (7.3), before considering the case of linguistic minorities and students with special needs (7.4) and issues of language in educational testing and assessment (7.5). We end with a discussion of roles that applied linguists can play in schools and other educational settings (7.6).

## 7.1  THE LANGUAGE OF HOME, COMMUNITY AND SCHOOL

Although free universal daycare in Canada and early education programmes in other countries have recently lowered the age at which children in these countries start school, many children begin their formal schooling at age five or six. At this age, children come to their initial school experiences with oral language competences that are nearly fully formed. With an increasingly sophisticated grammatical competence and a burgeoning lexicon, they already understand and speak the language(s) they have been exposed to and raised in at home. Depending on the extent of their contact and relationships with family members and people in and outside the home, young children will also have developed the ability to communicate beyond their immediate families. In multilingual communities, children's linguistic repertoires are thus likely to include knowledge of the other languages and language varieties they hear and see. Like Aumie, children come to school talking and sounding like the adults and other child members of their speech community. As we saw in Chapter 6, younger children are more likely to produce examples of decidedly non-adult performance especially in written language, but these are almost always developmental in nature, and should be regarded as further opportunities for language use and interaction rather than deficiencies to be remediated through explicit correction.

These basic facts of child language acquisition may be yesterday's news for linguists, but they merit greater attention in teacher preparation programmes, especially those devoted to preparing early childhood educators, bilingual educators, and teachers of additional languages and children with special needs. Here are some of the pressing questions about the home-to-school transition that are important for teachers to consider and that we take up in the remainder of this chapter:

- If homes are the places in which children develop their initial language abilities, what sorts of contexts do they provide for language use and development?
- What is the nature of language socialization in homes and families, and what aspects of language do children develop in these most intimate domains?
- What aspects of language and literacy development are not well supported in the home and would need to be promoted in school?
- Once children are in school and receiving formal instruction, do their teachers view their ways of speaking as resources to be built upon or as barriers to their academic success?
- How can educators build upon what children already know about language in order to support their language and literacy development in school?

## Language at home and in the community

While the cognitive processes of language acquisition unfold pretty uniformly under all but the most severely linguistically deprived and exceptional of conditions (see Chapter 13 for exceptions), the family and community groupings that humans are born into and grow up in vary considerably. Thus, as researchers such as Elinor Ochs (1988) have reported, child language socialization is not a universal process, but rather one which is shaped by specific cultural contexts. For example, features of family language use such as patterns of child-directed speech familiar to teachers raised in middle-class English homes may or may not be part of the earliest linguistic experiences of Panjabi- or Gujarati-speaking children attending school in Leeds or London.

The linguistic and related cultural differences between groups of students and between students and teachers are often cited as a cause for educational under-performance, especially in language minorities and working-class children generally. One well-known and controversial discussion of this mismatch was launched with the work of the sociologist Basil Bernstein. In trying to understand why working-class and immigrant children did poorly in British schools, Bernstein developed the notion that some working-class children entered school speaking what he described as **restricted code**, a tendency to speak in a way that takes knowledge of the specific topic and context of the talk for granted. Linguistic features of restricted code were said to include limited use of adjectives and adverbs; short and grammatically simple sentences; and 'poor syntactical construction', among others (Bernstein, 2003 [1972], pp. 42–3). Middle-class children, on the other hand, began school having already been socialized into the **elaborated codes** through which meanings are expressed more explicitly and with less context-specific language. Specific features of elaborated code were said to include more sophisticated use of adjectives and adverbs; grammatically complex and 'accurate' sentence-level syntax; conjunctions and prepositions indicating 'logical' relationships (Bernstein,

**Restricted** and **elaborated code** are terms Basil Bernstein developed to refer to two ways of using language: the former in situations in which interlocutors share knowledge, beliefs and assumptions, communicating much in few words (e.g. between farmers talking informally in a village pub); the latter in situations in which common ground is more limited and everything needs to be spelled out (e.g. between a farmer and bank manager discussing a loan in the bank manager's office).

2003 [1972], p. 53). Bernstein emphasized that these codes were social, rather than linguistic: 'Because a code is restricted it does not mean that a child is nonverbal, nor is he in the technical sense linguistically deprived, for he possesses the same tacit understanding of the linguistic rule system as any child' (Bernstein, 2003 [1972], p. 197).

There has been much discussion of what Bernstein meant by these divisions (Halliday, 2007 [1988]; Hasan, 1999). Bernstein (2003 [1975]) himself said that his two-code concept has been misinterpreted to mean that working-class speech is somehow linguistically deficient, its speakers linguistically deprived, and to argue that working-class children should be taught 'standard' grammar and to avoid using their 'non-standard' home dialect. This interpretation of Bernstein's notion has been used to support deficit theories of education and the formulation of curriculum with an emphasis on what children *cannot* do with language. Recall from Chapter 5 Payne's (2008) language of poverty argument, setting upper- and middle-class children's speech as language development norms for all pupils and blaming poor and working-class parents for miseducating their children. As school populations become more linguistically diverse as a result of immigration, such arguments are often extended to the children of immigrants and other pupils who are still learning the language(s) of the school (Extra, 2006). Since Bernstein's day, numerous studies of World Englishes have shown that varieties of English spoken in Hong Kong, throughout India, by Panjabis and Jamaicans in London and other cities in the UK and by Mexican Americans and African Americans in the US, turn out to be every bit as grammatically complex and functionally versatile as the forms spoken by users of more prestigious dialects (Mesthrie and Bhatt, 2008, chs 2 and 3).

Nevertheless, language differences – among students from different back-grounds and between students and their teachers – can be observed in many contexts. Where teachers belong to more prestigious class, ethnic and linguistic groups than their students, these differences are also cited as barriers to learning for students from certain groups. The exact nature of a cultural and linguistic mis-match (and thus its potential implications) depends, of course, on the backgrounds of the students and teachers and the languages and varieties they (don't) speak. Although educators by themselves cannot solve problems of child poverty or the structural inequalities that many immigrant and working-class families struggle against, teachers can use their applied linguistics expertise (analysing the discourse of classroom talk and student writing, for example, or having students compare the features of texts written in different languages, dialects or registers) to develop materials and propose instructional strategies aimed at building upon children's language resources rather than treating them as problems to be eradicated. Otherwise, as Bernstein (2003 [1972], p. 184) asked, if 'the schools are not made for these children, why should the children respond?'

Although most attention has been paid to the home and school language of young children, high school leaving, or drop-out, rates are leading educators and researchers to look more closely at language among the factors involved in access to education for adolescents and young adults (Darling-Hammond, 2010; Oketch and Rolleston, 2007). Higher education, because it often involves moving to urban areas to study or find work in one's chosen field, tends to pull people away from their communities of origin and doesn't do much to send them back, especially to rural areas. This is often the case in Indigenous and other language minority communities, where education authorities place newly trained teachers with little regard for their language background. Although conditions vary across and within regions and countries, many teachers find themselves teaching in areas where they don't or won't speak the languages or language varieties spoken by their students. Even where teacher mobility is influenced more by the job market and individual preference than by government assignment, an emphasis on 'proper' ways of speaking and writing in schools can lead teachers to reproduce language inequalities that they themselves may have faced and internalized as students. For example, in an ethnographic study of home and community language use among African American and white students in the south-eastern US, Shirley Brice Heath (2006 [1983]) found that urban teachers in a teacher preparation programme struggled to see their students' ways of speaking as legitimate for use in school.

## Language at school

Having addressed language in home and community domains, we now turn to schools as sites of language use and development. When children begin formal schooling, are they greeted with a radically different language environment or is the experience more of a friendly transition to new forms and new conventions for language use? Is the linguistic knowledge that children have already developed and which they bring with them respected and built upon by their teachers, or is it disregarded or even rejected in favour of other forms of speaking, writing or signing? As we consider language at school, it is important to bear in mind that teacher attitudes, beliefs and knowledge about language are not homogeneous and may vary even within a single school, and that local conditions (for example a pre-scriptivist curriculum or the opportunity to collaborate on projects with applied linguists from a local university) mean that every school is unique in this regard.

In his work on language vitality in bilingual communities, Joshua Fishman (2001 [1965]) asked, 'Who speaks what language to whom and when?', a question which applies equally to language varieties, and is central to the issue of language use in school. The division of students into same-age groups, a common practice in contemporary education, virtually guarantees that children will have as their primary interlocutors classmates of the same age and approximate level of cognitive development. From the perspective of child language socialization, this is quite different from the ways children grew up before the establishment of obligatory, state-sponsored education. The composition of most classrooms today, with one teacher and, with luck, an assistant for each group of 20–60 children, means that children are likely to have little time for extended individual interactions with teachers or interactions with older students who might serve as language models. An important exception is apparently India, where Alexander (2008, p. 14) reckons that more than three-quarters of the nation's one million schools contain **multi-grade classes**. Like all members of social groups, school children tacitly understand that situated language use is embedded in structures of hierarchy and respect which are, in turn, linguistically marked. In other words, they are learning how the main characters, students and teachers, should perform their talk in school. For this reason, multi-grade classrooms and other non-traditional arrangements which allow for increased interaction can provide conditions that foster language growth and development.

**Multi-grade classes** (also known as multi-age classrooms) are groupings in which learners of multiple ages and grade levels are taught in the same classroom. In addition to allowing pupils to work according to their ability levels in different subject areas, this arrangement has the further advantage of exposing younger children to the language and linguistic routines of more sophisticated speakers and writers, thereby using children's language as a resource for other learners.

A compelling example of children's early awareness and development of register comes from a study by Elaine Andersen (1990). Using puppets to role-play with children between the ages of four and seven, Andersen asked participants to act out the parts of child and adult characters in three distinct settings: family (with mother, father and child); a doctor's office (doctor, nurse and patient); and school (a teacher and two students). In the school setting, children first played the part of the teacher and one student and then were invited to play the two children, one of them an immigrant child new to the school. The researcher set up the scene as follows:

> Why don't I be the teacher now, and you can be the two children. Only this time, let's pretend that one of the children just came to this country from somewhere far away where they don't speak English. So she doesn't speak English very well. This is her first day at school, and she doesn't know what to do at school. So why don't you tell her what we do here, and maybe explain to her about a field trip we're going to go on. But remember, she only speaks a little bit of English.
>
> (Andersen, 1990, p. 11)

Using discourse analysis to examine the transcribed role-plays, Andersen found that across the three settings even the youngest participants were sensitive to differences in register and modified their use of language depending on the age, gender and occupation of their interlocutors. Degrees of familiarity (speaking differently within the family than at school) and hierarchy (doctors, teachers and parents in superordinate positions) were also reflected in the children's talk. In the school setting, children used more **directive** speech acts as 'teachers' than as 'students', and the frequency of directives by 'teachers' increased with the age of the children. Andersen interpreted this to mean that older children were less apt to treat school as an intimate, informal context for speaking. She also described a linguistically encoded hierarchy (teacher, student, immigrant student), with some children unwilling to assume the 'foreigner' role at all.

As it turns out, Andersen's young participants were quite knowledgeable about the ways language works in school. This linguistic authority – who speaks how to whom – is a robust feature built into many formal school contexts. Studies across linguistic contexts and with different students of different age groups show that classroom talk is typically dominated by adults. Student contributions are often relatively short and are directed mainly to the teacher in response to teacher-provided prompts and questions, rather than to questions or claims posed by classmates. This unbalanced system of linguistic interaction can be found around the world, having been dominant in schools in the West for over a century and exported through the colonial administration of education and teacher preparation programmes to other parts of the world (Willinsky, 1999).

In *The Pedagogy of the Oppressed* and other writings (1986 [1970], 1998), the Brazilian educator Paulo Freire claimed that schools in less wealthy nations function as colonizing agents, and that language regulation is instrumental in teaching students their 'place' in the economic and social system in which they are living. A similar theory of language and education was proposed by the French sociologist Pierre Bourdieu (1984; Bourdieu and Passeron, (1990 [1977]), in which

A **directive** is a speech act performed in order to make the addressee take some action. Examples include commands (*Shut the door behind you!*), requests (*Could you shut the door when you leave?*) and pieces of advice (*You should shut the door, or the cat'll get out*).

schools are viewed as institutions that structure language use in order to reproduce the status quo. Because aspects of language use such as vocabulary, pronunciation, grammar and handwriting are carefully measured and regulated in education, schools are often primary sites for language discrimination against children, particularly those from working-class and minority language backgrounds, and others whose ways of speaking are regarded as 'non-standard' and thus inappropriate for the task of teaching and learning. This notion is echoed by González *et al.*, who write that

> educational institutions do not view working class minority students as emerging from households rich in social and intellectual resources. Rather than focusing on the knowledge that these students bring to school and using it as a foundation for learning, schools have emphasized what these students lack in terms of the forms of language and knowledge sanctioned by the schools. This emphasis on so-called disadvantages has provided justification for lowered academic expectations and inaccurate portrayals of these children and their families.
>
> (González *et al.*, 1993, pp. 1–2)

In addition to the dubious pedagogical value of 'improving the quality of speech', as Aumie puts it at the beginning of the chapter (p. 156), the affective consequences for learners can clearly be detrimental. In the following example, a Mexican American woman studying to become a reading teacher in Texas recalled the lasting effects of the language discrimination she experienced as an adolescent:

> In eighth grade, my English teacher (who was all about Chicano power!!) told his students that people that had accents sounded uneducated. I looked up to him, so I took his warning to heart. I tried to sound as white as possible when I spoke English. I never knew that I had an accent until my teacher pointed it out to us. I felt ashamed of my Mexican heritage and tried to conquer the Spanish side of my tongue. Many years have passed, and although I have proudly embraced my Mexican heritage, I still catch myself trying to get rid of my accent.
>
> (Murillo and Smith, 2008)

## Bridging the languages of home, community and school

To this point, we've painted a rather gloomy portrait of language use in schools, in which curriculum and instruction are generally disconnected from and even in conflict with local ways of speaking. Educators and theorists of education alike have called for schools to become more closely connected to the communities they serve, and it is increasingly well understood that fostering this connection is essential if students are to master and be able to apply the academic norms and expectations of schooling, or even to care about them at all (Heller, 2006). This is the case particularly for immigrant students and others from non-dominant backgrounds, for whom school can be a strange new place. This has led to proposals for the development of culturally and linguistically relevant pedagogies (Darling-Hammond, 2010) that may, potentially at least, contrast with the ways language has been used in traditional schooling. Happily, much recent research has studied explicit ways of linking children's community and home language and literacy practices with the more academic forms cultivated in school.

An example of efforts to connect local forms of language with the language of instruction comes from a programme of research known as **Funds of Knowledge** for Teaching (González *et al.*, 2005). Originally proposed to familiarize teachers in the US Southwest with forms of knowledge held in the households and families of Mexican and Native American students, Funds of Knowledge approaches to teaching are becoming popular across the US, as well as in Australia and the UK. A typical project begins with teachers visiting the students' homes and getting to know the neighbourhoods where students live. Once a level of confidence and mutual trust has been established, the teacher-researchers interview parents and other family members in order to explore and understand the areas of everyday knowledge used in the home and to document the language forms and practices that family members engage in as they enact these forms of knowledge. Through the household visits, teachers can observe households engaged in, for example, running a family business (literacy and maths skills); operating a welding and automobile repair shop or making food to sell (science); and playing music professionally or for fun (art). By observing children's participation and apprenticeship in such activities with parents, siblings and other relatives, teachers gain a more complete sense of their students' abilities. In after-school study groups, teachers meet to discuss their observations and to design materials and lessons incorporating household forms of knowledge into subject area instruction, including mathematics, science, art and reading. In a sense, these teacher-researchers are engaged in mapping children's home knowledge onto the curriculum.

Smith (2002) describes a case of funds of linguistic knowledge to show how teachers in a Spanish–English dual language immersion programme in Arizona created a bridge between students' practical, out-of-school knowledge about language and the more abstract forms of language knowledge sought in academic settings. As we will see in Chapter 8, dual language immersion is a form of bilingual education in which children of two home language backgrounds are instructed together in both languages. The study focused on the oral and written modalities of language and included student-produced stories, letters to the editor, community radio announcements and other texts that teachers identified as culturally relevant, linguistically challenging and consistent with curriculum goals. Following a letter-writing project in which students wrote letters in Spanish to bilingual elders in the community, their teacher commented on the extra care and attention to audience and form taken by the emergent bilingual writers:

> What I saw was that the children were concentrating, that they wrote their letters like three times. Because they thought that the people they were writing to didn't read English. Because it was a person they didn't know, the students were a little more careful about how they presented themselves. Because of their eyesight, their age, to be clear, to write Spanish that could be easily understood . . . the students were taking more time and being more careful in their writing.
>
> (Smith, 2002, p. 176)

**Funds of Knowledge** is the term used by Luis Moll and colleagues to refer to the stock of knowledge, practices and skills that households develop over the generations, and which can provide rich resources for learning if tapped by schools. The Center for Applied Linguistics in Washington, DC, provides a report on how this model can be used in the context of linguistic minority students.

**www.7.2**

Another way that applied linguistics can promote language in education is through discourse analysis. Considering language in both its reflective and constitutive elements – that is, how language simultaneously reflects our individual understanding of the world around us and enables us to mediate our collective understandings – James Gee argues that the texts that people create and interpret in and out of school can be seen as reproducing, questioning and occasionally challenging discourses of power and dominance. The Soweto students' sign mentioned at the beginning of the chapter (p. 154) is a dramatic example of the latter, but of course more mundane examples abound in daily life. For example, in a controversial book on video games and their potential for language and literacy learning, Gee (2007) questioned the belief, held by many educators and parents, that playing video games is a waste of time. While learning to play a game called *No Need to Hide When It's Dark Outside* with his young son, Gee was surprised to find that

> it was fairly long and pretty challenging, even for an adult. Yet a very young child was willing to put in the time and face the challenge – and enjoy it, to boot. I thought, as someone who has spent the second half of his career working in education (the first half was devoted to theoretical linguistics): 'Wouldn't it be great if kids were willing to put in this much time on task on challenging material in school and enjoy it so much?'
>
> (Gee, 2007, p. 2)

Citing video games and the online gaming activities that many adolescents are engaged in as examples of new literacies that require higher-level thinking and skills than at least some of the traditional forms of reading and writing students do in school, Gee argued that teachers often fail to understand the complexity of games and the learning principles involved in playing them.

Figure 7.2 shows a screenshot from the multi-player online game *Deliantra*, in which players cooperate or compete for information and goods in a mediaeval fantasy world of the same name. After creating an identity by selecting from possible races (including dragons, elves and just plain human beings) and professions (alchemists, monks and warriors, but – alas – no applied linguists as yet), players navigate a continent represented by thousands of maps. In Figure 7.2 you can see a 'micro map' displaying an impressive density of language, which players must read and manipulate in order to achieve the goals they have set. Comparing these inviting and expressive uses of out-of-school language with the forms learners typically encounter in school, Gee and others have suggested that educators' continued focus solely on 'traditional' forms of written language is boring for many students and may even be holding learners back in their development of powerful new forms of literacy. Thus, another avenue for unifying home and school forms of knowledge is for teachers to explore and exploit the online practices their pupils are engaging with at home.

A final and fascinating example of the interconnections between language in home, school and community comes from Monica Heller's (1996) situated analysis of classroom talk in a French language high school in Ontario, Canada. As a student in a French immersion classroom composed of Anglo Canadians and immigrant students from Arabic, Farsi and Haitian Creole backgrounds, Mohamud

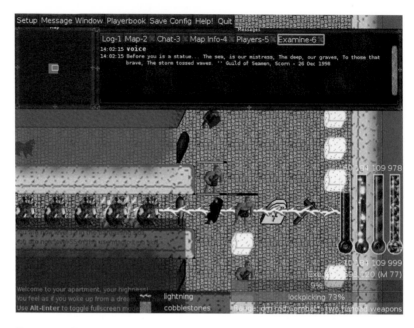

**Figure 7.2**   Screenshot from the online game *Deliantra* (*Source*: Wikimedia Commons)

is a first language speaker of Somali and a fluent speaker of Arabic whose impressive command of French is not the same variety promoted at school or by Lise, his French Canadian teacher. Nevertheless, Mohamud's sophisticated ways with words buy him extended talk time. Although he is eventually chastised by the teacher for swearing in class, and mocked by his classmates for speaking the variety of French he learned in private school in Somalia, Mohamud's fluency in the target language allows him to defend himself and even to temporarily challenge the teacher's linguistic authority by assuming the role of teacher at her invitation:

> Lise [the teacher] has decided that if Mohamud is unhappy with what she is doing in class, then she will briefly turn the class over to him. He has decided to do what for him is a more credible activity than group discussions and pen-and-paper activities, namely, a good old-fashioned dictee. He followed this with a lecture on the relations between men and women in Somalia. Throughout this episode, however, Mohamud had trouble acting and being taken seriously in the teacher role.
>
> (Heller, 1996, p. 154)

**Legitimate language** is a term used by **critical applied linguists** to describe the language or variety that is sanctioned for use in a given sphere or domain. Although it is not a term used in schools, pupils perceive very quickly which ways of speaking and writing are considered illegitimate.

Recalling Andersen's precocious puppeteers, but with many more cognitive and sociolinguistic arrows in his adolescent quiver, Mohamud's linguistic performance demonstrates that he understands how school 'works' and the role language plays in enacting student and teacher roles, even if he chooses not to follow them. Like the others we've presented in this section, this example underscores both the persistence of the notion of **legitimate language** in schools and the potential of

applied linguistics as a positive force for structuring meaningful learning opportunities for all pupils.

## 7.2  LANGUAGE AS A MEDIUM IN SCHOOL

Language also rules as a *tool* in school, as it does in other human endeavours and
spheres of interaction. Try to envision, if you can, a school without the medium of
language. Imagine, for example, Mohamud's dictation or lecture on gender relations
in the absence of speech. Obviously, very little of what we recognize as learning or
teaching could take place. Although weary teachers of adolescents might welcome
the occasional absence of 'off-task' language behaviour such as 'teasing, showing
off, competing, putting others down, duelling with the opposite sex' (Halliday, 2007
[1998], p. 52), they would also be hard pressed to develop their academic counterparts, forms of language such as debate, parody and satire. In addition to the
classroom, all other school domains – the dining hall, school playground, corridors
and other common spaces – would become eerie and pointless in our imagined
alinguistic institution. And what would a school be without written lunch menus,
announcements of sports events and club meetings, notes to and from parents
and doctors, end-of-term reports or signs proclaiming school rules like those shown
in Figure 7.3?

In the real world, of course, language is the primary medium of instruction and
learning. The language and discourses we encounter in school have profound
consequences for social justice. These meanings will depend on the language(s)
or variety(ies) used in instruction, those that students are best able to comprehend
and express themselves in, and how students understand and are understood by
their teachers and peers. This problem is hinted at by the school rules displayed in
Figure 7.3, which suggest that 'respect' is expressed universally and that 'quiet' is
the default for school behaviour. It is perhaps especially evident in situations where
instruction is not offered in the student's first or home language, such as for students
who cannot hear and so need sign interpreters, and for hearing students who are
still learning their teachers' language(s).

Applied linguistic research has also been invoked in debates over language
as a medium of instruction, including cases where teachers and learners arguably
share the same first language but not the same variety. For example, in the 1979
court case *Martin Luther King Junior Elementary School Children et al. v. Ann Arbor
School District* African American parents in Ann Arbor, Michigan, contended that
their children were receiving an inferior education because the members of the
primarily white teaching staff could not communicate with them. Although teachers
claimed to be unable to understand students (and thus unable to teach them
effectively), testimony provided by linguists demonstrated that the students, being
**bidialectal**, had little trouble understanding teachers (Labov, 1982). These expert
witnesses convinced the court that the varieties of English spoken by students at
the school were structurally comparable to the 'standard' variety of American English
used in instruction.

In finding that white teachers were not linguistically shut out from understanding children's talk, the Court concluded rather that teachers' objections to the
use of African American English in school were based on the subjective belief that

Someone is
**bidialectal** if they
are competent in two
dialects. For example,
most speakers of local
dialects in the UK are
bidialectal because if
they're literate they
also know the dialect
in which English
writing gets done
('standard English').

Figure 7.3   'Our school rules': an example of the ubiquity of language in school (Source: Whinney Banks Infant School, Middlesbrough, UK)

its use in school was culturally inappropriate and even linguistically inferior. Geneva Smitherman, a linguist who testified on behalf of the Ann Arbor children, wrote that

> Research on language attitudes consistently indicates teachers believe that Black English-speaking youngsters are non-verbal and possess limited vocabularies. They are perceived to be slow learners or uneducable; their speech is unsystematic and needs constant correction and improvement . . . These beliefs [are] linguistically untenable.
>
> (Smitherman, 2003, p. 141)

Events like the Soweto uprising and the Ann Arbor court case illustrate the extent to which decisions about language as a medium of instruction are often dependent on which varieties of language are judged to be suitable or legitimate for teaching. As we have seen in other domains of language use, such judgements are often based on social attitudes about particular groups rather than on any evidence from applied linguistics.

## 7.3  LANGUAGE AS AN OBJECT IN SCHOOL

Our second lens for looking at language in this chapter brings into focus its use as an object of school study. Instruction focusing on language in this way is known by many different names, and programmes vary according to individual factors, including the learners' age, home background and learning aptitudes, as well as collective factors such as national or disciplinary-based standards, official learning objectives and local conditions. In the UK, for example, under the National Curriculum adopted in the early 1990s all students between the ages of five and sixteen study 'English' as a compulsory subject, and this general convention is reflected in the national education schemes of Commonwealth countries and others influenced by the UK. In the US system state departments of education have historically enjoyed considerable autonomy in establishing curriculum, and remnants of this autonomy can be seen in the fact that students study 'English Language Arts' in New York, 'Reading/Language Arts' in California and 'Reading and English Language Arts' in Texas despite an increasingly standardized language curriculum at the national level.

Languages and varieties of power, almost always those that are written, are fostered and sometimes imposed in schools. Thus, in the epigraph with which we began this chapter (p. 154), Soweto students, who spoke Zulu, Sotho or other African languages at home, resisted the imposition of Afrikaans, the unpopular language of over half the country's ruling white minority, as a language of instruction. Throughout the world, schoolchildren are expected to master arbitrary conventions of usage in unfamiliar and often disconcerting languages and language varieties, including preferred pronunciation (as in Aumie being expected to 'talk properly'), pragmatic features like appropriate forms for requests, written language conventions such as spelling and punctuation, and **metalinguistic skills** like naming the parts of speech or diagramming the structure of sentences.

Some issues surrounding language as an object of education apply to both first (L1) and additional language (L2) teaching (the latter gets extensive solo coverage in Chapter 9). One of the main questions regarding how languages are taught is whether they are presented to learners with emphasis on the components of the linguistic code and their manipulation (for example naming the parts of speech, conjugating verb tenses, learning vocabulary lists, writing sentences with key words) or with more of an emphasis on interaction with whole texts (reading or listening to stories, singing along with songs, writing poems, etc.). Our point here is not to express a preference for one approach over the other (indeed, we believe that both are important), but rather to show that in each approach language functions as an object of study. Diagramming sentences involves one type of analysis, but so does translating an essay or composing a haiku.

 **www.7.3**

**Metalinguistic skills** are those things that learners and other language users can do with language that are not strictly linguistic, for example knowing how to begin a speech or, in writing, when to capitalize certain letters or use end punctuation. Since these abilities are often highly visible, they sometimes are used, inappropriately, as proxies for gauging linguistic knowledge.

## 7.4 EDUCATING LINGUISTIC MINORITIES AND LEARNERS WITH SPECIAL NEEDS

In Chapter 3, we pointed out that clients of applied linguistics are almost always members of multiple groups, each with distinct yet overlapping strengths and needs. Nowhere is this truer than in the field of education, where pupils are typically described, grouped and educated in same-age groups but simultaneously characterized by salient features, including gender, ability, previous schooling, parents' level of formal education, class, language background, immigration status, etc. Key groups here include:

- migrants, refugees and asylum seekers from countries where different languages are used at home and in education;
- language minority students whose home language(s) are different from the language(s) of instruction;
- students with learning difficulties, such as autism spectrum disorders;
- students with language impairments, such as dyslexia (recall Chapter 6);
- deaf and blind students.

Within schools, as rural to urban migration and immigration bring new languages to many communities, and as acknowledgement and acceptance of language rights (we hope) continue to increase, there is a pressing need for subject area assessment tools that are appropriate for linguistically diverse learners. International trends in the development of programmes to fit the needs of special populations are less effective if language differences are allowed to become a barrier to sensible identification and correct placement of learners who need these services. Similarly, there is a need to avoid the incorrect placement of learners who *don't* need them, as in the historic over-representation of Spanish speakers and other English language learners in special education programmes in the US (Reynolds and Fletcher-Janzen, 2007). Applied linguistics can help educators differentiate between students with genuine special needs and those whose low scores on assessments are more likely to be a result of their still-developing linguistic competence in the home or additional language.

As we'll see further in Chapter 8, on bilingual education, schools employ a range of practices with regard to subject area instruction in majority and minority languages. For example, if the curriculum of a school in Spain attended by North African students is intended to encourage students to develop advanced academic language proficiency in Arabic, educators must be hired or trained to identify and develop materials suitable for this purpose, and must be capable of assessing student learning based on these materials. In transitional bilingual education programmes, where the students' home language is used as the language of instruction only until academic proficiency is reached in the language of the school, educators need to be able to determine when students have reached this level of specialized linguistic competence. Classroom teachers who are responsible for these assessments are implementing a kind of applied linguistics. Not all classroom teachers will have the time, the language expertise needed or the desire to create instruments in multiple languages, but an awareness of the place of language as an aspect of a particular 'problem', together with knowledge of the theory and tools for describing the problem and designing a solution, can help teachers and administrators select textbooks, exams and other materials that are appropriate for certain types of language learners.

Since language and language-based assessment of knowledge and learning pervade the educational process, any gap between the child's linguistic abilities and the curriculum's linguistic demands will lead to serious consequences, affecting the child's development of fundamental skills. Children with language-related disabilities (Chapter 13) will be particularly challenged. Bashir, Conte and Heerde (1998, pp. 4–13) identify five ability sets that they might struggle with:

- participating in school scripts;
- interacting socially;
- learning through instructional discourse exchanges;
- acquiring knowledge and language;
- developing literacy skills.

Historically, of course, most children who have struggled in one or more of these areas were unlikely to receive any special treatment or accommodation at all, a condition that continues to be true in many places. Even in contexts where national education policy specifies the rights of differently abled learners, actual practice – whether due to attitudes toward people with language disabilities or a lack of resources and training – may result in children being left to get along as best they can within the confines of the 'regular' classroom and without the benefit of special instruction, or considered 'uneducable' and thus excluded from school altogether. Although the methods and frequency of diagnosis vary greatly, children with language impairments are increasingly taught under a specialized curriculum often referred to as **special needs education** (McConkey, 2001). Generally speaking, educators take one of two approaches in teaching learners who have been identified as needing some form of specialized instruction, depending on the severity of the impairment and the school's resources and ability to provide what is needed:

- **inclusion approaches**: children with language impairments are educated in the mainstream classroom along with their age-peers;
- **exclusion approaches**: children with language impairments are grouped together and taught separately from other learners.

Deaf and blind children face particular challenges in gaining equal access to instruction. Increasingly, governments and educators recognize the ethical and pedagogical importance of providing specialized instruction to meet their particular language needs by taking steps to ensure, for example, that all deaf people have access to education in the sign language used in their country or region.

An inclusion approach to education is now greatly preferred, following international proclamations such as UNESCO's Salamanca Statement (1994, p. ix) recommending that all children attend their local community mainstream school 'unless there are compelling reasons for [them] doing otherwise'. One such reason, of course, would be having a teacher who has not been prepared to work with linguistically impaired learners. How schools provide for this, whether through inclusion in mainstream classes or through special schools and classes, often

**Special needs education** is the provision of dedicated arrangements for students with an enduring disability which prevents or restricts them participating fully in, and benefiting fully from, the educational process. The SEN TEACHER website provides a wealth of free resources for teachers of pupils with special educational needs.

 **www.7.4**

**Inclusion approaches** and **exclusion approaches** to working with children with special needs refer to the practices of integrating such learners into the regular classroom (e.g. with non-special needs learners) or segregating them in separate classes.

 **www.7.5**

depends on their resources. Teachers involved in first language education will likely find themselves teaching children with a variety of language impairments and language-related needs. This may require them to work closely, individually or in teams, with special needs educators, sign interpreters, dyslexia specialists, speech language pathologists (whose work is discussed in Chapter 13) and others; another reason for advocating a broad training in applied linguistics for all language professionals.

Last but not least in our discussion of school populations with special language needs, we'll take up the issue of minority and Indigenous learners. In section 7.1 we described several approaches to teaching that aim to connect local forms of language with the language of instruction. A well-known example comes from Hawaii, where Hawaiian Creole was banned as a language of instruction in the late 1800s. Frustrated that English-only instruction was not helping Hawaiian children to succeed at school, despite the fact that most had grown up as English monolinguals, educators at the Kamehameha Early Education Program (KEEP) experimented with restructuring language arts instruction to incorporate the discourse patterns of the Hawaiian oral tradition known as *Talk Story* (Figure 7.4). As described by Katherine Au and her colleagues at the University of Hawaii, the central feature of this tradition is the co-construction of stories and narratives. By allowing multiple students to share the floor and take turns much more than in the mainstream instructional patterns they had been trained to use (in which only one person is supposed to speak at a time), the KEEP teachers elicited considerably more student participation in talking and writing (Au, 1993), and were able to connect them to the development of the features of written discourse valued in schools. *Talk Story* has since become an integral feature of the way writing is taught in Hawaiian schools, and its success in promoting language and literacy development has been cited as a factor in the widespread reintroduction of Hawaiian to schools and the state constitution, as we saw in Chapter 5.

If You Can Write Your Own Life Story,
You Can Write Your Own Happy Ending

 **www.7.6**   Figure 7.4   The Talk Story project in Hawaii (Source: http://www.kidstalkstory.com/)

## 7.5  LANGUAGE, TESTING AND ASSESSMENT

And then there is the field of testing and assessment, one of the most complex aspects of the nexus between language and formal schooling. The convergence of increased linguistic diversity in school populations, coupled with the standards movement that has become dominant in educational contexts in the English-speaking world and is spreading globally (Alexander, 2008), has produced an unprecedented demand for tests and measures in school. Some of these are intended to measure language proficiency (elaborated upon in Chapter 9) and others aim to measure subject area knowledge or achievement, something that – again highlighting the ubiquity of language in schools – is very difficult to do satisfactorily without the medium of language. One indication of the importance of assessment for language professionals is the rapidly growing membership of the European Association for Language Testing and Assessment (EALTA). Founded in 2004 with support from the European Community, EALTA has members in 41 countries in Europe and 24 countries outside Europe, including Expert Members who are hired to consult with government ministries and 'non-state schools' to design appropriate programmes of testing and assessment.

So what are the (applied) linguistic features of testing that concern educators? A critically important macro-level question is which languages and varieties are selected as the test medium, for example the choice of Chinese (based on the 'standard' Beijing variety) for testing the maths knowledge of Uyghur-speaking children in the Xinjiang Autonomous Region of China (where the home language belongs to the Turkic family and uses a form of Arabic script). We'll address this in Chapter 8 in greater depth. At the micro level, effective assessment of mother-tongue/first language learning and subject area knowledge is inherently dependent upon awareness of myriad features of language and their possible influence on the test-takers' ability to demonstrate learning. At the risk of oversimplifying matters, we'll consider two types of assessment:

1   tests which seek to measure learners' mastery of and level of attainment on discrete points of knowledge in specific subject areas;
2   tests which aim to describe learners' abilities to integrate and apply knowledge, including discrete skills, to concrete problems and tasks.

For our readers whose educational experiences embrace no such jargon, or who have simply been away from school too long to remember any, it may be helpful to envision the differences between a multiple choice test based on this chapter (type 1) and an essay summarizing its main points (type 2).

Both of these two basic types can be effective ways to assess what learners know, but each poses particular linguistic requirements for producers (teachers and test writers) and consumers (test-takers). These differences also have to do with how the results are intended to be used. Teachers should be able to use student test results as feedback to inform and improve instruction. For example, if half the pupils in a class miss a particular question on a biology quiz, an analysis of student errors can reveal whether the difficulty is likely to have been caused by the learners' level of subject knowledge (suggesting that the same information should be taught again but perhaps in a different format) or by the fact that the test instructions or wording of the question were confusing (no need to re-teach, but rather to assess differently). When tests are meant to situate learner knowledge relative to members of a group (e.g. grade level or key stage) as compared to members of similar groups in other places (e.g. across an entire country), they are usually delivered in standardized formats developed by education agencies and private testing companies.

The same is true of international comparisons of learning such as the Progress in International Reading Literacy Study (PIRLS, taken by nine- to ten-year-olds in approximately thirty countries every five years) and the Trends in International Math and Science Study (TIMSS, taken every four years by students of various ages in nearly ninety countries). Due to the great effort and expense of developing acceptably reliable and valid tests (*of* language and *through* language), a background in applied linguistics would be invaluable for test developers who must ensure that a question about science or maths 'means' the same thing to test-takers in Toronto as to their fellow students in Vancouver, as well as for policymakers charged with comparing learning across countries.

## 7.6  ROLES FOR APPLIED LINGUISTS

In this chapter we have described the central place of language in schools, as a school subject, and as a tool for organizing and delivering education. Because education is a critically important domain of language use, we believe that applied linguists should be closely involved in decisions about how to organize, present and assess the ways language is used in schools, whatever the curriculum or educational system. In this final section, we outline key roles applied linguists can play in this broad area. For example, a recent job posting for a Test Development Specialist at **www.7.7**  the Center for Applied Linguistics (CAL) in Washington, DC, sought an applied linguist to develop a large-scale English language assessment for Grades One to Five English language learners. Job responsibilities included ensuring content accuracy and grade-level appropriateness of test items and writing test materials and instructions. Another opening at CAL sought an applied linguist familiar with communities of English language learners from the Middle East and North Africa, South Central Asia and East Asia to conduct research on heritage language communities in the US.

Applied linguistics knowledge can also inform the development of measures to assess learners' abilities to integrate and apply knowledge to concrete problems and tasks. For example, under England's National Curriculum, teachers of 'English' at Key Stage 2 (ages seven to ten) are expected to help pupils learn how to 'talk effectively as members of a group' through use of the following language **www.7.8**  functions:

- mak[ing] contributions relevant to the topic and tak[ing] turns in discussion;
- vary[ing] contributions to suit the activity and purpose, including exploratory and tentative comments where ideas are being collected together, and reasoned, evaluative comments as discussion moves to conclusions or actions;
- qualify[ing] or justify[ing] what they think after listening to others' questions or accounts;

- deal[ing] politely with opposing points of view and enabl[ing] discussion to move on;
- tak[ing] up and sustain[ing] different roles, adapting them to suit the situation, including chair, scribe and spokesperson;
- us[ing] different ways to help the group move forward, including summarising the main points, reviewing what has been said, clarifying, drawing others in, reaching agreement, considering alternatives and anticipating consequences.
(QCA, 2009)

These examples reveal the opportunities for students and practitioners trained in applied linguistics. Drawing on their understanding of discourse analysis (Chapter 4), for example, they could:

- help students develop and practise the linguistic and pragmatic features to support brainstorming in a group (turn-taking, eliciting contributions from 'quiet' students);
- offer exploratory and tentative comments where ideas are being collected together;
- acknowledge and accommodate opposing points of view;
- shift between different roles in the resolution of a group task (chair, scribe and spokesperson).

With cultural and linguistic diversity on the increase in many schools, the ability to identify and foster these desirable forms of language use and practice in learners from diverse backgrounds is indeed a benefit of applied linguistics education.

Applied linguists also shape the ways languages are used in educational domains beyond the classroom. Although the exact phrase 'applied linguist wanted' is rarely found in actual job postings (the CAL positions mentioned above are an exception), knowledge of applied linguistics is extremely useful to professionals engaged in developing and evaluating textbooks, test instruments, websites and other educational materials. Consider the following example, from an advertisement seeking an editor to oversee development of an early literacy curriculum for children between five and nine years old. The position called for candidates prepared to:

- edit manuscript of teacher materials for content, accuracy, grammar, style and length;
- provide innovative content input for manuscript preparation;
- review manuscript for editorial quality in preparation for production.

While some of these functions might be within the skill set of applicants without training in applied linguistics (for example editing manuscripts for style), knowledge of the range of children's cognitive and linguistic abilities in the target age group, knowledge of early literacy development and experience with how materials translate into actual use in real-life classrooms are all areas in which a background in applied linguistics would presumably confer an advantage.

Finally, a good number of applied linguists devote at least part of their professional practice to preparing future and practising teachers to work in classrooms and schools at different levels and with learners from diverse groups. **Teacher**

**Teacher education** is the teaching of teachers. It takes place pre-service, most often at the undergraduate level, and continues in professional development throughout a teacher's career.

**education** is a very broad field, and includes, among other areas: bilingual education, early childhood education, special education and literacy education. As we have noted in previous chapters, not all teacher educators working in these fields view themselves as engaging in applied linguists, but certainly many teacher preparation activities draw on applied linguistics as an important part of the professional knowledge base.

In this chapter we have attempted to map the expansive and contested territory of language and education. By contrasting language as developed and used in the intimate domains of family, home and community with how it is used in school, we've considered language as both medium and object of education. We also examined the role language plays in the assessment of learning and academic achievement. In keeping with our concern for multilingualism, we've examined how changes in school populations are leading to new approaches to educating students with special needs and to the education of linguistic minorities, the topic we develop further in Chapter 8.

## activities

1   The Funds of Knowledge for Teaching programme (section 7.1) aims to develop teaching materials and techniques that draw on the knowledge and skills found in students' homes and communities. As an experiment in using household resources in the classroom, think about a piece of music or a song you learned at home as a child. How old were you and what were the circumstances in which you heard the music/song? Ask an older relative to choose a piece of music or a song they remember learning as a child and get them to tell you in detail what it reminds them of. If you are working in a group, share all the song/music titles, lyrics (if available) and accompanying stories with your group. Could this activity be adapted for use in a school classroom with which you are familiar? What might the instructional aims or learning outcomes of the activity be?

2   In section 7.3 we consider various ways in which language is treated as an object of study in schools. As a way of exploring your own local, regional or national context, find a curriculum document that describes what should be taught (content and attainment targets) about (one of) your national language(s). Or, if you can't find any suitable documents, try an internet search for the UK National Curriculum for English at Key Stage 1 (for children ages five to seven), on the Qualifications and Curriculum Authority website. Once you have located a suitable curriculum document, look at what the documents says about what children *need to be taught*. Ask yourself what assumptions are being made about:

**www.7.9**

■   the variety(ies) of language that is (are) useful (or prestigious) and which should be able to be used by pupils;
■   the variety(ies) of language that pupils experience at home and whether it is (they are) the same as the variety(ies) considered to be useful or prestigious.

3    In section 7.2 we ask you to imagine what could and couldn't be accomplished in schools in the absence of language. To further explore this idea, find a syllabus, textbook or test for teaching or assessing a 'non-language' subject like science, maths or geography. Are there any activities which pupils could perform without using language? Does the extent to which these activities require language differ? How? If you can't find a syllabus, textbook or test to consider, try an internet search for the New South Wales (Australia) K-6 syllabus for Science and Technology and look at the *Outcomes and Indicators* document. To what extent do the activities from this document test children's abilities to use *language* to:

 www.7.10

- develop a structure that can support itself after experimenting with a variety of materials such as sticks, string and Plasticine;
- use building blocks to model part of the school environment and label its important features;
- interpret maps, charts, graphs and time lines.

4    Ask a school-age child to describe their favourite games or hobbies to:

- a teacher in a one-to-one conversation in class (none of the other classmates will be able to hear the answer);
- a friend in a one-to-one conversation in the playground;
- a teacher in a whole-class activity (all the classmates will be able to hear the answer).

Following Andersen's (1990) study described in section 7.1, try role-playing the teacher or friend and ask the child to role-play their response. Do the content and language of the child's response vary depending on the intended audience? How? What does this variation tell you about the child's awareness of what constitutes legitimate content and language in their school context? Is the child able to comment on their own awareness and use of 'legitimate' language? Can they explain how they learned to talk 'differently' in different situations?

## FURTHER READING

Farr, M., Seloni, L. and Song, J. (eds) (2010). *Ethnolinguistic diversity and education: Language, literacy and culture*. New York: Routledge.

Halliday, M. A. K. (2007 [1988]). *Language and education*. London: Continuum.

Li, G. (ed.) (2009). *Multicultural families, home literacies, and mainstream schooling*. Charlotte, NC: Information Age Publishing.

Lindfors, J. W. (2008). *Children's language: Connecting reading, writing, and talk*. New York: Teachers College Press.

Scott, J. C., Straker, D. Y. and Katz, L. (eds) (2009). *Affirming students' rights to their own language: Bridging language policies to teaching practices*. New York: Routledge/National Council of Teachers of English.

**CHAPTER 8**

# Bilingual and multilingual education

We should not be in the business of making children forget what they know.

(Joseph Lo Bianco, 2009)

This chapter is concerned with education in multiple languages, a pressing issue in many communities around the world. In Chapter 7 we saw that the choice of which language(s) to use in school settings can be complex, so it's not surprising that the practice of bilingual or multilingual education is well accepted in some contexts and controversial in others. Although instruction in two or more languages is increasingly common, the term 'bilingual education' is often poorly understood, as the following quotation from a primary school teacher from Tucson, Arizona, illustrates:

> 'Bilingual ed' is a term that has such a negative connotation, which is partly the reason we've decided to call our model 'dual language'. It's helped a lot. When people think of bilingual education, the general opinion is, 'Oh, you're teaching Spanish to the Spanish kids, English to the English kids.' It's almost the opposite with dual language. These kids are receiving not just one education, they're receiving two. And if you explain this to parents, it's like, 'Wow! That's really great!' Whereas before if you had said it's bilingual ed, people didn't want to hear about it.

> (Smith, 2000, p. 118)

One source of misunderstanding is the fact that supporters and detractors seldom share the same definitions of bilingual and multilingual schooling or agree about its goals. A related problem is that until quite recently much of the available research and information about bilingual education has described practices in English-speaking contexts, particularly in the UK, the US and Canada, and may therefore seem inappropriate or irrelevant to educators working in other multilingual contexts. For example, a recent report on bilingual education in sub-Saharan Africa observed that (mis)use of the term bilingual education in North America 'has been transported to many countries in Africa where people label programmes bilingual where there is very little L1 medium in place' (Alidou et al., 2006, p. 5).

Students and practitioners of applied linguistics will no doubt find irony in the fact that research in this area has been dominated by some of the very nations in which education in multiple languages has been unpopular with large and powerful segments of the population. However, with the impetus of globalization, international migration, and increasing awareness and concern for the rights of

Indigenous groups and other ethnic and cultural minorities, the study and practice of bilingual and multilingual education are beginning to acquire a much needed international flavour (Creese and Martin, 2003; Gándara and Hopkins, 2010; García, 2009; Gregory *et al.*, 2004). In the European context, Extra and Yağmur argue that:

**www.8.1**

> [t]here is a great need for educational policies . . . that take new realities into account. Processes of internationalization have brought European nation-states to the world, but they have also brought the world to European nation-states . . . This language diversity is considered to be a prerequisite rather than an obstacle for a united European space in which all citizens are equal (but not the same) and enjoy equal rights . . . The maintenance of language diversity and the promotion of language learning and multilingualism are seen as essential elements for the improvement of communication and for the reduction of intercultural misunderstanding.
>
> (Extra and Yağmur, 2005)

Clearly, the monolingual lens that has long characterized state education systems in the UK and US, and that has resulted in a monolingual/bilingual paradigm underlying the ways we conceptualize, talk and practise education, is unsuitable for viewing and mapping a terrain that is increasingly multilingual. In this chapter, we refer generally to bilingual *and* multilingual education in order to present the knowledge base, issues and choices that applied linguists should be familiar with, whatever their current geographic location. To reflect local, contextualized practice, we use *bilingual education* or *multilingual education* separately where it describes a particular case. As we've done in previous chapters, we invite you to consider how the issues and examples we present fit with practice in your own setting.

We begin our discussion with an overview of the varied definitions and purposes of bilingual and multilingual education (section 8.1), and then present three frameworks for understanding the subject: *language-based* (8.2), concentrating on how the languages are used and what happens to them developmentally; *content-based* (8.3), where the emphasis is on what the languages are for; and *context-based* (8.4), in which national and local conditions are the key factors. In 8.5 we draw the three frames together, before highlighting key characteristics of effective programmes (8.6) and ending the chapter with a review of roles for applied linguists (8.7).

## 8.1 DEFINITIONS AND PURPOSES

Bilingual and multilingual education mean different things in different places. In Chinese schools, for example, bilingual education refers to the rapidly growing number of Mandarin/English programmes for the Han majority, as well as to programmes that use a combination of Mandarin and a regional language such as Yi in Hunnan and neighbouring regions in the south of the country (Feng, 2005) or Uyghur in the Xinjiang Autonomous Region in the west (Schluessel, 2007). Similarly, in schools along the US–Mexico border the term describes:

- programmes that teach Spanish–English bilingual children in a single language (typically English in the US and Spanish in Mexico);
- programmes that teach in both English and Spanish, even if students are home language speakers of only one of these languages;
- programmes which intentionally group together pupils of two distinct language backgrounds.

**www.8.2**

And in South Africa, a nation with eleven official languages (PanSALB, 2009a), 'bilingual education is understood as mother tongue instruction (L1 medium) throughout school, plus a second language taught as a subject to a high level of proficiency' (Alidou *et al.*, 2006). In other words, the criterion for what makes a programme *bilingual* or *multilingual* in a particular context can be the language backgrounds of the learners and/or the language(s) they are taught in. Here, unless otherwise specified, we refer to programmes in which at least two languages are systematically employed as languages of instruction, including for the purposes of teaching academic content.

The purposes of bilingual and multilingual education programmes are similarly diverse, ranging from development of advanced levels of proficiency and academic achievement in both target languages to the promotion of academic skills in a dominant language but not in the pupils' home language. Similarly, some programmes aim to help learners develop knowledge about a particular cultural group in addition to their own, while others have as their primary orientation and mission the promotion of assimilation and acculturation of linguistically diverse learners into a mainstream or dominant culture. We note increasing interest in programmes seeking to develop 'multilingual, culturally adept citizens who can prosper and contribute to our increasingly global society' (Gándara and Hopkins, 2010, p. 4). In this chapter we will look at examples of programmes with a variety of goals and purposes.

We present here a three-part framework for understanding how education in multiple languages is commonly organized (Figure 8.1). We begin by distinguishing between frames that are (1) *language-based*, (2) *content-based* and (3) *context-*

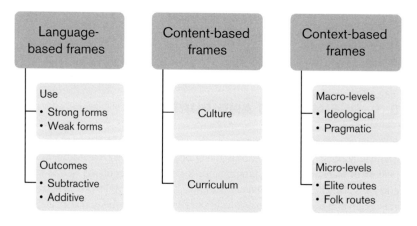

Figure 8.1   Three frameworks for understanding bilingual and multilingual education

*based*. These ways of looking at programmes are not mutually exclusive, of course. To some extent, all programmes must take into account the language and subject matter learning needs of their students, as well as the contextual features and constraints of the larger context in which they are based. We argue that much more can be learned about particular schools and programmes by examining them from all three frames.

## 8.2 LANGUAGE-BASED FRAMES

One key way of looking at bilingual and multilingual programmes is in terms of language use and language outcomes. A clear example of a focus on use is the distinction between 'strong' forms – in which two or more languages are used systematically for academic purposes, including reading and writing in subject areas such as maths, science and history – and 'weak' forms, where the non-dominant languages are used sparingly, typically to clarify instructions or for interpersonal communication only (Baker, 2006). Despite its apparent simplicity, the **strong–weak dichotomy** reminds us to pay close attention to the manner in which and the extent to which bilingual and multilingual programmes actually use each of the target languages. Asymmetry in the use of the dominant and non-dominant languages is problematic for many programmes, and human, material and technological resources tend to be concentrated in the dominant language unless special steps are taken to address this imbalance. This is especially true for combinations that include a language of wider communication, such as English, French or Mandarin, with less prestigious or less widely spoken languages.

Achieving even a relative degree of symmetry between target languages is no simple task. Some of the reasons for this imbalance are economic; where appropriate materials exist in both languages, schools may lack the funds needed to purchase them, or they may wish to devote scant resources to other aspects of the curriculum, including instruction in the dominant language. Where commercially prepared materials are unavailable, as is the case for many Indigenous and other non-dominant languages, local curriculum writers – typically classroom teachers or their bilingual assistants – must create them. Because opportunities to develop strong literacy skills in non-dominant languages are often scarce, a common problem for bilingual and multilingual programmes is finding materials developers whose subject area knowledge is matched by strong literacy skills in the target language(s). Even in programmes which 'simply' translate the curriculum from the **dominant language** into a **minority language**, the quality of the result is not a foregone conclusion, as we'll see in Chapter 10, on translation.

Perhaps the greatest potential barrier to symmetry can be found in attitudes towards one or both of the target languages or feelings about bilingualism and multilingualism, though these attitudes are changing over time. For example, when they began in the late 1930s, Welsh-medium schools were intended only for children of Welsh-speaking families; eventually they were opened to all children in Wales (Mejía, 2006). A similar shift in attitudes towards education in immigrant languages in Europe is evident in statements by the Council of Europe calling for multilingual education in immigrant communities and support for immigrants learning the language of the area where they live (Beacco and Byram, 2003).

The **strong–weak dichotomy** in bilingual education refers to the balance in classroom usage between the two languages involved. Strong bilingual education involves balanced usage of both languages across all subject areas, in order to reinforce the minority language in its role as a medium of instruction. In weaker forms, the minority language is used for less central curricular functions.

In bilingualism, a **minority language** is distinguished from a **dominant language** according to what it's used for (its functions) and where it's used (its contexts). For example, Urdu is a minority language in Leeds (in the UK) but a dominant language in Lahore (in Pakistan).

A **heritage language** is the language of a minority community viewed as a property of the group's cultural history, and is often in danger of loss as third generations grow up being un- or underexposed to the language. So heritage language bilingual education focuses on the uses of the minority language as a tool to promote group identity, solidarity and language revitalization. (The UCLA Center for World Languages publishes the (free) *Heritage Language Journal* online.)

**www.8.3** 🌍

**Biliteracy** is literacy in two (or more) languages. The word is analogous to *bilingual* (in Latin *bi-* means 'having two', *litteratus* means 'lettered' and *lingua* means 'tongue').

**Subtractive** bilingual education leads to the loss of the first language (the second replaces the first), whereas **additive** bilingual education leads to competence in two languages (the second augments the first).

In other contexts, speakers may be ambivalent about, or even outright opposed to, having children learn to read and write their **heritage language**. Members of some Indigenous communities, such as the Arhuaco in Colombia (Murillo, 2009) and Maori in New Zealand (Smith, 2006), express strong reservations about whether and how their home language should be used in schools. In other words, **biliteracy** may be viewed as appropriate and desirable for heritage language learners but not for others. Thus, any categorization and analysis of strong and weak programmes needs to take into account contextual factors that are economic and attitudinal (ideological) in nature. This includes consideration of localized forms of diglossia in bilingual and multilingual communities that have developed shared beliefs and practices concerning the proper roles and functions each language should play (Fishman, 2000 [1967]).

A second type of language-based frame concerns the linguistic outcomes of schooling in multiple languages. This perspective compels us to ask about the changes in pupils' abilities to use their first and additional languages after completing a bilingual or multilingual programme of study. **Subtractive** programmes (e.g. Figure 8.2) are those in which the student's home language is not used at all as a medium of instruction or its use is progressively diminished as early as the first year of school. Although students in such programmes *may* learn new vocabulary, develop stronger reading and writing skills, and be introduced to new genres in the mother tongue, these gains are often the result of *out-of-school* learning and experiences. In more extreme cases, where schools actively discourage or even ban the use of non-dominant languages outright, interpersonal and even intergenerational communication can suffer, with children eventually becoming unable or unwilling to communicate in the home language with older family members (Wong Fillmore, 1991). Even in cases where students have two (or more) first languages,

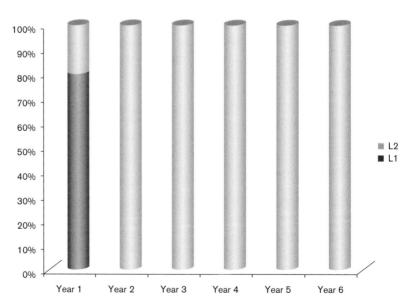

Figure 8.2   Language of instruction in an educational programme which leads to subtractive bilingualism

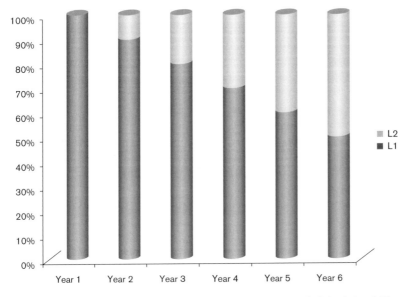

Figure 8.3   Language of instruction in an educational programme which leads to additive bilingualism

for example Hindi-, Gujarati- and English-speaking students in India enrolled in either English-medium or Vernacular-medium schools, there may be tension between the two languages as a result of how, in different contexts, either English or the Vernacular is emphasized and valued (Ramanathan, 2005).

In contrast, **additive** bilingual and multilingual programmes (e.g. Figure 8.3) aim to support and extend the student's home language and additional language(s) through the systematic and sustained use of both/all as languages of instruction. Such programmes typically have as a goal that learners will leave the programme as more fully developed speakers, readers and writers of their home language across a variety of genres, discourses and contexts. Thus, learners in additive programmes are expected to add a new language without the expectation that they will give up their home language.

## 8.3  CONTENT-BASED FRAMES

Although controversies about bilingual and multilingual education typically assume a language-based frame, in those contexts where schooling in multiple languages is more widely accepted, educators often emphasize the acquisition of academic content. In such cases, the languages of instruction are portrayed primarily as *vehicles* for intercultural communication and content learning rather than as the *defining feature* of the programme, as reflected in statements by the Council of Europe (2007).

There is also growing awareness that the forms of knowledge that linguistically diverse learners bring to school are a valuable resource to be tapped in bilingual and multilingual programmes. Implicit use of students' existing conceptual and content knowledge has been described as *de facto* **bilingual education**

Children engage in *de-facto* **bilingual education** when they and their teachers implicitly draw on subject knowledge acquired previously in a language which is different from the language of instruction. For example, a Hong Kong student who learned elementary mathematics through the medium of Cantonese will be familiar with mathematical concepts even when they're presented by a Mandarin Chinese-speaking teacher.

(Krashen, 1998), in recognition of the fact that students with a strong educational background in their first language are better able to transfer or apply the conceptual knowledge developed through L1-medium education to learning in additional languages. This lesson was brought home very clearly to Patrick while teaching history with students from South-East Asia and the Caribbean. During a **sheltered English** lesson on Columbus' voyages to the Americas, Rithy, a Cambodian youth whose formal education to that point had been limited to English language and US culture classes in refugee camps in Thailand, asked why Columbus had taken several months to cross the Atlantic. Why, Rithy wanted to know, did the Spaniards travel in sailing ships, rather than in an aeroplane as he and his family had done? Some Colombian and Puerto Rican students in the class laughed, but the question made good sense based on Rithy's understanding of things. His classmates understood that Columbus could not have flown across the Atlantic because aeroplanes had not yet been invented in 1492. They understood this not because their English was better than Rithy's, but because their school experience included the formal study of history and, more specifically, stories about the European conquest of the Americas that they were able to bring to bear on learning history through a new language.

A **sheltered English** programme is one in which school pupils with limited proficiency in the target language get instruction in English as an additional language along with other subjects taught in English, until they can join students who have the proficiency required to engage in mainstream classrooms.

In the following sections we describe the most common forms of bilingual and multilingual schooling. We will revisit some of these notions in our discussion of additional language education in Chapter 9. We remind the reader that the terms for programme types that we use here are not the only ones used to talk about education in multiple languages. For more extensive discussion, see Baker (2006) and García (2009).

## Submersion education

Also known as *sink-or-swim*, submersion programmes make little or no effort to acknowledge or accommodate the special needs of second language learners

Figure 8.4   Sink-or-Swim submersion programmes

(Figure 8.4). Pupils are placed in classes with students who are native/proficient speakers of the dominant language, and their academic progress is evaluated using measures designed to assess the performance of native speakers and for comparison with the norms established for them. Whether the pupils' home languages are relatively recent arrivals (as in the case of children who have recently migrated across linguistic borders) or have been long present and historically undervalued (the case of most Indigenous and sign languages), submersion education remains the most common form of schooling for language minority students (García, 2009).

## Transitional bilingual education

**Transitional bilingual education** programmes, known in some contexts by the acronym TBE and in the UK as *bilingual support* (Martin-Jones and Saxena, 2003), feature the temporary use of the students' L1 or another regional language as an academic bridge to highly proficient users of the dominant language. Unlike submersion programmes, transitional programmes often feature at least some content instruction in the home language and may also include initial literacy instruction in the students' L1. An important factor in the organization of TBE programmes is the length of time that students are permitted to study in their L1 before being moved into classes designed for native speakers of the dominant language. In many cases, this decision is based on political expediency rather than evidence from second language acquisition research. Thus, despite scholarly consensus that most students need at least seven years in order to fully develop academic language proficiency in English as a second language (Collier and Thomas, 2007), some US states stipulate that students must be 'mainstreamed' into English-only instruction with native English-speaking classmates after a maximum of one year of native language or sheltered instruction. California, Arizona and Massachusetts, where such programmes are labelled 'structured English immersion', are well-known examples. Variations on the TBE model are also known as 'early exit' or 'late exit', depending on the number of years of L1 instruction students receive before moving into monolingual instruction in the dominant language. Typically, emphasis is placed on literacy skills and achievement in the dominant language, and the development of academic skills in the students' L1 receives less attention.

> **Transitional bilingual education** is subtractive, using the first language as a temporary medium for gaining proficiency in the (dominant) second language; whereas **maintenance bilingual education** is additive, aiming to complement and strengthen, rather than replace, the (minority) first language.

## Maintenance bilingual education

**Maintenance bilingual education** refers to upkeep of the non-dominant language. We know of few contemporary programmes under this name, but the notion of pupils maintaining rather than being forced to 'forget what they know' by giving up their home languages contrasts sharply with the linguistic assimilation goals of the submersion and transitional models we have seen. It is also consistent with aims of the two-way immersion and community language teaching models described on pp. 184–8.

   The maintenance bilingual education model is intended for immigrant pupils thought likely to return to their home countries and whose successful return would ideally include being able to participate in schools there. An early example of education for language maintenance was developed in the (now) very multilingual city of Miami when Cubans who fled their country in the early 1960s created private schools to provide Spanish language instruction so that their children would still be able to speak Spanish upon their planned return to schools in Cuba (Mackey and Beebe, 1977). Although history has proved otherwise in this case, maintenance of the home language remains a goal of programmes serving the children of guest workers in numerous host countries around the world. Notable contemporary examples include the language conditions experienced by Turkish speakers in German schools and ethnic Japanese living in Brazil. Students of applied linguistics reading this book who are currently outside their home countries will be particularly aware of the difficulties that might face children who return 'home' after being schooled, primarily or exclusively, in a different language in their host country.

Whatever the conditions, key questions in such situations include what exactly is meant by 'maintenance' and who is responsible for helping pupils achieve it. Generally speaking, the size of the student population matters, as does duration, that is, how long pupils are expected to remain in the host country.

## Immersion

In **immersion** bilingual education programmes, pioneered in Canada, learners are immersed in the second language. In **one-way immersion**, the pupils typically share an L1, whereas in **two-way immersion** (TWI) speakers of both languages study content together, and the language of instruction for a particular subject may be either language. (For a wealth of online resources, visit the Immersion page at the University of Minnesota's Center for Advanced Research on Language Acquisition.)

**www.8.4**

The term **immersion** refers to programmes designed to teach content in the target language, but in a way that does not (intentionally) harm the learner's L1. The target language may be the dominant language or a minority language which has become economically viable and/or socially prestigious, as was the case of Spanish in Miami following the arrival of a large elite and highly educated Cuban population. Support for children's other languages is often available. Key variables in immersion programmes include the language(s) of instruction and the home language(s) of the students, with **one-way** and **two-way immersion** programmes being common variations.

Perhaps the best-known examples of one-way immersion are the French language programmes for children of English-speaking homes first developed in Montreal in the early 1960s and now common across Canada (Heller, 2006). Studies of programmes following this well-documented and influential model suggest that children from a majority language background can develop content knowledge (history, science, mathematics, etc.) in a second language to a degree comparable or superior to peers schooled exclusively in their L1, and that they do so with no apparent cost to academic development in the majority language. A primary attraction of such programmes is, of course, that students typically develop much higher levels of L2 proficiency than are attained in traditional foreign language classrooms. Reading test scores and other measures of academic proficiency in English sometimes lag behind those of children schooled monolingually, but the delay seems to be temporary, with bilingually schooled children of dominant language backgrounds eventually 'catching up' with their monolingual peers on measures of achievement, such as reading and maths, even when tested in the dominant language.

In Europe, the teaching of content in additional languages has been identified as an education priority by the European Commission (2008), which states that all schools in European Union (EU) countries should aim to be teaching in their students' mother tongue, plus two additional languages, so that every European citizen will have 'meaningful communicative competence' in at least three languages. In the Content and Language Integrated Learning (CLIL) approach, learners engage in the task of learning content and an additional language simultaneously because these dual objectives are integrated in materials and instruction. While many CLIL programmes teach content through English, an increasing number of schools teach content in other languages. For example, Serra (2007) describes a programme in which German-speaking elementary school pupils in Switzerland study mathematics in Italian or Romansch. Baetens Beardsmore (2009) cites the case of a Scottish teenager who claimed his life had been changed by learning technical subjects through French. This model is quickly becoming popular across Europe, in part because it offers a means of reaching the goal of multilingualism through formal education, and also because the approach is sufficiently flexible to fit the diversities of multilingual, multi-state Europe (Coyle, 2007). It is too early to tell whether CLIL will enjoy the long-term successes of the Canadian immersion programmes on which it is modelled, but by seeking to promote additional languages CLIL programmes are contributing to bi- and multilingualism.

Two-way immersion (TWI) programmes (also known as *dual language* or *bilingual immersion*) involve students from two language communities in a single classroom or academic programme. For example, in Korean–English TWI schools like those found in Los Angeles, English-speaking children and Korean-speaking children study all or most of their subject area classes together, rather than being segregated on the basis of language as happens in many programmes. Depending on the particulars of the curriculum, children could study mathematics and science in Korean and history and geography in English. Initial reading instruction is usually, but not always, done through the child's first language, and this is generally the only time during the school day that learners are divided by home language. Another critical feature of TWI programmes is the teacher's language competence and ability to teach subject area knowledge in each language. Even in widely spoken language pairs (such as Spanish and English) it is often difficult to find sufficient numbers of teachers capable of teaching in both languages. For this reason, children in TWI programmes sometimes have two teachers, each teaching in his or her dominant language. Programmes following this model have become popular in the US, thriving even in states such as California and Arizona where other types of bilingual education have been banned (see Figure 8.5).

Research on learning outcomes in TWI programmes generally show excellent results for achievement in the areas of additional language learning, literacy development in L1 and L2, subject area knowledge and intercultural communication skills when compared with student achievement in other types of bilingual education programmes and with monolingual teaching (Collier and Thomas, 2007). Advocates claim that this model is responsible for higher student achievement, but it's also true that such programmes are atypical in that they are often attended by children from privileged homes (*elite bilinguals*; see p. 189), and that parents who choose bilingual and multilingual education for their children may have higher levels of formal education and are also more able to push for high quality instruction and educational resources.

The teacher comments we quoted the beginning of this chapter (p. 176) suggest that two-way immersion or dual language programmes are also attractive

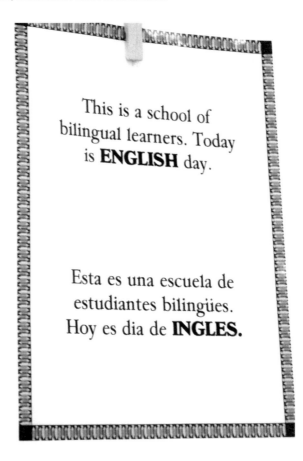

Figure 8.5    Bilingual sign in a US school with a two-way immersion programme

for some dominant language parents when other forms of bilingual or multilingual education are not. A particular challenge faced by such programmes is that they require the participation of comparable numbers of dominant language speakers. Thus, under this model minority language learners may not be able to receive schooling in their home language unless pupils from dominant language backgrounds are also willing and allowed to participate (Valdés, 1997).

In terms of the additional language proficiency, it is important to note that although pupils in both types of immersion programmes build a broad foundation for academic bilingualism, particularly literacy skills in the minority language, expectations vary with respect to the oral language proficiency they develop in the L2. Educators often 'market' programmes with the goal of sounding like a 'native speaker', but results in this area are not uniform. Studies of French immersion programmes in Canada and two-way immersion programmes in the US show that children who begin these programmes as monolingual speakers of the minority language end up talking and sounding like their dominant language counterparts. However, research suggests that it is less likely for children who begin school as monolingual speakers of the dominant language to achieve native-like proficiency in minority languages, even after many years of instruction (Cummins, 2008).

There are several factors at play here, beginning with the likelihood that some minority language speakers are actually emergent bilinguals with substantial exposure to the dominant language (through television, older siblings already in school, etc.) before they begin school. We need to remember that models of language distribution in teaching don't necessarily reflect children's actual language practices in school. In other words, a seven-year-old being taught 80 per cent in Spanish and 20 per cent in English (see Figure 8.3) is unlikely to follow this pattern in her classroom talk or when interacting with friends in the playground. Furthermore, although the promise of their child 'sounding like a native speaker' may seem attractive to parents considering immersion programmes for their children, it may also be that the native speaker goal is an unrealistic and unnecessary one (an issue we discussed in Chapter 2 and take up again in Chapter 9).

## Community language teaching

Recent immigration is also the driving force behind **community language teaching** (CLT). Not to be confused with *Community Language Learning*, a method of language instruction popular in adult foreign language teaching in the 1970s and 1980s, the term has been proposed to describe the growth of immigrant language teaching in cities across Europe. CLT incorporates programmes sometimes referred to as *mother-tongue teaching* and *home language instruction*, but has the advantage of accounting for the effects of language shift (e.g. not all pupils speak the same first language as their parents and older family members) and the inclusion of non-migrants (dominant language speakers) who want to study migrant languages (Extra and Yağmur, 2005). In Sheffield, in the UK, for example, some fifty languages are supported, with primary school languages including Somali, Arabic, Urdu, French, Spanish, Italian and German. The Multilingual Cities Project, a study of urban multilingualism and CLT in six large cities in EU member states (Göteburg, Hamburg, The Hague, Brussels, Lyon and Madrid), found that primary education was largely monolingually oriented and that CLT had higher status at the secondary level (but even here had to compete on the curriculum with more established and prestigious 'foreign languages'). Although the demand for CLT is growing, teacher training has not been able to meet it. A government report from the UK, for example, notes that

> In parts of England where community languages are widely taught in schools, no [training] courses are available. In 2006/07, there were only 35 trainees nationally studying to teach Arabic, Bengali, Japanese, Mandarin, Panjabi, Turkish, or Urdu with one of five initial teacher training providers.
>
> (Ofsted, 2008, p. 5)

 **www.8.5**

**Community language teaching** is an approach to heritage language education adopted in the UK, Australia, the Netherlands and other countries in which the home languages of ethnic minorities are taught and used as languages of instruction in schools and community centres. The *Our Languages* Consortium in the UK shares experiences and promotes good practice.

 **www.8.6**

## Heritage language programmes

Although they come in many different 'flavours' and forms, heritage language programmes share the assumption that there is educational value in teaching students in and about the historic language(s) of their community. The specific purposes vary, from promoting oral fluency to foster intergenerational communication (between children and grandparents and other elders), to developing academic literacies as a motor for advanced biliteracy and university study. Across programmes, pupils' linguistic background is valued and instruction is sensitive to the marginalization of local ways of speaking and writing. For example, the French heritage language programmes developed in a collaboration between the French government and the Center for Applied Linguistics (CAL) in the USA have had to be rethought and extended with the arrival of thousands of Haitian refugees to Canada and the US following the 2010 earthquake.

 **www.8.7**

Strong examples of heritage language programmes have evolved in many places, although they are not always known locally by this name. Duff and Li (2009, p. 4) note that other names for heritage language programmes include *community, complementary, ancestral, ethnic, immigrant, minority, original, non-official* and *second/third languages.* Pioneering sites include Hawaii and New Zealand, where advocates of Hawaiian and Maori as a medium of instruction have developed programmes that cover all levels of education, from kindergarten to university (Reyhner and Lockhard, 2009). Indigenous groups in Canada and the US also draw on the concept of heritage language education in diverse attempts to revitalize community languages that are at risk of being lost. A condition facing many heritage language educators is the fact that their students' stronger academic language is often a dominant language or language of wider communication, particularly in the area of literacy. This has prompted calls for such programmes to learn more about pupils' language learning aspirations and to structure heritage language learning to match them more closely (Callahan, 2010).

## 8.4  CONTEXT-BASED FRAMES

Our third frame for considering bilingual and multilingual education is based on the nature of the contexts in which programmes are designed, enacted and evaluated. This frame can be further divided into *macro-* and *micro-*level contexts.

### Macro-level contexts

At the national level, ideological stance leads to considerable diversity in public and official attitudes to bilingual and multilingual education. Consider the following statement by Argentine–US scholar Maria Brisk, comparing perceptions of bilingual education in the US and in other nations:

> Much of the debate on bilingual education [in the US] is wasteful, ironic, hypocritical, and regressive. It is wasteful because instead of directing attention directly to sound educational practices, it has led to advocating specific 'models' based solely on what language should be used for what purpose. It is ironic because most attacks on bilingual education arise from an unfounded fear that English will be neglected in the United States, whereas, in fact, the rest of the world fears the opposite; the attraction of English and interest in American cultures are seen by non-English speaking nations as a threat to their

own languages and cultures. It is hypocritical because most opponents of using languages other than English for instruction also want to promote foreign language requirements for high school graduation. Finally, it is regressive and xenophobic because the rest of the world considers ability in at least two languages to be the mark of a good education.

(Brisk, 1998, p. 160)

We would take issue with the assessment that 'the rest of the world considers ability in . . . two languages to be the mark of a good education': historically, there has been considerable resistance to bilingual schooling by authorities in Britain and China (Feng, 2005), for example, and many primary schools in Europe still feature a 'monolingual habitus' (Extra and Yağmur, 2005). But the ideological imbroglio in the US contrasts sharply with more pragmatic approaches of other nations. In Malawi, for instance:

It is clear . . . that the introduction of indigenous languages in the primary school curriculum makes a lot of academic sense and has, ideally, some benefits for the pupils, the ethnolinguistic groups whose languages are used in the schools, and the education system as a whole.

(Matiki, 2006, pp. 245–246)

So, although national-level characterizations may have some value in their own contexts, in many instances they unhelpfully oversimplify the complexity of regional and local situations.

## Micro-level contexts

Perhaps a more helpful way of thinking about the importance of context in bilingual and multilingual education is by examining conditions at more micro levels. Applied linguists can accomplish this by examining local conditions in which specific programmes operate. To do this, we borrow Suzanne Romaine's distinction between **elite** and **folk bilingualism** in children. According to Romaine (1999, p. 61), much of what linguists know about the development of childhood bilingualism is based on studies of 'middle-class and relatively privileged populations', whereas much less is known about the more numerous cases of bilingual and multilingual development in 'folk' contexts. Adapting this distinction to our consideration of education, we find that, in elite contexts, bilingual and multilingual programmes involve at least one major European language, or another language of wider communication such as Mandarin (see Figure 8.6), and that such programmes are commonly sought out by families who recognize the prestige of knowing multiple languages and who are able and willing to devote considerable financial and personal resources to raising bilingual or multilingual children.

In contrast, as Romaine points out, we know relatively little about how the majority of the world's children become bilingual or multilingual. In 'folk' contexts, including immigrant schools in Europe and North America and in Indigenous communities worldwide, children seldom enjoy the high levels of economic and educational resources common among their 'elite' counterparts. Their home

**Elite** and **folk bilingualism** are terms used by Suzanne Romaine to label the difference in socioeconomic circumstances and motivations between those who seek to become bilingual out of choice, often for increased prestige, and those who seek to become bilingual out of necessity, often for survival. So an example of elite bilingualism would be Polish children sent to English-medium schools in Poland, and an example of folk bilingualism would be Polish immigrant children attending English-medium schools in the UK.

Figure 8.6    Elite Mandarin–English bilingual education programme in Edmonton, Canada

language is seldom the prestige language of the community and, in most cases, acquisition of the dominant language is regarded as a matter of economic survival rather than choice. The home languages of these young bilinguals are often underutilized and frequently ignored in school. Thus, 'bilingual' education becomes a subtractive process in which pupils may lose aspects of competence in one language while attempting to gain competence in another.

A word of caution is in order here. Rather than categories or labels to attach to specific programmes, we believe the 'elite/folk' distinction is more useful for understanding the conditions in which programmes develop and function, and in which pupils live and study. Elite conditions are generally associated with greater opportunities to complete more years of formal schooling and greater access to multimedia and internet technology (in and outside school). The world knowledge that results from these extra years at school and greater access to knowledge through digital technology is more likely to lead to success in learning environments in which academic performance in an additional language is required. In other words, it is not (a certain kind of) education that leads to academic success but the wider context in which bilingual and multilingual programmes are situated.

## 8.5  INTEGRATING THE FRAMEWORKS

The wide range of practices we've reviewed above reflects the fact that bilingual and multilingual programmes are not only linguistic and learning endeavours, but also political and economic arrangements, a point we return to in Chapter 14. In response to this complexity, applied linguists need to be able to understand programmes of bilingual and multilingual education from the multiple and overlapping perspectives of language, content and context, with special attention to global and local situations.

Essentially, we can think of bilingual and multilingual programmes as being organized along one or more of three primary orientations:

■  language as problem;
■  language as right;
■  language as resource.

As we saw in Chapter 5, the notion of language orientations was proposed by Richard Ruiz (1984) as a tool for thinking about how languages are perceived and employed in language planning efforts. So, for example, a dominant world language

Table 8.1  Some major features of bilingual education programmes

| Type of programme | Support for L1 | Elite/folk | Primary orientation |
|---|---|---|---|
| Submersion | None | Folk | Language as problem |
| Transitional | Temporary, until dominant language is mastered | Typically folk | Language as right |
| Maintenance | Strong, although mixed access to quality materials and well-trained teachers | Mixed | Language as right and resource |
| One-way immersion | Varies, but L1 not denigrated or threatened | Typically elite | Language as resource |
| Two-way immersion/ dual | Strong | Elite/folk | Language as resource |
| Community language teaching | Strong, particularly at secondary level | Folk | Language as resource |
| Heritage language education | Pupils' L1 is often a dominant language | Elite/folk | Language as resource |

like English is considered inherently desirable in many places and is therefore usually welcomed as a valuable resource for teaching and learning, alone or in combination with other languages, such as in French immersion programmes for English speakers in Canada. In contrast, in many education contexts minority and less prestigious languages are viewed as problems. Arguments against using them in schools vary – it is claimed that bilingual education in these languages is expensive (in terms of the costs of books, course materials and teacher education) or politically divisive. But when speakers of minority languages appeal to governments or to UNESCO's International Declaration of Human Rights and other international policy statements that recognize the rights of peoples to be educated in a language they understand, they are advocating for bilingual and multilingual education on the basis of language as a right, like the Soweto youth we read about it in Chapter 7.  **www.8.8**

Table 8.1 attempts to correlate some of the main features of bilingual and multilingual education discussed in this section, combining insights from each of our three conceptual frameworks.

## 8.6  CHARACTERISTICS OF EFFECTIVE PROGRAMMES

Applied linguists are often asked whether bilingual and multilingual education works and what makes programmes successful. We hope to have made clear that answers to this question will depend greatly on the expectations placed on individual programmes. For example, programmes following the tenets of CLIL are likely to be concerned with the integration of language and content and with the learner's development of both. In contrast, as we have seen, submersion and transitional bilingual programmes in the US have as a primary aim the assimilation of pupils into

English language instruction. Using this limited criterion, a school that places speakers of other languages into English-only instruction would be judged a success, despite possibly negative implications for academic failure and language loss that many educators and applied linguists view as unacceptable. The same programme, evaluated using any or all of the criteria of advanced academic bilingualism, biliteracy (or multiliteracy) and intercultural understanding for all learners would likely be judged a failure.

Conversely, two-way immersion, community language teaching and heritage language programmes typically set forth more ambitious goals. In addition to learning a new *language*, bilingually schooled children are simultaneously expected to master *subject matter* material, such as history, science and maths, to the same degree and often at the same rate as children whose first language is used for instruction. Increasingly, they must show evidence of their achievement via standardized tests designed for native speakers of the dominant language, a game that educational linguists have likened to 'chasing a moving target' (Cummins, 2009, p. 24). And, whether they are bilingually schooled or not, all children who come to the dominant language through the avenue of schooling simultaneously grapple with the intangibles of the dominant culture, or at least enough of it to be able to get along in institutions operating with rules and understandings that may be very different from their home culture.

Our reading of the research on bilingual and multilingual education suggests that the most effective programmes are those that have the support and involvement of students, families and teachers, and in these exceptional cases individual programmes develop and adopt practices that best fit their needs. Ultimately, then, responsible answers about the effectiveness of education via two or more languages are possible only after close examination of individual programmes to ensure that their objectives recognize and reflect local realities and stakeholder expectations. With this caveat, some key features of successful programmes can be offered here:

- All pupils learn best in a language they understand. Programmes that teach children in a language or languages they comprehend have a greater chance of success, particularly as regards subject matter learning.
- Teacher preparation – in terms of language proficiency, the ability to teach content in both languages and sensitivity to local language ideologies – is fundamental.
- School autonomy is a condition for success. Rules and expectations developed for monolingual schools are generally unsuitable for bilingual and multilingual programmes.
- Parents and other care-givers, teachers, administrators and school staff should be in agreement about providing support for advanced bilingualism and, especially, should have respect for the minority language.
- Programmes should challenge students to work at high academic levels, because low expectations don't foster academic success in any language.

## 8.7  ROLES FOR APPLIED LINGUISTS

This final section suggests ways that applied linguists can contribute to successful bilingual and multilingual teaching and learning, both in and out of school settings.

## In schools

Around the world, finding sufficient numbers of linguistically proficient and well-trained language professionals poses a critical challenge to the success of bilingual and multilingual schooling. In addition to the obvious need for classroom teachers, programmes may require:

- bilingual assistants for monolingual teachers;
- writers and designers able to produce curriculums, forms of assessment, and print and digital materials in non-dominant languages;
- school administrators able to communicate the special needs of bilingual learners to those education and public authorities which regard monolingualism and monolingual schooling as 'normal' and bilingual or multilingual learners as something of a mystery or a nuisance.

For applied linguists working in these positions, it is important to acknowledge from the outset that the majority of colleagues, administrators and parents are not applied linguists (yet), which means that the fundamentals of bilingualism, language acquisition and other aspects of applied linguistics, however clear and compelling to you, may be neither to your uninitiated counterparts and other stakeholders. However, your knowledge, training and experience in applied linguistics can support school-based efforts on behalf of language pluralism. For example, an applied linguistics background would allow you to identify where, and be able to explain why, certain materials are linguistically troublesome, insensitive or otherwise inadequate to meet the specific needs of bilingual or multilingual pupils.

Likewise, applied linguists understand that language proficiency in itself is not the same thing as intelligence, and that second language speakers often have difficulty with measures of intelligence and school readiness that have been designed for native-speaking students or students who are speakers of a different variety of the target language (see dead ends 6 and 7 in Chapter 1, pp. 10 and 11). Applied linguists working in bilingual and multilingual programmes can help ensure that judgements of pupils' abilities are based on cognitive or developmental assessments rather than on language proficiency (recall section 7.4; and see Chapter 13). Applied linguists should also be able to scrutinize the participation of non-dominant language speakers in special programmes for students with learning difficulties (where they are often over-represented) and in classes for gifted and talented youth (where they may be under-represented). By identifying which learners truly require and can benefit from special services, applied linguists can contribute to the education of linguistically diverse learners.

## Outside schools

Not all applied linguists are classroom teachers or work in schools, of course, but there are also valuable contributions that they can make with the remit of informing the education profession and the general public. Conducting and reporting research on bilingualism in non-scholarly forums is particularly important, because the results of research on bilingualism and learning in actual programmes too rarely find their way into public discourse on, or policy about, bilingual and multilingual education. This is not because pertinent research is not being done – it is arguably one of the richest areas of exploration by applied linguists. Rather, because school programmes for multilingual pupils are typically designed and run by educators and administrators who lack applied linguistics knowledge, they are often conceived and operated under the influence of the anti-bilingual 'dead ends' we deconstructed in Chapter 1. Thus, as practised in many places, the schooling of bilingual and multilingual children seems to ignore and even resist evidence that researchers find compelling, and stakeholders often base decisions (about which languages to use, for which subject areas, at what points in the curriculum, etc.) more on issues of power and identity than on matters of instruction or pedagogy. Walt Wolfram, a sociolinguist who has written extensively about linguistic and cultural diversity in education, tells a story that exemplifies this problem. After giving a workshop on dialect diversity for teachers, he was approached by one of the participants, who reminded him that he had done a similar workshop in the very same school on the topic nearly twenty years before. Wolfram recalls:

> the startling revelation was not my forgetfulness, but the fact that there was no indication from the responses of the participants that my earlier workshop had any effect on the perspective or the policy of the school with respect to dialect diversity . . . While the teachers understood the need to be tolerant and respectful of different cultures and the diverse ways of speaking represented by their students, they firmly insisted that their primary if not exclusive task as educators was to get their students to speak 'correct', 'proper', or 'Standard English' – and that any compromise of this objective was at best frivolous and at worst misguided education.
>
> (Wolfram, 2010, p. 129)

We end with the observation that, to be truly 'applied', research and practice in bilingual and multilingual schooling must include thoughtful consideration of how to address educators and members of the public accustomed to viewing education and language from different, often conflicting, perspectives. As Wolfram and others have noted, this will require great patience and persistence. The stakes are too high to do otherwise.

1   Type the words *bilingual education*, *multilingual education* and *news* into an internet search engine and read some of the reports concerned with bilingual education in your country or another region you are interested in. How do the objectives of these programmes fit those described in section 8.1? Do the reports provide enough detailed information to allow you to find a match with the types of programmes outlined in this chapter? Are the reports mainly positive or negative about the purposes and outcomes of bilingual and multilingual education? What sort of evidence do the reports' authors provide for their claims about programme effectiveness? How do these views compare to the ideas about bilingual and multilingual education we've seen in Chapter 8?

2   Create a brief bilingual education profile for yourself using the following questions:

(a)  How would you describe your own language education to date, in terms of the points discussed in this chapter?

(b)  At what age and in what conditions were you first exposed to instruction in an additional language? Did it change the ways you were taught in your L1?

(c)  What was the purpose of the additional language programme and what language expectations did you and your parents/family have when you began? How were these expectations the same as or different from what your teachers expected you to learn?

(d)  Have you become as bilingual or multilingual as you intended?

(e)  What do you think that you, your family or your teachers might have done differently in terms of promoting bilingualism or multilingualism?

When your profile is complete, consider sharing it with colleagues or other members of your class. How do their experiences with bilingual and multilingual education differ from yours?

3   In this chapter we discuss some of the common arrangements by which bilingual education programmes are known (*mother-tongue, home language instruction, community language teaching, heritage language education,* etc.), but there are many others. Make a list of the ways in which bilingual students are taught in your community or city and the featured languages of instruction. What are the advantages and disadvantages of each, in your opinion?

4   Imagine that you are a candidate for a teaching position at a primary school in a multilingual city with a rapidly growing immigrant population. During the job interview, the headteacher (school principal) asks you to share your philosophy of educating learners whose home language is different from the language of instruction. What can you say that will convince her that your background in applied linguistics has prepared you for this important task?

## FURTHER READING

Baker, C. and García, O. (eds) (2007). *Bilingual education: An introductory reader.* Clevedon, UK: Multilingual Matters.

Creese, A. and Martin, P. (eds) (2003). *Multilingual classroom ecologies: Inter-relationships, interactions and ideologies.* Clevedon, UK: Multilingual Matters.

García, O. (2009). *Bilingual education in the 21st century: A global perspective.* Oxford: Wiley-Blackwell.

Ovando, C. and Combs, M. C. (2010). *Bilingual and ESL classrooms*, 5th edn. Boston: McGraw-Hill.

Skuttnab-Kangas, T., Phillipson, R., Mohanti, A. K. and Panda, M. (eds) (2009). *Social justice through multilingual education.* Clevedon, UK: Multilingual Matters.

Wei, L. and Moyer, M. (eds) (2008). *The Blackwell handbook of research methods on bilingualism and multilingualism.* Oxford: Blackwell.

# CHAPTER 9

# Additional language education

> Who this booke shall wylle lerne may well entreprise or take on honde marchan-
> dises fro one lande to anothir, and to knowe many wares which to hym shal be good
> to be bougt or solde for riche to become. Lerne this book diligently; grete prouffyt
> lieth therein truly.
>
>     (Anyone who wishes to study this book will have business success in inter-
> national trade. It has all the key terms and phrases you will need for the goods you
> are buying and selling, goods that will make you rich. Get this book and you are
> guaranteed great profit.)
>
> (William Caxton, c. 1483; an early example of a<br>publisher's blurb for an English–French phrasebook)

Since the origins of the discipline in the 1950s, the area of applied linguistics which has received most attention from both scholars and practitioners is without doubt that of additional language education. Early applied linguists working in language education looked to linguistics and to psychological theories of learning for solutions to the practical problem of how and what to teach. Despite (or perhaps because of) the failure to solve the problem of how to learn an additional language, a broader, more complex discipline has gradually emerged.

Additional language learners, teachers and researchers (some of us are all three) continue to think about the problem of *what* bits of which variety of the language to learn (or teach) and *how* best to learn (or teach) these bits. In English language teaching, the World Englishes movement is challenging teachers and learners to think carefully about their target variety (what to learn/teach). As the number of speakers of English as an additional language continues to grow and communication between them increases (Graddol, 2006), learners in China, for example, may prefer to be taught by a speaker of Indian English, as a more relevant (and possibly cheaper) alternative to a speaker of American or British English (D'Mello, 2004). Teachers of languages other than English are also exploring the question of target variety; for an example, recall the Somali student Mohamud learning French in Montreal in Chapter 7; or see Tew (2004) on the teaching of Moroccan French to secondary school pupils in the UK with special educational needs. As for the question of how *best* to learn (or teach), the search is still on, though the relevant research is more likely to be conducted on and in specific learning contexts, even specific classrooms, by teachers engaged in action research, rather than with large groups of randomly selected students specially convened for the purposes of an experiment.

 **www.9.1**

 **www.9.2**

 **www.9.3**

Before introducing the contexts in which additional languages are learned, we'll defend the terms we use for this chapter's topic: *additional*, instead of *second*

or *foreign*, and *education*, instead of *learning* or *teaching*. The use of *second* or *foreign* involves issues of scholarly convention, theory and sociopolitical context (as discussed in section 9.1), so we use *additional* because it encompasses both. And language *teaching* tells only half the story: learning can happen without teaching. In fact, teaching is often just a catalyst for self-directed learning, and in many cases people learn languages despite teaching. *Education* includes both learning and teaching and implies other things that may have an impact on additional language learning: government policy, the educational materials publishing business, folk beliefs about the personal and professional benefits of language learning; and so on. It is specifically classroom-based learning, rather than additional language acquisition in general, that we aim to explore here, though if you are interested in this related field (usually known as second language acquisition, or SLA), we have

**www.9.4**

a brief introduction to some of the main themes on our companion website and two SLA-related suggestions for further reading at the end of this chapter (p. 219). On balance, we think that additional language education is the best description of our topic.

Bearing in mind that the big questions for additional language education are still *what* and *how*, we begin this chapter by taking a step back to look at the contexts of language learning (section 9.1). Then we move on to the question of *how*, including the problem of method (9.2) and the issue of individual learner differences (9.3). Next we look at the question of *what*, including assessment (9.4) and, finally, we consider some of the economic, cultural and political aspects of additional language education (9.5).

## 9.1 CONTEXTS OF ADDITIONAL LANGUAGE EDUCATION

Additional languages are learned in a wide variety of circumstances, which we may define according to overlapping clusters of factors. Perhaps the most significant of these are the following quartet: place, age, manner and purpose.

### Place

Starting with place, let's think about how the experience of learning a language is partially conditioned by cultural geography, as we observed in Chapter 2: Japanese, for example, is primarily learned as a foreign language in locations where the main language is not Japanese, for example in Pakistan or France; it is learned as a second language in locations where it is a principal language of the surrounding community, namely in Japan. This is not just a technicality. Here are some typical fundamental differences between the two contexts.

In an instructed foreign language (FL) situation, it's likely that all learners will share a common mother tongue (L1), since they will typically come to a local classroom from a single location. In a second language (SL) environment, however, it is distinctly possible that a wide variety of L1s will be represented in the classroom, since what identifies the learner is her need for the local language: she may be an immigrant, or be combining language learning with a short holiday in a country where the target language is spoken, and her classmates may come from many different language backgrounds.

In an FL context, exposure to the target language, and hence learning and practice opportunities, will typically be restricted to classroom meeting times and homework sessions. In the SL context, however, the wider community (at least outside the immigrant learner's immediate neighbourhood) may speak only the target language, and thus the learner will have many more opportunities, as well as possible pressures, to learn the new language. Indeed, SL learning may be a matter of national identity, economic opportunity, of conflict or of pride, whereas FL learning can typically be more an individual process, undertaken as an optional part of schooling, for example, or for personal growth, or to prepare for work or travel to places where the target language is spoken.

In FL contexts, it is more likely that a learner's L1 will be used as a vehicle for learning and teaching, since teachers and other learners are likely to be speakers of the same language. Most internationally distributed teaching and testing materials for English, however, assume an SL context, are written solely in the target language and are published by a small number of big UK and US publishing companies. Where such materials are used by teachers in FL contexts, some of the cultural markers of groups living in those particular places become embedded in the language learning experience.

One domain in which cultural geography is perhaps less central to the task of additional language learning is the World Wide Web. Resources for online language learners designed to give students practice in listening, reading, grammar and vocabulary have proliferated in the last decade, and speaking and writing practice has been made much easier by blogging (and other web-based writing formats) and internet telephony. Until very recently, such resources have been only superficially place-based (for example a webpage which uses the Union Jack to mark a programme aimed at students and teachers wishing to learn and teach British English), but even the disembodied domain of the internet is now being mapped through the creation of virtual 'villages', 'islands' and other spaces for language learning (for example in *Second Life*, a virtual world in which more than 30,000 users were logged on at any one time in 2008).

# Age

Turning now to age, we might recall the reference to a biologically determined 'critical age' for language learning in Chapters 1 and 3. There we pointed out that although children may be better equipped in biological terms for learning an additional language, they may lack the attention span, motivation, social strategies and confidence that some adults are able to deploy. We'll have more to say about the individual outcomes of additional language learning in section 9.3, but for the moment let's settle the related terminological issue raised at the beginning of the chapter: the difference between **acquisition** and **learning**. The former term has been used most in the context of the unconscious, dedicated cognitive processes by which linguistic knowledge and abilities unfold in infancy on the basis of input from the environment. Language development in this sense is innately driven, resembling the ability to walk on two feet or the ability to recognize individual faces,

**Acquisition** is the mental process by which knowledge and/or behaviour emerges naturally on the basis of innate predisposition and/or triggers from environmental input (e.g. walking on two feet). **Learning**, on the other hand, requires conscious effort and leads to skills which cannot be part of our genetic make-up (e.g. walking on stilts).

which emerge very early in life. Language *learning*, on the other hand, has been used to refer to the consciously deployed general problem-solving processes used in the kind of language study typically undertaken by adults (Krashen, 1981; Bley-Vroman, 1989).

Given that (1) the learning/acquisition distinction is still a hypothesis, rather than an indisputable fact; and (2) *learning* is the more general of the two terms in non-technical usage; and (3) applied linguists can in any case influence deliberate learning processes more than they can unconscious, automatic acquisition, we prefer to use the adjective *learning* to label here the process of coming to know and use an L2, irrespective of age.

## Manner

The third factor, manner, refers to *how* additional languages have been learned and taught in different places and different times. While scholarly research on additional language education (in the field commonly known as second language acquisition) may have influenced practice in many contexts from the second half of the twentieth century onwards, other significant factors have always included more practical issues, such as:

- teachers' and learners' *beliefs* about teaching and learning (including, for example, the benefits of drilling, the best way to teach grammar or whether and how to correct students' mistakes);
- the availability of well-trained *teachers*;
- the availability of *resources* (for example: class size and classroom furniture; number and origin of textbooks and study materials for students; access to learning technologies such as a photocopier, an audio/video player, a computer, the internet);
- achievement and proficiency *tests*, where practice test exercises are used in lessons or as part of independent study.

We return to manner, and the problem of method, in section 9.2.

## Purpose

And finally purpose. An example of what we mean here can be found in the metaphor of 'command and demand' motivations for English language education (Maguire, 1996). Command-motivated programmes are those in which the state or national curriculum obliges students in government schools to study in a particular language or languages. In contrast, programmes motivated by demand are privately organized and funded, market-driven schools that arise and thrive where individuals want language-in-education services that are not provided by government schools and colleges. Here's an example from one Indonesian city, Bandung (population around two million). Command-motivated programmes require English, Sundanese (the regional language of West Java) and an additional language, usually Mandarin, as compulsory primary and secondary school subjects. Demand-motivated programmes are offered by private primary and secondary schools teaching core subjects, such as science and mathematics, in English. There are also numerous privately owned English language schools, for children and teenagers who learn the language in the hope that their school marks or future prospects may be bettered, business people who attend classes as part of a compulsory in-service training programme or voluntarily after work, and students hoping to study at a university in another country. Finally, as in most countries, there are many freelance language teachers offering a wide range of languages for one-to-one tuition.

Place, age, manner and purpose are four of the many overlapping and interacting variables in any additional language learning context. Of these variables, manner, the subject of section 9.2, is perhaps of greatest interest to researchers and practitioners alike.

## 9.2  THE PROBLEM OF METHOD

Changes in methods for teaching languages are underpinned by the assumption that the fragments of language we teach, and the way in which we teach them, facilitate (or, put more strongly, *cause*) learning. Not only do methods facilitate learning, the assumption goes, but some methods are better at facilitating learning than others. Indeed, if we could only find it, there would be a 'best' method, a method that would 'fix' the language learning problems of all those students who currently struggle to get anywhere with a second language. In an attempt to discover this 'best method', a number of research projects (often referred to now as the 'methods comparison studies') were conducted in the 1960s against a backdrop of enthusiasm for the latest development in educational technology, the language laboratory. The methods comparison studies aimed to find out whether **audiolingual** methods, with an emphasis on listening and speaking, were more effective than traditional **grammar translation** methods. The findings of one study of almost 1,800 US schoolchildren learning French and German are typical: children taught an additional language over a period of two years using 'new' audiolingual methods were no better at listening, speaking or writing, and worse at reading, than their peers who had been taught using traditional methods. The study concludes that differences in classroom methodology are not associated with difference in attainment and that language labs are unlikely to be cost effective, given that they were not shown to accelerate learning and that there were cheaper ways of recording students (Smith and Baranyi, 1968).

Despite the failure of the methods comparison studies to provide evidence for an association between method and attainment, the lure of the 'best' method continued to exert its influence over subsequent decades of educators. For a vivid example, look on YouTube for the short extract from the television documentary *A Child's Guide to Language* (BBC, 1983). In the extract, James Asher, an early proponent of the **Total Physical Response** (TPR) method, suggests that it will, in future, make it feasible for pupils to leave primary school with three or four additional languages, which could then be 'fine-tuned' for grammar, reading and writing at secondary school. More than twenty-five years after this documentary was made, the promise of TPR, and of a 'best' method in general, has not been realized. Indeed, the very idea that there is a single, best method that will facilitate learning

The **audiolingual** method of teaching an additional language is characterized by repeated oral grammar drills and the outlawing of the L1. Maximilian Berlitz was a pioneer, using the method to teach French and German in the USA. But over 130 years later the company he started now favours a less rigid learning regime.

The **grammar translation** method of teaching an additional language focuses on memorization of L2 grammatical rules and translation of texts from the L2 into the L1. The method's origins lie in the European tradition of teaching schoolchildren the great works of ancient Greek and Latin.

 **www.9.5**

 **www.9.6**

**Total Physical Response** (TPR) is the compelling name given by James Asher to the additional language teaching method he developed.

It attempts to recreate for learners the conditions of first language acquisition by getting them to listen and respond with appropriate physical action to spoken instructions. They do this for an extensive period before attempting to speak themselves.

in widely varying teaching situations is falling out of fashion (although not always out of practice) and has gradually been replaced with a concern for the unique characteristics of individual learners and classrooms, discussed in more detail in the sections that follow.

## What is a method?

The word *method* has been variously defined (for example Pennycook, 1989; Prabhu, 1990). Figure 9.1 shows one way of conceptualizing the components of a method and their relationship with each other. In this model, *method* is an umbrella term that includes an *approach* (based on theories of language and language learning), a *design* (the organization of the teaching laid down in syllabi and lesson plans) and a *procedure* (what happens in the classroom). Describing a lesson using this model can help teachers to externalize their beliefs about language and learning, as well as to examine the consistency of what course documents say about a method (its approach and design) and the realization of the method in the classroom (the procedure). So, as a descriptive tool, the model is quite useful. However, there is a danger here of appearing to claim that all a teacher (or a syllabus or coursebook writer) needs to do is to assemble her chosen method, based on the framework above, apply it to any teaching situation and, hey presto, her students will learn in the optimal manner. In reality, pre-existing variables will all interact with the method to shape how teaching and learning actually take place: the students' expectations of classroom language learning, the size of the room, the climate, the perceived status of the teacher, the importance attached to assessment, the degree of surveillance of teachers' practice by managers or inspectors, etc., will all conspire to create specific local contexts in which methods must be shaped. It is this relationship between learning contexts and teaching methods that provides the backdrop for the rest of this section.

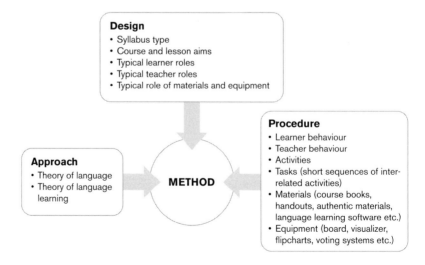

Figure 9.1   What is a method? (adapted from Richards and Rodgers, 2001, p. 33)

# Appropriate methods in different contexts

Bearing in mind that contexts of additional language learning vary according to the place and manner in which learning takes place, should language teachers be looking for the most appropriate *fit* between a (variety of) method(s) and their teaching context? What would looking for a 'best fit' involve anyway? At least the following:

- acknowledging that no single method or combination of methods has been comprehensively validated by research;
- attempting to understand students' (and possibly parents' and school managers') expectations of their teacher, the methods and the learning outcomes;
- considering the feasibility of the method (does it require any special equipment, a large teaching space, noisy group work in an otherwise quiet learning environment?);
- becoming aware of the assumptions about language and learning that underpin the method;
- thinking through any messages conveyed by the method about language communities, the students' (lack of) participation in these communities and the possible social and economic consequences of this.

Writers in the critical pedagogy tradition have strongly suggested that it is the responsibility of all language teachers, including those working in the context where they themselves learned, to think very carefully about their own cultural, social and political contexts and how these influence their beliefs and classroom practices – and also to encourage their students to do the same (Canagarajah, 1999; Pennycook, 1994b; Phillipson, 1992, 2009).

Three final cautions. First, generalizations about regions, countries, speakers of a language and even specific groups of students are inevitably inaccurate. Differences *within* groups of students mean that providing the 'best fit' between context and method involves using a *variety* of methods, in the belief (or hope) that some will be appropriate for some students some of the time. Second, such eclecticism must be principled, and the effects of the method on students carefully evaluated. Finally, it is important to remind ourselves that what some authors have pointed to as the 'unravelling' or 'decomposition' of certainties about additional language teaching (Larsen-Freeman and Freeman, 2008) might not be welcomed by everyone, for example by novice teachers or traditionally minded supervisors and students. A colleague of ours once wasted his students' time by asking them to write a sentence on a piece of paper suggesting how he could improve his teaching. To his dismay, all the pieces of paper he collected were blank, except one that said, 'Please wear a belt.' Where the value of talking to students about methods is unclear to them, our students might find it would be inappropriate (or pointless) to comment.

# 9.3  INDIVIDUAL LEARNER DIFFERENCES

Research in second language acquisition has highlighted some of the cognitive resources that all learners bring to the task of additional language learning, especially those developed during first language acquisition. One powerful resource is the mind's capacity to automatically assimilate new information into the networks of knowledge already stored in long-term memory. It is this ability that underlies universal processes of **cross-linguistic influence**, whereby first language features appear in the learner's developing second language (e.g. a 'foreign' accent). It is also reflected in the fact that translation between L2 and L1 is the inevitable process occurring in learners' minds in the beginner or intermediate classroom, whatever the teacher or the curriculum says about 'banning' L1 use (see Cook, 2010). But although there are commonalities across learners, they are normally beyond the reach of the classroom teacher and, in any case, are often positive in their effects. It is the *differences* between individual learners that present the greatest challenges for teachers.

Interest in the **individual differences** between language learners has been a feature of SLA studies since the 1960s. Early research on this topic took place in the field of language psychology, where, for example, attempts were made to understand the contribution of an 'aptitude' for learning additional languages – an attractive proposition for admissions boards and policy-makers hoping to avoid wasting money on those less likely to learn. In the 1970s, research into the 'good language learner' suggested that, in addition to 'who they are' (including what were considered 'fixed' qualities such as age, aptitude and motivation), 'what they do' also matters. Successful learners were those who used a range of learning techniques (strategies – like keeping vocabulary records and using memorization techniques) to help themselves learn. In this section, we return to the issue of age, and assess the contribution of aptitude, motivation and language learning strategies.

## Age

All of the individual learning differences discussed in this section interact with each other to some extent. Age, however, is probably the one which most affects all the others. The theory that there is a relationship between ultimate success in language attainment and age is known as the **critical period hypothesis** (CPH). Lenneberg (1967) suggested that, for reasons to do with the way the brain develops, the optimum age for language acquisition is between two years old and puberty. Most researchers now agree that there is a critical period for first language acquisition, though there is more controversy about the relationship between age and additional language acquisition, because of the difficulty of controlling for other possible factors. Research by Long (1988), however, suggests that the critical period for acquiring 'native-speaker'-like pronunciation is before the age of about six, and that 'native-speaker'-like grammar can be acquired up to the age of puberty. Consistent with Chomsky's theory of Universal Grammar, it seems that children have a mental toolkit for extracting regularities from linguistic input, which adults have lost.

Of course, the fact that many children are ultimately more successful at learning an additional language than most adults does not mean that adults are never successful learners, that *all* children are successful or that the best time to learn a new language is in primary school. Despite these important caveats, the idea of teaching an additional language to children has proved an irresistible one to policy-makers keen to promote multilingualism as a marketable advantage of their country or region, as we saw in Chapter 8. This policy preference is one manifestation of popular ideas about children being language 'sponges', as we discussed in Chapter 1.

Overall, research has shown that age is a critical factor in ultimate attainment in an additional language but that younger is not always better and that there are important intervening variables such as: access to quality instruction; informal opportunities for language input and production; motivation, time management and willingness to study; other languages spoken, their influence on the additional language; and aptitude. These intervening variables make research findings about age difficult to generalize between different learning contexts.

## Aptitude

Like age, aptitude has proved an attractive individual difference to policy-makers tasked with making decisions about additional language education. Generally, language aptitude tests have been used to identify and exclude those students who are likely to make slower progress in learning an additional language than others. Dörnyei (2005) describes how aptitude tests were used in the 1920s and 1930s in the USA with the intention of improving the overall success of language teaching in schools by excluding from language classes those students who were predicted to learn at a slower rate. In the 1950s and 1960s, when two widely used tests, the Modern Language Aptitude Test (MLAT) and the Pimsleur Language Aptitude Battery (DeKeyser and Juffs, 2005), were developed, the rationale for testing was the same: how to maximize the cost-effectiveness of additional language education.

What exactly language aptitude is has long been a matter of debate. One of the originators of the MLAT, John Carroll (1981), has described language aptitude as a combination of:

- phonetic coding ability (being able to distinguish between different sounds and remember them);
- grammatical sensitivity (being able to work out what each word is for in a sentence);
- rote learning ability (memorization);
- inductive language learning ability (being able to identify patterns or relationships of meaning or form).

Scholars currently working in the field of language aptitude are debating whether working memory (where information is initially processed and temporarily stored) may be one, or even the most important, component of language aptitude (Robinson, 2002).

Most schools around the world are unlikely to be able to afford the language aptitude tests that are commercially available. Anyway, for teachers, proficiency is probably of more interest than aptitude: they may be able to move between classes students who are not at the 'right level', but they are unlikely to be able to exclude students altogether for being hopeless learners. Many language teachers are, however, interested in the related area of cognitive **learning styles**, and although scholars continue to disagree about what learning styles are and even whether they exist, many teachers try to plan lessons with a variety of activity types to appeal to different learners (for example, so-called visual learners versus experiential learners). Finally, for some language education planners and managers, aptitude continues to be an appealing concept. The US Department of Defense, for example, uses aptitude testing to decide which of its new recruits will be trained as military linguists. Other users include: intelligence agencies and religious organizations, to identify the candidates most likely to be successful learners of the new language(s) needed for international posting as spies and missionaries; educational psychologists who are working with students who have failed in efforts to learn an additional language; and school managers who wish to select students for an accelerated language learning programme.

**Learning styles** are the different approaches people are believed to take to the acquisition of new information. The popular distinctions between 'visual' and 'tactile' learners, or between 'thinkers' and 'doers', illustrate the concept. Some scholars believe that if learners can identify their preferred style(s) they will be able to optimize their learning. Decide for yourself using North Carolina State University's online *Index of Learning Styles* questionnaire.

**www.9.8**

## Motivation

Ask any language teacher what makes a successful language learner and you will probably hear 'good motivation'. Ask the students on the other hand, and you might hear that the key to success is a teacher who motivates them! Where motivation comes from, what it is and what kinds of motivation are the most helpful in language learning have been a matter for discussion in social and educational psychology and applied linguistics for at least half a century.

In research that continues to influence the ideas of language teachers today, Robert Gardner, a social psychologist, together with his students and associates, developed a framework for linking the reasons people learn additional languages with their success in learning. Conducted in Canada, this research used attitude questionnaires to measure the strength of what was conceived of as an individual, mind-based phenomenon. Gardner (1985) suggested that for some learners the desire to become part of a target-language-speaking community (**integrative orientation**; see Figure 9.2) was more strongly associated with success, while for others the usefulness of the target language within the learner's own community was more effective (**instrumental orientation**). Other research in educational psychology, mainly conducted outside Canada in the 1990s, developed the concepts of **intrinsic** and **extrinsic motivation**, self-confidence and effectiveness, as well as the situation-specific motivations associated, for example, with feelings about the teacher, the course and fellow students. Research methods included the measurement of learners' actual classroom behaviour (rather than asking them to complete surveys, as Gardner and his colleagues had done), including: observing attention spans, choice of tasks and changing levels of participation in groups and whole-class work.

More recently, research using learners' verbal reports of their behaviour and attitudes has led to greater emphasis on the interaction between reasons for wanting to learn, the strength of the desire to learn, the kind of person a learner is and the specific situation she finds herself in. Dörnyei's (2001, 2005) concept of

**Integrative** and **instrumental orientations** to additional language learning result in different types of motivation to learn. Learners may desire to learn the language to integrate themselves into the community of L2 speakers or to use it as an *instrument* for some other benefit. An example of the former would be someone who learns Arabic after converting to Islam. An example of the latter would be someone who learns Arabic in order to win a contract to build a mosque.

Figure 9.2   Integrative motivation reinforced for an Italian immigrant to the USA in 1918
(Source: National Geographic)

Additional language learners have **intrinsic motivation** when the process itself is perceived as rewarding (for example the intellectual satisfaction they may gain from fathoming a complex verb conjugation). They have **extrinsic motivation** when success provides external rewards or is coerced (for example when they need to learn the conjugation in order to pass a test).

a second language 'motivational self system' proposes three main sources of the motivation to learn a language: the learner's vision of him/herself as an effective user of the additional language; social pressures on the learner to succeed or to discourage success; and positive learning experiences.

Many of the ways in which many teachers already try to motivate their students are consistent with Dörnyei's concept. Depending on the learning context, they may include:

- creating a positive rapport with students by being friendly and interested in their learning, taking care to plan relevant, challenging lessons;
- observing which activities students seem to enjoy or work harder on than others;
- using examples in the class of interesting or famous target-language speakers and places where the target language is spoken;
- encouraging students to work towards tests as a way of recording progress;
- recommending self-study activities;
- playing songs and showing films in the target language;
- stressing the benefits of an additional language and the disadvantages of speaking only one language;
- creating a feeling of obligation to attend and participate in the class.

## Learning strategies

Individual learners seem to differ in how they go about learning additional languages; for example, some people like to make and memorize lists of words, others prefer to find or create situations in which they can speak the language, and others like to do both. When a learner chooses to do something that facilitates learning, this

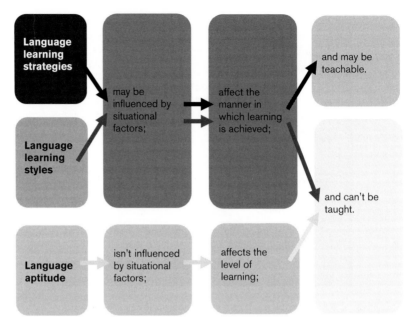

Figure 9.3   The relationship between language aptitude, language learning styles and language learning strategies

action is known as a learning strategy. What *causes* different learners to use different learning strategies, as well as how to classify and *measure* these strategies and whether they can and should be *taught* to learners, is, however, controversial. So why do learners seem to differ in their choice of learning strategies? Consciously chosen learning strategies are often presented as the surface manifestation of more stable, unconscious learning styles, part of individual cognition. Figure 9.3 illustrates some of these points, relating styles and strategies to aptitude.

How far learning strategies are related to cognitive factors and to what extent they are the approved learning behaviours that arise in interaction with a particular learning context or culture is not clear. In part because of this confusion over what strategies are, their measurement has also proved difficult. Measurement instruments have tended to rely on questionnaires which students themselves answer, introducing problems of self-awareness and social desirability bias. Whether teaching students to use new learning strategies is worthwhile is another cause of controversy, with reasons in favour including: increased self-awareness and ability to self-direct learning; arming students with a greater range of tactics for dealing with the demands of new learning situations; and providing the basis for a fun classroom discussion on themselves (everyone's favourite topic). On the other hand, reasons for not teaching students to use new learning strategies include: the impracticality of providing class time for learning strategies to suit all students, especially in large classes; the possibility that learners may already be using the learning strategies that suit them best and may not want to or be able to change; and the problem of not really knowing how learning strategies interact with other individual learner differences, including the possibility that the manner in which you learn may not affect your level of achievement.

Another group of strategies that it may be useful to draw students' attention to are **compensatory strategies** (Tarone, 2005). Compensatory (or simply communication) strategies are ways of talking that are aimed at avoiding misunderstanding (for example not mentioning or abandoning a problematic topic) and/or achieving understanding (for example monitoring for signs that the listener has understood, using a description or example of a thing where the specific word or phrase is not known). For information about the relevance of compensatory strategies for people with language-related disabilities, see Chapter 13.

## 9.4  ASSESSING ADDITIONAL LANGUAGES

Can language really be tested? To non-linguists, this might seem like a silly question. After all, job seekers routinely use test results to quantify their linguistic knowledge in some form or other (e.g. 'near-native speaker of Korean', 'reading knowledge of Portuguese', etc.). And governments around the world seek to assess whether immigrants and asylum seekers have sufficient knowledge of the host language(s) to be permitted entry and/or settlement (Shohamy and McNamara, 2009). People are taking countless different language tests around the world  which, like the compulsory College English Test for all university  students in China who wish to graduate, can make a huge difference to the life chances of the test-takers.

But what about applied linguists? Given increasing sophistication in appreciating the complexities of additional language use, can we truly measure with confidence and precision 'how much' or what aspects of a given language a person has attained? And, following our deconstruction of 'language' in Chapter 2 and discussion of standards and varieties throughout this book, which 'Chinese' or 'English' would we expect learners to show they know? For applied linguists, then, the question 'Can language *really* be tested?' presents a serious challenge. Some linguists claim that the additional language knowledge cannot be measured by tests at all (Troike, 1983), but rather only through regularly observing, over time, the real-life tasks that learners perform in the language they are learning (order a takeaway meal by telephone, write a job application letter, read an applied linguistics textbook), avoiding the kind of decontextualized assessment that we come back to in Chapter 13. An informed and honest answer to the question of whether language proficiency can be reliably and validly measured is probably 'not really' or 'not very easily'. Despite this, as we'll explore in this section, a large and powerful language testing industry has developed to meet the (perceived) needs of individuals and institutions to establish what learners 'know' about additional languages. In this section, we take the position that assessment is a necessary fiction that both we, as additional language teachers, and our students maintain through our daily practice.

The aim of additional language assessment is to judge attainment using, for example, a test, a learning journal, project work, a portfolio, observation or peer- and self-assessment. What makes additional language assessment interesting to applied linguists is the interaction between its psychological and social aspects, including ongoing debate on questions such as:

- What should (and shouldn't) language assessment measure (the **construct**)?
- How should learners be made to demonstrate the construct being measured?

Speakers use **compensatory strategies** when linguistic interaction is compromised in some way, because one or more of the interlocutors lacks relevant linguistic knowledge or ability. For example, circumlocution can compensate for word-finding difficulties.

A **construct** in testing is the ability, skill or knowledge that the test is (supposedly) testing.

■ How should this demonstration be quantified and measured in a way that doesn't distort the construct and is understandable to the public?

■ How can tools be developed so that learners can assess their own attainment?

■ How should (especially large-scale) assessment be organized fairly and efficiently?

■ What are the consequences of testing for learners in their ongoing learning and general life chances?

Although there is no current consensus on the best answers, anyone who is interested in creating an additional language assessment, or in using assessment scores to make decisions about users of additional languages must be prepared to consider these questions. In this section, we'll review some possible answers to the first and the last of our questions, as the ones which have generated the most recent debate. We'll finish with some thoughts on ways in which the questions might interact with each other in complex and intractable ways.

## Reasons for testing and models of language

So, what should (and shouldn't) language assessment measure? Your answer will partly depend on your reason for testing in the first place. Possible reasons for testing include:

■ *Placement*: to match a learner's current level of knowledge with an appropriately challenging course.

■ *Diagnostics*: to find out what a learner knows and doesn't know, perhaps to provide input into the design of a course or plan individualized instruction.

■ *Achievement*: to find out which of the planned learning outcomes of a course have been met by a learner. Achievement tests can usually be 'passed' or 'failed' and are sometimes used to decide whether a student is allowed to continue to the next level of proficiency, while on other occasions they can be used to motivate learners by providing proof of progress.

■ *Proficiency*: to get a general idea of a learners' current knowledge of the language. Proficiency tests may be 'pass or fail' where they are part of a suite of tests, like the five Cambridge ESOL General English exams. Other proficiency tests, like the International English Language Testing System (IELTS) or the Test of English as a Foreign Language (TOEFL), are not pass or fail tests but are scored at different levels (e.g. from non-user to expert, low to high or weak to strong). Although such tests are not marked on a pass or fail scale, a candidate who fails to achieve the score required for university entry or immigration purposes will most likely feel she has failed the test.

Of course, two or more of the reasons for testing mentioned above can be combined in a single test. For example, a test might be used to place students in a suitable class *and* show the teacher what the student does and doesn't know. Or, to show which learning outcomes have been achieved *and* diagnose which ones haven't (and so need to be addressed through instruction or covered in subsequent courses). While your answer to the question 'What should (and shouldn't) language assessment measure?' will partly depend on your reason for testing, as we suggested above, it will also depend upon your model of language, that is, the language feature(s) or abilities that you are actually aiming to assess. One way to look at proficiency levels, then, is to see them as based on definitions of ability, performance, interaction and hierarchical frameworks.

## Ethics and the consequences of testing

The last on our list of 'must-ask' questions was 'What are the consequences of testing for learners in their ongoing learning and general life chances?' This question raises the important issue of ethics in testing. Up until about twenty years ago, a fair assessment was generally considered to be one that was *valid* (measures what it says it measures, its **construct validity**) and *reliable* (produces consistent results between test-takers and across multiple administrations of the same test). More recently, however, the concept of validity has been broadened beyond that of a test-internal measure to include consideration of the social, educational and political contexts of tests, and the problems that assessment might cause. Issues include:

- the positive or negative effect **(washback)** of the assessment on the test-takers' learning;
- the kind of test-taker for whom the assessment is (un)suitable;
- the myth that there is one form of the language being assessed and that there are 'correct' and 'incorrect' versions of this language;
- how the method of assessment (including the interlocutor in a speaking test) might affect test-takers' scores;
- the uses to which the results of the assessment will be put, including whether they will limit the test-takers' access to opportunities for self-improvement and whether the test-takers are aware of this;
- the creation of a lucrative market for tests, test preparation materials and test preparation courses;
- whether it's possible to avoid the results of additional language assessments being confounded by intervening variables such as socioeconomic status, perseverance, conformity, test practice, peer or parental influence, background knowledge of the topic, etc. (Shohamy, 2001; McNamara and Roever, 2006).

It's not altogether clear how additional language assessment will deal with the serious ethical issues that a broader concept of validity has drawn our attention to. Where assessment decisions are made by language teachers, in conjunction with their students, innovative forms of assessment that are supportive of learning are likely to emerge. Less supportive might be the decisions made by the commercial organizations that organize and profit from large-scale testing (useful though their services are to the gate-keepers of opportunities for study and work).

**Construct validity** refers to how well some measurement system correlates with the construct it is designed to measure. You might, for example, have an opinion on the construct validity of the online *Index of Learning Styles* questionnaire, which uses multiple questions with two-option answers to assess your learning styles on four scales.

 **www.9.9**

In testing, **washback** refers to the positive and negative effects of testing on learning and teaching. So, for example, tests might boost self-confidence if they give learners the opportunity to show what they know (positive), or restrict what they learn if the constructs tested are known in advance and are allotted unbalanced study time (negative).

## 9.5  ECONOMIC, CULTURAL AND POLITICAL ASPECTS OF ADDITIONAL LANGUAGE EDUCATION

### The critical language teacher

Critical approaches to language teaching are those which demand careful thought about the connections between why (and how) a language is being learned (and assessed) and the social, economic and political contexts of additional language use (and assessment). Importantly, the critical language teacher doesn't just think about these connections; she encourages her students to think about, and act to change, attitudes and practices that disadvantage them as additional language learners and users (see also the sub-section on critical discourse analysis in Chapter 4, on pp. 88–9). Having a critical approach to teaching, learning and assessment has become known as **critical pedagogy** (CP). Advocates are very clear that as a method of teaching CP is necessarily sensitive to specific language learning (and using) contexts. This means that, while we can describe what CP is at the level of *approach* (see Figure 9.1), the *design* and *procedure* of this method will vary from classroom to classroom (Norton and Toohey, 2004).

**Critical pedagogy** is an approach to teaching which encourages students to develop critical awareness of, and to challenge, explicit or implicit systems of social injustice and oppression. It is particularly associated with the work of Paulo Freire.

### Are language teachers (un)critical?

Language teachers don't always worry about the connections between their classroom work and the wider social implications of learning, teaching and assessment in additional languages. One rationale for not worrying is that students are 'empty vessels' into which a new language can be simply poured, with no other consequence than the eventual achievement of 'proficiency'. Another rationale is that (for some students anyway) learning an additional language is a personal choice which provides them with access to jobs and study opportunities that might otherwise not have been available. A further rationale is that teaching the world's most frequently spoken languages constitutes a possible channel for increased mutual understanding between groups, maybe even improving the likelihood of peaceful relations within or between countries. These three reasons for not needing to worry about the social implications of why and how additional languages are taught and assessed can be summed up thus: 'the beneficiaries of my teaching are the students who are gaining good communication skills; making them more employable and more accepting of other people and other cultures.'

But the teaching of English, and, by implication, any of the world's most frequently taught languages, has been shown to result in financial, diplomatic and trade benefits to English-speaking countries, and the business of English language teaching conceals a complicated picture of influence by already powerful and influential groups over less powerful groups encouraged to feel in need of (an) additional language(s) (Phillipson, 1992, 2009).

Still, language teachers often work under considerable pressure: teaching for long hours and being held responsible both for maintaining students' motivation and for ensuring good results on the end-of-course test. Where schools or students can afford them, published materials with glossy pictures and extensive teacher's notes, and tests which claim to be 'standardized' and 'international', might seem like an attractive solution to some of these problems. The critical language teacher, however, will use these materials and tests with caution, asking themselves and their students questions about who is benefiting from (and who is disadvantaged by) any particular version of the language and the language learning experience. Specifically, the critical language teacher will insist on asking difficult questions, such as:

- What do my students bring to their lessons (beliefs about learning, language learning goals, expectations of interaction in the additional language, judgements about my personality and professional competence and so on)?
- What is the social and economic status of my students in target-language situations and how might this affect their opportunities to interact in the target language, as well as the ways in which these interactions will be judged?
- Who is allowed to decide what I teach, how I teach it and how learning is assessed? What are the consequences of these decisions for my students? In addition to my students, who benefits or is disadvantaged by these decisions?

## Native-speakerism

Becoming (or at least sounding and writing) indistinguishable from a monolingual native speaker of the 'standard variety' is commonly believed to be the aim of most (if not all) additional language learners (see Chapter 2). This assumed aim continues to exert a strong influence over the hiring practices, pay structure, marketing, materials selection and testing regimes of additional language education around the world, despite what we know from linguistics about: the lexico-grammatical and phonological variation within all languages (depending on the age, location, job, hobbies, religion, ethnicity, subculture, gender, etc. of the speaker); the absence of an accent-free version of any language; variation within individual speakers (depending on their role in the conversation and their relationship with their interlocutor); and the extent to which multilingual speakers sometimes mix their languages and varieties for maximum communicative effect.

In an effort to more accurately reflect this speaker- and situation-dependent variation, Constant Leung, Roxy Harris and Ben Rampton (1997) suggest that the idea of monolithic **native-speakerism** be finessed by consideration of speakers' linguistic repertoire in terms of: *expertise* (the ability to achieve specific tasks in specific situations); *inheritance* (the age at which a language in the repertoire began to be used, under what circumstances it was learned); and *affiliation* (level of comfort in using the language, feelings of belonging to a community of language speakers). Vivian Cook (1993) points out that the whole point of learning a new language is to *add* to an existing linguistic repertoire, that is, to achieve communicative goals in new situations for which the languages in the existing repertoire would be unsuitable or not ideal. Psycholinguistic research shows us that the original languages continue to exist in the learner's mind alongside the new language as an interconnected system, and are jointly activated in multilingual situations. Thus, even under the most ideal circumstances, the goal of native-speakerness is likely to be

**Native-speakerism** is the rarely challenged assumption that the desired outcome of additional language learning is, in all cases, 'native' competence in the 'standard' variety, and that native speakers have, therefore, an inbuilt advantage as *teachers* of the language. 'Nativeness' is also often conflated with nationality (note the ambiguity of *German*, *Chinese*, etc.), but since national borders are not consistent with linguistic ones, the geography-based native/second/ foreign typology is problematic as a system to classify language learners and teachers.

an irrelevant and reductive one for learners who have needs for different kinds and levels of expertise in their different languages.

## The benefits of learning an additional language

Caxton's introduction to his fifteenth century English–French phrasebook (from which we took the epigraph for this chapter (p. 197)) suggests that language learners may profit by being better able to buy, sell and transport goods internationally – an early form of languages for international business. Today, depending on who and where you are and the language you are learning, the benefits might include: meeting new people; being accepted into a university; getting a job or promotion; sounding like an intelligent, sophisticated person; or, in the case of immigrants and language minorities, access to formal education or simply survival.

Although some of these benefits are impossible to measure, language economists have attempted to explore the possible *financial* benefits of having an additional language. In Switzerland, for example (where less than 1 per cent of the population speak English as a first language), research has demonstrated a strong, positive link between an individual's earnings and their English language skills (Grin, 2001). However, other factors, such as type of job and other languages spoken, were important intervening variables: people in export-oriented jobs showed the greatest benefits, and German was more valuable than English for individuals who spoke French as a first language.

It seems likely that where speaking an additional language is considered part of a 'good' general education it is the demonstration of this 'good' education through additional language qualifications which 'causes' higher earnings, rather than proficiency itself. It is also possible that higher earnings create more chances for language learning (travel or a more 'international' job), suggesting that financial benefits might well 'cause' language learning, and not the other way round.

As with all other skills or qualifications, the advantage of an additional language may decrease as more and more individuals acquire the same skill. So, is learning an additional language likely to provide a good return on your investment? The answer depends on a number of factors, including what you want to achieve, what your job is, where you are and the level of skills in the pool of people you are competing with. Of course, this assumes a completely rational market for language skills. Sadly, the value of your languages probably depends more on the attitude of potential employers to the languages you speak (are they considered 'useful', or prestigious in some other way) and on their general attitude to you or the group they see you as representing.

## Teaching language varieties

As we saw in the introduction to this chapter (p. 197), the question of which variety of an additional language to teach is one which is increasingly debated. Regional and social variation within languages has, of course, always existed. But the spread of languages of wider communication such as Arabic, Chinese, Spanish, French and English through colonialism, migration and diffusion of new technologies has resulted in the development of a wide variety of norms to satisfy local communicative needs in different geographical settings. This profusion of varieties, and the endless possibilities for mixing with other languages already spoken by local users, does not, as might have been feared, seem to have created problems for interaction outside local contexts. On the contrary, the more linguistic resources a user has at her disposal and the greater her experience of monitoring and accommodating the language proficiency and choices of her interlocutors, the better she may be at communicating in an variety of social, regional and global contexts (Canagarajah, 2007). In fact, it has been suggested that being a monolingual speaker of even a widely used language may turn out to be a disadvantage (Smith, 1983; Rajagopalan, 2004).

How can teachers of languages of wider communication respond? Options include:

- reflecting on which varieties of the language their students are most likely to need, and want, to use;
- exposing students to a wide range of varieties to give them practice in accommodating differences in accent, lexicon, grammar and discourse strategies, as advocated in World Englishes and English as a lingua franca approaches to English teaching (for example Kirkpatrick, 2007; Matsuda, 2006);
- using dictionaries, grammar books and corpora that represent different varieties of the language;
- using world literature, popular music, TV and the internet as sources of texts for reading, listening, and presenting and practising varieties of the additional language;
- asking students (to think) about the varieties they are already using and/or aiming to use, and who they plan to use them with.

For an example of an awareness-raising activity that aims to draw students' attention to how they communicate in mixed language groups, see Wicaksono, (2009).

 **www.9.10**

## Additional language learning and identity

Early work that proposed a role for the learner's *identity* in the language learning process (for example Gardner and Lambert [1972] on instrumental and integrative motivation) tended to characterize identity as a fixed product of the relationship between an inherited language and culture, located in the mind of a learner. More recently, identity has been re-characterized as a more fluid process of a learner's actions and beliefs acting on, and being acted on by, his/her various situations and experiences (Norton, 2000). Allocating other people to groups can be an attempt to understand, manage (with their knowledge and consent) or control them (without their consent, and with or without their knowledge). Claiming or resisting a group identity can be an attempt to understand or manage others' impressions of oneself or take control over others.

An example of the allocation of identity is the effect of placing learners in classes based on their score in a target language proficiency test; subsequently a certain standard of proficiency will be expected by their teacher and variations from the target variety will be judged against 'what they should know by now'. Their opportunities to benefit from the input of more proficient students may thus be limited and they may be judged to be 'not ready' for specialist vocabulary or certain authentic texts. These same intermediate learners may not attempt to pronounce certain sounds that they feel make them look 'uncool' in front of their peers, or they may experiment with colloquial language when interacting with peers in the target-language community. The point is, the way a learner identifies with an additional language will depend on how, when, where and why she learned (or is learning) it and the assumptions that are made about her by the people she associates with.

In work by Celia Roberts, Michael Byram and their colleagues (Roberts *et al.*, 2001), university students of languages trained to become 'ethnographers of language' in preparation for study abroad experiences. The authors suggest that teachers interested in raising the issue of additional language effects on learner identities can consider encouraging their learners to: notice a variety of styles (register, genre, sociocultural variation) in the target situations they are preparing for; discuss how their languages can be mixed to achieve certain effects in some situations; reflect on how other people, both inside and outside the class, respond to their use of the target language; and consider how 'signs' other than their use of language (clothes, ethnicity, facial expressions, gestures, gaze, stance, etc.) are responded to by others.

## Culture in the classroom

Culture is a product of both society and the processes or sets of actions by which society creates, maintains and transforms itself. Culture is something we 'do', and therefore appears to be something we 'have', but does it therefore follow that it is possible to talk about monolithic 'cultures'? Describing the culture of the Indian subcontinent (or Sri Lankan culture, or Tamil culture, or Tamil student culture, or the culture of agricultural students at the Eastern University in Vantarumoolai, Sri Lanka) requires us to notice, select and prioritize differences between people. What we notice, select and prioritize depends on our situation, current activity, time and what we are making important now.

Having said all this, additional language education has generally presented culture as a product, rather than a process; something that is internally consistent and fixed, that 'belongs' to the speakers of the language being taught. Thus, languages are often conflated with 'national cultures', when, for example, English is associated uniquely with 'British' or 'American' culture and Mandarin is seen as reflecting 'Chinese' culture. This product-based approach to culture in the language classroom typically takes the form of 'representative topics' – aspects of 'the culture' that are considered by the teacher or syllabus designer to be useful, important, attractive or different from the culture of the learner. Here are a couple of examples of this 'representative topics' approach to culture:

■  A British university course for pre-undergraduate students called 'British Culture and Society': Food (fish and chips, roast beef and Yorkshire pudding),

Government (three main political parties, 'first past the post' voting system), Sport (rugby, cricket), Media, Health, etc.
■ A textbook for Indonesian children in West Java learning Sundanese, the regional language, at primary school: Inside the House (cassava, stinking bean, fermented cassava, bucket, duck, satay, chair, table, cupboard, potted plant, television, radio, bookshelf, shoes, ashtray, umbrella, etc.).

While this approach to culture in the language classroom can be interesting for learners, it can also:

■ over-generalize and over-emphasize difference (how often does a UK house-hold eat roast beef and Yorkshire pudding or a Sundanese household eat fermented cassava? In Britain curry (any vaguely spicy dish) is more often eaten than roast beef, and Sundanese families probably eat just as many packets of dried noodles as any other Indonesian family);
■ under-generalize and disguise interesting regional, class and age group differences, as well as changes over time;
■ be a way of promoting a particular impression of the additional language speakers (by sticking to certain attractive topics and avoiding others, or vice versa, depending on the power relations between the community of additional language learners and those who speak the additional language as a first language);
■ be a way of justifying unequal teacher employment conditions (for example paying a French national more to teach French in Sri Lanka than an equally competent and qualified Sri Lankan).

So, if a language teacher wants to raise her students' awareness of 'culture' but go beyond a superficial and inherently misleading 'list of things you need to know about the speakers of language A' approach, what can she do? Claire Kramsch (1993) lists ways in which teachers have tried to help students make sense of the new possibilities and challenges that an additional language may offer, including:

■ discussing whether differences between groups and individuals will diminish as the interconnectedness of the world's economies (globalization) increases;
■ increasing opportunities to experience cultural difference by encouraging student exchanges across national boundaries;
■ giving greater attention to ways in which we are all affected by international migration and the spread of information technologies;
■ raising awareness of the language and behavioural factors that can lead to people being judged as 'foreign', as well as how these judgements will be applied to them and whether they want to (or are able to) do anything to change the way they are judged.

The last point on the list above brings us back to our original definition of culture at the beginning of this section. In addition to (or instead of) having culture presented as something they 'have', language learners can also consider how culture is something they 'do' (and have done to them). Encouraging learners to focus on the *process* of doing the various cultures they belong to could involve, for example, noticing (and perhaps making an audio recording of – with the permission of the people being recorded) when and how they and other people:

■    mix languages;
■    slow down, simplify, rephrase something they have said, use (or consciously avoid) slang or jargon, alter their accent to match the person they are talking to;
■    use more, fewer or different gestures, nod, smile, back channel ('yeah, right', 'uh huh') or listen in silence, make or avoid eye contact;
■    take responsibility for starting a new topic of conversation, interrupt, pause, talk a lot, mainly listen, abandon a topic;
■    ask for clarification, agree and disagree, correct (or ignore) their own or others' language 'mistakes';
■    say that they dislike or like the way that someone else speaks, say that they think they are a better or worse communicator than the person they're speaking to.

## 9.6  ROLES FOR APPLIED LINGUISTS

Applied linguists can contribute to the area of additional language education by doing any or all of the following:

■    maintaining a critical stance, involving an awareness of the social, political, economic and commercial contexts of additional language learning, and how these might affect why, how and what students learn;
■    keeping up to date with major trends and new ideas in the theory of second language acquisition;
■    collaborating with applied linguists in other fields and developing an awareness of their aims and methods, especially language pathologists, educators working in literacy and bilingual environments, translators and lexicographers;
■    keeping up to date with changes in language use around the world and in different modalities, as well as (but with a critical eye for) developments in language teaching methods and educational technology;
■    advocating for fair access to, and assessment of, additional language learning;
■    being active researchers in their own classrooms, generating and testing hypotheses, and assessing outcomes (something language teachers have in common with other applied linguists, for example the speech and language pathologists in Chapter 13).

Before and since Caxton's fifteenth century English–French phrasebook, learners of additional languages have profited from, but also been disappointed and disadvantaged by, the results of their learning. As long as the potential for both profit and disadvantage in language learning remain, applied linguists will continue to play an important role in learners' endeavours.

1   Your supervisor at the school where you work asks you to write a report comparing two recently published additional language textbook series, for possible adoption by your school. What headings and sub-headings will your report contain? Make an outline.

2   Read section 9.1 again, where we illustrate the metaphor of 'command and demand' motivations for additional language education using the example of Bandung. Can you do the same with your own home town or city, or the nearest one to you?

3   Look at the second list of bullet points in section 9.4, 'Reasons for testing and models of language'. Take a language assessment (or a section of one) with which you are familiar and use this bulleted list to consider in what ways the assessment is and isn't valid. If you don't have access to a local language assessment, use an internet search engine to find the IELTS or the TOEFL website and consider the validity of the sample papers you can find there.

 **www.9.11, 9.12**

4   Search the internet for online news reports written or spoken in different varieties of your first language, or an additional language you are learning. For major stories, it may be possible to find multiple reports on the same event, for example the Swine Flu pandemic as reported by the BBC *World Service*, the *South China Morning Post* in Hong Kong and the *Deccan Chronicle* in India. When you have a collection of articles, think about how this collection, or corpus, could be used in an additional language class. If you are working in a group, you could compile your lists, perhaps using a social bookmarking site (such as www.delicious.com).

# FURTHER READING

Doughty, C. and Long, M. H. (2003). *The handbook of second language acquisition.* Oxford: Blackwell.

Hedge, T. (2000). *Teaching and learning in the language classroom.* Oxford: Oxford University Press.

Hinkel, E. (ed.) (2005). *Handbook of research in second language teaching and learning.* Mahwah, NJ: Lawrence Erlbaum Associates.

Kumaravadivelu, B. (2006). *Understanding language teaching: From method to post-method.* London: Routledge.

McKay, S. L. (2002). *Teaching English as an international language: Rethinking goals and approaches.* Oxford: Oxford University Press.

Saville-Troike, M. (2006). *Introducing second language acquisition.* Cambridge: Cambridge University Press.

# PART C

# Language and expert uses

In this penultimate part of the book, we map applied linguistics as practised in four key and rapidly changing domains. In Chapter 10, we tackle 'mission impossible': the problem and practices of *translating* (and interpreting) ideas across mutually unintelligible languages. In Chapter 11, we examine the process of dictionary-making, the role of dictionaries in contemporary societies and other elements of the field of *lexicography*. Chapter 12, on *forensic linguistics*, deals with the role of language as a medium of the law, as legal subject matter and as evidence in civil and criminal investigations and court cases. Chapter 13 maps the territory that applied linguists cover in the diverse field of *language pathology* as they seek to help clients with language-related disabilities to (re)build their linguistic capacities and cope with the worlds of discourse around them.

All the chapters in Part C deal with the complex (and often invisible) interplay between social and psychological factors. The first three map specialized areas of applied linguistics which focus on potential problems related to the social mani-festations of language – as barrier and bridge between individuals and groups in Chapter 10, as community resource in Chapter 11, and as a medium for group standards of behaviour in Chapter 12. In Chapter 13, we focus more closely on the language code itself, to describe how language pathologists confront problems related to what we describe as the 'ultimate stuff of language': the neural circuits underlying grammar and lexicon, and the motor and perceptual systems which allow us to externalize and internalize linguistic messages.

Taken collectively, the topics addressed in Part C represent some of the most dynamic and rapidly evolving areas within our field. They include areas with long traditions of practice and scholarly inquiry (translation and interpretation and, to a lesser extent, lexicography), and areas with much briefer trajectories (forensic linguistics and the study of language pathologies). Reflecting these different trajectories, we move from consideration of areas regarded as squarely within the field of applied linguistics, in the first couple of chapters, to examination of areas that have only recently been considered by applied linguists, in the second two chapters.

As we have done throughout the preceding chapters, we insist here that many complex problems faced by applied linguists can be solved only through attention to the cognitive and sociocultural dimensions of language and language users. Translating and interpreting are both psycholinguistic processes, yet have social motives and consequences; dictionaries are codified records of the shared aspects of language users' lexical memory stores; forensic analyses of writing and speech are used by lawyers, judges and juries to draw conclusions about intentions and meanings in defendants' minds; and many language pathologies involve cognitive impairments which impact on fundamental social processes. Recognizing these two interlocking facets of language, we stress the transdisciplinary nature of applied linguistic practice, as scholars and practitioner employ knowledge and tools developed in other fields. Similarly, as those in other fields recognize the centrality of language in their work, new problems are coming within the purview of the applied linguist, and interdisciplinary teamwork is becoming the norm.

In each chapter, we examine the contributions, limitations and promise of new forms of technology, as tools for understanding and solving problems in applied linguistics. Thus, in Chapters 10 and 11 we examine how computer and digital technologies have revolutionized the work of translators and dictionary-makers through advances in machine translation and electronic corpora, respectively. We also observe how new challenges are presented by the application of new technologies, such as voice analysis using spectrograms (Chapter 12) and the choice of whether or not profoundly deaf children should undergo cochlear implant surgery (Chapter 13).

In each chapter, we:

- present some of the main issues dealt with by applied linguistic specialists in these fields;
- identify and explain key concepts and terms;
- exemplify and explain the different approaches proposed, and practices adopted, to tackle the problems of each domain;
- describe the roles currently, and potentially, played by applied linguists.

At the end of each chapter, we supply, as usual, activities to encourage you to reflect on the issues covered, in your own contexts and those you may be preparing to work in. The activities are open-ended, encouraging you to apply the insights gained by identifying similar problems and exploring the nature of possible solutions. The suggested readings and companion website offer a wealth of resources for exploring all the issues in greater depth.

# CHAPTER 10

# Translation

It were as wise to cast a violet into a crucible that you might discover the formal principle of its colour and odour, as seek to transfuse from one language into another the creations of a poet.

(Percy Bysshe Shelley, *Defence of Poetry*, 1821)

A major objective of applied linguists is to confront the kinds of problems (and embrace the opportunities) that arise when groups or individuals speaking different languages interact. Few people have communicative competence in more than two or three languages, at most, and yet there are perhaps as many as 7,000 languages still being spoken around the planet. Communication between speakers who don't share a common language is a universal and – so far! – permanent problem faced by humanity, and thus falls within the scope of applied linguistics. One solution has been the adoption of a **lingua franca** (see, for example, Knapp and Meierkord, 2002). Mandarin Chinese, for example, has been established over the centuries by the rulers in Beijing as the national *Putonghua* ('common tongue') of China, enabling communication between mutually unintelligible linguistic groups in this vast country. Over the past few decades, European Union documents have increasingly been drafted in English (DGT, 2007a). But the other option is, of course, translation, and bilinguals have served as translators and interpreters since time immemorial. Indeed, in practice lingua franca usage often works hand in hand with translation. In the European Union, for example, a document written in Swedish is unlikely to be translated directly into Portuguese, but rather 'relay-translated' from Swedish to English and then from English to Portuguese. And in East Asia, English as a Lingua Franca is often the intermediary through which speakers of regional languages like Russian and Japanese understand each other (Proshina, 2005).

Although many practising translators and interpreters, as well as theorists who are specialists in the area of **Translation Studies**, may not in fact identify themselves as applied linguists, the root problem is clearly – and centrally – related to the concerns of the discipline. In this chapter we review the nature of the translation problem, in both linguistic and cultural terms, and sketch some of the ways in which language professionals from different traditions provide or propose solutions.

Before going any further, let's identify and define some fundamental concepts. For example, the term *translation* refers to both a process and a product. The *process* is embedded within four communicative components:

1  the original *expression* of the message in a **source language** (SL) text;
2  the *comprehension* of this SL text;

---

**Translation Studies** is the academic field concerned with the systematic study of the theory and practice of translation and interpreting. Research and teaching in the area are interdisciplinary, and closely aligned with Intercultural Studies (the largest professional organization is the International Association for Translation and Intercultural Studies).

 **www.10.1**

**Source language** (SL) and **target language** (TL) are terms used in translation and interpreting to refer to the 'translated-from' and 'translated-into' languages, respectively. They are appealing terms because they implicitly assume a focus on interlinguistic meaning, and the process of moving from one language to another.

3    the *expression* of the message derived from the SL text in a **target language** (TL) text;

4    the *comprehension* of this TL text.

Translators are always responsible for at least two of the components (2 and 3). In some cases, however, a speaker/writer may translate his or her own text, so may be the agent in component 1 too. Samuel Becket originally wrote *Waiting for Godot* in French and only later translated it into his native English. Translators are always also constantly reading what they have written. Thus, Becket presumably *read* (component 2) the original text he *wrote* (component 1) before he *wrote* (component 3), and then *read* (component 4), the English translation.

How to define the *products* of translation is not so straightforward, and indeed how the TL text might or should correspond to the SL text and the original message will be a major topic in this chapter. One thing is certain: translation is almost never a mere TL recodification of a message originally expressed in the SL. We might claim that a particular word in one language has a **translation equivalent** in another language, such that English *cat* is equivalent to French *chat*. But a word is not the same thing as a message. For applied linguists, the translation problems of interest arise in actual communicative acts, where language is used on the basis of the underlying beliefs, intentions and interpretations of the various participants in the translation process. Translation is therefore not uniquely a process of linguistic substitution, but rather also a semantic, pragmatic and cultural process, in which 'equivalence' is elusive.

**Translation equivalents** are (often ideal or elusive) pairs of terms across languages which have the same meaning, to a greater or lesser degree. They may perhaps best be thought of as cross-linguistic synonyms.

In her memoir *Reading Lolita in Tehran*, the Iranian scholar Azar Nafisi (2003, p. 265) describes '[dancing to] music that was filled with stretches of *naz* and *eshveh* and *kereshmeh*, all words whose substitutes in English – *coquettishness*, *teasing*, *flirtatiousness* – seem not just poor but irrelevant'. If she is right, how would a translator render these Persian words into English? The example demonstrates that translation is inevitably a cultural object, by definition one which is the joint product of two or more different linguistic cultures. Translations are thus texts and discourses in and of themselves, the products not only of grammatical and lexical resources, but also of sociopragmatic processes and judgements. One consequence of this is that, as sociocultural acts and objects, translations will have sociopolitical ramifications, a theme we pick up throughout the chapter.

In this chapter we first look at some of the contexts in which translation happens (section 10.1), before discussing the various manifestations that translation processes and products take (10.2 and 10.3). We then focus in on the knowledge and skills needed by professionals in the field (10.4), before exploring the question of genres of translation and the interrelated issue of modality of expression (10.5 and 10.6). These sections allow us to ponder some of the sociopolitical questions surrounding the role of translation in the lives of disparate groups of language users. From human users we then turn to the rapidly expanding role of IT in translation (10.7). The chapter ends with a discussion of potential roles for graduates of applied linguistics programmes (10.8).

## 10.1  CONTEXTS OF TRANSLATION

Translation is happening all the time, all over the planet, and has been since our earliest language-endowed forebears split into mutually unintelligible speech communities but stayed in contact for trade, war or mutual protection. In Mexico, the most famous of translators was *La Malinche*, the Indigenous interpreter for the Spanish conquistadors who conquered the region under Hernán Cortés (see Figure 10.1). She actually started out translating as the enslaved half of a relay-translation team, providing the linguistic bridge between the Maya spoken by Cortés' original interpreter, Jeronimo de Aguilar, and Nahuatl, the main language of the Aztec empire.

La Malinche is a powerfully iconic figure in Mexico, representing, on the one hand, the phenomenon of *mestizaje*, the dominant mixed-race (Indigenous and Spanish) ethnicity in the modern nation, as a source of rich social history and national identity; and, on the other hand, the enduring shame and anguish stemming from the original people's perceived submissiveness. This duality is reflected in the two other names by which La Malinche was known: *Doña Marina* in Spanish and *Malintzin* in Nahuatl. La Malinche provides a powerful metaphor of the defining context of translation: as a meeting point not only of languages, but also of cultures, and very often of unequal partners.

La Malinche was not, of course, a professional or trained translator, although she is better remembered than many who were, as suggested by her inclusion in the *Translator Interpreter Hall of Fame* (Conner, n.d.). But then again much, probably

Figure 10.1   La Malinche interpreting for Cortés in Xaltelolco (Source: Wikimedia Commons)

most, translation, occurs outside the professional realm. In the many multilingual cities, towns and villages of the world (many of them lying beyond the native lands of the world's regional and global powers), translation is a daily communication tool, more often than not oral. In India, over 400 languages are spoken, and in Papua New Guinea over 800. In Paraguay, Guarani is spoken by over 90 per cent of the population, but almost everyone in the capital uses it *and* Spanish in their daily lives. In South Africa, many people speak English as well as Xhosa, Zulu and other regional languages. In such multilingual communities (which, recall, are the rule rather than the exception), few members have access to *all* the languages they need, so translation is likely to be a very frequent occurrence.

Translation also happens in language classrooms all over the planet as an inevitable component of learning, sometimes under the guidance of the teacher, but probably more often involuntarily (Cook, 2010; see Chapter 9). Studies of language learners, especially those in the earlier stages of target language development, show that translation into the native tongue is an automatic, cognitive process, not susceptible to conscious control. Scholars who conduct research on vocabulary development in language learners have shown that the mind automatically forges memory connections between lexical entries which are perceived as translation equivalents (cf. Hall, 2002). Learners 'translate' into the L1, by activating perceived equivalents, whether they intend to or not! Recent research (for example Laufer and Girsai, 2008) also suggests that translation harnessed as a teaching tool can deliver significant benefits in vocabulary learning.

For linguists working to understand languages which are not well known outside the communities where they are spoken, translation is a fundamental tool, used to analyse the way the language works. In applied contexts, the knowledge derived from such translations provides evidence for linguistic recommendations regarding literacy education and language revitalization measures, or at least for the documentation and preservation of endangered languages and the cultures they express (see Chapter 5).

Here is an example from the US linguists Carolyn Mackay and Frank Trechsel's volume on Misantla Totonac, a language spoken in the Mexican state of Veracruz (La Malinche's homeland):

(1) 'tuut lakáachu nalh taayaaní' laawaní
    que NEG-ya FUT aguanta-DAT 3OBJ.PL-dice.x-DAT
    'ese no lo va aguantar' dice (él que era gavilán)
    'He's not going to handle/bear/stand it' says he (the one who was the sparrowhawk)

(Mackay and Trechsel, 2005, p. 96)

A **morphemic gloss** is an interlinear, morpheme-by-morpheme presentation in the reader's language of the grammatical information and lexical meaning expressed in lines of text from another language.

**www.10.2**

In their analysis of the story from which this tiny fragment is taken (which is about a sparrowhawk which changes places with a man), Mackay and Trechsel give four versions of the original spoken Totonac. First, in a practical orthography based on Spanish (the first line in our example), then phonetic and morphophonological transcriptions (not shown here), followed by a **morphemic gloss** (our third line: see the *Leipzig Glossing Rules* for a key) and, finally, a rendering in the Spanish dialect used in the region (not the national 'standard' variety). The last line is our translation of the Spanish. Now Mackay and Trechsel are native English-speaking general linguists rather than professional translators, and their informant is neither (although he is a bilingual Spanish–Totonac speaker). But their painstaking collaboration leads to a rich and informative descriptive analysis of Misantla Totonac, which, although designed to be used principally by linguists, is also made accessible to community members through practical orthography and the use of local Spanish varieties.

Translation is being used by Mackay and Trechsel as a linguistic (and applied linguistic) resource. But most work in translation studies, most courses in translation training programmes and most of the day-to-day toil of practitioners is concerned with *translation as communication*: producing a text to make comprehensible its content, not its form. Perhaps the most visible professional translation products of this kind are written: novels and poems written originally in other tongues (Shelley's caution notwithstanding); menus and hotel notices seen on vacation; search results from Google or Altavista's Babel Fish. For those who live outside the mainly monolingual Anglophone nations, translations are encountered even more frequently, delivered through college textbooks, newspaper articles, consumer product instructions, sacred writings, international legal codes and a whole host of other imported texts. Spoken translations – the products of the interpreting process – are heard most widely through the TV, radio and film, although ever-larger numbers of globetrotting conference attendees will hear simultaneous interpretations. Users of some sign languages will be especially familiar with the products of simultaneous interpretation (see section 10.5).

With the information technology revolution of the past few decades, professional translation has become a thriving service industry, worth over $9 billion annually in 2002, according to one report (ABI Research, 2002). But outside big international organizations like the UN and European Union (or internet giants and other multinational corporations), the most frequent context for the translation process is still that of the freelance worker, operating from home, either independently or through a small agency. Most translators join the profession because they happen to be or become bilingual and circumstances lead them to realize that their everyday bilingual competence is also a marketable skill. What applied linguistics can tell us about the development and effective deployment of this skill is our major concern here.

## 10.2  TRANSLATABILITY AND TRANSLATION EQUIVALENCE

The original Latin word *translatus* (the past participle form of the verb *transferre*) meant 'carried across'. Here, the translation process 'carries across' an intended message or meaning from one text to a second text in another language. Now when an object, let's say a Mandarin–English bilingual dictionary of the sort discussed in Chapter 11, is carried from one place to another it is the same object, before and after carrying. But can we really say this about the meaning expressed by an SL text and its TL translation? Is translation a process which transforms linguistic expression but leaves meaning untouched? Such a view assumes 'translation equivalence', a belief in which underlies the efforts of most beginning language learners, but one which very soon becomes untenable if held too tightly.

In his efforts to learn Latin and Greek, the English novelist Thomas Hardy's character Jude, from *Jude the Obscure*, hoped for 'a secret cipher, which, once known, would enable him, by merely applying it, to change at will all words of his own speech into those of the foreign one' (Hardy, 1998 [1895], p. 30). The Spanish philosopher José Ortega y Gasset (1992 [1937], p. 109) likened this vain hope to the Roman Catholic doctrine of transubstantiation, the process through which the bread and wine are miraculously transformed into the body and blood of Christ by the priest during mass: 'Should we understand [translation] as a magic manipulation through which the work written in one language suddenly emerges in another language? If so, we are lost, because this transubstantiation is impossible.'

Although absolute equivalence at all levels is impossible, translated messages don't necessarily suffer the drastic fate of Shelley's violet in the crucible. Let's see at what levels this 'impossible' process can happen. We noted on p. 224 that translation is simultaneously a linguistic, semantic, pragmatic and cultural process. To what extent can we expect a translation to approach equivalence to the SL text at these levels? We'll take the linguistic level first. Clearly, phonological equivalence must normally be surrendered. The dual trick language uses to combine mean-ingless phonemes on one level and meaningful words on the other makes the achievement of phonological equivalence between source and translation impos-sible, except in the case of historical cognates or loan words (the concept 'taxi', for example, is expressed as something very close to /taksi/ in most – perhaps all – languages). This presents problems when the sound is important in the original, for example in poetry or punning. Let's look at two examples of the latter.

Like many bilinguals living in a multilingual city, Chris became an accidental translator in Mexico City in the late 1980s (a clear case of native-speakerism; see Chapter 9). He was asked to translate into English a book on Mexican identity (Roger Bartra's *The Cage of Melancholy*, 1992). In one section (p. 9), the author refers to the concept of postmodernity (*posmodernidad*), but remarks in a footnote that he prefers 'the reverberations of the Spanish term *desmodernidad*'. He goes on to observe that '[i]n English it might be termed "dismothernism", but only Latin Americans would understand the *desmadre* implied in the translation'. This left the novice translator in a difficult position. The reader of the translation might not be familiar with the Spanish term *desmadre*, but understanding it is crucial for understanding the author's own English pun. In the end, Chris added (rather lamely) 'Translator's note: *desmadre* (lit. "dismother") means roughly "mess, ugly predicament"'.

Our second example is from English translations of *The Satyricon*, originally written by the Roman courtier Petronius (in Latin) a couple of millennia ago. At one point during a lavish feast, a servant boy is imitating the god Bacchus and the host, Trimalchio (a nouveau riche financier), makes a pun. In the original it is on the Latin word *liber*, which is both an alternative name for Bacchus and also the word for *free*. What should the translator do? In some early English versions, translators have faithfully explained the pun using parentheses. William Burnaby's version (made three hundred years ago) renders the passage in clunky, almost impenetrable prose, as follows:

(2)  'Dionysius,' said he, 'be thou Liber,' (i.e.) free, (two other names of Bacchus)
     . . . Trimalchio added, 'You will not deny me but I have a father, Liber.'
                                                                    (Petronius Arbiter, n.d.)

Frederic Rafael's contemporary translation, on the other hand, uses only the name Bacchus, and makes the pun on that name:

(3) 'Now you won't question that I never lacked backers. Bacchus, geddit?'
(Petronius Arbiter, 2003, p. 52)

Readers will surely agree with us that this sly rendering, which maintains a pun (*backers*/*Bacchus*) but dispenses with the original phonology, is much funnier than Burnaby's.

What these two examples show is that when a decision is made about equivalence on the lowest rung of our linguistic competence – i.e. that of form – it will have effects further up at the level of function. In the Bartra example, clarity was judged more important than mirth, so explanatory devices were used, but in *The Satyricon*, mirth is central to the writer's intention and the reader's expectation up to that point, so Rafael modifies semantic content to produce the appropriate literary sound effect.

At the lexical and grammatical levels, structural equivalence will rarely give you an authentic or effective TL version, since languages differ in the way meanings are mapped onto words, morphemes and syntactic structures. For example, the single Spanish word *lustro* must be rendered into English as two words in a syntactic relationship: $_{NP}[_D[\text{five}]\ _N[\text{years}]]$; in contrast, many English compound nouns, like *textbook*, must be expressed in Spanish as nouns modified by prepositional phrases, like $_{NP}[_N[\text{libro}\ _{PP}[_P[\text{de}]\ _{NP}[_N[\text{texto}]]]]]$.

Different lexico-grammatical mappings can also lead to loss of equivalency at semantic and pragmatic levels. Again, take English and Spanish. The English pronoun *you* covers three different second person pronouns in Mexican Spanish: *tú*, *usted* and *ustedes*. The use of *tú* and *usted* reflects differences in intimacy and/or power relations with the addressee (a distinction common in other languages, such as the Indonesian *kamu*/*anda*). For example, *usted* is typically used with a stranger and *tú* with a child. The third form, *ustedes*, is used for more than one addressee and does not indicate level of formality. Thus, where an English SL text uses *you* the translator into Spanish must not only choose an appropriate lexico-grammatical form, but also make an appropriate sociopragmatic judgement not expressed in the original. Sometimes the original text will be ambiguous on purpose (when, for example, someone says, 'I hope you can come to dinner', and they really mean just *one* member of a couple because they can't *bear* the partner but are too polite to say so).

The reverse case, where English must include semantic information that is not necessarily expressed in Spanish, is exemplified by the so-called 'null subject' phenomenon, whereby Spanish need not mention the subject of a verb but English must. And this can also have *sociopolitical* consequences: Spanish can ask (4B) about a university dean, a doctor or a government minister without indicating their gender, as the gloss on the second line shows. In English, on the other hand, one often uses either *he/his* or *she/her* in conversation (though *they/their* is increasingly common, even for singular subjects).

(4) A: Mi jefe despidió a diez personas ayer.
POSS-1P-SG boss fire-PAST-3P-SG to ten person-PL yesterday

*My boss fired ten people yesterday*
B: ¿Consultó a los miembros de su departamento?
consult-PAST-3P-SG to the-MASC-PL member-PL of POSS-3P-SG
    department
*Did he/she consult the members of his/her department?*

Translators run the risk of an accusation of sexism if they choose one gender over the other in English.

At the cultural level, equivalence will again, inevitably, be illusory, since cultures are defined by their differences, through time and space. We look again at translations of Petronius' *Satyricon*. At a later stage of the banquet, the revellers are interrupted by the arrival of another of the host's servants, who reads aloud from a report of the day's affairs at one of his employer's estates. In Alfred R. Allinson's translation, the fragment goes as follows:

> (5)  ... the historiographer, who read out solemnly, as if he were reciting the public records: 'Seventh of Kalends of July (June 25th) ...'
>
>                           (Petronius Arbiter, 1930, verse LIII)

This is problematic for modern readers, given the cultural distance between ancient Rome and contemporary Anglophone societies. Rafael's solution is again to move from the original Latin and its linguistic equivalents and to use instead concepts from contemporary British culture. Thus, Rafael's translation talks of

> (6)  ... an accountant who came in and read out, as if from *The Financial Times*: 'Twenty-sixth of July ...'
>
>                             (Petronius Arbiter, 2003, p. 62)

Note the anachronisms: accountancy is a modern profession, the British newspaper was founded in 1888, and the date is given according to our Gregorian calendar, introduced in 1582. But the sentence says something to the modern reader that the more 'equivalent' versions do not.

## 10.3 THE TRANSLATION PROCESS

We claimed earlier that translation is happening all the time, throughout history and around the planet. We also claimed that this activity is not achieving the absolute equivalence between SL text and TL text envisaged in Jude the Obscure's secret cipher or Ortega y Gasset's transubstantiation. So what really happens in the translation process? What kind of translation products *are* possible? The unmagical process has been described as having three distinct stages (see, for example, Roberts, 2002, pp. 433–434). These stages connect together the four communicative components described at the beginning of the chapter (pp. 223–4) and may be summarized as follows:

- comprehension of the original SL text, the end (product of which is a non-linguistic, conceptual representation in short-term memory);

■ expression of the comprehended message in the TL;
■ revision of the TL text on the basis of a re-reading of the SL text and deeper consideration of the TL-speaking audience.

Look at Figure 10.2, where the basic psycholinguistic process is diagrammed. It shows the essential flow of information and its transformation in the translation process. Outside the area defined by the dotted line, on the left, we have the original expresser's message, the context in which it was formulated and the language in which it was encoded. This produces the actual physical manifestation of the linguistically encoded message: the SL text (which could be a poem, a novel, an instruction manual, a speech, a conversational turn signed in a sign language, etc.). The translator uses her linguistic knowledge of SL and her non-linguistic (contextual) knowledge and beliefs about the circumstances of the text's creation to comprehend the text. Then, using her knowledge of the TL and her understanding of the contextual circumstances and cultural knowledge available to TL speakers, she encodes the comprehended message in the TL, thus producing the TL text. If we added a receiver to this diagram (the reader of the translated poem, the interlocutor in the conversation between British Sign Language and English speaker, etc.) we'd end up with three conceptualized messages. As our examples and arguments above have demonstrated, these three messages will not be identical.

This is, of course, something of an idealization, since many translators (especially non-professional, non-balanced bilingual ones) will not wait for a full conceptual representation of the message to be built in the mind, and will read off translation equivalents at levels of processing which precede the final state of

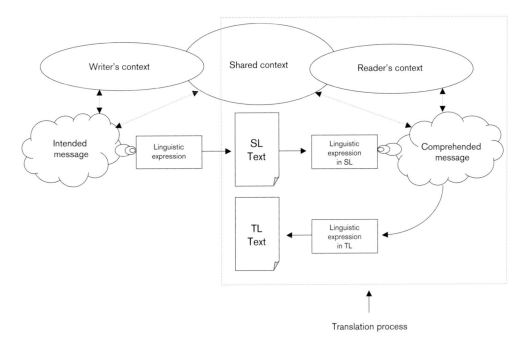

Figure 10.2   The translation process

comprehension. An example is word-for-word translation (like the glosses used by descriptive linguists), which will often produce a very foreign-sounding – probably incoherent – TL text, with the word order of the SL and none of the meaning derivable from contextual cues. A subsequent level of translation, centred around the sentence or clause, will correspond to the propositional level of semantics: the literal, but not the pragmatically interpreted meaning. For the translation to be effective, it will need take into account the whole gamut of linguistic, contextual, cultural and encyclopaedic information available. In order to achieve this, translators need to know, or come to know, an awful lot.

## 10.4  WHAT DO TRANSLATORS NEED TO KNOW?

Professional translators clearly bring to their task a broad range of linguistic and applied linguistic knowledge, ideally including all of the following:

- grammatical competence and fluency in the relevant TL variety(ies);
- grammatical competence and fluency in the relevant SL variety(ies);
- (access to) a large and varied vocabulary in both languages, including specialized terminology tied to often very narrow professional or cultural domains;
- explicit metalinguistic knowledge about the grammars of both languages and about areas of grammatical overlap, alignment or disparity;
- knowledge of the pragmatic routines through which SL and TL map communicative intention and effects onto linguistic expressions;
- knowledge of a range of styles, genres, registers, dialects and international varieties associated with both languages;
- knowledge of literacy and the ability to read and to write (and speak or sign) clearly and elegantly (i.e. knowledge of the conventions of appropriate style for a range of contexts);
- knowledge of translation theory and the range of professional resources and strategies that may be employed to translate effectively.

As we've seen repeatedly, much intended meaning goes unexpressed through linguistic form, being presupposed by SL expressers on the basis of shared context and locally or universally shared knowledge of the world and our social roles and practices within it. So translators must also bring to bear a considerable amount of non-linguistic knowledge, in order to understand the SL text, locate appropriate expressions in the TL and compensate for gaps in the TL receiver's knowledge. Among other things, they're likely to need:

- knowledge of the cultural background of the expresser and of the knowledge the expresser assumes the SL receiver to have (the expresser is writing for speakers of the SL, not the TL, and so assumes knowledge which the TL receiver may not possess);
- knowledge of the subject matter of the SL text and the extent to which aspects of it are limited to the expresser's cultural context;
- knowledge of the social and political practices, and the moral and behavioural norms, of the expresser's and receivers' cultures;

- 'research intelligence': the skills required to find appropriate terminology and identify reliable sources (especially on the internet);
- a clear understanding of the specific needs of the client (both the commissioner of the translation and its end-users), as well as professional credibility and personal trustworthiness in the clients' eyes (Edwards *et al.*, 2006).

These areas of knowledge must often also extend to earlier epochs, especially in the case of non-contemporary literature, historical documents, ancient inscriptions and the like. A famous example of the latter is that of the 2,200-year-old Rosetta Stone, a granite tablet found in el-Rashid (Rosetta) in Egypt in 1799, on which is inscribed a decree issued by the priests of Ptolemy V. The decree is written three times: in hieroglyphs, common (or demotic) Egyptian and Greek (see Figure 10.3). This gave scholars an opportunity to compare three versions (translations) of the same original message, and thus crack the hieroglyphic code, which had gone out of use and become forgotten some 1,400 years before. It took over two decades to interpret the inscriptions, and the final breakthrough was made by Jean-François Champollion early in the 1820s. If you take a look at the English translation on the British Museum website, you will appreciate how crucial it must have been for the translators to possess detailed knowledge of the political and social history of Ancient Egypt.

 **www.10.3**

Figure 10.3   The Rosetta Stone (Source: Wikimedia Commons)

## 10.5  TYPES OF TRANSLATION

The range of translation types is as broad as the range of discourse types. Just as discourse analysis (Chapter 4) distinguishes between genres on the basis of formal linguistic properties of texts and the social and communicative purposes to which they are put, one can classify translation tasks and products according to the linguistic and functional challenges they present to the translator. Technical translation is often treated as the poor relative in the family of translation types. For example, the index to Venuti's (2004) anthology of seminal writing in translation studies includes only seven brief references to the topic, compared to over twenty more extensive ones to the translation of literature. Literary translation is certainly less constrained by the SL text, giving greater power of decision to the translator and providing almost unlimited scope for creativity, inventiveness and imagination. The Argentine writer Jorge Luis Borges (2004 [1935], p. 45) celebrates Mardrus' 'luxurious' translation of *The Thousand and One Nights*, claiming that 'it is his infidelity, his happy and creative infidelity, that must matter to us'. With technical translation, on the other hand, that licence must be sacrificed in favour of complete fidelity. The translator's responsibility here is enormous: on his or her shoulders rests the well-being of patients taking foreign drugs, the proper functioning of machinery in factories and homes, the financial stability of companies and countries, the good health and effective training of workforces, the balance of justice in legal proceedings, and the outcomes of millions of other situations in which the mis-translation of a word or expression may have adverse effects.

Here's one revealing example, which also nicely illustrates the importance of explicit metalinguistic knowledge and subject matter knowledge (cf. section 10.4). The website of the US-based technical translation service RIC International tells of a mistranslated motorcycle manual they had to put right:

> One of the more interesting errors, though far from being the most egregious, was in the translation of the original English instruction: 'Loosen the eccentric bearing carrier pinch bolt.' In the Italian version of the manual, the sentence was referring to an eccentric bearing; in the French manual, it was referring to the eccentric bearing carrier; and the Spanish translation referred to the eccentric pinch bolt!
>
> (RIC International, n.d.)

For those unfamiliar with this use of the word *eccentric* (as we were until we looked it up), it means here 'not concentric' or 'not placed centrally' (the literal meaning of its ancestor in Greek) (see Figure 10.4).

What's special about this example is that it wasn't just the technical vocabulary that led to the mistranslations, but also the linguistic analysis of modification relations between adjectives and compound nouns (structures which are very uncommon in the Romance languages). In order to understand the SL text and thus provide a faithful TL version, the translator must have (1) awareness of linguistic modification ambiguities (so-called 'bracketing paradoxes') and (2) the subject matter knowledge which will permit them to make the right choice between alternative interpretations. If they don't, users of the resulting manual will end up rotating the wrong bit of the motorcycle, or be unable to locate the correct piece in the first place.

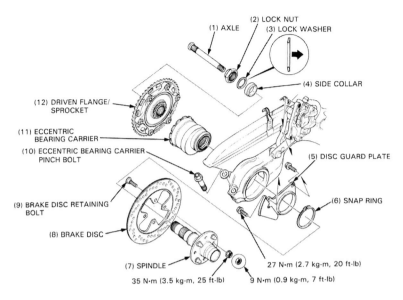

(2) LOCK NUT
(1) AXLE
(3) LOCK WASHER

(4) SIDE COLLAR

(12) DRIVEN FLANGE/
SPROCKET

(11) ECCENTRIC
BEARING CARRIER

(10) ECCENTRIC BEARING CARRIER
PINCH BOLT

(5) DISC GUARD PLATE

(9) BRAKE DISC RETAINING
BOLT

(6) SNAP RING

(8) BRAKE DISC

(7) SPINDLE

27 N·m (2.7 kg-m, 20 ft-lb)

35 N·m (3.5 kg-m, 25 ft-lb)        9 N·m (0.9 kg-m, 7 ft-lb)

Figure 10.4    Loosening the eccentric bearing carrier pinch bolt

Technical and literary translation are often correlated with opposite poles on a continuum of translation types defined by their fidelity to the original language and culture of the SL or, put differently, whether they are text-focused or reader-focused. Different terms, reflecting different but overlapping parameters of fidelity, have been used to label the poles of the continuum. Table 10.1 lists some of the more commonly used terms and their focuses.

The *formal–functional* dichotomy (Nida, 2004 [1964]), for example, will be apparent in the translation of poetry, or any other literary text in which linguistic form (rhyme, metre, alliteration, etc.) may be an integral component of the poet's intended effect. How should one render in Japanese, for example, Dylan Thomas's (2006 [1954]) 'play for voices' *Under Milk Wood*, which contains expressions like '. . . the sloeblack, slow, black, crowblack, fishingboat-bobbing sea'? In other cases, the purpose of the translation may dictate the focus. A translation of an ancient text for the general reader may focus on function, but the same text intended for scholars may focus more on form, using extensive footnotes or parenthetical explanations to compensate for the semantic and cultural opacity that might result from the reader's cultural and temporal displacement. The first type, then, the product of *text-based* translation, will be more *communicative*, resulting in *shifts*, whereas the second type, the product of *word-based* translation, will be more *semantic*, striving to maintain *equivalence*.

We have already seen a number of examples of these differences in focus. MacKay and Trechsel's (2005) grammar of Misantla Totonac uses formal, semantic, word-for-word translation equivalences in the literal glosses intended for linguists seeking to understand the structure of the SL, but also more communicative translations into colloquial Spanish for members of the local Indigenous community. Over the centuries, the various translators of *Satyricon* have moved from a text-focused to a reader-focused orientation, as changes in society have accelerated, moral

Table 10.1   Types of translation at the poles of a continuum defining greater focus on the text vs greater focus on the reader

| Reader-focused types (least faithful to SL) | Text-focused types (most faithful to SL) |
| --- | --- |
| *Functional*<br>The translation seeks to render the functions of the SL text, independently of its original linguistic form. | *Formal*<br>The translation seeks to render as close as possible the form of the SL text, which might sometimes require sacrificing aspects of its function. |
| *Communicative*<br>The translation seeks to communicate the original expresser's message, whether it enjoyed explicit linguistic expression in the SL text or not. | *Semantic*<br>The translation seeks to render the literal meaning of the original text, leaving unexpressed any meaning which was only implicit in the original. |
| *Text-based*<br>The translation process operates on the meaning of the whole text. | *Word-based*<br>The translation process operates on the level of the sentence. |
| *Shift*<br>The translation modifies the content of the SL text in the interests of the reader's – and translator's – localized cultural knowledge and needs. | *Equivalence*<br>The translation does not contain any meaning which is not in the original. |
| *Domesticating*<br>The translator adapts the translation to local conditions. | *Foreignizing*<br>The translation maintains as many elements of the SL and source culture as possible, even when the result does not sound colloquial in the TL or familiar in the target culture. |

positions have become more relaxed and readerships have expanded far beyond the erudite elites. Certain kinds of texts, most often technical ones like the motor-cycle manual retranslated by RIC International, are intended for universal application and so are inevitably text-based. Others are so tied to the cultural setting and epoch of their original creation that some translators have sought to make them more accessible by domesticating them. Rafael's translation of *Satyricon* is again a good example. (Apart from the reference to the UK daily the *Financial Times*, he mentions two other non-Roman institutions – the United Nations and Mickey Mouse – elsewhere in the text.)

But domesticating a text is not only the semantic process of replacing outdated concepts with contemporary ones or local ones with foreign. At the discourse level, translators may also implement shifts of a higher order, which adapt an SL text to the predominant ideologies and moral attitudes of the TL readership. Perceived obscenity in the SL text, for example, can in certain epochs and cultures tempt translators to perpetuate drastic domesticating shifts in the translated text, in order to protect their local readers from moral outrage. Borges tells of Edward Lane's nineteenth century translation of *The Thousand and One Nights*, describing it as 'scrupulous' (recall his use of 'luxurious' to describe Mardrus' less inhibited version).

But, he goes on, '[t]he most oblique and fleeting reference to carnal matters is enough to make Lane forget his honor in a profusion of convolutions and occutations' (Borges, 2004 [1935], p. 36). Perhaps more honourable is the strategy taken by the translator of the words of Orff's *Catulli Carmina* (the second work in the series which starts with *Carmina Burana*) in the 1954 Vox LP recording, part of which we faithfully reproduce in the following:

| | |
|---|---|
| O tui oculi, ocelli lucidi,<br>fulgurant, efferunt me velut specula<br>O tua blandula, blanda, blandicula,<br>tua labella ad ludum ad ludum<br>prolectant<br>O tua lingula, usque prerniciter<br>vibrans ut vipera<br>(cave, cavete meam viperam nisi te<br>mordet)<br>Morde me, basia me.<br>O tuae mammulae. . . | O your brightly shining eyes, how<br>they exalt me! O your charming,<br>alluring lips! O your nimble tongue!<br><br>*For obvious reasons the translation<br>of the following lines has been<br>omitted.* |

The reasons for the absent translation may not be all *that* obvious to the reader who knows no Latin, but at least he or she is not misled!

Other translators have domesticated their products so that they serve purposes which may be different from those of the original expresser's, such as missionaries who introduce concepts from local religions in order to mask conversion as continuity, or political activists who introduce local concepts which correspond to their own agenda. Venuti (2004, p. 471), however, draws attention to the fact that this kind of shift is often an inevitable consequence of freer translation, rather than being a conscious objective of the translator: 'The foreign text is rewritten in domestic dialects and discourses, registers and styles, and this results in the production of textual effects that signify only in the history of the domestic language and culture.' Ideological motives also often underlie the opposite stance, that of foreignizing the translation in order to make the non-local and/or non-contemporary characteristics of the SL text more transparent.

The process inevitably results in non-colloquial TL forms, but this is seen as an inevitable price to pay for conceptual fidelity. The exiled Russian novelist and translator Vladimir Nabokov (2004 [1955], p. 115), for example, proclaimed that '[t]he clumsiest literal translation is a thousand times more useful than the prettiest paraphrase'. He believed this, according to Venuti (2004, p. 68), because '[h]e nurtures a deep, nostalgic investment in the Russian language and in canonical works of Russian literature and disdains the homogenizing tendencies of American consumer culture'. A very different rationale has underlain the practice of Chinese literary translators since the 1980s, according to Xianbin (2007). He observes that Chinese translators tend to foreignize their translations from English into Chinese and to domesticize their translations from Chinese into English, which he explains as an effect of the respect which globally dominant English now has in China, so that Chinese texts will be made as accessible as possible to English speakers, but English texts will be tampered with as little as possible when rendered in Chinese.

Finally, from a postmodern, feminist perspective, Spivak (2004 [1992]) argues that many (especially English) translations of postcolonial literature fail to reflect an 'intimacy' with the rhetorical context of the original, resulting in the use of bland Western 'translatese'. As an example, she mentions the Bengali novelist Mahasweta Devi's *Stanadāyini*, translated as *The Wet-nurse* in one version, but in another as the more faithful, but less neutral, *Breast-giver*. The first comfortably domesticates, the second uncomfortably foreignizes.

## 10.6   INTERPRETING AND AUDIOVISUAL TRANSLATION

So far in this chapter we have concentrated on translation as a deliberate, reflective process, displaced in time and space from the creation of the original SL text. This is due fundamentally to the success story of literacy (see Chapter 6): writing leaves permanent records, both of SL texts that may be translated multiple times and of translated texts that may be studied and critically discussed again and again. The modalities of speech and sign, on the other hand, leave transitory footprints which are more likely to be local in significance, are normally accessible only to those in the immediate vicinity and are thus less available to critical analysis.

But professional **interpreting** of oral and signed SL discourse is becoming an increasingly common and important aspect of global translation activity. We see three main reasons for this. One is that international travel has become so much cheaper and easier, resulting in more frequent and more varied multilingual encounters: for business people, professionals, academics, politicians, NGOs, special interest groups, artists, students on holiday and others. A second reason is the growth in transnational migration, also involving increased mobility but often motivated by economic needs or personal security rather than choice. A third and related reason is the growing recognition in many countries that residents who do not have access to one of the languages in which public affairs are typically conducted nevertheless have the right to participate fully in the affairs of their local and national communities. This is especially the case for linguistic minority groups such as Indigenous communities, immigrants and deaf people, so **community interpreting** is increasingly taught in training programmes and researched in translation studies departments.

It is now common to see professional interpreters in schools, courtrooms, hospitals and countless other public domains, including TV and the theatre. Interpreting is an extremely complex and cognitively taxing skill, given its inherent temporal constraints. This goes for both **simultaneous/whispered** and **consecutive interpreting**. In the former cases, the interpreter must perform the psycholinguistic task diagrammed in Figure 10.2 *in real time*, without the luxury of preparing multiple drafts and consulting dictionaries. For this reason, in university classrooms, conferences and increasingly also in courtrooms, teams of interpreters are employed, working for thirty-minute stints. Given increasing globalization, relay-interpreting is becoming common, with English (or occasionally French) as the lingua franca. In the UN at Geneva, for example, Arabic- and Chinese-speaking interpreters will translate from and into English or French, the UN's two working languages, and German-speaking interpreters will render original Chinese or Arabic

---

**Interpreting** is the process of translating from and into spoken or signed language. It's **simultaneous** when the speaker or signer doesn't pause for the interpreter to translate what they've expressed, for example when making an address at a conference (in a private meeting the translation may be **whispered**, also known as *chuchotage*). Interpreting is **consecutive** when the speaker/signer produces a stretch of discourse and then pauses while the interpreter translates it, and alternating phases of SL and TL ensue until the whole message is interpreted.

**Community interpreting** is interpreting for residents of a multilingual community rather than between members of different language communities: in doctor–patient encounters, job interviews or court proceedings, as opposed to international conferences and diplomatic or commercial meetings.

**www.10.4**

content through the English or French versions (UNOG, n.d.). In consecutive interpreting, other challenges present themselves, especially the need in some contexts to accurately store lengthy fragments of the accumulating SL discourse in working memory, so that nothing is lost or substantially modified in the subsequent TL product. In this case, note-taking skills can be extremely important.

In both types of interpreting there is also an important ethical dimension, which does not present itself so frequently in written translation; this is because the spoken or signed SL discourse is often spontaneous (or at least not fully prepared or revised in advance), resulting in slips of the tongue or hand and apparent redundancies or inconsistencies in content, all of which are frequent distinguishing features of real-time discourse. Does the interpreter faithfully reproduce such mistakes, even if they are pretty sure they were unintended and they have a good guess at what was really meant? Ethical guidelines from the US Registry of Interpreters for the Deaf (RID) suggest that they shouldn't, recommending in their Code of Professional Conduct that interpreters '[r]ender the message faithfully by conveying the content and spirit of what is being communicated, using language most readily understood by consumers, *and correcting errors discreetly and expeditiously*' (NAD-RID, 2005, p. 3; emphasis ours).

In community interpreting the ethical issues go way beyond error-correction. Using the example of medical discourse, Sandra Beatriz Hale (2007) describes the long-standing debate in the field between the view of interpreters as brokers or mediators who may consciously modify, omit or add elements of the message, and the view taken by Hale herself, that a more direct 'invisible' approach is safer, given the high stakes of the discourse and the difference in status between the doctor and interpreter, on one hand, and the patient, on the other. When the interpreter takes an active role, crucial information may be lost or distorted, as the following example (with the Russian SL here rendered in TL italics) illustrates:

| | |
|---|---|
| *Doctor:* | Ah, are you uh having a problem with uh chest pain? |
| *Interpreter:* | *Do you have a chest pain?* |
| *Patient:* | *Well how should I put it, who knows? It . . . sometimes it does happen.* |
| *Interpreter* (to patient): | *Once a week? Once every two weeks?* |
| *Patient:* | *No, this thing happens then depending on . . . on circumstances of life.* |
| *Interpreter* (to patient): | *Well at this particular moment do your life circumstances cause you pain once a week, or more often?* |
| *Patient:* | *Sometimes more often, sometimes more often.* |
| *Interpreter* (to doctor): | Once or twice a week maybe. |

(Bolden, 2000, pp. 396–397, cited in Hale, 2007, p. 55)

Hale points out how important it is for interpreters to understand the crucial role of the doctor's linguistic skills, especially in questioning, in order to make a full and informed diagnosis. In the example given here, the interpreter effectively deprives the doctor of his tools, and misrepresents the client.

As we saw in Chapter 6, ethnic minority children often serve as 'language brokers', informal translators and interpreters in communications between their parents and older relatives and representatives of the dominant culture (teachers at school, doctors, landlords, immigration lawyers and others). Although they are not paid for their services, the products of these translations can have important economic and legal consequences for the young interpreters and their families (Orellana *et al.*, 2003). This phenomenon, in which bilingual children draw on their linguistic and pragmatic knowledge, also raises the ethical question of whether it is wise to have children play this role in matters that could cause them emotional harm (as might be caused by having to relay a doctor's message to a sick parent), and to what extent it is the obligation of the state or government to provide translation services so that children are protected. A similar situation often holds for deaf people too, where relatives or friends serve as interpreters because professional interpreters are unavailable or too costly. Smeijers and Pfau (2009) report, for example, that most deaf users of Sign Language of the Netherlands (*Nederlandse Gebarentaal*, NGT) don't book a state-funded interpreter for medical consultations because there are few available at short notice and yet appointments must be made on the day of the consultation. They suggest (Smeijers and Pfau, 2009, p. 10) that more resources might be available if NGT were to be granted 'official language' status.

Another ethical issue relates to the confidentiality of the information contained in the interpreted message. This arises from the fact that real-time language use is more often conducted in the private sphere than is the case with writing, which tends to have more public currency. Maintaining confidentiality is especially relevant for language minority members requiring interpreting at school (for example regarding academic performance), in consultation with medical professionals, and particularly so in legal proceedings. In the latter case, it is not uncommon for interpreters to be subpoenaed and called to give evidence in court about what someone has allegedly said or signed (Mathers, 2002).

There are also purely *linguistic* challenges for interpreters which are not shared to the same extent by translators. For example, German syntax places main verbs at the end of the sentence, requiring interpreters to wait or anticipate. And in typologically similar languages or a language with many loan words, cognates will get activated in the interpreter's mind faster than perhaps more accurate translation equivalents (the 'false friend' problem familiar to additional language teachers). In both cases language structure combined with time pressure can lead to loss of translation quality. In the case of some sign languages and less common languages which lack codified standards and extensive lexicons (see Chapter 5) there may not be a ready term in the TL, resulting in loss of specificity or extensive circum-locution, both of which will place cognitive strains on the interpreter and so potentially compromise the quality of subsequent performance. Curiously, inter-preting between sign and speech may be slightly easier than between two spoken languages, given the fact that in the former case comprehension and production are not competing for the same phonological system (one is vocal-acoustic, the other is manual-visual). We are not aware of any research on this; however, the fact that sign interpreters regularly work for longer than the thirty-minute cross-modal interpreting stint is suggestive.

Speech-to-sign interpreting is not the only cross-modal translation process, of course. In the sub-field of **audiovisual translation**, SL discourse in one or more modalities is rendered into corresponding or different modalities in the TL. The main context for this is the screen (TV, movie, computer, game console, mobile

**Audiovisual translation** encompasses all translation involving multiple modalities (including multimedia), but typically involves subtitling or dubbing for screen-based language in film, TV and video games.

phone, etc.), hence the alternative name *screen translation*, and the typical process involved is subtitling, with dubbing (and non-lip synchronized voice-over) being other options. Subtitling is the dominant method because it's cheaper than dubbing and doesn't interfere with the original product. The downside, however, is that the TL version has to be considerably abridged from the original SL message, because the viewer needs time to both read the text and experience the sight and sound of the main attraction (this loss of information can be as much as 70 per cent, according to Chiaro, 2009, p. 148). Dubbing, which can retain much more of the SL message, is the preferred practice in a small number of countries and regions where official language pride is important, either in the context of major world languages vying with English (e.g. in China, Japan, Latin America and the French-, Italian-, German- and Spanish-speaking nations of Europe) or in the context of regional minority languages seeking greater presence in society (e.g. Catalonia, the Basque Country and Wales).

Subtitling is expanding, even in traditionally dubbing countries, especially for movies, where there is high demand for a fast release of Hollywood products after their US premiere. Despite the high demand for translation of screen products, quality is often compromised in the rush to release and the lack of involvement of translators in the production process. An interesting exception here is, however, video games, which represent a massive global market. Chiaro (2009, pp. 153–154) reports that, at least in the Japanese sector of the market, translators are involved from the outset and are given considerable freedom to adapt and modify SL text and speech so that it has maximum entertainment value for TL users (to the extent that the process is often called *transcreation* instead of translation).

The worldwide spread of English and US dominance of the film and TV industries means that people the world over are reading a lot of English subtitles. This can make translation a very effective teaching tool for additional language education (as we noted in Chapter 9), but it also has profound cultural and political effects, effectively disseminating the Englishes and cultures of Kachru's 'Inner Circle' around the globe at the expense of local languages and local content. The translation theorist Henrik Gottlieb points out how TV companies in non-English speaking countries are trapped by economics here:

> Today, American, British and Australian imports are so much more affordable to TV stations than domestic productions – as long as these remain difficult to export because neighboring countries keep filling their shelves with anglophone imports. Vicious or not, this circle needs to be broken, at least for the sake of linguistic and cultural diversity.
>
> (Gottlieb, 2004, p. 89)

Dubbing is the standard practice for imported children's films and programmes around the world, so at least the onslaught of English is delayed, even if the rest of the 'polysemiotic' code is going to reinforce Anglo-Saxon cultural hegemony. And at least with subtitling the translation is automatically 'foreignizing' in effect, if not in form: by presenting the TL at the same time as the SL whilst at the same time detaching the two through shifting the modality, subtitles interfere with the screen illusion, despite their familiarity in much of the non-Anglophone world.

# 10.7 TECHNOLOGY IN TRANSLATION

**Automatic translation** (also known as machine translation, MT) is the study and practice of translation via computer software (now increasingly embedded in online applications on the internet). Like additional language teaching (Chapter 9), the MT enterprise is often characterized by its lack of success, but actually it's only unsuccessful to the extent that it can simulate human ability, and this is an impossible yardstick when you consider the extent to which real language use depends on non-linguistic context.

Communication with extraterrestrials has never presented much of a problem in the science fiction canon. Fans of the genre know that many authors and screen writers have eliminated the intergalactic communication gap by conveniently assuming that all aliens speak fluent English! In more sophisticated treatments, it is almost universally assumed that technological advances will sooner or later result in the design of a gadget which will automatically translate between all galactic language combinations. Unless the Babel fish is discovered first:

> 'The Babel fish,' said the Hitch Hiker's Guide to the Galaxy quietly, 'is small, yellow and leech-like, and probably the oddest thing in the Universe. It feeds on brainwave energy received not from its own carrier but from those around it. It absorbs all unconscious mental frequencies from this brainwave energy to nourish itself with. It then secretes into the mind of its carrier a telepathic matrix formed by combining the conscious thought frequencies with nerve signals picked up from the speech centres of the brain which has supplied them. The practical upshot of all this is that if you stick a Babel fish in your ear you can instantly understand anything said to you in any form of language. The speech patterns you actually hear decode the brainwave matrix which has been fed into your mind by your Babel fish.
>
> (Adams, 1979, pp. 49–50)

**Back-translation** is a way of assessing translation quality. You take a translation from

**www.
10.5, 10.6**

Language A to Language B and obtain an independent translation back into Language A. The degree of discrepancy between the SL text of the first translation and the TL text of the second allows you to assess the quality of the original TL text. It's basically the game known variously as *Chinese Whispers*, *(Broken) Telephone*, *Arab Phone* or *Stille Post*, but with alternating languages.

The Babel fish is, of course, a fanciful notion, the product of the wild imagination of British author and humourist Douglas Adams, creator of *The Hitch Hiker's Guide to the Galaxy*. But surely technology can succeed where biological evolution will – in this case – undoubtedly fail. **Automatic translation** has steadily progressed since its beginnings half a century ago. Many users of the internet will be aware of online tools like Google Translate or Altavista's appropriately named Babel Fish. Both are powered by SYSTRAN, one of the major commercial developers of machine translation, whose products represent the state of the art.

But how close does the software get to actually performing like Adams' original Babel fish or a skilled human translator? As an example, we fed the last line of the *Hitch Hiker's Guide* quotation ('The speech patterns you actually hear decode the brainwave matrix which has been fed into your mind by your Babel fish') into the Altavista system and it gave us the following Spanish TL text:

(7)  El discurso le modeló oye realmente para descifrar la matriz del brainwave que ha sido alimentada en su mente por sus pescados de Babel.

In order to test the quality of this translation, we then asked a balanced bilingual scholar of the Spanish language, and Altavista's Google Fish itself, to **back-translate** the Spanish TL text into English. The results were (8) and (9) respectively:

(8)  The discourse shaped him listens really to decipher the matrix of the brainwave that has been fed in his mind by his fish of Babel.

(9)  The speech modelled really hears to decipher the matrix to him of brainwave that has been fed in its mind by its fish of Babel.

The back-translations in (8) and (9) reveal some major problems with the output in (7), most of them the result of the software's lack of linguistic knowledge and insensitivity to context. For example, the erroneous use of the word *discurso* comes from the ambiguity of the original English word *speech* (meaning both 'spoken language' and 'public address') and the system's inability to disambiguate it. Human translators would be sensitive to the subsequent verb *hear* (used more with the first reading than the second) and the context of the preceding text. The garbage in the first part of the sentence reflects the complex subordination rules used in the original, and *brainwave* remained untranslated presumably because it wasn't there in the translation corpus.

This is a symptom of a larger difficulty in handling language faced by **artificial intelligence** (AI), the interdisciplinary field which designs machine-based intelligent systems. The fact that human languages use such complex bio-computational systems, coupled with the fact that they may be used to communicate an infinite range of messages which are almost always interpretable only when combined with vast sources of non-linguistic knowledge, makes the complete simulation of any one of them by a computer well nigh impossible, at least for the foreseeable future. And if this is the case, you can imagine the extent of the challenge presented by machine translation programmes, which require knowledge of *more than one language* and *more than one set of cultural and contextual knowledge*.

As a result, although machine translation software may be relied upon by end-users when all that is needed is a rough-and-ready sketch of the meaning of the original SL text, it is normally only used professionally as a support tool. For example, the European Commission makes available its own version of SYSTRAN software as an IT aid for staff who need to quickly browse or draft documents in a language they do not speak. But when it is used by the Commission's translation service, the output must be extensively edited by hand (DGT, 2007b, p. 11), requiring knowledge of the SL text.

Recent developments in linguistics and computer science, however, suggest that the Babel fish ideal may be swimming closer, even if it will probably never actually arrive. The 'father of modern linguistics' Noam Chomsky has always stressed that human language is a system with infinite expressive potential obtainable through (1) a finite set of grammatical rules and (2) a finite lexicon. Modelling the lexicon is not the toughest nut to crack for AI, given modern computers' enormous memory capacity and the growing tendency to create programmes which mimic the massive interconnectedness of neural networks. Ignorance of a term (like *brainwave* in our Babel Fish example) is easy to put right: you just add an entry to the lexicon. There are now extremely large specialized **terminology banks** and multilingual dictionaries available for different subject areas, many available online. And through interconnected lexical entries you can simulate context effects by, for example, making stronger connections between *hear* and 'speech as spoken language' and between *listen to* and 'speech as public address.'

It is the unfathomable complexity of grammatical rule-systems that has stymied AI language projects in the past (and currently available machine translation systems, as we saw with the subordinate clauses of our Babel Fish sentence). But what if the 'easy' lexicon could be souped up and the 'difficult' rule-system made redundant? Non-Chomskyan linguists have recently begun to propose that the central role of the rule-system in human language has been exaggerated, and

**Artificial intelligence** (AI) is the interdisciplinary field which develops theory on, and designs and tests, machine-based intelligent systems, like those telephone helpline systems that (fail to) understand your spoken instructions. We don't recommend the Spielberg movie of the same name.

 **www.10.7**

**Terminology banks** provide searchable bilingual or multilingual glossaries of technical or specialist vocabulary for use by translators. A good example is the government of Quebec's *Grand dictionnaire terminologique* in French, English and Latin. Another is Nuclear Threat Initiative's Chinese–English glossary of arms control and nonproliferation terms.

 **www.10.8**

that in fact much of language behaviour may be accounted for by the production and comprehension of memorized chunks: precisely what the lexicon is good for.

There are now massive computational databases of already-used bits of language, namely the *language corpora* that we explored in Chapter 9. So a new approach to machine translation exploits these resources in the form of alignment between attested fragments of discourse and their known equivalents in other languages. This is a modern-day version of what Champollion did with the Rosetta Stone: recall that he used the three aligned inscriptions on the stone to interpret (translate) hitherto undeciphered hieroglyphic texts. **Statistical translation** does the same with SL texts by searching for the statistically most probable matches in a **translation corpus**, – say, the combined database of translated documents at the United Nations. The advantage over earlier translation programmes which sought to simulate human rule-governed language processing is evident. For one thing, the output will be real, human, translator-produced language, rather than pseudo-language generated by machines. For another, such systems will be able to translate vast quantities of documents incredibly rapidly, without compromising inter-document consistency of terminology and style (a perennial problem when human translators work as a team on longer texts). Given the size, scope and impact of the internet, there's a lot more information out there now which needs to be translated. The linguist Richard Sproat (2010, p. 241) concludes his discussion of these developments with the following observation: 'the gap in quality between machine translation and human translation has narrowed. But equally importantly, the information needs of the world have changed.'

But by turning their backs on Chomsky's insight regarding the infinite expressivity of language, the developers and promoters of statistical translation leave no options for the automatic translation of novel material. As Kirsten Malmkjær puts it:

> Language use must . . . be deferential to future users, and although past usage constitutes a monumental corpus that guides and informs future usage, it can neither determine nor reflect future usage. Seen in this light, translating is a display of creativeness.
>
> (Malmkjær, 2005, p. 185)

The point here is that automatic statistical translation will never replace the human translator, since a great deal of language output *is* both novel and unpredictable.

By this we don't, of course, mean to suggest that stored, aligned translation fragments will not be a useful tool to translators: on the contrary, they have already eliminated much of the drudgery and redundancy implicit in technical and non-literary translation. At the European Commission's Directorate-General for Translation, for example, their *Euramis* suite of translation tools includes a huge database of more than 88 million 'translation units' in all of the European Union's twenty official languages (DGT, 2007b, p. 9). At the human translator's request, the software can simultaneously display both identical and 'fuzzy' matches from this huge **translation memory**, together with SYSTRAN's machine translation output. Figure 10.5 gives an example of *Euramis* in action. The lower pane shows the ongoing translation (from Dutch to French), and in the upper pane you can see

**Statistical translation** (or **probabilistic translation**) is a procedure which identifies already-existing translations of chunks of texts and yields the most likely match. An example is Google Translate, which uses millions of pages of translation from the United Nations.

**www.10.9**

A **translation corpus** is a computerized database of existing pairs of SL and TL text fragments in phrase-, sentence- and paragraph-sized chunks, for use in translation software, also known as a **translation memory**.

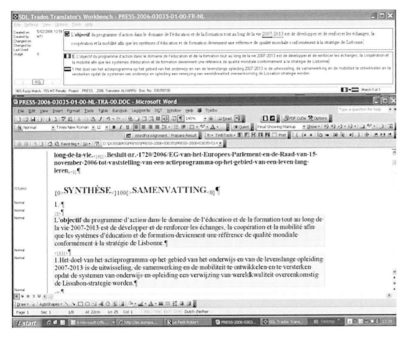

Figure 10.5    Example from *Euramis* of combined retrieval from translation memory and machine translation (Source: DGT, 2007b, p. 22)

the SL fragment sent for matching to the translation memory, and below it the matched SL and TL pair retrieved.

Some freelance translators use *Euramis*, and it has transformed their work, while others may be much happier reaching for their battered bilingual dictionaries or consulting peers online (e.g. in one of the forums at WordReference.com); as we saw in Chapter 5, an overly 'mechanistic' approach to translation in the EU has been accused of constituting a threat to quality (Tosi, 2006). But whatever the reaction by individual translators, the role of IT is set to grow enormously over the next decades. Although Ortega y Gasset's concept of magical transubstantiation, Hardy's secret cipher and Adams' Babel fish will remain forever elusive, all three writers would be truly amazed at how close technology is getting to achieving their impossible dreams.

 **www.10.10**

## 10.8  ROLES FOR APPLIED LINGUISTS

The many 'accidental translators' who take on translation projects because they are bilingual or have a high proficiency in another language are often surprised by the challenges that translation poses, and are unprepared for the subtle judgements and breadth of linguistic and non-linguistic knowledge that the process requires in order to deliver a high quality product. But their prevalence in the industry is often aided and abetted by clients, for two main reasons: accidental translators normally charge much less for their products than trained professionals and in many cases clients cannot evaluate the product because they lack proficiency in the TL.

The discipline of applied linguistics can play a major role in the professionalization of the industry as a whole and of individual members working within it, even though many practitioners and even academics in the area may not recognize this (e.g. Townsley, 2007). Look once more, for example, at the list of knowledge areas sketched in section 10.4. The kind of sensitivity to linguistic and cultural factors represented in these areas, together with the ability to use them in a practice which directly involves clients and other agents who are unversed in linguistics, is precisely the balanced, integrated view that applied linguistics is good at focusing. Thus, a thorough grounding in applied linguistics is excellent preparation for professional accreditation as a translator or an interpreter, or for enrolment in a Translation Studies postgraduate programme which focuses on specific methods, techniques, strategies and resources.

Translation studies programmes in the universities are normally at the master's degree level and are offered in different academic contexts, most commonly: (1) in association with comparative literature or literary studies; (2) in foreign language departments; (3) with linguistics or applied linguistics; or (4) as separate entities, often in combination with intercultural studies. Undergraduate applied linguistics degree programmes will sometimes offer courses in translation studies, but even when they don't, such a degree will provide the sensitivity to language in its cognitive and sociocultural contexts that translators and interpreters must possess.

Applied linguists must also play a role from outside the profession, sensitizing both translators and their clients to a range of applied linguistic issues, such as:

- the urgent need for translated materials into and from minority languages, especially Indigenous languages that are in danger of disappearing;
- the need to educate politicians and policy-makers about the linguistic rights of citizens and non-citizens, who may, in order to exercise these rights, require interpreting and/or translation services they can easily access, and trust;
- the need to carefully consider educational materials such as curriculums and tests which have been translated from one language to another but which are not culturally relevant to target users;
- the need to point out the necessary, and useful, role that translation processes and products play in additional language learning;
- the need to inform educators and other public speakers who work with deaf learners and audiences to provide visual and pragmatic cues that will simplify the job of sign interpreters (e.g. face the audience, stay in one place, speak more slowly, etc.).

For Shelley's violet to survive the crucible, applied linguists certainly have their work cut out. But they have a much better chance of successfully meeting the practical challenges of translation than those who assume that bilingualism is all you need.

1  Type *translate* in to an internet search engine and choose one of the free online machine translators listed. Try the exercise described in section 10.7: type in a couple of sentences in English and use the software to translate them into another language (preferably one with which you are familiar, or you could enlist the help of a classmate or friend who speaks the language you are interested in). Look carefully at the translation offered. Are there any problems with it? What are they? Now, do the exercise in reverse: ask the software to translate the sentences *back* to English. What happens? Are you able to get back to the sentences you originally entered? If not, can you suggest why?

2  If you were asked to translate an academic journal article from another language into English by a friend, would you use automatic translation exclusively, or at all? Why? Consider your proficiency in the SL and the TL, the length of the text, the level of detail needed by your friend, etc.

3  You live in a linguistically diverse city and the mayor asks you to advise on what percentage of the city's budget should be spent on any, or all, of the following:

  (a)  providing classes in the majority language (for people who either are not able to use the majority language at all or only have a very basic level of proficiency);
  (b)  providing classes in a range of minority languages (for people who either are not able to use the minority language offered at all or only have a very basic level of proficiency);
  (c)  translating local government documents into minority languages;
  (d)  providing interpreters who can translate between the majority and minority languages.

  What questions would you need to ask the mayor before starting to formulate your advice?

4  The mayor asks you to join an interview panel for the post of translator/interpreter. What are the linguistic, social and personal skills necessary for the job? Make a list of six interview questions that will help you judge who is the best candidate for the job.

# FURTHER READING

Baker, M. and Saldanha, G. (eds) (2008). *Routledge encyclopedia of translation studies*, 2nd edn. London: Routledge.

Cook, G. (2010). *Translation in language teaching.* Oxford: Oxford University Press.

Gouadec, D. (2007). *Translation as a profession.* Amsterdam: John Benjamins.

Hale, S. B. (2007). *Community interpreting*. Basingstoke, UK: Palgrave Macmillan.

Munday, J. (ed.) (2009). *The Routledge companion to translation studies*. London: Routledge.

Venuti, L. (2004). *The translation studies reader*, 2nd edn. London: Routledge.

# CHAPTER 11

# Lexicography

> The idea that all that work by so many different people will one day be neatly compressed into one oblong book and look as though it just fell out of a tree – that is really a wonder.
>
> (Landau, 2001, pp. 229–230)

Lexicography, the science and practice of dictionary-making, is a vibrant field, currently experiencing rapid growth as a result of the spectacular advances in technology of the last few decades. Dictionaries are no longer fusty tomes compiled by grey-bearded Victorian enthusiasts, who pinned down words like the corpses of exotic butterflies as though desiring to embalm the language itself. Dictionary-makers these days can be pretty savvy, maybe even hip, striving to outdo each other in the authenticity, contemporaneity and accessibility of their wordware. Indeed, although lots of dictionaries are still bought in book form, they are more likely to be consulted nowadays via pre-installed desktop computer applications, websites with online look-up and hand-held devices (Li, 2005).

Dictionaries are perhaps the most *popular* manifestation of applied linguistic labour, found in most homes that have books and used by millions of the planet's literate majority to solve lexical problems that stretch from language learning and translation to crossword solving and technical-report writing. How dictionaries are constructed and how they are used is therefore seen by many as a central area of applied linguistics (although once again there are many lexicographers who would not consider themselves members of the club).

Lexicography is closely associated with an area of descriptive linguistics called **lexicology**. In twentieth century linguistics, lexicology was largely neglected, as the emphasis shifted to phonology, morphology, syntax and semantics. But it hasn't disappeared. As the influential British linguist M. A. K. Halliday (2004) presents it, the goal of lexicology is to produce descriptions of the words of a language, and these descriptions are then published as dictionaries. Thus, dictionary-making starts as lexicology, the study and description of a body of words, and ends as lexicography, the compilation of these descriptions into a single reference work.

Following this logic, we start out this chapter (section 11.1) with a more theoretical discussion of the nature of words as both mental and social objects, before moving on to more applied concerns, such as the changing role of dictionaries (11.2), the variety of forms and functions they take (11.3), how they are compiled (11.4), their central role in language learning (11.5) and, finally, the involvement of technology in the lexicographic process (11.6). By the end of the chapter, you should have a keener understanding of some of the key issues in the theory

**Lexicology** is the academic study of words: their spoken and written forms, their syntactic and morphological properties, and their meanings; in a particular language or in human language in general; both at a fixed point in history and as they change through time.

and practice of lexicography and, in particular, will be able to assess potential contributions of lexicographers to the solution of a variety of applied linguistic problems, as addressed in 11.7.

# 11.1  WORDS IN THE MIND AND IN SOCIETY

Let's start with the problem of what a word is and isn't. Here are some questions to get the ball rolling:

- How many words are there in the title to this sub-section (*Words in the mind and in society*)? Is it six or seven?
- Is *words* the same word as *word*?
- Is *mind* the noun a different word from *mind* the verb (as in 'I don't mind if I do')?
- How do we define words like *in* and *the* such that our definitions also cover the same words in '*in the* know' or '*in the* Taj Mahal'?

These are not easy questions, because the concept of 'word' is not at all an easy one to define, despite its familiarity. In the last century, as general linguistics turned its central attention away from the description of languages as formal systems divorced from mind and society, and began to focus instead on language as mental representation and socially situated action, the old lexicological certainty about wordhood was eroded. Linguists now question the stability of the concept of word, asking among other things whether word *meaning* is really 'part' of the word, or is found in social usage or in the mind's conceptual memory; whether words have single canonical forms or belong to fuzzy, overlapping sets shared between speakers and situations; whether words have any limits on their length or internal structure; whether they can be counted, and so whether vocabularies can be quantified (Hall, 2005, ch. 3).

In general linguistics, some (e.g. Hall, 2005, p. 83) claim that words as single entities don't really exist . . . But *applied* linguists can't afford to wallow in such epistemological luxury. As we explained in Chapter 1, they need to mediate between theory and practice, between the inherent uncertainty of scientific hypothesis-testing and the 'faith-based' certainty of folk belief. In other words, applied linguists need a working definition of 'word' so they can help solve non-linguists' problems with what *they* think of as words. For example:

- experts in language teaching need to connect with *learners'* conceptions of vocabulary and how it is learned, despite the attractiveness and plausibility of more radical, research-based lexical approaches (e.g. Willis, 1990; Lewis, 1993);
- translators often need to work with the conventional notion of translation equivalents at the word level, even if psycholinguistic and sociolinguistic research suggests that absolute translation equivalents don't exist (see Chapter 10);
- language pathologists need to deal with the real problems people with aphasia have with word-finding in ways which will be meaningful to both patients and their families (see Chapter 13).

Perhaps foremost among the applied linguists, lexicographers have to embrace a working definition of 'word', since their task is to collect, analyse and codify what language users treat as words, so that those users can have a permanent record of them, as reference and guide.

In order to operationalize the notion of word for lexicography in a way which is at least compatible with the complexities of the linguistic view, we should probably start by acknowledging the dual mental and social existence of words. These are concomitant and complementary realities: words must be both mental and social in order to do their job. Let's take each in turn.

## Words as mental networks

First, from the psycholinguistic perspective, words are interconnected memory representations in individual minds, linking together a mass of information in addition to form and core meaning. Here are some of the less intuitive bits:

- fragments of grammar (parts of speech, kinds of complement, etc. – for example that *hold* is a 'transitive verb' and that *furniture* is a non-count noun in some speakers' minds and a count noun in others');
- pointers to **lexical phrases** and **collocations** in which the word form habitually participates, like *take* in the entry for *umbrage*;
- activation levels (how fast the form can be accessed in memory when you need it for speaking, listening, reading or writing), determined by **frequency** and recency of usage (for example high frequency *rain* versus low frequency *precipitation*);
- indices of pragmatic force, situational appropriateness, sociocultural value and other connotations of usage, for example *problem* versus *issue* versus *dilemma*.

From this perspective, words are not neat pairings of forms and meanings (like the two sides of a coin in the famous metaphor of the Swiss linguist Ferdinand de Saussure); rather they are fuzzy sets of disparate kinds of knowledge connected up in multifarious ways. Here is a tiny selection of some of the causes of blurred lexical boundaries:

- There are, at least in English, multiple **homonyms**, either homophones like *red* (the colour) and the past tense of *read*, represented as a single phonological word form connected to two different spellings and meanings, or homographs like *lead* (the verb) and *lead* (the metal), a single orthographic word form with two different pronunciations and meanings.
- Some words with purely grammatical functions (like the *of* in 'think of' or the *to* in 'I want to be alone') have form and part of speech but no meaning.
- Many (perhaps most) word forms express more than one related meaning, a phenomenon known as **polysemy**. For example, *get* as in *get old* ('become'), *get a new car* ('obtain'), *get talking* ('begin gradually'), *get the joke* ('understand'), etc.
- Some (potential) word meanings have no single word form to express them: these are **lexical gaps**, like the absence in English of a single word for 'five

**Lexical phrases** are chunks of language consisting of strings of words which are regularly spoken, signed and/or written together, like *Take care!* or *To whom it may concern.*

**Collocations** are frequently occurring sequences of words. You can search for sample collocations for words that you input at *The Collins WordbanksOnline English Corpus.*

 **www.11.1**

**Word frequency** is an estimation of the regularity with which a word occurs in speech and/or writing, normally calculated on the basis of large samples of language, such as those provided by corpora. The *Compleat Lexical Tutor*, a suite of tools from Tom Cobb at the Université du Québec à Montréal, contains a frequency profiler for texts you can input yourself, and is available on the companion website.

 **www.11.2**

**Homonyms** are two or more words that are pronounced and/or written the same way (e.g. *site*, *sight*, and *cite*; a sycophantic *bow* to the Queen vs. a *bow* in your hair; *case* as 'baggage' and 'instance').

www.11.3

www.11.4

**Polysemy** refers to the very frequent situation in which a single word form does many semantic jobs, expressing a series of related meanings. There will be a core concept underlying the several meanings, but it's normally context which provides the specific sense (e.g. *run* in *Tears ran down his face* and *A shuttle runs from the airport every hour*).

**Lexical gaps** occur in a language when it lacks a word for a concept (which may be expressed lexically in another language).

The **mental lexicon** is the component of memory where we store the vocabulary we know and use. We access its entries at lightning speed every time we speak, listen, sign, read or write.

years' (where Spanish has *lustro*) or for 'aunts and uncles' (where Spanish has *tíos*). Douglas Adams, creator of the Babel fish (see Chapter 10), also wrote (with John Lloyd) *The Meaning of Liff*, a 'dictionary of things that there aren't any words for yet', available in its entirety online (Adams and Lloyd, 1983).

And the list could go on (see the companion website for the full version). The upshot is that words seen as entries in the **mental lexicon** are not unitary notions. In lexicography, on the other hand, their waywardness must be acknowledged but also tamed, if dictionaries are to serve their users in an effective manner.

## Words in social use

Now we turn to words as social objects, because they don't figure only in lexical memory, but also out there in groups, identities and events. Sociolinguists, like psycholinguists, see words as inherently variable, hard to pin down in lexicographical collections. From the social perspective their variability is seen in the situations in which they are used and the identities of the groups who use them, rather than in the intricacies of their mental storage. As we have seen again and again, language doesn't operate in a vacuum. It is always contextually mediated. Word forms and their core meanings are not on their own sufficient to communicate the rich kinds of meaning that we human beings need in order to negotiate our daily lives. Much of word meaning is actually derived from contexts of use, and these are infinitely variable and can't be recorded in the finite limits of dictionaries. Furthermore, some pronunciations of word forms, or the forms themselves, are associated with particular groups of speakers. Others carry different meanings when used by certain speakers in certain social contexts.

Take the following text: 'I've done a lot of drugs in my time, but these days if I do a load of charlie or pills on Friday, I'm monged out till about Wednesday and I can't think straight while making a tune' (from *Q magazine*, 2002, cited in Dent, 2003, p. 77). The verb *do* when used with drugs means the same as *take*, but with the additional meaning component 'regularly', and for recreational rather than medicinal purposes. But the difference is not just a semantic one. 'Doing' drugs is associated also with an informal social register: it will not be used in medical textbooks or legal codes, for example. The word form *charlie* will be known by most speakers probably as a proper name, but here is an insider term for cocaine. Then there is the phrase 'monged out', which appeared in UK street slang in the last decade and means 'under the influence of drink or drugs'. It is not yet in most dictionaries, although Grant Barrett's online dictionary of 'words from the fringes of English' (Barrett, 2006) lists it as coming from the noun *monging*, dating from as far back as 1992. Finally, consider the verb *make*, used here with 'a tune' where the more specific verb *compose* might be expected. The verb is used by a musician, quoted in a rock music magazine, so it may be that 'making tunes' is favoured over 'composing tunes' because of its less pretentious, more 'hip' tone.

www.11.5

The sociolinguist will thus see words as functions of social contexts, acquiring meaning from context (*doing* drugs), marking group identities (*charlie*), reflecting social trends (*monged out*) and marking speaker roles and attitudes (*making* tunes).

All this causes potential problems for dictionary-makers, who must present a static, inevitably context-reduced record of what is a dynamic social phenomenon.

## Capturing words

If words represent a moving target, both psychologically and socially, how are the lexicographers to capture them? Here are a few initial criteria, which we'll develop as the chapter progresses:

1   First and foremost, they must maintain the necessary fiction that words do exist as unitary objects rather than as random nodes spread over mushy networks.
2   They must view them as collective linguistic resources, rather than as properties of individuals – that is, they must be seen as subject to codification in the sense discussed in Chapters 2 and 5. (This has ideological implications, e.g. in World Englishes, a point we'll take up later in section 11.2.)
3   They must be selective in the information they present. This may be achieved by:

- restricting meanings to core senses or frequently attested senses;
- providing contextual elements only when they recur with frequency;
- limiting information about pronunciation and spelling to one or at most two varieties;
- packaging the lexical spaghetti of homophones, polysemes and the like into mouth-sized spoonfuls (called *entries*).

4   They need to determine some kind of index of currency, so they can decide which word forms and related meanings to include and which to exclude or label as 'dated', 'archaic', etc.
5   Finally, they must take a position – in effect an ideological stance – on whether they wish to record actual usage, present an 'expert opinion', report some kind of consensus about usage or actively seek to influence usage.

The first four criteria, relatively technical issues, can be put off for later. But we really can't postpone discussion of the last criterion, which still grabs headlines on a regular basis and seems to annoy clients of applied linguistics (in this case, the dictionary users) as much as any other area we cover in this book.

## 11.2  AUTHORITY OR RECORD?

In *The Devil's Dictionary* (2003 [1911]), the US writer Ambrose Bierce starts off the entry for *lexicographer* as follows:

 **www.11.6**

**LEXICOGRAPHER**, *n.*
A pestilent fellow who, under the pretense of recording some particular stage in the development of a language, does what he can to arrest its growth, stiffen

its flexibility and mechanize its methods. For your lexicographer, having written his dictionary, comes to be considered 'as one having authority,' whereas his function is only to make a record, not to give a law.

(Bierce, 2003 [1911], p. 178)

Bierce's view looks like quite an enlightened one for the time, since he appears to be arguing for descriptivism over prescriptivism ('a record, not . . . a law'). But he is still deeply conservative at heart, worrying later in the same entry about linguistic 'impoverishment' and 'decay' and extolling the 'golden prime and high noon of English speech; when from the lips of the great Elizabethans fell words that made their own meaning and carried it in their very sound' (Beirce, 2003 [1911], p. 179). The idea that the lexicographer should provide a full and faithful record of English speech as it falls from the lips of uneducated labourers, unruly teenagers, rural dialect users, 'non-native' speakers, gang members and others who may not aspire to the epithet 'great' would probably have appalled him.

Almost a century later, many educated speakers in countries with long literacy traditions still succumb to the 'spell' of language (Hall, 2005), allowing the monolithic myth of a single correct version of each language to mould our attitudes to vocabulary. When we exclaim, 'But it isn't in the dictionary!' to affirm that some word or other 'doesn't exist', we continue to 'invest [lexicographers] with judicial power'. As Carter (1998, p. 151) puts it, 'the dictionary is a trusted and respected repository of facts about a language. And an important part of its good image is that it has institutional authority'. But although ordinary speakers insist on treating dictionaries as repositories of the one true version of the language, few English language lexicographers would now feel comfortable with the role of custodian of linguistic purity.

The publication of *Webster's Third New International Dictionary* in the US in 1961 marked a watershed for lexicography, with its 'permissive' (i.e. descriptivist) stance. It included so-called 'non-standard' forms like *ain't*, *groovy* and *irregardless*, and cited as sources people like Elizabeth Taylor and Bob Hope as well as William Shakespeare and Henry James. This was a major shift from the original intention of Noah Webster himself. In his *An American Dictionary of the English Language* (1828), Webster patriotically set out to codify the English of the United States as an independent variety, distinct from British English. Although he had no wish to hinder the natural growth of the language and welcomed lexical innovation, he still had strong ideas about what was acceptable and what was not, omitting 'indelicate' words like *turd* and *fart*, which had appeared in Samuel Johnson's and other more liberal dictionaries of the previous century (Landau, 2001, p. 69).

The reception by the critics and the language mavens was – perhaps unsur-prisingly for the times – extremely negative. Finegan (1980, pp. 116–128) recounts the 'hysterical alarm' with which the *Third* was met, citing review articles with titles like 'The Death of Meaning'. The main criticisms were that it was too 'democratic' and 'permissive', and – interestingly for us – that it 'was thought a 'hostage' of the new science [of linguistics]', which in its objective, non-judgemental approach to language variation was perceived as promoting linguistic anarchy. The American Heritage publishing company was so outraged that it sought to buy Merriam-Webster in order to suppress the *Third*. Failing in its attempt, it published its own in 1969: *The American Heritage Dictionary* (AHD). The AHD adopted what Finegan and Besnier (1989, p. 500) call a 'custodial' position, like that of the national language academies, which 'has limited respect for what even reputable writers do; instead it places a premium on what such writers and others (including the prescriptivists themselves) say *ought* to be done'. The arbiters were a usage panel of the great and good, including 'distinguished writers, critics, historians, editors and journalists, poets, anthropologists, professors of English and journalism, even several United States senators' (Finegan, 1980, p. 136). Ironically, given their implicit desire to constitute the definitive authority on lexical usage, the panel agreed unanimously on only one of the more than 200 cases they were called upon to adjudicate.

Let's take a look at the corresponding sample entries for the verb *finalize* in the *Third* and *AHD*, respectively:

> **fi•nal•ize** [. . .] *vb* -ed/-ing/-s vt : to put in final or finished form : finish, complete, close <soon my conclusions will be *finalized* –D.D. Eisenhower> <the couple ~ plans to marry at once –S. J. Perelman> <empowered to . . . ~ the deal –James Joseph> : give final approval to <the list has not been *finalized* by the deputy, but it won't be changed now –Robertson Davies><ties up the day's loose ends, *finalizing* the papers prepared and presented by his staff –*Newsweek*> ~ vi : to bring something to completion <if we don't ~ tonight, those two . . . will get suspicious and sell to someone else –I.L. Idriess>.
>
> (*Webster's Third New International Dictionary*, 1961)

> **fi•nal•ize** [. . .] *tr.v.* –**ized, -izing, -izes.** To put into final form; to complete
> ***Usage:*** *Finalize* is closely associated with the language of bureaucracy, in the minds of many careful writers and speakers, and is consequently avoided by them. The example *finalize plans for a class reunion* is termed unacceptable by 90 per cent of the Usage Panel. In most such examples a preferable choice is possible from among *complete, conclude, make final,* and *put in final form.*
>
> (*The American Heritage Dictionary*, 1969)

Note how the *Third* simply lays out the series of meanings illustrated by their citation evidence, using definitions, near-synonyms and examples, blithely listing the verb as both transitive and intransitive, and allowing social contexts of use to emerge from sentence context. The AHD's approach is the polar opposite, providing only one definition, for the transitive verb only, and a lengthy usage section characterized by implicit social judgements about groups of speakers and explicit advice regarding the word itself and how to deal with it: 'careful' users associate the word with bureaucracy, and so 'consequently' they avoid it; the Usage Panel explicitly disapproves (with 90 per cent of them finding it unacceptable!), so 'preferable' alternatives are offered. The contrast between the approaches could not be sharper.

So what has changed since this 'war of words' of the 1960s? One thing is certain: linguistics has not had much of an impact on the general public's belief in the authority of dictionaries. But applied linguistics, including lexicography, has matured, and language professionals now know better than to ignore their clients' views by practising naïve 'linguistics applied' (cf. Chapter 1). Much contemporary lexicography manages both to remain true to the linguistic view of language and also to satisfy clients' perceived need for guidance, by recording all common usage

**www.11.7**

while at the same time indicating 'appropriate' contexts of that usage. So, for example, the Merriam-Webster Online now has a usage note for *finalize*, which tells us that the verb 'is most frequently used in government and business dealings; it usually is not found in belles-lettres'. It is still deemed unacceptable by over one-quarter of the AHD Fourth Edition's Usage Panel, however (revealing that not all lexicographers are equally hip!).

Significantly, the applied linguistic perspective has not sought to eradicate *all* vestiges of prescriptivism in contemporary lexicography. As we saw in Chapters 2 and 6, a uniform written variety of the language may still be defended, and is in fact assumed in all general purpose dictionaries, with variants clearly labelled as such. Take for example the social conventions of spelling. The FAQ (frequently asked questions) section of the OED's AskOxford website states the following:

**www.11.8**

> Most lexicographers are good spellers, if only owing to lots of practice. Lexicographers take the same view of language as other linguists. They know that language use varies widely in space and time, and they spend much of their time charting its changes through history. They are therefore not shocked or surprised to encounter variation in spelling. At the same time, they recognize that there is a standard set of conventional spelling rules to which we all mostly conform, and which assist good communication.
>
> (AskOxford, 2010)

Furthermore, you may recall from Chapter 5 that dictionaries play an important role in codifying the vocabulary in newly literate languages and languages in the process of revitalization through literacy, as a tool of both corpus and status planning. This applied linguistics enterprise is essentially prescriptivist: providing a 'standard' list of word forms and meanings which may be used in official documents and other national forums, both oral and written. Dictionary projects in language planning are also often charged with formulating terminology to serve new cultural, technological, scientific and economic challenges. The Maori Language Commission, charged by legislation from 1987 to promote the use of Maori in New Zealand, sees lexical expansion as a major language planning goal. *Te Matatiki*, a monolingual dictionary, is an important part of that process, and the prescriptivist component is confirmed on the Commission's website in a reference to new words being '*validated* by the Commission' (Maori Language Commission, n.d., emphasis ours).

In groups of users which are already literate in at least one majority language, the publication of a dictionary to preserve a minority language may actually backfire, especially when applied linguistics expertise is not sought. Liddicoat (2000, p. 428) reports that a grass-roots dictionary project for Jersey Norman French (JNF) has 'actually given an impetus to language shift rather than to language maintenance', because the orthographic codification of what was a collection of oral varieties led to feelings of linguistic inadequacy, especially among its younger speakers. He continues:

> The development of a dictionary, with a standardised spelling system, is not an ideologically neutral act . . . The presentation of an authoritative, normative, but unexplained orthographic system had an ecological impact. Native speakers of JNF, who are literate in at least one language [English and/or French],

now express a lack of proficiency in JNF because they do not know how to write the language – they have become illiterate.

(Liddicoat, 2000, p. 428)

This case illustrates once more our contention that applied linguistics cannot operate in a social vacuum: lexicography affects language ecology, and so must be conducted with foresight, sensitivity and extensive knowledge of associated issues in general and applied linguistics.

In some of the world's more 'powerful' language communities, dictionaries may play a much more overtly prescriptivist role in the language management process, responding to the spread of English and the perceived 'sullying' of the national tongue through loan words. As Finegan and Besnier point out in the passage quoted on p. 255, the dictionaries of the revered national language academies are often the major instruments in this endeavour. The academies consciously adopt a clearly ideological lexicographical policy, though their ecological impact on speakers' usage has been negligible. The Académie Française was founded in 1635 by Cardinal Richelieu, as part of broad efforts to centralize royal power so as to counter internal and external threats. In the face of new perceived threats from English, the Academy clearly affirms that the purpose of its dictionary is to 'fixe l'usage de la langue' (fix language usage) (Académie Française, n.d.). Other academies take their lead from the French. The Spanish Royal Academy, for example, was founded in 1713 with the motto 'Limpia, fija y da esplendor' (cleanse, fix and make resplendent). The stated aim of its dictionary is to 'confer normative value in the entire Spanish-speaking world' (Real Academia Española, 2006, our translation).

Using dictionaries as instruments of 'lexical cleansing' is not restricted to the wealthy, former imperial powers of Europe. Smaller nations, hosting smaller languages, asserted their postcolonial identities also through the exclusion of foreign words. According to Spolsky (2004, pp. 37–38), the Iranian Academy of Language proposed 35,000 new Persian words to replace foreign ones before the revolution of 1979, and after the Soviet occupation Estonia published 100 terminological dictionaries to counteract the pressure from Russian. And Quechua, an Indigenous language spoken by millions in Peru and Ecuador and in the Andean regions of Bolivia and Colombia, has been subject to attempts to 'fix and cleanse' by the Cusco-based Academy of the Quechua Language (Hornberger and King, 1998; Marr, 1999).

Dictionaries can, of course, also be used as tools of resistance to prescriptivism. The online *Coxford Singlish Dictionary*, for example, provides a satirical antidote to the Singapore government-sponsored 'Good English Campaign', which, you may recall from Chapter 5, attempts to stifle the local, indigenized variety of English (*Coxford Singlish Dictionary*, n.d.). But even in postcolonial World Englishes contexts where one might expect a more radical, anti-prescriptivist attitude, the Inner Circle (Anglo native-speaker) models are being replaced in the Outer Circle by new norms determined by *local* 'educated' usage. Kachru and Smith state the following about Asian ELT professionals:

 **www.11.9**

[They] are used to norms presented in [American and British] dictionaries and as mature users of the language, they rely on their prior experience. However, they are also aware of the local norms of usage and are familiar with words and expressions that even highly educated people in their own community use regularly. These local words and expressions, of course, are not listed in the dictionaries they are familiar with. The dilemma that they face is whether to consider the local items *legitimate* and *acceptable* in educated English.

(Kachru and Smith, 2008, p. 105, emphasis ours)

These authors provide references to various dictionary projects for Englishes of the Outer and Expanding Circles (Kachru and Smith, 2008, p. 103), highlighting the success of the ongoing *Macquarie Dictionary* project for South and Southeast Asia. But the main criteria they cite for inclusion of items are: (1) occurrence and frequency in the corpus being assembled; and (2) 'opinion of local experts with regard to the item's status, i.e. is it used in "standard" regional English – both formal and informal – or is it restricted to informal colloquial language use only?' (Kachru and Smith, 2008, p. 110). There are clear echoes of the *American Heritage* approach here. But while linguistic hegemony exists at global levels – US and UK standard Englishes globally, Russian in the ex-USSR, Spanish in Latin America – lexicographical prescriptivism is an inevitable factor in local language planning.

## 11.3 USES AND TYPES OF DICTIONARIES

When asked to name a dictionary, English speakers in the UK will probably mention the *Oxford*, and in the US *Webster's*. French speakers will go for *Robert*, *Larousse* or that of the Académie Française; German speakers might plump for *Duden*; and most Spanish speakers will unquestioningly commend that of the *Real Academia*. When prompted to tell you what they use these dictionaries for, they will in all likelihood tell you that they use them to look up the meaning or spelling of a word they're unsure of. But there are many thousands of dictionaries in the world's major languages, presenting different kinds of words in many different ways – and for many different purposes. Amazon.com lists over 28,000 titles in its category of dictionaries and thesauri.

Lexicographical typologies have been proposed which classify dictionaries into a whole host of types, defined by anything from age of user to number of words included. Landau (2001) mentions an extensive range. In the following sub-sections we explore some of the huge variety of formats and objectives which dictionaries adopt, starting with issues of access and structure, and then moving on to specialized lexicographical content.

The internal organization of a dictionary's entries is called its **microstructure**. The way the whole dictionary is put together (with words listed in alphabetical order, for example) is called the **macrostructure**.

## Differences in macrostructure

A distinction is drawn in lexicography between a dictionary's **microstructure**, the internal organization of individual word entries, and its **macrostructure**, the organization of the whole work. We'll concentrate on the latter here, leaving the former until later. Oxford University Press publishes over 200 titles with the word *dictionary* in the title, but many of them, such as *A Dictionary of Chemistry* or the *Oxford Dictionary of Dance* are actually encyclopaedias, reference works in which concepts are the focus, rather than the words that label them. Encyclopaedias

closely resemble dictionaries because our principal means of transmitting information about concepts is through the words associated with them. Although pictures
can help immensely, we still have no conventional method for ordering visual
information, thus making word-based, alphabetically ordered entries the current
standard for easy access. Dictionaries focus on words, even though it's often the
concept conveyed by the word that dictionary users are looking for: if you come
across a word form you don't recognize (e.g. *metamer*), or one that you do but
whose exact meaning you don't know or recall (e.g. *polymer*), you may well reach
for your dictionary. However, if you want to know more about chlorophyll, the novels
of Naguib Mahfouz or China's Qin Dynasty you're more likely to consult Wikipedia
on the internet or a print encyclopaedia in your local library.

What happens if you have the concept more or less clear in your mind but it's
the word's *form* which escapes you? Say the form is *polymer* (you need it because
you're telling a neighbour about the anti-corrosive polymer coating on your new car),
but it's not even on the tip of your tongue. You can't use a traditional dictionary or
encyclopaedia to find the word because the *word form* is the access point and
that's precisely the information you lack. You might, however, have in mind a related
but more general word, such as *chemical*. The dictionary entry for *chemical* is
unlikely to mention the word *polymer*, but a thesaurus entry will. Although the word
*thesaurus* is sometimes used to describe other kinds of dictionary, most people now
use it to refer to the kind of work first compiled by the French lexicographer Peter
Mark Roget, published in 1852 and still perhaps the most widely used work of this
kind. It contains over a quarter of a million terms, organized thematically into over
a thousand 'idea categories', which themselves are grouped into eight conceptual
'classes': abstract relations, space, physics, matter, sensation, intellect, volition and
affections.

To find the word *polymer*, for example, the user starts by looking up a semantically related word in the alphabetical index. Thus, the first reference in the index
entry for *chemical* points you to section 379.1 in the main list, the first of thirteen
sub-categories of the category 'chemicals', part of the sub-class 'matter in general',
in the fourth idea class, namely 'matter'. There, you read:

> nouns **chemical**, chem(o)- *or* chemi-, chemic(o)-; organic chemical, biochem-
> ical, inorganic chemical; fine chemicals, heavy chemicals; **element**, chemical
> element; **radical**; **ion**, anion, cation; atom 326.4,21; **molecule**, macromole-
> cule; **compound**; isomer, pseudoisomer, stereoisomer, diastereoisomer,
> enantiomer, enantiomorph, alloisomer, chromoisomer, metamer, polymer,
> copolymer, interpolymer.
>
> (*Roget's Thesaurus*)

Note that no meanings are indicated, although terms closer in meaning are grouped
between semicolons and more general terms appear in boldface.

A thesaurus like *Roget's* helps users not only to find a word form for a known
concept, but also to choose alternative word forms for aesthetic reasons (hence the
reference to 'literary composition' in *Roget's* original title) or for the expression of
finer meaning distinctions or for better contextual 'fit' with the text being written. In
this sense, a thesaurus resembles a dictionary of synonyms and antonyms, which
is like a regular dictionary but lists words with close meanings and opposing

meanings, rather than giving definitions or illustrating usage. Take the *Collins Paperback Thesaurus in A-to-Z Form*, to be found on many bookshelves; this is more a dictionary of synonyms and antonyms than a thesaurus in the sense of *Roget's*. In the latter, the category 'conciseness' is found between 'plain speech' and 'diffuseness', but in the former the entry for *concise* appears between the semantically unrelated *conciliatory* and *conclave*. So the Collins thesaurus differs from *Roget's* in both its macrostructure and microstructure. The alphabetical arrangement of a synonym and antonym dictionary provides one-step rather than two-step access to entries, and the entries themselves contain possible substitutes for the headword as well as opposite meanings, rather than all associated words.

A **rhyming dictionary** is a dictionary organized according to the end of the word rather than the beginning. Some use spelling as the organizing principle (so *sew* is near *dew*), but the best use sound (so *sew* is near *dough*).

A further, rather uncommon, kind of macrostructure is that followed by **rhyming dictionaries**. In this type, the focus is exclusively on the word form, and meaning is irrelevant. Although rhyming dictionaries will principally be of use to poets or songsters who use rhyming couplets, they are also of use to linguists, when they need to find lists of words which all share the same suffix, for example. Of course, technological advances are making macrostructure a dynamic rather than a fixed dimension of dictionaries. So, for example, you can find rhymes, homophones, synonyms and polysemes (even pictures!) all through the same search engine at rhymezone.com, and you can get lists of words all ending with the same letter sequences, along with definitions and translations, at onelook.com. (See section 11.6 for more on technology.)

**www.11.10**

**www.11.11**

Finally, there is an expanding range of dictionaries published for deaf and blind users, client areas often neglected in lexicography (although Hartmann [2001, p. 73] acknowledges the former). For ASL users, the *Gallaudet Dictionary of American Sign Language* (with DVD; Valli, 2005) is the biggest, containing over 3,000 signs and English translations. Brien's (1992) dictionary, using photographs and including extensive grammatical information, remains the most complete for British Sign Language. For the blind, Braille dictionaries are costly to produce and remarkably unwieldy. Since Braille takes up over three times the space of printed letters, a college dictionary using this alphabet can run to over seventy volumes (Hartz, 2000)! For those with residual vision there are large print dictionaries, such as Oxford's, which covers over 90,000 words and was designed with advice from the UK's Royal National Institute for Blind People. More common now, however, are speaking dictionaries such as those produced by Franklin Electronic Publishers, which deliver the contents of Merriam-Webster dictionaries in the spoken modality.

## Specialized dictionaries

The dictionary types described in the previous pages respond to different user needs by adapting access route and macrostructure, but their coverage of words is not restricted to a particular usage domain, oral variety or genre of discourse. Some dictionaries are designed for use by a subset of the speech community, defined by age, profession, language proficiency, cultural identity or other group membership. Examples include second language learners' and children's dictionaries (which we look at in greater detail in section 11.5) and dialect dictionaries.

Still others are designed for any social group, but specialize in some subset of a language's vocabulary. Dictionaries of slang, for example, record the informal words and phrases associated with particular subcultures (normally 'minority' sub-cultures like teenagers, gangs or gay people) or simply with 'non-standard' usage which goes beyond regional or social dialect (especially items relating to sex and sexuality, drugs and 'embarrassing' bodily functions). Such dictionaries provide data for social historians, sociolinguists and others, but are perhaps mostly browsed for entertainment by general readers. Technical and professional dictionaries, on the other hand, contain the jargon associated with the concepts, processes, theories and practices of, say, electrical engineers, horticulturalists or psycholinguists. Jargon dictionaries also exist for other realms of human activity, from football to folk music, web-surfing to wine-tasting. Such works may be consulted by members of the associated community or group, in order to ensure consistent usage and thus maintain group cohesion, as well as by outsiders interested in cracking the users' linguistic code.

Another important type of dictionary is the bilingual (or, less common, the multilingual) dictionary. Users of such dictionaries stretch all the way from beginning learners at one extreme to professional translators at the other (as we saw in Chapters 9 and 10). Bilingual and multilingual dictionaries are often also used as tools of language policy and planning, in order to provide bridging points between speakers and texts operating in different national languages. *Afrilingo*, for example, is a translation software package which incorporates a dictionary of over 3,000 translation equivalents in the eleven official languages of South Africa (Afrikaans, English, isiNdebele, isiXhosa, isiZulu, Sepedi, Sesotho, Setswana, siSwati, Tshivenda, Xitsonga). It is being co-sponsored by the government's Pan South African Language Board, to complement a more ambitious project to compile monolingual dictionaries for each language (PanSALB, 2009a).  **www.11.12**

In the compilation of bilingual and multilingual dictionaries the problem of translation equivalence we came across in Chapter 10 must be met head-on. Whereas in translation, more or less precise equivalents may be selected so as to render the specific contextualized meaning (or may be avoided altogether in 'freer' translations), in lexicography the equivalents must be of general application, because once recorded in print they become fixed, codified, decontextualized. The need for example sentences is thus paramount, especially for learners, as we'll see in further detail in section 11.5.

In this section we've seen examples of various types of dictionary, designed for different users with different purposes. And yet they're not so different from each other in structure, and all share a common process of compilation, as we'll see in section 11.4, which takes a look at the complex process of dictionary-making, from initial plans to final production.

## 11.4  DICTIONARY COMPILATION

Compiling a dictionary used to take a very long time. The OED saga, for example, was initiated by the Philological Society of London in 1857, but the last volume of the first edition didn't appear until 1928, over seventy years later. Advances in technology over the past few decades have sped up the glacial flow of earlier lexicographical practice, but still the path from inception to publication is a slow one. The French Academy's website (Académie Française, n.d.), for example, reveals  **www.11.13**

that the entries corresponding to the second volume of the ninth edition of their magnum opus were completed according to a rather unhurried schedule, as shown below:

*fatigable à filon, n°44, 26–5–1994*
*filoselle à formation, n°36, 28–3–1995*
*forme à frontignan, n°72, 8–8–1995*
*frontispice à gendarmerie, n°1, 16–1–1996*

. . .

*parfum à patte, n°10, 4–10–2006*
*patté à périodiquement, n° 3, 21–3–2007*
*périoste à piécette, n°16, 26–10–2007*
*pied à plébéien, n°13, 24–9–2008*

That's less than one letter of the alphabet per year, indicating that even with modern tools lexicography remains a lengthy process.

What takes so long? Well, to a certain extent this will depend on the type of dictionary being written (see section 11.3), and this, in turn, will normally depend on an identified demand or need. But most dictionary projects will pass through a series of seven cascading (rather than discrete) stages, as depicted in Figure 11.1. As in all complex tasks, the desired outcomes and the appropriate inputs and procedures required to achieve them must be planned. The final outcome is, of course, the production of the dictionary, be it in paper and ink or LCD and pixels. In

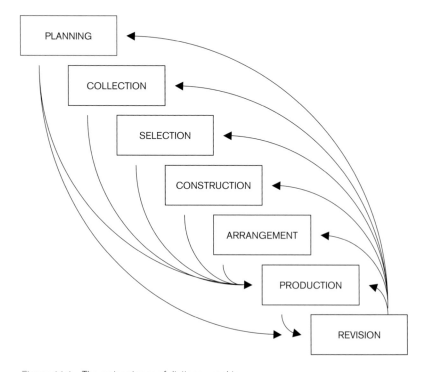

Figure 11.1   The major stages of dictionary-making

between come the core phases of the lexicographical process: (1) *collection* of words and contexts of their use; (2) *selection* of the words to be included; (3) *construction* of the entries in which the words will appear, i.e. microstructure; and (4) their *arrangement* together in the dictionary, i.e. macrostructure (cf. Zgusta, 1971). The seventh stage in Figure 11.1 is the all-important and never-ending revision stage, as the dictionary-makers constantly try to keep up to date with the hurtling dynamism of the language.

The arrows in the diagram reflect the fact that these stages may overlap and interact with each other. For example, each stage must be planned, including revision, and each stage must be revised, including planning.

## Planning

Market research will probably precede other kinds of planning. Lexicography is unique in applied linguistics in that the ultimate objective is, almost always, the design of a commercial product. Aside from the most well-known titles, dictionaries have not traditionally had very high profit margins, although technology is changing this (the licensing of digital rights to the AHD, for example, has made millions for its owner, the Houghton Mifflin Company, over the past few years). Unlike most other kinds of books, dictionaries cost a lot of money early in the editorial process and their actual production can be relatively cheap. Hence, although publishers don't always require that their lexicographers research the market directly, they will insist from the outset that the scholars have clearly identified future users' preferences and requirements.

Knowledge of their clients will assist lexicographers in making decisions about the size and scope of the product, the time frame for compilation, and the resources needed, such as the design of database systems (where increasingly they will work alongside software engineers). Such knowledge will also allow them to plan the word lists themselves, locate the best sources for definitions and examples, determine policy on the amount and type of guidance on usage, and decide on layout and conventions of presentation. A pioneer in the employment of user research was the lexicographer Clarence Barnhart, who applied a systematic questionnaire to US college teachers almost half a century ago to establish students' preferences for different kinds of information included in college dictionary entries (Hartmann, 2001, pp. 81–82). (Perhaps unsurprisingly, he found that students used dictionaries most to check spelling and meaning, and were least concerned with etymology.)

## Collection and selection

But before resolving what to put in each entry – for example whether or not to include etymologies – one must decide which words to give entries for in the first place. Words must be collected, and then a subset selected for inclusion. Barnhart pointed out that if a project for a college dictionary did not establish limits on the number of words before compilation, the estimated page length would be entirely used up before the letter E was reached (Landau, 2001, p. 357). Landau (2001, p. 360) reports using Thorndike's system of proportions of words per initial letter

Table 11.1 Proportions of English words per initial letter in Thorndike's block system, where one block represents just under 1 per cent of the total number of words

| Number of blocks | Words beginning with: |
| --- | --- |
| 1 | j, k, q, xyz |
| 2 | n, u, v |
| 3 | o, w |
| 4 | e, g, h, i, l |
| 5 | f, m, r, t |
| 6 | a, b, d |
| 8 | p |
| 10 | c |
| 13 | s |

for some of his own English dictionaries. Thorndike divided the lexicon into 105 blocks, with each block containing roughly the same number of words. His proportions are given in Table 11.1.

This means, for example, that words beginning with *x, y* and *z* should between them account for just under 1 per cent of the words in the dictionary; that words beginning with *c* should account for roughly 9.5 per cent; and that the highest number of words (just over 12 per cent) should start with *s*. But it won't be enough just to establish the projected *number* of words in advance: the *actual* words themselves need to be listed before definitions are written, since the definitions can't include words that are not themselves defined! (See the sub-section on construction and arrangement of entries on pp. 266–70.) Where, then, do lexicographers get their words from? Do they just snuggle up in an armchair with a cup of tea and a notepad and start writing down all the words they know, perhaps starting with *aardvark* and moving through the alphabet?

No, of course not. For languages with a codified literacy tradition, lexicographers, like all scholars, 'stand on the shoulders of giants' and use the wealth of scholarship already in place. For their purposes it will be lexical material compiled previously in the form of simple word lists, whole dictionaries, computerized corpora or citation indices. Word lists may be forthcoming from frequency studies like the famous Thorndike and Lorge list of the 1960s. Corpora are either commercially available to lexicographers or, for the bigger outfits, are developed as part of the dictionary-making process (see section 11.6).

Pre-existing dictionaries are, however, still the main starting point for many lexicographical projects, providing words and also citations. The venerable OED, for example, intended as an unabridged record of the entire wordstock of English from Anglo-Saxon onwards, mined extensively the word lists, glossaries and dictionaries of the Renaissance, including the first monolingual dictionary of English – Robert Cawdrey's *A Table Alphabeticall*, from 1604 – Samuel Johnson's Dictionary of 1755 and Randle Cotgrave's influential *A Dictionarie of the French and English Tongues*, from 1611. Almost a century after the initiation of the OED project, *The Random House Dictionary of the English Language* appeared, compiled on the basis of Barnhart's *American College Dictionary*, for which his editors had trawled the OED and the semantic frequency list published by Lorge and Thorndike (1938). The OED project did use 'armchair' sources too, through its public Reading Programmes dating back 150 years, which collected citations from volunteers around the world.

Figure 11.2 shows an index card used by J. R. R. Tolkien, author of *Lord of the Rings* and, during 1919–1920, a contributor to the OED, responsible for the entries spanning *waggle* and *warlock*. The (unused) quotation reads: '1896 *Cosmopolitan* xx. 356/2. Near Herbert Island I secured a goodly number of walruses – cows, calves, yearlings and two-year-olds. (See cutting *walrus-calf*.)'

The OED, like most other modern dictionaries, also uses the internet, technical databases and lexical corpora to provide evidence of its words in use. Expert consultants, normally users of specialized terminology who reveal the jargon of their craft in interviews or surveys, are also used. This kind of fieldwork is, of course, more extensively used at both selection and definition-writing stages.

We turn now to the criteria used to determine which words are selected for inclusion and which are left out. The principal factors are:

- space restrictions;
- frequency and currency of the word;
- purpose/uses/users of the dictionary;
- lexicographical ideology.

These factors overlap. Let's use a single set of synonyms to elucidate the criteria:

*chocka, farctate, full (up), FURTB, replete, stuffed*

These six adjectives all mean roughly 'full (up)'. Although an 'unabridged' dictionary should have entries for all of them, a pocket dictionary will probably only include one or two (at least with the sense intended here). In between, a concise

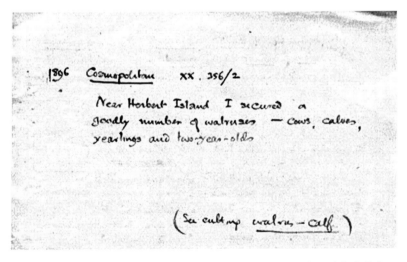

Figure 11.2   A suggested quotation for the OED entry for *walrus* from J. R. R. Tolkien (Source: Oxford University Press)

or college dictionary may have entries for some of them, but not all. The pocket edition will no doubt include *full (up)* and maybe *stuffed* on the grounds that they are the most frequent words used for the concept in common usage. But the latter may not appear if the dictionary editors have what we might call a 'conservative lexicographical ideology' and decide not to include terms they consider to be slang or vulgar (e.g. out of a desire to 'protect' target users who are, say, schoolchildren or language learners). Other words may appear in concise or college dictionaries if they are old-fashioned but still used in formal, written contexts, such as *replete*, but the inclusion of the very rare *farctate* is highly improbable. The word *chocka*, from Australian English, is unlikely to be found outside regional dictionaries, although related *chock-full* and *chock-a-block* are likely to be included in larger dictionaries of British English. *FURTB* is the acronym of 'full up ready to burst' and is included in the online *Chat Slang Dictionary* of 'slang words, acronyms and abbreviations used in websites, chat rooms, blogs, internet forums or text messaging with cell phones'. Such specialist or jargon terms are no doubt very current in the lexicons of some bloggers and web-surfers, but may not be judged pervasive or durable enough to find a place even in the largest unabridged dictionary.

## Construction and arrangement of entries

Once the words have been selected and evidence of their use recorded, the micro-tructure of each entry must be constructed, arranged together into the dictionary's macrostructure and woven together through cross-references (the **mediostructure**; Hartmann, 2001, p. 65). Let's look first at the structure of an entry in a typical general dictionary, a monolingual, medium-sized work for native-speaking adults, produced for commercial purposes. As we've pointed out, many dictionaries are now available in electronic format. We'll therefore use as an example the *New Oxford American Dictionary* (NOAD, 2001), as bundled with recent versions of the Apple Macintosh operating system (a 'portable version' which comes with the print edition may also be downloaded to a mobile phone or PDA). The NOAD contains a quarter of a million entries (around the same number as the *Concise Oxford* (2006) or 100,000 more than *Merriam-Webster's Collegiate* (2003)). Figure 11.3 shows the entry for *polymer*.

Entries in general dictionaries mimic the entries in our mental lexicons, pro-viding a much-abbreviated graphical sketch of the kinds of wordhood information we loosely and partially described in section 11.1. The example entry in Figure 11.3 is typical. It begins with the **headword**, providing spelling and syllable divisions, and is followed by a representation of the pronunciation, in this case set to 'British IPA' (International Phonetic Alphabet) in the application preferences. Next the gram-matical properties of the word are given (namely N, indicating 'noun'). Usage is indicated in this example simply by labelling the genre (Chemistry). The meaning of the word is given as a definition, followed by an example, but not, in this case, a **citation** or example of its meaning in use. Morphologically related forms are often included as 'run-on' entries, as here with the adjective *polymeric*. Finally, etymological information is given, presenting the history of the word (its earliest recorded origins, here from Ancient Greek, and its first recorded usage in English). The etymology is the only element of the entry that has no counterpart in the mental lexicon.

Cross-referencing between dictionary entries is called **mediostructure**. In electronic dictionaries the mediostructure takes the form of (hyper-)links.

The **headword** is the form of the word which appears at the beginning of its dictionary entry. It is normally uninflected and often gives syllabic information. So, for example, the headword for the entry corresponding to the word *is* will be *be* and for *corresponding* will be *cor•res•pond*.

A **citation** in a dictionary entry is an authentic example of the word's use in context, to provide meaning. The citations for the first meaning of word *citation* in the NOAD is 'there were dozens of citations from the works of Byron | recognition through citation is one of the principal rewards in science'.

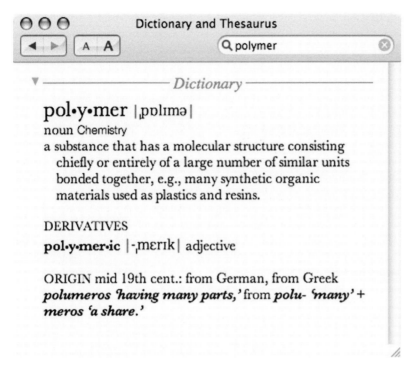

Figure 11.3   Entry for *polymer* in the *New Oxford American Dictionary* (Source: Apple Macintosh Dictionary application version 1.0.1)

So far, the core elements of the dictionary's microstructure are:

- headword;
- grammatical properties;
- usage;
- meaning;
- related forms;
- etymology.

(A seventh, *citation*, should be added, even though our example from NOAD doesn't employ it.) Although there are interesting things to say about each element, let's focus in on meaning here, along with form, which constitute the two sides of the Saussurian word coin. Meaning is far more challenging than form for the lexicographer, because although spelling and pronunciation can vary greatly across users and contexts, they are observable phenomena which can be recorded in conventional ways (most commonly using orthographic symbols, with the option of audio files for electronic dictionaries). Meanings, on the other hand, are ultimately mental representations which may be infinitely modulated by social contexts of use and are constantly shifting as we create and share new experiences of the world.

For many of us, a dictionary definition is the closest we can get when asked to think about the concept of word meaning. And lexicographers are not immune to the dilemma: Hartmann (2001, pp. 10–14) spends four pages defining the words *lexicography* and *dictionary* via reference to a series of definitions in dictionaries – including, ironically, his own *Dictionary of Lexicography* (Hartmann and James, 1998)! Although definitions are really no more than a string of further word forms which themselves require meanings to be associated with them (see Hall, 2005, pp. 96–97), lexicographers can't afford the philosophical luxury of this unpalatable truth. Instead, they must buy into the folk fiction held by most of their clients, that definitions themselves 'provide' meaning (as we pointed out back in section 11.1). Hence, the 'meaning' of *polymer* may be represented in NOAD as 'a substance that has a molecular structure consisting chiefly or entirely of a large number of similar units bonded together'. The phrasal meaning derived from this string of 124 characters and spaces allows the user to come to an understanding of the concept underlying the string of letters *p, o, l, y, m, e, r*.

One important principle of dictionary definition arising from the convenient folk fiction we have just explained is that each word in the definition must itself be defined (cf. Landau, 2001, pp. 160–162). In NOAD, one may double-click on each word in a definition and be transported to the corresponding entry along invisible mediostructure. So clicking on *substance*, the first noun in the definition of *polymer*, takes us to the entry reproduced here in Figure 11.4.

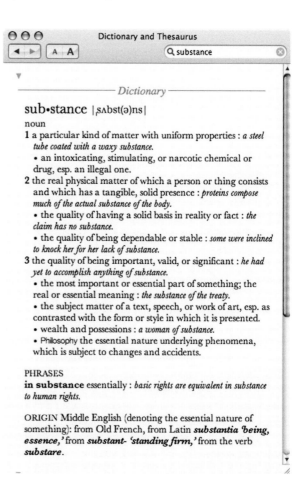

Figure 11.4   Entry for *substance* in the *New Oxford American Dictionary* (Source: Apple Macintosh Dictionary application version 1.0.1)

The first informative noun in the definition of *substance* is *matter*. But then *matter* is defined as 'physical substance in general, as distinct from mind and spirit'. Which brings us back to *substance*. Landau (2001, pp. 157–163) lists a number of principles for dictionary definitions, including the one requiring each word used in the definition to have its own entry in the dictionary. But a more important one for him is the following:

> *Avoid circularity*: 'No word can be defined by itself, and no word can be defined from its own family of words unless the related word is separately defined independently of it'.
>
> (Landau, 2001, p. 158)

Landau criticizes the definition of *sleep* in the *Longman Dictionary of American English* (1983) as a case where a word is used to define itself: the definition given is 'to be asleep' and *asleep* is defined as 'sleeping'. He would surely applaud NOAD's solution, which takes us from *asleep*, the adjective, to *sleep*, the verb, and thence to *sleep*, the noun, where the circle is broken with the following *sleep*-free definition: 'a condition of body and mind such as that which typically recurs for several hours every night, in which the nervous system is relatively inactive, the eyes closed, the postural muscles relaxed, and consciousness practically suspended'.

The NOAD entry for *polymer* illustrates another way of indicating meaning: to give an example or instance alongside the definition ('e.g., many synthetic organic materials used as plastics and resins'). A third option is to follow the synonymy route, as in the entry for *concise* in the *Collins Paperback Thesaurus*: 'brief, compact, compendious, compressed, condensed, epigrammatic, laconic, pithy, short, succinct, summary, synoptic, terse, to the point.' Like definitions, though, synonyms are just more words you need to know the meanings of in order to know the meaning of the words they are used to explain.

A fourth way of showing meaning was championed by Ayto (1983) and later by Carter (1998), and this focuses on the linguistic and sociopragmatic contexts in which the word is used, yielding connotative-associative aspects of meaning rather than the conceptual-denotative aspects revealed through definitions and synonyms. Some citation contexts (e.g. 'some were inclined to knock her for her lack of substance' in the entry for *substance*) are designed to augment definitions by distinguishing denotative senses. But Ayto and Carter are thinking beyond this, for example considering positive and negative associations, degree of formality, social identity of likely users, ideological presuppositions of use, stylistic implications, etc. Ayto's example of *man* in phrases like *Be a man* well illustrates these dimensions: does the meaning of the word form *man* include (in such uses) a sense of courage and resolution? Two main tools would seem to be required for the unpacking of these subtleties of meaning: (1) user surveys; and (2) lexical corpora. We will be looking at corpora in section 11.6, so we end this section highlighting once more the importance of the client in applied linguistics, this time as a direct source of evidence for the ways words are used to mean. Carter (1998, pp. 270–275) provides a useful discussion of the challenges and potential rewards of such informant work. In anticipation of the discussion of technology in section 11.6, we note here that data on English word associations are now available to lexicographers online: the *Edinburgh Word Association Thesaurus* has association norms for over 8,000 words, collected from 100 different speakers for each word.

 **www.11.14**

We'll now turn briefly to the arrangement stage of dictionary compilation, but since most of the relevant issues have been covered in section 11.3 we'll confine ourselves to the problem of meaning here. Notice the way polysemy is handled in the entry for *substance*. Typical of word forms in all languages, this one expresses a set of related meanings, each with one or more sub-meaning (or 'sense'). In NOAD, these are listed as separate numbered or bulleted sub-entries. Lexicographers need to make decisions about where polysemy ends and homonymy begins, i.e. whether to follow form and stack up sub-entries under a single headword or go with meaning and repeat the headword in a series of numbered entries. Some cases are clearly homophones, e.g. *lean* the verb (as in *lean on me*) and *lean* the adjective (as in *lean meat*). Some are trickier: the third sense of meaning 2 of *substance* is no doubt a metaphorical extension of meaning 1, since emotional dependability and stability are like physical dependability and stability, a function of 'matter with uniform properties'. But in other cases the metaphorical connection is more obtuse. NOAD treats *peer* (as in 'judged by one's peers') and *peer* (as in 'peer of the realm') as polysemes, although few users will know of or be able to work out the metaphorical relationship (*Burke's Peerage Online* tells us that '[t]he term peerage derives from the Latin word for equal (*par*) and to the extent that all peers with seats in the [UK] House [of Lords] have tended to be summoned to it irrespective of their relative rank, importance or wealth, the term still has some relevance'). Some lexicographers have argued that instead of attempting the impossible in identifying all word *senses*, it makes much more sense to identify different *uses*, using corpora (Stock, 2008 [1984]; Kilgarriff, 1997).

## 11.5  DICTIONARIES AS TOOLS FOR LEARNING

The earliest lexicographical works were lists of words in two different languages, and had a clear educational objective: to allow users to study texts written in another language, be it Sumerian for speakers of Akkadian in Babylon 4,000 years ago or Latin for Anglo-Saxons in Kent 3,000 years later. In China around 3,200 years ago, lexicographers developed word lists to teach students learning to write Chinese characters. Monolingual dictionaries with the aim of teaching people the 'hard' words in texts written in their own language came much later in Europe and other parts of the world. In England, the first such text appeared as the glossary at the end of Edmund Coote's *English Schoole-Maister* in 1596, with Robert Cawdrey's *Table Alphabeticall of Hard Usual English Words*, appearing eight years later, as the first proper dictionary (incorporating much of Coote's material). Both books were written principally for schoolboys, although they soon came to have more pervasive influence on adult readers. Coote's volume consists of a series of exercises, rules and readings, followed by a list of words with definitions normally comprising single synonyms or short circumlocutions, and resembling the entries of many earlier bilingual dictionaries. Here are some examples from the letter *p*:

> *pirate* sea robber.
> *piety* godlines.
> *pillage* spoyle in warre.
> *pilot* maister, guider of a shippe.

*plaintife* the complaynant.
*planet* wandring starre.

The 'pedagogical dictionary' tradition continues to lead much lexicographical work today. Hartmann sees the design of such works as truly applied linguistics, because they are 'linguistic in orientation, interdisciplinary in outlook and problem-solving in spirit' (Hartmann, 2001, p. 33). Learner dictionaries require particular care with elements of both macrostructure and microstructure, since their users are characterized by an underdeveloped lexical competence in the target language. Typically, these users are children or young adults learning their first language and additional language learners. The former group are given dictionaries to help them amass a fuller vocabulary than simple exposure to discourse would achieve. The latter group, additional language learners, having acquired at least one vocabulary, are using dictionaries to create or develop knowledge of another group's wordstock. Then of course there are the millions who straddle both groups: children learning an additional language because their parents are immigrants, refugees or expatriates – or simply have brought them up in multilingual environments.

Children's dictionaries are characterized by the selection of words included, the simplicity of the language they use in definitions, and normally the use of illustrations to maintain interest and support understanding. They tend to be visibly more attractive, with larger type (and more often than not pictures of large animals on the cover!). Student and college dictionaries used to look just like 'adult' versions, but with some simplifications and emphasis on the vocabulary of school subjects or academic writing. Now they are much more likely to come in electronic format (see section 11.6): increasingly popular among Chinese, Korean and Japanese students are e-dictionaries, handheld devices which often also incorporate voice recorder, MP3 player, video-streaming, etc. Li (2005) reported that over 70 per cent of Hong Kong Polytechnic students were using e-dictionaries more than printed versions, and this figure must be much higher now.

## 11.6   CORPORA, COMPUTERS AND THE INTERNET

Like so many areas of applied linguistics, lexicography has been transformed by technology. Chris recalls visiting the OED offices in Oxford in 1985 to see a friend who worked there, and being shown the six inch by four inch index card with the word and citation she had been assigned to work on that day. It was less than twenty years ago that computers were first used to manage the massive database of words and citations amassed since the London Philological Society began collecting words and examples of their use in 1857. Landau (2001, p. 285) recalls that although he and his team were able to edit a medical dictionary's entries on computer by 1984, they still had to be sent on tape to the publishing company to be processed on the mainframe computer.

These twenty years have revolutionized the field in many ways. Editing copy is only one, rather pedestrian, area in which technology has reshaped dictionary-making. The use of corpora has brought astounding improvements (and challenges) to the lexicographical process, and the development of affordable and portable multimedia has generated a range of dictionary products that would have dazzled, or more likely terrified, Webster and Murray. Figure 11.5 illustrates one of the new incarnations of the modern dictionary. This is a dictionary of British Sign Language for young learners of the language who can read English. Imagine the benefits for deaf kids of being able to see signs actually performed in front of them by an engaging cartoon figure, rather than having to leaf through printed pages to find the static photos or line drawings using arrows that you'd find in traditional sign dictionaries (you can see the movement for yourself online). Meanwhile, the Scottish Sensory Centre at Edinburgh University is constructing a series of BSL glossaries for school subjects, using Quicktime video.

www.11.15

www.11.16

Aside from transforming access routes, format and multimedia resources in the end result, technology has had a massive impact on the core processes of collection, selection, construction and arrangement through the creation of lexical corpora and the development of associated software. We saw in section 11.1 that the mind automatically records the number of times a particular mental representation is accessed, but that is ultimately a private matter, depending on each individual's circumstances: obstetric nurses might use the word *mother* hundreds of times a year more than other adults. A speaker of Aboriginal English in Australia might use the word *mother* more frequently than other speakers if she has many maternal aunts, since the form can be used to refer to a mother's sisters too in that variety (Eades, 2007). Young speakers of some varieties of American English might notch up much higher frequencies of the form if they use it as a short form of the common insult and sometimes term of endearment *motherfucker*. Since *mother* is quite a formal term for female parent, some speakers may never use it at all,

Figure 11.5  Screenshot from a British Sign Language/English online dictionary for children (Source: BSL Dictionary developed by Dunedin Multimedia for the Scottish charity Stories in the Air; reproduced with permission)

preferring *mom, mam, mum, ma* instead. And we could go on: the contents of one speaker's lexicon will only ever *resemble* those of another, especially in the number of times particular form–meaning mappings have been traversed. Only a massive and representative collection of recorded usages will yield robust estimates of aggregate word frequencies across a speech community, and only computers can deliver the storage and processing capacity required to count the high numbers required and keep track of the syntactic, semantic and sociopragmatic circumstances of usage.

Hunston (2002, pp. 96–109) discusses the main impact of corpora on applied linguistic theory and practice in terms of a new focus on the following five features:

- frequency;
- collocation and phraseology;
- variation;
- lexis in grammar;
- authenticity.

For lexicography, data on frequency of occurrence and co-occurrence in different genres of real usage has transformed the field. As we saw in the Chapter 9, a corpus is required if we are to assess empirically how commonly a word form is used with a particular meaning in the speech and writing of members of a speech community (instead of relying on armchair intuition). This is important for dictionary-writing at collection and selection stages (see section 11.4), in order to discard **nonce words** and rank priorities for inclusion by identifying highly infrequent words (like *farctate*), **hapax legomena** and emerging **neologisms** (see Crystal, 2000, for an estimation of the challenges this poses). At the construction stage, corpus data can be used to ensure that in entries more frequent usage is listed first, and more frequent meanings are given more attention through definition, exemplification and/or citation. (But corpus data are only as good as the corpora from which they are drawn, of course.)

## 11.7  ROLES FOR APPLIED LINGUISTS

The role of lexicographers in the broader project of applied linguistics extends far beyond the range of activities involved in the design and compilation of dictionary and thesauri we have mapped in this chapter:

- In educational contexts, applied linguists can contribute to language learners' and users' understanding of the role and purpose of dictionaries, for both vocabulary development and guidance regarding social conventions of usage in particular domains.
- In additional language situations, applied linguists can guide users about how to use dictionaries as effective tools for learning and teaching.
- For translators, applied linguists can be involved in the development of lexicographical databases (e.g. for specialized terminology) as aids in manual and (semi-)automatic translation.
- Applied linguists can cooperate on the design and use of dictionaries as tools for language codification (in the case of minority languages and varieties),

---

**Nonce words** are one-off coinages, created for a specific purpose and not likely to gain common currency. David Crystal (2000, p. 219) gives the example of *chopaholic*, which he overheard said of someone who likes lamb chops.

**Hapax legomena** (from the Greek for 'said once'; also known simply as *hapax*) are words with a single occurrence in a corpus. In a large corpus, around 50 per cent of words are likely to be hapax legomena. For example, the word *haptic* is a hapax legomenon in the British National Corpus (whereas *hapax* itself occurs three times).

A **neologism** is a newly coined word which is intended to gain or appears to be gaining common currency in the language. There are many examples at Birmingham City University's *Neologisms in Journalistic Text* website.

🌐 **www.11.17**

maintenance (in the case of endangered languages) and historical-cultural record-keeping.

Most broadly, applied linguists can promote lexicographical practices which avoid prescriptivism, for example by questioning belief in 'the dictionary' as monolithic repository of 'the language', and stressing the dynamic, boundless and non-monolithic nature of a language's wordstock. In short, applied linguistics can help clients and members of the public understand that even dictionary-makers, for all their impressive attainments in creating records of language use and usage, cannot achieve Landau's 'wonder', a single book containing all the words of a people.

activities

**www.
11.18**

1   Figure 11.5 illustrates one of the new products of contemporary lexi-cography, a dictionary of British Sign Language for young learners of the language who can read English. How might access to information about signs change for deaf children when they are able to see signs actually performed in front of them by an engaging cartoon figure, rather than having to leaf through printed pages to find the static photos or line drawings using arrows typical of traditional sign dictionaries?

**www.11.19**

2   Go to the *Collins Wordbanks Online English Corpus* (made up of 56 million words of contemporary British and American English written and spoken text). Type in the word *like* to get forty lines of concordance, each with a maximum width of 250 characters. Look at the different uses of *like* and compare them with the entry for the word *like* in your dictionary (or in any online dictionary). Does your dictionary include all the uses illus-trated in the forty concordance lines? Why (not)?

3   What information would you like to see included in your ideal dictionary entry? Why? (Consider: the language of the dictionary and your reasons for using it; how you will access the dictionary; and the information that is typically stored about words in the mental lexicon.)

4   An additional language teacher asks you whether her learners should be allowed to use dictionaries in class. What do you say about the benefits, and any possible drawbacks, of different types of dictionaries? Are there certain instances or tasks in which you would especially recommend or discourage the use of dictionaries in class?

## FURTHER READING

Atkins, B. T. S. and Rundell, M. (2008). *The Oxford guide to practical lexicography.* Oxford: Oxford University Press.

Fontenelle, T. (2008). *Practical lexicography: A reader.* Oxford: Oxford University Press.

Halliday, M. A. K., Teubert, W., Yallop, C. and Cermáková, A. (2004). *Lexicology and corpus linguistics.* London: Continuum.

Landau, S. I. (2001). *Dictionaries. The art and craft of lexicography*, 2nd edn. Cambridge: Cambridge University Press.

Svensen, B. (2009). *A Handbook of lexicography: The theory and practice of dictionary-making*. Cambridge: Cambridge University Press.

**CHAPTER 12**

# Forensic linguistics

> You have the right to remain silent. Anything you say will be misquoted, then used against you.
>
> (Bumper sticker)

For lots of people, the word *forensic* will evoke images of white-coated scientists conducting lab tests on guns to see if they've recently been fired or dusting for fingerprints at the scene of a murder – the stuff of TV shows like *CSI* or *Waking the Dead*. Although in the USA the term *forensics* is normally associated with criminal investigation, it is used more broadly in the UK to refer to any activity or process related to the law enforcement and justice systems. In this sense, forensic linguists are those who study or interpret language use in the legal process, from crime scene to courtroom, either in the pursuit of justice or for general or applied linguistic scholarship (for examples of the latter, see Atkinson and Drew, 1979; Goodwin and Goodwin, 1997).

Forensic linguistics is a booming sub-field of applied linguistics, with inter-national professional organizations, journals, research centres and conferences (see Coulthard and Johnson, 2007, pp. 5–7, for a brief history). From its roots in English language scholarship in the 1960s, it is now fast becoming a truly global area of scholarship and professional practice. According to a list from 2007 (Blackwell, 2008), the subject is taught at over forty institutions in more than fifteen countries, from Hong Kong to Kenya, Malaysia to Malta, Israel to Australia. In some it may be a single course on legal language in a law programme; in others it may be a complete master's degree. In the couple of years since that list was compiled, new courses have opened in the Czech Republic, Singapore and beyond. Of course, all this activity in the universities does not guarantee that the judiciaries of the world have accorded the field full legal recognition, as we shall see as the chapter proceeds.

We begin our exploration by acknowledging the dual nature of forensic lin-guistics as scholarship concerned with language as both the medium of the law and also often as its subject matter (section 12.1). We map the field by essentially following the chronology of events in the legal process. In 12.2, we look at the language of the law itself, then turn in 12.3 to the role of language in the inves-tigation of cases where the law has been broken. In subsequent sections we move to the courtroom, taking a brief look at how language itself may be put on trial (12.4) and at how trials are actually conducted through the medium of language in different legal traditions (12.5). The chapter ends (12.6) with a brief, critical look at the growing role of applied linguists as expert witnesses.

# 12.1 LANGUAGE AS LEGAL MEDIUM AND MATTER

In Chapter 3 we made a distinction between language as a medium for the law – in statutes, case transcripts, arrest warrants, the reading of rights, courtroom proceedings, etc. – and language as legal matter, either as evidence (used by detectives in criminal investigation or by lawyers and judges in court) or as the actual subject matter of a case, for instance in brand name disputes, accusations of plagiarism or defamation proceedings. Some have proposed that forensic linguistics properly covers only the former, but in line with the broader view of applied linguistics adopted in this book, we cover both areas here.

To provide a context for this broader view, let's start out with an example involving language as both medium and subject matter: the Miranda warning, familiar to many from TV cop shows. In the US, a person apprehended by the police will be advised, among other things, that: 'You have the right to remain silent. Anything you say can be used against you in a court of law.' These are the first words of the warning named after Ernesto Miranda, a defendant freed by the Supreme Court in 1966 after being convicted of kidnap and rape, on the basis largely of a confession made to police without a lawyer present (he was found guilty in a second trial). In the UK, the suspect would be cautioned with the more awkward sequence: 'You do not have to say anything. But it may harm your defence if you do not mention when questioned something which you later rely on in court. Anything you do say may be given in evidence.'

These words constitute linguistic formulae, frozen chunks of language which, if not spoken, may invalidate all prosecution proceedings that follow. As such, they epitomize the concept of 'language as medium of the law'. The utterance of these formulae by police officers is regularly assumed to constitute a performative speech act (see Chapter 4): the linguistic act itself is supposed to bring about a new state of affairs in the world for those citizens who may not already be aware of their rights. But of course the critical issue for the effective exercise of justice is not just that the words of these formulae have been spoken, but that they are heard and *understood*, i.e. that the desired perlocutionary effect is achieved, *and* that law enforcement officials believe that this is so.

With this in mind, imagine now a suspect who is a monolingual Spanish speaker, recently arrived in the US, and that the police officer giving the warning has only limited proficiency in Spanish. Similar scenarios are becoming more and more common in our increasingly multilingual cities and towns (and problems with communicating the rights of suspects are not necessarily obviated by the presence of an interpreter; see section 12.5 and Nakane, 2007). One Mexican man accused of sexual abuse in California in 2001 was interviewed in Spanish by the native-English-speaking detective. According to the detective's report, the accused 'agreed to speak to me about this case and why he was arrested' (McMenamin, 2002, p. 251). But the transcript of the taped interview suggests otherwise:

| *Spanish original* | *English translation* |
|---|---|
| *Detective*: Ok, ¿y sí gusta hablar con nosotros de por qué estuvo arrestado? | *Detective*: Ok, and you do want to speak with us about why you were arrested? |

| | |
|---|---|
| *Defendant*: Pues, sí me gustaría saber por qué. Yo no sé por qué, me cae de sorpresa, verdad. | *Defendant*: Well, I *would* like to know why. I do not know why, it comes as a surprise to me, truly. |

From his words, it seems that the man was not waiving his right to silence, but was demanding that his arrest be explained to him. The detective's misinterpretation may have been wilful, or caused by his insufficient Spanish proficiency: since Spanish *sí* indicates agreement ('yes') as well as the positive emphasis intended, he may have interpreted the accused as saying:

*Pues sí. Me gustaría saber por qué.*
Well yes. I would like to know why.

This example illustrates how, on the one hand, language provides the medium for the legal process (the reading of the Miranda formula) and also becomes – as it subsequently did – a subject of legal proceedings, namely the question of whether the accused waived his right to silence and so allowed his statements to be used against him as evidence.

## 12.2  THE LANGUAGE OF THE LAW

The eighteenth century English philosopher and legal commentator Jeremy Bentham defined the law as 'an assemblage of signs' (Bentham, 1988 [1776], p. 1). In more recent times, jurists have followed linguists from the fields of semantics and pragmatics in questioning this. Endicott (2002), for example, argues that 'when a law is made by the use of signs, that law is a standard for conduct, and not an assemblage of signs'. Bentham implied that the law is the linguistic instrument (the 'assemblage of signs') through which conduct is prescribed or proscribed, rather than the standard of conduct itself. Essentially, what's at stake in this (perhaps typically lawyerly) argument is the difference between *what is said* (the linguistic instrument) and *what is meant* (the standard of conduct): between linguistic form and linguistic meaning. In other words, is the law what it says or what it means? This question gives rise to others: to what extent do the two fail to coincide? Can justice be said to be done when the law is expressed but not understood? Can we say, for example, that the law has been duly exercised when the Miranda warning is read to a suspect without intent to *mean* (when delivered in garbled form, for instance)? Or when it is spoken clearly but not understood?

In Susan Philips' enlightening ethnographic study of Arizona trial judges' handling of guilty pleas (Philips, 1998), one judge proves to be particularly sensitive to this problem. In a post-trial interview the judge states:

if I don't get feedback that suggests that [defendants] are understanding and going with me, I will modify, until I start to get feedback . . . Some [judges] are so concerned with what they are saying and whether they're saying it in the right way . . . that they miss whether they're communicating at all.

(Philips, 1998, p. 59)

The same judge goes on to explain why he always asks questions about the defendant's personal background, even when the written law doesn't require it:

> I suspect, if I left that out, did not make that inquiry, if I use the magic words at the end, 'knowingly, intelligently and voluntarily enters a plea', [then a higher appeal] court might say this: 'that's what the judge found. There must have been something from the demeanor and appearance of the defendant at the time that suggested that he was intelligently making this plea though we can't find anything in the record . . . See here's his magic words at the end. So he must have found that.' And they would perhaps put aside that argument on appeal on that basis.
>
> (Philips, 1998, p. 59)

Comments such as these highlight the central role played by language in the exercise of the law. Without language, law is impossible. But language also brings indeterminacy: in the meaning intended in the original code or case precedent, the meaning interpreted by the courts, and the meaning understood by the parties in dispute.

Now in the absence of telepathy, we're stuck with an external channel (language) for communicating thought. A consequence of this is that we have developed written law – Bentham's 'assemblage of signs', the existence of which is independent of the situated meanings it is intended or construed to mean. Recall from Chapter 4 that there is no simple one-to-one correspondence or identity between linguistic expressions (code or signs) and their underlying meanings. Furthermore, there is indeterminacy in both form and meaning: a word or sentence may be ambiguous and a thought or intention or message may be incomplete or vague. Even more importantly, we don't always say what we mean, or mean what we say. All this presents major obstacles to the pursuit and practice of justice.

This problem of the slipperiness of form and meaning can be seen at the levels of language as both medium and matter of the law: indeterminacy in the codified law itself and in the linguistically encoded evidence presented on particular occasions of its interpretation, enforcement or possible violation. Codified law – law as an 'assemblage of signs' – may be open to different interpretations in different circumstances, especially when the language used is itself vague or ambiguous. Hence the need for maximum explicitness: the use of a register marked by redundancy (e.g. repetition of full noun phrases instead of pronouns), technical terms with precise definitions (to reduce ambiguity), complex sentence structures (through which information otherwise available from non-linguistic context is given expression) and formulaic expressions (to assure consistency across cases).

The downside of this need for explicitness and precision is that legal language tends to be extremely user-unfriendly for its non-expert consumers. An example we've already seen is the UK equivalent of the Miranda warning, which sacrifices clarity for accuracy and informativeness, and consequently is not as easy to comprehend (or remember!) as the US version. But in this regard the US is not a paragon of simplicity either. Susan Philips begins her book on Tucson judges with an admission that '[w]hen I began observing in the courts . . . much of what went on was unintelligible' (Philips, 1998, p. 3). In fact, she decided to go to law school for a year in order to gain access to the mysteries of the profession. Relative unintelligibility appears to be a feature of all uses of legal language, including legislation, case law (the official record of cases serving as legal precedent), legally binding documents such as wills and contracts, and the patterns of talk in lawyers' chambers or in the courtroom.

It's apparent that legal language is not the way it is solely because it must avoid ambiguity. Take, for example, the following clause from a contract we once signed with a publisher:

### 19 FORCE MAJEURE

The time for fulfillment by the Publishers of any of their obligations under this Agreement (including the obligation to publish the Work) shall be suspended during and delayed for such period of time in which the fulfillment of such obligation is prevented or delayed by war strikes lock-outs fires Acts of God governmental restrictions or controls or any circumstances whatsoever beyond the Publishers' control.

Here are a few questions for the drafters of this clause:

- What makes the French term *force majeure* less ambiguous than the English 'unforeseeable circumstances'?
- Why is *shall* clearer than *will*?
- Why both 'suspended during' *and* 'delayed for'?
- Logically, can a time be suspended or delayed 'for [a] period of time'?
- How does the absence of commas in the list of unforeseeable circumstances decrease ambiguity?
- What constitutes an 'Act of God'?
- What does the formula 'any X whatsoever' add that 'any other X' would not?

There don't appear to be reasonable explanations for these arcane choices of expression, other than that 'this is just the way we do it'! (Coulthard and Johnson [2007, p. 37] do rightly point out, though, that some 'formulaic formality' can serve to indicate that '"high stakes" activity' is occurring, and so help participants orient themselves appropriately.)

Some elements of legal language are likely to be a consequence of the state's social and political history. Legal language will probably be more conservative than that of other public activities, given the need for stability and consistency over time. Hence the archaic flavour of much legal language, including in English legalese a large number of French words and phrases, like *force majeure*, which have survived from the time when French was the language of the law in England (a period which began with the Norman Conquest in 1066 but did not end, remarkably, until a few years before Jeremy Bentham was born, almost 700 years later). Figure 12.1 shows one of the first summaries of English law, compiled by Anthony Fitzherbert early in the sixteenth century: *La Graunde Abridgement* ('the great summary'), written in French, not English.

But not all obscurity in current legalese can be explained by the inertia of history or the diligent insistence on precision and elimination of ambiguity. Like other professionals, including doctors and (yes, we admit it) academics, the lawyers have been accused of using their jargon as verbal armour-plating, to protect their

Figure 12.1 Frontispiece of an edition of *La Graunde Abridgement*, a sixteenth century summary of English law, written in French (Source: Wikimedia Commons)

monopoly over the exercise of their profession (and in some cases to justify high fees). And like other branches of government, the judicial system has been charged with using legalese to restrict public accountability and to maintain the status quo.

Such considerations become particularly disturbing when the state maintains the right to execute its citizens, as is still the case in many parts of the US and in over seventy other countries. Tiersma and Solan (2002, pp. 235–237) describe three cases in which prisoners sentenced to death were executed, despite evidence that the juries did not fully understand the instructions they had been given regarding the role of mitigating factors. Two of the cases come from Illinois, where the statute states:

> If the jury determines unanimously that there are no mitigating factors sufficient to preclude the imposition of the death sentence, the court shall sentence the defendant to death.

Unless the jury unanimously finds that there are no mitigating factors sufficient to preclude the imposition of the death sentence the court shall sentence the defendant to a term of imprisonment.

(cited in Tiersma and Solan, 2002, p. 235)

Note the complex structure of both sentences. The first has an 'if . . . then' structure within which there is an issue of quantifier scope ('unanimously') interacting with double negation ('*no* mitigating factors sufficient to *preclude*'). The second sentence has an almost parallel structure, but further impedes comprehension by imposing another layer of negation, using 'unless . . . then' instead of 'if . . . then'. The result, in the words of Tiersma and Solan (2002, p. 236), is 'phrasing that suggests that a death verdict is the desired outcome'. In each of the three cases, an appeal was rejected on the grounds that juries are 'presumed' as a 'rule of law' to understand and follow their instructions. Tiersma and Solan conclude (2002, p. 235) that in such cases, 'the politics are palpable'.

There has been increasing recognition in recent years of the need to simplify legal language in the interests of social and criminal justice and participatory democracy. A number of more liberal lawyers, together with the judiciary and government, have collaborated with applied linguists, communication scientists and design specialists in the promotion of simplified English in legal and other official documents and procedures. In the US, California jury instructions have recently been translated into 'plain English'. For example, the phrase 'Innocent misrecollection is not uncommon', containing three negatives, has been replaced by the longer but simpler: 'People sometimes honestly forget things or make mistakes about what they remember.' In the UK, new regulations from the Office of Fair Trading require companies to replace unclear language in legal contracts. For example:

> *Old clause*: Title to property in the goods shall remain vested in the Company (notwithstanding the delivery of the same to the Customer) until the price of the Goods comprised in the contract and all other money due from the Customer to the Company on any other account has been paid in full.
> *New clause*: We shall retain ownership of the goods until you have finished paying for them.

Governments around the world have launched simplification campaigns, many of them based on UK and US models. An international society of lawyers, called *Clarity*, is active in the promotion of plainer legal language. Many private companies now offer plain language editing services, such as the Plain Language Commission. The Commission's research director, Michael Cutts, together with Emma Wagner from the European Commission's translation service, have shown how the Commission's regulations could be presented in much more accessible style, without compromising their legal content (Cutts and Wagner, 2002). The possibilities for linguistic form and meaning to become disconnected are endless, and yet in law this can have grave consequences for individuals' liberty and financial well-being – and, where capital punishment still exists, for their very lives. The increasing cooperation between lawyers, forensic linguists and translators is clear evidence of applied linguistics as a force for good in the world!

## 12.3  LANGUAGE AND CRIMINAL INVESTIGATION

Detectives will often use language data as evidence to solve or prevent a crime, and here language will constitute the subject matter, rather than the medium, of the law. A text or recording of speech might be used in the same way as an eyewitness description, phone records, a fingerprint or other evidence, to establish issues of fact which may lead to the apprehension of a suspect and subsequently support the case for the prosecution or for the defence. In criminal investigation, language evidence comes in the form of written documents (normally on paper or electronic media), as audio or video recordings of spoken (or signed) language use, or as witnesses' *memories* of such language events. The evidence is used primarily to identify and/or eliminate suspects, but can also be used for threat assessment and other aspects of psychological profiling. In this section, we'll look first at writing, then at speech.

### Written language as evidence

Documents can include ransom letters in kidnapping cases, threats or warnings about intended violence (such as a terrorist attack), or suicide notes and wills in cases of suspected forgery. In cases like these, forensic linguists might be called in to compare the document with one or more of known authorship, in order to help establish the identity of the author of the questioned document or to rule out one or more of the authors of the known documents. In the case of a ransom note or, say, a bomb threat, the work of a forensic document examiner may be crucial not only in subsequent court proceedings where language data are presented as evidence of guilt or innocence, but also in the apprehension of suspects in the first place, thereby preventing further crimes, avoiding false accusations of innocent persons and possibly saving lives.

The skills involved in document analysis may be more or less linguistic in nature. At the non-linguistic end of the spectrum, the identification of a typewriter or computer font, of a particular brand of paper or photocopying machine, may, in combination with other evidence, be a critical factor in the identification of a suspect or a subsequent case against them. But the training and experience you need for such tasks will not include linguistics. Closer to forensic linguistics proper is handwriting analysis, used to establish authorship or at least an identity profile. Here it may be important for the analyst to have some conception of idiolect and individual or regional variation in written language form and style. Chapters in McMenamin (2002) on letters written in Gujarati, Korean and Japanese, for example, demonstrate that there is significant variation across writers, due to a combination of knowledge of literacy conventions, stylistic choices and localized norms.

Much forensic analysis of texts has its origins in studies of disputed literary authorship. Perhaps the most well-known literary case in the English-speaking world is that of Shakespeare: did he really write all those plays and poems, or was it Christopher Marlowe, Francis Bacon, the Earl of Derby or the Earl of Oxford? In many early cases of disputed authorship, language analysis was rather subjective, relying on impressionistic studies of the somewhat vague concept of 'style'. But over

**Forensic stylistics** (sometimes known as **stylometry**) is the measurement of linguistic style through the analysis of the frequency with which given linguistic variables occur in a sample of texts, normally in cases of unclear or disputed authorship. A famous example is the authentication by the Netherlands Institute for War Documentation of Anne Frank's diaries in the 1980s (Barnouw and Stroom, 2003).

**www.12.1**

the past couple of decades a more rigorous, scientific approach has been taken, and it is this approach, sometimes known as **forensic stylistics** or **stylometry**, that has been applied to forensic cases, given the need for legal evidence to be objective and verifiable (Coulthard, 2004; Solan and Tiersma, 2004).

The approach treats style as a linguistic, more than a literary, phenomenon. It uses quantitative techniques and statistical measures from discourse analysis and corpus linguistics to provide evidence of authorship. One method is to analyse the documents in question and isolate groups of distinctive linguistic variables which appear to co-occur, so that documents containing these elements are identified as likely to be authored by the same person and documents that don't exhibit them are likely to be written by someone else. The linguistic variables analysed might include the use of rare or unusual words or collocations, variations in spelling and punctuation, particular syntactic structures or degree of subordination and other idiosyncrasies of expression, including recurrence and type of metaphorical devices or of archaisms. On their own, the variables analysed may not distinguish between authors, but when they are taken together a profile might emerge for the questioned document, which may either closely match one of the other samples or significantly differ from them.

The pioneering forensic linguist Malcolm Coulthard reports a case he was involved in which uses this technique (Coulthard, 2007; you can also see him talk about the case in an online video). The police suspected a man of sending messages to himself from the mobile phone of his niece after she had disappeared, as a *post hoc* alibi. Coulthard examined sixty-five text messages she had sent from the phone in the days before she disappeared. He found features in the final, questioned texts which did not occur in the previous ones. Here's a sample:

HIYA STU WOT U UP 2. IM IN SO MUCH TRUBLE AT HOME AT MOMENT EVONE HATES ME EVEN U! WOT THE HELL AV I DONE NOW? Y WONT U JUST TELL ME TEXT BCK PLEASE LUV DAN XXX

In the 'reference corpus' of texts known to have been written by the missing girl, the abbreviation she used of *what* was always *wat*, never *wot*; *one* was always *1* (even in her abbreviation for *everyone*); *the* was never omitted from a prepositional phrase, unlike *at moment* here; *text* was never written in full, unlike here; etc. On the basis of evidence like this, Coulthard concluded that she was not the author of the last two messages.

Of course, the method is not foolproof: forensic linguistics has no equivalent of DNA profiling or fingerprinting. First, a particular constellation of linguistic variables co-occurring at certain frequency levels for any specific individual might only be register-specific, activated in certain situations or contexts. Second, elements of style, either alone or in combination, can be properties of groups as well as of individuals, when they define regional and social dialects, or mark ethnic identity, age and/or sex, language proficiency, occupation or hobby. Although many of the style elements which mark group identity are more apparent in speech than in writing, some variables consistently show up in writing, such as regional differences and unconventional spelling (see Figure 12.2) or lexical choices influenced by profession. Thus, coincidence of stylistic features in two writing samples may indicate that they were written by two members of the same population, but not necessarily the same person. As Coulthard, puts it:

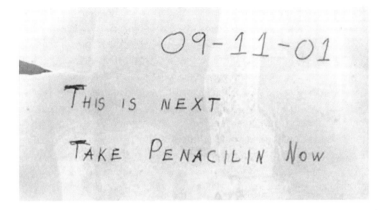

Figure 12.2   Example of a spelling error on an anonymous letter accompanying anthrax powder sent to the editor of the *New York Post* in 2001 (Source: US Department of Justice)

[t]he task [is] never one of identifying an author from millions of candidates on the basis of the linguistic evidence alone, but rather of selecting (or of course *de*selecting) one author from a very small number of candidates, usually fewer than a dozen and in many cases only two.

(Coulthard, 2004, p. 432)

A third problem, particularly acute in forensic linguistics, is sample size. Normally, the writing samples available (the ransom note, the threatening letter, the will) are short. Furthermore, many individuals have few natural writing samples available for comparison. For prolific writers like Shakespeare and Marlowe, who have been studied extensively for centuries, and for professional writers, who use word processors and keep backups of everything, one might be able to factor out extraneous variables such as genre (sonnet or play? scholarly article or lecture notes?) in order to make an informed decision about authorship probability. But with only a paragraph or two, can the forensic linguist draw any useful conclusions?

In certain cases a reference corpus from the general population can be useful. Coulthard has pioneered this method, using it in a number of 'cold cases' which had been closed before witness statements were audio-recorded. A famous example involved the use of the time adverbial *then* in nineteen-year-old Derek Bentley's 'confession' in 1952 to the murder of a police officer (Coulthard, 1994a). Coulthard used corpus data to show that the sentences attributed to Bentley were more likely to have been written by police. First, he showed that the use of temporal *then* in the 'confession' was much higher than in small corpora he constructed from other witness statements and in the COBUILD Corpus of Spoken English. Second, he showed that the positioning of temporal *then* after the grammatical subject in the 'confession' (e.g. *Chris then jumped over*) was almost a thousand times less frequent than the reverse order in the COBUILD corpus. Finally, he showed that the subject–adverbial order was common in a corpus he constructed from police-authored statements. Bentley was exonerated posthumously in 1998.

So far we have seen that the examination of bundles of co-occurring features in individuals and tell-tale features in groups can be useful in the forensic analysis of text. We have highlighted the fact that, as in so many other areas of applied linguistics, corpora play an important role in this method. But you may recall that in the last couple of chapters we have also noted how corpus data give only a snapshot of past usage, and can't characterize the unrealized expressive potential of a language, which gives speakers/writers an 'open choice' to produce new expressions (see Widdowson, 2000). With this in mind, we can appreciate the importance forensic linguists attach to what Coulthard (2004) calls 'single identical strings': stretches of discourse which are repeated in two (or more) texts, but which are alleged to have been produced by different authors (for example in plagiarism cases). Coulthard suggests that the 'open choice' that speakers/writers have in creatively exploiting the resources of their language can yield evidence about disputed authorship. Writers' frequent deployment of previously unattested strings of words constitutes phrasal versions of the hapax legomena we encountered in lexicography. The longer a phrase is, 'the more likely it is that at least some of its components have been created by the open choice principle and consequently, the less likely that the occurrence of this . . . sequence in two different texts is a consequence of two speakers/writers coincidentally selecting the same chunk(s) by chance' (Coulthard, 2004, pp. 440–441). So, for example, a search on Google for the subject noun phrase of our penultimate sentence in this paragraph (*Writers' frequent deployment of previously unattested strings of words*) produced zero hits. It's a hapax legomenon, and if you see it in a student essay without quote marks you can be pretty sure it wasn't written by the student.

A **spectrogram** is a visual representation of speech (or other acoustic token) produced by an instrument called a spectrograph. It measure frequency and amplitude as they change through time. To try your hand at reading one, visit Rob Hagiwara's *Monthly Mystery Spectrogram Webzone* at the University of Manitoba, Canada.

**www.12.2**

Acoustic energy (sound), including speech, comes at different levels of **amplitude** (loudness) and **frequency**. The way these change through time is captured by a spectrograph and displayed as spectrograms. For some excellent animations of sound waves (including those produced by beer bottles being knocked together), visit Dan Russell's *Acoustics and Vibration Animations* page at Kettering University.

**www.12.3**

## Spoken language as evidence

Speaker identification presents different challenges from writer identification, and there are challenges and opportunities associated with the interpretation of evidence in this modality. Text, as a durable, visual record of language use, is relatively easy to manipulate after being produced, and so it's easier to forge and consequently harder to identify with a specific individual. Although some people have very distinctive handwriting styles, the dimensions of variation are fewer than for speech, and so forgery (of a signature, for example) through tracing or sustained practice is a real possibility. Conversely, speech is a transitory signal produced by an inherently more complex instrument (the vocal tract) and thus is more variable: no two voices are identical (though some may be hard to tell apart), and effective imitators are few and far between. Speech, then, holds the advantage here in terms of identifiability.

Given this modality difference, one might think that speech records would be closer to DNA samples and fingerprints in the uniqueness of their 'signature'. And yet the apparent forensic blessing of variance is actually also a curse, since the speech signal varies also greatly *within* the individual, making positive matches between samples of the same person sometimes difficult. For an 'earwitness' attempting to pick out a voice from a 'line-up' on the basis of a memory trace which is invariably weeks or months old, the potential for error is high. Even the objective and permanent record of speech provided by **spectrograms** can be of questionable utility. A spectrogram (illustrated in Figure 12.3) provides a visual representation of three distinguishing properties of a particular speech token: **frequency**, **amplitude** (or loudness) and how these change through *time*.

The trouble is that no two acoustic tokens of the same word type are identical, and once words are uttered in the company of other words (linguistic context) and other noises, spectrograms of known and questioned voices become harder and harder to match (note that the repeated syllable in Figure 12.3 is different on each utterance). Intercepted telephone conversations and covert recordings, which represent ever more common formats for spoken language evidence these days, will often provide only limited information about the all-important vowel frequencies, and usually also are marred by substantial interference from background noise and signal instability (Broeders, 2001).

Still, a large amount of casework for forensic linguists these days is in the area of forensic phonetics, and there have been considerable advances in methodology over the past decade. **Earwitness** evidence from voice line-ups may be used in court cases, and according to some estimates (e.g. Nolan and Grabe, 1996) such **naïve speaker identification** can be quite robust, especially when care is taken to match the 'foil' voices phonetically and the circumstances under which they are recorded. But where witnesses are unreliable or absent, or to complement their evidence, voice recordings may be subjected to increasingly sophisticated analyses. One of the major problems in the past has been the identification of suitable cues for distinguishing between speakers, and this has been hampered by the lack of statistics for background speaker populations. Among recent work which seeks to address this gap in the research is that conducted by Nolan and his team in the *Dynamic Variability in Speech* (DyViS) project (Nolan *et al.*, 2009). They have assembled a database of 100 male speakers of educated Southern British English, recorded with studio quality in various modes, and including simulated police interviews, telephone conversations and reading. One set of 'voiceprint' features they identify as having the potential to distinguish individual speakers are points of rapid transition in the speech signal. For example, instead of looking for acoustic signatures by comparing the spectrograms of different speakers' articulations of a syllable, for example [ta] in Figure 12.3, it appears to be more profitable to compare the dynamic *transition* from vowel to vowel, for example in a word like *tying*. (For writing, Chaski [2001] pioneered a similar approach, in which grammatical aspects of verb use are demonstrated to represent robust diagnostic features.)

**Naïve speaker identification** is when a lay witness (an **earwitness**) (attempts to) identifies (or attempts to identify) a speaker by recognizing their voice from a single recording, a set of recordings or a voice 'line-up' of speakers.

 **www.12.4**

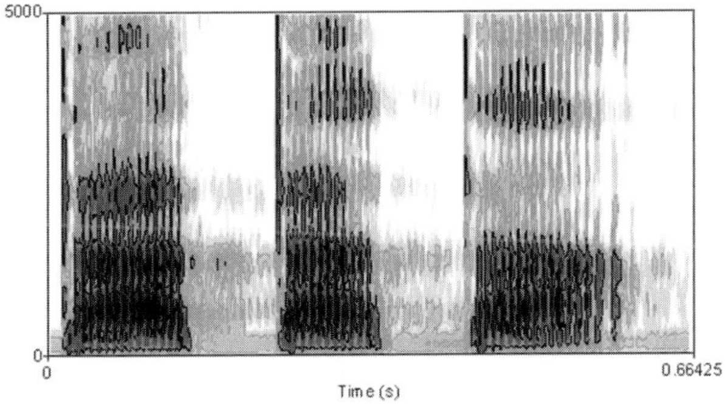

Figure 12.3   A spectrogram of a male voice repeating the syllable [ta] (Source: Wikimedia Commons) (*Note*: Frequency is indicated on the vertical axis, time on the horizontal axis, and amplitude as depth of grey)

Given the evident and unsurprising knowledge gap between technical findings in forensic phonetics, on the one hand, and actual legal practice, on the other, applied linguists in this area have placed a great deal of emphasis recently on how to articulate the status of the evidence they provide in court. For example, a group of UK forensic phoneticians have published a position statement which calls for the adoption of a conservative framework for disputed voice analysis which emphasizes not speaker *identification*, but speaker *comparison* (*Position Statement . . .*, 2007). In Figure 12.4, you can see that the five-point scale of *Distinctiveness* (for cases where the comparison reveals consistency) presents a more nuanced assessment of how similarities between samples might be taken by the court as evidence for same or different speakers.

**www.12.5**

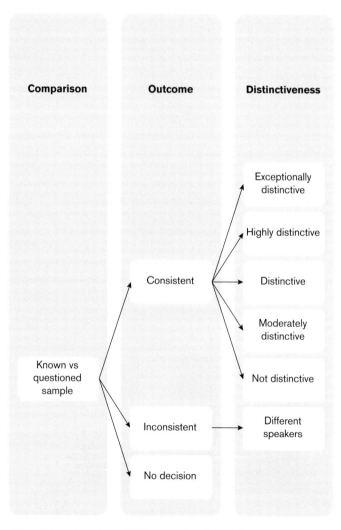

Figure 12.4  Schematized view of UK forensic phoneticians' *Position statement concerning use of impressionistic likelihood terms in forensic speaker comparison cases* (2007)

Of course speech contains more than just information about voice quality. Even more than written documents, which may contain linguistic cues to authorship going below the orthographic surface, recorded speech can indicate the population the speaker may belong to through sociolinguistic markers in accents, dialects and registers. In October 2005, news services announced that a man had been charged in connection with the notorious 'Yorkshire Ripper' case which had gripped the UK thirty years earlier. Between 1975 and 1980, thirteen women were murdered, recalling Jack the Ripper's terrorizing of London a century before. In 1979, the shocked nation heard on the news a recording of a voice which Assistant Chief Constable George Oldfield, the senior detective investigating the case, claimed was that of the Ripper. The recording began: 'I'm Jack. I see you are still having no luck catching me. I have the greatest respect for you, George, but, Lord, you are no nearer catching me now than four years ago when I started. I reckon your boys are letting you down, George. They can't be much good, can they?'

Stanley Ellis, a linguist from the University of Leeds, subsequently analysed the voice and identified the accent as that used in a specific locality of the small northern town of Sunderland. Oldfield immediately moved his investigation – the biggest manhunt ever seen in Britain – to that region. But the murders continued. Two years later, in 1981, the actual culprit, a Yorkshireman who had been questioned but then eliminated on the basis of the dialect evidence, was arrested in Sheffield. A quarter of a century later, the linguist has been vindicated: the hoaxer, identified through DNA samples on the letters, was arrested at his home in Sunderland (see French *et al.*, 2007).

Controversially, analysis of spoken language has been used in Australia, Belgium, Germany, the Netherlands, Sweden, Switzerland and the UK in cases where people have been required by a court to prove their nationality in order to qualify for refugee status. In such cases, documentary evidence may also include passports, identity cards, letters from friends and family, notes taken by police or immigration officials during interviews, as well as lists and drawings supplied by the claimant (see Blommaert, 2005, for examples of these in the case of an asylum seeker in Belgium claiming to be from Burundi in East Africa). Where the documentary evidence is limited or unconvincing, governments may also request an analysis of the claimant's spoken language, known as LADO: *Language Analysis for the Determination of the Origin (of asylum seekers)*. Examples of such cases are available on the website of the Australian Legal Information Institute (try a search for 'refugee review tribunal'). In a number of them, the courtroom discussion has concerned whether a claimant can be proved, by virtue of their spoken language, to be from Afghanistan (in which case they would be more likely to be granted refugee status) or from Pakistan (in which case they would not). In a review of LADO in such cases, Eades (2005) accepts that spoken language does contain clues about places in which a person has lived, but argues strongly against the use of this evidence to make judgements about *nationality* (the Hazaragi variety of the Dari language, for example, is spoken by ethnic Hazaras on both sides of the Pakistan/Afghan border).

 **www.12.6, 12.7**

Eades and other applied linguists have published a set of guidelines to counter potential injustices of LADO (available on the companion website). But she cautions (Eades, 2005, p. 514) that awareness-raising doesn't guarantee justice for those potentially misjudged or discriminated against on linguistic grounds. However, there

 **www.12.8**

is at least one decision record of the Refugee Review Tribunal of Australia (2004) which references her work in this area. In this particular case, the Tribunal dismisses the language analysis reports, noting, amongst other limitations, that they fail to provide information about the analysts' professional qualifications, expertise or relevant skills. This area is still a controversial one in applied linguistics. At its 2009 annual conference, the International Association for Forensic Phonetics and Acoustics passed a resolution which acknowledges LADO and the contribution to be made by:

- linguists and trained native speakers with the latter working under the guidance and supervision of the former;
- linguists with in-depth research knowledge of the language(s) in question.

(IAFPA, 2009)

Evidently this controversial zone of professional practice has profound implications for social justice among many accidental clients of applied linguistics around the world.

## Discourse as evidence

Discourse analysis can sometimes reveal the difficulties involved in identifying a particular intention in a speaker's utterances, by identifying Gricean implicature or pointing out the phatic use of certain expressions. For example, when somebody in a covert recording is heard to say 'yeah' or 'uh-huh', this doesn't necessarily imply complicity in a conspiracy: such utterances are commonly used as feedback devices intended to acknowledge that the other interlocutor still maintains the floor (Shuy, 1993). The Mexican suspect's use of *sí*, discussed at the beginning of the chapter (pp. 277–8), represents a similar case, where emphasis seems to be intended rather than the affirmative 'yes'.

Furthermore, discourse practices vary considerably, and implicit anglocentric or eurocentric bias in this regard can distort the record, especially given the diversity of World Englishes used in legal proceedings around the world. Forensic linguistics must concern itself not only with the form and interpretation of linguistic expressions, but also with the cultural practices in which language is used as a channel of identity construction and maintenance as much as a medium of communication. For example, 'yes' doesn't necessarily indicate affirmation or emphasis when used by Indigenous Australians, as Eades points out:

> when Aboriginal people say 'yes' in answer to a question it often does not mean 'I agree with what you are asking me'. Instead, it often means 'I think that if I say "yes" you will see that I am obliging, and socially amenable and you will think well of me, and things will work out between us'.
>
> (Eades, 1992, cited in Neate, 2003, pp. 25–26)

And an Australian judge (Gray 1995, cited in Neate 2003, p. 23) has suggested that the answer 'don't know' may conceal one of a number of propositions:

- This is not my country, so I can't speak about it.
- Although this is my country, it is not appropriate for me to speak about it when someone more senior is present.
- Although this is my country, it is not appropriate for me to speak about it, but someone else should be approached for the information.
- This is not a matter about which I can speak in front of people who are present, e.g. women or men or children.
- I cannot say the name because it is the name of a person recently deceased.
- I cannot say the name because it is the name of my sibling of the opposite sex.
- I don't know.

Neate (2003), in an informative discussion of language and land claims by Indigenous peoples in Australia, points out the cultural dissonance that literate Anglophone trial systems can cause for aboriginal Australians, and the numerous misunderstandings that arise as a result. He cites such a misunderstanding from a case in which Jimmy, the witness, must in addition rely on a court interpreter:

*Mr Howie*:    When you go hunting on that country, do you have to ask anybody or can you go there any time you want to?

*Jimmy*:    I ask somebody

*Mr Howie*:    When you ask somebody, who do you ask?

*Jimmy*:    I might ask Japaljarri, my son, I might ask Jampijinpa about we go hunting.

. . .

*The Interpreter*:    The answer is that he might ask anyone, including his son, or he might ask Jampijinpa.

*His Honour*:    It is not a matter of asking anyone, is it?

*Mr Howie*:    As I understand what he is saying, your Honour, he is asking in terms of inviting people to come rather than asking for permission.

*The Interpreter*:    Yes – 'Let's go hunting.'

(Neate, 2003, p. 26)

Sociopragmatic factors which transcend technical issues of language form will play an increasingly vital role in forensic linguistics as the field continues to expand its impact beyond the monolingual societies of Europe and North America. A final example from Australia will serve to illustrate the nature of 'postcolonial' forensic linguistics. In land claims by Indigenous peoples before courts which impose what for them is still a 'foreign' social practice, the evidence that a witness might give regarding 'ownership' of the land can depend on who has the 'right' to speak. Neate points out that

[t]he dissemination of information is tightly controlled and regulated and is hedged about with restrictions according to factors such as age, kinship, descent categories, locality or gender . . . Local rules will govern who can speak and what they can speak about. It is therefore important to determine first which people are fully knowledgeable about the land and have special responsibilities towards it.

(Neate, 2003, p. 18)

To our readers studying and working in mainly monolingual contexts, this kind of information may seem interesting but irrelevant. But in an increasingly globalized world, for which monocultural rules and conventions are inadequate, an under-standing of 'other' practices is indispensable and will enable 'Indigenous' applied linguists in, for example, China, Japan, Britain, the US, France and Germany to understand, respect and assist ethnic minority communities at home, as well as the growing numbers of fellow citizens involved in legal cases abroad.

## 12.4   LANGUAGE AS THE SUBJECT MATTER OF LAW

Occasionally in the courts, it is language itself which is on trial. One such occasion is when written works such as scholarly articles or novels are alleged to have been plagiarized. Nowadays, the detection of simple copy–paste plagiarism (or 'textual borrowing', as Coulthard and Johnson (2007), perhaps less sensationally, refer to it) can be relatively straightforward, given the widespread digitalization of written documents and the ready availability of dedicated software and internet search engines. You can see the results of such an analysis on Sue Blackwell's forensic linguistics website, in which David Wools identified the British government's pla-giarism of an article by Ibrahim al-Marashi in its dossier on Iraq published prior to the last Gulf War. But such technology represents a double-edged sword, since it is harder to date an electronic document than a written one, and contestants in a plagiarism case will need to prove who was the original author by demonstrating earlier publication or composition of the material. A forensic linguist might get involved in such a case if the kind of author identification methods we looked at earlier can be applied to a disputed text to adjudicate between the opposing parties' authorship claims.

**www.12.9**

Another situation placing language in the dock can arise when something said or written is construed as being defamatory, libellous, slanderous, blasphemous, racist, sexist or otherwise criminally obnoxious. In such cases, it is normally the 'finder of fact' (the judge or jury) who interprets the words used and reaches a decision regarding the extent of their obnoxiousness. But sometimes a linguist may be called upon by the defendant's or plaintiff/claimant's lawyer to assist the fact-finder in determining the range of possible intentions underlying the words used. Linguists who specialize in discourse analysis will normally be best prepared to offer such testimony, although in some cases a sociolinguist or dialectologist may be more appropriate (for example in the use of an expression which may be innocent in one variety but not in another, such as the popular term *motherfucker*, considered sarcastic and even complimentary between certain speakers in some urban dialects of US English, but highly offensive in many variants).

Finally, there are the numerous cases involving trademark or proprietary name disputes. Two cases discussed by Tiersma and Solan (2002, p. 228) are particularly illuminating. The first, from 1989, involved a product called *Aveda*, presumably pronounced a-vee-da. Another company subsequently launched a similar product and called it *Avita*. In the ensuing lawsuit, a linguist testified to the extremely close phonetic similarity between the names, given that the *t* of *Avita* is often pronounced in the US with a 'flap' consonant resembling [d], rendering the two words almost homophonous. The judge ruled that the second company must discontinue using the name. The second example drew on evidence from productivity in morphology. Quality Inns planned to open a chain of budget motels which it wanted to call 'McSleep', and was challenged by McDonald's, who alleged that the *Mc-* prefix belonged to them. In a subsequent court case, linguists testified on both sides. The winning argument, perhaps unsurprisingly, was that the morpheme had acquired a new dominant meaning associated with the hamburger company, and was no longer just a generic Scottish prefix. Entrepreneurial applied linguists take note – a distance education course entitled *McLinguist* might meet the same legal fate.

## 12.5   DISCOURSE AND DIFFERENT LANGUAGES IN THE COURTROOM

Courtroom discourse has been the subject of much work in discourse analysis. Some of this work has been theoretical, but much of it is also motivated by practical concerns about the fairness of judicial proceedings. Jury instructions, mentioned in section 12.1, are one such discourse component. Others include cross-examination by lawyers (who may be coercive) and plea-taking by the judge (who may not follow due process). This latter discourse unit was the object of Susan Philips' (1998) extensive ethnographic study referred to on p. 279. She contrasted Arizona judges' handling of guilty pleas, using courtroom observation, interviews with the judges, and intertextual analysis correlating what they said with the written requirements from the relevant procedural rules and case law. She concluded that judges may be placed on a continuum from 'procedure oriented' to 'record oriented'. The former vary their discourse structure and style according to how they assess the defendant's ability to fully comprehend their rights and the consequences of pleading guilty. The latter follow the letter of the law, rarely elaborating on the minimal requirements provided in written guidelines and assuming that the overall written record will show that the defendant's rights were respected. Philips also uses quantitative measurements to make her case, counting variables such as the number of 'wh-' questions addressed to the defendant and the number of responses elicited from the defendant (both higher in the case of procedure-oriented judges). Her ultimate interpretation of this dichotomy is that it is *ideologically* driven, and hence that US trial judges' claims to be mere deciders of fact are not tenable.

Another aspect of courtroom discourse which is becoming ever more significant is where more than one language is involved. We have already seen what can happen in police investigations where suspect and authority do not share the same mother tongue. Interpreters have become regular participants in court proceedings, but their presence does not always guarantee that the interests of justice are served. As we noted in Chapter 10, there is controversy about the extent to which interpreters can and should be invisible conduits of meaning. In courtrooms, interpreters often lack the common ground of the (alleged) facts of the case shared by participants in lengthy trials, but are often more familiar with the cultural contexts of witnesses and defendants than are the juries and legal professionals who need to understand what they say. Lee (2010) shows how Korean–English interpreters in Australia were reluctant to faithfully reproduce inexplicit portions of witnesses' utterances, preferring instead to modify them so that they were grammatically and pragmatically consistent with the unfolding English discourse. For example, in Korean the omission of the subject is common, and so in the absence of relevant context this can result in potential ambiguities about who is doing what. In Lee's analysis of courtroom discourse, some interpreters supplied incorrect or arbitrary subjects (e.g. *someone* or *they*), and only one disclosed to the court a problem with inexplicit language.

Where the context outside the courtroom is bilingual, other ethical problems of a sociolinguistic nature can arise. In an infamous case in New York from the beginning of the 1990s (cf. Valdés, 1995), potential jurors were excluded from service because they were bilingual Spanish–English speakers and could not convince the court that they would listen only to the Spanish–English interpreter, rather than directly to Spanish-speaking witnesses. The motive for this decision may have been purely one of fairness – given that monolingual English-speakers were also inevitably involved in the process, the court and the jury would all need to base their interpretation of evidence on a common source of information, namely the interpreter. But there were two major problems with this, one cognitive and one sociocultural, which an applied linguist would have anticipated from the outset. The cognitive problem is that it is impossible for someone *not* to hear and interpret a message directed to them in a known language. The sociocultural problem is that knowing a language is inevitably a cultural (here an ethnic) phenomenon: in the largely Hispanic community where the trial took place, barring bilinguals would render the jury ethnically unrepresentative. Despite the contentiousness of the original court's decision, it was upheld by the Supreme Court in 1991.

So far in this chapter we have been assuming the kind of legal system which operates in the UK and USA, familiar to many from hundreds of English language TV and film dramas. This criminal system is adversarial – a verbal contest between defence and prosecution to convince a jury in open court, with a judge as umpire and a presumption of innocence until guilt is proven. The law is interpreted for the jury by the judge and the lawyers on the basis of precedents in similar cases, tried in earlier courts. This is the so-called 'common law' tradition. But in many parts of the world the legal process works differently, following an 'inquisitorial' process and departing not from precedent but directly from written codes and statutes. This system, known as 'civil law', found its most articulated expression in the so-called 'Napoleonic Code' (see Figure 12.5) adopted by post-revolutionary France to replace the almost feudal set of customs, edicts and charters which held sway previously. A number of other European countries occupied by Napoleon's forces followed France in the adoption of such a code, including Spain and the Netherlands, and many other nations' legal systems were influenced by it, including those of Germany and some European colonies.

In Indonesia (a Dutch colony until 1945) a civil code was adopted in 1847: the *Burgerlijk Wetboek*. Today, although there are several unofficial translations into Indonesian, the only authoritative version of the code is the original, in Dutch (Lindsey, 2008). This has several implications for present-day Indonesian law and lawyers: Dutch language is still a compulsory class for university law students; Indonesian lawyers are dependent on their (more proficient in Dutch) law professors for explication of the code; and amendment of the law is problematic (new articles would need to be written in Dutch for consistency). One result of this tangle of law

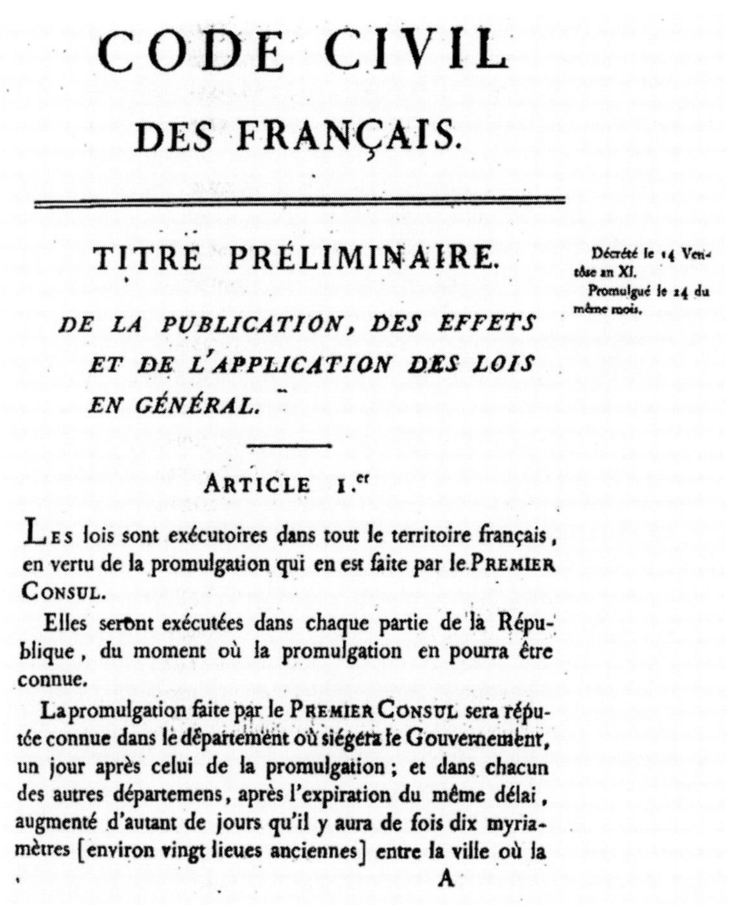

# CODE CIVIL

## DES FRANÇAIS.

### TITRE PRÉLIMINAIRE.

Décrété le 14 Ven-
tôse an XI.
Promulgué le 24 du
même mois.

#### DE LA PUBLICATION, DES EFFETS
#### ET DE L'APPLICATION DES LOIS
#### EN GÉNÉRAL.

##### ARTICLE 1.er

LES lois sont exécutoires dans tout le territoire français,
en vertu de la promulgation qui en est faite par le PREMIER
CONSUL.

Elles seront exécutées dans chaque partie de la Répu-
blique, du moment où la promulgation en pourra être
connue.

La promulgation faite par le PREMIER CONSUL sera répu-
tée connue dans le département où siégera le Gouvernement,
un jour après celui de la promulgation ; et dans chacun
des autres départemens, après l'expiration du même délai,
augmenté d'autant de jours qu'il y aura de fois dix myria-
mètres [environ vingt lieues anciennes] entre la ville où la

A

Figure 12.5   The first page of the 'Napoleonic Code', published in France in 1804 (Source:
Wikimedia Commons)

and language is that Indonesian contract law, for example, has not been updated
since 1847 and remains documented in a language that very, very few Indonesians
today can understand.

The laudable ideal behind the original introduction of a code in Europe was to
harness the fixing power of the written word in order to eliminate the indeterminacy
and arbitrariness which had characterized much of the orally based judicial
processes of Europe's law courts. Ironically, bearing in mind the current obscurity
of the code in Indonesia, complete and explicit codification of the law was intended
to provide all citizens with an objective recourse, independent of the whim of
individual judges or their patrons in royal palaces and feudal chateaux.

In section 12.2 we described the 'push-me pull-you' tension between the need
for precise codification of the law and efforts to make it accessible to citizens. We
assumed there that one of the major problems was the interpretation of the written
code in the context of an orally conducted trial. What happens, however, when
the trial itself is conducted through the submission of written documentation, rather
than through verbal contest in open court? This is the situation that holds in many

countries which have inherited a legal system based on the Napoleonic Code. In Mexico, for example, evidence is first submitted in writing and verified by the *Ministerio Público* (the office responsible for marshalling evidence and bringing a case). Subsequently, the plaintiff and defendant, accompanied by their lawyers, attend a session in the presence of the court secretary, during which each party has fifteen minutes to present their case orally. The secretary reviews the evidence and statements and emits both verdict and sentence, which are then submitted in writing to a judge for confirmation. The process is designed to facilitate the objective implementation of the written law, with no room for variable interpretation, opinion or belief.

An unwelcome by-product of doing justice almost exclusively through documents, however, is that the process is very long and complicated. The number of different documents required is daunting. They include: (1) the indenture of accusation; (2) the official instrument initiating the action; (3) the bill of indictment; (4) the report of evidence from the *Ministerio Público*; (5) the endorsement of the bill of indictment by the court secretary; (6) the endorsement of the bill of indictment and report of evidence by the judge; (7) the report registering the verdict (and sentence, if the defendant is found guilty) endorsed by the court secretary; and (8) the final report (ratifying the secretary's report), endorsed by the judge. In the absence of computerized document-management systems, files tend to get misplaced, inconsistencies between reports go unnoticed, and when significant questions arise they often remain unpursued for long periods (if they are pursued at all). Recent proposals for judicial reform at the federal level place oral trial proceedings at centre stage. The goal of the proposals is 'to implement accusatory, oral and public criminal procedures, in the obligatory presence of the judge during hearings, resulting in the resolution of most legal disputes in the court itself, as a guarantee of juridical invulnerability and openness' (Presidencia de la República, 2006, p. 8; translation ours). The immediacy of oralcy will present great administrative challenges to the Mexican legal system. Its promoters hope it will enhance the pursuit of justice for ordinary Mexicans.

Remarkably, we have yet to hear a commentator remark on one consequence of oral trials which to applied linguists will be patently obvious: after centuries of exclusion, the many thousands of functionally illiterate Indigenous Mexicans will be able to *participate* in legal decision-making which can significantly affect their lives. At the same time, however, the particular oralcy practices of the English adversarial system will not necessarily guarantee equal rights before the law for Indigenous peoples or anyone else. The cross-examination 'information elicitation' ritual, in which lawyers craft questions to which witnesses and defendants must give precisely focused answers, doesn't accommodate cultures which value other forms of communication. In the context of Indigenous nations in Australia, Neate once again notes that such a system

> [does not] afford Aboriginal witnesses the opportunity to give their evidence in a narrative form. Witnesses find that they are required to provide answers to specific questions. They also find that they are often interrupted, and the sometimes aggressive tactics of counsel will normally be interpreted as a prelude to verbal confrontation.
>
> (Neate, 2003, p. 28)

Among their many roles, forensic linguists need to impress upon judicial reformers around the world the need for sensitivity to differing language and discourse practices in cross-cultural and cross-linguistic legal proceedings.

## 12.6  ROLES FOR APPLIED LINGUISTS

The applied linguists among us who dream of providing expert witness testimony in courts of law are unlikely to get the chance, because linguistic evidence is not yet accorded the same status in the courtroom as old-fashioned fingerprinting or twenty-first century DNA profiling, and the jobs are few and far between. There are a number of reasons why forensic linguistic evidence is in limited judicial demand, including the following:

- The inherent problems of variance in individual language use, discussed in section 12.3, guarantee that forensic findings on speaker/writer identity will never be 100 per cent reliable.
- Courts are sometimes reluctant to recognize that anything as commonplace and apparently straightforward as human language use could be in need of expert testimony (a consequence of the Language Spell; see Chapter 1).
- Some judges appear to feel that linguists may usurp the traditional role of juries, which in large part is to interpret evidence expressed through writing or speech (recall the death penalty example in section 12.1).
- Some judges also perceive that their own role as interpreters of the law as an 'assemblage of signs' (law as language) is being questioned when a linguist is present.

Rules on expert testimony around the world vary substantially. In the UK and Australia, for example, courts recognize individual expert witnesses, independently of the methods they use. The British Civil Evidence Act 1972 (OPSI, n.d.) states that 'where a person is called as a witness in any civil proceedings, his opinion on any relevant matter on which he is qualified to give expert evidence shall be admissible in evidence'. In the US, expert evidence must be based on testable, peer-reviewed theories and techniques, susceptible to statistical error analysis. The current standard was established in a 1993 products liability case (*Daubert vs Merrell Dow Pharmaceuticals, Inc.*). Some forensic linguists (e.g. Tiersma and Solan, 2002, p. 225; Solan and Tiersma, 2004) are quite confident that linguistic evidence will, in general, meet these standards, whereas others (cf. Olsson, 2004, p. 42) are more cautious.

 **www.12.10**

In any case, not all courts follow the Daubert ruling strictly, and expertise from forensic linguistic consultants is clearly in demand, if the number of suppliers on the internet is any indication. Among the numerous specialist Language and Linguistics categories in one internet directory of expert witnesses (*JurisPro*) one finds: 'conversational analysis', 'foreign accents', 'second language acquisition', 'inter-cultural communication', 'interpreting and translating', 'speech pathology', 'language planning', 'language policy' and 'trade name/generic name issues'. A dozen different commercial forensic practices are listed as experts in these areas. Tiersma and Solan (2002, p. 223) estimate that in the US there may be annually 'a thousand

 **www.12.11**

trial-court cases in which linguistic expertise was involved in some way'. But with this increased participation by applied linguists in legal cases comes a new set of ethical responsibilities. As we have seen in previous chapters, professionalization of the field, involving the establishment of codes of ethics (like the guidelines mentioned in section 12.3 above), practitioner certification procedures, professional organizations, peer-referenced journals, etc., is an urgent theme in the discourse of applied linguists today.

To conclude, then, we list some of the main roles for applied linguists in this field in the near future:

- quality control through the establishment of codes of ethics and guides for good practice;
- advocacy of the linguistic rights of those involved in legal proceedings, especially marginalized minority language speakers or speakers of 'non-standard' or 'non-native' varieties;
- explanation and promotion of the tenets of general and applied linguistics to appropriate government agencies, to people involved in administering justice such as lawyers and judges, and to NGOs providing support to refugees and asylum seekers;
- continued collaboration with other applied linguists and legal professionals in the simplification of legal language;
- consultancy work and, maybe occasionally, service as an expert witness.

Human beings in many societies have the right to remain silent . . . but it's hard, and once the words flow, the linguist's job begins and – hopefully – justice prevails.

activities

**www.**
**12.12**

1   Do you know of any legal cases in your country in which language issues have been central to the case, or of cases in which linguists have been called upon to give evidence? To look for such cases online, type the words 'linguistics', 'news' and the name of your country into an internet search engine and browse the results. The News link on Webster's Forensic Linguistics Homepage, hosted by the University of Birmingham in the UK, has examples of cases from the USA, UK, Australia, etc. If you find any interesting examples, let us know via the companion website.

2   Ask your friends and family about ways in which language and the law might be connected. Make a list of the issues they mention. Compare your list with the sub-headings in this chapter. Do they mention any issues not covered by the chapter? If they do, email us via the companion website and let us know. Are there any issues covered in this chapter which are not mentioned by the people you have surveyed? What are they?

3   The careers service at your local high school asks you to come and talk to pupils aged sixteen to eighteen about how an awareness of language issues is important for anyone considering a legal career. Look through

this chapter again and make brief notes on the issues you will include in your presentation, bearing in mind what you found out in activity 2 about public awareness of these issues. Could you use any of the legal cases you found in activity 1 to illustrate your points? Which ones?

4    In section 12.6 we mentioned the Language Spell, the idea that the complex mechanisms of language mainly operate without any need for conscious awareness of them (see Chapter 1 for more details). Two important consequences of the Spell are that we tend to equate language with thought itself and that we identify languages with the groups who speak them. Both of these consequences of the Spell could have serious (possibly negative) results for defendants in a legal case. What might they be?

## FURTHER READING

Coulthard, M. and Johnson, A. (2007). *An introduction to forensic linguistics: Language in evidence*. London: Routledge.

—— (eds) (2010). *The Routledge handbook of forensic linguistics*. London: Routledge.

Eades, D. (2010). *Sociolinguistics and the legal process*. Bristol, UK: Multilingual Matters.

McMenamin, G. R. (2002). *Forensic linguistics: Advances in forensic stylistics*. Boca Raton, FL: CRC Press.

# CHAPTER 13

# Language pathology

Someone's cut the string
between each word and its matching thing.

(Gwyneth Lewis, *Aphasia*)

In the other chapters of Part C we have mapped specialized areas of applied linguistics which focus on potential problems related to the *social* manifestations of language – as an obstacle to be negotiated in Chapter 10, as a community resource in Chapter 11 and as a medium for group standards of behaviour in Chapter 12. We end our guide to the themes and practices of applied linguistics by returning to the language code itself, its *cognitive* form. For unlike many areas of contemporary applied linguistics which can adopt a largely or uniquely socio-linguistic orientation, language pathology must grapple with the ultimate physical forms of language: the neural circuits which underlie grammar and lexicon, and the motor and perceptual systems which allow us to externalize and internalize the messages which grammar and lexicon jointly encode.

In focusing on the biological reality of language here, we must not – cannot – lose sight of its fundamental social and communicative purpose. Language pathologists, in common with all applied linguists, must always remain aware that they are dealing with broader human issues: that the disorders they diagnose and treat affect the very core of their clients' lives as social beings. As we have seen with all the other areas of applied linguistics mapped in this book, language pathology is therefore inherently multidisciplinary. It employs the research findings, practical experience and expertise not only of linguists, but also of cognitive, developmental and social psychology, education and the health sciences.

There is a profusion of names associated with this area of applied linguistics. The specific application of linguistics to problems of language disability has been called 'clinical linguistics' by David Crystal (1981), whereas the broader term 'language pathology' is generally used to cover the whole professional/scientific enterprise relating to language-related disorders, from neurolinguistic theory to therapeutic practice. Practitioners whose main work is in clinics, schools, hospitals and patients' homes, rather than in research laboratories, call themselves 'speech and language *therapists*' in the UK and 'speech and language *pathologists*' in the USA (see Crystal and Varley, 1998, p. 1, for names used in other countries). We opt for language pathology as a cover term here.

The chapter is organized as follows. First, in section 13.1, we'll stress once again the dual nature of human language, as both an individual, cognitive system rooted in human biology and a shared resource embedded in, and articulating, sociocultural beliefs and practices. Then, after a brief tour of the biological landscape of human language, we describe some of the major types of language disability (13.2) and other disorders that can affect language use (13.3). This essential background knowledge will allow us to proceed to an account of the clinical and community-based practice of language pathologists at both the assessment (13.4) and treatment stages (13.5). As usual, a brief roll call of other roles for applied linguists closes the chapter in 13.6.

## 13.1  BIOLOGICAL AND SOCIAL FOUNDATIONS OF LANGUAGE

We have seen in previous chapters that language without social meaning is as unnatural as fish without water. Language evolved in the human species as a tool to share meaning in society. By sharing meaning through language, we were able to become progressively more social, ultimately cultural. Our creation of cultural groups and identities, with their own characteristic practices and beliefs, was accompanied by a remarkable growth in brain power: we became prodigious thinkers, and sharing meaning through language gave us progressively more to think about. A key component in the emergence of this unique way of being was the mystery of human consciousness: the awareness we have of ourselves and of the world around us. Luckily, this consciousness is limited to the important stuff. Much of the boring legwork of life is not available to our conscious minds, including most of language. This is what Hall (2005) has called being under 'the Language Spell', a metaphor we have exploited throughout this book.

But the blithe state of efficient ignorance that the Language Spell bestows on us becomes compromised once the subconscious mental apparatus that supports our language capacity breaks down or our children are born with apparatus which is faulty. If we are to help people solve problems arising from these situations, we must come to grips with the internal structure and functioning of language in the brain and the physical channels it uses to mediate understanding in the external world – as speech, sign, Braille and writing. Given this, we need to take a brief tour of language as it resides in, and is enacted by, the human body.

Even though almost all people use the vocal channel to communicate linguistically, and despite the use of terms like *tongue* and *speech* to refer to language, the central location of our linguistic capacity is clearly the brain, rather than the speech or hearing organs. Because we possess no telepathic power to share meaning directly with each other, we have to rely on an external channel, like speech, to do the job of message delivery. But speech doesn't have a monopoly on this sociophysiological function: for sign languages, the same range of linguistic messages find outlet essentially through the hands. So we know that the vocal tract is not a necessary component of human language, but that language without brain is impossible. Furthermore, we know that language resides in the brain because we can measure the electrochemical activity generated there when people speak and listen or produce and comprehend sign languages (see Ingram, 2007, for a comprehensive overview of the research), and we can see the effects on language when the brain is damaged.

The **cerebral cortex** is the 'grey matter', the 2–4 mm layer of neural tissue covering the two cerebral hemispheres of the human brain, containing the neural networks responsible for 'higher cognitive functions' like language and visual processing.

The **cerebral hemispheres** are the two halves of the cerebrum, the principal component of the human brain. You can take a 3D tour of the brain at the US Public Broadcasting System's website for its series *The Secret Life of the Brain* . Eric Chudler's *Neuroscience for Kids* site at the University of Washington has a page on language and the brain, and is also available in several languages, including Chinese and Spanish.

**www.13.1**

**www.13.2**

**Broca's area** is a region of cerebral cortex associated with language production, located above the **Sylvian Fissure**, the deep crevice in each cerebral hemisphere running backwards from above the ear. **Wernicke's area** is a region of cerebral cortex below the inner

# Neurological underpinnings of the language faculty

Over the past century and a half we have come to understand a good deal about how language is represented in the neural tissue which constitutes the brain's grey matter (the **cerebral cortex**). It's too complicated to be located all in one particular region of the brain, like the blood-pumping function is located in the valves of the heart. In fact, language knowledge and activity are distributed throughout the neural tissue of the cortex. But certain regions around the **Sylvian Fissure** (the deep crevice running roughly from temple to ear) on the left side of the brain appear to be especially important for language processing (see Figure 13.1).

A few people (especially left-handers) may have language function concentrated in the right **cerebral hemisphere**, or across both, but this is rare. Damage to **Broca's area** on one side of the Sylvian Fissure or to **Wernicke's area** on the other side will more often than not affect aspects of language production or comprehension, respectively. And yet the kinds of impairment resulting from damage to one of these areas can vary greatly, and damage to other areas can produce similar effects.

So on the one hand, language appears to be *localized* to some extent, but on the other hand it also appears to be widely *distributed* throughout the brain. This apparently contradictory architecture makes sense, though, if you think about how it effectively minimizes the effects of brain damage. Not having *all* your linguistic eggs in one basket means that a lesion (injury) to an area of the brain lying outside the region of the Sylvian Fissure is less likely to result in a language deficit. And distributed representation means that if a language area *is* damaged, not all language functions and knowledge will be knocked out, and other areas may be able to compensate.

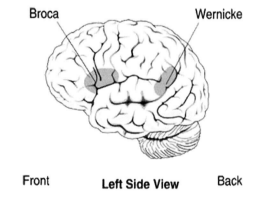

Figure 13.1   Broca's and Wernicke's areas on either side of the Sylvian Fissure in the left cerebral hemisphere (side view, facing left) (Source: US National Institute on Deafness and Other Communication Disorders)

# Language in other parts of the brain and the body

Apart from the linguistic areas of the brain, damage to other areas of neural tissue can compromise language functions. We've argued that the essential function of language is to express meaning in a format that can be externalized as physical energy, with social objectives. So at least four other brain functions will be involved in successful language use: conceptual and social processes at one end, and perceptual and motor control processes at the other. We know very little about the neural correlates of conceptual knowledge (meaning) or of sociocultural beliefs and actions, but cognitive neuroscience has revealed a lot in recent decades about the sensory and muscular systems which allow us to produce and receive linguistic signals (Gazzaniga, 2009). We know, for example, that visual input from sign and writing is processed in the occipital lobes at the very back of the brain, and that acoustic input from speech is initially dealt with close to Wernicke's area. For production, we know that the relevant motor routines required to engage the speech articulators in the vocal tract, together with the sign and writing articulators in the upper limbs, are controlled and coordinated by the 'motor strip' along the Fissure of Rolando, stretching roughly from the region behind the ear to the top of the head.

end of the Sylvian Fissure, which plays a major role in language comprehension.

Furthermore, over a century of sustained scientific enquiry into the organic-muscular systems of the language modalities has revealed a lot of knowledge about the vocal tract and the speech processing system, although relatively less about reading and writing, and only a meagre amount about sign articulation and perception. Studies in articulatory phonetics have shown how language is externalized through the expulsion of air from the lungs through the continually morphing resonating chamber of the vocal tract, between the larynx (Adam's apple) and the lips, nostrils, palate and teeth. Work in acoustic phonetics has taught us how the linguistically structured sounds produced by the contortions of the vocal tract are reconstructed on the basis of salient cues in the input. For example, sudden changes in **amplitude** and relative **frequency** help us identify sibilants, like the [s] or [z] sounds which produce energy at the highest levels of pitch, and distinguish vowels, like low [u] and high [i].

It's an unfortunate truth that in our precarious existence any of the complex biological subsystems from which we are built may be compromised by malfunctions and accidents which occur as we develop as embryos, enter the world as independent organisms, mature into adulthood, interact with our physical and social environments, and decline in old age. The myriad components associated with language use are no exception. Actually, it's a wonder that so many of us manage to survive with language intact for so long! One of the responsibilities of applied linguistics is to contribute expertise to aid those who are not as lucky in this regard.

## 13.2  TYPES OF LANGUAGE PATHOLOGY

Given that a defining characteristic of applied linguistics is its practical engagement with the language-related *problems* faced by individuals and groups, we need to address here the nature of the problems with which language pathology is concerned. But it's not our purpose to describe language disorders comprehensively or in any great detail here. Following the rationale we set out in Chapter 1, we focus here on the *practice* of language pathology, rather than the theory and description of the disorders themselves – just as we focused on language *teaching* in Chapter 9, and left a summary of second language acquisition processes to other authors. But we do in this section map some of the descriptive territory, so as to be able to follow a number of principal routes in professional practice.

A simple way to start would be to claim that client issues in this area are 'communication problems'. But this would admit too broad a range of phenomena, from miscommunication between groups because they don't share a common language or dialect, through temporary breakdowns in communication because of a slip of the tongue or a noisy environment, to misinterpretations of gestures, facial expressions or other non-linguistic communication channels. A more limiting focus, then, so we can distinguish language pathologists from translators and other applied linguists, is reflected in the term 'individual language-related disabilities'. One of the major issues for clinicians in the field is to recognize the vastly heterogeneous

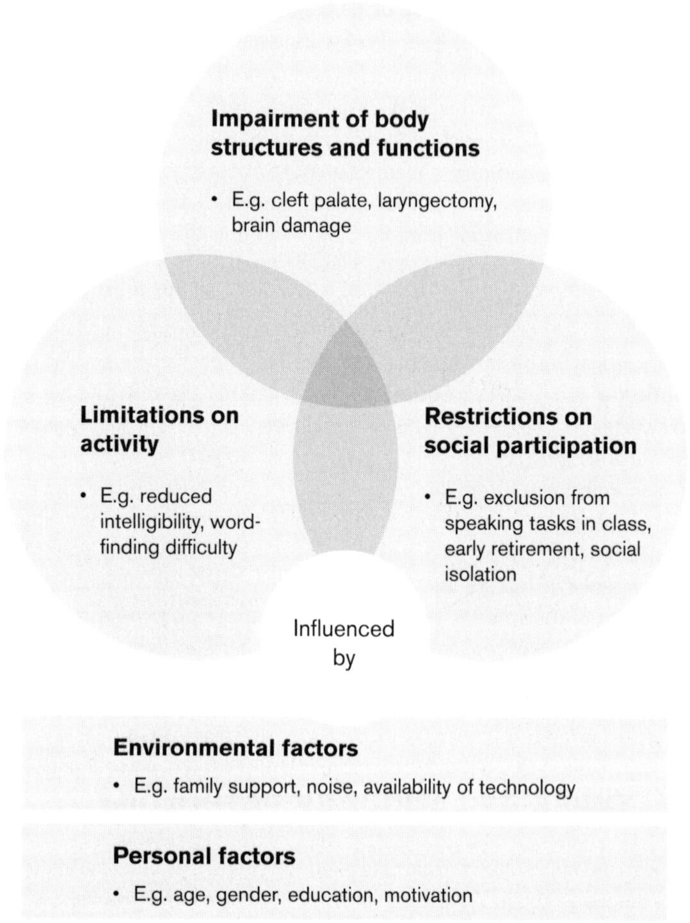

**Impairment of body
structures and functions**

- E.g. cleft palate, laryngectomy, brain damage

**Limitations on
activity**

- E.g. reduced intelligibility, word-finding difficulty

**Restrictions on
social participation**

- E.g. exclusion from speaking tasks in class, early retirement, social isolation

Influenced
by

**Environmental factors**

- E.g. family support, noise, availability of technology

**Personal factors**

- E.g. age, gender, education, motivation

Figure 13.2   The International Classification of Functioning and Communication Disorders (ICF) (adapted from Ferguson and Armstrong, 2009, p 29)

Table 13.1   Some central dichotomies used to categorize dimensions of individual
language-related disability

| Dichotomy | Example |
|---|---|
| System vs modality | *Aphasia* results in damage to, or loss of, the neurally encoded language system, independent of modality; *deafness* leaves the system intact but affects one of the modalities of language use |
| Reception vs production | *Wernicke's aphasia* can impair the reception of linguistic messages; *Broca's aphasia* has greater impact on language production |
| Congenital vs acquired | *Developmental dyslexia* is congenital (either inherited or developing in the foetus); *acquired dyslexia* is normally the result of injury to the left hemisphere |
| Neurological vs non-neurological | *Dysarthria* impairs neurological control of the speech articulators (muscles used in speaking); *cleft lip and palate* affects the articulators themselves |

nature of such disabilities. Our knowledge of language and the brain is still very limited, but data from people with language-related disorders reveal an enormous variety of conditions, affecting one or more of the diverse processing mechanisms and knowledge structures that underlie the functioning of the language faculty.

One of the central tenets of language pathology is that each client must be viewed individually and therefore diagnosed and treated according to their own unique psycho- and sociolinguistic profile, and their own communicative and social needs. The perspective of the client and their needs is central to the World Health Organization's *International Classification of Functioning and Communication Disorders* (ICF) (WHO, 2001). Their scheme, summarized in Figure 13.2, 'takes into account the social aspects of disability and does not see disability only as a 'medical' or 'biological' dysfunction'.   **www.13.3**

For our expository purposes here, we need to focus first on the disabilities, so that later we can pan out to appreciate the broader view. One way to form an impression of the scope of individual language disabilities is to identify them in terms of a series of central dichotomies in the dimensions of linguistic knowledge and/or linguistic processing affected. Some of these dimensions, with some examples of disabilities, are summarized in Table 13.1.

Before looking at three of these dichotomies in greater depth, let us just clarify once again that 'dimension of disability' doesn't define individual *clients*: as we noted in Chapter 3, people with language disabilities, like all clients of applied linguistics, seldom – if ever – fall into neat typological categories.

## System vs modality

As we've repeatedly seen, language as a system of grammar and lexicon relies on speech and other external channels to get in and out of people's minds. If the modality of delivery is damaged, language can become unusable to a greater or lesser extent, even if the internal system itself is completely spared. Consider deafness. If you have trouble hearing sounds, you will inevitably have trouble with hearing speech. Speech, though, is not language, but rather 'language spoken', which must be heard in order to be understood. Being deaf does not mean that you have anything wrong with your language capacity: your linguistic *system* will develop and be used as normal if you also use another language modality which does not depend on speech, such as sign. An example of damage to the system, on the other hand, is **aphasia**, the range of disorders resulting from damage to areas of the brain responsible for specifically linguistic functions. Aphasias are caused by prolonged interruption to the flow of oxygen to the brain through the blood supply (often through strokes or haemorrhage) or destruction of neural tissue (through disease or injury, for example). You will not have aphasia if the damage or disease bypasses the language areas completely and affects only the areas of the brain responsible for auditory processing.

But the two concepts cannot be separated completely. If a child is born deaf and the parents and/or other care-givers use only spoken languages as opposed to sign languages, then the child will not acquire a fully fledged linguistic system, since for this to happen linguistic input is required from the environment to trigger the system's growth. Also, damage to the system may be intimately related to issues of modality too. It's no coincidence, for example, that aphasias which affect the processing of grammatical structure in incoming speech involve damage to areas of the brain which are also associated with auditory processing in general. It is possible, too, that some aphasic individuals may be able to use language almost normally in the written modality but not the spoken, or vice versa (Crystal and Varley, 1998, pp. 170–171).

**Aphasia** is an impairment or loss of linguistic knowledge or ability. It may be due to congenital or acquired brain damage. It is sometimes called *dysphasia* when language loss is not total.

## Developmental vs acquired disabilities

Children may, in effect, be born with a language disorder, either due to a traumatic event or disease occurring during gestation/birth, or possibly because of some inherited trait or condition (see the sub-section on specific vs general on pp. 307–8). Alternatively, the disorder may have been caused by the environment, any time from infancy to old age. A major difference between the two is that developmental disorders affect the acquisition of linguistic knowledge and processes, whereas acquired disorders affect the knowledge and processes previously acquired. This will clearly have important consequences for treatment, since the child with a developmental disorder will need a therapist's help to *learn*, whereas an adult or older child with an acquired disorder will require assistance to *recover* what they have already acquired. Although aphasia, for example, is normally defined as an acquired state and is most often associated with older adults who have had a stroke, early damage to the brain's language centres can affect the development of the emerging language system or the ways we process it.

One language-related impairment that comes in both developmental and acquired versions is dyslexia, affecting reading and writing (among other non-linguistic processes). This complex range of conditions, experienced by significant numbers of people in some literate societies, is not yet fully understood by psycho-

or neurolinguists. There's broad consensus, though, that at the root of many of the dyslexic syndromes is a problem with the use of phonology in the encoding and decoding of writing (although science moves fast, and other possibilities are currently being investigated – see, for example, the research review authored by Rice with Brooks (2004, pp. 42–70)). A dysfunction in the 'metalinguistic' ability to focus conscious attention on naturally acquired phonology is not going to affect speech itself, cocooned as it is by the Language Spell. But it *will* show up in the socially learned 're-representation' of spoken language required by glottographic (sound-based) writing systems. This is especially so when the relationship between the elements of the writing system and the elements of the phonological system is supposedly one-to-one but is not exclusively so. For example, fewer cases of dyslexia surface in Spanish speakers than in English speakers. This is presumably because the spelling conventions of Spanish represent in a more or less direct way the phonemic sequences that make up spoken word form, whereas in the latter spelling is sometimes rather arbitrary. In Spanish you can confidently pronounce almost any newly encountered written word, but in English how would you know how to pronounce the newly coined word *zough*? (Think of the *o u g h* sequence in *dough*, *thought*, *rough* and *plough*.)

www.13.4

Some kinds of dyslexia may be present at birth, through either genetic inheritance or processes of hormonal development at the early foetal stage. Other kinds of dyslexia may be acquired in adulthood, through injury to the left cerebral hemisphere (often resulting also in Broca-type aphasia). The development of literacy skills is an extremely variable process, influenced by socioeconomic and other factors (see Chapter 6) rather than running according to a biologically predetermined sequence. The disruption caused by developmental dyslexia is therefore particularly acute, since other neural circuits will not automatically compensate, as they do in the case of disruptions to the early development of innately based abilities. Early detection and treatment will therefore be critical. With acquired dyslexia, however, the problem is slightly different: it is likely that the patient will have already learned how to read and write, and additionally will have assumed the social abilities and attitudes which come with literacy. If the brain damage they suffer leaves other cognitive skills intact, their loss will hit them extremely hard, and a range of different kinds of therapies will be called for. See section 13.5 for more on treatment.

**Apraxia** is a motor planning disorder involving impairment or loss of the ability to make voluntary movements, such as the articulatory gestures involved in speech. **Dysarthria** is a speech articulation disorder caused by damage to the nerves that control muscles in the vocal tract and lungs.

## Specific vs general

A disorder may affect linguistic and non-linguistic capacities and skills, or language alone. The set of conditions called **apraxias** are specific to language modality, for example, leaving related motor functions unimpaired, whereas **dysarthria** will affect all activities carried out by the muscles controlled by the damaged areas of the nervous system. One set of language-specific disabilities that have provoked a lot of scientific interest (and considerable controversy) in recent years are those named collectively Specific Language Impairment (SLI), thought by some researchers to be caused by genetic factors involved in the emergence of grammar during language acquisition (Fisher and Marcus, 2006). One family of English speakers (reported in Gopnik *et al.*, 1997), exhibits three generations of individuals with grammatical rule disorders, from the grandmother down to twelve of her grandchildren

www.13.5

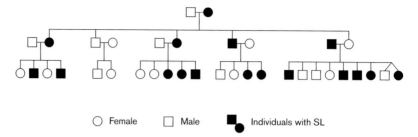

Female    Male    Individuals with SL

Figure 13.3   Family tree for three generations of a family affected by SLI (Source: reproduced with permission from Gopnik *et al.*, 1997)

(see Figure 13.3). The language-impaired members of the family reportedly have hearing and general cognition in the normal range, and although some have prob-lems with speech articulation, tests appear to show that these problems are not the cause of the grammatical problems.

In Down Syndrome, language acquisition and linguistic communication will also routinely be disrupted as the result of genetic mutation, in this case a mutation that involves an unexpected extra copy of certain information in the chromosomes. But the syndrome never affects language alone. It often has very wide-ranging effects across the whole spectrum of human attributes, from physical appearance to cognitive performance. A therapeutic programme for a child with Down Syndrome, then, may contain some of the treatments called for in SLI, but will go way beyond this, and language will be only one component in a complex set of communicative, psychiatric, social, health-related, educational and physiological concerns. It is not yet clear if the language problems of people with Down Syndrome are due to actual changes in the way language acquisition unfolds or merely to delayed language acquisition associated with non-linguistic aspects of the condition.

## Non-linguistic disorders which affect language

Some disorders involve damage to neither the language components of the brain nor the perceptual and expressive pathways of language modality. In our definition of language as a cognitive mechanism which evolved to transform sound into social meaning and social meaning into sound, we've stressed that it's the *social meaning* part of the equation which is all-important. Consequently, a pathological condition which limits a person's ability to make sense of the physical and social world in which they live and/or to conceptualize messages about themselves and their world may well be associated with language problems too. For theorists of language, one of the most interesting facts in this domain is that some general cognitive disorders of this kind *do* affect language, whereas others *don't*. This kind of 'double disso-ciation' has been argued to constitute further evidence for the cognitive modularity of the language faculty mentioned earlier: the idea that language, at some level, is a separate system from the rest of cognition.

A relevant (and very ironic) example of double dissociation is presented in the set of 'clinical tales' published in 1998 by the British (but US-based) neurologist Oliver Sacks, under the title *The Man Who Mistook his Wife for a Hat*. In a chapter called 'The President's Speech', Sacks describes the reactions of some of his patients to a televised speech by the US president. The aphasic patients, with damage to their language comprehension systems, do not take the president seriously, laughing at him for his insincerity. But how can they apprehend his mental state if not through what he says? Sacks explains that they develop an enhanced sensitivity to

> vocal nuance, the tone, the rhythm, the cadences, the music, the subtlest modulations, inflections, intonations, which can give – or remove – verisimilitude to or from a man's voice. In this, then, lies their power of understanding – understanding, without words, what is authentic or inauthentic. Thus it was the grimaces, the histrionisms, the false gestures and, above all, the false tones and cadences of the voice, which rang false for these wordless but immensely sensitive patients.
>
> (Sacks, 1998, p. 82)

Sacks compares their reactions with that of another patient, Emily D., who has tonal **agnosia**: she is unable to recognize the expressive qualities of voice, but processes the words in their grammatical sequences perfectly normally. She is a negative image of the aphasic patients, hence the double dissociation. Here is Sacks' description of her reaction to the president's speech:

> It did not move her – no speech now moved her – and all that was evocative, genuine or false completely passed her by. Deprived of emotional reaction, was she then (like the rest of us) transported or taken in? By no means. 'He is not cogent,' she said. 'He does not speak good prose. His word-use is improper. Either he is brain-damaged, or he has something to conceal.' Thus the President's speech did not work for Emily D. either, due to her enhanced sense of formal language use, propriety as prose, any more than it worked for our aphasics, with their word-deafness but enhanced sense of tone.
>
> (Sacks, 1998, p. 84)

In case you're wondering, Sacks does not mention the president's name . . . but the piece was written in 1984 (not 1998).

People with one of the many kinds of **agnosia** are unable to recognize selective aspects of what they perceive. So, for example, someone with *visual agnosia* might see a familiar object but not be able to make sense of what it is (like Sacks' real patient 'who mistook his wife for a hat'). Someone with *verbal agnosia* might hear words spoken to them but not know which words they are, even though they can read, write and speak them.

## 13.3 ASSESSMENT

We now turn from theory to practice, from decontextualized brains to contextualized whole people. Imagine that a fifty-eight-year-old man, let's call him Joban, arrives home from work one day in distress and unable to communicate with his wife. She takes him to the doctor, who refers him to a speech and language therapist. How does the therapist find out what's wrong? She will probably start by making an initial assessment on the basis of information gleaned from Joban's medical history, an interview with his wife and observation of, and interaction with, Joban himself. But the therapist will know that a much deeper investigation is needed in order to propose an effective treatment programme. Because language is many things at many levels – simultaneously biological, psychological, social, cultural and personal

– she cannot restrict herself to the traditional diagnostic practices of the medical profession, which normally seek first to identify the organic *causes* of the pathology. Joban's language problem may not have an evident physiological cause at all, and so treatments aimed at removing it would be pointless. The medical approach to assessment may well turn out to be more promising than other lines of investigation, of course: it's possible that Joban's condition could turn out to be due to an accident damaging his hearing and causing severe psychological trauma.

The therapist will be part of a team of professionals, each with a different area of expertise, and they must cast the diagnostic net more broadly than the physician, employing an ample battery of assessment tools drawn from medicine, linguistics, cognitive psychology, neuropsychology and social psychology. Let's say that a neurological analysis reveals blood clots in the perisylvian region of Joban's brain, providing evidence that his problem is indeed specifically linguistic: an aphasia caused by a stroke. It's tempting to suppose that an experienced therapist could assess the nature and extent of the damage simply by talking to him informally and analysing his answers. This option would clearly be the least stressful for Joban. But to be clear about the extent and nature of the linguistic problem, she might instead need to carry out a series of specialized tests, adapted from experimental methods used in psycholinguistics, designed on the basis of technical knowledge from descriptive and theoretical linguistics, and complemented by pragmatics research and conversation analysis. We now turn to a description of such measures.

## Tests and samples

**Anomia** is a type of aphasia in which word-finding is impaired. People with anomia might recognize objects but be unable to name them.

In section 13.2 we mentioned some of the multiple dimensions on which language-related disorders may vary. This is due in part to the way language is compartmentalized in the mind, in a series of modules dedicated to processing different kinds of linguistic information (phonological, morphological, syntactic, etc.). A very structured kind of linguistic assessment, informed by cognitive neuropsychology (e.g. Whitworth *et al.*, 2005), is therefore often necessary in order to pinpoint the underlying modular disruptions involved in any given surface deficit. Tasks using a range of words, controlled for frequency, grammatical features, concreteness of meaning, etc., can be very powerful, from picture-naming used to test the extent of **anomia**, to **nonword** repetition used to assess phonological short-term memory. In the UK, the most well-known battery of such tests is found in the *Psycholinguistic Assessments of Language Processing in Aphasia* (PALPA; Kay *et al.*, 1992), which contains sixty assessment tools targeting different combinations of modality, processing direction, grammatical level or function, etc. (Ferguson and Armstrong, 2009, ch. 10, provide a comprehensive list of other standardized tests, including the Western Aphasia Battery, used more widely in the USA.)

**Nonwords** are potential word forms of a language (like *splord* or *flobage* in English), normally devised by psycho- and neurolinguists for use in lexical processing experiments and the assessment of language-related disabilities which affect the use of words.

Here is an example of an assessment (number 38) from PALPA. It requires patients to supply a definition for regularly and irregularly spelled homophones in order to assess any impairment in access to word meaning from written input (Whitworth *et al.*, 2005, p. 72). If the patient typically confuses homophones like *bury* and *berry* (defining the first as 'something that grows on bushes' and the second as 'to put in the ground'), then the therapist can surmise that a common phonological route (via /bɛri/) is being used to access mental concepts and that the spelling disambiguation is not being exploited. If they confuse the regularly spelled *berry* but respond to irregularly spelled *bury* with 'that's not a word – /bjʊəri/', then the therapist can conclude that access to meaning is only available through letter-to-phoneme spell-out, the same way you would react to a nonword like *gury* or *mury*. Examples of similar tests can be seen (and even test-driven!) on the internet as part of the multimedia textbook on neuropsychology developed by Inglis, Newsome, Tang and Martin (2002) from Rice University in Texas.

 **www.13.6**

Stackhouse and Wells (1997, 2001) have developed a profiling scheme based on these psycholinguistic processing models to be used to assess children's difficulties with speech and spelling. The profile (Figure 13.4) is based on the broadly held position addressed earlier, that early alphabetic literacy development is dependent on phonological awareness: the child's ability to reflect on, recognize and manipulate phonological units such as phonemes and syllables (see Chapter 6). The pathways in the diagram characterize successive stages in the processes of speech reception (A–F) and production (G–K), with stages at the top more dependent on stored linguistic knowledge than stages lower down. Stage L represents the child's ability to self-monitor (i.e. to attend to their own output as input). Various data elicitation tasks are associated with each stage. For example, at Stage B the child should be able to tell whether two made-up words (nonwords) are the same or different; Stage F can be tested by asking the child to decide whether pairs of words rhyme or not; for Stage H the child might be asked to pronounce a word with the first consonant missing ('Can you say "spot" without the "s"?').

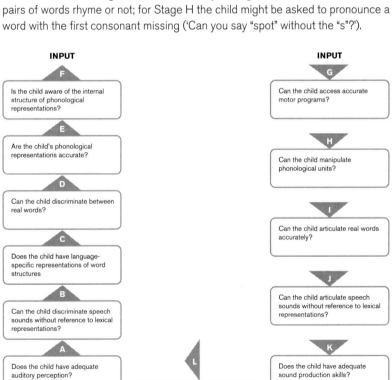

Figure 13.4   Speech Processing Profile (adapted from Stackhouse and Wells, 1997)

As useful as such carefully elicited quantitative data can be, though, they can't be used in isolation. Some of the tests have much in common with the evaluation instruments we talked about in Chapters 7 and 9, used to assess a learner's competence via discrete-point questions. One of the major shortcomings of such tests when used alone is that they are often decontextualized, completely unconnected with meaningful, motivated, socially embedded communicative acts (in which language itself is not part of the objective). As we mentioned earlier in the section, many of the speech and language pathologist's diagnostic tests have been adapted from psycholinguistic tasks employed to test hypotheses about language representation and processing under artificial laboratory conditions. Hence there's a real danger that, just as in second language testing, there could be either underdetermination or overdetermination of the patient's language abilities.

So as a complement to such test results the careful practitioner will collect and analyse a natural sample of discourse with the patient. Sometimes it will be appropriate that the interaction is with a family member or someone else familiar with the patient, rather than with a healthcare professional, who, no matter how sympathetic to the needs of the patient, may not be able to strike up a completely natural and unthreatening conversational relationship. For the same reasons, it might be more appropriate for the sampling and testing to be carried out in the familiar surroundings of the patient's home rather than the sterility of a clinic. Furthermore, the extent and nature of the disability may well only be assessable in language-modulated interaction, as in cases of **pragmatic language impairment**. To provide all potentially relevant data, then, samples would need to be collected in real or simulated social contexts. One useful tool for assessing children's ability to negotiate discourse and recover from inevitable temporary setbacks is to use a map task (Merrison and Merrison, 2005), similar to those used in task-based instruction for additional language learning. In this approach to assessment, the child draws a route on a map on the basis of instructions from the therapist, whose own copy of the map differs with respect to the location and/or inclusion of various landmarks. Conversation analysis techniques are then used to assess the nature of the pragmatic impairment and also as a basis for subsequent therapeutic interaction.

> People with **pragmatic language impairment** have a neurological disorder which affects their ability to use language for appropriate and meaningful communication in social contexts. It is associated with autism spectrum disorders (ASD).

## Assessment and linguistic diversity

In the urban centres of developed nations there will increasingly be large numbers of second language users, normally ethnic minorities. When members of these communities are referred to a language pathologist, he or she must be especially sensitive to aspects of linguistic and cultural variation which might, if ignored, compromise or derail effective assessment measures. The *Clinical Guidelines* of the UK's Royal College of Speech and Language Therapists, for example, are very clear on this danger:

■ Liaison with bilingual personnel will assist the Speech & Language Therapist in differentiating linguistic and cultural diversity from disorder.
■ Assessment of the individual's complete communication system will prevent confusion of normal bilingual language acquisition with communication disorders in bilingual children.

■  Cultural and linguistic bias have in the past led to the misdiagnosis of language and learning difficulties in bilingual populations. Bilingual children from ethnic minority populations may be unfamiliar with assessment procedures, may expect to speak a certain language in one situation and may respond only minimally to adult questions.

(RCSLT, 2005, p. 15)

As we saw in Chapter 8, it is sensible to view bilinguals as speakers with a single communication system which spans two languages, rather than as linguistic schizo-phrenics. Hence, in the assessment of language disorders the RCSLT goes on to recommend that '[a]ssessment of an adult's complete communication system will identify which elements are language specific and which elements are affected across the whole system' (RCSLT, 2005, p. 15). In line with our discussion of dialect and register variation in Chapter 2, assessment of language abilities and compe-tences should be conducted from the perspective provided by diglossia. In other words, language pathologists, like language teachers, test-writers and other applied linguists, need to appreciate that differences in clients' externalization of language do not imply language deficit or pathology. The US National Aphasia Association has a Multicultural Task Force which contributes to this endeavour by coordinating and disseminating information on aphasia and clinical practices in different lan-guages and cultures, including bilingual communities.

 **www.13.7**

Recognition of diglossic situations raises the general issue in diagnostic assessment of just what the 'benchmark' should be for 'normal' language, against which the patient's knowledge and abilities should be compared. (For obvious reasons, this will also be a problem in the measurement of recovery.) The idea might be confusing to non-linguists: surely it's obvious what 'normal English' or 'normal Korean' is? (And if the linguists haven't worked this out yet, then what have they been up to all this time?) Well, the answer – as so often in science – is that it's not so straightforward. Recall our discussion of 'standard English' in Chapter 2, where we attempted to establish that there is not just 'one' English, and that it's even less tenable to suppose that there are 'correct' and 'incorrect' versions of any language. For example, if Joban were a speaker of Panjabi in the UK, he might use a version of the language which differs from the 'standard' form used in print and by privileged groups in Pakistan and India. Martin *et al.* (2003), for example, suggest that the novel lexical and lexicogrammatical forms they found in the spontaneous speech of Panjabi-speaking youngsters in the West Midlands (mostly due to influence from English) make language assessment difficult. They conclude (Martin *et al.*, 2003, p. 262) that '[t]raditional descriptions of Panjabi can no longer be used as target forms for "normative" comparison with speakers of new varieties of British Panjabi'. And it's a two-way street, of course: the global presence of World Englishes, influ-enced reciprocally by L1 phonological and grammatical substrates, ensures that the issue will be high on the agenda for language pathologists throughout the Inner and Outer Circle countries.

## Assessing children's problems with language

In the case of developmental disorders, additional assessment problems arise, since the benchmark of 'the language' is unavailable not only for the reasons just discussed, but also because the patients – children – haven't had the chance to fully acquire it yet! You may be thinking that the appropriate yardstick might then be supposed to be what is 'normal' for a child of that age. But this can sometimes be a difficult standard to judge, especially in the early years of acquisition, when the detection and assessment of language disorders can actually lead to the most positive outcomes. This is because of the great variability and pacing of language acquisition: although psycholinguistic research has shown clearly that children follow the same series of milestones (in roughly the same order and at roughly the same intervals), the maturational plan unfolding in the child's brain is not a computer programme, and the social contexts in which each child grows and learns are unique. Detailed guidance for parents is abundant on the internet and in self-help books, and, although useful, can give the impression that these milestones are universal laws rather than average tendencies (Harris, 2004). The US National Institute on Deafness and Other Communication Disorders (NIDCD, 2010) provides a lengthy checklist in its 'How Do I Know If My Child Is Reaching the Milestones?' section, which parents can use to determine whether their child's language and speech are developing 'on schedule'. If any points on the lengthy list are answered in the negative, the parent is advised to talk to their doctor. So, for example, they state that a child between twelve and seventeen months '[s]ays two to three words to label a person or object', and yet the research shows that many normal kids don't start to produce their first words until after eighteen months (Fenson et al., 1994).

**www.13.8**

The upshot for language pathologists is that, in the case of babies and infants, where any case history will be brief, a really comprehensive assessment is going to be paramount following diagnosis of a language-related disability. Since a child is not yet a mature human being, their motor control, language system, general cognition, socialization and theory of mind will all be underdeveloped or at only a rudimentary stage of development. It is thus impossible to carry out the kinds of diagnostic and assessment procedures we saw in the case of Joban, since they presuppose a preceding state in which the person was a 'normal', fully developed language user.

## 13.4  TREATMENT

The whole point of viewing language pathology as a component area of applied linguistics is, of course, that the collected knowledge and experience of the relevant academic disciplines and health professions may ultimately be used by practitioners to alleviate the many serious language-related problems faced by people with the sort of disabilities we've seen so far in this chapter. We therefore spend this section looking at the kinds of intervention available and the extent to which they are effective.

The range of treatment and management programmes is, perhaps unsurprisingly, almost as varied as the array of disorders identified. The degree of success of any particular intervention will depend, in part, on the accuracy of the specific diagnosis and integrated assessment of the client. And vice versa: '[assessment should] contribute to a measurable baseline for treatment against which the outcome of any intervention can be measured' (RCSLT, 2005, p. 15). Thus assessment and treatment go hand in hand, and both must be individualized and flexible, rather than routinized and dogmatic. This in turn requires that practitioners be 'action researchers' in their own clinics, testing hypotheses and assessing outcomes, just as we saw with language teachers in their classrooms (Chapter 9). Lesser and Milroy make this point eloquently in their book on aphasia treatment:

> [T]he hypothesis-testing method . . . sees the work to be carried out with each patient as a mini-research exercise . . . The only gap between the 'researcher' and the 'applier' . . . is in the time each can devote to this study. The practising clinician contributes to the development of the field, and brings to it the benefit of an extending and intimate knowledge of the continuing nature of the disorder, rather than receiving and applying prescriptions formulated elsewhere.
>
> (Lesser and Milroy, 1993, p. 240)

Treatments can tackle different aspects of the client's language-related problem, and it's important to clarify at the outset that they're not all carried out by speech and language therapists. In the case of disorders with a clearly identified organic cause, surgical procedures or pharmacological therapies will often be recommended and will be administered by physicians, not linguists. Cleft lip and palate, for example, can be treated through reconstructive surgery. For other options, little more than self-help advice may be needed from the experts who make up the professional team. Take **augmentative and alternative communication** (AAC) resources, such as the use of technology which makes linguistic messages coded in one modality available in another. These may deliver a potential solution (if only partial) for people who have loss of, or damage to, one of the modalities. Although there are many language pathologists whose primary expertise and occupation is with AAC aids, some quite sophisticated technology is now available to anyone with a computer and connection to the internet: the BBC's 'My Web, My Way' website, for example, shows blind and sight-impaired users how to convert text to speech or to make text larger. Adobe Reader and Microsoft Word both convert text into speech. Working in the other direction, the latest voice recognition software can 'train' a computer to transcribe oral language into written form, although current versions still require a bit of punctuation assistance from the speaker – check out *NaturallySpeaking 10* on the internet (Nuance, 2008). Another company sells 'scanning pens' for dyslexics, which read aloud words from printed text, display them in larger text in the barrel of the pen and also read aloud definitions (and cross-references within them) from the *Concise Oxford English Dictionary*.

Much speech and language therapy happens in schools, and these days it is teachers and teaching assistants who often take on 'front-line' assessment and treatment responsibilities (usually in coordination with therapists, working according to a 'consultative model' of provision; see Law *et al.*, 2002). In most developed nations, for example, students with dyslexia are educated along with their peers, according to the 'inclusive model' championed in UNESCO's Salamanca Statement, as discussed in Chapter 7. Effective management of dyslexia in the primary classroom has contributed to the popularity of phonics, especially in UK schools, as we

**Augmentative and alternative communication** helps people with communication impediments to communicate more effectively, using alternative modalities (such as gesture), specially designed symbol systems (like Braille) and/or communication devices (e.g. speech synthesizers).

 **www.13.9**

 **www.13.10**

noted in Chapter 6. (We also observed there, however, that an over-emphasis on sound-based literacy learning is not in the interests of non-dyslexic students.) Teacher-led activities to aid children with dyslexia often emphasize multisensory activities, using colours, textures and movement, and can include tasks like the ones we saw used for assessment according to Stackhouse and Wells' (1997, 2001) psycholinguistic profile or the PALPA tests. They can be incorporated into games or play (Figure 13.5) and other motivating and entertaining activities.

The Serpentine Gallery in London, for example, has worked with the leading British charity Dyslexia Action and a local artist to create an online suite of 'learning resources' to create 'alternative learning spaces' in the classroom through art. Called *NEVERODDOREVEN* (a rather artistic palindromic play on words itself), the site provides numerous suggestions for activities in the regular classroom of children aged five to seven.

**www.13.11**

**www.13.12**

Therapists' more direct intervention with patients and carers may be separated into two broad types, associated by Lesser and Milroy (1993) with psycholinguistic and pragmatic models in linguistics. As we saw in section 13.4, it was psycholinguistic models of normal language processing that first led therapists to conduct the kinds of assessment tests we discussed there. Such tests also provide the basis for targeted *intervention* to restore and/or improve the specific aspects of language performance detected. Pragmatic approaches, on the other hand, adopting a 'social model' of therapy, take into account the whole spectrum of abilities required for successful social communication and stress the collaborative nature of language use. Bearing in mind once more that the objective of applied linguistics is ultimately to help people solve problems, we should be extremely wary of engaging in the kind of confrontational debates which drive advances in *theory*. It should be apparent that for the therapist it is not a question of *which* approach is the correct one (psycholinguistics in the white corner, pragmatics in the red!), but rather what combination of approaches and tools will best help a particular client. Of course such eclecticism must be principled and based on measurable outcomes (just as we insisted on in Chapter 9 for language teaching methods). But if we can liberate ourselves from the spell which makes us blind to the dual social-biological nature of language, we will no doubt reach the intuitive conclusion that more often than not a complementary psycholinguistic/pragmatic approach will hold the greatest potential benefits for patients. In what remains of this section we take a look at some of the options these approaches provide.

Thankfully, in no case of language disability is the entire linguistic system compromised. Since we (think we) know quite a lot about the various components and subcomponents of the system and how they interact with other domains, both social and psychological, it surely makes sense to exploit this knowledge and treat the specific mental processes directly if we can. There are two major provisos, however: (1) the assessment must be accurate; and (2) positive outcomes must be documented to justify the further use of the treatment. These points and caveats are illustrated well in Pascoe, Stackhouse and Wells (2005), reporting the case of a child whose speech is characterized (in part) by reduction of consonant clusters and missing final consonants, so that *fish* is pronounced [vɪ] and *pram* is pronounced [bæ]. The authors document the use of a psycholinguistic 'phonotactic [syllabic structure] therapy' which progresses from isolated words through to connected speech. The intervention programme pinpoints relevant details of phonological competence for intensive practice through games and activities. These correspond to performance-level deficits identified at the macro-level by the Speech Processing Profile discussed in section 13.4.

Although psycholinguistic, linguistic and medical approaches can often detect and sometimes successfully treat the specific linguistic problem of a given patient (or its cause), recovery is seldom complete. The 'pragmatic approach' responds to this concern and is thus 'pragmatic' in the non-specialist sense. But it is also con-sistent with the academic field of pragmatics, which analyses language as a system embedded in social contexts (rather than 'just' a fancy biological symbol-crunching machine). On a daily basis, language users experience not just the psycholinguistic encoding and decoding of messages, but also the use of language as a psychosocial and emotional resource, as well as a badge of personal identity and membership in a range of communities and groups. Thus, the effects of language disability go beyond the purely physiological and psycholinguistic.

Language pathologists must always take into account the whole person, and not just their specific organic or functional disorder. Take the case of a profoundly deaf two-year-old child of deaf parents who are fluent users of American Sign Language (ASL). The parents consider several options:

1   raise their child in ASL, their native language;

A **cochlear implant** is a tiny device embedded under the skin behind the ear, which is used to bypass the damage to the **cochlea** – the hollow, spiral bone structure in the inner ear which transforms acoustic energy into auditory nerve impulses – and transmit sound via an alternative route to the auditory nerve.

2   have him or her undergo **cochlear implant** surgery (NIDCD, 2006; see Figure 13.6);

3   use a combination of options 1 and 2.

Although the sound transmitted by a cochlear implant is not identical to normal speech sound, many users are able to hear almost normally. So which option should the parents opt for? The first will mean that their son will grow up as a member of the parents' language community, and probably also of the larger culturally Deaf community, adding English (in this case) as an additional language of wider communication through literacy. The second option (if the surgery is successful) is to have the child join the hearing community, and to become an ASL–English bilingual via sound.

Clearly, the decision has linguistic ramifications. A two-year-old start with speech is rather late and could have negative consequences, and the child may already have been exposed to sign, from her parents and others, from birth. In both cases, the child will have the capacity to start to learn language normally, either through speech (with the implant) or through sign (from the parents) or both (using

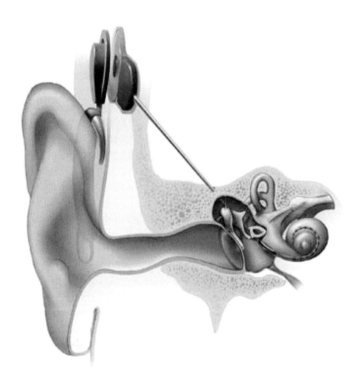

Figure 13.6   A cochlear implant (Source: US National Institute on Deafness and Other Communication Disorders)

resources like the sign language/spoken language online dictionaries for children mentioned in Chapter 10). But beyond language, this is also a pragmatic and cultural choice, including the promise of sign/aural bilingualism. For many in the Deaf community, it is also a profoundly political matter, and language pathologists and applied linguists working with deaf children and families will need to be sensitive to strong feelings about language and identity. (To find out more, the website *Inside Deaf Culture* provides a useful 'resource for the Deaf-friendly community' in the UK.)

 **www.13.13**

We used this example to illustrate the need for practitioners to consider factors that go far beyond specific impairments to the linguistic system or modalities for language use, but, of course, not all treatment options involve such stark choices. Treatments must take into account, and try to diminish, the personal frustrations that many patients will experience in their attempts to communicate. And this is especially so in cases like aphasia after a stroke, where often the rest of the person's cognitive capacities are left untouched. It's hard to imagine the levels of stress, anxiety and anger of a middle-aged person who from one day to the next finds herself unable to put her ideas into speech, after a lifetime of doing so. She can't wait for the research to provide therapies which will 'cure' or 'heal' her, because she needs to continue communicating with others on a daily basis. Hence she must develop compensatory strategies, a resource we have already discussed in the context of additional language learning, in Chapter 9. Patients can, for example, be helped to develop repetition strategies to be used in verbal interaction, so that they give themselves time to formulate an appropriate response. They may also be coached in formulaic responses, the same unanalysed chunks of language that can 'jump-start' effective discourse in beginning language learners and which serve as building blocks for the latest automatic translation systems. People with aphasia are pretty good at the appropriate use of discourse markers (Simmons-Mackie and Damico, 1995), a finding consistent with Oliver Sacks' observation that although his aphasic patients were language-impaired, they still conserved a strong notion of communicative effectiveness (indeed some have enhanced abilities in this sphere).

Finally, we should point out that within a 'social model' of therapy which views the client holistically, as a participant in social encounters and routines, barriers to communication are caused not only by the disability itself but also in the way others respond to it. A revealing demonstration of this is provided by Dijkstra *et al.*'s (2010 [2002]) analysis of nursing-home discourse between aides and residents with dementia. The study found that the aides used 'facilitative' techniques such as information cues, encouragements (like 'Go on') and repetitions more with early-stage than with late-stage dementia residents, 'where they are needed most' (Dijkstra *et al.*, 2010 [2002], p. 155). The authors suggest that aides might be trained to use more effective communication techniques to help residents with utterance-level cohesion and coherence.

## 13.5  ROLES FOR APPLIED LINGUISTS

Once more, knowledge, awareness and sensitivity regarding language and its use are key factors in the success of language pathology, and applied linguistics plays a major role in creating and disseminating the relevant knowledge, as well as promoting awareness and fostering sensitivity in the health and caring professions, the educational sector, government, the media and the public at large. Aside from training to become a language pathologist (for resources, see the companion website), applied linguists in general can take on some of the following roles and responsibilities:

**www.13.14**

- educating students, parents, teachers, the media, policy-makers and the public at large about the existence of language-related disabilities, how they affect the people that have them and how those who interact with them can, if necessary, modify their behaviour as appropriate to the situation;
- conducting research and making recommendations about how to modify institutional interactional behaviour and language practices to allow people with language-related disabilities to participate as fully as possible in public discourses and daily life, including school and the workplace;
- combating the prejudices surrounding disability and particularly the widespread beliefs which equate language disability with low intelligence or psychosis;
- contributing to the design and development of assessment and treatment instruments, including neuropsychological tests, discourse analysis and AAC aids;
- collaborating with other applied linguists – language planners, literacy teachers, bilingual educators, additional language teachers, interpreters, lexicography software developers, advocates for the reform of legal language, etc. – to take into account the needs of clients of language pathology and to understand that they are *their* clients too.

At the beginning of this chapter we pointed out that, of the various specialized disciplines that constitute the field of applied linguistics, it is language pathology that deals with the ultimate physical realities of human language: the 'string[s] between each word and its matching thing', in the words of the Welsh poet Gwyneth Lewis. As the chapter has progressed, we hope you have also come to appreciate that the biology of language can't be dissociated from the sociology of language. If we are to help solve problems experienced by people with language-related disabilities, we must abandon narrow orthodoxies (whether cognitively or sociologi-cally oriented) and strive to understand our clients from multiple perspectives. As we'll suggest in the final chapter (Chapter 14), a major role for all applied linguists will be to advocate this cooperative and inclusionary approach ever more widely and effectively.

activities

1    Do you, or does anyone you know, have a language-related disability? Use Table 13.1 in section 13.2 to briefly describe the dimensions of linguistic knowledge and/or linguistic processing that may be affected by this dis-ability. What solutions or interventions, if any, are being tried to ameliorate the problem (including educating the public), and how successful do you think these efforts have been?

2    Type the words 'augmentative alternative communication device' into an internet search engine and browse the various options. Choose one of the AAC devices you find and say how it could be helpful to a person with a language-related disability. Can you find an AAC device that might be helpful to the person you described in activity 1? How might it help? How would a person with a language-related disability obtain such a device? Is access (availability, affordability, training, etc.) an issue that needs to be considered?

3    The coordinator of additional language teaching at your local primary school has concerns about a number of children who she thinks may have some kind of language-related disability. She asks you to make a short presentation to teachers and support staff on the issues in language pathology that language teachers should be aware of. Look through the chapter again and make a list of the issues you would include in your presentation.

4    Are there any diagnostic and treatment services for people with individual language-related disabilities available in your local area? If there are, what are they? If you had a moderate (but not unlimited!) budget to improve these services, what additional services would you provide and why?

# FURTHER READING

Ball, M. J., Perkins, M. R., Müller, N. and Howard, S. (eds) (2008). *The handbook of clinical linguistics*. Oxford: Blackwell.

Ferguson, A. and Armstrong, E. (2009). *Researching communication disorders*. Basingstoke, UK: Palgrave Macmillan.

Oates, J. and Grayson, A. (eds) (2004). *Cognitive and language development in children*. Oxford: Blackwell/Open University.

Roddam, H. and Skeat, J. (2010). *Embedding evidence-based practice in speech and language therapy: International examples*. Chichester, UK: Wiley-Blackwell.

Whitworth, A., Webster, J. and Howard, D. (2005). *A cognitive neuropsychological approach to assessment and intervention in aphasia: A clinician's guide*. Hove, UK: Psychology Press.

# CHAPTER 14

# Prospects and perspectives

Those who have knowledge, don't predict. Those who predict, don't have knowledge.
(Lao Tzu)

The dynamism of applied linguistics that we've described throughout the book makes it difficult to resist casting ahead to the key issues that will shape and populate future maps of the field. So in this final chapter we take stock and identify some of the key features of contemporary applied linguistics as they are affecting research and practice in all its diverse arenas, all around the globe, today. We look at these developments with a critical eye, and try to estimate how they're likely to pan out in the short and medium terms. Inevitably, our own opinions figure more explicitly in this chapter than in the rest of the book (although of course no textbook provides a neutral, objective account of its field).

In order to explain and illustrate what these developments could mean for the study and practice of applied linguistics, we also depart somewhat from the organization and knowledge sources employed in earlier chapters. Where the discipline-specific chapters in Parts A, B and C have focused primarily on research findings from the scholarly literature, interspersed with examples from contemporary professional practice, here we focus on how an emerging generation of language professionals is bridging applied linguistic theory and practice. Complementing our own views, then, we call on the voices of practitioners from five countries who we were talking to as we wrote this chapter: *Khawla Badwan* from Gaza, *Chandy Charlton* from the UK, *Duan Yan* from China, *Liliana Fernández* from Peru and *Melissa Vasquez* from the US–Mexico border (see Figure 14.1).

Like many of our readers, these practitioners work in contexts that are attentive to, yet outside, the university-dominated world of applied linguistics scholarship. Although we present them as working primarily within one key area of the field (additional language teaching, language pathology, language planning, literacy and translation/interpreting) and within specific nation states, their work involves the constant crossing of political, linguistic and disciplinary boundaries and collaboration on projects with specialists from outside the field. In addition, their practice involves seeking solutions to specific client needs through encounters with other applied linguists via new communications technologies and virtual spaces unavailable even a few years ago. In order to capture the bottom-up dynamics of applied linguistic practice, we asked Khawla, Chandy, Liliana, Melissa and Duan Yan to tell us about the aspects of their work they see impacting our developing field. Their experiences will perhaps help you to see relevant connections between what we discuss here and your own contexts of practice and study.

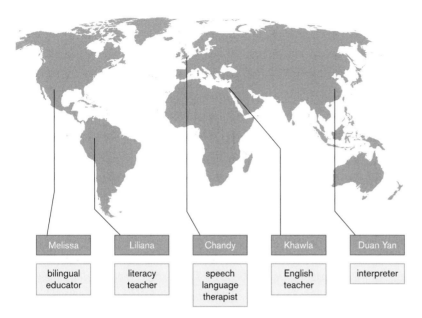

Figure 14.1    Five practitioners from around the world

So, at the risk of fulfilling Lao Tzu's prediction, we present here our estimation of pivotal issues in the present which may signal future directions for the field. Specifically, we address *the radical impact of new technologies* (14.1), *the dissolution of borders* political, linguistic, disciplinary and professional (14.2), and *the exercise of the profession*, including new ways applied linguists are working and their renewed focus on language, freedom and social responsibility (14.3). Before concluding, we hazard a series of key predictions of how we believe the field is changing and the developments that, in our estimation, will shape the future of the discipline (14.4).

# 14.1  THE IMPACT OF NEW TECHNOLOGIES

According to 'Moore's Law', which dates back to an article written by the computer scientist and entrepreneur Gordon Moore in 1965, the number of transistors on a chip will double about every two years (Intel Corporation, 2005). This prediction has held up. In 2009, the media reported that Intel, the company Moore founded, had released a new microchip that used fingernail-sized chips containing almost three billion transistors, measured in billionths of a metre (Shiels, 2009). It's these break-neck developments in microtechnology over the past half-century that have driven the information revolution, still very much in progress. Given the central roles of information and communication in applied linguistics, it isn't surprising that the revolution has had a massive impact on the *content* of the field, and not just the speed and ease with which we conduct our professional practice. Although we can say for certain that technology has already changed the ways in which many applied linguists work, as well as the ways in which they (or others) think they *should* work,

 **www.14.1**

it's hard to predict future impacts because we don't know for certain which new forms will become available or how quickly they will become accessible to all groups. In this section we illustrate some of the ways in which technology has had an impact on translation, literacy, additional language learning and language pathology, and recognize the challenges as well as the opportunities of this fundamental change in the way we interact with each other and the world we live in.

The tragedy in Haiti following the January 2010 earthquake provides dramatic evidence of how applied linguists can help people communicate across language borders using the technologies of corpus linguistics, machine translation and social networking through mobile phones. David Bellos of the *New York Times* wrote:

> When Haiti was devastated by an earthquake in January, aid teams poured in to the shattered island, speaking dozens of languages – but not Haitian Creole. How could a trapped survivor with a cellphone get usable information to rescuers? If he had to wait for a Chinese or Turkish or an English interpreter to turn up he might be dead before being understood. Carnegie Mellon University instantly released its Haitian Creole spoken and text data, and a network of volunteer developers produced a rough and ready machine translation system for Haitian Creole in little more than a long weekend. It didn't produce prose of great beauty. But it worked.
>
> (Bellos, 2010)

Translation, traditionally seen as a lone and painstakingly slow business, has, in certain contexts, been revolutionized by the opportunities for collaboration in virtual work environments and by the increased speeds of output made possible by developments in software and mobile devices, as this example shows. *Duan Yan* is aware of these advantages of technology for translators: she tells how corpus-based translation software increases her productivity and the acceptability of the results to the client, and how online discussion boards give her a dedicated community to consult when she has a problem. She will post a question on a website and it will be answered by a translator she has never met and whose geographical location she doesn't know.

> *Duan Yan* was born and grew up in the city of Chengdu, capital of Sichuan province, China. She studied English at university and is now close to completing an MA degree in interpreting and translating. She works with clients in business, education and government agencies, translating between English and Mandarin, and interpreting both face-to-face and online.

One very clear impact of new technologies, in the form of digital media, is their power to engage youth in literacy-rich virtual environments that are not part of the formal education system. Via the internet, learners are seeking information that is useful and interesting to them, and, in doing so, they read and hear self-selected texts, as well as easily and quickly being able to compose their own. A primary attraction of digital literacies for adolescents is their interactive nature and space for self-expression. In ways never before possible, young people (at least those

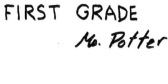

"Writing is just like texting except that you have to use
all of the letters in each word."

Figure 14.2  Bringing technology-driven textual energy into the classroom (Source: www.
CartoonStock.com)

with high-speed internet access) can create and display identities, and set controls
on who they allow to see what they create. Many teachers and researchers are
seeking to bring this textual energy to the literacies students must master at school
(see Figure 14.2).

This includes a level of dexterity with, and confidence in, using new technologies that often outruns that of their teachers, although this is less likely to be
true in rural communities. While literacy teachers will probably not, for example,
need or want to become proficient in the varieties of digital subcultures such as
'Leetspeak' (see Chapter 6), they should know that their students are likely to be
involved in new online literacy practices and be ready to assess how these practices
support (or threaten) their students' learning. So, for example, teachers might
enquire about the extent to which their students are using instant messaging during
homework time (see Lewis and Fabos, 2005), and then decide to assign collaborative projects and wikis, rather than inviting plagiarism.

As the literacy practices associated with a language evolve, so do the communicative goals of additional language learners aiming to participate in these practices with other users of their target language. This is now motivating learners and teachers to keep abreast of digital developments in target language use by:

- keeping up to date with new technology-related words (*twitter, tweet, twestival, twirgin* and so on);
- learning the grammatical and discourse features of new genres (texting, turn-taking in online text chat or in conference calls using internet telephony software, and so on);
- becoming aware of opportunities to switch between and blend languages and varieties.

On the latter point, *Khawla* has noticed how she updates her status on online social networking sites in various mixtures of Arabic (including 'standard' Arabic and Palestinian dialects, all transliterated into the Latin alphabet) and English, in an effort to be inclusive of her monolingual friends.

*Khawla Badwan* is a Palestinian who lived in Saudi Arabia for eleven years (where her mother was an English teacher) and now teaches English as an additional language, as well as training English language teachers and translators, in Gaza, Palestine. Khawla has an MA in TESOL from the UK.

In addition to offering new ways to communicate, technology is also being relentlessly promoted to teachers as a resource to deliver content in new ways. Calling on teachers to work as 'designers to create the most appropriate technologically inclusive learning plans in their subject areas with their students', the American Association of Colleges for Teacher Education (2008, p. 290) includes training in teaching with digital technology as a component of teacher certification. And although many teachers and students around the world may not have access to the newest technology, availability is growing and prices are falling, provoking dramatic changes in the way basic education and adult literacy instruction are provided, and in the economic and social development of the communities affected (Wagner and Kozma, 2005).

*Melissa* describes being encouraged to 'incorporate as much technology in the classroom as possible' through training sessions at work on how to create a web page, use a SMART Board, and use an online grading system for marking and recording students' grades. She also reminds us that new technologies are not

*Melissa Vasquez* is an independent language arts consultant in the border city of El Paso, Texas, in the US. Originally trained as an accountant, she returned to school to earn an MA as an Instructional Specialist in Reading and now works with Spanish/English-speaking secondary students. She comes from a family with several generations of teachers.

without potential drawbacks, however, telling familiar tales of promised tools being unavailable, broken or out of date.

Both *Liliana* and *Melissa* agree that much of their own learning to use new technologies has come from trial and error and from their own initiative, usually seeking information online. As *Liliana* put it, 'You teach yourself. The programs are available on the internet.'

Liliana Fernández is a Peruvian linguist whose work with Ashaninka/Spanish bilingual teachers was featured in Chapter 5. She has been engaged in descriptive linguistics and bilingual teacher training in the Amazon region of Peru and now develops materials to promote Spanish reading comprehension and teaches verbal reasoning to university students.

Schools and universities will find themselves under increasing pressure to be seen to be keeping up with developments in learning technology by investing in the latest interactive whiteboards, hand-held voting devices, visualizers, virtual learning environments and so on, despite the sparsity of evidence for their positive impact on learning. Furthermore, as *Liliana* and *Melissa* attest, teachers will be expected to find, and learn how to use, appropriate technologies *without* the help from professional technologists that they may have been able to count on in the past. While some practitioners may welcome the power to make decisions about technology, others will see this responsibility as an extra job, leaving them with less time to develop their subject-specific expertise.

In some domains of applied linguistics, the use of new technologies in content delivery is less controversial. For language pathologists, technology (both established and new) can provide access to detailed diagnoses and precisely focused treatments for clients. Observing a client with Parkinson's disease whose low volume was affecting her ability to communicate, *Chandy* observed how a decibel reader could provide the client with convincing evidence of progress and therefore motivation to continue with the treatment programme.

Chandy Charlton is a speech and language therapist in the UK who has also taught English as an additional language in Egypt, Spain and Indonesia. Her parents came to the UK in the 1960s from India and she grew up in the West Midlands with Panjabi as her main home language. She studied French and Russian at university.

On the other hand, the analysis of spectrograms that she learned on her training programme is something she has not yet had the opportunity to use in practice (see Chapter 12). She thinks this may be because the time required to do the analysis is more than most practising speech and language therapists have, and the cost of the equipment required is more than many clinical settings can afford (though this may be changing; see the next page).

New technology, as we've noted, is not equally distributed and nor is it guaranteed in its effects; but it is here to stay and it is getting steadily cheaper. Even in the most economically marginalized communities around the world, communications technology is becoming a familiar part of everyday life, sometimes at the expense of what might be considered more fundamental human needs. A new report from the United Nations University (UNU-INWEH, 2010), for example, reveals that many more Indians have access to a mobile phone than to proper sanitation facilities. More encouragingly, the One Laptop per Child project, which aims to supply the world's poorest children with a low-cost, networked PC, continues to make partnerships with countries and regional organizations. Having already distributed 1.6 million machines, they have now reached agreement with the East African Community to distribute thirty million machines in Tanzania, Rwanda, Kenya, Uganda and Burundi by 2015 and with the UN to provide a further 500,000 in the Middle East (of which thousands have already been recently distributed in Gaza).

**www.14.2**

**www.14.3**

In the wealthier nations of the developed world, access to technology is also increasing apace. When we started writing material for this book a few years ago, various drafts existed in Mexico, York and Texas, and on laptops and memory sticks elsewhere, depending on the location of the author who was currently working on them. We each used expensive, separately purchased copies of a word processing software package to write the text and produce the illustrations. But for a couple of years now we've all been able to simultaneously edit a single version of each chapter, stored on the web, with a variety of authoring tools, all for free. We've also benefited enormously from increased access to information in online encyclopaedias, a resource also highlighted by *Duan Yan* as a major way in which developments in technology have enabled her to prepare more easily and thoroughly for an interpreting job. More specialized technology is also becoming more readily available. Developments in digital audio players (for mixing and playing music), for example, have led to the availability of downloadable programmes with built-in spectrographs for under US$20 (see, for example, sharewareconnection.com). There is now mainstream access to specialized language corpora and the databases which mine them. The FrameNet database of English word meanings, for example, is available online and is being used by researchers and developers for translation, lexicography and natural language processing software projects, both commercial and non-commercial, around the world (an example is *Kicktionary*, the multilingual English–French–German dictionary of soccer [Framenet, 2009]).

**www.14.4**

**www.14.5**

**www.14.6**

Overall, it seems very safe to predict that applied linguistics practice will continue to be shaped (in unpredictable ways) by new technologies, and that scholars and practitioners will continue to be interested in, but often challenged by, the impact of different forms of technology on problems related to language. In the world at large, one of the main effects of information and communication technology is to make our global community more tightly knit and better informed than it ever has been, toward the erasing of borders: both horizontally between groups in different physical locations and vertically between groups in different social hierarchies. In section 14.2 we reflect on this conspicuous feature of today's applied linguistic landscape and how it is likely to reshape tomorrow's.

## 14.2  THE DISSOLUTION OF BORDERS

We have, in this book, used the metaphor of a map to explore the terrain of applied linguistics. At times the map we've presented has been more of the 'political' variety, with separate chapters, sections and sub-sections corresponding to national, regional and municipal jurisdictions. But throughout the book we've also stressed the fluid, richly textured, multifaceted nature of the activities and perspectives of applied linguists, the contexts in which they work, the skills and tools they use, and the colleagues and clients they work with. In this sense, our map of the discipline has looked more like a 'physical' one, showing intersecting bodies of water, land-scapes morphing gradually from desert to rainforest, rising and falling altitudes, erratic river flows and winding mountain passes. This kind of map has no lines drawn on it.

We believe that applied linguistics is set to continue dissolving borders of many kinds as it focuses on its client-driven, problem-solving trajectory. In this section we explore some of the effects for applied linguistics of the ease with which we can now cross *political* borders, the realization that as a species we've always been crossing *linguistic* borders, the stubborn persistence of *disciplinary* borders in scholarly practice, and the increasing need for applied linguists to cross borders between different *roles* in professional practice.

### Crossing political borders

The movement and flow of people, information, and capital across national bound-aries is growing at an unprecedented pace. In some places, like the Schengen Area in Europe, national borders themselves are more matters of legislation than physical landscape. Figure 14.3 shows the area, stretching from Scandinavia in the north to Spain, Italy and Greece in the south (with the UK and Ireland outside).  **www.14.7**

This global percolation is being amplified by the opportunities for cross-border communication afforded by the new technologies we discussed in section 14.1. Clients and practitioners from applied linguistics and many sister fields in the social sciences are dealing with the consequences of increased immigration, cross-border communication and economic integration, leading to a rethinking of society that is no longer automatically defined or confined by the nation state (Levitt and Glick Schiller, 2008). *Duan Yan*, for example, reports interpreting for an overseas ani-mation company that has outsourced much of its creative work to China: making cartoons for television and movie audiences is a globalized endeavour in ways which consumers may be only vaguely aware of, if at all.

Applied linguists accustomed to working in border regions may see these conditions as business as usual. For example, *Melissa* commented:

> Living on the border, I haven't seen much change that can be attributed to immigration as far as student demographics or teaching methods are con-cerned. Students still have differing levels of English proficiency and different backgrounds that I keep in mind as I develop activities to foster learning.

Figure 14.3   The effectively borderless Schengen Area of Europe (Source: Wikimedia Commons)

She points, however, to visits she has made to learn about schools and teaching in China and Japan; hosting Russian and German students and teachers in the US; and her ongoing conversation, via e-mail, with a teacher in Beijing about current events, the economy and educational practices in the US and China. Work with Indigenous communities in Peru highlights the challenges that migration is presenting for applied linguistics work in regions not traditionally regarded as borderlands. While collaborating on a dictionary project in Ese Ejja and training bilingual teachers of Ashaninka and Shipibo in the Amazon, *Liliana* discovered that internal migration from Andean regions of the country, along with intermarriage between speakers of various languages, means that efforts to develop resources for language learning and maintenance in particular regions do not easily keep up with the shifting linguistic identities of Indigenous communities.

The sociolinguist Monica Heller has pointed out a certain irony in the ways these globalizing processes are playing out for language groups: as previously all-powerful monolithic nation states have begrudgingly allowed linguistic minorities 'to mobilize to retain the right to self determination, that is, to set up their own nation states', globalizing forces and the movements of peoples are undermining 'the very logic of ethnic state nationalism' (Heller, 2006, p. 212). So, for example, while various European minority groups of the former USSR and its satellites obtained their political and linguistic autonomy after 1989, many of the new nations they form part of are submitting their sovereignty to pan-national organizations like the European Union, opening their borders as part of the Schengen Area, and using English as a working language for commerce and education. The changes associated with globalization not only are extremely far-reaching, but also undermine the taken-for-granted relationships between language and place that have underpinned the language policies of the modern nation state for the last couple of centuries (Williams, 2010). And not just the policies of the language planners, but also the attitude of citizens to their own linguistic identities and their right for these to be recognized, as the next section, on crossing linguistic borders shows.

## Crossing linguistic borders

The notion that languages are discrete, countable objects which are consistent with (and can be used to determine) the boundaries of ethnic populations, and the corollary that languages are contained by geopolitical borders, can be traced back to colonial and nationalistic relationships of dominance and power (Pennycook and Makoni, 2007). It's been a commonplace since then to assume a natural and indissoluble link between language, place and identity. This is something that *Khawla* comes across in her work as an English language teacher in Gaza. She reports feeling the need to display identifiably Palestinian aspects of herself to her students, in an attempt to allay their fears that speaking English will make them less authentically Palestinian. It is disquiet about language and national identity that perhaps motivates questions about language use in the census exercises of some nations. Although census information is vital to applied linguists in some of their endeavours (see pp. 119 and 135), they are aware of the over-simplicity of data-collection procedures, and often complain about the precision and representative-ness of survey data on home language use. Problems include:

- low response rates from immigrants and minority ethnic groups;
- under-reporting of Indigenous and other low prestige languages;
- the absence of any means to measure the validity of self-report data;
- a lack of sensitivity to the code-switching and code-mixing practices that often constitute most 'language use' in multilingual households.

These 'counting' problems underline the point we made about 'monolithic views' of languages back in Chapter 2, where we likened languages to beaches, clouds and galaxies: language use in multilingual households is not easily quantifiable, and even when householders are sensitive to the scope of use of each language, their impressions can't be contained in the check boxes of census forms.

For *Chandy*, the boundaries between two of her languages, Panjabi and English, in her speech and language therapy work with bilingual UK-based clients, are not always clear (see also Chapter 13 on the development of new varieties of Panjabi in the West Midlands and the challenge these developments pose for speech and language therapists). *Chandy* talks, for example, about her experience of translating an oral assessment from English to Panjabi, in an initial meeting with a child she had been told spoke only Panjabi. The assessment used the English word *dolls*, and *Chandy* says that, although she knows that there might be another word in Panjabi for 'doll', the word that she (growing up in the UK) has always used is *dolly*. In the course of the assessment she translated *dolls* for the Panjabi-speaking child as *dollyia*, using the Panjabi plural suffix *-ia*. What the child understood by *dollyia* will have depended on, at least, where he grew up, what he expected to hear from the professional addressing him (based on his opinion of her appearance, accent and job), and his understanding of the assessment task.

*Chandy*'s bilingual background, together with her experience of additional language learning and teaching, has undoubtedly contributed to her awareness of the translation and clinical diagnosis issues for a language pathologist working with minority language speakers in the UK. However, she is also aware that her multilingual experience and sensitivities could lead to an assumption by employers and peers that she should specialize in bilingual language pathology, when in fact this might not be what she would choose. To be restricted to working with minority language clients would not, she feels, be fair to bilingual speech and language therapists or to their monolingual peers, who would consequently be denied opportunities to further develop their own language awareness.

*Chandy*'s views reflect some of the complex social and professional issues surrounding the applied linguist's inevitable disposition to reveal the extent of linguistic diversity, despite the suspicion with which this is met in many powerful 'monolingual' states and the 'nuisance' it causes to the social accountants in our nations' bureaucracies, and even the challenge that it may provide to the firmly held beliefs of our clients (see *Khawla*'s example, on the previous page, of her students who associate speaking English with not being a proper Palestinian, or the phenomenon of native-speakerism, described in Chapter 9). Although applied linguists are increasingly aware of the shifting, multi-layered hybridity of most language communities, they know too that 'monolingual monolithism' is still seen as the preferred arrangement, the unmarked case. So *Chandy* is conscious of potentially being earmarked for specialized work on the basis of her own linguistic status, implicitly viewed as 'marked'.

Granting 'countable language' status to the practices of certain groups can, of course, lead to positive outcomes. For all their flaws, census figures on language use can, for example, provide important data for language planners seeking to project future needs for multilingual classrooms, courts, health care and other services. But the 'status' of language is often arbitrarily bestowed. *Liliana* speaks, for example, of how the Peruvian education ministry considers Ashaninka, Awajun (also known as Aguaruna), Shipibo and Quechua as languages for the purposes of planning for and providing bilingual education, whereas other Indigenous languages have not been as fully documented, have fewer trained teachers and published materials, or are treated as varieties or dialects and hence are not considered worthy of their own curriculum or textbooks.

## Crossing disciplinary borders

Coming from backgrounds in psycholinguistics, literacy, multilingual education and additional language teaching, we set out to write an introduction to applied linguistics that would freely cross the border between cognitive and sociocultural perspectives on language. Or so we hoped. As we read and discussed new works for each of the chapters, it became clear that some areas of applied linguistics operate under the assumption of a 'paradigm gap' (e.g. Sridhar and Sridhar, 1992) in which cognitive and social aspects of language are regarded as separate and unbridgeable areas. In language pathology, we've seen that socio- and psycho-linguistic approaches constitute dual pillars for both training and practice, as *Chandy* experienced on her undergraduate speech and language therapy programme in the UK. In forensic linguistics and translation too we saw how both academic per-spectives and their associated methodological tools are employed: *Duan Yan* mentions the importance of both cognitive-oriented research into short-term memory and sociocultural research into cross-cultural pragmatics as essential for successful interpreting. Indeed, this interdisciplinarity was a major feature of all the expert uses explored in Part C.

In Part B, however, where education was the common theme, dual engagement with mind- and culture-oriented scholarship was harder to identify. Expert opinion on literacy instruction and assessment for children has long been divided, for example, by those advocating more context-independent methods (meeting the challenge of literacy as 'psycholinguistic guessing game') and those for whom literacy is essentially a contextually driven social practice (see Chapter 6). *Melissa* notes that her training as a reading teacher was primarily cognitive, and that she has developed an appreciation of the importance of the sociocultural aspects of language and literacy learning mainly through practice. These polarities are in espe-cially sharp relief in the training of teachers of English as an additional language. *Khawla*, for example, trained to be an English language teacher in an academic environment that was dominated by psycholinguistic theory. She also talks about selection tests for teaching jobs in Gaza that focus exclusively on psycholinguistic theory and research. On the other hand, our experience suggests that in many contemporary applied linguistics and language-related programmes in higher education institutions it's psycholinguists who are in the minority, if they are present at all.

We've argued in this book that it's advisable for students and practitioners of applied linguistics to develop the broadest possible understanding of language learning and use. This, we think, must embrace the mental states that allow us to write, and now you to read, these words, as well as the social contexts which influence how and what people write and read. If this objective were to be fully embraced by applied linguists involved in education, it could lead the way to funda-mental changes in the discipline. For example, it might raise the prospect of radical reappraisals of the notion of proficiency and the practices of testing and assess-ment. This in turn would have knock-on effects in other areas of applied linguistics which use these skills and tools, such as diagnostic measures in language pathology and literacy assessment.

An integrated sociocognitive argument might go as follows. The traditional concept of proficiency held by almost all stakeholders presupposes monolithic views of languages through the assumption of a normed target variety, outside the learner's mind: an idealized system. This assumption and the corollaries that 'foreignness' is undesirable and that 'error' means deficiency are taken for granted by, for example, many English language and additional language teachers around the globe, and by many researchers too. According to a sociocognitive approach which seeks to 'disinvent' monolithically viewed languages, proficiency-based conceptions of language learning are inherently deficit models, for the following reasons. A 'target variety' is an unreal (invented) concept, neither socially nor psycho-logically accessible. Individual learners are expected to (and assume they must) internalize a named language, a monolithic body of knowledge which 'belongs to' others and is used for purposes that are not necessarily their own. Actual outcomes of instructed learning are internal mental representations that, if the learner is lucky, converge to a considerable extent with those of others with whom the learner needs/wants to interact. Very seldom do they approach convergence on the idealized 'target variety' itself (hence the popularity of designations such as 'native-like proficiency' and 'near-native speaker').

So, a more realistic position is to reconceptualize proficiency as a whole range of outcomes of language 'appropriation' leading to non-conformity (Widdowson, 1994), rather than as monolithic 'second language acquisition' (see Chapter 2). Some learners may aim to develop English resources associated with specific contexts (e.g. English as a lingua franca for an online IT customer service provider in the Philippines); others might want to approximate a native-speaker register (e.g. English for Academic Purposes for admission to an Australian university); still others might want an indigenized variety of English as an internal lingua franca (e.g. in India, for use between Tamil speakers in Chennai and Kannada speakers in Bangalore, just 200 miles away); etc.

In some cases, convergence of the linguistic code with some target group's norms may be important and would be tested; in many others, the linguistic code would be irrelevant, and what would be assessed would be the communicative success of interactions. This view, where the objectives of language learning and use are determined locally, represents a possible rapprochement between socially and cognitively oriented thinking in applied linguistics. But it also presents a massive challenge to established thought and practice in the profession, and the response from outside the profession (e.g. from national cultural agencies and publishing houses) is unlikely to be accepting, if indeed it is forthcoming at all.

This leads us to acknowledge another set of borders that are fast disappearing: those that demarcate roles and sub-disciplines, dividing the *creation* of content from the *communication* of this content to clients and the general public.

## Crossing professional borders

Throughout this book we have emphasized the shifting roles of applied linguists as theoreticians, mediators and practitioners. We have argued that applied linguists should be able to move between the different sub-disciplines of the field too, from language teaching to translation, from forensic linguistics to literacy practices, from language planning to lexicography. Some of the motivation for professional border-crossing is economic. For example, since training in linguistics at university, *Liliana* has worked as a field linguist, a teacher educator and a materials developer. In Peru, she notes that other applied linguists are working as teachers, editors and therapists. In her current job as a materials developer, working with teachers whose backgrounds are in literature and composition, *Liliana* sees her responsibilities as including teaching her colleagues about language and its contributions to their collaborative project.

But applied linguists will not only need to be ever more knowledgeable about each other's practice and to collaborate on joint projects, they will all – no matter what their sub-discipline – need to become (1) publicists for their profession and (2) online communication technologists. The first of these additional roles, that of publicist, fills a position that is currently vacant in the field. Applied linguists share with scholars in related disciplines (especially general linguistics and sociology) a credibility deficit (see, for example, Cameron, 1995; Kretchmar, 2008). The 'Language Spell' ensures that much that is language-centred or language-mediated in our lives is interpreted and dealt with in the complete absence of insights from language-related scholarship. The views of general and applied linguists are subject to general ridicule when aired in the media, or when we're brave enough to express them at family dinners or at the hairdresser's. We desperately need to get the word out on the complex issues we deal with, but in a way that is maximally accessible to clients, opinion-formers and decision-makers. Educating clients and the general public is part of our collective professional project across disciplinary and national boundaries.

Second, as technological tools become more and more mainstream, we will be expected to cross the border between making and managing the content of applied linguistics, on the one hand, and communicating this content, on the other. In section 14.1, we noted the impact of technology on the job specifications of practitioners working in education. As learners turn to the online environment to supplement or replace their classroom learning, some teachers are being expected to add 'digital technologist' to their CV skills list. Indeed, for applied linguists in general, cheaper and easier-to-use communications hardware and the popularity of online social spaces will increasingly mean that we are able (and indeed may want or be expected) to communicate more effectively with more people than ever before. *Duan Yan*, for example, reports the increased use of teleconferencing work for interpreters, requiring familiarity with rapidly developing and often competing or incompatible software options.

## 14.3  THE EXERCISE OF THE PROFESSION

In this third and last section on what we consider the hottest topics of today's and tomorrow's applied linguistics, we concentrate on the directions of flow of professional responsibility, both internally, within the exercise of the profession at academic and practitioner levels, and externally, in engagement with the domains of clients, governments, commercial enterprises and society at large. In particular, we observe a growing unease and even non-compliance with the volume and nature of top-down, discipline-external proclamations and stipulations regarding: (1) our professional standards; (2) the methods we are to use; and (3) the objectives we are to meet. We address each of these areas in turn, assessing the prospects for a more 'bottom-up' exercise of our profession in coming years.

## Standards of practice and quality assurance

The codification of standards and the execution of quality assurance processes appear to be increasing rapidly across all the language professions, as we've noted in several chapters. Underlying this trend are several factors. As the scope of applied linguistics broadens to include a wider range of jobs in publicly funded institutions, exercised across national boundaries, professional standards can be used to ensure that clients receive equitable services independently of geographical locations, social connections, economic conditions and language backgrounds. Also, as we've repeatedly observed, many contemporary language-related problems involve applied linguists working in multidisciplinary teams with other professionals. In such cases, clients should be able to expect coordinated attention from the team, and so practitioners should expect their work to be shaped not only by their own professional standards but also by those of colleagues working on the same problem from different disciplinary perspectives.

**www.14.8** 🌐

Professional and academic organizations play a major role in codifying these standards of practice. A number of them have been referred to in this book and more can be found on the companion website. They cover the whole gamut of applied linguistics, from the provision of home language services offered in counselling and family health programmes mentioned in Chapter 5, to the acceptability of expert linguistic testimony in courtrooms and legal cases discussed in Chapter 12. Standards and codes of practice are not only developed and governed by professional bodies, of course. Increasingly too, aspects of our professional practice are determined by governments' economic policies. But they also emerge 'bottom up' from academic proposals and debates in scholarly publications and conferences, and are disseminated through educational programmes, notably in MA degree programmes.

*Khawla* thinks that it is the professional practices she learned about while at university that will enable her to mediate between the practitioners she works with in Gaza and the research of applied linguists around the world. She sees the emergence of more research that is more context-sensitive, in her own and other researchers' settings, as a development that will have a positive impact on her professional practice in the future. *Duan Yan* is motivated to measure her interpreting skills against a Chinese government national professional certificate, though she is also aware that her actual interpreting practice is not neutral but is influenced by her own loyalties to the person or company who hires her. She goes as far as saying that her client-employers sometimes expect, as part of her interpreting services, behaviours more usually associated with marketing, public relations or just plain socializing.

The economic climate at the turn of the century has featured multiple attempts around the globe to shift the financial costs of language-related services to the private sector. In practice, business and corporate interests shape public policy, but often without guaranteeing the funds needed to meet established mandates. In the US, the 'No Child Left Behind' federal education law for the past decade has been perhaps the most celebrated and reviled example of imposed standards that ignore practitioner input and pay little attention to underlying issues of poverty and language background. It is also an example of how efforts to comply with standards can spend vast sums of taxpayers' money with very little to show for it (National Center for Education Statistics, 2009). At the end of the spending cycle, failing schools are under the threat of 'takeover' by private firms that receive government funding to run them. In the UK, *Chandy* worries that possible future reductions in funding for speech and language therapists working in schools will result in an attempt to pass responsibility for children with communication needs onto class-room assistants, who are paid lower salaries. Lower salaries associated with lower status will probably mean less power to influence issues of professional standards and practice imposed from the top down.

Despite these conditions, it will probably remain true that an advanced academic degree in applied linguistics or a related area will provide practitioners with at least some degree of autonomy from the imposition of standards and quality assurance schemes that aim to regulate practice from outside the profession. But there is another source of models for codes of practice and quality assurance from the bottom up: namely the evidence-based, informed and reflective experiences of individual academics and professionals in their own unique contexts. We see the technological and ontological developments discussed in sections 14.1 and 14.2 being harnessed to make the field increasingly collegiate and participative: doing applied linguistics truly from the bottom up through community activity. Figure 14.4 illustrates the flows of responsibility for standards that we see being consolidated,

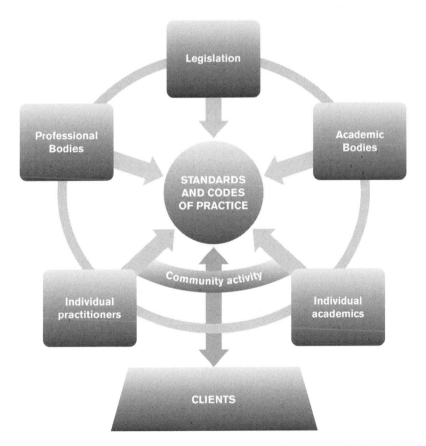

Figure 14.4   Flows of responsibility for standards and codes of practice in applied linguistics

with bottom-up sources of practice permanently engaged with top-down codification, and client needs and experiences benefiting from, but also contributing to, these standards.

## Ways of doing applied linguistics

Practitioners may, at times, feel bound by the methods, materials and tools they are obliged or expected to use, or have been trained to use. An ongoing challenge that all applied linguists face is to judge how well their suggested or required professional tools work in their own context, for their own clients, and what to do if they don't seem to work very well. In Chapter 4 we suggested that practitioners can increase their understanding of language problems in their own professional contexts through the careful analysis of discourse (speaking, writing and images) produced by and surrounding their clients. Discourse analysis can shed light both on the nature of the language problems under scrutiny (including how certain language behaviours come to be thought of as a problem in particular contexts) and on the risks and benefits of possible courses of treatment. Many practitioners will be aware of the benefits of action research for the design and testing of solutions to local problems and will already be engaging in cycles of observation, reflection and action, individually or in teams of clients and professionals. But *Chandy* comments on the potential for conflict between practices based on locally generated evidence and institutionally sanctioned practices (which may or may not be) based on research (perhaps conducted by professional researchers or government bodies) in other contexts.

In the diagnosis and treatment of language problems, we suspect that many, if not most, practitioners' loyalties lie with their clients, rather than with their employing institutions, a coursebook, their manager or their trainer. When it comes to methods, they are most concerned with 'what actually works' in their own experience, rather than what their coursebook or manual suggests should work. Many applied linguists work hard to develop their practice in local contexts, from the bottom up. This is not to say that they don't also read research, try new materials, use new tools when they become available, exchange ideas with other practitioners or occasionally even do what they're told by a manager! But, as *Liliana* points out, the knowledge of how to respond to specific questions is also developed through practice. On the whole, we think that applied linguists will continue to develop their locally appropriate practices from the bottom up, sometimes even in defiance of institutional guidance.

For example, during an education project in Ucayali, Peru, *Liliana* collaborated with teachers, lawyers, engineers and psychologists, many of whom had no previous experience working with Indigenous students, which led to difficulties in communication. Through workshops on Indigenous cultures and ways of thinking, *Liliana* used her knowledge of applied linguistics to 'build bridges' between the students and non-Indigenous professionals. She points out that this practice was something she developed on site and in response to communication problems that arose, rather than a technique she learned from her formal training at university. The challenge for individual applied linguists, and for the discipline, is to look for and to provide opportunites for findings such as *Liliana*'s to be contributed to the general knowledge base.

## Language, freedom and social responsibility

Language is the primary human tool for expressing, interpreting and commenting on the meanings of things, including how they are now, how they came to be that way and how they might be different in the future. Thus, in all its forms, language has at least the potential to liberate and to oppress, to preserve the conditions which privilege some and marginalize others, or to disrupt or undermine those conditions. Because our work deals directly with people facing different language-related problems in diverse communities, applied linguists are witnesses to how language shapes lives, including access to information and resources, and to basic services such as education, health care and legal protections. *Chandy* mentions, for example, the well-documented links between unmet needs in the area of speech, language and communication, on the one hand, and lower educational attainment, behavioural problems, emotional and psychological difficulties, challenges to mental health and, in some cases, increases in criminal behaviour, on the other (for more details, see UK Department for Children, Schools and Families, 2008). Many teach-  **www.14.9** ers see language as a tool for fostering social justice, like *Melissa*, whose ultimate goals in educating El Paso youth are to help students stay in school, become critical thinkers and active community members, and prepare for a university education.

The notion that academic language study can have an effect on the law, education, public policy and public opinion is not new. In 1979 the sociolinguist William Labov provided expert testimony in the famous court case concerning the use of 'Black English' in public schools in Ann Arbor, Michigan discussed on pp. 165–7. In subsequent writings, he urged linguists to uphold what he called 'the principle of linguistic democracy', arguing for them to support the use of a standard dialect as a means of wider communication, but 'oppose its use as a barrier to social mobility' (Labov, 1982, p. 186). He went on to formulate further, more general, 'principles of commitment' that, he argued, would lead to linguists taking social action. His 'principle of the debt incurred' mandated a commitment to sharing data with the communities and individuals from which they were gathered. He noted, however, that linguistic data, and the scholarly interpretations and conclusions derived from them, are often opaque (read 'useless') to non-linguists. He therefore proposed a stronger version of the principle, according to which '[a]n investigator who has obtained linguistic data from members of a speech community has an obligation to use the knowledge based on that data for the benefit of the community, when it has need of it' (Labov, 1982, p. 173). The principle is seen in practice in the example from Chapter 10 of language maintenance and literacy education materials being developed from Mackay and Trechsel's (2005) descriptive work on Misantla Totonac in Mexico.

Other ways in which applied linguists can be socially responsible researchers and practitioners have been proposed by the psycholinguist-turned-discourse analyst James Gee. Gee (2008) claims that applied linguists have an ethical obligation to base their practices on what they believe is the best available evidence, as opposed to mandates from above, such as legislation and other voter initiatives proposed and imposed by non-linguists. He also points out that, often, viable recommendations for best practice are formed through a consideration of *conflicting* evidence and *alternative* viewpoints. Other discourse analysts (for example those doing critical discourse analysis or interactional sociolinguistics; see Chapter 4) are also concerned with exposing the (often invisible) ways in which perceptions about language interact with the judgements that individuals and institutions make about other people.

Finally, applied linguists are increasingly aware of the potential liberating effects of the knowledge they can mediate and generate. *Khawla* is currently working with a group of English language teachers in Israeli-occupied and academically isolated Gaza, to explore the local relevance of linguistic theory and research taught and published in almost inaccessible locations abroad. This is a role which involves her summarizing and paraphrasing research findings, facilitating group discussion of context-specific elements and assumptions, replicating parts of the research locally in order to work with her colleagues to test and extend the original findings, and then providing important feedback to the studies' authors.

In sum, we agree that applied linguists have responsibilities to their clients and to the wider society. We would like to suggest the following four commitments for socially responsible students and practitioners:

- to consider and compare multiple sources of evidence, opinions and traditions, in order to avoid unthinking practice, in the hope that someone else (our line manager, tutor, government, professional organizations, etc.) will know what the right thing is for our clients;
- to share our own research findings in accessible ways with the speech communities from which we collect data;
- to use our research findings to create solutions which meet the needs of the speech communities we research, when and where needs arise;
- to disseminate knowledge about, and increase public understanding of, the many ways in which language shapes lives, making it more difficult for the dead-end patterns of thinking and belief described in Chapter 1 to be used against vulnerable and marginalized groups.

The fact we feel compelled to make our own recommendations more than thirty years on from Labov's call to action suggests that socially responsible practice in its widest sense is still not easily achieved. As we saw in section 14.2, public understanding of how language shapes lives remains limited. Applied linguists with heavy workloads may find that they have very little time to respond to commitments like the ones we propose. Opportunities to reflect on such commitments may be limited for practitioners with rigidly prescribed work routines, or for those working with clients and employers whose world views are resolutely based on the monolithic view of languages and other 'dead ends' of linguistic belief.

There may also be structural issues that create inequities in practitioners' abilities to manage their own work and disseminate their findings. For example, *Chandy* is concerned that the experiences and opinions of the many female, part-time speech and language therapists do not necessarily get the attention they deserve from policy-makers and budget-holders, perhaps partly because part-time and female therapists tend to be juggling a wide range of personal as well as professional responsibilities. And *Melissa* talks about damaging assumptions many educators continue to hold about the intelligence of poor and multilingual students based on their ways of speaking, reading and writing. She sees applied linguistics as fundamental to learning how to teach against deficit views of students and also to meet the needs of her adolescent students: 'By educating ourselves about the complexities of language and the changing nature of literacy, we can better serve the needs of our students.'

So, although most applied linguists would probably agree with the commitments we've outlined, it would be unethical and impractical of us to suggest that the opportunity to exercise our profession in a socially responsible fashion lies solely in the hands of individual practitioners. As we were finishing this chapter, for example, prospective and practising teachers in Texas and Arizona were being challenged by state education departments to pass 'accent' tests as a symbolic measure of speaking English 'properly'. According to a proposed state law in Arizona, teachers 'whose spoken English it deems to be heavily accented or ungrammatical must be removed from classes for students still learning English' (Jordan, 2010). In practice, then, the power to liberate and oppress, privilege and marginalize will continue to be distributed in complex, and often invisible, ways throughout the whole of society (individuals and groups; clients and their families; practitioners and their employers; governments and voters). Accordingly, commitments to social responsibility made by applied linguists will continue to play themselves out in complicated and often frustrating ways for the foreseeable future. Given these constraints, we find it helpful to think of applied linguistics practice as bottom-up community activity, in which we address language-related problems with knowledge and methods from our own and related fields, and we constantly interpret and react to regulation.

www.14.10

## 14.4  KEY PREDICTIONS

Mindful of the wise words of Lao Tzu quoted in the epigraph (p. 322), but unable to resist the temptation, we here provide our view of the prospects for the field in the decades to come. We are upbeat, but cautious.

- Technology will become seamlessly embedded in our daily lives, with communication devices becoming as portable and unobtrusive as a wristwatch or a necklace. This will open up to billions of people a vast and complex network of information and communication possibilities. Applied linguists will need to keep their balance as we continue hurtling through cyberspace towards this species-transforming state.

www.14.11

- At the same time, unpredictable inequalities of opportunity for applied linguists and their clients will continue to exist. While recognition by applied linguists of these inequalities will grow, society at large may be more difficult to convince of the crucial role played by language, and attitudes to groups of language users, in the creation of social inequalities.
- Borders between the different roles of applied linguists and their different objects of study will become increasingly fuzzy. We will all become language learners and users, researchers and practitioners, content creators, providers and communicators. Hybrid linguistic systems and 'non-standard' varieties will become more apparent to more people and will begin to be adopted as linguistic mediums to be taught and tested.
- Global integration will continue, but the consequent recognition of minorities will result in new polities with their own structures of power. Increased integration will lead to greater challenges for localism. Linguistic snobbery and

resistance to hybridity and non-conformity will continue, as will intense language loyalty and linguistic nationalism.

- applied linguistics will become more engaged with issues of freedom and social justice via bottom-up community activity, much of it facilitated by new technologies. But threats to professional autonomy (in the guise of national and international testing regimes, business-oriented approaches to the practice of applied linguists, government-enforced quality assurance schemes, etc.) will continue to restrict the choices made by individual practitioners. Codes of practice will be more widely disseminated and upheld, raising professionalism.

- Bottom-up community activity might also foster broader, more integrated, less ontologically narrow approaches to applied linguistic problem-solving. Advances in cognitive science will help break the 'Language Spell', making the cognitive workings of language more visible and publicly available to counter the monolithic myth. But resistance to science will continue in some broadly shared ideologies, so dead-end thinking and versions of the monolithic myth which serve the interests of powerful parties will continue to circulate.

- Practitioners will develop new methods of researching the needs of, and designing ways of working with, clients in their own contexts, from the bottom up. These will challenge, for example, the commercial wisdom of national and international publishing companies to sell one-size-fits-all coursebooks, the power of governments to design and attempt to enforce curriculums through top-down testing and inspection regimes, and the inevitable hubris of big-name scholars who use their access to influential forums to push untested but seductive panaceas.

## 14.5  FINAL THOUGHTS

> When someone (such as a map maker) attempts to measure a coastline, the often jagged line of where water meets shore can actually be measured by many perspectives, ranging from the height of a satellite to the very close viewpoint of a person kneeling on the shore.
>
> (Grandgenett, 2008, p. 148)

Like Grandgenett's map-maker, we have explored the terrain of applied linguistics from a variety of perspectives. We've tried to create a map of applied linguistics that is more inclusive of practice around the world and less focused only on contexts and concerns in the UK and the US (although, inevitably, these still predominate). We've also examined boundaries and fissures, circumnavigating some, such as the Language Spell, and attempting to build bridges across others, such as the gap between cognitive and sociocultural accounts of language.

For now, we have arrived at the boundaries of our map, although we invite you to follow its development, and perhaps add your own ideas to shape it further, on the website that accompanies this book. We would remind readers that the book is only one of many possible maps that could serve as an introduction to the field of applied linguistics. We've recommended plenty of resources for further reading and provide more learning materials and activities on the website. In closing, we ask you to indulge us one more time as we invoke an image created by Jorge Luis

Borges and Adolfo Bioy Casares in the very short story 'Of Exactitude in Science'. Describing a cult of map-makers in a fictional nation, the authors relate how the cartographers' obsession with detail and precision led them to create an enormous map representing every geographic feature to an exact scale. Eventually the map grew so large that it was no longer useful as a guide to the territory and was dispersed into 'tattered Fragments . . . sheltering an occasional Beast or beggar'. Avoiding the temptation to be overly exact – and knowing when to stop – we are proud to offer our map as a guide to the vital and exciting discipline of applied linguistics.

To learn more about the developing issues discussed in this chapter, identify and interview an applied linguist or language professional in your community or a context where you hope to work. We've listed below all the questions we asked our five practitioners, but you should select those that are most interesting to you. You may also want to revise some questions or add new ones to fit your actual or eventual context of practice. With your interviewee's permission, you could audio- or video-record the interview (or ask your interviewee to respond in writing) to make sure you've captured their ideas before you share them. Alternatively, if you are already a practising applied linguist, you might want to create a 'talking head' video in which you respond to the same questions, and post your interview to the companion website. See the companion website for examples.

1    *Background*

    (a)  Where did you grow up and go to school?
    (b)  What's your job title and what aspect(s) of language are most central to your work?
    (c)  Why did you want to become an applied linguist/language teacher/language pathologist/etc.?
    (d)  What does your family think of your job and what you do for work?
    (e)  What kinds of formal preparation have you had? What do you know about the clients you work with or plan to work with?
    (f)  What kinds of language-related problems do you help solve?
    (g)  Does your work involve working with applied linguists or language professionals whose background and training are different from yours?
    (h)  How do you think your work helps people?

2    *The impact of new technologies*

    (a)  How has your work been influenced or affected by new technologies?
    (b)  What are the forms of technology you use in your job?
    (c)  How did you learn to use them? What technological developments do you think are still needed in your field?
    (d)  Is access to these tools and training open to all?

*activities*

3   *Crossing political borders*

(a)   Has your work been influenced or affected by immigration or other aspects of globalization?
(b)   As an applied linguist, how do globalization and economic integration affect your work?

4   *'Disinventing' languages*

(a)   Does your practice involve identifying or registering clients' languages?
(b)   Why do you need this information?
(c)   How do clients describe themselves linguistically?
(d)   Are there some language identities that don't seem to fit pre-established categories?
(e)   What categories would make sense in your context of practice?

5   *Incorporating cognitive and sociocultural aspects of applied linguistics*

(a)   Has your training as an applied linguist been markedly more oriented toward either cognitive aspects or sociocognitive aspects of language?
(b)   What about in your practice?
(c)   Do you ever have to work with colleagues whose understanding of language and professional tools are very different from your own?
(d)   How do you handle these differences?

6   *Professional standards*

(a)   Are there professional standards or codes of practice in your area of applied linguistics?
(b)   Who are the authors of these standards or codes of practice?
(c)   How do these expectations influence your work?
(d)   Are there issues you would like to see added to or removed from these professional standards?

7   *Language, freedom and social responsibility*

(a)   How do you share the results of your findings with clients?
(b)   What kinds of questions have they asked you about your work?
(c)   What kinds of social justice or equity issues are important in your practice?

8   *Gaining new knowledge in applied linguistics*

(a)   Have you experienced any situations when you are not sure how to solve a problem in your work? If so, what were they and what did you do about them?

(b)   How do you obtain the information you need to solve new kinds of problems?

(c)   Who do you consult with in order to gain the new knowledge you need (for example colleagues, professors or teachers, your employers, professional groups, the internet, specific websites)?

(d)   Do you use social networking sites or other digital literacies to communicate with other applied linguists or language professionals in your field? If so, what kinds of questions have you been able to resolve in this way?

(e)   Are your contacts for finding new information mostly local or mostly located far away from where you live?

9   *Final thoughts*

(a)   How do you feel about your future as an applied linguist?

(b)   How is the field going to change, in your opinion?

(c)   Is there anything else about your applied linguistics practice that you would like to share with readers of *Mapping Applied Linguistics*?

# Glossary

**Acquisition** is the mental process by which knowledge and/or behaviour emerges naturally on the basis of innate predisposition and/or triggers from environmental input (e.g. walking on two feet). Contrasted with LEARNING.

**Acquisition planning** involves direct instruction, independent language study and other efforts to motivate people to acquire or learn a particular language or VARIETY.

**Action research** is a form of self-reflective enquiry (which may include discussion and reading) undertaken by participants in social contexts with the aim of improving their situation in some way. Action researchers often organize their activities in ongoing cycles of reflection and action.

**Additive**: see SUBTRACTIVE

People with one of the many kinds of **agnosia** are unable to recognize selective aspects of what they perceive. So, for example, someone with *visual agnosia* might *see* a familiar object but not be able to make sense of what it is. Someone with *verbal agnosia* might *hear* words spoken to them but not know which words they are, even though they can read, write and speak them.

An **alphabetic writing system** uses (ideally) single symbols for each phoneme (speech sound) in the language.

Acoustic energy (sound), including speech, comes at different levels of **amplitude** (loudness) or extent of vibration, and is measured in decibels (*dB*).

**Anomia** is a type of APHASIA in which word-finding is impaired. People with anomia might recognize objects but be unable to name them.

**Aphasia** is an impairment or loss of linguistic knowledge or ability. It may be due to congenital or acquired brain damage. It is sometimes called *dysphasia* when language loss is not total.

**Apraxia** is a motor planning disorder involving impairment or loss of the ability to make voluntary movements, such as the articulatory gestures involved in speech.

**Artificial intelligence** (AI) is the interdisciplinary field which develops theory on, and designs and tests, machine-based intelligent systems, like those telephone helpline systems that (fail to) understand your spoken instructions.

The **audiolingual** method of teaching an additional language is characterized by repeated oral grammar drills and the outlawing of the L1.

**Audiovisual translation** encompasses all translation involving multiple modalities (including multimedia), but typically involves subtitling or dubbing for screen-based language in film, TV and video games.

**Augmentative and alternative communication** (AAC) helps people with communication impairments to communicate more effectively, using alternative modalities (such as gesture), specially designed symbol systems (like Braille) and/or communication devices (e.g. speech synthesizers).

**Autism** is a complex developmental condition that typically appears during the first three years of life and is the result of a neurological disorder which affects the normal functioning of the brain, impacting development in the areas of social interaction and communication skills (e.g. THEORY OF MIND).

**Autism spectrum disorder** (ASD) refers to an array of related disabilities (such as Asperger's syndrome) that share many of the core characteristics of the classical form of AUTISM. The term is now used more frequently than autism alone, in order to emphasize the diverse nature and extent of individuals' symptoms and experiences.

**Automatic translation** (also known as *machine translation*, MT) is the study and practice of translation via computer software (now increasingly embedded in online applications on the internet).

According to Brian Street's **autonomous model**, literacy is a set of skills for encoding and decoding language in the written modality. According to his **ideo-logical model**, it is viewed as competence in forms of social practice.

**Back-translation** is a way of assessing translation quality. You take a translation from Language A to Language B and obtain an independent translation back into Language A. The degree of discrepancy between the SOURCE LANGUAGE text of the first translation and the TARGET LANGUAGE text of the second allows you to assess the quality of the original target language text.

Someone is **bidialectal** if they are competent in two dialects. For example, most speakers of local dialects in the UK are bidialectal because if they're literate they also know the dialect in which English writing gets done ('standard English').

**Biliteracy** is literacy in two (or more) languages. The word is analogous to *bilingual* (in Latin *bi-* means 'having two', *litteratus* means 'lettered' and *lingua* means 'tongue').

**Braille literacy** is the ability to read and write using the tactile system of raised dots that represent the Roman alphabet, as well as other alphabetic writing systems such as Korean.

**Broca's area** is a region of CEREBRAL CORTEX associated with language production, located above the SYLVIAN FISSURE.

**Causality** is the relationship between causes and effects. The causality of two events describes the extent to which one event happens as a result of the other.

The **cerebral cortex** is the 'grey matter', the 2–4 mm layer of neural tissue covering the two CEREBRAL HEMISPHERES of the human brain, containing the neural networks responsible for 'higher cognitive functions' like language and visual processing.

The **cerebral hemispheres** are the two halves of the cerebrum, the principal component of the human brain.

**Child-directed speech** is the linguist's term for the distinctive patterning of language used by some care-givers with babies. It is characterized by cooing intonation and short, simplified words.

A **citation** in a dictionary entry is an authentic example of the word's use in context, to provide meaning.

The **cochlea** is the hollow, spiral bone structure in the inner ear which transforms acoustic energy into auditory nerve impulses.

A **cochlear implant** is a tiny device embedded under the skin behind the ear, which is used to bypass the damage to the COCHLEA and transmit sound via an alternative route to the auditory nerve.

**Code-switching** is the ability to form utterances using elements of multiple languages in real-time discourse, and the practice of doing so.

A **codex** (plural **codices**) is an ancient manuscript in book form. The Mexican codices were painted on deerskin or bark paper.

**Cognitive discourse analysis** is an approach which takes into account the PROCESSING of discourse, including the role of socially shared knowledge stored in individuals' long-term memory and the capacity and limitations of their short-term (working) memory.

**Collocations** are frequently occurring sequences of words.

The **communicative approach** in additional language teaching stresses that the aim of learning a language is COMMUNICATIVE COMPETENCE. Teachers who base their lessons on a communicative approach may follow a syllabus based on functions or topics, teaching the language needed to perform a variety of authentic tasks and to communicate appropriately in different situations.

**Communicative competence** is not only the ability to form utterances using grammar, but also the knowledge of when, where and with whom it is appropriate to use these utterances in order to achieve a desired effect. Communicative competence includes the following knowledge: grammar and vocabulary; the rules of speaking (how to begin and end a conversation, how to interrupt, what topics are allowed, how to address people and so on); how to use and respond to different SPEECH ACTS; and what kind of utterances are considered appropriate.

**Community interpreting** is interpreting for residents of a multilingual community rather than between members of different language communities: in doctor–patient encounters, job interviews or court proceedings, as opposed to international conferences and diplomatic or commercial meetings.

**Community language teaching** is an approach to HERITAGE LANGUAGE education adopted in the UK, Australia, the Netherlands and other countries in which the home languages of ethnic minorities are taught and used as languages of instruction in schools and community centres.

Speakers use **compensatory strategies** when linguistic interaction is compromised in some way, because one or more of the interlocutors lacks relevant linguistic knowledge or ability. For example, circumlocution can compensate for word-finding difficulties.

**Conceptual blending theory** looks at how the meaning of texts is comprehended in real time by a listener or reader prompted by linguistic cues to activate MENTAL MODELS. These models allow speaker-listeners to distinguish between different elements of a text and understand where there is a relationship ('blending') between these elements.

INTERPRETING is **consecutive** when the speaker/signer produces a stretch of discourse and then pauses while the interpreter translates it, and alternating phases of SOURCE LANGUAGE and TARGET LANGUAGE ensue until the whole message is interpreted.

**Consonantal** writing systems have symbols for the consonants but not for the vowels. Context supplies the words' identities. (For example, *Cn y rd ths*?)

A **construct** in testing is the ability, skill or knowledge that the test is (supposedly) testing.

**Construct validity** refers to how well some measurement system correlates with the CONSTRUCT it is designed to measure.

**Contrastive rhetoric** compares the organization of texts written in different languages, based on the assumption that there are characteristic patterns of writing associated with culturally determined ways of thinking.

**Convergence** in talk is when a person changes the way they speak in order to sound more like the person they are talking to (or more like the way they *think* the other person speaks). For example, an additional language teacher may use less complex syntax when she is talking to a group of beginning learners. Contrasted with DIVERGENCE.

**Conversation analysts** are interested in the organizational structure of spoken interaction, including how speakers decide when to speak in a conversation (rules of turn-taking) and how the utterances of two or more speakers are related (adjacency pairs like A: 'How are you?' B: 'Fine thanks'). As well as describing structures and looking for patterns of interaction, some analysts are also interested in how these structures relate to the 'doing of' social and institutional roles, politeness, intimacy, etc.

A **corpus** (plural **corpora**) is a digital collection of authentic spoken or written language. Corpora are used for the analysis of grammatical patterns and estimations of the frequency of words, word combinations and grammatical structures. The results are useful in, for example, additional language education, translation, lexicography and forensic linguistics.

**Corpus linguistics** is the creation and analysis of (normally large, computerized) CORPORA of language composed of actual texts (speech and writing), and their application to problems in descriptive and applied linguistics.

**Corpus planning** refers to language planning that attempts to modify in some way the code of a given variety. Not to be confused with CORPUS as a digital collection of authentic language.

**Covert prestige** is a term describing instances in which language pride goes underground due to social pressures. For example, when schools and other institutions frown upon the use of a certain language or VARIETY, speakers often continue to use it as an expression of in-group solidarity and resistance to authority, and it often spreads widely as a result.

**Creoles** are complete languages that have evolved from more basic PIDGIN languages, in some cases in a matter of two or three generations.

**Critical applied linguistics** is the practice of applied linguistics grounded in a concern for addressing and resolving problems of inequality.

**Critical discourse analysts** study the ways in which social power, dominance and inequality are enacted, reproduced and resisted by text and talk in social and political contexts.

**Critical language planning** involves questioning the social causes and ramifications of language plans and policies and their implementation. In line with CRITICAL APPLIED LINGUISTICS generally, language planning from a critical perspective means asking why and in whose interests decisions about language(s) are made.

**Critical pedagogy** is an approach to teaching which encourages students to develop critical awareness of, and to challenge, explicit or implicit systems of social injustice and oppression. It is particularly associated with the work of Paulo Freire.

According to the **critical period hypothesis**, there is a limited window of opportunity for language ACQUISITION, during which input must be received and PROCESSED, before the innate cognitive mechanisms responsible for the process 'shut down'.

**Cross-linguistic influence** is when the knowledge or use of one language affects the learning or use of another (typically, L1 influencing L2). The traditional term for this phenomenon is *transfer*. Another term, *interference*, wrongly implies that all L1 influence on L2 learning has negative effects.

Children engage in ***de facto* bilingual education** when they and their teachers implicitly draw on subject knowledge acquired previously in a language which is different from the language of instruction. For example, a Hong Kong student who learned elementary mathematics through the medium of Cantonese will be familiar with mathematical concepts even when they're presented by a Mandarin Chinese-speaking teacher.

**Decreolization** occurs when a CREOLE begins to merge with varieties of the SUPERSTRATE language through (renewed) contact with it.

**Descriptive linguistics** documents and describes what people say, sign and write, and the grammatical, lexical and phonological systems they use to do so.

**Diacritics** are the 'extra' marks required in many orthographies, including the ALPHABETS of French, German, Spanish and the CONSONANTAL writing system of

Arabic. Placed over, under, next to and even through individual letters or syllabic elements, diacritics change the phonetic value of what they mark.

A **dialect** is a VARIETY of a language determined normally by geographical and/or social factors. The term is normally used in the context of languages which have been extensively documented and have a recognized 'standard' dialect against which others are compared.

**Diglossia** is the (perhaps universal) use of (normally two) different languages, VARIETIES or registers of differing levels of prestige for different situations and/or purposes. So, for example, in a Welsh bank the cashiers might use Welsh with their customers but English when requesting approval for leave from the area manager.

A **directive** is a SPEECH ACT performed in order to make the addressee take some action. Examples include commands (*Shut the door behind you!*), requests (*Could you shut the door when you leave?*) and pieces of advice (*You should shut the door, or the cat'll get out*).

**Discursive psychologists** are interested in how (and which) ways of talking and behaving are understood by people to mean that a person is (being) friendly, aggressive, loving and so on: how we 'do' friendliness, for example, and what we recognize as friendliness when we see and hear it.

**Divergence** occurs when a person changes the way they speak to sound less like the person they are talking to, like the local who exaggerates his accent in order to differentiate himself from the incomer. Contrasted with CONVERGENCE.

**Dominant language**: see MINORITY LANGUAGE

**Dysarthria** is a speech articulation disorder caused by damage to the nerves that control muscles in the vocal tract and lungs.

**Dyslexia** is a heritable, neurodevelopmental condition involving impairment or loss of phonological awareness, which shows up as a range of difficulties in learning to read, write and spell, especially in languages which use LOGOGRAPHIC systems or have significant opacity in phonetic-based spelling (like English). These difficulties tend to persist despite the provision of appropriate learning opportunities. They do not reflect an individual's general cognitive abilities and may not be typical of performance in other areas.

**Earwitness**: see NAÏVE SPEAKER IDENTIFICATION

**Elaborated code**: see RESTRICTED CODE

**Elite bilingualism** is a term used by Suzanne Romaine to label the kind of bilingualism of those who seek to become bilingual out of choice, often for increased prestige. An example would be Polish children sent to English-medium schools in Poland. Contrasted with FOLK BILINGUALISM.

The term **emergent literacy** refers to knowledge and behaviours involving reading and writing that children develop before formal schooling.

An **emoticon** is a representation of a facial expression using the punctuation marks and letters available on a keyboard. They range in complexity from the simple :) to the rather more elaborate Japanese d(*⁻▽⁻*)b, both of which mean 'happy'.

**Endangered languages** are those which are at risk of being lost due to massive LANGUAGE SHIFT or the death of their remaining speakers.

**Epigraphers** study and interpret written inscriptions on hard surfaces, such as stone.

**Epistemology** is the study of forms of knowledge and how we come to know them.

**Ethnographic** enquiry seeks to understand cultural situations and activities from the richly contextualized perspectives of the participants themselves. Ethnographers record what they observe from a holistic perspective, with no preconceived expectations about what to look for and what to ignore.

**Exclusion approaches**: see INCLUSION APPROACHES

The **Expanding Circle** is Braj Kachru's (1985) term for the regions where English is used mainly as a FOREIGN LANGUAGE, and where most of its users may now be found. The **Outer Circle** is his term for where English is used mainly as a SECOND LANGUAGE, in former colonies of the UK and USA, where new norms may be developing. English is used mainly as a native language in the **Inner Circle**: England and the regions where English native speakers effectively displaced local populations.

**Extrinsic motivation**: see INTRINSIC MOTIVATION

**Folk bilingualism** is the term used by Suzanne Romaine to label the kind of bilingualism of those who seek to become bilingual out of necessity, often for survival. An example would be Polish immigrant children attending English-medium schools in the UK.

**Foreign language**: see SECOND LANGUAGE

**Forensic stylistics** (sometimes known as **stylometry**) is the measurement of linguistic style through the analysis of the frequency with which given linguistic variables occur in a sample of texts, normally in cases of unclear or disputed authorship.

The **frequency** of acoustic energy (sound) is its rate of vibration, measured in cycles per second (*Hz*). Speech is a combination of many frequencies.

**Funds of Knowledge** is the term used by Luis Moll and colleagues to refer to the stock of knowledge, practices and skills that households develop over the generations, and which can provide rich resources for learning if tapped by schools.

**Glottographic** writing systems use symbols which represent sounds, either individual phonemes (as in ALPHABETIC codes like the one used for English) or syllables (as in the SYLLABARY used for Inuktitut in Canada or the Japanese hiragana and katakana scripts).

A **glyph** is a symbol or character used in a writing system, especially that of the ancient Mayan civilization in what is now Mexico. Ancient Egyptian hiero*glyph*ics provide another example.

The **grammar translation** method of teaching an additional language focuses on memorization of L2 grammatical rules and translation of texts from the L2 into the L1. The method's origins lie in the European tradition of teaching schoolchildren the great works of ancient Greek and Latin.

**Graphophonic** relations hold between the symbols of GLOTTOGRAPHIC writing systems (the *grapho-* bit) and the sounds they represent (the *-phonic* bit).

**Hapax legomena** (from the Greek for 'said once'; also known simply as *hapax*) are words with a single occurrence in a CORPUS. In a large corpus, around 50 per cent of words are likely to be hapax legomena. For example, the word *haptic* is a hapax legomenon in the British National Corpus (whereas *hapax* itself occurs three times).

The **headword** is the form of the word which appears at the beginning of its dictionary entry. It is normally uninflected and often gives syllabic information. So, for example, the headword for the entry corresponding to the word *is* will be *be* and for *corresponding* will be *cor•res•pond*.

A **heritage language** is the language of a minority community viewed as a property of the group's cultural history, and is often in danger of loss as third generations grow up being un- or underexposed to the language. So heritage language bilingual education focuses on the uses of the MINORITY LANGUAGE as a tool to promote group identity, solidarity and LANGUAGE REVITALIZATION.

Bakhtin's theory of **heteroglossia** suggests that a text can't be reduced to a single, fixed, self-enclosed, 'true' meaning which is determined by the intention of its author. Instead, the meanings of the words in the text, and the ways in which these words are combined, are linked to conditions of cultural production and reception. What texts mean, therefore, depends on the multitude of understandings, values, social discourses, cultural codes and so on of all their potential readers and hearers.

**Homonyms** are two or more words that are pronounced and/or written the same way (e.g. *site*, *sight* and *cite*; a sycophantic *bow* to the Queen vs a *bow* in your hair; *case* as 'baggage' and 'instance').

**Ideological model**: see AUTONOMOUS MODEL

**Ideologies** are shifting and sometimes contradictory sets of ideas about power and social structures that shape the way we view the world, including the ways we use and talk about language.

An **idiolect** is the unique form of a language represented in an individual user's mind and attested in their discourse.

**Illocutionary**: see LOCUTIONARY

In **immersion** bilingual education programmes, pioneered in Canada, learners are immersed in the second language. In **one-way immersion**, the pupils typically share an L1, whereas in **two-way immersion** (TWI) speakers of both languages study content together, and the language of instruction for a particular subject may be either language.

**Inclusion approaches** and **exclusion approaches** to working with children with special needs refer to the practices of integrating such learners into the regular classroom (e.g. with non-special needs learners) or segregating them in separate classes.

**Individual differences** between learners are those which potentially account for the wide variety of paths followed and ultimate outcomes achieved in additional language learning.

**Inner Circle**: see EXPANDING CIRCLE

**Inner speech** is spoken (or signed) language that doesn't get expressed.

**Instrumental orientations**: see INTEGRATIVE ORIENTATIONS

**Integrative** and **instrumental orientations** to additional language learning result in different types of motivation to learn. Learners may desire to learn the language to *integrate* into the community of L2 speakers or to use it as an *instrument* for some other benefit. An example of the former would be someone who learns Arabic after converting to Islam. An example of the latter would be someone who learns Arabic in order to win a contract to build a mosque.

The work of **interactional sociolinguists** focuses on the fleeting, unconscious, and culturally variable conventions for signalling and interpreting meaning in social interaction. Using audio or video recordings, analysts pay attention to the words, prosody and REGISTER shifts in talk, and what speakers and listeners understand themselves to be doing with these structures and processes.

**Interpreting** is the process of translating from and into spoken or signed language.

Additional language learners have **intrinsic motivation** when the process itself is perceived as rewarding (for example the intellectual satisfaction they may gain from fathoming a complex verb conjugation). They have **extrinsic motivation** when success provides external rewards or is coerced (for example when they need to learn the conjugation in order to pass a test).

**Language death** is the dramatic and unfortunate fate currently facing most of the world's smallest languages. Linguists sometimes view language death as a process (a language is said to by 'dying' when people stop using it) and sometimes as a final state of linguistic rest (i.e. the last living native speaker has died).

**Language maintenance** implies a focus on keeping a language vital within a given speech community or region. This term is sometimes used to describe bilingual education programmes that aim for learners to retain or further develop their home language while gaining an additional language.

**Language of wider communication** (LWC) refers to a language or VARIETY that is used across communities and regions. The term is completely relative and context dependent, of course; Kiswahili is an LWC in East Africa, but not in Asia or Europe. Similar to LINGUA FRANCA.

**Language orientations** refers to the idea that language planning efforts of all types can be characterized as approaching language from one or more of three primary stances: language as problem, language as right and language as resource.

**Language revitalization** is the name given to efforts to stop or slow down language loss and simultaneously increase the VITALITY of a language in a given community or region.

**Language shift** refers to the process in which speakers, individually or collectively, abandon one language in favour of another. 'Reversing language shift' entails efforts to change the conditions that contribute to language loss (in other words, LANGUAGE REVITALIZATION).

**Language vitality** is a construct used by language planners to gauge the long-term health of a language or variety. Although there are many ways to operationalize this construct, the central feature concerns the transmission of a language from one generation to the next.

**Language-in-education planning** refers to instances of language planning that take place within the domain of education and schooling.

**Learning styles** are the different approaches people are believed to take to the acquisition of new information. The popular distinctions between 'visual' and 'tactile' learners, or between 'thinkers' and 'doers', illustrate the concept. Some scholars believe that if learners can identify their preferred style(s) they will be able to optimize their learning.

The mental process of **learning** requires conscious effort and leads to skills which cannot be part of our genetic make-up (e.g. walking on stilts). Contrasted with ACQUISITION.

**Legitimate language** is a term used by CRITICAL APPLIED LINGUISTS to describe the language or VARIETY that is sanctioned for use in a given sphere or domain. Although it is not a term used in schools, pupils perceive very quickly which ways of speaking and writing are considered illegitimate.

**Lexical gaps** occur in a language when it lacks a word for a concept (which may be expressed lexically in another language).

**Lexical phrases** are chunks of language consisting of strings of words which are regularly spoken, signed and/or written together, like *Take care!* or *To whom it may concern.*

**Lexicology** is the academic study of words: their spoken and written forms, their syntactic and morphological properties, and their meanings; in a particular language or in human language in general; both at a fixed point in history and as they change through time.

A **lingua franca** is a language used as a medium of communication between speakers of different languages.

**Linguistic deficit** is a fictional creature that has, nonetheless, been the subject of much discussion and lament by non-linguists, particularly when applied to the language abilities of children from marginalized groups.

**Linguistic landscapes** are visual representations of language use in a community. By mapping the presence of signs, posters and other publicly displayed texts, applied linguists form a picture of the relative VITALITY of languages at a particular place and point in time.

In speech act theory, utterances involve two kinds of meaning: a **locutionary** meaning, which is the literal meaning of the words and structures being used; and an **illocutionary** meaning, which is the effect the utterance is intended to have on the listener. A **perlocutionary** act is the effect or result of the utterance.

**Logographic** writing systems use symbols which represent whole words or ideas. They normally encode no (or only limited) information about how the symbols are pronounced (compare the logographic symbol & with ALPHABETIC *and*) and no (or only limited) iconic information about what the symbol *means* (so ☺ is not a logographic symbol, but 面 *is* – it's a word for 'face' in Chinese script).

**Macrostructure**: see MICROSTRUCTURE

**Maintenance bilingual education** is ADDITIVE, aiming to complement and strengthen, rather than replace, the (MINORITY) first language. Contrasted with TRANSITIONAL BILINGUAL EDUCATION.

Cross-referencing between dictionary entries is called **mediostructure**. In electronic dictionaries the mediostructure takes the form of (hyper)links.

The **mental lexicon** is the component of memory where we store the vocabulary we know and use. We access its entries at lightning speed every time we speak, listen, sign, read or write.

**Mental models** are representations of situations in the mind which are constructed on the basis of sensory and linguistic input, general knowledge, beliefs, attitudes and intentions. They are the starting point for writing and speaking and the endpoint for listening and reading. Mental models contain far more detailed information than can be mapped onto the linguistic expressions we use to produce (encode) and comprehend (decode) them.

**Mentalese** is the abstract 'language of thought' in the mind: *what we are consciously or unconsciously thinking*, independent of whether it is expressible or expressed using the 'linguistic language' of speech, writing and sign.

**Metalinguistic skills** are those things that learners and other language users can do with language that are not strictly linguistic, for example knowing how to begin a speech or, in writing, when to capitalize certain letters or use end punctuation.

The internal organization of a dictionary's entries is called its **microstructure**. The way the whole dictionary is put together (with words listed in alphabetical order, for example) is called the **macrostructure**.

In bilingualism, a **minority language** is distinguished from a **dominant language** according to what it's used for (its functions) and where it's used (its contexts). For example, Urdu is a minority language in Leeds (in the UK) but a dominant language in Lahore (in Pakistan).

A **morphemic gloss** is an interlinear, morpheme-by-morpheme presentation in the reader's language of the grammatical information and lexical meaning expressed in lines of text from another language.

**Morphology** is the systematic patterning of meaningful word parts, including prefixes and suffixes.

**Multi-grade classes** (also known as *multi-age classrooms*) are groupings in which learners of multiple ages and grade levels are taught in the same classroom.

In addition to allowing pupils to work according to their ability levels in different subject areas, this arrangement has the further advantage of exposing younger children to the language and linguistic routines of more sophisticated speakers and writers, thereby using children's language as a resource for other learners.

**Naïve speaker identification** is when a lay witness (an EARWITNESS) identifies (or attempts to identify) a speaker by recognizing their voice from a single recording, a set of recordings or a voice 'line-up' of speakers.

**Native-speakerism** is the rarely challenged assumption that the desired outcome of additional language learning is, in all cases, 'native' competence in the 'standard' variety, and that native speakers have, therefore, an inbuilt advantage as *teachers* of the language. 'Nativeness' is also often conflated with nationality (note the ambiguity of *German*, *Chinese*, etc.), but since national borders are not consistent with linguistic ones, the geography-based native/second/foreign typology is problematic as a system to classify language learners and teachers.

A **neologism** is a newly coined word which is intended to gain or appears to be gaining common currency in the language.

**Nonce words** are one-off coinages, created for a specific purpose and not likely to gain common currency. David Crystal (2000, p. 219) gives the example of *chopaholic*, which he overheard said of someone who likes lamb chops.

**Nonwords** are potential word forms of a language (like *splord* or *flobage* in English), normally devised by PSYCHOLINGUISTS and neurolinguists for use in lexical PROCESSING experiments and the assessment of language-related disabilities which affect the use of words.

**One-way immersion**: see IMMERSION

**Oracy** is COMMUNICATIVE COMPETENCE in spoken interaction. The word was coined by analogy with *literacy* in the 1960s.

**Orthographies** are symbolic systems for representing language in visual form (or tactile form, in the case of Braille). They can include ALPHABETIC and syllabic elements, and are the focus of applied linguists working with literacy development in written and previously unwritten languages.

**Outer Circle**: see EXPANDING CIRCLE

**Perlocutionary**: see LOCUTIONARY

**Phatic communion** is a term used by Malinowski to refer to communication which is not intended to convey information but which functions as a way of creating or maintaining social contact. In English 'How are you?', 'Have a nice day!' and 'Terrible weather!' are examples of phatic communion.

The **phonology** of a spoken language is the system of sounds that it uses, both individual units (consonants and vowels) and combinations of these units (stress and intonation). The phonology of a sign language is the system of manual and facial gestures that it employs.

**Pidgins** are very basic linguistic systems which sometimes emerge in situations in which speakers of different languages find themselves in frequent contact and need to communicate.

**Polysemy** refers to the very frequent situation in which a single word form does many semantic jobs, expressing a series of related meanings. There will be a core concept underlying the several meanings, but it's normally context which provides the specific sense (e.g. *run* in *Tears ran down his face* and *A shuttle runs from the airport every hour*).

People with **pragmatic language impairment** have a neurological disorder which affects their ability to use language for appropriate and meaningful communication in social contexts. It is associated with AUTISM SPECTRUM DISORDERS.

**Pragmatics** aims to understand what spoken (or signed) language means in specific contexts of use, through a description of the relationship between speaker, hearer, utterance and context.

**Praxis** is educational jargon for 'practice' or 'enaction', from the Greek verb *prattein*, 'to do'.

**Probabilistic translation**: see STATISTICAL TRANSLATION

Language **processing** research investigates how the linguistic knowledge that is stored in the mind/brain is used in real time (as the cognitive events unfold) to produce and understand utterances.

**Psycholinguistics** is the study of the psychology of language and the nexus of language and mind/brain.

**QWERTY** is the name of the standard keyboard layout devised by Christopher Sholes in Milwaukee, Wisconsin, in the USA in 1878, so called because of the order of the first six letters.

**Received Pronunciation** (RP) is a way of pronouncing English which emerged in the late nineteenth century as the accent of England's privileged classes. It is considered by many to have very high prestige and is still used as a target for teaching and a benchmark for phonetic description of other accents, despite its rarity.

A **register** is a way of using the language in certain contexts and situations, often varying according to formality of expression, choice of vocabulary and degree of explicitness. Register variation is intrapersonal because individual speakers normally control a repertoire of registers which they deploy according to circumstances.

In conversation analysis, **repair** refers to the ways in which speakers correct unintended forms and non-understandings, misunderstandings or errors (or what they perceive to be such) during a conversation. A self-initiated repair is when the speaker corrects themself: 'You know Jim, *erm, what's his name*, John?' An example of an *other*-initiated repair is when the listener replies: '*Hmm?*'

**Restricted** and **elaborated code** are terms Basil Bernstein developed to refer to two ways of using language: the former in situations in which interlocutors share knowledge, beliefs and assumptions, communicating much in few words (e.g. between farmers talking informally in a village pub); the latter in situations in which common ground is more limited and everything needs to be spelled out (e.g. between a farmer and bank manager discussing a loan in the bank manager's office).

A **rhyming dictionary** is a dictionary organized according to the end of the word rather than the beginning. Some use spelling as the organizing principle (so *sew* is near *dew*), but the best use sound (so *sew* is near *dough*).

Additional languages may be classified as **second languages** when they are routinely *used* in a country outside the context in which they are *learned* (for example in bilingual countries) and as **foreign languages** when they are not so used. English is learned extensively as a second as well as a foreign language, whereas Icelandic is always learned as foreign language, unless the learner is in Iceland.

A **sheltered English** programme is one in which school pupils with limited proficiency in the target language get instruction in English as an additional language along with other subjects taught in English, until they can join students who have the proficiency required to engage in mainstream classrooms.

INTERPRETING is **simultaneous** when the speaker or signer doesn't pause for the interpreter to translate what they've expressed, for example when making an address at a conference.

**Sociolinguistics** is the study of language in social contexts.

**Source language** (SL) and **target language** (TL) are terms used in translation and INTERPRETING to refer to the 'translated-from' and 'translated-into' languages, respectively. They are appealing terms because they implicitly assume a focus on interlinguistic meaning, and the process of moving from one language to another.

**Special needs education** is the provision of dedicated arrangements for students with an enduring disability which prevents or restricts them participating fully in, and benefiting fully from, the educational process.

**Specific Language Impairment** (SLI) refers to problems in the acquisition and PROCESSING of language, typically in the situations where there are no other developmental disorders, hearing loss or acquired brain injury.

A **spectrogram** is a visual representation of speech (or other acoustic token) produced by an instrument called a *spectrograph*. It measure FREQUENCY and AMPLITUDE as they change through time.

**Speech acts** are utterances which operate as a functional unit in communication; for example: promises, requests, commands and complaints. In additional language education (especially lesson planning and syllabus design), speech acts are often referred to as *functions*.

**Statistical translation** (or **probabilistic translation**) is a procedure which identifies already-existing translations of chunks of texts, and yields the most likely match.

**Status planning** refers to efforts to increase or decrease the prestige of a particular language or VARIETY.

The **strong–weak dichotomy** in bilingual education refers to the balance in classroom usage between the two languages involved. Strong bilingual education involves balanced usage of both languages across all subject areas, in order to reinforce the MINORITY LANGUAGE in its role as a medium of instruction. In weaker forms, the minority language is used for less central curricular functions.

**Stylometry**: see FORENSIC STYLISTICS

**Substrate**: see SUPERSTRATE

**Subtractive** bilingual education leads to the loss of the first language (the second replaces the first), whereas **additive** bilingual education leads to competence in two languages (the second augments the first).

In a language contact situation, the **superstrate** language is the one spoken by the politically and socioeconomically dominant group. The **substrate** language is spoken by less powerful speakers, and influences the development of grammatical features in an emerging VARIETY based on superstrate vocabulary.

A **syllabary** is a writing system in which each symbol represents a syllable (in English we can simulate this by using *Q* for monosyllabic *cue*, *I-V* for bisyllabic *i.vy*, *F-E-G* for trisyllabic *e.ffi.gy*, etc.)

The **Sylvian Fissure** is the deep crevice in each CEREBRAL HEMISPHERE running backwards from above the ear.

**Systemic functional linguistics** (SFL) is interested in the social context of language. In SFL, language is analysed as a resource used in communication, as opposed to a decontextualized set of rules. It is an approach which focuses on functions (what language is being used to *do*), rather than on forms.

**Target language**: see SOURCE LANGUAGE

**Teacher education** is the teaching of teachers. It takes place pre-service, most often at the undergraduate level, and continues in professional development throughout a teacher's career.

**Terminology banks** provide searchable bilingual or multilingual glossaries of technical or specialist vocabulary for use by translators.

**Theoretical linguistics** builds theories about the nature and limits of grammatical, lexical and phonological systems.

**Theory of mind** refers to humans' (and perhaps other primates') innate knowledge that the minds of other members of the species have intentional states, including beliefs and desires. In other words: the mental faculty of *empathy*. People with AUTISM might have impaired theory of mind.

**Total Physical Response** (TPR) is the compelling name given by James Asher to the additional language teaching method he developed. It attempts to recreate for learners the conditions of first language ACQUISITION by getting them to listen and respond with appropriate physical action to spoken instructions. They do this for an extensive period before attempting to speak themselves.

In **transactional** views of reading, the process involves not simply the passive extraction of meaning encoded in the text, but also the active contribution of the reader's own knowledge and beliefs in constructing meaning.

**Transitional bilingual education** is SUBTRACTIVE, using the first language as a temporary medium for gaining proficiency in the (DOMINANT) second language. Contrasted with **maintenance bilingual education**.

A **translation corpus** is a computerized database of existing pairs of SOURCE LANGUAGE and TARGET LANGUAGE text fragments in phrase-, sentence- and paragraph-sized chunks, for use in translation software, also known as a **translation memory**.

**Translation equivalents** are (often ideal or elusive) pairs of terms across languages which have the same meaning, to a greater or lesser degree. They may perhaps best be thought of as cross-linguistic synonyms.

**Translation memory**: see TRANSLATION CORPUS

**Translation Studies** is the academic field concerned with the systematic study of the theory and practice of translation and INTERPRETING. Research and teaching in the area are interdisciplinary, and closely aligned with Intercultural Studies.

**Two-way immersion** (TWI): see IMMERSION

In linguistics, a **variety** refers to the systematic ways in which an identified group of speakers uses a language's sounds, structures and senses. The term allows linguists to recognize the distinctiveness of a group's shared linguistic system and usage, without making claims about its status as a 'full language' or 'just a dialect'.

In testing, **washback** refers to the positive and negative effects of testing on learning and teaching. So, for example, tests might boost self-confidence if they give learners the opportunity to show what they know (positive), or restrict what they learn if the CONSTRUCTS tested are known in advance and are allotted unbalanced study time (negative).

**Wernicke's area** is a region of CEREBRAL CORTEX below the inner end of the SYLVIAN FISSURE, which plays a major role in language comprehension.

**Whispered interpreting** is simultaneous INTERPRETING *sotto voce*, often in a private meeting. Also known as *chuchotage*.

**Word frequency** is an estimation of the regularity with which a word occurs in speech and/or writing, normally calculated on the basis of large samples of language, such as those provided by CORPORA.

**World Englishes** refers to the phenomenon of English as an international language, spoken in different ways by perhaps one-third of the world's population spread across every continent. The term also indicates a view of English which embraces diversity and questions the assumption that contemporary native speakers have inherent stewardship of, or competence in, the language.

# Bibliography

Abbas, S. (1993). The power of English in Pakistan. *World Englishes*, 12, 147–156.

ABI Research (2002). *Language translation, localization and globalization*. 29 October. Online. Retrieved 11 August 2006 from: http://www.abiresearch.com/abiprdisplay.jsp?pressid=192.

Academie Française (n.d.). *Le rôle*. Online. Retrieved 6 September 2006 from: http://www.academie-francaise.fr/role/index.html.

Adams, D. (1979). *The hitch hiker's guide to the galaxy*. London: Pan Books.

Adams, D. and Lloyd, J. (1983). *The meaning of Liff*. London: Pan Macmillan.

Adetunji, J. (2009). Pip . . . pip . . . pip . . . bleep! Radio 4 stalwart to leave after four-letter outburst. *Independent*, 16 September. Online. Retrieved 8 January 2010 from: http://www.independent.co.uk/news/media/tv-radio/pip-pip-pip-bleep-radio-4-stalwart-to-leave-after-fourletter-outburst-1787955.html.

Agheyisi, R. and Fishman, J. A. (1970). Language attitude studies. A review and proposal. *Anthropological Linguistics*, 12, 131–157.

Alexander, R. (2008). *Education for all, the qualitative imperative and the problem of pedagogy*. Consortium for Research on Educational Access, Transitions and Equity, Research Monograph 20. Institute of Education, University of London.

Alidou, H., Boly, A., Brock-Utne, B., Diallo, Y. S., Heugh, K. and Wolff, H. E. (2006). *Optimizing learning and education in Africa – the language factor: A stock-taking research on mother tongue and bilingual education in sub-Saharan Africa*. Paris: UNESCO/Association for the Development of Education in Africa (ADEA). Online. Retrieved 15 June 2010 from: http://www.adeanet.org/adeaPortal/adea/downloadcenter/Ouga/B3_1_MTBLE_en.pdf.

American Association of Colleges of Teacher Education (eds) (2008). *Handbook of technological pedagogical content knowledge for educators*. New York: AACTE/Routledge.

*American heritage dictionary of the English Language* (1969). Boston: Houghton Mifflin.

American Speech–Language–Hearing Association (ASHA) (2010). *Accent reduction*. Online. Retrieved 8 January 2010 from: http://www.asha.org/public/speech/development/accent_mod.htm.

Amnesty International (2009). *Fatal flaws: Barriers to maternal health in Peru*. London: Amnesty International Publications. Online. Retrieved 18 November 2009 from: http://www.amnesty.org.uk/uploads/documents/doc_19530.pdf.

Andersen, E. S. (1990). Acquiring communicative competence: Knowledge of register variation. In R. C. Scarcella, E. S. Andersen and S. D. Krashen (eds),

*Developing communicative competence in a second language*. New York: Newbury House.

Asif, S. I. (2005). Siraiki language and ethnic identity. *Bahauddin Zakariya University Journal of Research*, 7, 9–17.

AskOxford (2010). *Are lexicographers good spellers?* Online. Retrieved 14 June 2010 from: http://www.askoxford.com/asktheexperts/faq/aboutdictionaries/spellers?.

Atkinson, J. M. and Drew, P. (1979). *Order in court: The organisation of verbal interaction in judicial settings*. London: Macmillan.

Au, K. (1993). *Literacy instruction in multilingual settings*. Fort Worth, TX: Harcourt Brace.

Austin, J. L. (1975). *How to do things with words*, 2nd edn. London: Clarendon Press.

Ayto, J. R. (1983). On specifying meaning. In R. R. K. Hartmann (ed.), *Lexicography: Principles and practice*. London: Academic Press.

Baetens Beardsmore, H. (2009). Language promotion by European supra-national institutions. In O. García (ed.). *Bilingual education in the 21st Century: A global perspective*. Oxford: Wiley-Blackwell.

Baghat, A. and Mogel, L. (eds) (2008). *An atlas of radical cartography*. Los Angeles, CA: Journal of Aesthetics and Protest Press.

Baker, C. (2006) *An introduction to bilingualism and bilingual education*, 4th edn. Clevedon, UK: Multilingual Matters.

Baker, P. (2006). *Using corpora in discourse analysis*. London: Continuum.

Bakhtin. M. M. (1981). *The dialogic imagination: Four essays* (trans. C. Emerson and M. Holquist; ed. M. Holquist). Austin, TX: University of Texas Press.

Bambgose, A. (1998). Torn between the norms: Innovations in World Englishes. *World Englishes*, 17, 1, 1–14.

Baquedano-López, P. (2004). Traversing the center: The politics of language use in a Catholic religious education program for immigrant Mexican children. *Anthropology and Education Quarterly*, 35, 2, 212–232.

Barbour, S. and Carmichael, C. (2000). *Language and nationalism in Europe*. Oxford: Oxford University Press.

Barnouw, D. and Stroom, G. van der (2003). *Who betrayed Anne Frank?* Amsterdam: NIOD. Online. Retrieved 6 February 2006 from: http://www.niod.nl/annefrank/Who%20betrayed%20Anne%20Frank.pdf.

Barrett, G. (2006). *Double-tongued word wrestler dictionary*. Online. Retrieved 4 September 2006 from: http://www.doubletongued.org/.

Barton, D. (2007). *Literacy: An introduction to the ecology of written language*, 2nd edn. Oxford: Blackwell.

Bartra, R. (1992). *The cage of melancholy: Identity and metamorphosis in the Mexican character* (trans. C. J. Hall). New Brunswick, NJ: Rutgers University Press.

Bashir, A. S., Conte, B. M. and Heerde, S. M. (1998). Language and school success: Collaborative challenges and choices. In D. D. Merritt and B. Culatta (eds), *Language intervention in the classroom*. San Diego, CA: Singular Publishing Group.

Batibo, H. M. (2009). Language documentation as a strategy for the empowerment of the minority languages of Africa. In M. Matondo, F. McLaughlin and E.

Potsdam (eds), *Selected proceedings of the 38th Annual Conference on African Linguistics*. Somerville, MA: Cascadilla Proceedings Project.

BBC (1983). *A child's guide to language* [*Horizon* Video]. London: BBC.

BBC World News (2009). *The misunderestimated president?* Online. Retrieved 14 June 2010 from: http://news.bbc.co.uk/1/hi/world/americas/7809160.stm.

Beacco, J. C. and Byram, M. (2003). *Guide for the development of language education policies in Europe: From linguistic diversity to plurilingual education.* Council of Europe, Language Policy Division: Strasbourg. Online. Retrieved 18 June 2007 from: http://www.coe.int/t/dg4/linguistic/Source/FullGuide_ EN.pdf.

Bellin, W. (2009). Reconsidering the role of older speakers in language planning. In S. Pertot, M. S. Priestly and C. H. Williams (eds), *Rights, promotion and integration issues for minority languages in Europe*. London: Palgrave Macmillan.

Bellos, D. (2010). I, translator. *New York Times*, 21 March. Online. Retrieved 14 June 2010 from: http://www.nytimes.com/2010/03/21/opinion/21bellos.html? scp=1&sq=&st=nyt.

Beninatto, R. S. (2009). New Brazilian Portuguese in effect. *Global Watchtower.* Online. Retrieved 20 February 2010 from: http://www.globalwatchtower.com/ 2009/01/06/new-brazilian-portuguese-spelling-in-effect/.

Bentham, J. (1988 [1776]). *A fragment on government* (ed. J. H. Burns and H. L. A. Hart). Cambridge: Cambridge University Press.

Bernstein, B. (2003 [1972]). *Class, codes and control. Volume I: Theoretical studies toward a Sociology of Language*. London: Routledge.

— (2003 [1975]). *Class, codes and control. Volume III, Towards a theory of educational transmission*. London: Routledge/Taylor and Francis.

Bickford, J. O. (2004). Preferences of individuals with visual impairments for the use of person-first language. *RE:view*, 36, 3, 120–126.

Bierce, A. (2003 [1911]). *The Devil's dictionary*. London: Folio Society.

Blackwell, S. (2008). *Webster's forensic linguistics home page*. University of Birmingham. Online. Retrieved 9 February 2009 from: http://web.bham.ac.uk/ forensic.

Bley-Vroman, R. (1989). What is the logical problem of foreign language learning? In S. M. Gass and J. Schachter (eds), *Linguistic perspectives on second language acquisition*. Cambridge: Cambridge University Press.

Blommaert, J. (2005). *Discourse: A critical introduction.* Cambridge: Cambridge University Press.

Bloomfield, L. (1984 [1933]). *Language*. Chicago: University of Chicago Press.

Borges, J. L. (2004 [1935]). The translators of *The Thousand and One Nights*. In L. Venuti (ed.), *The translation studies reader*, 2nd edn. London: Routledge.

Bourdieu, P. (1984). *Distinction: A social critique of the judgment of taste*. London: Routledge and Kegan Paul.

Bourdieu, P. and Passeron, J. C. (1990 [1977]). *Reproduction in education, society and culture*, 2nd edn. Thousand Oaks, CA: Sage.

Braber, N. (2006). Use of language: A sign and cause of alienation. In C. Leung and J. Jenkins (eds), *Reconfiguring Europe: The contribution of applied linguistics. British Studies in Applied Linguistics. Volume 20*. London: British Association for Applied Linguistics/Equinox.

Bradley, H. (ed.) (1900). *Dialogues in English and French by William Caxton*. Early English Text Society. London: Kegan Paul, Trench, Trübner and Co., Ltd. Reprinted 2007 Kessinger Publishing.

Bremer, K., Roberts, C., Vasseur, M., Simonot, M. and Broeder, P. (1996). *Achieving understanding: Discourse in intercultural encounters*. Harlow: Longman.

Brien, D. (1992). *Dictionary of British Sign Language*. London: Faber and Faber.

Brisk, M. E. (1998). *Bilingual education: From compensatory to quality schooling*. Mahway, NJ: Lawrence Erlbaum.

Broeders, A. P. A. (2001). *Forensic speech and audio analysis. Forensic linguistics 1998 to 2001. A Review*. Paper presented at the 13th INTERPOL Forensic Science Symposium, Lyon, France, October.

Brown, R. (2009). In Nashville, a ballot measure that may quiet all but English. *New York Times*. Online. Retrieved 1 February 2010 from: http://www.nytimes. com/2009/01/11/us/11english.html?_r=2&ref=us.

Brumfit, C. J. (1995). Teacher professionalism and research. In G. Cook and B. Seidlhofer (eds), *Principle and practice in applied linguistics*. Oxford: Oxford University Press.

Burke's Peerage Online (2005–2007). *A to Z definition guide*. Online. Retrieved 15 July 2007 from: http://www.burkes-peerage.net/articles/peerage/page 66-peerage.aspx.

Burns, A. (2009). *Doing action research in English language teaching: A guide for practitioners*. London: Routledge.

Callahan, L. (2010). U.S. Latinos' use of written Spanish: Realities and aspirations. *Heritage Language Journal*, 7, 1, 1–26.

Cameron, D. (1995). *Verbal hygiene*. London: Routledge.

—— (2002). Globalization and the teaching of 'communication skills'. In D. Block and D. Cameron (eds), *Globalization and language teaching*. London: Routledge.

—— (2005). Language, gender, and sexuality: Current issues and new directions. *Applied Linguistics*, 26, 4, 482–502.

—— (2007). *The myth of Mars and Venus*. Oxford: Oxford University Press.

Canagarajah, A. S. (1999). *Resisting linguistic imperialism in English teaching*. Oxford: Oxford University Press.

—— (2007). Lingua franca English, multilingual communities, and language acquisition. *Modern Language Journal*, 91 (focus issue), 923–939.

Carroll, J. B. (1981). Twenty-five years of research on foreign language aptitude. In K. C. Diller (ed.), *Individual differences and universals in language learning aptitude*. Rowley, MA: Newbury House.

Carter, R. (1997). *Investigating English discourse: Language, literacy, and literature*. London: Taylor and Francis.

—— (1998) *Vocabulary: Applied linguistic perspectives*. London: Routledge.

Carter, R. and McCarthy, M. (2006). *Cambridge grammar of English: A comprehensive guide, spoken and written English, grammar and usage*. Cambridge: Cambridge University Press.

Casas-Cortes, M. and Cobarrubios, S. (2008). Drawing escape tunnels through borders: Cartographic research experiments by European social movements. In A. Baghat and L. Moge (eds), *An atlas of radical cartography*. Los Angeles, CA: Journal of Aesthetics and Protest Press.

Castles, S. (2007). The factors that make and unmake migration policies. In A. Portes and J. DeWind (eds), *Rethinking migration: New theoretical and empirical perspectives*. New York: Berghahn Books.

Chafe, W. and Danielewicz, J. (1987). *Properties of spoken and written language*. Technical Report No. 5, National Center for the Study of Writing. Washington, DC: US Department of Education. Online. Retrieved 12 June 2010 from: http://www.nwp.org/cs/public/download/nwp_file/142/TR05.pdf?x-r=pcfile_d.

Chaika, E. (2008). *Language: The social mirror*, 4th edn. Boston, MA: Heinle.

Chaski, C. (2001). Empirical evaluations of language-based author identification techniques. *Forensic Linguistics*, 8, 1–65.

Chen, Z. (n.d.). Language law bewilders bilingual educators. *China.org.cn*. Online. Retrieved 22 February 2010 from: http://www.china.org.cn/english/2002/Apr/31210.htm.

Chiaro, D. (2009). Issues in audiovisual translation. In J. Munday (ed.) *The Routledge companion to translation studies*. London: Routledge.

Chomsky, N. (1986). *Knowledge of language: Its nature, origins and use*. New York: Praeger.

CILT (2006). *Positively plurilingual*. London: The National Centre for Languages. Online. Retrieved 15 June 2010 from: http://www.cilt.org.uk/pdf/pubs/positively_plurilingual.pdf.

Cintron, R. (1997). *Angels' Town: Chero ways, gang life, and rhetorics of the everyday*. Boston, MA: Beacon Press.

Clair, R. S. and Phipps, A. (2008). Ludic literacies at the intersections of cultures: An interview with James Paul Gee. *Language and Intercultural Communication*, 8, 2, 91–100.

Clark, C. and Dugdale, G. (2008). *Literacy changes lives: The role of literacy in offending behaviour – a discussion piece*. London: The National Literacy Trust. Online. Retrieved 12 January 2010 from: http://www.literacytrust.org.uk/research/Literacy_changes_lives_prisoners.pdf.

Clear, J. (1996). Technical implications of multilingual corpus lexicography. *International Journal of Lexicography*, 9, 3, 265–273.

Codó, E. (2008). *Immigration and bureaucratic control: Language practices in public administration*. Berlin: Mouton de Gruyter.

Coffin, C. and O'Halloran, K. (2010). Finding the global groove: Theorising and analysing dynamic reader positioning using APPRAISAL, corpus, and a concordancer. In C. Coffin, T. Lillis and K. O'Halloran (eds), *Applied linguistics methods: A reader*. London: Routledge.

Cole, M., Levitin, K. and Luria, A. R. (2005). *The autobiography of Alexander Luria: A dialogue with the making of mind*. London: Taylor and Francis.

Collier, V. P. and Thomas, W. P. (2007). *Predicting second language academic success in English using the Prism Model*. In J. Cummins and C. Davison (eds), *International handbook of English language teaching, Part 1*. New York: Springer.

Collins, J. and Blot, R. K. (2003). *Literacy and literacies: Texts, power and identity*. Cambridge: Cambridge University Press.

Collins, J. and Slembroucke, S. (2007). Reading shop windows in globalized neighborhoods: Multilingual literacy practices and lexicality. *Journal of Literacy Research*, 39, 3, 335–356.

Commission of the European Communities (2003). *Promoting language learning and linguistic diversity: An action plan 2004–2006.* Brussels. Online. Retrieved 15 June 2010 from: http://europa.eu/legislation_summaries/education_ training_youth/lifelong_learning/c11068_en.htm.

— (2008). *An inventory of community actions in the field of multilingualism and results of the online public consultation.* Online. Retrieved 28 September 2010 from: http://ec.europa.eu/education/languages/pdf/com/inventory_en.pdf.

*Concise Oxford English Dictionary* (2006). 11th edn. Oxford: Oxford University Press.

Conner, R. M. (n.d.). *La Malinche: Traitor or creator?* The Translator Interpreter Hall of Fame. Online. Retrieved 2 March 2009 from: http://www.tihof.org/honors/ malinche.htm.

Connor, U. (2002). New directions in contrastive rhetoric. *TESOL Quarterly,* 36, 4, 493–510.

Cook, G. (2010). *Translation in language teaching.* Oxford: Oxford University Press.

Cook, G. and North, S. (2010). *Applied linguistics in action: A reader.* London: Routledge.

Cook, V. (1993). *Linguistics and second language acquisition.* London: Macmillan.

Cooper, R. L. (1989). *Language planning and social change.* Cambridge: Cambridge University Press.

Coote, E. (1997 [1596]). *The English schoole-maister* (transcribed by Lancashire, I.). Toronto: Web Development Group, University of Toronto. Online. Retrieved 15 June 2010 from: http://www.library.utoronto.ca/utel/ret/coote/coote.html.

Coulmas, F. (1989). *The writing systems of the world.* Oxford: Blackwell.

Coulson, S. and Oakley, T. (2000). *Blending basics.* Online. Retrieved 11 June 2010 from: http://www.case.edu/artsci/engl/Library/Oakley-CoulsonBlendBasics. pdf.

Coulthard, M. (1994a). Powerful evidence for the defence: An exercise in forensic discourse analysis. In J. Gibbons (ed.), *Language and the law.* London: Longman.

— (1994b). On the use of corpora in the analysis of forensic texts. *Forensic Linguistics: The International Journal of Speech, Language and the Law,* 1, i, 27–43.

— (2004). Author identification, idiolect, and linguistic uniqueness. *Applied Linguistics,* 45, 4, 431–447.

— (2007). By their words shall ye know them: On linguistic identity. In C. R. Caldas-Coulthard and R. Iedema (eds), *Identity trouble.* London: Palgrave Macmillan.

Coulthard, M. and Johnson, A. (2007). *An Introduction to forensic linguistics: Language in evidence.* London: Routledge.

Council of Europe (2007). *Language education policy profiles: Guidelines and procedures.* Online. Retrieved 18 June 2010 from: http://www.coe.int/t/dg4/ linguistic/Annex_EN.asp#P100_11154.

*Coxford Singlish Dictionary* (n.d.). Online. Retrieved 1 March 2009 from: www.talkingcock.com/html/lexec.php?op=LexView&lexicon=lexicon.

Coyle, D. (2007). Content and Language Integrated Learning: Towards a connected research agenda for CLIL pedagogies. *International Journal of Bilingual Education and Bilingualism,* 10, 5, 543–562.

Creese, A. and Martin, P. (eds) (2003). *Multilingual classroom ecologies: Inter-relationships, interactions and ideologies.* Clevedon, UK: Multilingual Matters.

Crystal, D. (1981). *Directions in applied linguistics*. London: Academic Press.

— (2000). Investigating nonceness: Lexical innovation and lexicographic coverage. In R. Boenig and K. Davis (eds), *Manuscript, narrative and lexicon: Essays on literary and cultural transmission in honor of Whitney F. Bolton*. London: Associated University Presses. Online. Retrieved 8 June 2010 from: http://www.davidcrystal.com/DC_articles/Lexicography4.pdf.

— (2002). *The English language*. London: Penguin.

— (2008). Two thousand million? *English Today*, 24, 1 3–6.

Crystal, D. and Varley, R. (1998). Introduction to language pathology, 4th edn. London: Whurr Publishers.

Cummins, J. (2008). Foreword: Multilingualism and minority languages. *AILA Review*, 21, 1–3. Amsterdam: John Benjamins.

— (2009). Fundamental psycholinguistic and sociological principles underlying educational success for linguistic minority learners. In T. Skutnabb-Kangas, R. Phillipson, A. K. Mohanty and M. Panda (eds), *Social justice through multicultural education*. Clevedon, UK: Multilingual Matters.

Cutts, M. and Wagner, E. (2002). *Clarifying EC regulations*. High Peak, UK: Plain Language Commission. Online. Retrieved 6 February 2006 from: http://www.clearest.co.uk/index.php?id=20.

D'Mello, A. (2004). India's English lesson for China. *Times of India*. Online. Retrieved 2 June 2009 from: http://timesofindia.indiatimes.com/articleshow/903403.cms.

Da Pigin Coup (1999). *Pidgin and education*. Online. Retrieved 25 February 2007 from: www.hawaii.edu/sls/pidgin.html.

Darling-Hammond, L. (2010). *The flat world and education: How America's commitment to equity will determine our future*. New York: Teachers College Press.

Davies, A. (2007). *An introduction to applied linguistics*, 2nd edn. Edinburgh: Edinburgh University Press Ltd.

Davies, A., Hamp-Lyons, L. and Kemp, C. (2003). Whose norms? International proficiency tests in English. *World Englishes*, 22, 4, 571–584.

de Leon, F. M. and Macdonald, S. (1992). Name power: Taking pride, and control, in defining ourselves. *Seattle Times*, 28 June.

DeKeyser, R. and Juffs, A. (2005). Cognitive considerations in L2 learning. In E. Hinkel (ed.), *Handbook of research in second language teaching and learning*. Mahwah, NJ: Lawrence Erlbaum Associates.

Dent, Susie (2003). *The language report*. Oxford: Oxford University Press.

Diamond, J. (1997). The curse of QWERTY. *Discover*. Online. Retrieved 12 June 2010 from: http://discovermagazine.com/1997/apr/thecurseofqwerty1099/.

Dijkstra, K., Bougeois, M., Petrie, G., Burgio, L. and Allen-Burge, R. (2010 [2002]). My recaller is on vacation: Discourse analysis of nursing-home residents with dementia. In G. Cook and S. North (eds), *Applied linguistics in action: A reader*. London: Routledge.

Dilevko, J. (2001). *La Francophonie*: An emerging international governmental organization. In P. I. Hajnal (ed.), *International Information, Volume 2: Documents, publications, and electronic information of international organizations*, 2nd edn. Santa Barbra, CA: Libraries Unlimited.

Directorate-General for Translation (DGT) (2007a). *Transiaing for a multilingual community*. Brussels: European Commission. Online. Retrieved 1 March 2009 from: http://ec.europa.eu/dgs/translation/bookshelf/brochure_en.pdf.

— (2007b). *Translation tools and workflow*. Brussels: European Commission. Online. Retrieved 1 March 2009 from: http://ec.europa.eu/dgs/translation/bookshelf/tools_and_workflow_en.pdf.

Dörnyei, Z. (2001). *Teaching and researching motivation*. Harlow: Pearson Education Limited.

— (2005). *The psychology of the language learner: Individual differences in second language acquisition*. Mahwah, NJ: Lawrence Erlbaum Associates.

Drew, P. (2005). Foreword: Applied linguistics and conversation analysis. In K. Richards and P. Seedhouse (eds), *Applying conversation analysis*. Basingstoke: Palgrave Macmillan.

Duff, P. (2002). The discursive co-construction of knowledge, identity and difference: An ethnography of communication in the high school mainstream. *Applied Linguistics*, 23, 3, 289–322.

Duff, P. A. and Li, D. (2009). Indigenous, minority, and heritage language education in Canada: Policies, contexts, and issues. *Canadian Modern Language Review/La Revue canadienne des langues vivantes*, 66, 1, 1–8.

Duranti, A. (1997). *Linguistic anthropology*. Cambridge: Cambridge University Press.

Duranti, A. and Goodwin, C. (eds) (1992). *Rethinking context: Language as an interactive phenomenon*. Cambridge: Cambridge University Press.

Dworin, J. E. and Bomer, R. (2008). What we all (supposedly) know about the poor: A critical discourse analysis of Ruby Payne's 'Framework'. *English Education*, 40, 2, 101–121.

Eades, D. (1992). *Aboriginal English and the law*. Brisbane, Australia: Queensland Law Society.

— (2005). Applied linguistics and language analysis in asylum seeker cases. *Applied Linguistics*, 26, 4, 503–526.

— (2007). Aboriginal English. In *Language Varieties*. Online. Retrieved 28 February 2009 from: http://www.une.edu.au/langnet/definitions/aboriginal.html.

Edwards, D. and Potter, J. (1992). *Discursive psychology*. London: Sage.

Edwards, R., Alexander, C. and Temple, B. (2006). Interpreting trust: Abstract and personal trust for people who need interpreters to access services. *Sociological Research Online*, 11, 1. Online. Retrieved 14 February 2009 from: http://www.socresonline.org.uk/11/1/edwards.html.

Eggington, W. G. (2002). Unplanned language planning. In R. B. Kaplan (ed.), *The Oxford handbook of applied linguistics*. Oxford: Oxford University Press.

Endicott, T. (2002). Law and language. In E. N. Zalta (ed.), *The Stanford encyclopedia of philosophy* (Winter 2002 edn). Online. Retrieved 1 March 2009 from: http://plato.stanford.edu/archives/win2002/entries/law-language/.

Environmental Literacy Council (n.d.). Online. Retrieved 12 June 2010 from: http://www.enviroliteracy.org/index.php.

EpiGenesis (2007). *Inside deaf culture* website. Online. Retrieved 9 June 2010 from: http://insidedeafculture.com.

Extra, G. (2006). Dealing with multilingualism in multicultural Europe: Immigrant minority languages at home and in school. In C. Leung and J. Jenkins (eds), *Reconfiguring Europe: The contribution of applied linguistics*. London: Equinox/British Association for Applied Linguistics.

Extra, G. and Yağmur, K. (2005). Multilingual Cities Project: Crossnational perspectives on immigrant minority languages in Europe. *Noves SL, Revista de Sociolingüística*, spring–summer 2005. Online. Retrieved 15 June 2010 from: http://www6.gencat.net/llengcat/noves/hm05primavera-estiu/extra1_3.htm.

Fairclough, N. (1995). *Critical discourse analysis: The critical study of language*. London: Longman.

— (2001). *Language and power*. London: Longman.

Feng, A. (2005). Bilingualism for the minor or the major? An evaluative analysis of parallel conceptions in China. *International Journal of Bilingual Education and Bilingualism*, 8, 6, 529–551.

Fenson, L., Dale, P., Resnick, S., Bates, E. Thal, D. and Pethick, S. J. (1994). Variability in early communicative development. *Monographs of the Society for Research in Child Development*, 59, 1-73.

Ferguson, A. and Armstrong, E. (2009). *Researching communication disorders*. Basingstoke: Palgrave Macmillan.

Ferguson, C. A. (1971). *Language structure and language use: Essays*. Stanford, CA: Stanford University Press.

Ferreiro, E. and Gómez, M. P. (eds) (1997 [1982]). *Nuevas perspectivas sobre los procesos de lectura y escritura*. Mexico: Siglo Veintiuno Editores.

Ferreiro, E., Pontecorvo, C., Riebiero, M. and García Hidalgo, I. (1996). *Caperucita Roja aprende a escribir: Estudios psicolingüísticos comparativos en tres lenguas*. Barcelona: Gedisa Editorial.

Finegan, E. (1980). *Attitudes toward English usage: The history of a war of words*. New York: Teachers College Press.

Finegan, E. and Besnier, N. (1989). *Language: Its structure and use*. New York: Harcourt Brace Jovanovich.

Fisher, S. E. and Marcus, G. F. (2006). The eloquent ape: Genes, brains and the evolution of language. *Nature Reviews. Genetics*, 7, 9–20.

Fishman, J. A. (1991). *Reversing language shift: Theoretical and empirical foundations of assistance to threatened languages*. Clevedon, UK: Multilingual Matters.

— (2000 [1967]). Bilingualism with and without diglossia; diglossia with and without bilingualism. In L. Wei (ed.), *The bilingualism reader*. London: Routledge.

— (2001 [1965]). Who speaks what language to who and when? In L. Wei (ed.), *The bilingualism reader*. London: Routledge.

Flowerdew, J. (2000). Discourse community, legitimate peripheral participation, and the nonnative-English speaking scholar. *TESOL Quarterly*, 34/1, 127–150.

Foster-Cohen, S. (1999). *An introduction to child language development*. London: Longman.

Foundation for Endangered Languages (2009). *Manifesto*. Online. Retrieved 21 September 2010 from: http://www.ogmios.org/manifesto/index.htm.

Framenet (2009). *Welcome to Framenet*. Online. Retrieved 3 March 2010 from: http://framenet.icsi.berkeley.edu/index.php?option=com_content&task=view&id=40&Itemid=1.

Freire, P. (1986 [1970]). *Pedagogy of the oppressed*. New York: Continuum.

— (1998). *Teachers as cultural workers: Letters to those who dare teach*. Oxford: Westview Press.

Freire, P. and Macedo, D. (2001 [1987]). *Literacy: Reading the word and the world*. London: Routledge.

French, P., Harrison, P. and Windsor Lewis, J. (2007). R v John Humble: The Yorkshire Ripper hoaxer trial. *International Journal of Speech, Language and the Law*, 13, i, 289–298.

Gal, S. (1978). Peasant men can't get wives: Language change and sex roles in a bilingual community. *Language in Society*, 7, 1, 1–16.

Gándara, P. and Hopkins, M. (eds) (2010). *Forbidden languages: English language learners and restrictive language policies*. New York: Teachers College Press.

García, O. (2009). *Bilingual education in the 21st century: A global perspective*. Oxford: Wiley-Blackwell.

Gardner, H. (2005). A comparison of a mother and a therapist working on child speech. In K. Richards and P. Seedhouse (eds), *Applying conversation analysis*. Basingstoke: Palgrave Macmillan.

Gardner, R. C. (1985). *Social psychology and second language learning: The role of attitudes and motivation*. London: Edward Arnold.

Gardner, R. C. and Lambert, W. E. (1972). *Attitudes and motivation in second language learning*. Rowley, MA: Newbury House.

Garfinkel, H. (1967). *Studies in ethnomethodology*. Englewood Cliffs, NJ: Prentice Hall.

Gazzaniga, M. S. (ed.) (2009). *The cognitive neurosciences*, 4th edn. Cambridge, MA: MIT Press.

Gee, J. P. (2005). *An introduction to discourse analysis: Theory and method*. London: Routledge.

—— (2007). *What video games have to teach us about learning and literacy*. New York: Palgrave Macmillan.

—— (2008). *Social linguistics and literacies: Ideology in discourses*, 3rd edn. London: Routledge.

Gilbert, N. and Mulkay, M. (1984). *Opening Pandora's box: A sociological analysis of scientists' discourse*. Cambridge: Cambridge University Press.

Giles, H. and Billings, A. C. (2004). Assessing language attitudes: Speaker evaluation studies. In A. Davies. and C. Elder (eds), *The handbook of applied linguistics*. Oxford: Blackwell.

Giles, H., Coupland, N. and Coupland, J. (eds) (1991). *Contexts of accommodation: Developments in applied sociolinguistics*. Cambridge: Cambridge University Press.

Glewwe, P., Kremer, M. and Moulin, S. (2007). *How many children left behind? Textbooks and test scores in Kenya*. Abdul Latif Jameel Poverty Action Lab. Cambridge: MIT. Online. Retrieved 17 February 2010 from: http://www.povertyactionlab.com/projects/project.php?pid=33.

Goffman, E. (1981). *Forms of talk*. Oxford: Blackwell.

González, N. E., Moll, L. C. and Amanti, C. (2005). *Funds of knowledge: Theorizing practices in households, communities, and classrooms*. Mahwah, NJ: Lawrence Erlbaum.

González, N., Moll, L. C., Floyd-Tenery, M., Rivera, A., Rendon, P., Gonzales, R. and Amanti, C. (1993). *Teacher research on funds of knowledge: Learning from households*. Santa Cruz, CA: The National Center for Research on Cultural Diversity and Second Language Learning.

González, R. (2000). *Turtle pictures*. Tucson, AZ: The University of Arizona Press.

Goodman, K. (1993). *Phonics phacts*. Portsmouth, NH: Heinemann.

— (1996). *On reading*. Portsmouth, NH: Heinemann.

Goodwin, C. and Goodwin, M. H. (1997). Contested vision: The discursive constitution of Rodney King. In B. Gunnarsson, P. Linell and B. Nordberg (eds), *The construction of professional discourse*. New York: Longman.

Goody, J.R. (1977) *The domestication of the savage mind*. Cambridge: Cambridge University Press.

Gopnik, M., Dalalakis, J., Fukuda, S. E. and Fukuda, S. (1997). Familial language impairment. In M. Gopnik (ed.), *The inheritance and innateness of grammars*. New York: Oxford University Press.

Gottlieb, H. (2004). Language-political implications of subtitling. In P. Orero (ed.), *Topics in audiovisual translation*. Amsterdam: John Benjamins.

Graddol, D. (2006). *English next*. London: British Council. Online. Retrieved 16 January 2010 from: http://www.britishcouncil.org/learning-research-english-next_rev.pdf.

Graddol, D., Leith, D., Swann, J. Rhys, M. and Gillen, J. (eds) (2007). *Changing English*. London: Routledge.

Grandgenett, N. F. (2008). Perhaps a matter of imagination: TTPCK in mathematics education. In M. J. Koehler and P. Mishra (eds), *Handbook of technological pedagogical content knowledge for educators*. New York: AACTE/Routledge.

Gray, P. R. A. (1995). *Taking evidence of traditional Aboriginal rights to land*. Paper presented at the Supreme Court and Federal Court Judges Conference, Adelaide, January.

Green, L. (1998). Aspect and predicate phrases in African-American vernacular English. In S. S. Mufwene (ed.), *African-American English: Structure, history, and use*. London: Routledge.

Gregory, E. and Williams, A. (2000). *City literacies: Learning to read across generations and cultures*. New York: Routledge.

Gregory, E., Long, S. and Volk, D. (eds) (2004). *Many pathways to literacy: Young children learning with siblings, grandparents, peers and communities*. London: RoutledgeFalmer.

Grenoble, L. A., Rice, K. D. and Richards, N. (2009). The role of the linguist in language maintenance and revitalization: Documentation, training, and materials development. In W. Harbet, S. McConnell-Ginet, A. Miller and A. Whitman (eds), *Language and poverty*. Clevedon, UK: Multilingual Matters.

Grima, A. C. (2005). *Developing a whole school language policy*. Ensemble website. Online. Retrieved 21 February 2010 from: http://www.ecml.at/mtp2/ENSEMBLE/results/School-policy.htm.

Grin, F. (2001). English as economic value: Facts and fallacies. *World Englishes*, 20, 1, 65–78.

Gumperz, J. J. (1982). *Discourse strategies*. Cambridge: Cambridge University Press.

Hale, S. B. (2007). *Community interpreting*. Basingstoke: Palgrave Macmillan.

Hall, C. J. (2002). The automatic cognate form assumption: Evidence for the Parasitic Model of vocabulary development. *International Review of Applied Linguistics*, 40, 69–87.

— (2005). *An introduction to language and linguistics: Breaking the language spell*. London: Routledge.

Halliday, M. A. K. (1978). *Language as social semiotic: The social interpretation of language and meaning*. London and Baltimore, MD: Edward Arnold and the University Park Press.

— (1994). *An introduction to functional grammar*. London: Edward Arnold.

— (2004). Lexicology. In M. A. K. Halliday, W. Teubert, C. Yallop and A. Cermáková, *Lexicology and corpus linguistics*. London: Continuum.

— (2007 [1979]). Differences between spoken and written language: Some implications for literacy teaching. In J. J. Webster (ed.), *Language and education, 9, Collected works of M. A. K. Halliday*. London: Continuum.

— (2007 [1998]). *Language and education*. London: Continuum.

Hamel, R. E. (2003). Regional blocs as a barrier to English hegemony: The language policy of Mercosur in South America. In J. Maurais and M. A. Morris (eds), *Languages in a globalising world*. Cambridge: Cambridge University Press.

Harbert, W., McConnell-Ginet, S., Miller, A. and Whitman, A. (eds) (2009). *Language and poverty*. Clevedon, UK: Multilingual Matters.

Hardy, T. (1998 [1895]). *Jude the Obscure*. Harmondsworth: Penguin.

Harley, T. (2008). *The psychology of language: From data to theory*, 3rd edn. Hove, UK: Psychology Press.

Harris, M. (2004). First words. In J. Oates and A. Grayson (eds), *Cognitive and language development in children*. Oxford: Blackwell/Open University.

Hartmann, R. R. K. (2001). *Teaching and researching lexicography*. London: Longman.

Hartmann, R. R. K. and James, G. (1998). *Dictionary of lexicography*. London: Routledge.

Hartz, D. (2000). Literacy leaps as blind students embrace technology. *The English Journal*, 90, 2, 52–59. Online. Retrieved 14 June 2010 from: www.nfb.org/Images/nfb/Publications/fr/fr6/frw0103.htm.

Hasan, R. (1999). The disempowerment game: Bourdieu and language in literacy. *Linguistics and Education*, 10, 1, 25–87.

Heath, S. B. (2006 [1983]). *Ways with words: Language, life, and work in communities and classrooms*. Cambridge: Cambridge University Press.

Heffernan, C. H., Misturelli, F. and Neilsen, L. (2001). *Restocking and poverty alleviation: The perceptions and realities of livestock-keeping among poor pastoralists in Kenya*. Reading: University of Reading. Online. Retrieved 13 January 2010 from: http://www.smallstock.info/research/reports/R7402/RestockingAndPovertyAlleviation.pdf.

Heller, M. (1996). Legitimate language in a multilingual school. *Linguistics and Education*, 2, 8, 139–157.

— (2006). *Linguistic minorities and modernity: A sociolinguistic ethnography*, 2nd edn. London: Continuum.

Henry, A. (1995). *Belfast English and Standard English: Dialect variation and parameter setting*. New York: Oxford University Press.

Holm, J. (2000). *An introduction to pidgins and creoles*. Cambridge: Cambridge University Press.

Hornberger, N. H. and King, K. A. (1998). Authenticity and unification in Quechua language planning. *Culture and Curriculum*, 11, 3, 390–410.

Howatt, A. P. R. and Widdowson, H. G. (2004). *A history of English language teaching*. Oxford: Oxford University Press.

Hunston, S. (2002). *Corpora in applied linguistics.* Cambridge: Cambridge University Press.

Hurst, M. (2007). *Bit literacy: Productivity in the age of information and e-mail overload.* New York: Good Experience Press.

Hutjens, L. (1997). Life of Edmund Coote. In I. Lancashire (ed.), *Edmund Coote: The English schoole-maister.* Toronto: Web Development Group, University of Toronto. Online. Retrieved 15 June 2010 from: http://www.library.utoronto.ca/utel/ret/coote/ret2.html#bio.

Huws, C. F. (2009). Does legislation change perception and behaviour? Attitudes to and perceptions of the Welsh language in legal proceedings. In S. Pertot, T. M. S. Priestly and C. H. Williams (eds), *Rights, promotion and health issues for minority languages in Europe.* London: Palgrave Macmillan.

Hymes, D. (1972). Models of the interaction of language and social life. In J. J. Gumperz and D. Hymes (eds), *Directions in sociolinguistics: The ethnography of communication.* New York: Holt, Rinehart and Winston.

— (1974). *Foundations in sociolinguistics: An ethnographic approach.* Philadelphia: University of Pennsylvania Press.

IASSW (2009). *Language policy.* International Association of Schools of Social Work. Online. Retrieved 21 February 2010 from: http://www.iassw-aiets.org/index.php?option=com_content&task=blogcategory&id=59&Itemid=89.

Inglis, L., Newsome, M., Tang, Z. and Martin, R. (2002). Language. In D. M. Lane (ed.), *Multimedia textbook in behavioral neuroscience.* Online. Retrieved 21 June 2010 from: http://psych.rice.edu/mmtbn/.

Ingram, J. C. L. (2007). *Neurolinguistics: An introduction to spoken language processing and its disorders.* Cambridge: Cambridge University Press.

Intel Corporation (2005). *Moore's Law 40th Anniversary.* Online. Retrieved 3 May 2010 from: http://www.intel.com/pressroom/kits/events/moores_law_40th/index.htm?iid=tech_mooreslaw+body_presskit.

International Association for Forensic Phonetics and Acoustics (IAFPA) (2009). *Resolution – language and determination of national identity cases.* Online. Retrieved 8 June 2010 from: http://www.iafpa.net/langidres.htm.

ioyu.com (2006). *English-to-l33t Translator.* Online. Retrieved 14 June 2010 from: http://ioyu.com/io/javascript/l33t.asp.

Jackendoff, R. (1992). *Languages of the mind: Essays on mental representation.* Cambridge, MA: MIT Press.

Jaworski, A. and Coupland, N. (eds) (1999). *The discourse reader.* London: Routledge.

Jernigan, K. (2009). The pitfalls of political correctness: Euphemisms excoriated. *Braille Monitor,* 52, 3. Online. Retrieved 15 January 2010 from: http://www.nfb.org/images/nfb/Publications/bm/bm09/bm0903/bm090308.htm.

Jiménez, R. T. and Smith, P. H. (2008). Mesoamerican literacies: Indigenous writing systems and contemporary possibilities. *Reading Research Quarterly,* 43, 1, 28–46.

Johnson, D. C. (2009). The relationship between applied linguistic research and language policy for bilingual education. *Applied Linguistics,* 31, 1, 72–93.

Johnston, T. A. and Schembri, A. (2007). *Australian sign language (Auslan): An introduction to sign language linguistics.* Cambridge: Cambridge University Press.

Jordan, M. (2010). Arizona grades teachers on fluency. *Wall Street Journal*, 20 April. Online. Retrieved 5 June 2010 from: http://online.wsj.com/article/SB10001424052748703572504575213883276427528.html?mod=WSJ_hpp_MIDDLENexttoWhatsNewsTop#printMode.

JurisPro Inc. (n.d.) List of expert categories. *Language and linguistics*. Online. Retrieved 23 December 2005 from: http://www.jurispro.com/subcategory.asp?category=88.

Kachru, B. B. (1985). Standards, codification and sociolinguistic realism: The English language in the Outer Circle. In R. Quirk and H. Widdowson (eds), *English in the World*. Cambridge: Cambridge University Press.

— (ed.) (1992) *The other tongue. English across cultures*, 2nd edn. Urbana, IL: University of Illinois Press.

Kachru, B. B., Kachru, Y. and Nelson, C. L. (eds) (2006). *The handbook of World Englishes*. Oxford: Blackwell.

Kachru, Y. and Smith, L. E. (2008). *Cultures, contexts, and World Englishes*. London: Routledge.

Kaplan, R. B. (1966). Cultural thought patterns in intercultural education. *Language Learning*, 16, 1–20.

Kapperman, G. and Sticken, J. (2003). Using the Braille Lite to study foreign languages. *Journal of Visual Impairment and Blindness*, November, 704–709.

Karrow, R. W. (2007). Introduction. In J. R. Akerman and R. W. Karrow (eds), *Maps: Finding our place in the world*. Chicago: University of Chicago Press.

Kay, J., Lesser, R. and Coltheart, M. (1992). *PALPA: Psycholinguistic assessments of language processing in aphasia*. Hove, UK: Psychology Press.

Kayne, R. S. (2000). *Parameters and universals*. New York: Oxford University Press.

Kegl, J. and Iwata, G. (1989). Lenguaje de signos nicaraguense: A pidgin sheds light on the 'creole'?. In R. Carlson, S. DeLancey, S. Gildea, D. Payne and A. Saxena (eds), *Proceedings of the fourth meeting of the Pacific Linguistics Conference*. Eugene, OR: University of Oregon.

Kilgarriff, A. (1997). 'I don't believe in word senses'. *Computers and the Humanities*, 31, 91–113.

Kirkpatrick, A. (2007). *World Englishes: Implications for international communication and English language teaching*. Cambridge: Cambridge University Press.

Knapp, K. and Meierkord, C. (eds) (2002). *Lingua franca communication*. Frankfurt: Peter Lang.

Kong, K. (1998). Are simple business request letters really simple? A comparison of Chinese and English business request letters. *Text*, 18, 103–141.

Kramsch, C. (1993). *Language and culture*. Oxford: Oxford University Press.

Krashen, S. (1981). *Second language acquisition and second language learning*. Oxford: Pergamon.

— (1998). *Condemned without a trial: Bogus arguments against bilingual education*. Portsmouth, NH: Heinemann.

Krauss, M. (1992). The world's languages in crisis. *Language*, 68, 1, 4–10.

Kretchmar, W. A. (2008). Public and academic understandings about language: The intellectual history of Ebonics. *English World-Wide*, 29, 1, 70–95.

Labov, W. (1972). *Sociolinguistic patterns*. Philadelphia: University of Pennsylvania Press.

— (1982). Objectivity and commitment in linguistic science: The case of the Black English trial in Ann Arbor. *Language in Society*, 11, 2, 165–201.

Lakoff, R. T. (2000). *The language war*. Berkeley, CA: University of California Press.

Lambert, W. E. (2003 [1967]). A social psychology of bilingualism. In C. B. Paulston and G. R. Tucker (eds), *Sociolinguistics: The essential readings*. Oxford: Blackwell.

Landau, S. I. (2001). *Dictionaries. The art and craft of lexicography*, 2nd edn. Cambridge: Cambridge University Press.

Landry, R. and Bourhis, R. Y. (1997). Linguistic landscape and ethnolinguistic vitality: An empirical study. *Journal of Language and Social Psychology*, 16, 1, 23–49.

Lanza, E. and Woldemariam, H. (2009). Language ideology and linguistic landscape: Language policy and globalization in a regional capital in Ethiopia. In E. Shohamy and D. Gorter (eds), *Linguistic landscape: Expanding the scenery*. Oxford: Routledge.

Larsen-Freeman, D. and Freeman, D. (2008). Language moves: The place of 'foreign' languages in classroom teaching and learning. *Review of Research in Education*, 32, 147–186.

Laufer, B. and Girsai, N. (2008). Form-focused instruction in second language vocabulary learning: A case for contrastive analysis and translation. *Applied Linguistics*, 29, 4, 694–716.

Law, J., Lindsay, G., Peacey, N., Gascoigne, M., Soloff, N., Radford, J. and Band, S. (2002). Consultation as a model for providing speech and language therapy in schools: A panacea or one step too far? *Child Language Teaching and Therapy*, 18, 2, 145–163.

Lawson, A. (2010). *Last speaker of ancient language of Bo dies in India*. BBC News. Online. Retrieved 6 February 2010 from: http://news.bbc.co.uk/2/hi/south_asia/8498534.stm.

Le Page, R. B. and Tabouret-Keller, A. (1985). *Acts of identity: Creole-based approaches to language and ethnicity*. Cambridge: Cambridge University Press.

Lee, J. (2010). Interpreting inexplicit language during courtroom examination. In G. Cook and S. North (eds), *Applied linguistics in action: A reader*. London: Routledge.

Lenneberg, E. (1967). *Biological foundations of language*. New York: Wiley.

Lesser, R. and Milroy, L. (1993). *Linguistics and aphasia: Psycholinguistic and pragmatic aspects of intervention*. London: Longman.

Leung, C., Harris, R. and Rampton, B. (1997). The idealised native speaker, reified ethnicities, and classroom realities. *TESOL Quarterly*, 31, 3, 543–60.

Levitt, P. and Glick Schiller, N. (2008). Conceptualizing simultaneity: A transnational social field perspective on society. In A. Portes and J. DeWind (eds), *Rethinking migration: New theoretical and empirical perspectives*. New York: Berghahn Books.

Lewis, C. and Fabos, B. (2005). Instant messaging, literacies and social identities. *Reading Research Quarterly*, 40, 4, 470–501.

Lewis, G. (2003). *Keeping mum*. Tarset, UK: Bloodaxe Books.

Lewis, M. (1993). *The lexical approach: The state of ELT and a way forward*. Hove, UK: Language Teaching Publications.

Lewis, M. P. (2010). *Ethnologue: Languages of the world*, 16th edn. Dallas, TX: SIL International. Online. Retrieved 10 June 2010 from: http://www.ethnologue.com/.

Lewis, M. P. and Simons, G. F. (2010). Assessing endangerment: Expanding Fishman's GIDS. *Revue roumaine de linguistique*, 55, 103–20.

Li, L. (2005). The growing prosperity of on-line dictionaries. *English Today*, 83, 21, 3, 16–21.

Library and Archives Canada (LAC) (2008). *Official languages*. Online. Retrieved 22 February 2010 from: http://www.collectionscanada.gc.ca/notices/index-e.html#d.

Liddicoat, A. J. (2000) The ecological impact of a dictionary. *Current Issues in Language Planning*, 1, 3, 424–430.

Lindsey, T. (2008) *Indonesia, law and society*. Leichhardt, NSW, Australia: Federation Press.

Lippi-Green, R. (1997). *English with an accent: Language, ideology, and discrimination in the United States*. London: Routledge.

Lo Bianco, J. (2000). Multiliteracies and multilingualism. In B. Cope and M. Kalantzis (eds), *Multiliteracies: Literacy learning and the design of social futures*. London: Routledge.

— (2009). *Positively plurilingual: The contribution of community languages to UK education and society*. London: The National Centre for Languages. Online. Retrieved 14 June 2010 from: http://www.primarylanguages.org.uk/teaching_learning/community_languages.aspx.

Long, M. H. (1988). Instructed interlanguage development. In L. Beebe (ed.), *Issues in second language acquisition*. New York: Newbury House.

*Longman Dictionary of American English* (1983). New York: Longman.

Lorenz, G. (1998). Overstatement in advanced learners' writing: Stylistic aspects of adjective intensification. In S. Granger (ed.), *Learner English on computer*. Harlow: Longman.

Lorge, I. and Thorndike, E. L. (1938). *A semantic count of English words*. New York: Teachers College Press.

McConkey, R. (2001). *Understanding and responding to children's needs in inclusive classrooms: A guide for teachers*. Paris: United Nations Educational, Scientific and Cultural Organization, Division of Basic Education. Online. Retrieved 15 June 2010 from: http://unesdoc.unesco.org/images/0012/001243/124394E.pdf.

Mackay, C. and Trechsel, F. R. (2005). *Totonaco de Misantla, Veracruz*. Mexico City: El Colegio de México Press.

Mackey, W. F. and Beebe, V. N. (1977). *Bilingual schools for a bicultural community: Miami's adaptation to the Cuban refugees*. Rowley, MA: Newbury House.

McMenamin, G. R. (2002). *Forensic linguistics. Advances in forensic stylistics*. Boca Raton, FL: CRC Press.

McNamara, T. and Roever, C. (2006) *Language testing: The social turn*. Oxford: Blackwell.

McNiff, J. (2002). *Action research for professional development: Concise advice for new action researchers*. Online. Retrieved 11 June 2010 from: http://www.jeanmcniff.com/booklet1.html#2.

Maguire, P. L. (1996). Language policy and planning and the ELT profession in selected Central American countries. *TESOL Quarterly*, 30, 3, 606–611.

Maiaa Foundation (2009). *Health literacy*. Online. Retrieved 12 June 2010 from: http://themaiafoundation.org/health.htm.

Major, R. C. (2005). Chemehuevi revisited. *Journal of the Southwest*, 47, 3, 523–533.

Makoni, S. and Pennycook, A. (eds) (2007). *Disinventing and reconstituting languages*. Clevedon, UK: Multilingual Matters.

Malinowski, B. (1999 [1923]). On phatic communion. In A. Jaworski and N. Coupland (eds), *The discourse reader*. London: Routledge.

Malmkjær, K. (2005). *Linguistics and the language of translation*. Edinburgh: Edinburgh University Press.

Maori Language Commission (n.d.) *Maori language resources*. Online. Retrieved 4 September 2006 from: http://www.tetaurawhiri.govt.nz/.

Maragall rectifica y anuncia 'mediaciones' por la traducción al valenciano de la Carta europea (2009). *El País*, 5 November. Online. Retrieved 16 January 2010 from: http://www.elpais.com/articulo/espana/Maragall/rectifica/anuncia/mediaciones/traduccion/valenciano/Carta/europea/elpepuesp/20041105el pepunac_5/Tes.

Marr, T. (1999). Neither the state nor the grass roots: Language maintenance and the discourse of the Academia Mayor de la Lengua Quechua. *International Journal of Bilingual Education and Bilingualism*, 2, 3, 181–197.

Martin, D., Krishnamurthy, R., Bhardwaj, M. and Reeva, C. (2003). Language change in young Panjabi/English children: Implications for bilingual language assessment. *Child Language Teaching and Therapy*, 19, 245–265.

Martin-Jones, M. and Saxena, M. (2003). Bilingual resources and 'Funds of Knowledge' for teaching and learning in multi-ethnic classrooms in Britain. *International Journal of Bilingual Education and Bilingualism*, 6 (3&4), 267–282.

Mathers, C. M. (2002). To testify or not to testify: That is the question. *VIEWS*, October. Online. Retrieved 9 June 2010 from: www.rid.org/UserFiles/File/pdfs/ToTestifyorNot.pdf.

Matiki, A. J. (2006). Literacy, ethnolinguistic diversity and transitional bilingual education in Malawi. *International Journal of Bilingual Education and Bilingualism*, 9, 2, 239–254.

Matsuda, A. (2006). Negotiating ELT assumptions in EIL classrooms. In J. Edge (ed.), *(Re)locating TESOL in an age of empire*. Basingstoke: Palgrave Macmillan.

Maybin, J. and Swann, J. (2007). Everyday creativity in language: Textuality, contextuality, and critique. *Applied Linguistics*, 28, 4, 497–517.

Mejía, A. M. (2006). Review of Iolo Wyn Williams (ed.) Our children's language: The Welsh-medium schools of Wales, 1939–2000. Ceredigion, Wales: Y Lolfa Cyf, 2003. Reviewed in the *International Journal of Bilingual Education and Bilingualism*, 8, 6, 623–624.

Mendoza, M. (2004). *Latinos in Memphis and Tennessee*. Memphis, TN: University of Memphis.

*Merriam-Webster's Collegiate Dictionary* (2003). New York: Merriam-Webster.

Merrison, S. and Merrison, A. J. (2005). Repair in speech and language therapy interaction: Investigating pragmatic language impairment of children. *Child Language Teaching and Therapy*, 21, 2, 191–211.

Mertz, E. (1982). Language and mind: A Whorfian folk theory in United States Language Law. Sociolinguistics Working Papers, No. 93, Duke University.

Online. Retrieved 17 November 2009 from: http://ccat.sas.upenn.edu/~ haroldfs/540/theory/mertz1.html.

Mesthrie, R. and Bhatt, R. M. (2008). *World Englishes. The study of new linguistic varieties*. Cambridge: Cambridge University Press.

*The Michigan Corpus of Academic Spoken English*. (2010) Online. Retrieved 14 June 2010 from: http://lw.lsa.umich.edu/eli/micase/index.htm.

Ministry of Education, Singapore. (2008). *Good English the way to go*. Online. Retrieved 22 February 2010 from: http://www.moe.gov.sg/media/forum/ 2008/12/good-english-the-way-to-go.php.

Mitchell, R. E. and Karchmer, M. A. (2004). Chasing the mythical ten percent: Parental hearing status of deaf and hard of hearing students in the United States. *Sign Language Studies*, 4, 2, 138–163.

Mohanty, A. K. (2009). Perpetuating inequality: Language disadvantage and capability deprivation of tribal mother tongue speakers in India. In W. Harbert, S. McConnell-Ginet, A. Miller and J. Whitman (eds), *Language and poverty*. Clevedon, UK: Multilingual Matters.

Morton, G. R. (2002). *A history of human technology*. Online. Retrieved 14 June 2010 from: http://home.entouch.net/dmd/chron.htm.

Moss, G. (1989). *Un/Popular fictions*. London: Virago Press Limited.

Motolinía, F. T. de B. (1969). *Historia de los indios de la Nueva España*. Mexico: Editorial Porrua.

Murillo, L. A. (2009). 'This great emptiness we are feeling': Toward a decolonization of schooling in Simunurwa, Colombia. *Anthropology and Education Quarterly*, 40, 4, 431–450.

Murillo, L. A. and Smith, P. H. (2008). Linguicism and counter-pedagogies for teaching Chican@ students. Annual Texas Regional Conference of the National Assocation for Chicano and Chicana Studies, Edinburg, TX.

Myers, G. (2005). Applied linguists and institutions of opinion. *Applied Linguistics*, 26, 4, 527–544.

Nabokov, V. (2004 [1955]). Problems of translation: *Onegin* in English. In L. Venuti (ed.), *The translation studies reader*, 2nd edn. London: Routledge.

Nafisi, Azar (2003). *Reading Lolita in Tehran: A memoir in books*. New York: Random House.

Nakane, I. (2007). Problems in communicating the suspect's rights in interpreted police interviews. *Applied Linguistics*, 28, 87–112.

Nashville English First Charter Amendment (2009). *Ballotpedia*. Online. Retrieved 21 February 2010 from: http://ballotpedia.org/wiki/index.php/Nashville_ English_First_Charter_Amendment_(2009).

National Association of the Deaf and Registry of Interpreters for the Deaf (NAD-RID) (2005). *NAD-RID code of professional conduct*. Alexandria, VA: Registry of Interpreters for the Deaf. Online. Retrieved 13 January 2009 from: www.rid.org/UserFiles/File/pdfs/codeofethics.pdf.

National Center for Education Statistics (2009). *The nation's report card: Reading 2009* (NCES 2010–458). Washington, DC: Institute of Education Sciences, US Department of Education.

National Federation of the Blind (NFB) (2009). *The Braille literacy crisis in America. Facing the truth, reversing the trend, empowering the Blind. A report to the nation by the National Federation of the Blind*. Baltimore, MD: NFB. Online.

Retrieved 14 June 2010 from: http://www.nfb.org/images/nfb/documents/word/The_Braille_Literacy_Crisis_In_America.doc.

National Institute of Neurological Disorders and Stroke (NINDS) (2009). *Autism fact sheet.* Bethesda, MD: NINDS. Online. Retrieved 13 January 2010 from: http://www.ninds.nih.gov/disorders/autism/detail_autism.htm.

National Institute on Deafness and Other Communication Disorders (NIDCD) (2006). *Cochlear implants.* Online. Retrieved 12 May 2006 from: http://www.nidcd.nih.gov/health/hearing/coch.asp.

— (2008). *Aphasia.* Bethesda, MD: NICDC. Online. Retrieved 13 January 2010 from: http://www.nidcd.nih.gov/health/voice/aphasia.asp.

— (2010). *Speech and language.* Online. Retrieved 10 June 2010 from: http://www.nidcd.nih.gov/health/hearing/coch.asp.

Neate, G. (2003). *Land, law and language: Some issues in the resolution of Indigenous land claims in Australia.* Paper presented at the International Association of Forensic Linguists, Sydney, Australia, July. Online. Retrieved 9 February 2009 from: http://www.nntt.gov.au/News-and-Communications/Speeches-and-papers/Documents/2003/Speeches%20Land%20law%20and%20language%20Neate%20July%202003.pdf.

*New Oxford American Dictionary* (NOAD) (2001). Oxford: Oxford University Press.

New Zealand Ministry of Education (2005). *Kiwi phonics.* Online. Retrieved 7 June 2010 from: http://www.otago.ac.nz/press/kiwiphonics/index.html.

Nida, E. (2004 [1964]). Principles of correspondence. In L. Venuti (ed.), *The translation studies reader*, 2nd edn. London: Routledge.

Nolan, F. and Grabe, E. (1996). Preparing a voice line-up. *Forensic Linguistics*, 3, i, 74–94.

Nolan, F., McDougall, K., de Jong, G. and Hudson, T. (2009). The DyViS database: Style-controlled recordings of 100 homogeneous speakers for forensic phonetic research. *International Journal of Speech, Language and the Law*, 16, 1, 31–57.

Norton, B. (2000). *Identity and language learning: Gender, ethnicity, and educational change.* London: Longman.

Norton, B. and Toohey, K. (2004). *Critical pedagogies and language learning.* Cambridge: Cambridge University Press.

Nuance (2008). *Your digital life: Naturally speaking.* Online. Retrieved 3 March 2009 from: http://www.nuance.com/naturallyspeaking/resources/pogue video.asp.

O'Keeffe, A., McCarthy, M. and Carter, R. (2007). *From corpus to classroom: Language use and language teaching.* Cambridge: Cambridge University Press.

Ocean Literacy Network (2009). *Essential principles of ocean literacy.* Online. Retrieved 12 June 2010 from: http://oceanliteracy.wp.coexploration.org/.

Ochs, E. (1988). *Culture and language development: Language acquisition and language development in a Samoan village.* Cambridge: Cambridge University Press.

Office of Public Sector Information (OPSI) (n.d.). *Civil Evidence Act 1972.* Online. Retrieved 16 June 2010 from: http://www.opsi.gov.uk/RevisedStatutes/Acts/ukpga/1972/cukpga_19720030_en_1.

Ofsted (2008). *Every language matters.* London: Ofsted. Online. Retrieved 21 June 2010 from: http://www.ofsted.gov.uk/Ofsted-home/Publications-and-research/Browse-all-by/Education/Teachers-and-teacher-training/Routes-into-teaching/Every-language-matters.

Oketch, M. and Rolleston, C. (2007). Policies on free primary and secondary education in East Africa: Retrospect and prospect. *Review of Research in Education*, 31, 131–158.

Olsson, J. (2004). *Forensic linguistics: An introduction to language, crime, and the law*. London: Continuum.

Ong, W. J. (1982). *Orality and literacy: The technologizing of the word*. London: Taylor and Francis.

Orellana, M. F., Reynolds, J., Dorner, L. and Mesa, M. (2003). In other words: Translating or 'para-phrasing' as a family literacy practice in immigrant households. *Reading Research Quarterly*, 38, 1, 12–34.

Ortega y Gasset, J. (1992 [1937]). The misery and the splendor of translation (trans. E. G. Miller). In R. Schulte and J. Biguenet (eds), *Theories of translation: An anthology of essays from Dryden to Derrida*. Chicago: University of Chicago Press.

Pan South African Language Board (PanSALB) (2009a) *Index*. Online. Retrieved 15 June 2010 from: http://www.pansalb.org.za/index.html.

—— (2009b) *N/U Language*. Online. Retrieved 14 June from: http://www.pansalb.org.za/thenulanguage.html.

Park, J. (2007). Co-construction of nonnative speaker identity in cross-cultural interaction. *Applied Linguistics*, 28, 3, 339–360.

Pascoe, M., Stackhouse, J. and Wells, B. (2005). Phonological therapy within a psycholinguistic framework: Promoting change in a child with persisting speech difficulties. *International Journal of Language and Communication Disorders*, 40, 2, 189–220.

Paulson, E. J. (2005). Viewing eye movements during reading through the lens of chaos theory: How reading is like the weather. *Reading Research Quarterly*, 40, 3, 338–358.

Paulston, C. B. and McLaughlin, S. (1994). Language-in-education policy and planning. *Annual Review of Applied Linguistics*, 14, 53–81.

Payne, R. K. (2008). *A framework for understanding poverty*, 3rd edn. Highlands, TX: Aha! Processes.

Pennycook, A. (1989). The concept of method, interested knowledge, and the politics of language. *TESOL Quarterly*, 23, 589–618.

—— (1994a). Incommensurable discourses? *Applied Linguistics*, 15, 2, 151–138.

—— (1994b). *The cultural politics of English as an international language*. London: Longman.

—— (2007). The myth of English as an international language. In S. Makoni and A. Pennycook (eds), *Disinventing and reconstituting languages*. Clevedon, UK: Multilingual Matters.

Pennycook, A. and Makoni, S. (eds) (2007). Disinventing and reconstituting languages. Clevedon, UK: Multilingual Matters.

Petitto, L. A. (1997) In the beginning: On the genetic and environmental factors that make early language acquisition possible. In M. Gopnik (ed.), *The inheritance and innateness of grammars*. New York: Oxford University Press.

Petronius Arbiter (n.d.). *The Satyricon* (trans. W. Burnaby). Online. Retrieved 16 May 2006 from: http://www.gutenberg.org/etext/5611.

— (1930). *The Satyricon* (trans. A. R. Allinson). New York: The Panurge Press. Online. Retrieved 16 May 2006 from: www.sacredtexts.com/cla/petro/satyr/index.htm.

— (2003). *Satyrica* (trans. F. Raphael). London: The Folio Society.

Philips, S. (1998). *Ideology in the language of judges: How judges practice law, politics, and courtroom control*. Oxford: Oxford University Press.

Phillipson, R. (1992). *Linguistic imperialism*. Oxford: Oxford University Press.

— (2009). *Linguistic imperialism continued*. London: Routledge.

Piety, P. J. (2004). The language system of audio description: An investigation as a discursive process. *Journal of Visual Impairment and Blindness*, August, 453–469.

Pinker, S. (1994). *The language instinct*. New York: HarperCollins.

Pirsig, R. (1974). *Zen and the art of motorcycle maintenance*. New York: Harper Perennial.

Pohlandt-McCormick, H. (2000). 'I saw a nightmare. . . ': Violence and the construction of memory (Soweto, June 16, 1976). *History and Theory*, 39, 23–44.

Population Census Office (Pakistan) (1998). *Population by mother tongue*. Online. Retrieved 21 September 2010 from: http://www.statpak.gov.pk/depts/pco/statistics/other_tables/pop_by_mother_tongue.pdf.

*Position statement concerning use of impressionistic likelihood terms in forensic speaker comparison cases* (2007). Online. Retrieved 6 June 2010 from: http://www.forensic-speech-science.info/position.html.

Prabhu, N. S. (1990). There is no best method – why? *TESOL Quarterly*, 24, 161–176.

Presidencia de la República. (2006). *Presentación de la Iniciativa de Reforma al Sistema de Seguridad Pública y Justicia Penal*. Online. Retrieved 20 September 2006 from: http://fox.presidencia.gob.mx/multimedia/videos/?contenido=7835&pagina=98.

Preston, D. (2002). Language with an attitude. In J. K. Chambers, P. Trudgill and N. Schilling-Estes (eds), *The handbook of language variation and change*. Oxford: Blackwell.

Proshina, Z. G. (2005). Intermediary translation from English as a lingua franca. *World Englishes*, 24, 4, 517–522.

Qualifications and Curriculum Authority (QCA) (2009). *National Curriculum, Key Stages 1 and 2, Assessment in personal, social, and health education*. London. Online. Retrieved 15 June 2010 from: http://curriculum.qca.org.uk/key-stages-1-and-2/assessment/assessmentofsubjects/assessmentinpersonalsocialandhealtheducation/index.aspx.

Rajagopalan, K. (2004). The concept of 'World English' and its implications for ELT. *ELT Journal*, 58, 2, 111–117.

— (2005). The language issue in Brazil: When local knowledge clashes with global knowledge. In A. S. Canagarajah (ed.), *Reclaiming the local in language policy and practice*. Mahwah, NJ: Erlbaum.

Ramanathan, V. (2005). *The English–vernacular divide: Postcolonial language politics and practice*. Clevedon, UK: Multilingual Matters.

Rao, G. N. and Raman, U. (2005). Vision 2020: The right to sight, *Cataract and Refractive Surgery Today*, October, 41–42.

Real Academia Española (2006). Online. Retrieved 6 September 2006 from: http://www.rae.es/.

Refugee Review Tribunal of Australia (2004). Decision record N04/48762. Online. Retrieved 2 March 2009 from: http://www.austlii.edu.au/cgi-bin/sinodisp/au/cases/cth/RRTA/2004/701.html.

Reyhner, J. and Lockhard, L. (eds) (2009). *Indigenous language revitalization: Encouragement, guidance and lessons learned.* Flagstaff, AZ: Northern Arizona University. Online. Retrieved 13 June 2010 from: http://jan.ucc.nau.edu/~jar/ILR/.

Reynolds, C. R. and Fletcher-Janzen, E. (eds) (2007). *Encyclopedia of special education: A reference for the education of children, adolescents, and adults with disabilities and other exceptional individuals. Volume 3,* 3rd edn. Hoboken, NJ: John Wiley and Sons.

RIC International (n.d.). *Do technical translators really need to have an engineering background?* Online. Retrieved 21 August 2006 from: http://www.ricintl.com/subject_expertise.html.

Rice, M. with Brooks, G. (2004). *Developmental dyslexia in adults: A research review.* London: National Research and Development Centre for Adult Literacy and Numeracy. Online. Retrieved 3 March 2009 from: http://www.nrdc.org.uk/projects_details.asp?ProjectID=75.

Ricento, T. K. and Hornberger, N. H. (1996). Unpeeling the onion: Language policy and planning and the ELT professional. *TESOL Quarterly*, 30, 3, 410–427.

Richards, J. C. and Rodgers, T. (2001). *Approaches and methods in language teaching*, 2nd edn. Cambridge: Cambridge University Press.

Richards, K. and Seedhouse, P. (2005). *Applying conversation analysis.* Basingstoke: Palgrave Macmillan.

Ringbom, H. (1998). Vocabulary frequencies in advanced learner English: A cross-linguistic approach. In S. Granger (ed.), *Learner English on computer.* Harlow: Longman.

Riordan, B. (2005). Language policy for linguistic minority students in Japanese public schools and prospects for bilingualism: The Nikkei Brazilian case. *Indiana University Linguistics Club Working Papers Online, 5.* Online. Retrieved 14 July 2010 from: https://www.indiana.edu/~iulcwp/contents.cgi?which=5.

Roberts, C. (2005). English in the workplace. In E. Hinkel (ed.), *Handbook of research in second language teaching and learning.* Mahwah, NJ: Lawrence Erlbaum Associates.

Roberts, C. and Campbell, S. (2006). *Talk on trial.* London: Department for Work and Pensions.

Roberts, C., Byram, M., Barro, A., Jordan, S. and Street, B. (2001). *Language learners as ethnographers.* Clevedon, UK: Multilingual Matters.

Roberts, R. P. (2002). Translation. In R. B. Kaplan (ed.), *The Oxford handbook of applied linguistics.* Oxford: Oxford University Press.

Robinson, P. (2002). Effects of individual differences in intelligence, aptitude and working memory on adult incidental SLA: A replication and extension of Reber, Walkenfeld and Hernstadt, 1991. In P. Robinson (ed.), *Individual differences and instructed language learning.* Amsterdam: John Benjamins.

Romaine, S. (1999). Early bilingual development: From elite to folk. In G. Extra and L. Verhoeven (eds), *Bilingualism and migration.* Berlin: Mouton de Gruyter.

—— (2009). Biodiversity, linguistic diversity and poverty: Some global patterns and missing links. In W. Harbet, S. McConnell-Ginet, A. Miller and A. Whitman. (eds), *Language and poverty*. Clevedon, UK: Multilingual Matters.

Rose, J. (2006). *Independent review of the teaching of early reading: Final report*. London: Department for Education and Skills. Online. Retrieved 6 June 2010 from: http://www.standards.dcsf.gov.uk/phonics/rosereview/.

— (2009). *Identifying and teaching children and young people with dyslexia and literacy difficulties*. London: Department for Children, Schools and Families. Online. Retrieved 6 June 2010 from: http://www.dcsf.gov.uk/jimroseand dyslexia/.

Rosenblatt, L.M. (2005). *Making meaning with texts: Selected essays*. Portsmouth, NH: Heinemann.

Rosetta Project (n.d.). Online. Retrieved 18 January 2010 from: http:// rosettaproject.org.

Royal College of Speech and Language Therapists (RCSLT) (2005). *Clinical guidelines*. Bicester, UK: Speechmark Publishing.

Rubdy, R. (2006) Remaking Singapore for the New Age: Official ideology and the realities of practice in language in education. In A. M. Y. Lin and P. W. Martin (eds), *Globalization, de/neo-colonization and language-in-education: Policies and practices*. Clevedon, UK: Multilingual Matters.

Rubin, J. (1983). Evaluating status planning: What has the past decade accomplished? In J. Cobarrubias and J. A. Fishman (eds), *Progress in language planning: International perspectives*. Berlin: Mouton de Gruyter.

Rubin, J. and Jernudd, B. H. (eds) (1971). *Can language be planned? Sociolinguistic theory and practice for developing nations*. Honolulu: University of Hawaii Press.

Ruiz, R. (1984). Orientations in language planning. *NABE Journal*, 8, 2, 15–34.

Ryles, R. (1996). The impact of Braille reading skills on employment, income, education, and reading habits. *Journal of Visual Impairment and Blindness*, 90, 3, 219–226.

Sacks, O. (1998). *The man who mistook his wife for a hat*. New York: Simon and Schuster.

Saussure, F. de (1983). *Course in general linguistics* (trans. R. Harris; ed. C. Bally and A. Sechehaye). La Salle, IL: Open Court.

Saville-Troike, M. (2003). *The ethnography of communication: An introduction*. Oxford: Blackwell.

Schegloff, E. A., Koshik, I., Jacoby, S. and Olsher, D. (2002). Conversation analysis and applied linguistics. *Annual Review of Applied Linguistics*, 22, 3–31.

Schluessel, E. T. (2007). Bilingual education and discontent in Xinjiang. *Central Asian Survey*, 26, 2, 251–277.

Schmitt, N. and Celce-Murcia, M. (2010). An overview of applied linguistics. In N. Schmitt (ed.), *An introduction to applied linguistics*, 2nd edn. London: Hodder Education.

Scribner, S. and Cole, M. (1981). *The psychology of literacy*. Cambridge, MA: Harvard University Press.

Seedhouse, P. (2004). *The interactional architecture of the language classroom: A conversation analysis perspective*. Oxford: Blackwell.

Seidlhofer, B. (2001). Closing a conceptual gap: The case for a description of English as a lingua franca. *International Journal of Applied Linguistics*, 11, 2, 133–158.

Serra, C. (2007). Assessing CLIL at primary school: A longitudinal study. *International Journal of Bilingual Education and Bilingualism*, 10, 5, 582–602.

Shiels, M. (2009). *Intel shows chips can get smaller*. BBC News Online. Online. Retrieved 3 May 2010 from: http://news.bbc.co.uk/1/hi/technology/8269278.stm.

Shohamy, E. (2001). *The power of tests: A critical perspective on the uses of language tests*. Harlow: Longman.

Shohamy, E. and Gorter, D. (eds) (2009). *Linguistic landscape: Expanding the scenery*. Oxford: Routledge.

Shohamy, E. and McNamara, T. (eds) (2009). *Language testing for citizenship, immigration and asylum*. Special issue of *Language Assessment Quarterly*, 6, 1.

Shuy, R. W. (1993). *Language crimes: The use and abuse of language evidence in the courtroom*. Oxford: Basil Blackwell.

Simmons-Mackie, N. N. and Damico, J. S. (1995). Communicative competence in aphasia: Evidence from compensatory strategies. *Clinical Aphasiology*, 23, 95–105.

Sinclair, J. M. and Coulthard, R. M. (1975). *Towards an analysis of discourse*. Oxford: Oxford University Press.

Slobin, D. (1996) From 'thought and language' to 'thinking for speaking'. In J. Gumperz and S. Levinson (eds), *Rethinking linguistic relativity*. Cambridge: Cambridge University Press.

Smeijers, A. S. and Pfau, R. (2009). Towards a treatment for treatment: On communication between general practitioners and their deaf patients. *The Sign Language Translator and Interpreter*, 3, 1, 1–14.

Smith, F. (2004). *Understanding reading: A psycholinguistic analysis of reading and learning to read*, 6th edn. Mahwah, NJ: Lawrence Erlbaum.

Smith L. E. (ed.) (1983). *Readings in English as an international language*. Oxford: Pergamon Press.

Smith, L. T. (2006). *Decolonizing methodologies: Research and indigenous peoples*. London: Zed Books.

Smith, P. D. and Baranyi, H. A. (1968). *A comparison study of the effectiveness of the traditional and audiolingual approaches to foreign language instruction utilizing laboratory equipment*. ERIC document ED030013. Online. Retrieved 8 July 2009 from: http://eric.ed.gov/ERICWebPortal/custom/portlets/recordDetails/detailmini.jsp?_nfpb=true&_&ERICExtSearch_SearchValue_0=ED030013&ERICExtSearch_SearchType_0=no&accno=ED030013.

Smith, P. H. (2000). Community as resource for minority language learning: A case study of Spanish–English dual language schooling. Unpublished doctoral dissertation, University of Arizona.

—— (2002). 'Ni a pocha va a llegar': Minority language loss and dual language schooling in the U.S.–Mexico borderlands. *Southwest Journal of Linguistics*, 21, 1, 165–183.

Smitherman, G. (2003). *Talkin that talk: Language, culture, and education in African America*. London: Routledge.

Solan, L. M. and Tiersma, P. M. (2004). Author identification in American courts. *Applied Linguistics*, 25, 4, 448–465.

Spencer-Oatey, H. and Franklin, P. (2009). *Intercultural interaction: A multidisciplinary approach to intercultural communication*. Basingstoke: Palgrave Macmillan.

Spender, D. (1980). *Man made language*. London: Routledge and Kegan Paul.

Spivak, G. C. (2004 [1992]). The politics of translation. In L. Venuti (ed.), *The translation studies reader*, 2nd edn. London: Routledge.

Spolsky, B. (2004). *Language policy*. Cambridge: Cambridge University Press.

— (2009). Prolegmena to a sociolinguistic theory of public signage. In E. Shohamy and D. Gorter (eds), *Linguistic landscape: Expanding the scenery*. Oxford: Routledge.

Sproat, R. (2010). *Language, technology, and society*. Oxford: Oxford University Press.

Sridhar, K. K. and Sridhar, S. N. (1992). Bridging the paradigm gap: Second-language acquisition theory and indigenized varieties of English. In B. B. Kachru (ed.), *The other tongue. English across cultures*. Urbana, IL: University of Illinois Press.

Stackhouse, J. and Wells, B. (1997). *Children's speech and literacy difficulties 1: A psycholinguistic framework*. London: Whurr.

— (2001). *Children's speech and literacy difficulties 2: Identification and intervention*. London: Whurr.

Stock, P. F. (2008 [1984]). Polysemy. In T. Fontenelle (ed.), *Practical lexicography: A reader*. Oxford: Oxford University Press.

Street, B. V. (1984). *Literacy in theory and practice*. Cambridge: Cambridge University Press.

— (ed.) (2001). *Literacy and development: Ethnographic perspectives*. London: Routledge.

Tarone, E. (2005). Speaking in a second language. In E. Hinkel (ed.), *Handbook of research in second language teaching and learning*. Mahwah, NJ: Lawrence Erlbaum Associates.

te Molder, H. and Potter, J. (2005). *Conversation and cognition*. Cambridge: Cambridge University Press.

Tew, C. (2004). Rahal au Maroc. *MFL: CILT's bulletin for secondary language teachers*, Issue 5. Online. Retrieved 8 July 2009 from: http://www.cilt.org.uk/pdf/pubs/bulletins/mfl_5.pdf.

Thiong'o, N. wa (2009 [1986]). *Decolonising the mind: The politics of language in African literature*. Portsmouth, NH: Heinemann.

Thomas, D. (2006 [1954]). *Under Milk Wood: A play for voices*. Online. Retrieved 13 January 2009 from: http://gutenberg.net.au/ebooks06/0608221h.html.

Tiersma, P. and Solan, L. M. (2002). The linguist on the witness stand: Forensic linguistics in American courts. *Language*, 78, 2, 221–39.

Tolchinsky, L. (2003). *The cradle of culture and what children know about writing and numbers before being taught*. Mahwah, NJ: Lawrence Erlbaum:

Tollefson, J. W. (ed.) (2002). *Language policies in education: Critical issues*. Mahwah, NJ: Lawrence Erlbaum.

Tosi, A. (2006). The devil in the kaleidoscope: Can Europe speak with a single voice in many languages? In C. Leung and J. Jenkins (eds), *Reconfiguring Europe: The contribution of applied linguistics*. London: British Association for Applied Linguistics/Equinox.

Townsley, B. (2007). Interpreting in the UK community: Some reflections on Public Service Interpreting in the UK. *Language and Intercultural Communication*, 7, 2, 163–170.

Trillos, M. A. (1998). *Lenguas aborígenes de Colombia. Memorias. Educación endógena frente a educación formal.* Bogota: Universidad de los Andes y Centro Colombiano de Estudios de Lenguas Aborígenes.

Troike, R. C. (1983). Can language be tested? *Journal of Education*, 165, 2, 209–216.

Tsung, L. (2009). *Minority languages, education and communities in China.* New York: Palgrave Macmillan.

UK Department for Children, Schools and Families (2008). Bercow Review of Services for Children and Young People (0–19) with Speech, Language and Communication Needs. Online. Retrieved 7 April 2010 from: http://www.dcsf. gov.uk/bercowreview/docs/7771-DCSF-BERCOW.PDF.

UNESCO (n.d.a). *Literacy Assessment and Monitoring Programme.* Online. Retrieved 14 June 2010 from: http://www.uis.unesco.org/ev.php?ID=6411_ 201&ID2=DO_TOPIC.

— (n.d.b). *United Nations Literacy Decade.* Online. Retrieved 14 June 2010 from: http://www.unesco.org/en/literacy/un-literacy-decade/.

— (1994). *The Salamanca Statement and framework for action on special needs education.* Salamanca, Spain. Online. Retrieved 15 June 2010 from: http:// www.unesco.org/education/pdf/SALAMA_E.PDF.

UNESCO Institute for Statistics (2008). *International literacy statistics: A review of concepts, methodology and current data.* Montreal: UNESCO. Online. Retrieved 13 January 2010 from: www.uis.unesco.org/template/pdf/Literacy/Literacy Report2008.pdf.

— (2009). *Information sheet No. 2: The Literacy Assessment and Monitoring Programme (LAMP).* Montreal: UNESCO. Online. Retrieved 13 January 2010 from: http://www.uis.unesco.org/template/pdf/LAMP/Infosheet_No2_LAMP _EN.pdf.

— (2010). *Literacy.* Online. Retrieved 21 September 2010 from: http://www.uis. unesco.org/ev_en.php?ID=6401_201&ID2=DO_TOPIC.

United Nations Office at Geneva (UNOG) (n.d.). *Conference management. Interpretation.* Online. Retrieved 1 May 2010 from: http://www.unog.ch/ 80256EE60057CB67/(httpPages)/2C87D748E41A2E3880256EF80049 6BF2?OpenDocument.

UNU-INWEH (2010). Sanitation as a key to global health: Voices from the field. Hamilton, Ontario: United Nations University Institute for Water, Environment and Health. Online. Retrieved 21 April 2010 from: http://www.inweh.unu.edu/ documents/2010_Sanitation_PolicyBrief.pdf.

Vaillancourt, F. (2009). Language and poverty: Measurement, determinants and policy responses. In W. Harbert, S. McConnell-Ginet, A. Miller and J. Whitman (eds), *Language and poverty.* Clevedon, UK: Multilingual Matters.

Valdés, G. M. (1995). Bilingües y bilingüismo en los Estados Unidos: la política lingüística en una época antiinmigrante. *Alteridades*, 5, 10, 25–42.

— (1997). Dual language immersion programs: A cautionary note concerning the education of language-minority students. *Harvard Educational Review*, 67, 391–429.

Valdes, J. M. (ed.) (1986). *Culture bound: Bridging the cultural gap in language teaching.* Cambridge: Cambridge University Press.

Valli, C. (2005). *Gallaudet dictionary of American Sign Language.* Washington, DC: Gallaudet University Press.

Valli, C. and Lucas, C. (2000). *Linguistics of American Sign Language: An introduction.* Washington, DC: Gallaudet University Press.

Valls, F. (2004). Cataluña asume la traducción valenciana de la Constitución europea. *El País*, 29 October. Online. Retrieved 16 January 2010 from: http://www.elpais.com/articulo/Comunidad/Valenciana/Cataluna/asume/traduccion/valenciana/Constitucion/europea/elpepuespval/20041029elpval_11/Tes.

van Dijk, T. (2001). Multidisciplinary CDA: A plea for diversity. In R. Wodak and M. Meyer (eds), *Methods of Critical Discourse Analysis* (95–120). London: Sage.

Venuti, L. (ed.) (2004) *The translation studies reader*, 2nd edn. London: Routledge.

Vygotsky, L. (1986). *Thought and language.* Cambridge, MA: MIT.

Wagner, D. A. and Kozma, R. B. (2005). *New technologies for literacy and adult education: A global perspective.* Paris: UNESCO.

Walmsley, S. (1981). On the purpose and content of secondary reading programs: Educational ideological perspectives. *Curriculum Inquiry*, 11, 76–87.

Walsh, S. (2006). *Investigating classroom discourse.* London: Routledge.

Wardhaugh, R. (2006). *An introduction to sociolinguistics*, 5th edn. Oxford: Blackwell.

Waters, A. (2009). Ideology in applied linguistics for language teaching. *Applied Linguistics*, 30, 1, 138–143.

White, M. J. and Glick, J. E. (2009). *Achieving anew: How new immigrants do in American schools, jobs, and neighborhoods.* New York: Russell Sage.

Whitworth, A., Webster, J. and Howard, D. (2005). *A cognitive neuropsychological approach to assessment and intervention in aphasia: A clinician's guide.* Hove, UK: Psychology Press.

Wicaksono, R. (2009). *Introducing English as a lingua franca: An online tutorial.* York: York St John University. Online. Retrieved 12 June 2010 from: http://www2.yorksj.ac.uk/EnquiryCommons/elf/.

Widdowson, H. G. (1994). The ownership of English. *TESOL Quarterly*, 28, 2, 377–389.

— (2000). On the limitations of linguistics applied. *Applied Linguistics*, 21, 1, 3–5.

Williams, C. (2009). Governance without conviction. In S. Pertot, T. M. S. Priestly, and C. Williams (eds), *Rights, promotion, and integration of minority languages in Europe.* London: Palgrave Macmillan.

Williams, G. (2010). *The knowledge economy, language and culture.* Clevedon, UK: Multilingual Matters.

Willinsky, J. (1999). *Learning to divide the world: Education at empire's end.* Minneapolis: University of Minnesota Press.

Willis, D. (1990). *The lexical syllabus.* London: Collins.

Wilson, J. and Henry, A. (1998). Parameter setting within a socially realistic linguistics. *Language in Society*, 27, 1–21.

Wodak, R. and Meyer, M. (eds) (2001). *Methods of critical discourse analysis.* London: Sage.

Wolfram, W. (2010). Dialect awareness, cultural literacy, and the public interest. In M. Farr, L. Seloni and J. Song. (eds), *Ethnolinguistic diversity and education: Language, literacy and culture.* New York: Routledge.

Wolfram, W., Adger, C. T. and Christian, D. (1999). *Dialects in schools and communities.* Mahwah, NJ: Lawrence Erlbaum.

Wong Fillmore, L. (1991). When learning a second language means losing the first. *Early Childhood Research Quarterly*, 6, 323–346.

Wools, D. and Coulthard, M. (1998). Tools for the trade. *Forensic Linguistics*, 5, 33–57.

World Health Organization (WHO) (2001). *International Classification of Functioning, Disability and Health (ICF)*. Online. Retrieved 21 June 2010 from: http://www.who.int/classifications/icf/en/.

— (2006). *Deafness and hearing impairment*. Geneva: WHO. Online. Retrieved 15 January 2010 from: http://www.who.int/mediacentre/factsheets/fs300/en/print.html.

— (2007). *What is dyslexia?* Online. Retrieved 12 June 2010 from: http://www.dyslexia-international.org/WhatIs2.htm.

Xianbin, H. (2007). Power relations and translational inequality in China. *Language and Intercultural Communication*, 7, 3, 240–252.

Young, R. F. and Nguyen, H. T. (2002). Modes of meaning in high school science. *Applied Linguistics*, 23, 3, 348–372.

Zgusta, L. (1971). *Manual of lexicography*. The Hague: Mouton.

# Index

# Index of languages

# Index of places

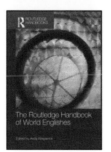